INTRODUCTION TO
American
Government

Robert J. Bresler
Pennsylvania State University

Robert J. Friedrich
Franklin and Marshall College

Joseph J. Karlesky
Franklin and Marshall College

D. Grier Stephenson, Jr.
Franklin and Marshall College

Charles C. Turner
Chico State University

North West Publishing LLC

PHOTO RESEARCHER: Turi Tenant

MARKETING MANAGER: Troy Fisk

TEXT DESIGN AND COMPOSITION: Archetype Book Composition

COVER DESIGN MANAGER: Lesli Haht

ISBN 1931910103
Copyright © 2002 by North West Publishing, LLC
Revision December 2002

Table of **Contents**

The Features

Politics and Ideas

Politics and Economics

Contemporary Controversies

The Preface

Economics, Ideology, and Politics

The need persists for widespread mastery of the political system John Quincy Adams once described as "the most complicated on the face of the globe." To this end, we offer today's students a comprehensive, readable, and balanced study of the context, structure, and process of American politics.

A distinguishing feature of this book is the explicit recognition that economics and ideology significantly influence American politics. No student or instructor in a course on American government is immune to the ideological and economic forces that help shape the perennial pursuit of power in a democracy. Nor is any class or instructor untouched by recurring problems ranging from budget deficits and health care to unemployment and the underclass. Economics and ideology, in one way or another, intersect nearly all of them.

This text highlights the importance of economics and ideology in the context of American government in several ways. Chapter 14, "Public Policy and Economics" explores the relationship between politics and *economics,* as does a series of "Politics and Economics" boxes (described below) throughout the rest of the book. Students see how economic decisions have political consequences and how political decisions affect the economy. This is essential information in a day when economic topics frequently dominate electoral campaigns, television news, and conversation at the dinner table. However, the text assumes *no* prior knowledge of economics, and references to economic policy are free of confusing jargon.

Understanding differences among political beliefs is likewise essential at a time when the labels "liberal" and "conservative," "left" and "right" are hurled about. Such terms can be baffling, particularly because their meaning has not been constant. Consequently, the text underscores the importance of *political ideology*—the ideas people have about what government should or should not do and what kind of government they should have. This emphasis is reflected in a series of "Politics and Ideas" boxes (described below), in Chapter 4, "Political Ideologies," and in Chapter 5, "Public Opinion and Political Participation." Chapter 4 is nearly unique among shorter volumes on American government because it draws a road map that guides students through intellectual debates, past and present, in American politics. Additionally, Chapter 3, "Civil Liberties and Civil Rights" probes ideological distinctions among Americans concerning fundamental freedoms. Such an encompassing survey of the spectrum of political ideas encourages students both to comprehend and to tolerate points of view other than their own, enabling them to gain further insight into political differences that exist nationwide.

Pedagogical Features

This textbook is not a "theme" or point-of-view book. Aside from emphasizing the importance of politics and political involvement, the book embraces no single ideological perspective; it does not attempt to make readers Democrats or Republicans, liberals or conservatives. To ensure a single voice in this presentation, one author has served as general editor.

The goals are knowledge of, and critical thinking about, American politics and government. Accordingly, we have designed the book to encourage students to *engage* the material. Passive reading is not enough. Understanding so important and complex a subject necessitates active intellectual involvement.

To aid in learning, this textbook incorporates several serviceable pedagogical features.

- **"Politics and ideas"** boxes appearing throughout the text explore ideological topics in depth. They demonstrate how ideological divisions generate different political consequences.
- **"Politics and Economics"** boxes appearing through the text highlight special economics topics, illustrating the relationship between economics and politics.
- **"Contemporary Controversies"** boxes are present in a few chapters to illustrate how the subject matter covered in the chapter carries over into disputes that divide the nation.
- Study questions conclude the special boxed features to encourage critical thinking and further inquiry.
- Tables, graphs, and maps appear throughout the text to display both quantitative and conceptual data. Some illustrations present new data, while others summarize information covered in the body of the chapter.
- A summary, key terms, and a description of suggested readings conclude each chapter. The summary contains in numbered form the main points presented in the chapter. Key terms, in boldface, are defined at the point at which they are introduced in the chapter. Suggested readings are widely available primary and secondary sources that students may consult in pursuing topics in the chapter.

Supplements

The following supplements are available from North West Publishing, LLC: Instructor's Manual, Test Bank, Transparencies, and Study Guide.

Acknowledgments

The authors express their gratitude for the many helpful criticisms and suggestions offered by colleagues who read various drafts of the manuscript. They include: Robert Albritton, Northern Illinois University; Peter Bergerson, Southeast Missouri State; Sam Hoff, Delaware State College; Willoughby Jarrell, Kennesaw State College; Gregory D. Lessig, Edinboro University of Pennsylvania; Alfreda McCullough, College of Charleston; Gerald Money, El Paso Community College; Richard K. Moore, Lewis-Clark State College; Daniel Sloan, University of Colorado, Boulder; Elliot Vittes, University of Central Florida; Mitchell Weiss, Mutt Community College; and Norman Zucker, University of Rhode Island.

Finally, special gratitude, as always, is owed to our families, whose love, encouragement, and understanding are essential ingredients in a project of this magnitude. Specifically, we thank Ellen, Todd, and Claire Stephenson; Jessica Bresler, Lin Carvell, and Jordan and Greg Rogoe; Rebecca, Philip, and Elizabeth Friedrich; and Audrey, Christopher, and Matthew Karlesky.

Robert J. Bresler

Robert J. Friedrich

Joseph J. Karlesky

D. Grier Stephenson, Jr

Charles C. Turner

The **Introduction**

This book is an introduction to American politics and government. Its objective is not to convince readers that a particular political position is "best." It does not celebrate the virtues of capitalism or socialism or the free market or a planned economy. Nor does this book argue that taxes are too high or too low, abortion is right or wrong, social welfare policies are too generous or too stingy, or government is too big or too small. This book is not designed to create more liberals or conservatives or capitalists or socialists. Its task is to examine the American political system and to stimulate informed critical thinking about politics and government.

A/P World Wide

The two fundamental goals of this book are: (1) to explain why understanding politics and government is crucial to making one's way in our complex society, and (2) to clarify how the actions of politicians and the consequences of governmental decisions affect people's lives. The book highlights the importance of ideas and economic concerns in the resolution of political issues. Toward this end, most chapters contain one or more of the following special feature boxes: "Politics and Economics," "Politics and Ideas," and "Contemporary Controversies."

What Is Politics?

What exactly is politics? For many people the word evokes negative feelings. "It's just politics," people say when they don't like a decision that's been made or when a friend loses out on a job promotion. The very mention of the word often conjures up the picture of a smooth-talking "wheeler-dealer" who uses cash to influence votes, or a corrupt officeholder who exploits his or her position for financial gain. But politics is not all graft and kickbacks. Despite much of the current disillusionment with the political process, politics can be an honorable and noble profession. At its best it is a moral activity reconciling social and economic differences and constructing a way of governing society without chaos, tyranny, or undue violence.[1]

---

[1]Bernard Crick, *In Defense of Politics* (Chicago: University of Chicago Press, 1963), ch. 1.

The ancient Greek philosopher Aristotle once called politics the "master science." He did not mean that politics explained all the mysteries of human life and nature. Rather, Aristotle meant that politics provided the means by which a community of people with differing views and interests could strive for collective survival and advancement. The drama of the American Civil War illustrated the importance of politics as a means of resolving differences without resorting to violence. All societies inevitably have differences; the issue is how a society copes with those differences. In this sense, politics is better described as the "necessary science."

With over 280 million people, the American nation is diverse. Some people are white and some are African American. Some Americans were born in other countries, and some have an American ancestry that dates back centuries. Some are religious fundamentalists and others liberal humanists. Some are young, paying Social Security taxes, and some are old, receiving Social Security benefits. Some earn high incomes and others have little or no income at all. Some live in fashionable town houses or suburbs and others live in blighted inner cities or on declining farms. Some make their living in high-tech industries and others in traditional smokestack industries,

The point need not be belabored. America is a complex, multicultural society in which consensus is often difficult to achieve. Different groups want different things and have different values. Such differences are at the root of the political process. In its best-known and most straightforward definition, **politics** is the study of "who gets what, when, and how."[2]

politics

The process of peacefully reconciling social and economic differences.

Politics and Economics

Many of the conflicts that arise in a society—who has and who has not, who gives and who gets, who gains and who loses—are economic in their origins or their manifestations. Because money and material resources are limited, and because human wants and demands are almost limitless, the need to make choices about spending money and using scarce resources becomes inevitable. Many of government's decisions are economic in nature because they affect the production, distribution, and consumption of wealth.

Even though our national government spends nearly $2 trillion annually, it still does not have enough capital to satisfy all the demands and expectations placed on it. Every year the president and Congress wrestle over the budget. Should we increase the funding for the development of a missile defense system or spend more on Medicare coverage? Not all programs can be funded to the complete satisfaction of their supporters. Nor will everyone agree on who should provide the taxes to pay for them.

Politicians must make these choices under the pressure of people who clamor to advance their own interests. The elderly are likely to press for increases in Social

[2]Harold Lasswell, *Politics: Who Gets What, When, How* (New York: McGraw-Hill, 1936).

Security, while the young are more likely to be interested in higher student aid grants for college expenses. Steel- and autoworkers favor quotas on foreign imports. Farmers who depend on the export market fear such quotas because foreign governments might retaliate against our agricultural products. Of course, not everyone takes predictable positions on every issue, nor is everyone motivated entirely by economic self-interest. Some of the wealthy are willing to pay higher taxes to help the poor, and some of the poor oppose higher social welfare spending. But, in general, when economic or occupational consequences are at stake, most people press for programs that serve their self-interest. Politicians must resolve the resulting conflicts.

In the face of scarcity, this task is difficult. Not all people will be satisfied, and few, if any, will be satisfied completely. Politics produces decisions that are almost guaranteed to be imperfect. Although the American system leaves most decisions about economics to the marketplace, it has never considered economic liberty an absolute right. Nor has America practiced any pure form of **capitalism**, an economic system based on private ownership of property and free economic competition among individuals and businesses. Minimum wage laws, child labor laws, and environmental regulations are a few examples of government restrictions on the functioning of the marketplace. From the beginning of the nation, government has provided certain infrastructural services (schools, roads, hospitals) in order for capitalism to flourish. And, since President Franklin D. Roosevelt's New Deal in the 1930s, the government has provided benefits for the elderly, the poor, and the unemployed. The American experience, particularly at the outset of the twenty-first century, has been witness to a strong central government that complements, coexists with, and regulates an economy largely in private hands. In the United States, economic and political power have historically been divided. But the line is always fluid and often hotly contested.

The genius of the American political experience comes from our ability, with the notable exception of the Civil War, to compromise claims and resolve differences without wrenching the system apart. But as the country grows more complex and diverse, the challenge becomes more formidable.

Politics and Ideas

Money and its uses have a magnetic attraction. But even if the supply of money were infinite (which it clearly is not), conflict would still be present. The political system is continually buffeted by debates over issues in which money and economic goods may be involved, but in which they do not play a central role. Such debates focus on the question of which political ideas and values should be reflected in a nation's laws and political institutions. In other words, many political disputes are ideological in origin. **Ideology**, used interchangeably in this book with the term *political ideas*, refers to the kind of government people think they should have. Ideology may also include ideas about the economic system. The

capitalism

An economic system based on private ownership of property and free economic competition among individuals and businesses.

Ideology

A set of ideas concerning the proper political and economic system under which people should live.

prevailing political ideas have a lot to do with shaping the kind of life Americans enjoy, and ideological differences among Americans spark many political controversies.

For example, should abortion be allowed or banned? What pro-choice groups see as the constitutional right of women to control their own bodies, pro-life groups see as the murder of innocents. Other examples of disputes over values include debates about the rights of homosexuals; the necessity and morality of capital punishment; the censorship of pornography and obscenity; and the teaching of evolution and sex education in the public schools.

Opposition to the sums of money spent on nuclear weapons, therefore, comes not just from the people who are concerned about the costs of defense, but also from those who believe the use of such armaments to be immoral. Likewise, others call for increased government aid to the homeless because they believe providing such aid is the humane thing to do.

No amount of money can bring people together on these issues, which involve fundamentally different views about what is right and just. In these matters, as in economic issues, politicians must get people to settle for less than their ideal in this imperfect world. Politicians are the brokers of the claims we make and the values we insist on. Politics becomes the art of reaching compromises when none seem possible.

Why Government?

government

The political and administrative organization of a state, nation, or locality.

People often use the words politics and government interchangeably. Politics is a process, however, and **government** is the set of organizations within which much of that process takes place.

But why government? What is its purpose? No better answer to that question can be found than in the Preamble to the Constitution of the United States. In 1787, the framers summarized the answer in one sentence:

> *We the people of the United States, in Order to form a more perfect Union, establish justice, insure domestic Tranquility, provide for the common defense, promote the general Welfare, and secure the Blessings of Liberty to ourselves and our Posterity, do ordain and establish this CONSTITUTION for the United States of America.*

"To Establish Justice, Insure Domestic Tranquility, . . . and Secure the Blessings of Liberty"

Government is essential to civilization. Restraint and decency among people are necessary prerequisites of a civilized society. To government falls the task of trying to ensure such behaviors. "Taxes," Justice Oliver Wendell Holmes (1902–1932)* wrote, "are what we pay for civilized society."[3] The English philosopher Thomas Hobbes wrote that in the absence of "the sovereign" or government, life among individuals would be "solitary, poor, nasty, brutish, and short."

Sovereign power is essential for protecting people from one another, by force if necessary. If people attempt to kill one another or steal from one another or assault one another, government must intervene. If it does not, civilization is simply not possible. People could not enjoy the fundamental pleasures of life—a walk in the park, a baseball game, a concert—if their physical well-being were constantly threatened by others whose violent acts went unhindered or unpunished. Although anarchists would disagree, government is essential to human liberty.

Yet government cannot by itself guarantee civil behavior. Civilization is a precious and fragile state of human existence that must be continually buttressed by the supporting values and beliefs of individuals in a society. Hobbes saw civilization as a thin veneer, beneath which surged a boiling caldron of human impulses.

Even in contemporary society the veneer is occasionally pierced. When civil tensions reach a breaking point, as they did during the World Trade Organization (WTO) meetings in Seattle in December 1999, antisocial forms of behavior frequently emerge—vandalizing, looting, assaulting, or battering. These threats to civil behavior must be resisted, and it is government that does the resisting.

"To Provide for the Common Defense"

Government must also protect its citizens against threats from other societies or governments. National defense is among the most important and visible functions of government. National security is essential to a society's preservation. The common defense has a long history, as any recounting of the wars in which the nation has engaged over the last two centuries will suggest. One of the principal concerns of the framers of the Constitution in 1787 was the creation of a stronger national government that could grapple more easily with the external threats and dangers of an uncertain world.

People may debate whether the government spends enough or too much on defense. But few will deny that the national government must be capable of defending the nation. Any organization or group calling itself a government that does not have that capability may be a symbol or a wish, but it is not a government.

---

*Throughout this book, dates in parentheses following the names of presidents and justices of the Supreme Court indicate their years in office.
[3]*Campanio de Tobacos v. Collector*, 275 U.S. 87, 100 (1904).

"To Promote the General Welfare"

Government also exists to organize cooperative public efforts. Although some people believe in the adage "the government that governs least, governs best," few believe that government should do nothing. Throughout history government has subsidized railroads, constructed dams, protected the wilderness, provided for the needy, and built space shuttles. Such enterprises are **collective goods**, available for the benefit of all citizens, whether or not they paid taxes for them. These enterprises are generally too massive for private undertaking. They require a government that can tax and spend on a large scale.

The ideological debate over the size and scope of governmental enterprises has endured since the founding of our nation. Advocates of the positive state argue that government should play an active role in providing the goods, services, and conditions for a prosperous and equitable society. Adherents of the **minimalist state** argue that government is too inefficient and coercive and should be restricted to producing only goods that individuals themselves cannot provide.

collective goods

Something of value that, by its nature, can be made available only to everybody or not to anyone at all.

minimalist state

A government that restricts its activities to providing only goods that the free market cannot produce.

What Is Democracy?

It is a basic axiom of American society that a government cannot be accountable merely to itself. The legitimacy of government in America rests on the consent of the governed. The Preamble to the Constitution states, "We the people of the United States . . . do ordain and establish this Constitution." We live in a representative democracy, a system of government in which political authority is vested in the people. The underlying ideology of a representative democracy supposes that people are capable of controlling their own destiny, selecting their own leaders, and cooperating in creating a peaceful and wholesome society. Alexander Hamilton, a delegate from New York to the Constitutional Convention in 1787, thought the new American nation could answer "the important question whether societies . . . are really capable or not of establishing good government from reflection and choice, or whether they are forever destined to depend . . . on accident and force."[4]

Democratic Values and Goals

democracy

A system of government based on majority rule, protection of minority and individual rights, and the equality of all citizens before the law.

What makes a government democratic? **Democracy** requires a system of government based on four precepts:

1. *Majority rule* expressed in free, periodic elections
2. Full protection of *minority rights* against an irrational or tyrannical majority

---

[4]*Federalist,* No. 1.

3. Protection of *individual rights* to freedom of speech, press, religion, petition, and assembly
4. *Equality* before the law for all citizens, regardless of race, creed, color, gender, or national origin

The four objectives can be reached in different ways. Governments can vary in form and still be labeled democratic. In the United States, the head of state and the head of government are combined in one president, elected by the people. In other lands these roles may be vested in two people.

These four objectives are, to a degree, in conflict with one another. The achievement of one can entail limits on another. Minority rights limit the kinds of laws majorities in Congress or in the state legislatures may pass. Being in control of government in the United States does not give a majority unlimited power. If, for example, the Republicans lose an election to the Democrats, the latter have no authority to seize the property of the former or to say that Republicans no longer have the right to vote. Nor can members of a majority silence their critics (as much as they might like to) simply because they won an election.

Likewise, the command of equality before the law places limits on what a majority may do. Democratic governments may not design election laws so that some people have more votes than others. But the rule that everyone's vote counts equally does not guarantee everyone the same influence in public affairs. Citizens with money to contribute to the campaigns of certain candidates often have more influence than those who have less or who choose not to contribute. Equality before the law is often difficult to achieve in the face of economic inequality. For example, wealthier school districts often provide a better education than poor districts. Educational opportunities relate to one's income potential and full development as an informed citizen.

Yet, efforts to achieve equality may involve restraints on individual liberty. Laws banning certain forms of racial and gender discrimination, thus ensuring equal treatment for employees in the workplace, decrease the liberty of employers to hire and fire whomever they please. In turn, the protection of certain liberties may result in economic inequalities. For example, the liberty to keep one's property and earnings (subject, of course, to taxation) may result in vast disparities in wealth and income.

constitutionalism
The belief in limiting government power by a written charter.

So, democracy American-style is not only, in Lincoln's immortal words, "government of the people, by the people, for the people." As we shall see in Chapter 1, American democracy also involves **constitutionalism**—the principle of limiting governmental power by a written charter. Our Constitution restricts the power of the state. It also establishes the basic idea that no official, no matter how high, is above the law. This point is reaffirmed on Inauguration Day each time a president promises to "preserve, protect, and defend the Constitution of the United States."

Making Democracy Work

For a democracy to function effectively, the people and their leaders must be willing to accept compromise and the notion that no one group will get all it desires. They must also accept democratic values and goals such as majority rule and minority rights. For democracy to work, the public must support the process by which agreement is reached. As one political scientist described it, "The American way is by compromise in little bits, by persuasion, by much talk and little bitterness."[5]

Through the avenues of open debate and free elections, those who lose a political battle generally get another opportunity. Minority factions in a democracy are more likely to accept defeat today if they know the way is open for them to become a majority tomorrow.

Why Do Politics and Government Matter?

Although Americans have had political institutions since colonial days, the nature of government in the United States has undergone radical change. Government at all levels—national, state, and local, but especially the national government—plays a much larger role in the life of the average citizen than it did 210 years ago during President Washington's administration, or even 140 years ago during President Lincoln's time.

Today, the national government pervades society, the economy, and the lives of its citizens. Its actions affect people all over the globe. Its $2 trillion budget creates work for over 2.7 million federal employees. Governmental involvement is pervasive, regulating products from prescription drugs to toys. It insures banks, protects the air and drinking water, and warns against cigarette smoking.

With so broad a reach, the national government dwarfs every other organization in American society, including huge corporations like Exxon and IBM. Everyone who makes money must send some portion of it to the government in the form of taxes. In short, few people can get through a single day without being touched by the actions of the national government. These actions result from the process called politics. As the chapters that follow show, politics pervades American society, economy, and culture.

---

[5]Frank Tannenbaum, "On Certain Characteristics of American Democracy," *Political Science Quarterly* 60 (1945): 350.

SUMMARY

1. Politics is about the resolution of conflict in society. Conflicts frequently arise over resource allocation and value preferences. Politicians, at their best, find compromises among these issues where none seem available.

2. Government is essential to a civilized society. Its tasks are to ensure a peaceful society, to provide for the national defense, to secure basic freedoms, and to undertake cooperative enterprises for the general welfare.

3. American democracy provides for a government based on the consent of the governed, the protection of individual rights, and the equality of rights before the law. The Constitution, the basic charter of our government, preserves the principle of government under law.

4. In contemporary America, the tasks of government are extensive and varied. The national government spends nearly $2 trillion dollars per year, and its activities pervade society. All Americans are directly affected by the policies and choices of government.

KEY TERMS

politics (2)

capitalism (3)

ideology (3)

government (4)

collective goods (6)

minimalist state (6)

democracy (6)

constitutionalism (7)

READINGS FOR FURTHER STUDY

Two classic discussions of politics can be found in Harold Lasswell, *Politics: Who Gets What, When, How* (New York: McGraw-Hill, 1936), and Bernard Crick, *In Defense of Politics* (Chicago: University of Chicago Press, 1963).

Richard Hofstadter, *The American Political Tradition* (New York: Vintage Books, 1954), remains a landmark study in American political history.

A searching examination of politics in theory and practice can be found in Samuel P. Huntington, *American Politics: The Promise of Disharmony* (Cambridge, MA: Harvard University Press, 1989).

CHAPTER 1

The Constitution of the United States

A/P World Wide

Chapter Objectives

The politics of a nation is given a special cast by the kind of government it has as well as by the values of its citizens. This country is no exception. American politics has been shaped mightily by the Constitution and the institutions this document summoned into being. This chapter reviews the purposes of a constitution and traces the origins of ours from the Revolutionary War and the first experiment with a national government under the Articles of Confederation. Attention to the Philadelphia Convention of 1787 sheds light on what the framers of the Constitution wanted to avoid, as well as what they wanted to achieve. Did they want to establish a democracy? What was the significance of dividing governmental authority among legislative, executive, and judicial branches? What is the unique relationship between the Supreme Court and the Constitution? How can a piece of parchment from the eighteenth century fit American needs at the dawn of the twenty-first century? Exploring such questions is essential to understanding American government today, particularly when one considers that the Constitution of the United States is the oldest written national charter still in force.

What Is a Constitution?

constitutionalism

The belief in limiting government by a written charter.

"What is a constitution?" asked Supreme Court Justice William Paterson (1793–1806) two centuries ago. "It is," he answered, "the form of government, delineated by the mighty hand of the people, in which certain first principles of fundamental laws are established." Like Paterson and his contemporaries, most Americans embrace **constitutionalism**: the belief in limiting governmental power by a written charter. This makes a constitution a very special document.

11

Constitutionalism

Constitutionalism has long been important in American politics. Each of the 50 states has a constitution. In January 2001, President George W. Bush (2001–   ), like all his predecessors back to George Washington (1789–1797), took an oath to "preserve, protect, and defend" the Constitution. Constitutionalism has also been contagious. Almost every country on earth has a constitution, but constitutions take different forms in different lands. Most, like the United States Constitution, are single documents, usually with amendments. A few, like the British Constitution, are made up of a series of documents and scattered major acts of Parliament (the British lawmaking body) that time and custom have endowed with paramount authority. The major difference between constitutionalism American-style and constitutionalism British-style is that the British Constitution can be changed by an act of Parliament. As described later in this chapter, the American Constitution can be formally altered only by an elaborate amendment procedure that includes the states, and not by Congress alone.

American-style or British-style, a constitution is more than pieces of paper. It is a living thing that embodies much more than mere words can convey — it embodies intangibles that enable it to work and to survive. Moreover, it provides clues to the political ideas that are dominant in a nation. The United States Constitution, for example, includes a cluster of values in its Preamble: "to form a more perfect *Union*, establish *Justice*, insure domestic *Tranquility*, provide for the common *defense*, promote the general *Welfare*, and secure the Blessings of *Liberty*" [italics added].

Constitutional Functions

Constitutions matter because of what they do (or do not do) and what they are. First, a constitution *outlines the organization of government*. The outline may be long or short, detailed or sketchy, but it answers key questions about the design of a government. Are executive duties performed by a monarch, prime minister, president, or ruling committee? Who makes the laws? A constitution will probably not answer all the structural questions about a political system. The American Constitution, for instance, makes no mention of political parties; yet a picture of American politics without them would be woefully incomplete. Thus, knowledge of a constitution may be a good starting place for a student of politics, but it is hardly the finishing point.

Second, a constitution *grants power*. Governments exist to do things, and under the idea of constitutionalism, governments need authority to act. For example, Article I of the Constitution (reprinted in the appendix) contains a long list of topics on which Congress may legislate, from punishing counterfeiters and regulating commerce "among the several States" to declaring war.

Grants of power imply limits on power. This is the principle of constitutional government in America: Rulers are bound by the ruled to the terms of a written charter. Thus, a constitution can also be *a mainstay of rights*. Constitutions commonly include a bill of rights or a declaration of personal freedoms that lists some of the things that governments may not do and proclaims certain liberties to be so valued that a society enshrines them in fundamental law.

Finally, a constitution may serve as a *symbol of the nation*, a repository of political values. When this happens, a constitution becomes more than the sum of its parts. More than a document that organizes, authorizes, and limits, it becomes an object of veneration. Americans have probably carried constitution veneration further than people of any other nation. Such emphasis on the Constitution has had an impact on the political system that can hardly be exaggerated. Frequently, people debate policy questions not just in terms of whether something is good or bad, wise or foolish, but whether it is *constitutional*. Debate may rage over the meaning of the Constitution, but contending forces accept the document as the fundamental law of the land. One group might argue that the Constitution bans state-sponsored prayer in public schools, for example, while another might argue just as vehemently that the Constitution permits it.

The Road to Nationhood

American government does not begin with the Constitution. Prior to 1787, there were many years of British rule, followed by the turbulence of revolution, and an experiment with national government under the Articles of Confederation.

The Declaration of Independence: The Idea of Consent

At least 13 years before the revolution, British leaders in London attempted to bring the American colonies under more direct control. Among other things, they wanted the colonials to pay a larger share of defense expenses. This policy, however, ran head on into colonial self-interest, revolutionary ideas, and a feeling of a new identity—an American identity as opposed to a purely British one. A series of events between 1763 and 1776 encouraged organized resistance to British authority and culminated in independence. Politics and reasoned debate within the British Empire soon gave way to armed revolt against it. Near the end of this period, colonial political leaders, meeting as the Second Continental Congress, considered a resolution moved by Richard Henry Lee of Virginia on June 7, 1776: "Resolved, that these United Colonies are, and of right ought to be, free and independent states." A declaration embodying the spirit of Lee's resolution and largely reflecting Thomas Jefferson's handiwork soon emerged from committee. Twelve states (New York abstaining) accepted it on July 2, with approval by all 13 coming on July 4.

A facsimile of the Declaration of Independence surrounded with medallions of seals of the thirteen original colonies. *(Library of Congress)*

At one level, the Declaration of Independence (reprinted in the appendix) itemized and publicized the colonists' grievances against British rule, personified in King George III. The revolutionists felt obliged to justify what they had done. Reprinted in newspapers up and down the land, the revolutionists hope that the document might, with luck, rally support at home and abroad to the cause of independence, especially for the military conflict under way. There was, after all, no unanimity within the colonies in 1776 on the wisdom of declaring independence. Loyalists were an active and hostile minority. Even among those who favored the break with England, some opposed fighting a war. Others were plainly indifferent.

In its goal of making the cause seem just and worth great sacrifice, the Declaration at another level said much about political thinking at the time. The authors of the Declaration were steeped in the thinking of English and Scottish natural rights philosophers, such as John Locke, who were trying to find a new source of legitimacy for political authority. Formerly, justification of authority stemmed from the belief that governments were ordained by God. Consequently, rulers governed on the basis of a covenant with the Deity, which implied limits to a power, or on the basis of "divine right," which did not. If government was to have a secular basis, however, rulers could govern only by consent—not as an agent of God but as an agent of the people.

American leaders were also aware of precedents for rebellion in British history. Tensions between the Crown and Parliament had climaxed in the Glorious Revolution of 1688, which secured the supremacy of Parliament over the monarchy. They knew also of the series of political battles large and small over the centuries that had won particular rights for English subjects. They were familiar with the writings of the seventeenth-century English jurist Sir Edward Coke (whose name rhymes with *look*), who maintained that even actions of Parliament had to conform to "common right and reason" as embodied in the law of the land. Ironically, Coke's ideas eventually took root in America but not in England.

The Declaration of Independence drew heavily on these traditions. At least four themes emerge from its text. First, *humankind shares an equality*. All persons possess certain rights by virtue of their humanity. The Declaration called them "unalienable rights" and mentioned three specifically: "Life, Liberty, and the Pursuit of Happiness." These rights were bestowed by the Creator and were "self-evident."

Second, *government is the creation and servant of the people*. It is an institution deliberately brought into being to protect the rights that all naturally possess. It maintains its authority by consent of the governed. When government is destructive of the rights it exists to protect, citizens have a duty to revolt when less drastic attempts at reform fail. Citizens would then replace a bad government with a good one.

Third, *the rights that all intrinsically possess constitute a higher law binding government*. Constitutions, statutes, and policies must be in conformity with this higher law. That is, they must promote the ends that government was created to advance. Natural rights would become civil rights.

Fourth, *governments are bound by their own laws*. These laws must be in conformity with the higher law. No officer of government is above the law. To make this point, the authors of the Declaration detailed violations of English law by the king in a list that consumes more than half the text.

By eighteenth-century standards, the Declaration of Independence advanced objectives that were far removed from reality. Some newspapers of 1776 reprinted the

The signing of the Declaration of Independence, by John Trumbull. *(Library of Congress)*

Declaration alongside advertisements for slaves. Moreover, as a statement of American ideology, the Declaration's objectives remain unattained even today.

The Articles of Confederation: The Idea of Compact

If the Declaration of Independence proclaimed separation from England, it did little to knit the former colonies into a nation. Central political control disappeared in 1776. Something would now have to take its place for successful execution of the war and for development of the nation once liberty was won. Only eight days after adoption of the Declaration of Independence, a committee of Congress chaired by John Dickinson placed before the entire body a plan of union. The **Articles of Confederation** became the first American national constitution. Meeting in York, Pennsylvania, a safe distance from the British who had occupied Philadelphia, Congress approved Dickinson's Articles in amended form in November 1777 and referred them to the states for approval. All states, save one, gave assent by May 1779, with Maryland holding out until March 1781 because of a land dispute.

The main provisions of the Articles of Confederation are summarized in Table 1.1. Several features distinguished the document. First, *the Articles preserved state autonomy*. The document read more like a treaty between nations than a device to link component states. Describing the compact as "a firm league of friendship," the Articles stated clearly that "each state retains its sovereignty, freedom and independence, and every power, jurisdiction and right which is not by this Confederation expressly delegated to the United States in Congress assembled." The word *confederation* accurately described the arrangement: It was a loose union of separate states.

Second, *the Articles guaranteed equal representation for the states*. Congress represented the states, not the people. Whereas a state's delegation could range in size from two to seven, each state had one vote. The delegates were to be appointed "in such manner as the legislature of each state shall direct," and the states reserved the right to recall and replace their delegates at any time.

Third, *the Articles granted the central government only a few important powers*. The central government was given control over foreign affairs and military policy, but it was denied taxing power completely, as well as the authority to regulate most trade. Revenues instead would be supplied by the states. If a state failed to make its proper payment, the Articles offered no remedy. Furthermore, most appropriations and laws of any significance required the affirmative vote of nine states.

Fourth, *the Articles provided for no separate executive branch and no national courts*. The rights of citizens lay in the hands of state courts. Congress was supposed to be the arbiter of last resort in disputes between states. The few executive duties permitted under the Articles were performed by officers appointed by Congress.

Articles of Confederation

The first plan of the national government for the 13 American states, which was replaced by the Constitution. Under the Articles, the states retained most political power.

TABLE 1.1

An Overview of the Articles of Confederation

The Articles of Confederation provided for the dominance of the states in the political system and granted only a few powers to Congress.

Article I	Name of the confederacy: the United States of America
Article II	Guarantee of the powers of the member states, except where the states expressly delegated powers to Congress
Article III	Purposes of the confederation; defense and protection of the liberties and welfare of the states
Article IV	As they traveled from state to state, citizens of the several states were to enjoy the privileges each state accord its own citizens; freedom of trade and travel between states
Article V	Selection by state legislatures of delegates to Congress; voting by states in Congress
Article VI	States prohibited from engaging in separate foreign and military policies or using duties to interfere with treaties; recognition that each state would maintain a militia and a naval force
Article VII	Appointment by state legislatures of all militia officers of or under the rank of colonel
Article VIII	National expenses to be paid by states to Congress, in proportion to the value of the land in each state; states retained sole power to tax citizens
Article IX	Sole power to make peace and war placed in Congress; restrictions on treaty-making power; Congress designated the "last resort" in all disputes between states: procedures spelled out for settling such disputes; power to establish a postal system and to regulate the value of money issued by state and central governments given to Congress; provision made for an executive committee of Congress called a "Committee of the States" to manage the government; stipulation that most major pieces of legislation would require the affirmative vote of nine states
Article X	Committee of the States authorized to act for Congress when Congress was not in session
Article XI	Provision for Canada to join the United States
Article XII	Debts previously incurred by Congress deemed to be obligations of the government under the Articles of Confederation
Article XIII	Obligation of each state to abide by the provisions of the Articles of Confederation and all acts of Congress; amendment by consent of the legislatures of every state

Fifth, *the Articles made amendment almost impossible.* Changes in the terms of the Articles needed approval not only of Congress but of the "legislatures of every state." For example, a single state could block any realignment of the balance the

Articles struck between central direction and local autonomy. The states seemed destined to hold the dominant position for a long time to come.

The Making of the Constitution

Defects in the Articles of Confederation soon became apparent. Citizens who wanted change built their case on either of two deficiencies, and often on both. First was *an absence of sufficient power in the central government*. Absence of national taxation meant that Congress was hard-pressed to carry out even the limited responsibilities it had, such as national defense. Absence of control over interstate commerce meant trade wars between the states, with some states prohibitively taxing imports from others. Congress could do little to promote a healthy economic environment. Absence of power to compel obedience by the states meant that foreign countries had no assurance that American states would comply with treaties agreed to by the national government.

The second deficiency often mentioned was *the presence of too much power in the hands of the state governments*. Local majorities, unchecked by national power, could infringe on an individual's property rights. Of particular concern were the "cheap money" parties that had been victorious in some of the states. The decade of the 1780s was generally one of economic depression. In the wake of the ravages of war and the loss of British markets, times were hard. In response, state legislatures suspended debts or provided for payment of debts in kind, not cash. Added to this was the circulation of different currencies issued by the states, even though the national government was supposed to have the monetary power. Printing additional money drove down its value, aiding debtors and hurting creditors. The economic picture was unsettled at best, chaotic at worst.

Prelude to Philadelphia

A revolt of farmers led by Daniel Shays in Massachusetts in 1786–1787, known as **Shays's Rebellion**, only heightened the concerns over the Articles of Confederation. When farmers in the Berkshire Hills failed to get the debt relief they had demanded from the legislatures, they closed local courts and forced the state supreme court at Springfield to adjourn before they were finally routed by a state military contingent of 4,400 men. Although it was a military failure, the rebellion demonstrated that the central government under the Articles was powerless to protect the nation from domestic violence.

In September 1786, on the eve of Shays's Rebellion, delegates from five states attended the **Annapolis Convention** in Maryland to consider suggestions for improving commercial relations among the states. Alexander Hamilton was a delegate from New York. Along with Virginia's James Madison, Hamilton persuaded the gathering to adopt a resolution calling for a convention of all the states in Philadelphia the following May to "render the Constitution of the Federal Government adequate to the exigencies of the Union." In

Shays's Rebellion

Revolt by Massachusetts farmers in 1786–1787 over the lack of economic relief. The rebellion led many to believe that a stronger central government was necessary.

Annapolis Convention

A meeting of delegates from five states in Annapolis, Maryland, in 1786 to consider a common policy for trade among the American states. It resulted in a recommendation for a constitutional convention the following year.

Northwest Ordinance

Major statute enacted by Congress in 1787 under the Articles of Confederation providing for the development and government of lands west of Pennsylvania.

http://www.yale.edu /lawweb/avalon/art conf.htm

Why did the founders call for a constitutional convention? See for yourself by comparing the Constitution printed at the back of your book to this web version of the Articles of Confederation.

February 1787, Congress authorized the convention. All the states except Rhode Island selected delegates, but limited them to considering amendments to the Articles of Confederation.

Even though the Constitution soon replaced the Articles, the nation's first experiment with central government was not a complete failure. In one of its last actions, the Congress established by the Articles enacted the **Northwest Ordinance** in June 1787. This statute provided for the government and future statehood of the lands west of Pennsylvania, laid the basis for a system of public education, and banned slavery in that territory.

James Madison, the fourth president of the United States. *(Library of Congress)*

The Philadelphia Convention

To appreciate fully what happened in Philadelphia in 1787, one must visualize America two centuries ago. Doing so may not be easy. Today our nation is a global power—economically, militarily, and politically—with a population exceeding 280 million people in 50 states stretching from the Atlantic into the Pacific.

By contrast, the America of 1787 was a sparsely settled, weakly defended, and internationally isolated nation of 13 coastal states with a combined population of under 4 million. Philadelphia boasted a population of 30,000, making it the largest city in the land. Virginia and Massachusetts were the most populous states, with 747,000 and 473,000 inhabitants, respectively. Rhode Island and Delaware were the smallest, with populations of only 68,000 and 59,000, respectively. Three other states had fewer than 200,000 inhabitants. The slave population, found mostly in the states from Maryland southward, numbered 670,000, or about 17 percent of the total.

It was in this context that the Philadelphia Convention assembled. By modern standards, the convention was not a large body: the legislatures of 12 states had selected 74 delegates, and 55 eventually took their seats. Of these, fewer than a dozen did most of the work. Quality amply compensated for numbers, however. Probably no other American political gathering has matched the convention in talent and intellect.

Who were the framers? Twenty-nine were college graduates, and the remaining 26 included notables such as George Washington and Benjamin Franklin. The youngest delegate, Jonathan Dayton of New Jersey, was 26. Franklin, of Pennsylvania, was the oldest, at 81. Thirty-four were lawyers; others were farmers and merchants. Some names were prominent by their absence. Thomas Jefferson was abroad. John Jay of New York was not chosen, even though he had been foreign affairs secretary for the Articles Congress. Patrick Henry of Virginia was chosen but declined because he "smelt a Rat." Richard Henry Lee, also of Virginia, and Samuel Adams of Massachusetts were likewise suspicious of what might happen and stayed away. Ten delegates were also members of the Articles Congress. Eight delegates had signed the Declaration of Independence, and the signatures of six appeared on the Articles of Confederation. But on balance, this was not a reassembling of the generation that had set the revolution in motion. Rather, the delegates came from a pool of men who were fast gaining a wealth of practical experience in the political life of the young nation. Most were also committed to making changes in the Articles of Confederation—otherwise they would not have sacrificed the time and effort to attend.

May 14, 1787, was the appointed day for meeting, but the ten delegates who convened that day at the Pennsylvania statehouse (now called Independence Hall) could do nothing until more arrived. Not only did the convention need its quorum of states, but each state delegation also needed a quorum because voting would be by state. Finally, on May 25 the Philadelphia Convention began its work. From then until September 17 the delegates conferred almost without pause, formally at the statehouse and informally at the City and Indian Queen taverns a short walk away.

In one of their first actions the delegates adopted a rule of secrecy. The delegates even closed the windows during the steamy Philadelphia summer to discourage eavesdroppers. Without secrecy, it is doubtful whether the group could have succeeded. With secrecy came the freedom to maneuver, explore, and compromise. Because no verbatim stenographic account was made at the time, knowledge of the proceedings has had to be recreated piece by piece over the years.[1] The official journal of the convention was not made public until 1818. James Madison's notes on the proceedings, which are the most extensive account of what occurred, were not published until 1840.

Virginia Plan

The first plan of union proposed at the Constitutional Convention in 1787; it called for a strong central government.

New Jersey Plan

Introduced in the Constitutional Convention in opposition to the Virginia Plan; it emphasized the dominance of the states.

On May 29 the Virginia delegation, led by Governor Edmund Randolph, seized the high ground for the discussion to follow. His 15 resolutions, largely Madison's handiwork, made it increasingly evident that replacement, not tinkering, awaited the Articles of Confederation. Called the **Virginia Plan** and depicted in Figure 1.1, the resolutions proposed a substantially stronger national government and a Congress based on numerical representation. This plan generated a counterproposal put forward by William Paterson of New Jersey. Known as the **New Jersey Plan** (see Figure 1.1), it called for only modest change in the Articles of Confederation, keeping the state governments dominant. What divided the delegates the most was the issue of representation, because in a legislature, representation translates into power. Would some states and interests have more votes than others in Congress? In late June and early July, the convention was deadlocked between delegates who favored representation in proportion to a state's pop-

[1]See Max Farrand, *The Records of the Federal Convention of 1787*, 4 vols. (New Haven, CT: Yale University Press, 1900).

FIGURE 1.1

The Virginia Plan, the New Jersey Plan, and the Constitution

In the form signed by the framers on September 17, 1787, the Constitution reflected some features of the Virginia and New Jersey plans. Other features of the two plans were discarded during the summer's debates. The Great Compromise settled the issue of representation, drawing from both plans.

VIRGINIA PLAN	NEW JERSEY PLAN
A two-house legislature, with numerical representation. Popularly elected lower house elects upper house.	A one-house legislature, with equal state representation.
Broad but undefined legislative power, with absolute veto over laws passed by state legislatures and taxing power.	Same legislative power as under Articles, plus power to levy some taxes and to regulate commerce.
Single executive elected by legislature for fixed term.	Plural executive, removable by legislature, on petition from majority of state governors.
National judiciary elected by the legislature.	Judiciary, appointed by executive to hear appeals on violations of national laws in state courts.
Council of Revision, composed of executive and judiciary, to review laws passed by national legislature.	A "supremacy clause" similar to that found in Article VI of present Constitution.

CONSTITUTION OF 1787

A two-house legislature, with numerical representation in popularly elected House and equal state representation in state-selected Senate.

Broad legislative power, including power to tax and to regulate commerce.

Single executive, chosen by electoral college.

National judiciary, appointed by president, confirmed by Senate.

Supremacy clause; no Council of Revision.

ulation and those who wanted to keep equality between the states. Without settling this matter, the convention could not proceed.

This division is sometimes seen as the less populous states versus the more populous ones (small against large). True, a state such as Delaware would lose voting strength in the national legislature if population became the basis for representation. But the divisions of opinion were not always based solely on state size. A majority of the New York delegation, for example, opposed numerical representation in either house because other states lay claim to extensive western lands with the potential for

Great Compromise

Agreement at the Constitutional Convention in 1787 to accept representation by population in the House and by states in the Senate. Sometimes called the Connecticut Compromise because it was arranged by the delegation from Connecticut.

three-fifths compromise

A temporary resolution to the controversy over slavery, this agreement allowed slaveholding states to count each slave as 3/5 of a person for purposes of congressional representation.

Federalists

Persons who advocated ratification of the Constitution in 1787 and 1788 and generally favored a strong central government. Also the name of the dominant political party during the administrations of Presidents George Washington and John Adams.

Antifederalists

Persons who opposed ratification of the Constitution in 1787 and 1788. In the first years of government under the Constitution, Antifederalists in Congress opposed policies such as a national bank associated with a strong central government.

significant population growth. Besides, the Virginia Plan meant a greatly reduced role *for states as states* in the Union. Local leaders viewed centralizing tendencies as a threat to their own influence, regardless of their state's population.

Credit for a breakthrough goes to Dr. William Samuel Johnson and Oliver Ellsworth, both delegates from Connecticut. Known as the **Great Compromise** or the Connecticut Compromise, their plan called for numerical representation in the lower house and equal state representation in the upper house. This compromise broke the deadlock, permitting the delegates to move along to other matters, and forms the basis of congressional representation today: by population in the House of Representatives, by states in the Senate.

There were other compromises as well. The most notorious was the **three-fifths compromise**, which permitted slave states to count each slave as three-fifths of a person, thus enhancing these states' representation in the House while denying slaves, who were legally classified as property, the right to vote. Moreover, the Constitution let each state decide who could vote in national as well as state elections. As a result, a majority of Americans (women and all slaves) were denied basic rights of political participation for years to come. Property qualifications that existed in some states for a time barred the poorest white males from the polling places as well.

Ratification

Formal signing of the Constitution took place on September 17, 1787—109 days after the convention first met. Thirty-nine names appear on the document. Three delegates (Elbridge Gerry of Massachusetts and George Mason and Edmund Randolph of Virginia) refused to sign. Others, such as New York's Robert Yates, had gone home early because the Constitution included too many changes.

Approval by the country was surely on the framers' minds. Just as the delegates had taken liberty with their instructions to revise the Articles of Confederation, they proposed to bypass the rule of legislative unanimity for amendment. Article VII of the Constitution stipulated in revolutionary fashion that the new government would go into effect when *conventions* in *nine* states gave their assent. On September 28, 1787, the Articles Congress resolved unanimously, though noncommittally, that the Constitution should be handed over to the state legislatures "to be submitted to a convention of Delegates chosen in each state by the people thereof." Ironically, approval by popularly elected conventions meant that ratification of the Constitution would be a more democratic process than adoption of either the Declaration of Independence or the Articles of Confederation.

Supporters of the proposed Constitution called themselves **Federalists** and dubbed the nonsupporters **Antifederalists**, thus scoring a tactical advantage by making it seem that opponents of ratification were against union altogether. Because ratification meant persuasion, both sides engaged in a great national debate in the months after the

Philadelphia Convention adjourned. Not since the eve of the revolution had there been such an outpouring of pamphlets and essays. Most prominent among the tracts was ***The Federalist***, a collection of 85 essays written by Alexander Hamilton, John Jay, and James Madison under the pen name Publius, that originally appeared between October 27, 1787, and August 15, 1788, in New York State newspapers. One of the most important expositions of American political theory, *The Federalist* achieved early recognition as an authoritative commentary on the Constitution.

Who were the Antifederalists? Most were not opposed to all change in the government. Some fought ratification because the Constitution was to become the supreme law of the land in an illegal manner, replacing the Articles of Confederation in violation of the Articles' own amendment procedure. For many, the Constitution was unacceptable because it would severely weaken state governments, leading eventually to a loss of local authority. Other opponents believed that individual liberty could be preserved only in "small republics," or states. If states were subordinated in the new government, it was only a matter of time before liberty would be lost, especially since the Constitution contained no bill of rights. As the governments closest to the people, states offered the best chance for self-government and so would promote, Antifederalists thought, a virtuous citizenry. Conversely, a distant government endangered not just popular rule but citizenship itself. Moreover, the Constitution seemed designed to promote a commercial empire. This prospect threatened the agrarian values many of the Antifederalists shared.

For a time, ratification by the requisite number of states was in doubt, causing John Quincy Adams to observe a half-century afterward that the Constitution "had been extorted from the grinding necessity of a reluctant nation."[2] Not until June 21, 1788, did the ninth state (New Hampshire) ratify. Practically, however, the new government could not have succeeded had the important states of Virginia and New York not signed on. These states ratified on June 25 and 26, respectively—the latter by the close vote of 30 to 27. Some states ratified only on the promise that a bill of rights would soon be added to the Constitution, which it was (see Chapter 3).

Meeting on September 13, 1788, the Articles Congress acknowledged ratification, set a date in February for electors to choose a president, and designated "the first Wednesday in March next . . . for commencing

John Quincy Adams, the sixth president of the United States. *(Library of Congress)*

The Federalist

A series of 85 essays written by Alexander Hamilton, John Jay, and James Madison and published in New York newspapers in 1787 and 1788 urging ratification of the Constitution.

---

[2]John Quincy Adams, *The Jubilee of the Constitution* (New York: Samuel Colman, 1839), p. 55.

TABLE 1.2

An Overview of the Constitution of 1787

In the form in which it left the hands of the framers in 1787, the Constitution stressed the powers of the national government and did not include a bill of rights.

Article I	Establishment of legislative departments; description of organizations; list of powers and restraints; election of legislators
Article II	Establishment of executive department; powers, duties, restraints; election of the president and vice-president
Article III	Establishment of judicial departments; jurisdiction of Supreme Court and other courts established by Congress; definition of treason; appointment of judges
Article IV	Relation of the states to the national government and to one another; guarantees of the states; provision for territories and statehood
Article V	Amendment of the Constitution; assurance of equal representation of the states in the Senate
Article VI	Guarantee of national debts; supremacy of the national constitution, laws, and treaties; obligation of national and state officials under the Constitution; no religious test for national office
Article VII	Ratification of the Constitution

proceedings under the said Constitution." The new House and Senate transacted their first business on April 2 and April 5, 1789, respectively, with George Washington's inauguration as president following on April 30. Legislation creating the Supreme Court and setting February 1, 1790, as the day of its first session was signed by Washington on September 24. Confirmation by the Senate of the first Supreme Court justices followed on September 26.

The Constitution is reprinted in the appendix. The main provisions of the Constitution, without amendments, are summarized in Table 1.2. Amendments, including the Bill of Rights, are summarized in Table 1.3.

Features of the Constitution

Several features, implicit or explicit in the document of 1787, plus its Bill of Rights, suggest why the Constitution was important for the framers. More important, these features help to explain how the Constitution shapes American government today.

Republicanism, Divided Powers, and Federalism

The framers deliberately chose a **republican** (or **representative**) **government** with divided powers. They feared the excesses of democracy, or pure majority rule, that

republican (or representative) government

Representative government wherein the representatives are elected by the people to make decisions in their place.

TABLE 1.3

Amendments to the Constitution by Subject

Since the Bill of Rights (Amendments 1–10) was added in 1791, only 17 formal changes have been made to the Constitution. Most have occurred in periods of reform and have affected the manner in which officials are elected and the operation and powers of the national government.

Individual Rights	I	(1791)	Free expression
	II	(1791)	Bearing arms
	III	(1791)	No quartering of troops
	IV	(1791)	Searches, seizures, and warrants
	V	(1791)	Criminal procedure and fair trial
	VI	(1791)	Criminal procedure and fair trial
	VII	(1791)	Jury trials in civil suits
	VIII	(1791)	No cruel and unusual punishment
	IX	(1791)	Recognition of rights not enumerated
	XIII	(1865)	Abolition of slavery
	XIV	(1868)	Restrictions on state interference with individual rights; equality under the law; also altered nation-state relations
Political Process	XII	(1804)	Separate voting by electors for president and vice-president
	XV	(1870)	Removal of race as criterion for voting
	XVII	(1913)	Popular election of U.S. senators
	XIX	(1920)	Removal of gender as criterion for voting
	XXIII	(1961)	Enfranchisement of District of Columbia in voting for president and vice-president
	XIV	(1964)	Abolition of poll tax in federal elections
	XVI	(1971)	National voting age of 18 in all elections
Nation-State Relations	X	(1804)	Powers of the states
	XI	(1798)	Restriction of jurisdiction of federal courts
Operation and Powers of National Government	XVI	(1913)	Income tax
	XX	(1933)	Shift of start of presidential term from March to January; presidential succession
	XXII	(1951)	Two-term presidency
	XXV	(1967)	Presidential disability and replacement of vice-president
	XXVI	(1992)	Limitation on timing of change in congressional salaries
Miscellaneous	XVII	(1919)	Prohibition of alcoholic beverages
	XXI	(1933)	Repeal of Eighteenth Amendment

they had seen in the politics of their own states. At the same time, recalling the Declaration's insistence on "the consent of the governed," they knew that government had to be generally responsive to the people if ratification was to occur and revolution to be avoided. So, the Constitution blended democratic and antidemocratic elements: popular election—voters, as qualified by their states, directly elected only the members of the House of Representatives; indirect popular election—state legislatures chose members of the Senate, while specially designated electors selected the president; and appointment—the president picked the national judiciary (with the approval of the Senate).

In addition, the Constitution placed limits on what government can do. Implicit in the idea of a written constitution is that a government does not have unlimited power. As described later in this chapter, courts in the United States have assumed the role of deciding what those limits are and when they have been crossed. The Bill of Rights contains some of those restrictions. Sections 9 and 10 of Article I contain others.

The Constitution also diffused and dispersed power. Clearly concerned with the necessity of strengthening government, the framers divided power even as they added it. They were aware of an old dilemma: How does one construct a government with sufficient strength without endangering individuals' freedom? Madison put it this way in *Federalist* No. 51: "In framing a government, . . . the greatest difficulty lies in this: you must first enable the government to control the governed; and in the next place oblige it to control itself." The solution, thought the framers, lay in design: dividing power both horizontally among the different parts of the national government and vertically between the national government and the states.

To be avoided at all costs was tyranny, which Madison defined as "the accumulation of all powers, legislative, executive, and judiciary, in the same hands, whether of one, a few, or many, and whether hereditary, self-appointed, or elective." This threat could take at least two forms: domination of the majority by a minority, or domination of a minority by the majority, with the latter running roughshod over the former in disregard of its rights. Ordinarily, the ballot box would give ample protection. The vote, after all, was the primary check on the rulers. But Madison saw the "necessity of auxiliary precautions."

Division of responsibilities at the national level among the three branches of government (Congress, president, and Supreme Court) would help but would not be enough. What was to keep one branch from grabbing all the power from the other two? Words on paper ("parchment barriers," Madison called them) would be inadequate, especially because experience had taught that the legislature might be too responsive to the popular will. The solution lay in juxtaposing power—"Contriving the interior structure of the government, as that its several constituent parts may, by their mutual rela-

http://lcweb2.loc .gov/const/fed query/html

Explore the classic defense of the U.S. Constitution by reading the searchable online version of the *Federalist Papers* at the above site.

tions, be the means of keeping each other in their proper places." Rather than counting on noble motives to ward off tyranny, the Constitution assumed the existence of less noble motives. "Ambition," wrote Madison, "must be made to counteract ambition."

checks and balances

The system of separate institutions sharing some powers that the Constitution mandates for the national government. The purpose is to keep power divided among the three branches: legislative, executive, and judicial.

This is the constitutional arrangement commonly called **checks and balances.** Power is checked and balanced because the separate institutions of the national government—legislative, executive, judicial—share some powers. As depicted in Figure 1.2, no one branch has exclusive dominion over its sphere of activity.

For example, a proposed law may pass both houses of Congress only to run headlong into a presidential veto, itself surmountable only by a two-thirds vote of each house. After scaling that obstacle, the law in question might well encounter a negative from the Supreme Court using its power of judicial review. Judicial review is not mentioned in the Constitution, but it soon joined the roster of Madison's "auxiliary precautions." Even the president's appointment and treaty-making powers require Senate cooperation. And although the president is designated commander-in-chief of the armed forces, Congress must declare war and appropriate money to finance the president's policies.

Securing liberty was also to be helped by federalism, the vertical division between national and state governments (explained in Chapter 2). The Constitution left the states with ample regulatory or police power—that is, control over the health, safety, and welfare of their citizens. As the second justice Harlan (1955–1971) argued many years later, "We are accustomed to speak of the Bill of Rights and the Fourteenth Amendment as the principal guarantees of personal liberty. Yet it would surely be shallow not to recognize that the structure of our political system accounts no less for the free society we have." Harlan echoed Alexander Hamilton's observation in *Federalist* No. 84 that the Constitution, even without amendments, "is itself, in every rational sense, and to every useful purpose, a Bill of Rights."

Coupled with divided power at the top, federalism was useful in guarding against majority tyranny. Some of the framers worried about "factions"—today we would call them tightly knit political parties or interest groups. The most productive source of factions, Madison acknowledged in *Federalist* No. 10, was economic inequality—rich versus poor, creditors versus debtors, and so forth. The Constitution was designed in part to limit the influence of factions. Minority factions could be outvoted. Majority factions would, with luck, exhaust themselves trying to fuse together what the Constitution had diffused. The Constitution would ultimately not prevent the majority from attaining its objectives, but the effort would have to be both long and hard. Short of this, the Constitution would work to insulate national policy from political fads that might capture majority sentiment in one or two states. The framers were especially concerned about movements like Shays's Rebellion that threatened the rights of political minorities.

Power was divided horizontally and vertically in order to check human ambition run amok. Measured by this standard, the Constitution has been largely successful, yet the

FIGURE 1.2

The Constitutional System of Checks and Balances

The framers designed the Constitution not just to divide governmental function among three branches, but to create a tension among the branches by allowing each one influence over the other two. American constitutional government means not just a separation of powers but separate institutions sharing certain powers. The objective was to safeguard liberty by preventing a concentration of power.

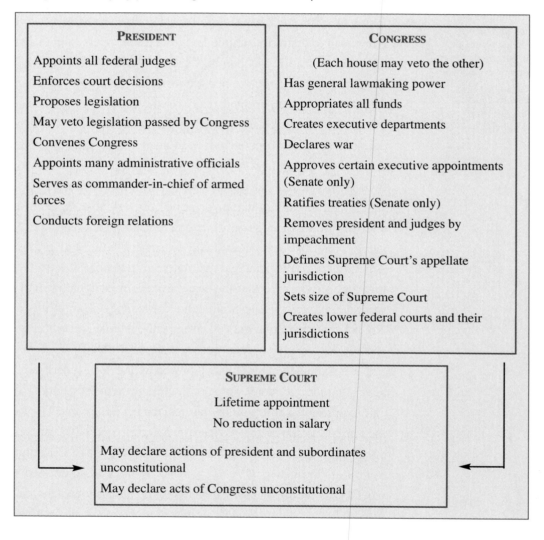

scheme is by no means foolproof. The vaccination against tyranny has had some unpleasant side effects. First, the arrangements that held off the threats to the nation that Madison feared have sometimes made dealing with threats to individual liberty in the states more difficult. As Chapter 3 describes, once the central government took a stand against continued racial and gender discrimination, fragmented powers and federalism hindered steps to alleviate existing wrongs. All checks, primary and auxiliary, failed to work for a long time.

Second, the constitutional legacy of the framers has sometimes made the task of governing a nation more than 200 years later a difficult one. Separate national institutions and federalism have contributed to weak political parties, all of which combine to tax the skills of any leader, including the president, who calls for concerted action. Power has to be amassed, it seems sometimes, in spite of the Constitution. The advantage tends to lie with those who would delay, deflect, or derail. The framers institutionalized tension within the government. Yet on balance, the benefits of fragmented power have been worth the costs. American constitutional government is now in its third century.

A Single and Independent Executive

Although few doubted that the Philadelphia Convention would make provision for a legislature, controversy converged on issues such as representation and manner of selection for the legislature. What is perhaps astonishing about the Constitution is that it provided for a single *and* independently elected executive. Neither the Virginia Plan nor the New Jersey Plan offered both, as Figure 1.1 illustrates. After 1776, executive authority was understandably suspect; determining the kind of executive branch to implement in the new government was thus a topic of debate throughout the summer. State constitutions of the day typically enhanced legislative power and kept governors on a short leash. Some delegates to the Philadelphia Convention favored a plural executive or a single executive responsible to a council or to Congress.

The framers in Philadelphia finally reached a compromise about the selection of a president the end of the convention. Their choice represented a compromise. Their creation of the electoral college, discussed in Chapter 8, meant that the delegates could avoid direct election by the people (a plan that allowed for too much democracy), election by Congress (a plan that would make the executive subservient to the legislature), and election by state legislatures (a plan that might make the executive a puppet of state governments). By allowing for selection of a single individual by specially chosen electors, the Constitution provided independence, strength, and, eventually, a popular base of power for the president.

Adaptability

The Constitution today is a living charter that plays a significant role in government. Yet the Constitution was written by eighteenth-century men, with eighteenth-century educations, for an obscure and fragile eighteenth-century nation. Formal amendment of the document, a process that we will discuss shortly, has taken place only 17 times since ratification of the Bill of Rights in 1791. How, then, does a document written in a by-gone era by a fledgling nation fit the needs of a world power at the outset of the twenty-first century? The answer is that the Constitution is adaptable. It is adaptable both because of

Contemporary Controversies
America Attacked

President Bush with firefighter while standing in front of the World Trade Center debris on Friday, September 14, 2001. *(AP Wide World)*

On September 11, 2001 America changed. The most violent single foreign attack on American soil in history left over 5,000 people dead and many more injured. Four domestic passenger planes took off from the east coast to begin cross-country flights, but were hijacked shortly after takeoff by terrorists wielding knives. The hijackers were believed to be connected to al Qaeda, an international terror organization headed by Osama bin Laden, a Saudi national being harbored in Afghanistan. Two of the planes crashed into New York's World Trade Center, completely destroying one of the tallest buildings in the world and an important symbol of global capitalism. Another plane crashed into the Pentagon, the nation's defense headquarters, and a fourth (possibly headed to Washington, D.C.) crashed in rural Pennsylvania. In one day the mood of the nation changed from one of security and confidence to one of grief, shock, fear, and anger.

Our government changed as well. Nearly every aspect of American government addressed in the pages of this textbook felt the shock of September 11th. The Constitution's war making powers were given new meaning as America embarked on a military response that President George W. Bush (2001–) declared a "war on terrorism" (Chapter 1). The emergency relief effort that followed the attacks raised federalism questions, as it required coordination of local, state, and national agencies (Chapter 2). The protection of civil rights and liberties became a concern as government officials

particular characteristics built into it, and because of the way the document has been regarded by successive generations.

The first factor in its adaptability is *brevity*. Including all 27 amendments, the Constitution of the United States contains fewer than 6,000 words, resulting in a shortage of detail and an absence of reference to many things the framers could conceivably have included. (By contrast, the constitutions of the 50 states today tend to be long and detailed; many are also short-lived.) Tactically, brevity was wise in the face of the ratifica-

America Attacked, *continued*

weighed the tradeoff between restricting freedom—through more invasive airport searches, for example—and providing Americans with a greater sense of security (Chapter 3). Political ideologies temporarily lost some significance when congressional leaders—liberal and conservative—passed nearly unanimous resolutions condemning the terrorist attacks and stating a need for armed response (Chapter 4). Media outlets responded by changing programming to increase coverage of the ongoing and developing acts of terror and American responses (Chapter 6). Established interest groups such as the American Red Cross and newly created organizations such as America's Fund for Afghan Children collected millions of dollars from concerned Americans who wanted to show their support for victims and families (Chapter 7).

The institutions of American government responded to change as well. On November 6, 2001, less than two months after the first attacks, New York City went to the polls and elected new mayor Michael Bloomberg. Bloomberg replaced the retiring incumbent Rudolph Giuliani, who earned acclaim for his leadership during the crisis (Chapter 8). Congress responded by drafting 123 pieces of emergency appropriation and anti-terrorism legislation in the first

seven weeks following September 11th; many of these bills and resolutions, including the Patriot Act, were quickly signed into law (Chapter 9). The recently elected and relatively untested president George W. Bush had perhaps the toughest job of all—reassuring a nation while pursuing an internationally supported military response (Chapter 10). Part of the president's response involved expanding the bureaucracy; on September 20th, President Bush created the Office of Homeland Security and named Pennsylvania Governor Tom Ridge as its head (Chapter 11). The U.S. court system provided the setting for several trials of individuals charged as accomplices or conspirators in terrorist activity (Chapter 12). Finally, the nation's budget, which had started the year with a strong economy, quickly found its surpluses turning to deficits as supplemental appropriations were approved to help pay for recovery and response efforts (Chapter 14).

Indeed, just as no American was left untouched by the events of September 11, no aspect of American government emerged unscathed either. How have these events affected you, and how have they affected your interactions with the American government? What further changes do you expect in the future?

---

tion debate—the less said, the less to arouse opposition. Later generations would have to flesh out the full potential of the document through interpretation and practice. For example, the "executive power" that Article II vests in the president is largely undefined.

Second, there is *elasticity* in the language of the Constitution. Some words and phrases do not have a precise meaning. Among Congress's list of powers in Section 8 of Article I is the regulation of commerce. But what does "commerce" include? In the

1960s Congress prohibited racial discrimination in hotels, restaurants, and other places of public accommodation. Its authority? The power to regulate commerce.[3]

Following the list of Congress's powers is the **elastic clause**, which authorizes Congress to pass "all Laws which shall be necessary and proper for carrying into Execution the foregoing Powers." Thus, an indefinite reservoir of implied powers was added to the scope Congressional authority. In different periods of American history this clause has enabled government to meet new challenges and the needs of a changing nation. For instance, as explained in Chapter 2, the Supreme Court long ago relied on the elastic clause to uphold Congress's authority to charter a national bank. According to Chief Justice John Marshall (1801–1835), the Constitution was "intended to endure for ages to come, and consequently to be adapted to the various crises of human affairs."[4]

Third, the Constitution exalts *procedure* over substance, containing far more about how policies are to be made than what policies are to be chosen. The Constitution stresses means over ends. The result has been to avoid tying the Constitution, for long periods of time at least, to a certain way of life—whether agrarian, industrial, or technological—or to a certain economic doctrine.

Amendment of the Constitution

The framers knew that the Constitution must allow for change in its terms if it was to be an enduring force. The near impossibility of amending the Articles of Confederation, after all, drove the framers to scrap the rule of unanimity that the Articles required. Formal amendment is thus another means of ensuring adaptability.

Yet, of the more than 5,000 amendments that have been introduced in Congress, only 27 amendments have been added to the document since 1789 (see Table 1.3). Article V of the Constitution mandates that only three-fourths of the states are needed to ratify an amendment to the Constitution. Compared with the Articles of Confederation, amending the Constitution is easier; however, it is still not an easy process. The national constitution is amended much less frequently than state constitutions.

As shown in Figure 1.3, the Constitution specifies two different tracks for its own amendment: initiation by Congress and initiation by state legislatures. Only the first has been employed successfully. Since 1789 Congress has submitted 33 amendments to the states for ratification. Until 1992, all but seven had been approved. Of those to fail, the two most recent were the District of Columbia Amendment, which would have given

---

elastic clause

The "necessary and proper" clause of Article I, Section 8, of the Constitution. This clause is the source of "implied powers" for the national government, as explained in *McCulloch v. Maryland* [17 U.S. (4 Wheaton) 36 (1819)].

---

[3]*Heart of Atlanta Motel v. United States*, 379 U.S. 274 (1964). This is a citation to a Supreme Court decision. "U.S" stands for the *United States Reports,* the official publication containing decisions by the Supreme Court. The number 379 preceding "U.S." and the number 274 following "U.S." indicate the volume and page, respectively, of the *Reports* in which the case can be found. For more information about Supreme Court decisions, see Chapter 12.

[4]*McCulloch v. Maryland*, 17 U.S. (4 Wheaton) 316, 415 (1819) (emphasis deleted). "Wheaton" was the name of the Supreme Court's reporter of decisions at this time. Until 1875, when the use of "U.S" became the rule, citations to Supreme Court decisions contained the reporter's name. Hence, this case was in volume 4 of the reports published by Henry Wheaton.

FIGURE 1.3

Formal Amendment of the Constitution

The formal amendment procedure is prescribed by Article V of the Constitution. The General Services Administration certifies the ratification and keeps tally of the states.

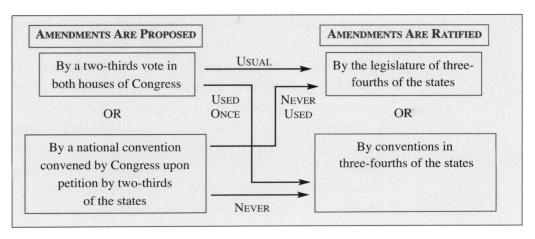

the district voting representation in Congress, and the Equal Rights Amendment, which would have banned discrimination by government on the basis of gender.

On May 7, 1992, the Twenty-seventh Amendment—long known as the "lost amendment"—became part of the Constitution upon ratification by Michigan, the thirty-eighth state (two additional states ratified it later in May). The Twenty-seventh Amendment declares: "No law, varying the compensation for the services of the Senators and Representatives, shall take effect, until an election of Representatives shall have intervened."

Ironically, this newest amendment is actually one of the oldest: It was among the 12 amendments Congress submitted to the states in 1789. (Ten of this group of amendments became the Bill of Rights. Another, dealing with apportionment of the House of Representatives, was never ratified and is obsolete.) By December 1791, when the Bill of Rights amendments were ratified, only six states had approved the pay amendment. Only one additional state ratified it during all of the nineteenth century, but a drive to revive the amendment began in the late 1970s as many people became increasingly frustrated with Congress.

Today, Congress sets a time limit for ratification, usually seven years. An amendment that fails to obtain the required three-fourths approval by the specified date then "dies." But no such limit applied to the early amendments. Critics say that accepting the lost amendment as part of the Constitution is a dangerous precedent because allowing the ratification process to be spread over so long a period of time does not guarantee a contemporary national consensus. Others reply that the amendment would not have been revived had there not been such support for setting the limits on congressional powers mandated by the amendment.[5]

The second track for amendment is the closest the Constitution comes to popular initiation of amendments. As depicted in Figure 1.3, the legislatures of two-thirds of the states first make application to Congress for an amendment. Congress then calls a convention, which in turn submits the amendment for ratification by the legislatures (or conventions) of three-fourths of the states. From time to time, people have attempted to amend the Constitution by campaigning for a second convention when Congress declined to propose the desired amendment in the usual way. Recently, efforts to obtain an amendment that would mandate a balanced budget for Congress proceeded along this second and untraveled track. By 1993, 32 states—two short of the required number— had petitioned Congress for a convention to propose such an amendment. This thrust from the states led the House of Representatives to pass a balanced-budget amendment on multiple occasions in the 1990s, most recently in March 1997. Had the proposal not fallen one vote short of a two-thirds majority in the Senate, the amendment would have been submitted to the states for ratification. Since 1997, bipartisan agreements to reduce spending and a robust economy have derailed the movement for the amendment. In this instance, Congress used track one of the amendment process to head off the drive along track two.

Grave doubts persist over the wisdom of summoning a second convention. Many questions understandably remain unanswered. *Must* Congress call a convention when two-thirds of the states request one? Would such a convention be limited to proposing the amendment sought by the petitioning states, or could a convention propose other changes in the Constitution? Would the delegates vote as individuals, or would they cast the vote of a state, as was done in 1787? The Constitution does not answer any of these questions.

Aside from formal amendment and judicial interpretation (which we will discuss next), the political system has also changed by custom. Even with the same words in the Constitution, the public's expectations of governmental institutions continue to evolve. Democratic values, socioeconomic conditions, industrialization, urbanization, and technology have all influenced attitudes and practices. For example, political parties, which developed early in our political history, are not mentioned in the Constitution. An even more obvious example of change by custom is the pledge of presidential electors to support their party's ticket, a practice the Constitution does not require. For a very long time members of the electoral college have been expected to register the choice of the voters on election day, rather than to exercise an independent choice for president and vice-president (voters would feel both anger and betrayal if the latter occurred).

---

[5]Marcia Coyle, "No Set Procedure for Amendments," *National Law Journal*, June 1, 1992, p. 10.

Judicial Review Comes to the Supreme Court

Most changes to the Constitution since its inception have resulted not in adding or deleting words, but in applying new meaning to existing words—a task that has largely fallen to the Supreme Court. Through its interpretative powers, the Supreme Court is rather like an ongoing constitutional convention. Thus, we must often look to court cases to interpret the meaning of various parts of the Constitution. Whether the framers intended the Court to occupy a place of such prominence in the political system is uncertain. For more about the Supreme Court and its power of judicial review, see Chapter 12.

Marbury v. Madison: The Case of the Undelivered Commissions

Following the presidential election in November 1800, the nation witnessed the modern world's first peaceful electoral transfer of political power from one party to another.[6] The "out group" of Democratic-Republicans led by Thomas Jefferson (1801–1809) captured the presidency and Congress, displacing the "in group" of Federalists led by President John Adams (1797–1801). Partisan tensions ran high.

In the wake of the Adams defeat, Oliver Ellsworth (1796–1800) resigned as the third chief justice of the United States. If Adams moved swiftly, he, and not Jefferson, would be able to make the new appointment. Adams offered the job to John Jay (1789–1795), who had been the first chief justice, but Jay declined because he doubted that the Court would ever amount to much. Adams turned next to his secretary of state, John Marshall, who accepted.

Several weeks before the switch in administrations, the Federalist-dominated Congress passed the District of Columbia Act, which authorized the appointment of 42 new justices of the peace. President Adams made the appointments, much to the displeasure of the Jeffersonians waiting in the wings. This series of events was possible because Congress convened annually in December in those days, which meant that members defeated in the November election (the "lame ducks") were still on hand to make laws. The newly elected Congress would not convene until after the presidential inauguration in March of the following year, a practice that was not changed until ratification of the Twentieth Amendment in 1933.

In the waning hours of the Adams administration, John Marshall, who was still serving as secretary of state, failed to deliver all of the commissions of office to the would-be justices of the peace. Upon assuming office on March 4, 1801, Jefferson held back delivery to some of the Adams appointees and substituted a few of his own. Later that year, William Marbury and three others whom Adams had named as justice of the peace filed suit against Secretary of State James Madison in the Supreme Court. They wanted the Supreme Court to issue a **writ of mandamus** to Madison, directing him to hand over the

writ of mandamus

Order by a court to a public official to perform a nondiscretionary or ministerial act.

---

[6]Richard Hofstadter, *The Idea of a Party System* (Berkeley: University of California Press, 1969), p. 128.

Marbury v. Madison

Landmark decision [5 U.S. (1 Cranch) 137 (1803)] by the Supreme Court in 1803 establishing the Supreme Court's power of judicial review.

undelivered commissions. (A writ of mandamus is an order issued by a court to a public official directing performance of a ministerial, or nondiscretionary, act.) Thus, a case was initiated that tested the power of the Supreme Court over another branch of government.

When the Court heard arguments in the case of *Marbury v. Madison* in February 1803, the Jefferson administration displayed its hostility to Marshall and the other Federalist justices by boycotting the proceeding.[7] It was by then apparent that Marshall and the five associate justices were in a predicament. If the Court issued the writ, Jefferson and Madison would probably disregard it. There would be no one to enforce the order, and the Court would seem powerless and without authority. For the Court to decide that Marbury and the others were not entitled to their judgeships would be an open acknowledgment of weakness and error.

Marshall's decision skillfully avoided both dangers and claimed added power for the Supreme Court, even though Marbury walked out the door empty-handed. First, in a lecture on etiquette to his cousin the president, Marshall made it clear that Marbury was entitled to the job. Second, he ruled that courts could examine the legality of the actions of the head of an executive department. Third, and dispositive, Marshall announced that Marbury was out of luck because the writ of mandamus he requested was not the proper remedy.

original jurisdiction

Authority of a court over cases that begin in that court. Courts of general jurisdiction have original jurisdiction over most criminal offenses. The original jurisdiction of the U.S. Supreme Court is very small.

appellate jurisdiction

Includes cases a court receives from lower courts. The appellate jurisdiction of the U.S. Supreme Court is defined by Congress.

Why? Marshall acknowledged that Section 13 of the 1789 Judiciary Act gave the Supreme Court authority to issue a writ as part of the Court's original, as opposed to appellate, jurisdiction. (A court has **original jurisdiction** when a case properly starts in that court, and **appellate jurisdiction** when the case begins elsewhere and comes to a higher court for review.) But, Marshall pointed out, the Supreme Court's original jurisdiction was specified in Article III of the Constitution and included no mention of writs of mandamus. By *adding* to the Court's original jurisdiction, Section 13 appeared unwarranted by the Constitution. Was the Court to apply an unconstitutional statute? No. To do so would make the statute (and Congress) superior to the Constitution. Section 13, therefore, was void, and the Court was obliged to say so.

The Significance of *Marbury*

Marbury v. Madison remains important because of what Chief Justice Marshall said about the Constitution and the Supreme Court. First, officers of the government were under the law and could be called to account in court. Second, statutes contrary to the Constitution were not valid laws. Third, the Court claimed for itself the authority to decide what the Constitution means and to measure the actions of other parts of the government against that meaning. This is the power of **judicial review**: An electorally responsible agency of government can be blocked by judges holding lifetime appointments. Alternatively, the lawmaking body (Congress) would be the judge of its own authority. Fourth, Marshall was

judicial review

The authority of courts to set aside a legislative act as being in violation of the Constitution.

---

[7]5 U.S (1 Cranch) 137 (1803).

Politics and Ideas
Whose Constitution Is It?

What standard should guide justices of the Supreme Court in deciding what the Constitution means? One approach criticizes the justices for too often substituting their own values in place of those the Constitution explicitly contains. Because the Constitution says nothing about abortion, for instance, and because there is no evidence that those who wrote either the document of 1787 or later amendments intended to include abortion as a protected liberty, they believe the Court was plainly wrong when it ruled in *Roe v. Wade* (1973) that the Constitution protects the right to abortion (see Chapter 3). In place of excessive judicial creativity, the Court relies on "original intent."[a] According to this view, the Supreme Court's task is to give the Constitution the meaning intended by those who wrote it. Whether abortions should be legal thus becomes a question for voters and legislators, not judges.

Others disagree and advance a different approach. Often the original intent is neither knowable nor clear, they argue. Even if it is, whose intent is supposed to matter most—those who wrote the words in the Constitution, those who voted on them at the Philadelphia Convention or (with respect to amendments) in Congress, or those in state ratifying conventions and legislatures? These questions aside, must the nation always be locked into an old way of thinking until the Constitution is formally amended? The Fourteenth Amendment, for example, commands that no state deny to any person the "equal protection of the laws." In its historic decision in *Brown v. Board of Education of Topeka* (1954), discussed in Chapter 3, the Supreme Court concluded that these words prohibited racial segregation in public schools. Yet the same Congress that wrote and proposed the Fourteenth Amendment almost a century earlier also mandated racially segregated schools for the District of Columbia. It is hard to argue that the framers of the Fourteenth Amendment intended to ban a practice they were themselves requiring. Does this mean that the 1954 decision was wrong? No—because the Constitution must be adaptive. According to opponents of "originalism," the Court's task should be one of applying principles, not specific intents. This approach sees in the Constitution the general principle of human dignity. One generation's understanding of human dignity will probably not be the same as another's. The question becomes not what the words meant in 1787 or 1868, but what the words mean in our own time.[b]

Even many proponents of original intent do not disagree with the result of *Brown*. Rather, they say that the Court can be faithful to the intent of the Fourteenth Amendment and still invalidate laws that require racial segregation because the framers of the Fourteenth Amendment, in laying down a command of "equal protection," did not foresee the harmful consequences of forced segregation.

If justices of the Supreme Court interpret the Constitution according to their understanding of the meaning of basic principles that the Constitution contains, how do they discover those principles? Why is their view of the values that the Constitution protects somehow superior to the views of state legislators or members of Congress? Should the fundamental law of the land be developed by elected representatives or by appointed judges?

[a] Robert H. Bork, *The Tempting of America* (New York: Free Press, 1990), pp. 143–160.

[b] William J. Brennan, Jr., "The Constitution of the United States: Contemporary Ratification," in Alpheus T. Mason and D. Grier Stephenson, Jr., *American Constitutional Law,* 8th ed. (Englewood Cliffs, NJ: Prentice Hall, 1987), pp. 607–15.

Kentucky and Virginia Resolutions

A challenge to national supremacy, these state documents declared states to be the final authority on the meaning of the Constitution.

answering the rumblings of dissent heard in the **Kentucky** and **Virginia Resolutions** of 1798. Written, respectively, by Jefferson and Madison (the latter had by now become a foe of strong central government) as an attack on Federalist party policies, these resolutions claimed for the states final authority to interpret the Constitution. In their words lay the seeds for dismemberment of the Union. Marshall's reply was that the Court would have the final say on the meaning of the Constitution.

Judicial Review and the Framers

The novelty of the *Marbury* case is that it marked the first instance in which the Supreme Court declared an act of Congress to be in violation of the Constitution. Did the framers intend the Court to have such power? The question cannot be answered with certainty. Some members of the Philadelphia Convention seemed to assume that the Court could set aside laws that ran counter to the Constitution. In *Federalist* No. 78, Alexander Hamilton made an argument in support of judicial review that Marshall followed closely in his *Marbury* ruling. References to judicial review abound in the records of the state ratifying conventions, and some state courts made use of the power well before Marshall did. Moreover, several Supreme Court decisions prior to *Marbury* assumed the existence of judicial review but neither explained nor applied it. Still, if the Court was to possess such a potentially important power, it is strange that the Constitution would not mention such powers. Neither does the Constitution say anything about how its words are to be interpreted, a question that still divides political leaders and legal scholars. (See "Politics and Ideas: Whose Constitution Is It?", p. 37.)

It is probably safe to say that Marshall's opinion in *Marbury* would not have come as a great surprise to the authors of the Constitution. But it is also probably true that they did not envision the Court's becoming a major policymaker, a role that the doctrine of judicial review makes possible and that the Court enjoys today, as Chapters 3 and 11 show. In fairness to Marshall, he viewed judicial review as a modest power. Whereas Marshall was not hesitant to strike down state laws that he felt conflicted with the Constitution, it was not until the infamous Dred Scott case in 1857, 22 years after Marshall's death, that the Supreme Court again set aside an act of Congress as violating the Constitution.[8] (Inflaming abolitionist sentiment on the eve of the Civil War, this decision denied congressional authority to prohibit slavery in the territories and asserted that African Americans were not intended to be citizens under the Constitution.)

Because of judicial review, the changes wrought by custom and formal amendment, and the needs of an expanding nation, what Americans mean by "the Constitution" today is vastly different from the document that emerged from the Convention in Philadelphia in 1787. Yet the Constitution, coupled with a commitment to constitutionalism, continues to play a vital part in the life of the third century of American government.

---

[8] *Scott v. Sanford*, 60 U.S. (19 Howard) 393 (1857).

SUMMARY

1. The Constitution of the United States is a living document, the charter of the nation, and thus has a presence that gives it a special place in American government.

2. The Declaration of Independence attempted to justify revolution against Great Britain by explaining the purposes of government. The Articles of Confederation represented the first effort at establishing a central government for the newly independent states, but the plan proved to be defective.

3. The Philadelphia Convention in 1787 produced a plan for a new national government that had to be approved by conventions in nine states before going into effect.

4. The Constitution was designed to achieve both effective and limited government: effective by granting powers sufficient for a strong union and limited by restraining and arranging those powers to protect liberty.

5. The possibility of amendment helps to explain how the Constitution remains current in its third century. The Constitution has also been remade through interpretation by the courts and through custom and usage.

6. *Marbury v. Madison* brought judicial review to the Constitution in 1803. As a result, the Supreme Court sits as the final authority on the meaning of the Constitution.

KEY TERMS

constitutionalism (11)

Articles of Confederation (16)

Shays's Rebellion (18)

Annapolis Convention (18)

Northwest Ordinance (19)

Virginia Plan (20)

New Jersey Plan (20)

Great Compromise (22)

three-fifths compromise (22)

Federalists (22)

Antifederalists (22)

The Federalist (23)

republican (or representative) government (24)

checks and balances (27)

elastic clause (32)

writ of mandamus (35)

Marbury v. Madison (36)

original jurisdiction (36)

appellate jurisdiction (36)

judicial review (36)

Kentucky and Virginia Resolutions (38)

READINGS FOR FURTHER STUDY

A Machine That Would Go of Itself, by Michael Kammen (New York: Knopf, 1986), explores the role of constitutionalism in American life.

Decisions of the Supreme Court interpreting the constitution are readily found in edited form in casebooks such as Alpheus T. Mason and D. Grier Stephenson, Jr., *American Constitutional Law*, 10th ed. (Englewood Cliffs, NJ: Prentice-Hall, 1993).

An explanation of the Constitution, section by section, appears in J. W. Peltason, *Corwin and Peltason's Understanding the Constitution*, 12th ed. (San Diego: Harcourt Brace Jovanovich, 1991).

Useful insight into American political thought in the founding era can be gleaned from Alpheus T. Mason and Richard H. Leach, *In Quest of Freedom*, 2d ed. (Englewood Cliffs, NJ: Prentice-Hall, 1973).

The Federalist essays are widely available in several editions.

The best collection of Antifederalist literature is Herbert J. Storing, ed., *The Complete Anti-Federalist*, 7 vols. (Chicago: University of Chicago Press, 1981).

Constitutional development since colonial days is the subject of Alfred H. Kelly, Winfred A. Harbison, and Herman Belz, *The American Constitution*, 7th ed., 2 vols. (New York: Norton, 1991).

CHAPTER 2

Federalism: States in the Union

A/P World Wide

Chapter Objectives

The Constitution established a national government with power dispersed among separate branches. The document also created a second kind of power diffusion: the sharing of power between the national government and individual states. This sharing of power is the principal characteristic of a "federal" system. At root, federalism is the product and symbol of the continuing struggle between the value of unity and the value of diversity as they compete for dominance in the political system.

This chapter considers the meaning of federalism and why comprehending it is crucial to a full understanding of American government. Continuing tension between national and state governments requires a look at the place of state governments in the Constitution and their role in American politics. The chapter discusses the legal, fiscal, and political relationships among national, state, and local governments. The national government has progressively become more dominant, but the chapter concludes by reviewing federalism as a complex, adaptable system of relationships in which states have begun to assume a more energetic and vigorous role in domestic policy.

The Idea of Federalism

Federalism

A system of government in which both the national and state governments share power within the same political system.

Federalism is a system of government in which the national government *and* state governments share governmental power within the same political system. As both the bombing of the Alfred P. Murrah Federal Building in Oklahoma City in 1995 and the terrorist attacks on the World Trade Center and Pentagon in 2001 demonstrated, a single event may trigger action by officials at both levels of government.

41

In a federal system, *both* the national and state governments have jurisdiction over individuals. For example, in preparation for the tax-filing deadline each year, individual citizens perform tasks resulting directly from the existence of a federal system. Taxpayers must file returns with the national government, and in most states (those that choose to have income taxes) they must file returns with state governments as well. The duty of filing national and state tax returns illustrates an important point about federalism: Individuals receive services both from Washington and their state capitals, and they must consequently send money to two different levels of governments.

The federal system is a compromise between a strong central government and a league of separate states. Because the states ultimately had to approve any change to the new constitution being created in 1787, the challenge for the framers was clear: How could a stronger national government be created without, at the same time, instilling so much fear in the states that the proposed new structure would be rejected? The states, after all, were already in place. The framers pressed for change, but not so much change that their efforts would fail. The result was a federal system.

Confederate, Unitary, and Federal Forms of Government

confederation

A loose association of states in which dominant political power lies with the member states and not with the central government.

As Figure 2.1 illustrates, the powers of states and the powers of a central or national government can assume different combinations in different political systems. A **confederation** is a loose collection of states in which principal power lies at the level of the individual state rather than at the level of the central or national government. Individual states, not the central government, have jurisdiction over individuals. As discussed in Chapter 1, the Articles of Confederation comprised such a system when it was in force during the decade before the Philadelphia Convention of 1787. Under the Articles, the states retained many important powers.

unitary system

A system of government in which principal power lies at the level of a national or central government rather than at the level of some smaller unit (a state or a province) within the political system.

In contrast to a confederation, a **unitary system** of government is one in which principal power within the political system lies at the level of a national or central government rather than at the level of some smaller unit, such as a state or province. Individual citizens have direct allegiance to the national or central government, which possesses ultimate power to make all political choices and determine public policy. The government of France is an example of a unitary system. The 50 American states are themselves unitary governments with respect to their own local governments. As later discussion in this chapter will make clear, principal power *within* each state lies with the state government rather than with local governments.

Confederations are founded on the political idea of diversity and local control. Such structures allow individual states to pursue diverse approaches to policy matters. On the matter of voting rights, for example, one state might allow every citizen over the age of 18 to vote, another might require that voters own property, and a third might make the right to vote contingent on passing a literacy test. According to the idea of di-

FIGURE 2.1

Unitary, Federal, and Confederate Systems

The central government has jurisdiction over individuals in a unitary government. If states or provinces exist, they are symbolic or administrative units with no real power. In a confederation, states are dominant and have jurisdiction over individuals. In a federal system, the central and state governments *both* have jurisdiction over individuals.

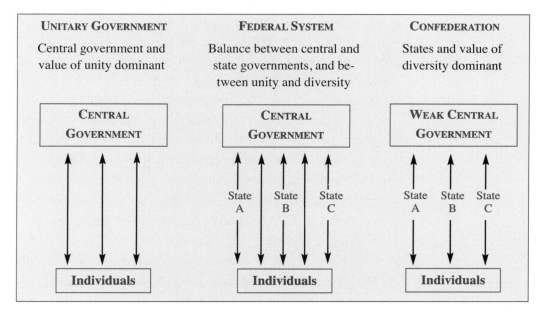

versity, individual states know best their own people and their own needs. Consequently, individual states ought to have their own powers to pursue individual approaches to the problems they face.

Unitary structures rest on the value of unity. Such structures assume that there is a national interest in meeting needs and problems in a particular way. Individuals are citizens of the nation (not separate states), and procedures and approaches to policy problems ought to be uniform rather than individualized and disparate. In the voting rights example, voter qualifications would be determined at the central level in the interest of a unified voting rights policy for all citizens of the nation.

In creating a federal system, the framers of the Constitution sought to change the political structure of a loose collection of states so that the value of unity might be more easily achieved. Although they were moved by a mix of considerations, the most important in the move to a national government were probably economy, foreign policy, and the military.[1] Foreign and military policies are areas in which centralized approaches are

[1]John P. Roche, "The Founding Fathers: A Reform Caucus in Action," *American Political Science Review* 55 (1961): 804; William H. Riker, *Federalism: Origin, Operation, Significance* (Boston: Little, Brown, 1964).

essential to success. Diverse approaches in these areas (e.g., if North Carolina and Massachusetts were to conduct their own foreign policies) would surely make any kind of union among the states impossible. Indeed, this was a major fault with the Articles of Confederation. The weak central government provided by the Articles had no real way to prevent the states from going in separate directions. At the same time, however, the framers had to acknowledge the continuing existence of diverse states and their diverse approaches in some areas of public policy.

Unity and Diversity in the Federal System

Diversity among the states can be measured in numerous dimensions. States differ in historical traditions, unemployment rates, economic development, ethnic composition, social welfare spending, federal funding, age distributions, religious affiliations, voter turnout rates, degrees of political party competitiveness, and even physical environments.[2] That states differ in physical size and population is readily evident. For example, Rhode Island is a state of just over 1,000 square miles; Alaska, by far the largest state, comprises more than 570,000 square miles. About 541 Rhode Islands could fit into Alaska. California, a state with 33 million people, has 68 times the number of people living in Wyoming.

Per capita income is another measure of state differences. For example, Connecticut in 2000 had a per capita income that was almost double the per capita income of Mississippi.[3] Such basic factors of wealth help to determine how much individual states can tax and how much they can spend on programs such as education and public assistance.

To what degree should physical, economic, and social differences among the states allow diverse public policies, and when should national values prevail? The minimum drinking age and highway speed limits are contemporary issues that illustrate the search for an appropriate balance between state and national approaches to public policy—two centuries after the framers originally wrestled with the problem. The repeal of Prohibition in 1933 granted to the states the power to regulate alcohol in whatever ways they saw fit. States had various minimum drinking ages ranging from 18 to 21. By the early 1980s, the problem of drunk driving had received national attention. People under the age of 21 were found to be responsible for a disproportionate number of alcohol-related traffic fatalities and injuries. In response to growing pressure from groups such as Mothers Against Drunk Driving (MADD), Congress enacted a measure

---

[2] For a seminal discussion of different political cultures among the states, see Daniel J. Elazar, *American Federalism: A View from the States*, 3d ed. (New York: Harper & Row, 1984), pp. 114–142.

[3] Bureau of Economic Analysis, U.S. Department of Commerce, "Annual State Personal Income," April 2001, http://www.bea.doc.gov /bea/regional/spi/drill.cfm (21 August 2001).

MADD President Millie Webb holds an image of her late 19-month old nephew Mitchell Pewitt, as she speaks during MADD's 20th anniversary rally. *(AP Wide World)*

withholding from individual states a portion of national highway funds unless the states raised their minimum drinking age to 21. Whether there should be a national drinking age or whether the individual states ought to decide their own minimum drinking age is a classic example of the types of debates that arise in a federal system. Is the value of unity of national approach more or less important than the value of diversity of individual state approaches in a matter that has been the states' own prerogative for more than half a century?

Debate over highway speed limits illustrates the same question. To conserve fuel in a time of oil shortages, in 1973 Congress mandated a 55-mile-per-hour speed limit throughout the nation. As concern over energy supplies dissipated, opponents of the law argued that a single national speed limit could not accommodate differences in highway conditions among the states. Some states, especially those in the West, have long stretches of straight, flat highways on which slower speeds contribute to driver boredom. In 1987 Congress passed a law allowing states to raise the speed to 65 miles per hour on interstate highways in rural areas. In 1995 Congress went even further, repealing the federally mandated maximum speed limits and completing the reversal of the course it had taken two decades earlier. Should there be a national speed limit, or should states decide for themselves speed limits within their borders?

A Comparative Perspective on Federalism

Federalism is not unique to the United States. Other countries having federal constitutional systems include Australia, Brazil, India, Malaysia, Nigeria, Pakistan, Switzerland, and Venezuela. Although such countries may differ in size, wealth, and military power, what is common to them is their attempt to pull together disparate groups while at the same time acknowledging the groups' separate identities. The search for the appropriate balance in power between the states and the national government in the United States resonates in other federal systems as well.

Daniel Elazar, the renowned federalism scholar, has written that "[f]ederalism has to do with the need of people and polities to unite for common purposes yet remain separate to preserve their respective integrities. It is rather like wanting to have one's cake and eat it too."[4] Groups in federal systems might be cultural or language minorities, people living in geographical units whose history predates the creation of the federal system, or different religious denominations in which no single one is dominant. Federal systems have pulled together, or tried to, French and English speakers, Lithuanians and Ukrainians, and Pennsylvanians and New Yorkers. Such groups get together for purposes such as a common defense or a common currency, but they retain their separate identities for other purposes, such as education or law enforcement.

The relative power of the central government and constituent groups will vary among countries. But federal systems generally have a dynamic quality in which there is a continuing search for the appropriate balance between national purposes and group needs. Some of the world's great political conflicts are essentially struggles to define this balance. For example, debate over the political status of French-speaking Quebec, the only one of Canada's ten provinces with a French majority, has strained Canadian politics for years. Whether Quebec can or will go it alone remains a troubling issue for Canada.

The dissolution of the Soviet Union is an illustration of how changes in a federal system can have momentous implications for world politics. A military superpower, the Soviet Union was comprised of 15 republics held together by the Communist Party backed by the threat of military force. Unchallenged central control made the system federal in name only. Worsening economic conditions, the emergence of ethnic demands, and attempts at liberal reforms showed cracks in the system. After an attempted coup by Communist Party hardliners failed in 1991, the central government's power over the 15 Soviet republics dwindled sharply. Individual republics declared their independence, and what was left of the Soviet Union quickly unraveled. The Soviet government officially disbanded several months after the failed coup and was replaced by a Commonwealth of Independent States in which the republics retained their independent

http://www.consti tution.org/afp/afp .htm

Despite their name, the Antifederalists actually favored federalism. A collection of their views on the need for strong government can be found at the above site.

---

[4]Daniel J. Elazar, *Exploring Federalism* (Tuscaloosa, AL: University of Alabama Press, 1987), p. 33.

status.[5] Today, the former Soviet republics are largely autonomous states, allying themselves when appropriate via international treaties and organizations, but displaying few traces of the once forced federal relationship.

States in the Constitutional System

That there are 50 states is a historical accident. If wars had been lost instead of won, if treaties and land purchases had not been made, if rivers coursed through different areas, the number, names, and sizes of states would be different. States are integral parts of our social and political consciousness. State boundaries are superimposed on satellite pictures of weather patterns. State universities enjoy great attention through the exploits of their athletic teams, and children in elementary schools throughout the land spend time trying to memorize the names of state capitals. The existence of states is simply assumed.

States play a crucial role in the American political system: they administer social welfare policies, grapple with regional problems, amend the Constitution, and shape electoral contests at the national level. States act in some measure as administrative units to help carry out national social welfare programs substantially funded by Congress, such as food stamps, Medicaid, and Temporary Assistance to Needy Families. Through the device of the **interstate compact**, states can enter into formal agreements with other states to deal with policy problems that cross state lines. An example is the agreement between New York and New Jersey to establish the New York Port Authority to regulate transportation in the New York City area. States also play a role in the process of formally amending the Constitution. Although controversy between states has raged over a variety of proposed amendments, including issues involving abortion, flag burning, and a balanced budget, no formal change to the Constitution can be made without the states considering, debating, and voting on the issue.

With the exception of the president and vice-president of the United States, *every* elected official in the country is chosen either by all the voters in a particular state (the governor or a U.S. senator) or by voters in part of a state (U.S. representatives or state legislators). Every elected official, except for the president and vice-president, has a geographic constituency that is either a state or part of a state, such as a county or a congressional district. This simple but crucial fact helps to explain much legislative behavior at the national level—for example, when members of Congress press for national legislation that helps industries in their home states or oppose the closing of military bases in their districts.

The **electoral college**, a political institution that, following the mandate in the Constitution, determines the winner in presidential elections, is another illustration of the

---

interstate compact

A formal agreement between states designed to solve a problem facing more than one state. Such an agreement is necessary when political problems are not limited by geographic boundaries.

electoral college

Institution established by the Constitution for electing the president and vice-president. Electors chosen by the voters actually elect the president and vice-president.

---

[5] See Gregory Gleason, *Federalism and Nationalism: The Struggle for Republican Rights in the USSR* (Boulder, CO: Westview Press, 1990) for discussion of Soviet federalism prior to the creation of the Commonwealth of Independent States.

role of the states. Presidents are elected not by a plurality (the highest number) of votes cast by voters throughout the United States, but by a majority of electoral college votes. Each state has a number of electoral votes equal to the number of its members in the House and Senate combined. Because the number of representatives is determined by population, the states with larger numbers of people have a larger number of electoral votes. California, for example, has 54 electoral votes, whereas Delaware has only 3. In every state but two, the presidential candidate receiving the largest number of popular votes in the state receives all that state's electoral votes.[6]

In effect, on the day of the presidential election, 51 separate elections are taking place (in the 50 states and the District of Columbia). Voters choose among slates of electors committed to one or another of the candidates. When the popular votes in each state are counted, state-by-state electoral college vote totals are combined to determine the presidential victor. After the election, victorious electors officially cast their presidential votes in their respective state capitals. From the perspective of federalism, the important point is that *states as states* play a crucial role in electing the person who holds the most important political office in the land. Presidential candidates must appeal not to an amorphous mass of citizens but to Texans, North Carolinians, Californians, and Virginians.

The center of the U.S. population changes as more and more people follow the sun in their moves to the South and the West. Florida, California, and Texas have gained population, while New York, Ohio, Pennsylvania, Illinois, and Michigan have suffered relative loss of residents. Such population changes have implications for power shifts in the U.S. House and in the electoral college. Figure 2.2 shows the shifts in regional power between 1942 and 1992. Since the 1990 census, almost one out of four members of the U.S. House has come from California, Texas, or Florida, and the presidential candidate winning California receives 20 percent of the electoral votes needed to win the presidency. The 2000 Census shows a continuation of this trend, as all three of those states will gain additional House seats after the next congressional apportionment.

The Rise of the National Government

As Chapter 1 made clear, the states were clearly dominant under the Articles of Confederation. The national government quite literally started out from nothing, yet we have today a national government whose actions, from delivering Social Security checks to regulating the safety of toys and nuclear power plants, pervades the daily lives of citizens. How did this change come about? Massive technological, communications, and economic changes have transformed the nation over the past two centuries. War and depression have made their own contributions to the shift in focus of demands and expectations.

---

[6]The two exceptions are Maine and Nebraska, which allocate electoral votes on the basis of candidate victories in congressional districts.

FIGURE 2.2

Shifts in Regional Power, 1942 and 1992, as Measured by the Size of State Delegations in the U.S. House of Representatives

Shifts and changes in population between 1942 and 1992 meant that over the past half-century parts of the East and the Midwest lost seats in the House of Representatives, while the West and South gained seats. The apportionment of the 435 House seats is calculated for each state following the census every 10 years. A state may increase its population but lose a seat if the rate of gain in other states is much greater.

SOURCE: U.S. Bureau of the Census.

REGION/STATE	1942	1992	REGION/STATE	1942	1992
MOUNTAINS AND PLAINS	29	31	**MIDWEST**	117	96
MT	2	1	MN	9	8
WY	1	1	WI	10	9
ND	2	1	MI	17	16
SD	2	1	IA	8	5
NE	4	3	IL	26	20
KS	6	4	IN	11	30
NM	2	3	OH	23	19
AZ	2	6	MO	13	9
UT	2	3	**EAST**	127	97
ID	2	3	ME	3	2
CO	4	6	NH	2	2
SOUTH	128	140	VT	1	1
WV	6	3	MA	14	10
VA	9	11	CT	6	6
OK	8	6	RI	2	2
AR	7	4	NY	45	31
KY	9	6	PA	33	21
NC	12	12	NJ	14	13
TN	10	9	MD	6	8
SC	6	6	DE	1	1
TX	21	30	**WEST**	34	71
LA	8	7	WA	6	9
MS	7	5	OR	4	5
AL	9	7	CA	23	52
GA	10	11	AK	N/A	1
FL	6	23	HI	N/A	2

The conflict between unity and diversity, which gave birth to the federal system, also shaped the relationships between the national and state governments in the early decades of the new nation. The national government cooperated with the states in a variety of areas. Because economic development was among the highest of priorities of the new nation, the national government provided funds and technical assistance to the states for construction of roads and canals. Land grants to states in the West for educational purposes signaled greater cooperation between the national government and the states to come.[7]

Despite the cooperation, however, sharp conflicts also occurred between the national government and the states in the early decades of the Republic. The Kentucky and Virginia Resolutions, adopted by the legislatures of those states in 1798, held that the Constitution created a compact among the states and that the power of the national government was sharply limited by the states. In 1819 the state of Maryland contested the right of the national government to establish a national bank. And in 1832 the South Carolina legislature declared a national tariff law null and void. The very existence of national power was at issue in these instances of national-state conflict.

The federal system was ultimately tested in war. The early skirmishes between the national government and the states paled in significance compared to the Civil War. At one level the war was about the question of slavery; but at another level the war was a question about federalism. Could a state (or several states) leave the Union and, in effect, unravel the work of the Constitutional Convention of 1787? From the perspective of federalism, the most important consequence of the war was preservation of the Union. President Lincoln is best known as emancipator of the slaves, but his sharp and unyielding refusal to allow dissolution of the Union was crucial in the evolution of federalism. The significance of Lincoln's stance cannot be overstated. Lincoln, the chief executive in a national government that did not even exist a century earlier, used *national* resources in a major war effort to resist by brute force the claims of the seceding states, four of which predated the national government itself.

The end of the Civil War marked the beginning of a rapid change in the character of the nation's economy. Transcontinental railroads pulled the nation together and brought farmers, producers, and sellers closer to buyers and consumers. Major new industries such as steel, oil, and, later, the automobile, began to emerge. With them came new forms of economic organization. Corporations crossed state boundaries in their activities and their effects. Control and regulation of economic matters increasingly eluded the grasp of any single state, resulting in political demands by the states that the national government confront the problems that economic monopolies left in their trail.

Later in the twentieth century, the economy plunged into the Great Depression of the 1930s. Farm and industrial prices collapsed, factories closed, banks failed, homes

---

[7]See Daniel J. Elazar, "Federal-State Cooperation in the Nineteenth-Century United States," *Political Science Quarterly* 79 (1964): 248–265.

A twenty-two year old mother with her children camped in a Resettlement camp for migrants during the Great Depression. *(Library of Congress)*

were foreclosed, and unemployment rates rose dramatically. State and local governments were overwhelmed by the needs and demands of millions of Americans who clearly needed help to survive. National problems seemed to require national solutions. As never before, the national government embarked on a series of social welfare policies that both improved the economic conditions of many and generated expectations that the national government could solve a variety of social problems in the future. Today many domestic programs administered by the states or their localities are funded by the national government.

Finally, the national government has responsibility for national security and relations with other nations. In the twentieth century, the Cold War and the increasing interdependence of the world economy combined to make the national government's conduct of foreign affairs important on a continuing basis. Though the Cold War has ended, demands for a revitalized military establishment remain strong, and the need for national government policies to enhance the nation's competitiveness in the global economy have become more acute.

The seemingly inexorable rise in the power of the national government has been accompanied by political demands that state and local governments assume a larger

New Federalism

A view of federalism that posits an expanded role for state and local governments and holds that state and local governments should be entrusted with greater responsibilities.

presence in the making of policy decisions affecting them. For example, **New Federalism,** a term most closely associated with the Republican administrations of Richard Nixon (1969–1974) and Ronald Reagan (1981–1989), calls for state and local governments to assume a much greater role than they traditionally had during the explosions of national policy initiatives in the Democratic administrations of Franklin Roosevelt (1933–1945) in the New Deal and Lyndon Johnson (1963–1969) in the Great Society.[8] New Federalism is taking on a new life during the George W. Bush (2001–) administration, this time in the form of calls for state self-reliance during crisis and scaling back of federal environmental regulations. New Federalism holds that state and local governments should not only be entrusted with greater responsibilities, but that they should also be allowed to follow their own best judgment in making decisions. Giving state and local governments more discretion in how they spend national grant money is an illustration. This view of federalism dovetails with the traditional Republican party "grass-roots" philosophy that the government in the best position to make good policy choices is the government "closest" to the people. But whether nationally defined policy goals, such as the amelioration of poverty, can (or should) accommodate state and local policies that may diverge from those goals is an old question in federalism.

Express and Implied Powers

delegated powers

Legal authority that the people in the states granted to the national government for certain purposes by ratifying the Constitution. Delegated powers can be either express or implied.

express powers

Powers specifically enumerated in the Constitution as belonging to the national government.

implied powers

Powers of national government not specifically cited in the Constitution but implicit in powers expressly granted by the Constitution.

The search for the right balance between state and national power remains an enduring issue in the federal system. What powers do the states have in their relationships to each other and to the national government? What powers does the national government have over the states? The Republic has struggled with these questions since 1787. The Constitution prohibits the exercise of some powers by one or both levels of national and state governments; for example, states may not coin money. In addition, national and state governments share some *concurrent* powers, such as the power each has to tax the same individual's income. However, the most important point about national and state powers is the distinction between *delegated* and *reserved* powers.

In accepting the Constitution, the people in the states through the ratification process *delegated* important new powers to the new national government. The statement of these powers is contained in Article I, Section 8, of the Constitution (see the appendix). **Delegated powers** are ordinarily divided into two types: express powers and implied powers. **Express powers** are specifically enumerated as belonging to Congress. Among these are the power to levy and collect taxes, to borrow money, to regulate interstate commerce, to coin money, to declare war, and to raise and support armies.

However, the last statement of power listed in Article I, Section 8, also delegates to the national government **implied powers**, which by their very nature have been

---

[8] For an examination on the differences between the Nixon and Reagan approaches to New Federalism, see Timothy Conlan, *New Federalism: Intergovernmental Reform from Nixon to Reagan* (Washington, DC: Brookings Institution, 1988).

subject to intense dispute. This provision is also known as the "elastic" or "necessary and proper" clause, and delegates to Congress the power "to make all Laws which shall be necessary and proper for carrying into Execution the foregoing Powers, and all other Powers vested by this Constitution in the Government of the United States, or in any Department or Officer thereof." Obviously, what is "necessary and proper" in a particular circumstance is a matter open to varying interpretations. A narrow interpretation would constrict the powers of the national government, whereas a broad interpretation would enlarge them.

The first time the clause was specifically interpreted was in *McCulloch v. Maryland*, one of the most famous and consequential Supreme Court decisions ever made.[9] The case represented an ideological division over the powers of the national government and the place of the states in the Union. Conflicting political objectives were sought in terms of opposing theories of federalism. Congress had chartered a national bank. Some states opposed the bank because it competed with state-chartered banks. Hoping to put the national bank out of business, Maryland imposed a tax on the new bank. McCulloch, its cashier, refused to pay. As part of its case, Maryland argued not only that a state could tax a nationally chartered bank but also that Congress had no authority to charter a bank in the first place, because banking was not a power delegated to Congress. Instead, Maryland claimed, banking was a subject the Constitution reserved for the states.

Contrary to Maryland's claims, Chief Justice John Marshall (1801–1835) declared that Congress possessed ample constitutional authority to charter a bank, even though such a power was not expressly listed in the Constitution. In Marshall's view, the power to establish a bank was implied in the express powers, such as the powers to tax and to coin money. A bank was a means to achieving the ends spelled out in the Constitution. Marshall's interpretation of the "necessary and proper" clause clearly allowed expansive power to the national government. In his memorable words,

> Let the end be legitimate, let it be within the scope of the constitution, and all means which are appropriate, which are plainly adapted to that end, which are not prohibited, but consistent with the letter and spirit of the constitution, are constitutional.

Furthermore, Marshall held that Maryland could not tax the bank because it was an instrument of the national government. In a conflict between an act of Congress and a state law, the former would prevail. No single part of the political community could be allowed to subvert a policy undertaken by the whole community represented in Congress.

Because of the brevity of the Constitution, many of its clauses and phrases are ambiguous and give little or no direction as to what is "legitimate" in a particular

---

[9] 17 U.S. (4 Wheaton) 316 (1819).

circumstance. The framers could not address every problem or clarify every uncertainty. According to Marshall's decision in *McCulloch*, the Constitution created a stronger national government by delegating to it express and implied powers. But exactly how strong it was to be or how it would evolve was left for later generations to decide.

Reserved Powers: What Do the States Do?

If the new government was to be more powerful and the states were nonetheless to continue to exist, what powers were left to the states? Although simpler in theory than in practice, the principle is that states can do all things not specifically prohibited to them and not delegated exclusively to the national government. These remaining powers are known as **reserved powers**. State and local governments are responsible for delivering the vast majority of public services. About 2.7 million civilian employees work for the national government, a number that has decreased slightly since a peak of 3.1 million in 1990. However, growth in government employment has occurred at the state and local levels. In 2000, state and local governments employed just over 15 million people, about five times the number of civilian employees working for the national government.[10] This number of employees indicates that states and localities play a large role in providing public services.

The **Tenth Amendment** states that "the powers not delegated to the United States by the Constitution, nor prohibited by it to the States, are reserved to the States respectively, or to the people." Politicians and groups whose political ideas are served by advocating "states' rights" have frequently pointed to the Tenth Amendment as support for their claims. However, that amendment, unlike the Articles of Confederation, does not contain the word *expressly* in citing powers delegated to the national government. Such delegated powers *include* the implied powers cited by Chief Justice Marshall in *McCulloch v. Maryland*.

Among powers reserved for the states are "police" responsibilities for the health, safety, and welfare of citizens. For civilized life to be possible, people must be able to carry on their day-to-day activities with the reasonable assurance that physical threats to their health and well-being are kept to an absolute minimum. For example, among the health responsibilities of states are those of dealing with outbreaks of contagious diseases, the disposal of wastes, cleanliness in public eating establishments, and the administration of networks of state hospitals and mental institutions.

In one of their most visible roles, the states also have primary responsibility for preventing and prosecuting criminal activities. Most of this work occurs at the level of local governments whose organization, powers, and functions are constitutionally subject to con-

reserved powers

Powers not specifically prohibited to the states and not delegated to the national government by the Constitution.

Tenth Amendment

An amendment ratified in 1791 that reserves to the states powers not prohibited to them and not delegated to the national government by the Constitution.

---

[10]U.S. Census Bureau, "2000 Public Employment Data," April 2000, http://www.census.gov/govs/apes/00stlus.txt (21 August 2001).

Workers sort through debris being dug up from an old Sandia National Laboratories chemical waste dump, near Albuquerque, New Mexico *(AP Wide World)*

trol by state governments. Some crimes, such as airline hijacking, kidnapping, tampering with the U.S. mail, and counterfeiting money, are violations of national law enforced by the national government. However, most law enforcement officers in the country are state agents and local personnel who act as agents of the state. From state police officers to county sheriffs who track down suspected criminals, to the local police who deal with matters such as burglary and domestic violence, most law enforcement responsibilities lie at the state and local levels. Most suspected rapists, murderers, thieves, burglars, muggers, and assorted swindlers are pursued only by state and local law enforcement personnel, prosecuted only in state courts, and incarcerated only in state prisons.

Most individuals encounter state power in a direct and personal way many times in their lives. A variety of inoculations and vaccinations may be required by the state before entrance into elementary school systems. The right to drive a car requires application for a state driver's license and the passing of a driver's test administered by a state officer. Individuals who wish to marry must apply for a (state) marriage license, and the ceremony is performed either by a public (state) official such as a justice of the peace or by a minister, priest, or rabbi who acts as an agent of the state in performing the ceremony. In divorce, the contesting parties must go through some (state) judicial proceeding to legally dissolve the relationship. And when the custody of children is at issue, state courts are called on to make the decisions.

States also play a regulatory role in a variety of matters having to do with business and commerce within the state. From laws on safety to zoning practices to requirements for filing periodic tax and information reports, practically no enterprise can escape the touch of the state. Entrance into many professions is controlled by state

http://www.consti
tution.org/afp/afp
.htm

Keep up to date on the latest developments in state politics at the Council of State Governments Web site.

licensing boards, which set rules, regulations, and standards that are supposed to ensure the quality of services delivered to citizens, but which also serve to limit entry into the profession. Such licensing procedures touch barbers, lawyers, medical specialists, dieticians, cosmetologists, real estate agents, and even taxidermists.

Perhaps the most visible and pervasive role of the state is in the area of public education. State policies of universal education have emerged from the belief in the importance of schools for improving literacy, inculcating civic and cultural values, and generally enhancing the capabilities of citizens. In administering educational systems, local school districts are agencies of the state. Curricula, certification of teachers, school year length, and policy on truancy are all matters of state power and concern. Some of the great policy debates of the past generation have focused on the role of the states in education. Should prayers be said aloud in the schools, or should a moment of silence for "meditation" be allowed at the beginning of each school day? Should schools be desegregated and, if so, how? Should the busing of schoolchildren be required to achieve integration? Should states be required to equalize expenditures among wealthier and poorer school districts? The *national* government can pursue *national* approaches, but its stress on unity can limit or threaten diversity among the states. Educational policy debates illustrate the vitality of the federal system. When shall the national government have its way, and when shall the states be allowed to go their separate ways?

Local Government: A Political Landscape of Contrasts

One of the reserved powers of the states is their control over the structure and powers of local governments. The Constitution makes no mention of city or other local governments, only for the nation's capital, the "Seat of Government." This fact makes local governments "creatures of the state." The relationships between state legislatures, traditionally with a rural bias, and local governments, especially those of larger cities, have frequently been stormy. Through much of the nineteenth century, state legislatures kept local governments on a tight rein by determining with great specificity their powers, functions, and procedures. In the late nineteenth century and the first half of the twentieth century, however, many local governments—particularly those of larger cities—were granted **home rule**, the power to determine, within broad limits, their own powers and functions. In the 1960s local governments (again, those of larger cities in particular) increasingly developed relationships—generally created by flows of cash—directly with the national government. Nonetheless, all local governments are, according to the Constitution, agents of the state performing what are constitutionally state functions.

As shown in Table 2.1, more than 87,000 local governments exist in the United States. These local governments perform many of the unglamorous services essential to

home rule

A legal status in which local governments, especially large cities, can determine for themselves within broad parameters their own powers and functions without interference from the state government.

TABLE 2.1

Governmental Units in the Federal System

The federal system contains many governments, but they do not all do the same things. The national government, all state governments, and many local governments are general-purpose governments; that is, they perform a wide variety of functions. A city government, for example, will typically provide police protection and numerous social services. School districts and special districts geographically overlap with general-purpose governments and perform only a single function, such as education, water distribution, fire protection, or sewage treatment. The largest growth in number of governmental units in recent years has occurred in special districts, due to the fact that they enable local areas to provide collectively services that they could not afford individually. Moreover, the particular tasks of special districts often stretch beyond the boundaries of local general-purpose governments. Finally, some local governments, such as towns or townships, have not been given power by their state constitutions and governments to perform such functions.

SOURCE: U.S. Census Bureau, *Statistical Abstract of the United States*, 2000, p. 299. Data are for 1997.

1	National Government
50	States
87,453	Local Governments
3,043	Counties (called parishes in Louisiana)
19,372	Towns and townships
13,726	School Districts
34,683	Special Districts

mayor-council

A form of government at the local level that mirrors the executive-legislative structure at the state and national levels. The mayor has executive powers and the council legislative powers.

civilized life, such as collecting trash, pursuing criminals, putting out fires, and providing drinking water. Local governments range in size from huge cities such as New York with more than 8 million people (more than in 39 states combined) to small villages and hamlets with fewer than 100 inhabitants. Governments at the local level differ in their structure. Some have a **mayor-council** form of government, which mirrors the executive-legislative structure at the state and national levels. Others have a council-manager form in which appointed managers look after the day-to-day operations of the government. Still others have a commission form of government in which power is diffused, and no single individual is in charge. Some local governments are "general purpose"—that is, they are responsible for a wide variety of functions including police protection, housing, social services, and parks administration. School districts and special districts overlap these general-purpose governments and are limited to a single function, such as education, mosquito control, fire protection, or transportation.

Although residents do not usually pay much attention to local government, they can and do get intensely interested during a local crisis or controversy. For example, when the water supply becomes polluted with toxic wastes, citizens get involved. School board meetings can be drab affairs, but they can become arenas of excitement and drama when matters such as AIDS education programs or higher taxes for a new school are at stake. Similarly, most local zoning board hearings are routine and sparsely attended. But a proposal by a hamburger chain to locate near a predominantly residential area, or the effort of a chemical company to place a toxic waste facility in or near a town, are issues that practically guarantee action by affected residents. In terms of size, structure, function, and degree of citizen interest, local governments are a mosaic of contrasts.

Government Relationships in the Federal System

The existence of different levels of government within a federal system means that federalism is about *relationships* among governments.[11] Because these governmental relationships are intangible and constantly shifting and changing, trying to understand them is not an easy task. Unlike the presidency, for example, federalism is not an institution with a physical place where its work is done. But one way to understand federalism is to picture it as a series of *legal, fiscal,* and *political* relationships among levels of government.

Models of Federalism

The federal system can at first appear to be a jumble of intangible relationships without obvious order or meaning. The effort to create models is an attempt to create pictures or portraits that bring some order to the complexity and chaos. Two models are particularly important.

dual federalism

A model of federalism in which national and state governments are separate and independent from each other, with each level exercising its own powers in its own jurisdiction.

The first is **dual federalism**, a model positing the view that national and state governments are separate and independent from each other, with each level exercising its own powers in its own jurisdiction. This model, supporting the rights of the states, was important as a judicial theory of federalism in the nineteenth and early twentieth centuries. In *Hammer v. Dagenhart*,[12] a decision the justices later overturned, the Supreme Court ruled that Congress could not ban shipment across state lines of products made with child labor because labor regulation was a state power only.

Dual federalism was never a completely realistic description of the relationship between the nation and the states. For example, in the nineteenth century the national

---

[11]For a comprehensive view of government relationships in the federal system on which this section draws, see Deil S. Wright, *Understanding Intergovernmental Relations,* 3d ed. (Pacific Grove, CA: Brooks/Cole, 1988), especially ch. 2.
[12]247 U.S. 251 (1918).

government gave land to the states to use for educational purposes. Indeed, some of the nation's great universities today are among the "land grant" institutions that resulted from this policy. But the model does reflect the fact that the state and national governments in much of the nineteenth and early twentieth centuries did not interact with each other with the regularity taken for granted today. Dual federalism is also known as the "layer cake" model because the separate levels of government in the model are likened to distinct layers of a cake.

marble cake federalism

A model of federalism in which the intertwining relationships between the national and state and local governments are likened to the intertwining flavors in a marble cake.

The second model is **marble cake federalism**, a view of federalism that likens intertwining relationships between the national and state and local governments to the intertwining flavors in a marble cake.[13] Across a wide range of public policies, despite occasional conflict, all levels of government work closely with one another. Minnesotans and Georgians are also Americans, and that fact helps to explain the intermingling of governmental functions. Interstate highways are largely funded by federal grants, but the highways are built and patrolled by the states. Medical care for the poor is jointly funded by national and state governments. National, state, and local law enforcement authorities regularly combine forces in pursuit of criminals such as drug smugglers, bank robbers, or suspected murderers whose escape routes take them across state lines. State and local health authorities call on the expert services of the national Centers for Disease Control when outbreaks of contagious or mysterious diseases threaten communities. State environmental and health agencies work with national units, such as the Environmental Protection Agency or the Nuclear Regulatory Commission, when problems with toxic or radioactive wastes arise.

The relationships are not always smooth and free of conflict. State and local officials criticize the national government for cuts in funding; FBI agents may run up against local police policies that in the agents' view hinder efficient law enforcement work; state and local officials may confront national regulations that they see as either pointless or unnecessarily encumbering. Nonetheless, marble cake federalism is a portrait of the federal system in which officials from different levels of government work together regularly.

Legal Relationships

One consequence of having different levels of government in the same political system is the potential for conflict over who has the power to do what. Legal conflicts between the national and state governments have both a rich past and a continuing vibrancy. The Supreme Court has played a major role in answering the questions such conflicts raise.

The Court has interpreted the Constitution to mean that diverse approaches among the states in some matters is constitutionally unacceptable. It has generally supported the national government and national constitutional values in conflicts with the

---

[13] The classic statement of the model can be found in Morton Grodzins, "The Federal System," in *President's Commission on National Goals, Goals for Americans* (Englewood Cliffs, NJ: Prentice-Hall, 1960), pp. 265–282.

states. Its interpretation of the interstate commerce clause is a good example. The "regulation of interstate commerce" is one of the most important powers that the Constitution grants to Congress. This provision has allowed Congress to shape national economic and even social policy. States do have a role to play. They can enact legislation affecting commerce to protect the health and safety of citizens. States can also act in the absence of congressional action or when not prohibited by Congress. But when Congress does act, the Supreme Court has generally allowed wide latitude to national legislation that limits state power in interstate commerce. For example, upholding the reach of congressional power in the Civil Rights Act of 1964, the Court held that hotels and local restaurants could not discriminate on the basis of race in their services because travelers and food served were part of interstate commerce.[14] More recently, however, the Court has indicated a willingness to restrict the definition of interstate commerce, thereby limiting congressional power to create gun-free school zones, for example, or to limit violence against women.[15]

Through its interpretation of the due process clause of the Fourteenth Amendment, the Court has also applied most of the limitations on the power of the national government contained in the first eight amendments to the activities of the states themselves. These amendments were added to the Constitution in the early years of the new government to assuage fears that the new national government might be a powerful threat to individual liberties. Ironically, the Court has applied these limitations to the states themselves. For example, states must now provide counsel for people accused of crimes and may not sponsor prayers in the public schools.[16]

The Court's interpretation of the Fourteenth Amendment's *equal protection* clause has also limited state power. For example, the Court's reapportionment decision that required equal populations in state legislative districts shifted political power from rural to urban areas.[17] The Court has even shaped the structure of local government. As an example, the Court found New York City's Board of Estimate, a local government body with substantial powers over land use, the city's budget, and other matters, in violation of its "one person, one vote" rulings.[18] The five boroughs of New York had equal representation on the Board, despite great population differences among the boroughs. The Court's decision was the impetus for elimination of the Board of Estimate and a major restructuring of New York City's government.

Using the equal protection clause the Court has also held that the states cannot exclusively determine for and by themselves the shape of their own school systems, even though public education has been traditionally among the reserved powers of the states. In *Brown v. Board of Education*[19] the Court unanimously declared that racially segregated

---

[14] *See Heart of Atlanta Motel v. United States*, 379 U.S. 274 (1964), and *Katzenbach v. McClung*, 379 U.S. 294 (1964).
[15] See *United States v. Lopez*, 514 U.S. 549 (1995), and *United States v. Morrison*, 529 U.S. 598 (2000), respectively.
[16] *Gideon v. Wainwright*, 372 U.S. 335 (1963); *Engel v. Vitale*, 370 U.S. 421 (1962).
[17] *Baker v. Carr*, 369 U.S. 186 (1962); *Reynolds v. Sims*, 377 U.S. 533 (1964).
[18] *Morris v. Board of Estimate*, 489 U.S. 103 (1989).
[19] 347 U.S. 483 (1954).

school systems are unconstitutional. Thus, some constitutional values have been deemed so important that they must be nationally determined and, if necessary, enforced by national power.

Despite the support the Court has generally given the national government, the constitutional power of the states in conflicts with the national government is not a predetermined issue. In recent cases the Court has weakened the power of the states and slighted the principle of federalism. But in others the Court has asserted a constitutional role for the states, protecting them from incursions of congressional power. The issue of who should set minimum wages and maximum hours for the employees of state governments and their political subdivisions is an example of a case that has gone back and forth with regard to who has jurisdiction. Although the Court upheld that private employers could set wages and hours a half-century ago, it declared in 1976 that states were immune to such requirements. But the Court reversed itself in 1985 by ruling in *Garcia v. San Antonio Metropolitan Transit Authority* that Congress *may* apply minimum-wage and maximum-hour legislation to state employees.[20] Three years later, in *South Carolina v. Baker*, Secretary of the Treasury, the Court ruled that Congress could tax state and local government bearer bonds,[21] a decision that limits the tax immunity of state and local governments. The *Garcia* and *South Carolina* decisions made state and local officials wonder whether the Court had "abandoned" Tenth Amendment protection of state powers.[22]

However, assuaging such fears, the Court ruled in 1991 that a congressional statute banning age discrimination does *not* overrule a provision in the Missouri Constitution requiring state judges to retire at age 70. In other words, the state of Missouri can reasonably determine for itself mandatory retirement policies for state officials.[23] The Court also ruled in 1992 that Congress cannot require a state to "take title" to radioactive waste produced within its borders if the state does not make provision for its disposal.[24] Additionally, in 1997 the Court struck down a congressional attempt to require local law enforcement officials to perform background checks on handgun purchasers and in 2000 ruled unconstitutional Congress's effort to prevent states from disclosing a driver's personal information without the driver's consent.[25] These cases indicate that states continue to draw on powers reserved to them in the Constitution.[26] The search for the proper legal balance between state and national power continues; the line between them has not disappeared.

---

[20] *National League of Cities v. Usery*, 426 U.S. 833 (1976); *Garcia v. San Antonio Metropolitan Transit Authority*, 469 U.S. 528 (1985).
[21] 485 U.S. 505 (1988).
[22] See, for example, David E. Nething, "States Must Regain Their Powers," *State Government* 63 (January–March, 1990): 6–7.
[23] *Gregory v. Ashcroft*, 59 U.S.L.W. 4687 (1991).
[24] *New York v. United States*, 60 U.S.L.W. 4603 (1992).
[25] See *Printz v. United States*, 521 U.S. 898 (1997), and *Reno v. Condon*, 528 U.S. 141 (2000).
[26] See Charles Wise and Rosemary O'Leary, "Is Federalism Dead or Alive in the Supreme Court? Implications for Public Administrators," *Public Administration Review* 52 (November–December 1992): 559–572.

Fiscal Relationships

Federalism is about more than just legal relationships. Cooperative *fiscal* relationships have become the single most important characteristic of federalism in the twentieth century, with money acting as a kind of glue that binds the different levels of government together. It is now commonplace to cite ratification in 1913 of the **Sixteenth Amendment**, which granted Congress the power to tax incomes, as a significant event contributing to the national government's unparalleled capacity to raise revenue. This capacity to raise funds reinforced the unprecedented emergence of public expectations for national government action in the Great Depression. The national government was cast in the role of a banker, doling out money to deal with social and economic ills that states had either ignored or found too large for local solutions.

The terms and conditions of specific programs vary enormously from one program to another, but cash grants from the national government to state and local governments are usually divided into two groups: categorical grants-in-aid and block grants. A **categorical grant-in-aid,** the predominant form of national aid, is a transfer of cash from the national government to state or local governments for some specific purpose, usually with the accompanying requirement that state and local governments match the national money with some funds of their own. The purposes of these grants are determined by the national government, and state and local governments have little or no discretion or flexibility as to how the funds can be spent. If the money is given for highways, it cannot be spent on libraries or airports. Some of these grants are given to state and local governments on the basis of formulas that take into account factors such as population, poverty, and income levels. Others distribute money for specific projects in response to applications from state or local governments.

Categorical grants are available in practically every policy area, including highways, health, education, and nutrition. The Catalog of Federal Domestic Assistance reported that there were 1022 categorical grant programs in 2001.[27] However, a small number of grants comprise a large proportion of total grant dollars. The grants for the Department of Health and Human Services, which includes Medicaid (medical benefits for the poor) and family support (welfare) payments, will make up 59.5 percent of the grant total in 2002. That amount is more than five times the allotment for any other agency.[28]

A **block grant** is a transfer of cash from the national government to state and local governments that allows the recipients greater discretion in its use. Instead of defining with great specificity how the money must be spent, the national government permits expenditures in some broad policy area, such as community development, social serv-

---

Sixteenth Amendment

Amendment to the Constitution, ratified in 1913, that gave Congress the power to tax incomes and thereby massively increase the potential revenue available to the national government.

categorical grant-in-aid

Transfers of cash from the national to state and/or local governments for some specific purpose, usually with the accompanying requirement that state and local governments match the national money with some funds of their own.

block grant

Transfers of cash from the national to state and local governments in which state and local officials are allowed discretion in spending the money within some broad policy area, such as community development or social services.

---

[27] The Catalog of Federal Domestic Assistance, "Types of Assistance," August 2001, http://www.cfda.gov/public/browse_by_typast.asp (22 August 2001).

[28] Office of Management and Budget, *Analytical Perspectives, Budget of the United States Government, Fiscal Year 2002* (FY 2002 Online via GOP access), pp. 195–211.

FIGURE 2.3

National Aid to State and Local Governments Since 1950, in Current and Constant Dollars, in Billions

National aid to state and local governments rose sharply after 1960 to a high point in 1980 of $168.5 billion in constant 1996 dollars, then fell in constant dollars through the 1980s. In the early 1990s, aid began to rise again, in both current and constant dollars. In 2000, the amount in constant dollars was nearly 17 times the amount of aid in 1950.

SOURCE: Office of Management and Budget.

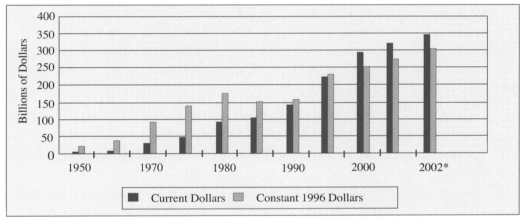

Note: *Data is estimated.

ices, or criminal justice. An increase in this type of grant has been a major federalism priority of the Republican Administration because block grants allow greater discretion at the state and local levels. In 1994 there were 16 block grants, which together accounted for almost 25 percent of the national aid total.[29] State and local governments prefer the flexibility allowed by block grants over the more rigid procedural requirements that accompany categorical grants.

In 1922 the national government granted to the states the relatively paltry sum of $122 million, the major proportion of which was spent on highway construction.[30] Figure 2.3 shows the sharp increase in such aid over the past four decades. Reflecting the explosion of Great Society grant programs in the 1960s, national aid in current dollars almost quintupled between 1965 and 1975, from $11 billion to $50 billion, and almost tripled again in the decade and a half after 1975.

Figure 2.3 shows that national aid is projected to continue rising in the early 2000s, but the growth area in national government dollars is in programs providing payments for individuals, such as Medicaid. In 1960, 35 percent of federal grant dollars were spent on payments for individuals.

---

[29] United States General Accounting Office, *Federal Grants: Design Improvements Could Help Federal Resources Go Further* (Washington, DC: GPO, 1996), p. 16.
[30] Advisory Commission on Intergovernmental Relations, *Categorical Grants: Their Role and Design* (Washington, DC: GPO, 1978), p. 16.

By 2000 that proportion increased to about 63 percent.[31] The proportional drop in grant programs that allow state and local governments to spend money, such as funding for capital projects and the discretionary dollars provided by the now defunct revenue-sharing program, forced those governments to depend increasingly on their own resources to support programs that had previously been aided by Congress. President George W. Bush's first budget proposal projected into the late 2000s the continuing trend of proportionally more dollars for individuals and proportionally less money for other programs.[32]

Political Relationships

The federal system can be viewed as a series of legal and fiscal relationships. However, a third way to look at the federal system is to see it as an arena for *political* relationships among officials at all levels of government who lobby and cajole one another, and who bargain and negotiate with one another. The cast of political players includes members of Congress representing states and local districts, the president, governors, state legislators, mayors, county and township commissioners, and national, state, and local bureaucrats. These officials band together into groups such as the National Governors' Association, the National Conference of State Legislatures, and the United States Conference of Mayors, all of which are among the participants in federal system politics.

The range and variety of political relationships are enormous because officials at all levels in the federal system press for their own interests as they see them. Scarce resources, the search for the appropriate balance between state and national power, and social and economic differences among the states all drive these political relationships. Sometimes local or state officeholders will make demands on the national government as a group. In the competition for dollars, for example, mayors want more federal money. In the battle over which level of government has the power to do what, governors want fewer federal regulations and more state flexibility in deciding regulatory policy.

But many of the political relationships in the federal system derive from economic differences among regions and states and their localities as they compete with each other to press their individual interests. Economic development and the creation of new jobs are always among the highest priorities of state officials. New businesses and jobs can bolster tax collections, help political incumbents keep their posts, and make the state more attractive to outsiders. Understandably, states are in constant competition with each other to attract new industry and to retain the industry they have. Domestic and foreign corporations that are planning new plant sites are wooed by governors, economic development staffs, and local officials, all of whom cite favorable tax provisions,

---

[31] Budget of the United States Government, *Fiscal Year 2002, Historical Tables*, p. 217.
[32] Ibid.

excellent physical facilities, and a skilled and dependable work force as reasons why the new plant should be located in their state.

State officials lobby to get what they see as their fair share of the huge budget expenditures of the national government. Associations of state and city officials and organizations such as the Northeast-Midwest Institute promote the economic interests of the regions they represent.

Members of Congress want for their states and districts the "plums" of national policy, such as military contracts, but not the undesirable consequences of national policy, such as nuclear waste dumps. Competition among the states for national defense dollars is especially keen. Military installations and work on new weapons systems may bring millions of dollars into a state each year, and efforts to close facilities or cut weapons development meet with predictable opposition from state officials and congressional representatives. Understandably, Mississippi's members of Congress think that naval ships built in Mississippi are better than ships built in Virginia.

Other policy examples beyond the struggle for money illustrate the conflicts among states and between states and the national government. The long history of slavery and discrimination against blacks in the South created epic battles between the southern states and the national government. Fights over school integration over the past generation illustrate the durability of the struggle. The issue did not reach the same intensity in states with different traditions and different avenues of economic development. Some of the great battles in Congress over environmental policy are conflicts between members of Congress trying to represent the interests of their states. Californians want stricter auto emissions standards to ameliorate their problem of dirty air, but autoworkers in Michigan fear the economic consequences of stricter standards for their industry. As these illustrations suggest, political relationships in the federal system shape many public policies.

Federalism in the Twenty-First Century

In the first decade of the twenty-first century, the federal system appears to be a curious blend of contrasts, as each level of government asserts its role. The states are now innovators in a variety of public policy areas, including education, welfare, and the environment. But policy innovation is not a new role for the states—they have in the past experimented with new ideas that were later accepted as national policy. For example, a variety of states enacted old-aged pension laws several years before Congress mandated Social Security as a national policy in 1935. Similarly, the state of Wisconsin had a program of unemployment compensation that predated national policy on the matter.[33]

---

[33] Arthur M. Schlesinger, Jr., *The Coming of the New Deal* (Boston: Houghton Mifflin, 1965), pp. 301–303.

Contemporary Controversies
Changing State Constitutions

In contrast to the U.S. Constitution, state constitutions are newer, longer, and more frequently changed. Of the 45 states admitted to the union before 1900, 13 have adopted one or more constitutions in the twentieth century. Of the 50 states, 31 have adopted two or more constitutions, with Louisiana having approved its eleventh in 1975. Among the most recent is the Georgia Constitution (the state's tenth) adopted in 1983. Only one state constitution still in force—Massachusetts's, adopted 1780—predates the U.S. Constitution.

With about 8,300 words, only Vermont's constitution is nearly as short as the U.S. Constitution. Alabama's has 310,000 words, Texas's 80,000, and Oklahoma's 79,000. Much of the length of the state constitutions is due to amendments. The length of the state constitutions means that they are usually far more detailed than the U.S. Constitution. Abundant detail is explained by a fundamental difference in the way Americans view

their national and state constitutions. The former has been largely concerned with the structure, operation, and powers of the government. Since the early nineteenth century the latter have reflected battles within the states over economic and social issues, matters of less interest to the national government before 1890. State constitutions also reflect struggles over legislative apportionment and the franchise. Since constitutions were more permanent than statutes, contending political groups attempted to write their preferred policies into a state's higher law. Moreover, state courts could not invalidate a constitutional provision as being in conflict with the state's constitution. This is why many state constitutions today read more like statutes.

The detail in state constitutions also means that they are changed frequently. The California Constitution has been amended 500 times, and even the new Georgia Constitution had 18 amendments added within six

Some states are now experimenting with market-like approaches in public education by allowing parents to choose the schools their children will attend; in others state courts are mandating more equal educational expenditures across school districts. The latest round of welfare reform, requiring welfare recipients to work, was actually presaged by states that had already begun to experiment with such programs.[34] And across a range of environmental policies, including auto and power plant emissions, recycling, and water quality, some states have set more stringent standards than the national government. Federal budget cuts help to explain this increased vigor of the states. As the national government has wrestled with its own budget deficit, the states have expanded their policy role.

During the early 1990s tensions grew between the national and state and local governments. The national government cut funding going to state and local governments

[34] Elaine Stuart, "Roaring Forward," *State Government News* (January/February 1999): 10–14.

Changing State Constitutions, *continued*

years of its adoption. Since 1776, some 232 constitutional conventions have been held by the states to propose new constitutions or major alterations to existing ones. Between 1900 and 1997, 43 of the 50 states took some kind of official action to amend their constitutions, resulting in the adoption of 644 constitutional amendments—an average of nearly 13 per state. Approximately one-sixth of the 644 were "local" amendments that affected only part of a state, but the remaining amendments had statewide application. In both categories, the amendments typically involved finance, taxation, and debt.

States vary in the way constitutional amendments are proposed, although each state makes *proposing* an amendment a separate step from *ratifying* it. While all allow the legislature (like Congress) to propose amendments, 18 permit a *constitutional initiative*. This allows voters to begin the process of constitutional change by collecting the required number of signatures on a petition. Some states, however, restrict the kind of amendment that may be proposed by an initiative. Amendments may also be proposed by convention. Indeed, the constitutions of 14 states now require the periodic submission to the voters of the question as to whether a constitutional convention should be held. By whatever means proposed, ratification of amendments in almost all states occurs following a majority vote by the electorate.

This chapter explains that much of the change in the national Constitution has come about not through formal amendment but by judicial interpretation. Should Americans prefer more frequent change of the national Constitution by amendment, as is now done in the states? Should the people vote directly on changes to the national Constitution as they routinely do on changes to state constitutions?

while, at the same time, it increased the number of regulations applied to state and local governments. Critics of this strategy called the national actions "unfunded mandates." Examples of these regulations, which result in higher costs that state and local governments must pay, include the federal mandate that local school districts remove asbestos materials from school buildings and the requirement that municipalities monitor a large list of pollutants in drinking water.[35] Protecting water supplies and the health of schoolchildren are worthwhile objectives, but which level of government should pay to meet the costs of national policy mandates?[36] States were being asked to do more to achieve policy objectives set by the national government but with fewer federal resources. By 1995, however, the national government seemed to have gotten the message. Congress

---

[35] Elaine Stuart, "Roaring Forward," *State Government News* (January/February 1999): 28–29.
[36] Timothy J. Conlon, "And the Beat Goes On: Intergovernmental Mandates and Preemption in an Era of Deregulation," *Publius* 21 (Summer 1991): 50–53.

passed the Unfunded Mandates Reform Act that year and, though not a panacea, the legislation led to the review of over 350 intergovernmental mandates during its first five years of operation. The Congressional Budget Office reports that the number of mandates that could be defined as unfounded declined steadily over that time period.[37]

Governors, state legislators, and mayors are more active, but many of them believe that the national government is curtailing their powers and responsibilities and denying them sufficient resources to perform the tasks they are asked to do. The national government has increasingly preempted state and local action in a variety of areas. For example, the national government has told the states to stay out of the economic regulation of buses, trucks, and airlines.[38] The rise in federal demands and the scarcity of dollars at all levels have increased tensions among governments in the federal system. State and local governments have assumed a prominent role in policy-making, but the lively debate over which level of government should have the power to do what, whether national or state action is more appropriate, and who should pay the costs in light of budget deficits, illustrates the continuing vitality of the federal system.

---

[37] Congressional Budget Office, *CBO's Activities Under the Unfunded Mandates Reform Act, 1996–2000* (May 2001).
[38] *Federal-State-Local Relations*, pp. 34–31.

SUMMARY

1. Federalism is a system of government in which a central or national government and regional or state government exercise governmental power within the same political system. Federalism is a compromise between a confederation, in which states hold principal power, and a unitary form of government, in which a central government is dominant. Countries throughout the world have federal systems, and some of the most bitter and consequential conflicts in other countries are battles to redefine the shape of federal systems.

2. In policy, the amendment process, and elections, states play an important role, but the national government has become more dominant in the federal system over the past two centuries. The Constitution delegates express powers to the national government, and the Supreme Court has given expansive interpretation to the implied powers clause in the document. Powers not delegated to the national government are reserved for the states and include police powers ensuring the health, safety, and education of citizens. Also among state powers is control over local governments, which vary greatly in size, structure, and functions.

3. Two models of the federal system are dual federalism and marble cake federalism. The federal system can be seen as a series of legal, fiscal, and political relationships among governments. Through its interpretation of the Constitution, the Supreme Court has generally supported national constitutional values and the national government. At the expense of support for capital and other programs, an increasingly greater proportion of national aid to state and local governments goes to payments for individuals. Officials at all levels press for the interests of their governments in political relationships with other officials in the federal system.

4. States are now vigorous policy innovators, but budget deficits and the rise in national regulations have increased tensions in the federal system.

KEY TERMS

Federalism (41)

confederation (42)

unitary system (42)

interstate compact (47)

electoral college (47)

New Federalism (52)

delegated powers (52)

express powers (52)

implied powers (52)

reserved powers (54)

Tenth Amendment (54)

home rule (56)

mayor-council (57)

dual federalism (58)

marble cake federalism (59)

Sixteenth Amendment (62)

categorical grant-in-aid (62)

block grant (62)

READING FOR FURTHER STUDY

Thomas J. Anton's *American Federalism and Public Policy: How the System Works* (Philadelphia: Temple University Press, 1989) offers a contemporary view of federalism in which coalitions seek policy benefits.

The Council of State Governments (Lexington, Kentucky) publishes biennially *The Book of the States,* a compendium of demographic, structural, and policy data about the states.

Articles describing and analyzing state and local governments in the federal system can be found in the journals *Publius* and *National Civic Review*.

The Advisory Commission on Intergovernmental Relations, a bipartisan group created by Congress to study the federal system, compiles data and publishes reports on a variety of issues in American federalism.

David Osborne provides case studies of policy vigor in the states in *Laboratories of Democracy: A New Breed of Governor Creates Models for National Growth* (Boston: Harvard Business School Press, 1990).

Carl E. Van Horn, ed., *The State of the States* (Washington, DC: Congressional Quarterly, Inc., 1989) provides a series of informative essays on the significance of contemporary changes in state government.

Alice Rivlin's *Reviving the American Dream: The Economy, the States and the Federal Government* (Washington, DC: The Brookings Institution, 1992) presents provocative proposals to reorder policy responsibilities between the national and state governments.

CHAPTER 3

Civil Liberties and Civil Rights

A/P World Wide

Chapter Objectives

Chapter 1 explained that a constitution can be a mainstay of rights. Beyond organizing and granting authority, constitutions place limits on what governments may do. Collectively, these limits are known as civil liberties and civil rights. Civil liberties are legally enforceable freedoms to act or not to act and to be free from unwarranted official intrusion into one's life. They include (but are not limited to) the First Amendment's guarantees of free expression and religious freedom and the Fourth, Fifth, Sixth, and Eighth Amendments' strictures governing police and courts in fighting crime. Civil rights encompass participation—citizens' rights under the law to take part in society on an equal footing with others. They embrace the guarantees of the three Civil War amendments to the Constitution (the Thirteenth, Fourteenth, and Fifteenth), as well as laws passed to give those amendments meaning and force. Civil rights are assurances that people are not penalized because of criteria (such as race or gender) that society decides should be irrelevant in making public policy. Yet, even after more than 200 years' experience as a nation, we continue to disagree over what liberty and equality mean in practice.

The Bill of Rights: Securing the Blessings of Liberty

As explained in Chapter 1, when the Constitution left the hands of the framers in 1787, there appeared to be too few restrictions on what the national government could do, leaving individual liberty without sufficient protection. Several of the state conventions that ratified the proposed Constitution did so with the provision that a "bill of rights" would soon be added. In 1791, the Bill of Rights, comprising the first ten amendments, was ratified (see Table 3.1).

TABLE 3.1

Content of the Bill of Rights

Consisting of barely 450 words, the Bill of Rights (Amendments I through X) was intended to remedy a defect critics found in the Constitution of 1787. In September 1789 Congress proposed 12 amendments for approval by the states. As the eleventh state (three-fourths of 14), Virginia's ratification in December 1791 made the Bill of Rights officially part of the Constitution. The remaining three states—Connecticut, Georgia, and Massachusetts—did not ratify until the 150th anniversary of the Bill of Rights in 1941. One amendment was never ratified. It dealt with apportionment of the House of Representatives and is now obsolete. The other amendment was not ratified until 1992—203 years after it was proposed! The Twenty-seventh Amendment—called the "lost amendment"—delays any increase in congressional salaries until a congressional election has intervened.

Amendment I	Nonestablishment of religion; free exercise of religion; freedoms of speech, press, petition, and peaceable assembly
Amendment II	Keep and bear arms
Amendment III	No quartering of troops
Amendment IV	No unreasonable searches and seizures; standards for search warrants
Amendment V	Indictment by grand jury; no double jeopardy or self-incrimination; no deprivation of life, liberty, or property without due process of law; compensation for taking of private property
Amendment VI	Speedy and public trial by impartial jury in state and district where crime was committed; nature and cause of accusation; confrontation of accusers; compulsory process for witnesses; assistance of counsel
Amendment VII	Jury trial in certain civil cases
Amendment VIII	No excessive bail or fines; no cruel and unusual punishments
Amendment IX	Recognition of the existence of rights not enumerated
Amendment X	Reserved powers of the states

Applying the Bill of Rights to the States

Nearly 180 years elapsed before most of the rights spelled out in the Bill of Rights applied fully to state governments. This was because, as Chief Justice John Marshall (1801–1835) held for the Supreme Court, the Bill of Rights was not intended to apply to the states.[1] As a result, at first disputes between states and their citizens were controlled

---

[1] *Barron v. Baltimore*, 32 U.S. (7 Peters) 243 (1833).

Fourteenth Amendment

Ratified in 1868, the amendment altered the nature of the Union by placing significant restraints on state governments.

by the federal constitution to only a small degree. For most abuses of power, citizens had recourse only to their state constitutions and state courts. But ratification of the **Fourteenth Amendment** (see appendix) in 1868 laid the groundwork for a drastic change in the nature of the Union. First, its language is directed to *state* governments, so aggrieved persons have the federal constitution as an additional shield between themselves and their state governments. Second, the words of the amendment are ambiguous. What, for instance, is the "liberty" the amendment protects?

The Supreme Court was initially hesitant to use the Fourteenth Amendment as a vehicle through which to make the Bill of Rights applicable to the states. Within a century, however, the Court did just that. Without additional formal amendment of the Constitution, the Court "incorporated" or absorbed the Bill of Rights into the Fourteenth Amendment in a series of about two dozen cases beginning in 1897 and concluding in 1969. Today almost all the provisions of the first eight amendments, whether involving free speech or the rights thought necessary for a fair trial, apply with equal rigor to both state and national officials and the laws they make. Only the Sixth Amendment stipulation about a trial's location, the Seventh's stipulation for a jury trial in most civil suits, the Eighth's ban on excessive bail and fines, and the Second and Third Amendments still apply only to the national government. Of these, only the Second and Eighth are substantively important (the Ninth and Tenth Amendments, although part of the Bill of Rights, do not lend themselves to absorption into the Fourteenth Amendment).

The Fragility of Civil Liberties

Charters of liberty, like a bill of rights, are commonplace today in the constitutions of many governments. Yet even a casual observer of world affairs knows that civil liberties are more likely to be preserved (or suspended) in some countries than in others. Even in the United States, the liberties enshrined in the Bill of Rights have meant more in some years than in others because of changing interpretations by the Supreme Court. For example, the Fourth Amendment's ban on "unreasonable searches and seizures" did not apply for a long time to electronic surveillance unless police physically trespassed on a suspect's property. This meant that state and federal agents could eavesdrop electronically in many situations without fear of violating the Constitution. In 1967, however, the Court ruled that the Fourth Amendment covered most electronic searches too, as long as there was a "reasonable expectation of privacy."[2] The words in the Bill of Rights have not changed, but the meaning attributed to those words has changed in the context of Supreme Court decisions.

Exactly why civil liberties thrive in one place or time and not another is a complex phenomenon. But this much is certain: Civil liberties are fragile. The most frequent

---

[2] *Katz v. United States*, 389 U.S. 347 (1967), overruling *Olmstead v. United States*, 277 U.S. 438 (1928).

and sometimes the most serious threats to civil liberties have come not from people intent on throwing the Bill of Rights away but from well-meaning and overzealous people who find the Bill of Rights a temporary bother, standing in the way of objectives, often laudatory ones, they want to reach. Put another way, constitutional protections are sometimes worth the least when they are needed most. When public opinion calls for a "crack down" on certain rights, such demands are felt in judicial chambers just as they are heard in legislative halls. Unsupported, courts and the Bill of Rights alone cannot defend civil liberties.

First Amendment

Part of the Bill of Rights containing protections for political and religious expression.

Free Expression: Speech, Press, and Assembly

The place of the **First Amendment** in the Bill of Rights is symbolic. Its liberties are fundamental because they are essential to the kind of nation the framers envisioned.

The Value of Free Expression

Free expression serves several important objectives. First, *free expression is necessary to the political process set up by the Constitution*. It is difficult to imagine government being responsive to a majority of the political community if the members of that community are afraid of saying what they think. It is even more difficult to imagine members of a political minority trying to persuade the majority without the right to criticize political officeholders. For democratic politics to work, free speech must prevail.

Second, in politics, as in education, *free expression allows the dominant wisdom of the day to be challenged*. Open discussion and debate aid the search for truth and thus foster intelligent policymaking. Whether the question is safeguarding the environment or probing the causes of birth defects, free speech encourages both investigation of the problem and examination of possible solutions.

Third, *free expression aids self-development*. Intellectual and artistic expression may contribute to realizing one's full potential as a human

Street artist Robert Lederman wears an anti-Mayor Rudolph Giuliani shirt while he paints outside the Metropolitan Museum in New York. He has been arrested 29 times for what he calls "free speech-related activities." (*AP Wide World*)

being. If government has the authority to define what kind of art is "acceptable," other kinds will be discouraged or suppressed altogether. Freedom of expression does not guarantee success as a poet, artist, or composer, but it does guarantee each person's right to try.

Free expression has its risks, however. There is no assurance that open debate and discussion will produce the "correct" answer or the wisest policy. Letting people speak their minds freely will surely stretch out the time it takes for a political community to decide what to do. Free speech can also threaten social and political stability. Although there are risks in silencing dissent, risks exist in permitting it too. Nations in upheaval rarely tolerate vocal dissent against official policy. But on balance, the American people, through their public officials and judges, seem willing to accept these risks most of the time.

The Test of Freedom

Even though the First Amendment has been part of the Constitution from almost the beginning, freedom's record has not been free of blemishes. The ink had hardly dried on the Bill of Rights when Congress passed the Sedition Act of 1798, making it a crime to publish "false, scandalous, and malicious" statements about government officials. The law was not challenged in the Supreme Court even though at least ten individuals were convicted before it expired in 1801. Scattered instances of suppression occurred on both sides during the Civil War, but the next major nationwide attacks on speech were directed at virtually anyone or anything pro-German during World War I, and on socialist ideas during the "red scare" that followed.

Only then did the Supreme Court first interpret the free speech clause of the Constitution. During World War I, Charles Schenck was found guilty of violating the Espionage Act by printing and circulating materials designed to protest and obstruct the draft. Announcing the **clear and present danger test**, Justice Holmes (1902–1932) ruled that the First Amendment provided no shield for Schenck's words. "The question . . . is whether the words are used in such circumstances and are of such a nature as to create a clear and present danger that they will bring about the substantive evils that Congress has a right to prevent. It is a question of proximity and degree."[3]

Although Schenck lost his case, Holmes's reasoning remained important. Only when harmful consequences of speech were imminent could government act. As Justice Brandeis (1916–1939) later declared, "If there be time to expose through discussion the falsehood and fallacies, to avert the evil by the processes of education, the remedy to be applied is more speech, not enforced silence."[4]

clear and present danger test

Guideline devised by the Supreme Court in *Schenck v. United States* [249 U.S. 47 (1919)] to determine when speech could be suppressed under the First Amendment.

---

[3] *Schenck v. United States*, 249 U.S. 47 (1919)
[4] *Whitney v. California*, 274 U.S. 357, 377 (1927), Justice Brandeis concurring.

bad tendency test

Guideline devised by the Supreme Court that allowed suppression of speech under the First Amendment if it might promote a harmful result.

incitement test

The Court's current test for First Amendment restrictions. It asks whether a speech act attempts to or is likely to incite lawless action.

prior restraint

Official censorship before something is said or published, or censorship that halts publication already under way. Usually judged unconstitutional today under the First Amendment.

obscenity

As applied by the Supreme Court, certain pornographic portrayals of sexual acts not protected by the First Amendment. The Supreme Court's current definition of the legally obscene appeared in *Miller v. California* [413 U.S. 5 (1973)].

For a while, however, the Holmes-Brandeis view of free speech was rejected by most justices on the Supreme Court, who preferred to apply the **bad tendency test**. Under this rule, government could silence unpopular speech, even if harmful consequences were not immediate.[5] Fortunately for the vitality of free speech, the bad tendency test was replaced in later cases by the clear and present danger test. The major exception since World War II occurred in cases involving suspected communists, mainly in the 1950s,[6] although as late as 1961 the Court maintained that someone who vigorously advocated actions to overthrow the United States government by force could be sent to jail.[7] Otherwise, the Supreme Court has been highly suspicious of restrictions on the *content* of speech. With few exceptions, such restrictions are now presumed to be at odds with the First Amendment. Since 1969 the clear and present danger test has evolved into the **incitement test**, stressing the Court's insistence that harmful consequences (such as a riot) be exceedingly imminent.[8]

Gags

Of the possible restrictions on speech today, the Court is least likely to approve a **prior restraint**. This is official censorship *before* something is said or published, or censorship that halts publication already under way. Prior restraints are especially dangerous to free expression because government does not have to go to the trouble of launching a prosecution and convicting someone at a trial. Even when *The New York Times* and the *Washington Post* reprinted verbatim parts of a purloined classified study of Defense Department decision-making on Vietnam, the Supreme Court, in the "Pentagon Papers case," refused to ban further publication.[9] Most of the justices admitted that the government could make it a crime to publish such materials, but concluded that there could be no restraints in advance. Likewise, the justices will only rarely approve a pretrial gag on newspaper and television reports about a crime, even if such suppression would help protect another constitutional right, the right to a fair trial.

Obscenity and Libel

Descriptions and depictions of various sexual acts have presented a special problem. Unlike cases involving other types of speech, the Court has required no evidence that obscene materials are in fact harmful. Yet the Court steadfastly regards **obscenity** as unprotected speech because of the widespread public view that exposure to obscenity is deleterious. But the justices have had a hard time writing a clearly understood definition

---

[5]*Pierce v. United States*, 252 U.S. 239 (1920).
[6]For example, see *Dennis v. United States*, 341 U.S. 494 (1951), and *Yates v. United States*, 354 U.S. 298 (1957).
[7]*Scales v. United States*, 367 U.S. 203 (1961).
[8]*Brandenburg v. Ohio*, 395 U.S. 444 (1969).
[9]*New York Times Co. v. United States*, 403 U.S. 713 (1971).

of what is obscene. Justice Stewart (1958–1981) once admitted, "I know it when I see it." Under the current standard, the Court will uphold an obscenity conviction if

> (a) "the average person, applying contemporary community standards," would find that the work, taken as a whole, appeals to the prurient interest, (b) . . . the work depicts or describes, in a patently offensive way, sexual conduct specifically defined by the applicable state law, and (c) . . . the work, taken as a whole, lacks serious literary, artistic, political, or scientific value.[10]

The target seems to be "hardcore" pornography. Within limits, the "community" to which the Court refers is local and not national, making the definition of obscenity variable. The policy thus allows one locale to suppress sexually explicit materials while another tolerates them. For example, the Court recently upheld a city ordinance that prohibited nudity in public places, including erotic dancing establishments.[11] Obscenity continues to trouble the nation. Films, videotapes, and magazines portraying explicit sex are big business. Many think the Supreme Court's definition is both too lax and insufficiently enforced. Although reluctant to advocate censorship, some feminists object to obscenity because it degrades women and may even contribute to sexual crimes against them.

libel

Defamation of a person's character or reputation, not protected by the First Amendment. *New York Time Co. v. Sullivan* [376 U.S. 254 (1964)] makes it difficult for public figures and officials to bring successful libel suits against their critics.

Like obscenity, **libel** is not protected by the First Amendment. Involving published defamation of a person's character or reputation, libel may subject a publisher or television network to damage suits involving thousands or even millions of dollars. Beginning in 1964, however, the Supreme Court made it very difficult for public figures and public officials to bring successful libel suits against their critics, because it felt that the democratic process needs robust and spirited debate, which might be muted by threat of legal action. In such situations, public figures and officials initiating libel suits must be able to prove "actual malice"—that is, that the author published information knowing it was false or not caring whether it was true or false.[12]

Freedom of Assembly and Symbolic Speech

symbolic speech

A speech act that centers on action or performance to communicate a point rather than on words.

People often convey ideas and attempt to build support for a cause by holding a meeting or a rally. This is an example of the freedom of assembly that the First Amendment protects. Sometimes assembly involves **symbolic speech** in which words, pictures, and ideas are not at issue but action is. A person may *do* something to send a message, usually in a dramatic, attention-getting manner. It might be a sit-in at the mayor's office to protest a budget cut or a sit-down on a public road leading to a nuclear power plant under construction. In some instances, demonstrators may be constitutionally punished for such nontraditional forms of expression, not because of the ideas expressed but

---

[10] *Miller v. California*, 413 U.S. 5, 8 (1973).
[11] *Erie v. Pap's A.M.*, 529 U.S. 277 (2000).
[12] *New York Times Co. v. Sullivan*, 376 U.S. 254 (1964).

because of the harm that results from the *mode* of expression. It is not the message but the medium that can be the basis of a legitimate arrest.

Yet in a 1989 decision that generated a storm of controversy, the Supreme Court overturned the conviction of Gregory Lee Johnson for burning the American flag in violation of a Texas law.[13] In a demonstration at the Dallas City Hall during the Republican National Convention in 1984, protestors chanted, "America, the red, white, and blue, we spit on you," as Johnson doused the flag with kerosene and set it ablaze. Short of a protest that sparks a breach of the peace or causes some other kind of serious harm, the Court held (five to four) that a state may not criminalize the symbolic act of flag burning. The Court's reasoning was that government protects the physical integrity of the flag because the flag is a symbol of the nation. Just as people may verbally speak out against what they believe the nation "stands for," they may also express the same thought by defacing or destroying the symbol of the nation. The following year, the Court held that the First Amendment also barred Congress from criminalizing flag burning, a decision that sparked a renewed drive to amend the Constitution.[14] The drive failed in 1990 when Congress failed to pass a constitutional amendment by the required two-thirds vote in both houses.

The Court has also invalidated a city ordinance that outlawed cross burning and other forms of symbolic hate speech directed against certain minorities.[15] The ordinance was defective because it was content-based: Some, not all, hate-messages were banned. The decision may be far-reaching because it calls into question the constitutionality of similar bans at public universities.

Religious Freedom

Guarantees of religious freedom form the first lines of the First Amendment. Ahead of other protections are an assurance of free exercise and a prohibition of an establishment of religion. Removing religion from the reach of political majorities reflected practical needs in 1791. The United States was already one of the world's most religiously diverse countries.

Religion and the Constitution

The Constitution is intentionally a non-sectarian document. It had to be if the framers were to secure ratification after 1787 and if the new government was to avoid the religious divisiveness that had plagued Europe before and after the Reformation, as well as the American colonies. Even though a few states still maintained established (state-supported)

---

[13]*Texas v. Johnson*, 491 U.S. 397 (1989).
[14]*United States v. Eichman*, 496 U.S. 310 (1990).
[15]*R.A.V. v. City of St. Paul*, 60 U.S.L.W. 4667 (1992).

churches in 1791, the First Amendment said that the nation could not have one.

The United States is even more religiously diverse today. About three-fifths of the population are members of churches, synagogues, and mosques. More than 90 distinct religious groups claim more than 50,000 members each. Within this context, the religion clauses have the same objectives, but work in different ways. The **free exercise clause** preserves a sphere of religious practice free of interference by government. The idea is that people should be left to follow their own dictates of belief or nonbelief. The **establishment clause** keeps government from becoming the tool of one religious group against others. Government may not be a prize in a nation of competing faiths.

Churchgoers return to church *(AP Wide World)*

Even though both religion clauses work to guard religious freedom, they concern different threats and so at times seem to pull in opposite directions. Rigorous protection of free exercise may appear to create an establishment of religion. Rigorous enforcement of the ban on establishment may seem to deny free exercise.[16]

Aid to Sectarian Schools

The Supreme Court has never limited the First Amendment's ban on the literal establishment of an official state church. But how much involvement between church and state is too much? Coins, for example, display the motto "In God We Trust." A troublesome area for almost a half-century has been public financial support for sectarian schools. The current standard for determining when government has violated the establishment clause in this context dates from a 1971 decision by the Supreme Court.[17] To pass scrutiny under the **Lemon test**, a law must have, first of all, a *secular purpose*. Second, the primary effect of the law must be *neutral*, neither hindering nor advancing religion. Third, the law must not promote *excessive entanglement* between church and state by requiring government to

free exercise clause

Provision of the First Amendment guaranteeing religious freedom.

establishment clause

Provision of the First Amendment barring government support of religion.

***Lemon* test**

A standard announced in *Lemon v. Kurtzman* [403 U.S. 602 (1971)] to determine when a statute violates the establishment clause. The law in question must have a secular purpose and a neutral effect and must avoid an excessive entanglement between church and state.

---

[16] For example, see *Westside Community Schools v. Mergens*, 496 U.S. 226 (1990).
[17] *Lemon v. Kurtzman*, 403 U.S. 602 (1971).

become too closely involved in the affairs of a religious institution. Using these criteria, the Court has upheld some, but not most, forms of state aid that have been challenged. Generally, direct grants of money from a government agency to a religious institution are the least likely to be found acceptable under the Constitution.

Prayer in the Public Schools

Whether religious observances can take place in public schools is another thorny issue. Because of strong emotions on both sides, the Court's decisions have stirred up controversy. In 1962 the justices outlawed a nondenominational prayer prescribed by the Board of Regents for opening daily exercises in the public schools of New York State. The following year, a Pennsylvania statute mandating daily Bible readings in public schools met a similar fate.[18] Reaction to these decisions in Congress and the nation was anything but dispassionate. After the New York prayer case, the U.S. House of Representatives unanimously passed a resolution to have the motto "In God We Trust" placed behind the Speaker's desk in the House chamber. The motto is still there for all to see during televised sessions of Congress.

Of course, the Supreme Court has never said that students cannot pray in school—students have been doing that before exams for years. But the Court has remained firm in its opposition to state-sponsored religious activities in public schools. For example, an Alabama statute authorizing a period of silence at the start of the school day for "meditation or voluntary prayer" was seen by most justices as constitutionally defective because the law endorsed religion as a preferred activity.[19] A bare majority of the Court even found constitutionally objectionable an invocation offered by a rabbi at a public middle school commencement. Although student attendance at the ceremony was optional, the prayer nonetheless carried "a particular risk of indirect coercion" of religious belief, according to justice Anthony Kennedy.[20] For the four dissenters, Justice Antonin Scalia asserted that the nation's long tradition of prayer at public ceremonies was a compelling argument that the school had not violated the establishment clause. In 2000, the Court maintained course by finding a student led prayer played over a public address system prior to a school football game to be in violation of the establishment clause.[21]

Religious Observances in Official Settings

Because of the impressionable nature of children, the Court has been quickest to strike down religious influences in elementary and secondary schools. Elsewhere, the justices sometimes wink. In 1983 the Court approved Nebraska's practice of paying the state

---

[18] *Engel v. Vitale*, 370 U.S. 421 (1962); *School District of Abington Township v. Schempp*, 374 U.S. 203 (1963).
[19] *Wallace v. Jaffree*, 472 U.S. 38 (1985).
[20] *Lee v. Weisman*, 60 U.S.L.W. 4723 (1992).
[21] *Santa Fe Independent School Dist. v. Doe*, 530 U.S. 290 (2000).

legislature's chaplain out of public funds.[22] (Both houses of the United States Congress also have chaplains who pray at the beginning of each day's session.) The following year, a bare majority allowed city officials in Pawtucket, Rhode Island, to erect a municipally owned Christmas display, including a crèche, in a private park. However, the Court has placed some limits on official observances of religious holidays, finding unacceptable a privately owned crèche displayed in the county courthouse in Pittsburgh, Pennsylvania. Above the crèche was a banner proclaiming "Gloria in excelsis Deo" (Latin for "Glory to God in the highest"). Yet in the same case, the Court found acceptable a nearby display that combined an 18-foot menorah and a 45-foot tree decorated with holiday ornaments. The justices explained that the crèche and banner impermissibly "endorsed" religion, but that the menorah and tree only "recognized" the religious nature of the winter holidays.[23] Such decisions point to the difficulty in deciding how much separation the establishment clause commands between government and religion.

Free Exercise of Religion

Contemporary free exercise problems typically arise from application of a law that by its own words has nothing to do with religion, yet works a hardship on some religious groups by commanding them to do something that their faith forbids or by forbidding them to do something that their faith commands. This kind of conflict often occurs with small separatist groups whose interests are overlooked when laws are made. Relying on the free exercise clause, they ask to be exempted on religious grounds from obeying the law. For example, a nearly unanimous bench in 1972 exempted members of the Old Order Amish and the Conservative Amish Mennonite churches from Wisconsin's compulsory school attendance law.[24] Like most states, Wisconsin required school attendance until age 16. The Amish were religiously opposed to formal schooling beyond the eighth grade. The justices found a close connection between the faith of the Amish and their simple, separatist way of life. The law not only compelled them to do something at odds with their religious tenets but also threatened to undermine the Amish community. On balance, in the Court's view, the danger to religious freedom outweighed the state's interest in compulsory attendance.

Recently, however, the Court has become less hospitable to free exercise claims. In 1990, the justices ruled against two members of the American Indian Church who were fired from their jobs as drug counselors in a clinic in Oregon after they ingested peyote (a hallucinogen) as part of a religious ritual. Oregon officials then denied them unemployment compensation because their loss of employment resulted from "misconduct." Under state law, peyote was a "controlled substance" and its use was

---

[22] *Marsh v. Chambers*, 463 U.S. 783 (1983).
[23] *Allegheny County v. American Civil Liberties Union*, 492 U.S. 573 (1989).
[24] *Wisconsin v. Yoder*, 406 U.S. 205 (1972).

forbidden. The two ex-counselors cited scientific and anthropological evidence that the sacramental use of peyote was an ancient practice and was not harmful. The Court, however, decided that Oregon had not violated the First Amendment. When action based on religious belief runs afoul of the criminal law, the latter prevails.[25] Though Congress attempted to reverse this ruling with the Religious Freedom Restoration Act in 1993, the Court found that this act exceeded congressional authority.[26]

Fundamentals of American Criminal Justice

legal guilt

The concept that a defendant's factual guilt be established in accordance with the laws and the Constitution before criminal penalties can be applied.

The American system of criminal justice insists not simply that a person be proved guilty, but that the guilt be proved in the legally prescribed way. This is the concept of **legal guilt**, inherent in the idea of "a government of laws and not of men."[27] Courts sit not just to make sure that wrongdoers are punished but to see that law enforcement personnel obey the commands of the Bill of Rights. The precise meaning of these commands at a given time represents the prevailing judgment on the balance to be struck between two values: the liberty and the safety of each citizen. The first focuses on fairness to persons accused of crimes, and emphasizes that preservation of liberty necessitates tight controls on law enforcement officers, even if some guilty persons go unpunished. The second focuses on crime control, emphasizing that too many rules hamstring police and judges, give lawbreakers the upper hand, and disserve honest citizens. Tension between the two values persists.

Inconvenient as they may be, the strictures of the Bill of Rights deliberately make government's crime fighting tasks harder to perform. Yet, holding police to standards of behavior set by the Constitution protects the liberty of everyone. Otherwise, officials would have the power to do whatever they wanted to whomever they wanted, whenever they wanted. Without limits to authority, America would be a far different place in which to live.

Presumption of Innocence and Notice of Charges

presumption of innocence

A concept in criminal procedure that places the burden of proof on the government in establishing guilt.

The idea that a person is "innocent until proved guilty" is often misunderstood. It does not mean that the police and prosecuting attorney think that the accused person is innocent, for putting obviously innocent people through the torment of a criminal trial would be a gross injustice. Instead, the **presumption of innocence** lays the burden of proof on the government. It is up to the state to prove the suspect's guilt "beyond a reasonable doubt." Along with a convincing case of factual guilt, the prosecution must also demonstrate criminal intent, or *mens rea*.

---

[25] *Oregon Employment Division v. Smith*, 494 U.S. 872 (1990).

[26] *City of Boerne v. Flores*, 521 U.S. 507 (1997).

[27] This phrase was popularized by John Adams shortly before the Revolutionary War and was later incorporated into the Massachusetts Constitution, the oldest of the American state constitutions still in force.

ex post facto laws

Laws that make an act a crime after it was committed or increase the punishment for a crime already committed. Prohibited by the Constitution.

bill of attainder

A law that punishes an individual and bypasses the procedural safeguards of the legal process. Prohibited by the Constitution.

Fourth Amendment

Part of the Bill of Rights that prohibits unreasonable searches and seizures of persons and their property.

warrant

Official authorization for government action.

probable cause

A standard used in determining when arrests and searches can be conducted by police.

A suspect is entitled to know what the state intends to prove and, therefore, what he or she must defend against. The state must go beyond saying merely that someone is a thief. The charge must explain, among other things, (1) what was stolen, (2) approximately when it was stolen, (3) by whom, and (4) from whom it was stolen. This principle also means that criminal laws must be as specific as possible so that citizens can have fair notice of what conduct is prohibited. The greater the vagueness in a law, the greater the danger of arbitrary arrests and convictions.

The basic fairness component of advance notice is why the Constitution prohibits **ex post facto laws**, criminal laws that apply retroactively. The Constitution also forbids a bill of attainder for a similar reason. A **bill of attainder** is a law that imposes punishment but bypasses the procedural safeguards of the legal process. Thus, a person might not have the opportunity for even a simple defense.

Limits on Searches and Arrests

The **Fourth Amendment** denies police unbounded discretion to arrest and search people and their possessions. Many searches and some arrests cannot take place at all until a judge has issued a **warrant**, or official authorization. To obtain a warrant, the police must persuade a judge that they have very good reason (called **probable cause**) for believing that someone has committed a crime or that evidence exists in a particular location. Warrantless searches of arrested suspects or automobiles are permitted in certain circumstances, but police officers who have made a warrantless search must still convince a judge afterward that they had probable cause to act.

Electronic surveillance is also usually considered a search in the constitutional sense. Under current law, practically all such "bugging" must be done on the authority of a warrant, except for exceptional situations involving agents of foreign powers.[28] Advances in surveillance technology continue to push the boundaries of the Fourth Amendment. In 2001, the Court held that heat sensing equipment that detects whether a private home is radiating abnormal levels of heat (which might indicate the use of heat lamps for growing marijuana plants) could not be used without a warrant.[29]

What happens when a judge concludes that police officers have acted improperly when making an arrest or conducting a search? In such instances, the exclusionary rule may come into play. This judge-made rule puts teeth into the Fourth Amendment by denying government in many situations the use of evidence gained as a result of violation of the suspect's rights. The rule lies at the heart of the clash between the values of fairness and crime control.[30]

---

[28]*United States v. U.S. District Court*, 407 U.S. 297 (1972).
[29]*Kyllo v. United States*, 533 U.S. 961 (2001).
[30]See *Mapp v. Ohio*, 367 U.S. 643 (1961), and *United States v. Leon*, 468 U.S. 897 (1984).

Assistance of Counsel and Protection Against Self-Incrimination

Other constitutional restraints are at work in the police station and in the courtroom. As interpreted by the Supreme Court, the Fifth Amendment denies government the authority to coerce confessions from suspects or to require suspects to testify at their own trials. These restraints conform with the presumption of innocence. The state must make its case—it may not compel the suspect to do its work. Under *Miranda v. Arizona*,[31] judges exclude almost all confessions, even if no physical coercion is present, unless police have first performed the following actions:

1. Advised the suspect of a right to remain silent (that is, a right not to answer questions)
2. Warned the suspect that statements he or she might make may be used as evidence at a trial
3. Informed the suspect of a right to have a lawyer present during the interrogation
4. Offered the services of a lawyer free of charge during the interrogation to suspects financially unable to retain one

If a suspect refuses to talk to the police, the police may not continue the interrogation. If a suspect waives these *Miranda* **rights** and agrees to talk, the state must be prepared to show to a judge's satisfaction that the waiver was done "voluntarily, knowingly, and intelligently." As it is, many "streetwise" suspects decide that it is in their interest to talk as part of a **plea bargain**—a deal with the prosecutor to obtain a lighter sentence in exchange for a guilty plea. Guilty pleas allow most criminal cases to be settled without going to trial, so the legal use of confessions continues.

For a long time, the **Sixth Amendment**'s assurance of counsel, or legal assistance, remained more promise than substance. Many defendants simply could not afford to hire an attorney, and some courts provided free counsel for the poor only in **capital cases** (cases in which the death penalty might be imposed). Until the 1970s, for example, 75 percent of people accused of **misdemeanors** (less serious offenses, punishable by a jail term of less than one year) went legally unrepresented. Since the 1930s the Supreme Court has greatly expanded the Sixth Amendment right. Today all persons accused of **felonies** (serious offenses, punishable by more than one year in jail) and all accused of misdemeanors for which a jail term is imposed must be offered counsel, at the government's expense if necessary.[32]

Still, none of the right-to-counsel rulings creates full equality in access to legal assistance. The Constitution, after all, does not guarantee a "perfect" trial, only a "fair" one. Indigents must be content with public defenders and court-appointed attorneys paid from public funds. Public defenders carry heavy case loads, their time is spread thin, and

---

Miranda rights

Requirements announced in *Miranda v. Arizona* [384 U.S. 436 (1966)] to protect a suspect during a police interrogation.

plea bargain

A deal with the prosecutor to obtain a lighter sentence.

Sixth Amendment

Provision of the Bill of Rights assuring, among other things, the right to counsel.

capital case

A criminal proceeding in which the defendant is on trial for his or her life.

misdemeanor

Less serious criminal offense, usually punishable by not more than one year in jail.

felony

A serious criminal offense, usually punishable by more than one year in prison.

---

[31]384 U.S. 436 (1966). See also *Dickerson v. United States,* 530 U.S. 428 (2000).
[32]*Powell v. Alabama,* 287 U.S. 45 (1932); *Gideon v. Wainwright,* 372 U.S. 335 (1963); *Scott v. Illinois,* 440 U.S. 367 (1979).

Contemporary Controversies
How Much Affirmative Action?

Suppose that a school board and a teachers' union agree to increase the number of minority faculty members in the public schools. In this district there has been no prior racial discrimination; the union and the school officials simply conclude that it is good publicity to hire more minority teachers. Suppose also that the agreement protects minority teachers by providing that if layoffs become necessary, the percentage of minority teachers would not be reduced. Next assume that budget reductions force layoffs, with the result that white teachers with greater seniority are laid off before minority teachers with less. In a 1986 case with similar facts from Jackson, Michigan,[a] the Supreme Court ruled that racially preferential *firing* was not permissible unless identifiable victims of past discrimination were being protected. Most justices thought the Michigan plan went too far by imposing undue burdens on particular individuals in order to achieve the laudable objective of racial equality. Yet, a majority believed that racially preferential *hiring* was permissible under certain circumstances. According to Justice O'Connor, "a public employer, consistent with the Constitution, may undertake an affirmative action program which is designed to further a legitimate remedial purpose and which implements that purpose by means that do not impose disproportionate harm on the interests, or unnecessarily trammel the rights, of innocent individuals. . . ."

In another situation, suppose that a city government requires contractors receiving city business to subcontract out a certain percentage of the dollar amount of each contract to one or more minority-owned businesses. Called a set-aside quota, the plan is designed to assist minorities by overcoming their exclusion in past years from the construction trades. Modeling its program on a ten percent set-aside mandated by Congress and upheld by the Supreme Court in 1980,[b] the city council in Richmond, Virginia, adopted a 30% set-aside plan in 1983. In 1989, however, the Supreme Court ruled that the quota violated the Fourteenth Amendment's equal protection clause.[c] According to Justice O'Connor, "To accept Richmond's claim that past societal discrimination alone can serve as a basis for rigid racial preferences would be to open the door to competing claims for 'remedial relief' for every disadvantaged group. The dream of a Nation of equal citizens in a society where race is irrelevant to personal opportunity and achievement would be lost in a mosaic of shifting preferences based on inherently unmeasurable claims of past wrongs. . . ." The ruling in the Richmond case has had a widespread impact—36 states and 190 cities had similar remedial programs.

In a situation like the Michigan case, should consideration of race be permitted in hiring but not in firing? In his dissent in the layoff case, Justice Stevens compared the Michigan plan to a contract that gives added job protection to computer science or foreign-language teachers. Should race-based classifications be regarded differently from those that are skill-based? In the Richmond case, do you agree with the Court's decision? Should it make any difference that a bare majority of Richmond's city council was African American at the time the council adopted the set-aside quota?

[a] *Wygant v. Jackson Board of Education*, 476 U.S. 267 (1986).

[b] *Fulliloce v. Klutznick*, 448 U.S. 448 (1980).

[c] *Richmond v. J.A. Croson Co.*, 488 U.S. 469 (1989).

compared to others in their profession, they are underpaid. In federal courts they are now responsible for over half of all defense work. They can cope with their caseloads only with the help of plea bargains. Defendants retaining counsel at their own expense also fare differently. Only a few can "afford the best."

Limits on Punishment

Eighth Amendment

The part of the Bill of Rights that prohibits "cruel and unusual punishments." This constitutional provision is often at issue in death penalty cases.

Guilty verdicts by juries or guilty pleas usually result in punishment for the accused. Generally, the Constitution leaves the particular sentence to legislators and judges, subject to the **Eighth Amendment's** prohibition of "**cruel and unusual punishment**." In the Supreme Court's view this means, first, that certain kinds of penalties (torture, for example) may not be imposed at all; second, that certain acts or conditions (such as alcoholism) may not be made criminal;[33] and third, that penalties may not be imposed capriciously. Indeed, the Eighth Amendment comes into play most frequently when someone has been sentenced to death. In only two noncapital cases has the Court overturned a sentence because it was too extreme.[34]

cruel and unusual punishment

Prohibited by the Eighth Amendment; at issue in capital cases.

Between 1930 and 2000 there were approximately 4,542 legal executions in the United States, with 85 percent of these occurring before 1972. Today, 38 of the 50 states, as well as the federal government, allow capital punishment, but the states vary widely in terms of the number of executions carried out, as Figure 3.1 shows. Nationally more than 3,500 persons were on "death row" as of the end of 1999. Opponents of the death penalty would like the Supreme Court to impose more restrictions on the states. Even if executions are not inherently "cruel and unusual," many believe that they are racially discriminatory because African Americans are more likely than whites to be sentenced to die, as are killers of whites versus killers of African Americans.[35] Others conclude that the sentencing process is fundamentally flawed because it results in caprice. One study found little or no difference between the facts of murder cases in which the death penalty was imposed and in which it was not.[36]

A Right to Privacy

Ninth Amendment

Part of the Bill of Rights that cautions that the people possess rights not specified in the Constitution.

Some liberties Americans enjoy are not specifically mentioned in the Constitution, as the **Ninth Amendment** cautions. One such judicially discovered civil liberty is the right to privacy, announced in 1965.[37] With far-reaching implications, this decision invalidated a Connecticut statute that prohibited the use of birth control devices.

---

[33]*Robinson v. California*, 370 U.S. 660 (1962).

[34]*Weems v. United States*, 217 U.S. 349 (1910); *Solem v. Helm*, 463 U.S. 277 (1983). *Harmelin v. Michigan*, 59 U.S.L.W. 4839 (1991), which upheld a mandatory sentence of life imprisonment without the possibility of parole for possession of more than 650 grams of a substance containing cocaine, means that legislatures have almost complete discretion in setting punishments for noncapital offenses.

[35]David C. Baldus, George Woodworth, and Charles Pulanski, "Comparative Review of Death Sentences: An Empirical Study of the Georgia Experience," *Journal of Criminal Law and Criminology* 74 (1983): 661; see *McCleskey v. Kemp*, 481 U.S. 279 (1987).

[36]Victor L. Streib, "Executions under the Post-*Furman* Capital Punishment Statutes," *Rutgers Law Journal* 15 (1984): 443.

[37]*Griswold v. Connecticut*, 381 U.S. 479 (1965).

The Abortion Controversy

Roe v. Wade

Supreme Court decision [410 U.S. 113 (1973)] establishing a constitutional right to abortion.

Several decisions that followed led to ***Roe v. Wade,***[38] the landmark abortion case. Throwing out the abortion laws of almost all the states, the Court recognized a woman's interest in terminating her pregnancy, the state's interest in protecting her health, and the state's interest in protecting "prenatal life." According to the seven-justice majority, the Constitution prohibited virtually all restrictions on abortions during the first trimester of pregnancy, allowed reasonable medical regulations to guard the woman's health in the second trimester (but no outright prohibitions of abortion), and permitted the state to ban abortions only in the third trimester after the point of fetal "viability" (except when the pregnancy endangered the woman's life). For 15 years after *Roe*, Congress and some state legislatures tried to limit the availability of abortion and to discourage its use, but the Supreme Court invalidated most restrictions, reasoning that the right to an abortion was a fundamental right, and thus the government had to show compelling reasons when the right was curtailed.

In 1989 opponents of abortion won a significant victory in the Supreme Court. In a case from Missouri, five justices upheld, among other things, a requirement for fetal viability testing prior to the twenty-fourth week of pregnancy, something which the Court previously would have doubtless struck down.[39] Moreover, the Court discarded *Roe*'s trimester-based analysis of the abortion right, but stopped short of overruling *Roe*. In 1992 the Court upheld parts of a Pennsylvania statute that imposed several conditions before a woman could obtain an abortion.[40] These included informed consent provisions, a 24-hour waiting period, parental consent for minors, and record-keeping regulations for medical personnel. However, the Court refused to accept a requirement for spousal notification because it imposed an "undue burden" on the abortion right.

Norma McCorvey, left, who was Jane Roe in the 1973 *Roe v. Wade* Supreme Court case that gave women the right to an abortion, walks with her attorney outside the Supreme Court. *(AP Wide World)*

---

[38]410 U.S. 113 (1973).
[39]*Webster v. Reproductive Health Services*, 492 U.S. 490 (1989).
[40]*Planned Parenthood of Southeastern Pennsylvania v. Casey*, 60 U.S.L.W. 4795 (1992).

The decisions in the Missouri and Pennsylvania cases have led to four conclusions. First, abortion is no longer a fundamental right, but it does enjoy modest constitutional protection. Second, and as a consequence of the first, total or near-total bans on abortion are almost certainly unconstitutional. Third, it remains to be seen what additional abortion regulations the Court is prepared to accept. Fourth, except for outright bans, a woman's freedom to terminate a pregnancy now depends largely on what her state legislature, Congress, and the executive branch allow. That being said, in 2000 the Court further defined the scope of legislative restrictions by ruling unconstitutional a Nebraska statute that criminalized the procedure known as "partial birth" abortion.[41]

Personal Autonomy and Sexual Orientation

For many people, the principle of personal autonomy, which lies at the heart of privacy cases, suggests that government should leave people alone in their choices about sexual relations, including homosexuality. Nonetheless, all states today have laws regulating private behavior and personal relations to some extent. Homosexual marriages, for ex-

[41]*Stenberg v. Carhart*, 530 U.S. 914 (2000).

FIGURE 3.1

Executions by State, 1976–2000

(See following page.) In *Furman v. Georgia,* 408 U.S. 238 (1972), the Supreme Court ruled five to four that the death penalty, as then administered, was cruel and unusual punishment in violation of the Eighth Amendment. Too much discretion in the hands of juries and judges had made application of the death penalty capricious. Most states then reinstated capital punishment (as did Congress for aircraft hijacking) with more carefully drawn statutes to meet the Court's objections in *Furman*. In *Gregg v. Georgia,* 428 U.S. 152 (1976), a majority of the Supreme Court concluded that the death penalty was not inherently cruel and unusual and upheld a two-step sentencing scheme designed to set strict standards for trial courts. A jury would first decide the question of guilt and then in a separate proceeding impose punishment.

Of the 38 states that now permit capital punishment, one (New Hampshire) sentenced no one to death between 1976 and 2000. Of the 37 states in which death sentences have been imposed, executions were carried out in only 31 states during this period. The states of Texas, Virginia, Florida, and Missouri accounted for approximately 61 percent of the executions. Twenty states executed 98 convicted capital felons in 1999, the largest number of executions in a single year since 1951, when 105 persons were put to death. Of the 85 executions in 2000, 40 occurred in Texas.

SOURCE: U.S. Department of Justice.

Figure 3.1—Executions by State, 1976–2000

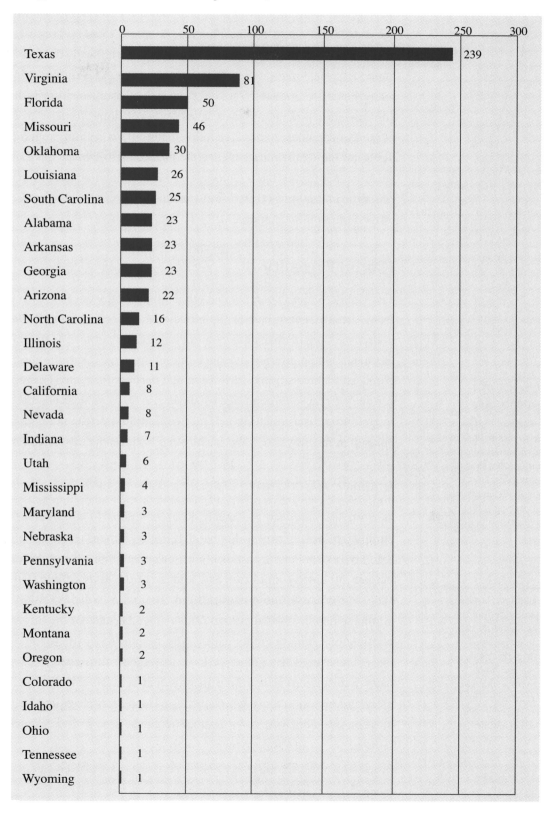

ample, are not officially recognized by any state, and in 1996 Congress passed the Defense of Marriage Act, which provides a federal definition of marriage that specifically excludes same-gender couples. In some locales, homosexual couples may not adopt or have legal custody of children. While eighteen states and numerous cities have banned sexual orientation discrimination in public employment, it remains legal in many places to engage in sexual orientation discrimination in housing and public accommodation practices.[42] Five states outlaw sodomy (oral or anal sex) between persons of the same gender, and twelve more states outlaw sodomy regardless of gender. Though the Supreme Court found such policies acceptable under the Constitution in 1986, ten years later it found that a Colorado constitutional amendment that prohibited laws barring discrimination against homosexuals was in violation of the Equal Protection Clause of the Fourteenth Amendment.[43]

Racial Equality

The United States is racially and ethnically wealthy because of centuries of immigration from virtually every part of the globe. The nation's motto (*E Pluribus Unum*—"out of many, one") symbolizes this coming together of peoples as much as it does the union of the states. Some groups have encountered massive discrimination, however; racial, religious, and ethnic stigmas have been real barriers for many. Perhaps because of color and certainly because of centuries of slavery, African Americans have had the hardest time overcoming discrimination in America. Latinos, whose numbers in this nation have increased in recent years, have faced some of the same obstacles to equality.

Equality: A Concept in Dispute

equality of opportunity

A standard that calls for government to remove barriers of discrimination, such as segregation laws or racially exclusive hiring practices, that have existed in the past.

equality of condition

A standard, beyond equality of opportunity, that requires policies, such as redistribution of income and other resources, that seek to reduce or eliminate the effects of past discrimination.

A word like *equality* can mean different things to different people. For believers in **equality of opportunity**, it is enough if government removes barriers of discrimination that have existed in the past. If life is like a marathon, all people should be allowed to participate by having a number and a place at the starting line. Others think government should promote **equality of condition**. To do this, policies should seek to reduce or even eliminate handicaps that certain runners face because of the lingering effects of past discriminations. The marathon can hardly be fair, they say, if some runners start out with their shoelaces tied together or have to wear ill-fitting shoes. Accordingly, the government will have to redistribute income and resources, collecting from those who have more and giving to those who have less. Head Start programs for preschool children and need-based scholarships for college students are obvious devices intended to further

---

[42]Wayne van der Meide, *Legislating Equality: A Review of Laws Affecting Gay, Lesbian, Bisexual, and Transgendered People in the United States* (Washington, DC: National Gay and Lesbian Task Force, 2000).
[43]*Bowers v. Hardwick*, 478 U.S. 186 (1986) and *Romer v. Evans*, 517 U.S. 620 (1996).

Segregated drinking fountains symbolized the separate worlds of the South until the 1960s. *(Library of Congress)*

equality of result

A standard, beyond equality of condition, that requires policies such as affirmative action or comparable worth, that places some people on an equal footing with others.

Thirteenth Amendment

The first of the Civil War amendments to the Constitution. Adopted in 1865, it banned slavery throughout the United States.

equal protection clause

Part of the Fourteenth Amendment that is the source of many civil rights, and declares that no state shall deny to any person "the equal protection of the laws."

equality of condition. Some find such policies inadequate. The effects of inequality, whether of wealth or race or gender, are too strong and pervasive. Government must therefore pursue **equality of result**. In the marathon, government may have to carry some runners to the finish line if they are to get there at all. Some affirmative action programs are aimed at achieving equality of result.

The Legacy: Slavery and Third-Class Citizenship

Shortly after the Civil War ended, ratification of the **Thirteenth Amendment** in 1865 banished slavery and "involuntary servitude" from the country. Following quickly were ratification of the Fourteenth and Fifteenth amendments in 1868 and 1870 and passage of several civil rights acts. Collectively these conferred rights of citizenship on the newly freed slaves and officially removed race as a criterion for voting. Especially significant was the **equal protection clause** of the Fourteenth Amendment: ". . . nor shall any State deny to any person within its jurisdiction the equal protection of the laws" (see Table 3.2).

By the end of the nineteenth century, however, it was clear that the nation had abandoned the promises of full citizenship for the former slaves. Enforcement of civil rights laws became lax, and the Supreme Court made it clear that the Constitution would not stand in the way of racially discriminatory policies. In *Plessy v. Ferguson*, for example,

TABLE 3.2
Chronology of Major Civil Rights Decisions, Laws, and Amendments

The drive for political equality for all Americans has been a long process and remains incomplete. Congressional statutes and Supreme Court decisions since the Civil War have been important in achieving equality.

1865	Thirteenth Amendment abolishes slavery and "involuntary servitude."
1868	Fourteenth Amendment prohibits state action denying any person "the equal protection of the laws."
1870	Fifteenth Amendment removes race as a qualification for voting.
1875	Civil Rights Act bans racial discrimination in places of public accommodation.
1883	Civil Rights Cases hold 1875 statute unconstitutional.
1896	*Plessy v. Ferguson* upholds constitutionality of state law requiring racial segregation on trains in "separate but equal" facilities.
1920	Nineteenth Amendment extends franchise to women.
1954	*Brown v. Board of Education of Topeka* declares unconstitutional racially segregated public schools; *Plessy v. Ferguson* reversed.
1957	Congress establishes the Civil Rights Commission.
1963	Congress passes the Equal Pay Act.
1964	Congress passes the Civil Rights Act: Title II outlaws racial discrimination in places of public accommodation; Title IV allows the Justice Department to sue school districts on behalf of African American students seeking integrated education; Title VI bans racial discrimination in federally funded programs; Title VII prohibits most forms of discrimination (as on the basis of race or gender) in employment and creates the Equal Employment Opportunity Commission. Twenty-fourth Amendment eliminates poll taxes in federal elections.
1965	Congress passes the Voting Rights Act. President Johnson bans racial discrimination by federal contractors.
1968	Civil Rights Act's Title VIII prohibits most forms of discrimination in sale or rental of housing.
1971	Twenty-sixth Amendment lowers national voting age to 18.
1972	Congress submits Equal Rights Amendment to states for ratification.
1978	*Regents v. Bakke* invalidates a medical school admissions program that reserved a specific number of seats for minority applicants.
1979	*Steelworkers v. Weber* upholds legality of a voluntary affirmative-action plan for industrial apprenticeships that gives preference to African American workers over white workers with greater seniority.
1982	Ratification of Equal Rights Amendment fails. Congress extends and amends Voting Rights Act. Title IX of Educational Amendments bars sex discrimination in "any education program or activity receiving Federal financial assistance."
1989	*Richmond v. J. A. Croson Co.* invalidates a municipally mandated 30 percent set-aside quota for racial minorities.
1990	Congress enacts the National Hate Crimes Statistics Act, which requires the Justice Department to gather data on crimes motivated by prejudice about race, religion, ethnicity, or sexual orientation. The Americans with Disabilities Act becomes law.
1991	Congress enacts a civil rights bill designed to modify several 1989 Supreme Court decisions that had made on-the-job discrimination more difficult to prove, and affirmative-action plans easier to challenge in court.

separate-but-equal doctrine

A standard announced by the Supreme Court in *Plessy v. Ferguson* in 1896 that allowed racially separate facilities on trains (and by implication in public services such as education), as long as the separate facilities were equal. Overturned by *Brown v. Board of Education of Topeka* in 1954.

http://www.civil rightsmuseum.org/

The National Civil Rights Museum was established in Memphis, Tennessee in 1991. Visit the above site for an interactive tour of the museum.

the Court announced the **separate-but-equal doctrine** in upholding a Louisiana law that required racial segregation on trains.[44] As long as racially separate facilities were "equal," the Court maintained, the Constitution had not been violated.

Three kinds of policies then developed that denied many African Americans their rights until after the middle of the twentieth century. First, virtually every aspect of life in the South (the region of the nation in which most African Americans lived) became racially segregated by law. Elsewhere, segregation existed too, but it was enforced more by custom than by law. No section of the nation was immune to racist attitudes and racially motivated violence, including riots and lynchings. Segregated neighborhoods became fixtures in the North and South alike.

Second, Southern politicians systematically excluded African Americans from the political process. To get around the Fifteenth Amendment, legislatures turned to devices such as poll taxes, good character tests, and literacy tests to keep African Americans away from the ballot box. Until its use was declared unconstitutional by the Supreme Court,[45] the "grandfather clause" allowed whites to vote who would otherwise have been disfranchised by those same barriers. Of all the discriminatory devices, the white primary was probably the most effective. Because one party, the Democratic, was dominant in the region after 1900, the real electoral choices in state, local, and congressional races were made in the primary, not in the general election. White Democrats thus excluded African Americans from meaningful political participation by adopting party rules that allowed only whites to vote in the Democratic primaries. Even though the white primary seems an affront to the Fifteenth Amendment, it was not until 1944 that the Supreme Court ruled that such deception violated the Constitution.[46] Still, for two decades afterward most African Americans were kept from voting in many places.

Third, without the vote African Americans were shortchanged across the board in the delivery of public services such as education. Favors are rarely extended to entire groups that are permanently disfranchised, especially when they bear racial or religious stigmas as well. Thus, the spirit of *Plessy* was honored only in part; although separate, services and facilities were only rarely equal.

The Counterattack

Opponents of racism saw little hope of victory through the legislative process. At the local level, African Americans were politically powerless in the areas in which segregation was most pervasive. At the national level, Congress operated racially segregated schools in Washington, D.C., and provided separate eating and working places for African American civil servants. Even Uncle Sam's toilets were marked "Whites Only"

---

[44]163 U.S. 537 (1896).
[45]*Guinn v. United States*, 238 U.S. 347 (1915).
[46]*Smith v. Allwright*, 321 U.S. 649 (1944).

NAACP

National Association for the Advancement of Colored People: an organization founded to improve the social, economic, and political condition of African Americans.

Brown v. Board of Education of Topeka

Landmark Supreme Court decision [347 U.S. 483 (1954)] that overturned the separate-but-equal standard of *Plessy v. Ferguson* [163 U.S. 537 (1896)] and began an end to racial segregation in public schools.

and "Colored." The armed forces remained racially segregated until President Truman (1945–1953) ordered an end to the practice in 1948.

Thus, the counterattack against racism looked to the federal judiciary and was led principally by the National Association for the Advancement of Colored People. Known by its initials, the **NAACP** was founded in 1909 to improve the social, economic, and political condition of African Americans. A separate division for litigation, called the Legal Defense Fund (LDF), began work in 1939 and had the primary responsibility of pressing the desegregation drive in courtrooms in the 1940s, 1950s, and 1960s. One prominent African American attorney in the LDF was Thurgood Marshall, later the first African American justice on the Supreme Court (1967–1991).

The assault on racial segregation reached a climax in the landmark decision of May 17, 1954: ***Brown v. Board of Education of Topeka***.[47] "Does segregation of children in public schools solely on the basis of race, even though the physical facilities and other 'tangible' factors may be equal, deprive the children of the minority group of equal educational opportunities?" asked Chief Justice Earl Warren (1953–1969). "We believe that it does. . . . In the field of public education," he concluded, "the doctrine of 'separate but equal' has no place. Separate educational facilities are inherently unequal." *Plessy* was overruled.

Putting *Brown* to Work: The Law and Politics of Integration

The Court had made its decision. What was to happen? Rather than order an immediate end to segregation, the justices announced that integration was to proceed "with all deliberate speed."[48] In most places "deliberate speed" proved to be a turtle's pace. A decade after the Court's historic pronouncement, less than one percent of the African American children in the states of the old Confederacy were attending public school with white children. In six border states and the District of Columbia the figure was much higher: 52 percent.

Several factors severely hampered quick implementation of *Brown*, making the 1954 decision a test case of the Supreme Court's power. First, some federal judges in the South were themselves opposed to integration. They did little to press for *Brown*'s speedy implementation. Second, state legislatures and local school boards usually reflected strong white opposition to *Brown*'s enforcement. Third, fear of hostile reaction by the local white community discouraged litigation. It was economically and physically risky for parents of African American children to sue local officials. Fourth, the Court received little initial support from Congress, the White House, and a large part of the organized legal community.

Significant enforcement of *Brown* and the lowering of other racial barriers did not come until civil rights activists such as Martin Luther King, Jr. riveted the nation's

---

[47]347 U.S. 483 (1954).
[48]*Brown v. Board of Education of Topeka* (II), 349 U.S. 294 (1955).

**Civil Rights Act
of 1964**

Comprehensive legis-
lation to end racial
segregation in access
to public accommo-
dations and in em-
ployment in the
public and private
sectors.

attention on injustices that persisted and called for action. Congress then enacted two important pieces of legislation: the **Civil Rights Act of 1964** and the Elementary and Secondary Education Act of 1965. The importance of the first for *Brown* came in Title VI: Every federal agency that funded local programs through grants, loans, or contracts was required to press for an end to racial discrimination. The 1965 school aid act was the first massive federal appropriation for local school systems. But to keep the money, school systems had to move swiftly on integration. The 1964 act was the hook, and the 1965 act was the bait. Ironically, public schools in the South are now among the most in-tegrated in the nation, whereas schools in the Northeast are among the most segregated.

The Continuing Effects of *Brown*

**de facto
segregation**

Programs or facilities
that are racially seg-
regated by private
choice or private dis-
crimination, not be-
cause of law or
public policy.

Supreme Court decisions about school integration since 1971 have come largely from states outside the South. Nonsouthern school systems had segregated schools, but rarely had they been recently segregated by law. The racial composition of these schools re-flected decades of residential segregation that had resulted from economic inequities and private discrimination. This kind of "unofficial" segregation was called **de facto segregation**. But in a pair of decisions from Ohio in 1979,[49] the Supreme Court decided that "racially identifiable schools" in any district probably resulted from school board policy. What many had thought to be de facto segregation was now considered **de jure segregation**: racial separation caused by government policy. Because of the 1979 rul-ing, local officials now have the affirmative duty of redrawing attendance zones and busing pupils from one part of town to another.

**de jure
segregation**

Programs or facili-
ties that are racially
segregated because
of law or public
policy.

Large metropolitan areas present a special problem. Typically, a city will have a single school district in which racial minorities are already a majority or well on their way to becoming a majority of the school population. Around the city, however, exist heavily white suburban school districts. Segregation is commonly between districts, not merely within a single district. In a Michigan case,[50] the Court (by a vote of five to four) rejected a metropolitan integration plan involving busing among more than 50 school districts spread over the city of Detroit and three suburban counties. Only when there is evidence that school boards have caused the segregation between districts will the Court find a constitutional violation.

Busing itself remains controversial. Many parents, African American and white alike, object to having their children transported farther than seems necessary. Many prefer neighborhood schools. Aside from achieving integration, scholars disagree on the effects of busing and similar measures on the schoolchildren involved, debating whether integration improves the educational performance of African American students. Although integrated schools often mean that African American parents lose control over

---

[49]*Columbus Board of Education v. Penick*, 443 U.S. 449 (1979); *Dayton Board of Education v. Brinkman*, 443 U.S. 526 (1979).
[50]*Milliken v. Bradley*, 418 U.S. 717 (1974).

schools in African American neighborhoods, integrated education probably prepares all students better for living in a racially diverse society. Moreover, many believe that "green follows white"—that the presence of white students assures more generous economic support of a school by local officials. Nonetheless, the Supreme Court has now taken the position that once a school district has eliminated segregation, the district may cease to be under a constitutional obligation to continue the policies that produced the integrated system, even if "re-segregation" might result.[51]

Whatever the progress with school integration, social segregation remains a fact in many areas of the nation. Even though the Civil Rights Acts of 1964 and 1968, respectively, prohibit racial discrimination in employment and in the sale or rental of housing (as do the laws in most states and hundreds of municipalities), African Americans remain the most segregated minority group—the group most isolated from whites.

Affirmative Action

affirmative action

Positive steps taken by public or private institutions to overcome the remaining effects of racial or sexual bias. Affirmative action programs attempt to achieve equality of result.

Many people believe that ending discrimination is not enough. They believe that positive steps called **affirmative action** are also needed to overcome the residual effects of generations of racial bias. Others oppose affirmative action if it involves preferential treatment for minorities. They argue that jobs and university scholarships, for example, are finite. To give to one means to withhold from someone else. The nonminority applicant who loses out because of race has been hurt just as much as a minority applicant in earlier years who was kept out because of race. One side says that two wrongs make a right; the other side answers that they do not.

If a national consensus has developed against racial discrimination in its old forms, no firm consensus exists on affirmative action. Even the Supreme Court has been divided, as *Regents of the University of California v. Bakke*[52] illustrates. In this landmark affirmative action case, the Supreme Court invalidated the use of a racial quota for medical school admissions at the Davis campus of the University of California but said that race could still be taken into account. Admissions officers may use race as one of several criteria in evaluating the record of an applicant but may not admit or exclude solely on the basis of race. In an important 1996 decision that the Supreme Court declined to review, a federal appellate court ruled that race could not be used as a consideration in public college admissions. Although the case did not set national policy, the decision suggested that the breadth of affirmative action laws has decreased since the *Bakke* decision.[53] In other cases, the Court has allowed governments and private businesses wide latitude in personnel decisions. Title VII of the Civil Rights Act of 1964 bans job discrimination on the basis of "race, color, religion, sex, or national origin." Even with such sweeping language, the

---

[51]*Freeman v. Pitts*, 60 U.S.L.W. 4286 (1992).
[52]438 U.S. 265 (1978).
[53]*Hopwood v. State of Texas*, 78 F3d 932 (Fifth Circuit, 1996).

Court has reasoned that a law intended to end discrimination against racial minorities and women should not be used to prohibit programs designed to help those groups.[54]

What, then, are the limits under the law to affirmative action? There is no clear answer to this question. Generally, policies by an employer to overcome the effects of its own past discrimination are permissible; indeed, they may be required. Even some policies by an employer to alleviate general "societal discrimination" for which the employer is not responsible are permissible. Policies that look like "quotas" have the best chance of being struck down.[55]

Voting Rights

Two centuries ago most Americans were denied the right to vote. The Constitution left voting qualifications to the states, with the result that women, African Americans, and some white adult males were left out. Since the 1820s the national trend has been to chip away at these restrictions so that today almost all adult citizens in the United States have the right to vote.

Voting Rights Act of 1965

Major legislation designed to overcome racial barriers to voting, primarily in the southern states. Extended in 1982 for 25 years.

As late as 1964, however, African Americans in particular were systemically denied the right to vote in most parts of the South. The response to this situation was the **Voting Rights Act of 1965**, the most important voting legislation ever enacted by Congress. Besides removing many barriers to voting, the act requires that any change in a "standard, practice, or procedure with respect to voting" in certain parts of the United States (most of them being in the South) can take effect only after being cleared by the attorney general of the United States or by the United States District Court for the District of Columbia. The Supreme Court has interpreted "standard, practice, or procedure" to include any change in a locale's electoral system. This advance clearance requirement is satisfied only if the proposed change has neither the *purpose* nor the *effect* of "denying or abridging the right to vote on account of race or color." This means that African American voting power can in no way be weakened or diluted by any change in local election practices.

Congress made an important change in the law in 1982, banning *existing* electoral arrangements with a racially discriminatory effect anywhere in the United States. Conceivably, this addition to the law may produce a realignment of political power in sections of the country in which African Americans and Latinos amount to at least a sizable minority of the population, and in which local political practices dilute the political influence of these minorities. More recently, the Court ruled in 1993 that reapportionment schemes may violate the Equal Protection Clause if they are drawn based solely on race, even when the intent is to increase racial minority representation.[56]

---

[54]For example, see *United Steelworkers of America v. Weber*, 443 U.S. 193 (1979) and *Johnson v. Transportation Agency*, 480 U.S. 616 (1987).
[55]*Richmond v. J.A. Croson Co.*, 488 U.S. 469 (1989).
[56]*Shaw v. Reno*, 509 U.S. 630 (1993).

The Voting Rights Act has had a far-reaching impact. African Americans in the southern states now vote at a rate approximating that of whites. In the 2000 election for the U.S. House of Representatives, voters nationally chose 38 African American and 19 Latino members, a number that amounts to about 13 percent of the chamber. There are currently no African Americans or Latinos serving in the U.S. Senate.

Sexual Equality

Because the political system has been the battleground for so many years in the fight for racial equality, it is easy to suppose that sexual equality has occupied the attention of Congress and the courts for just as long. However, such has not been the case: Making the nation free of discrimination based on gender has been a national priority for less than four decades.

The Legacy

Until recently the legal status of women in the United States was one of substantial inequality. Legally a wife had no existence apart from her husband. Without his consent, she could make no contracts binding either of them. In response to such attitudes, the first convention on women's rights was held in 1848 in Seneca Falls, New York. Change in attitudes came slowly, however. Even the Fourteenth Amendment spoke of "male inhabitants." The Nineteenth Amendment, extending the franchise to women, was not ratified until 1920, after a long and turbulent suffrage movement. Not until 1971 did the Supreme Court first invalidate a law because it discriminated against women.[57] And as late as 1973 there were 900 gender-based federal laws still on the books.

Gender to the Forefront

Attacks on racial discrimination during the 1950s helped to turn attention to laws that penalized women because they were women. Sex discrimination became a political issue few politicians could ignore after publication of books such as Betty Friedan's *Feminine Mystique* in 1963 and Kate Millett's *Sexual Politics* in 1971, and after the formation of the National Organization for Women (NOW) in 1966. At about the same time, the female half of the postwar "baby boom" entered college, graduate schools, and the work force. There were more women than ever before at an age and place in their lives and careers for whom questions of gender discrimination were very important.

Responding to inequities that had become obvious, Congress passed the Equal Pay Act in 1963, which commanded "equal pay for equal work." Title VII of the 1964 Civil Rights Act outlawed sexual (as well as racial) bias in employment and promotion

---

[57]*Reed v. Reed*, 404 U.S. 71 (1971).

practices. Title IX of the 1972 Educational Amendments banned sex discrimination in education programs and activities at colleges receiving federal financial aid. (Title IX remains contentious because of its applicability to how universities allocate dollars between male and female athletic teams.)

As a result of changes in both laws and attitudes, sex-based retirement plans, for example, may no longer require women to make higher contributions or to receive lower monthly benefits than men just because women as a group live longer than men as a group.[58] States may no longer operate single-sex schools of nursing (and probably any other kind), even if coeducational public nursing schools also exist.[59] In the workplace, not only has sexual harassment been judged to be a violation of Title VII, but the Supreme Court holds employers responsible under the law for not taking steps to prevent it.[60] Despite such remedies, sexual harassment continues to be a problem in many settings, as the reaction to Anita Hill's accusations against Supreme Court nominee Clarence Thomas in 1991 revealed (see Chapter 12).

Many people believe that real economic equality between the sexes will not be achieved without **comparable worth** (equal pay for jobs of equal value), a policy not required by federal law. Otherwise, they say, full-time female workers will continue to earn on average no more than about two-thirds the pay of full-time male workers.

Other Americans and Civil Rights

Discrimination against women and African Americans has occupied a prominent place on the public agenda in recent years, but discrimination has claimed other victims as well. American Indians, Latinos, immigrants, and Americans with disabilities have all demanded, with varying degrees of success, that public officials take steps to remedy years of neglect and unequal treatment. (Sexual orientation has also been the basis for discrimination by governments, businesses, and individuals, and was discussed as an aspect of privacy earlier in this chapter.)

American Indians

From an estimated sixteenth-century population of perhaps two million or more[61] (no one knows for certain), American Indians (also called Native Americans) numbered barely a half million in 1900 as war, disease, and systematic slaughter took their toll. Today, there are nearly 2.5 million, just less than one percent of the total U.S. population. As a group, American Indians suffer disproportionately high rates of sickness, poverty, illiteracy, and unemployment. Not until 1924 did Congress recognize them as citizens.

comparable worth

An employment policy, designed to overcome the economic inequities of sexual discrimination, mandating that persons holding jobs of equal responsibility and skill be paid the same.

---

[58]*Los Angeles v. Manhart*, 435 U.S. 702 (1978); *Arizona v. Norris*, 463 U.S. 1073 (1983).
[59]*Mississippi University for Women v. Hogan*, 458 U.S. 718 (1982).
[60]*Mentor Savings Bank v. Vinson*, 477 U.S. 57 (1986).
[61]*Historical Atlas of the United States* (Washington, DC: National Geographic Society, 1988), p. 34.

Many American Indians have understandably resisted assimilation into the rest of the population, insisting instead on preserving their culture and heritage. Approximately half live on 275 semiautonomous reservations and, in Alaska, in 223 native villages under the supervision of the Bureau of Indian Affairs in the Department of the Interior. The Indian Self-Determination and Education Assistance Act of 1975 granted American Indians greater control over their own affairs, and the Indian Bill of Rights of 1968 gave American Indians living on reservations protections similar to those found in the Constitution.

Recent policy reflects resurgent ethnic pride and new political awareness asserted by activist groups such as the National Indian Youth Council and the American Indian Movement. Not only have such groups protested inadequate national assistance and the plight of the reservation population, but they have also attempted, with some success, to recover through litigation ancient tribal fishing and land rights, sometimes worth millions of dollars. Over the last two decades, several American Indian tribes have been granted state authorization to operate gaming facilities on reservation land, providing an important source of revenue for their communities.

Latinos

Numbering more than 35 million and making up about 12.5 percent of the population, Latinos are the nation's fastest-growing minority. In the 2000 census, the number of Americans identifying themselves as Latino was larger than the number identifying themselves as African American. A majority originally came from Mexico; most of the others came from Puerto Rico, South America, and parts of Central America. Mexican-Americans reside mainly in the Southwest, Cuban-Americans in Florida, and Puerto Ricans in the Northeast.

For decades, Latinos have encountered the same discriminations in voting, education, housing, and employment that have confronted African Americans, compounded by a language barrier. Amendments to the Voting Rights Act of 1965 require ballots to be printed in Spanish as well as English in areas in which Spanish-speaking people number more than five percent of the population. (Partly as a result of this act, Latino voter registration jumped 52 percent nationwide between 1972 and 1996; yet Latinos are still less likely than African Americans and whites to register to vote.) Moreover, Title VI of the Civil Rights Act of 1964 requires public schools to provide bilingual instruction to students deficient in English. Both education and political participation are important to any group seeking to maintain ethnic identity in a diverse culture. Policies to lower language barriers have sparked a backlash among those who see non–English-speaking (particularly Spanish-speaking) persons as a threat to an American cultural identity.

http://www.aclu.org

The American Civil Liberties Union is a nonprofit and nonpartisan organization that fights vigorous court battles to defend the civil rights and liberties guaranteed by the Constitution. To find out more about the organization and the issues they are currently addressing, visit the above Web site.

Immigrants

The Statue of Liberty signifies that America is a land of immigrants, but some have been more welcome than others. Until 1921 entry into the United States was virtually unlimited, but in that year Congress established the first of a series of ceilings on immigration that discriminated against persons from Eastern Europe and Asia, a bias not eliminated until 1965. Today the law sets a ceiling of 675,000 immigrants per year, including those admitted because of job skills and family relationships. Exceptions to the ceiling for refugees and others means that the total number of immigrants admitted annually easily exceeds 800,000.

Immigrant family looking at the Statue of Liberty from Ellis Island. *(Library of Congress)*

Thousands more—no one knows the exact number—successfully enter the country illegally, putting pressure on public services and, many people believe, taking jobs from citizens and others who legally reside in the United States. In response to these issues, Congress passed the Immigration Reform and Control Act in 1986. Among other things, the law requires employers to verify the American citizenship or legal status of all job applicants and provides stiff penalties for employers who hire illegal aliens. The 1986 law has had an unintended consequence: discrimination against persons of Latino or Asian descent. A study by the General Accounting Office (an investigatory agency of Congress) found that one in five of the 4.6 million employers surveyed admitted that the law encouraged them to discriminate against job applicants who were "foreign-appearing" or "foreign-sounding."[62]

Disabled Americans

The nation's largest minority group consists of the more than 43 million Americans with a physical or mental disability. Long victims of bias in both the public and private sectors, disabled Americans were not covered by the Civil Rights Act of 1964, the most comprehensive anti-discrimination legislation ever enacted by Congress.

---

[62]Paul M. Barrett, "Immigration Law Found to Promote Bias by Employers," *Wall Street Journal*, March 30, 1990, p. A18.

In 1990 Congress passed the Americans with Disabilities Act, which bans discrimination in employment (in businesses with more than 15 employees) and in places of public accommodation (including not only restaurants and hotels but establishments as varied as physicians' offices, zoos, sports arenas, and dry cleaners). Called a bill of rights for disabled Americans, the law also stipulates that newly manufactured buses and railroad cars be accessible to persons in wheelchairs and that telephone companies provide service for those with hearing and speech impairments. The law's definition of Americans with disabilities goes beyond those who rely on wheelchairs or who have difficulty seeing or hearing; it includes people with mental disorders and those with AIDS (Acquired Immune Deficiency Syndrome) and HIV (the virus that causes AIDS), but not those who use illegal drugs or who abuse legal drugs such as alcohol. Although in 2001 the Supreme Court ruled that the Americans with Disabilities Act required the PGA to allow disabled persons to use golf carts during the PGA tour, the Act suffered a major setback when the Court held that state employees could not sue states for failing to comply with the Act.[63]

Liberties and Rights in the Constitutional Framework

Civil rights and liberties, the subjects of this chapter, are part of the framework of American constitutional government. Freedoms of political and religious expression, limits on the police, protection of privacy—all examples of civil liberties—are not only essential components of the political process, but also help to define the quality of life Americans enjoy. Civil rights in turn are inspired by the bold assertion of the Declaration of Independence that "all men are created equal." Against a legacy of toleration of inequality, much of what government and private citizens have done in recent decades has been driven by an intolerance of inequality. Through application of constitutional provisions, laws, and policies, many people have tried to make the Declaration's words a reality, for women as well as men, for African Americans as well as whites. Their efforts employ the tools of politics and the major institutions of government, described in the chapters that follow.

---

[63]*PGA TOUR, Inc. v. Martin*, 532 U.S. 355 (2001); *Board of Trustees of Univ. of Ala. v. Garrett*, 531 U.S. 356 (2001).

SUMMARY

1. Civil liberties are freedoms, protected by law, to act or not to act and to be free from unwarranted governmental intrusion in one's life. Civil rights encompass participation in society on an equal footing with others.

2. Initially the Bill of Rights restrained only the national government, but, using the Fourteenth Amendment, the Supreme Court has applied most of the protections of the Bill of Rights to the states.

3. Free expression is necessary to the democratic political process. Only in rare instances today will the Court approve restrictions on the content of what a person says.

4. The free exercise and establishment clauses have two main objectives: separation of church and state and toleration of different religious faiths.

5. Other parts of the Bill of Rights guard liberty by placing limits on what officials may do in the process of fighting crime.

6. By interpretation, the Constitution includes a right of privacy, giving people the right to make basic decisions about procreation without undue interference by government. Abortion continues to be a divisive national issue.

7. Only since the landmark case of *Brown v. Board of Education of Topeka* in 1954 has the nation made significant progress toward removing discrimination on the basis of race from American life. The Voting Rights Act of 1965 has enabled African Americans (as well as others) to participate more equally in the political process.

8. Most discriminations based on sex are generally forbidden by statute and by the Supreme Court's interpretation of the Fourteenth Amendment.

9. American Indians, Latinos, immigrants, and Americans with disabilities are other groups who face discrimination and present special needs.

KEY TERMS

Fourteenth Amendment (73)

First Amendment (74)

clear and present danger test (75)

bad tendency test (76)

incitement test (76)

prior restraint (76)

obscenity (76)

libel (77)

symbolic speech (77)

free exercise clause (79)

establishment clause (79)

Lemon test (79)

legal guilt (82)

presumption of innocence (82)

ex post facto laws (83)

bill of attainder (83)

Fourth Amendment (83)

warrant (83)

probable cause (83)

Miranda rights (84)

plea bargain (84)

Sixth Amendment (84)

capital case (84)

misdemeanor (84)

felony (84)

Eighth Amendment (86)

cruel and unusual punishment (86)

Ninth Amendment (86)

Roe v. Wade (87)

equality of opportunity (90)

equality of condition (90)

equality of result (91)

Thirteenth Amendment (91)

equal protection clause (91)

separate-but-equal doctrine (93)

NAACP (94)

Brown v. Board of Education of Topeka (94)

Civil Rights Act of 1964 (95)

de facto segregation (95)

de jure segregation (95)

affirmative action (96)

Voting Rights Act of 1965 (97)

comparable worth (99)

READINGS FOR FURTHER STUDY

The Bill of Rights by Irving Brant (Indianapolis: Bobbs-Merrill, 1965) remains one of the best treatments of the origins of the liberties protected in the Constitution.

The rapidly changing field of criminal procedure can be followed in George Cole, *Criminal Justice: Law and Politics*, 6th ed. (Pacific Grove, CA: Brooks-Cole, 1992).

Efforts to achieve racial equality are fully described in Richard Kluger's *Simple Justice* (New York: Knopf, 1976).

Abigail M. Thernstrone's *Whose Votes Count?* (Cambridge, MA: Harvard University Press, 1987), discusses reform in voting rights.

Gender Politics by Ethel Klein (Cambridge, MA: Harvard University Press, 1984) looks at the political concerns of women.

CHAPTER 4

Political Ideologies

A/P World Wide

Chapter Objectives

Politics is about power and influence—who gets what, when, and how. But politics is also about ideas. Political ideology is an integrated set of political ideas about what constitutes the most equitable and just political order. Political ideologies are concerned with the proper function of government, the issues of liberty and equality, and the distribution of goods and services.

All of the ideological perspectives discussed in this chapter and given any serious attention by Americans accept the basic ideas of democracy—representative government and individual liberty. They do not question the fundamental precepts of American political life, but they differ on matters of emphasis and degree. Although most Americans do not think in rigid ideological terms, ideology does influence how Americans think about political leaders. Politicians and policies tend to be labeled liberal, conservative, radical, or reactionary, and with some frequency we hear the terms *neoconservative* and *neoliberal* (*neo* being Greek for "new"). This chapter introduces the landscape of contemporary American political ideas and movements—liberal, conservative, neoliberal, neoconservative, socialist, and libertarian.

American Political Ideologies

Ideology "spells out what is valued and what is not, what must be maintained and what must be changed."[1] Most political leaders and most Americans share elements of or identify with mainstream ideologies. Generally identified as *liberal* or *conservative*, these ideological positions do not challenge the existing political order. For example,

---

[1]Roy C. Macridis, *Contemporary Political Ideologies* (Boston: Little, Brown, 1983), p. 9.

neither liberals nor conservatives want to make major changes in our political and social order. They accept capitalism American-style as a successful economic system, and the economic marketplace as the chief instrument for the distribution of economic goods. At the same time, liberals and conservatives accept most of the economic reforms of the New Deal (explained later in this chapter)—Social Security, unemployment insurance, and farm price supports—as a permanent part of our political system. Their differences are over matters of emphasis and degree. By contrast, radical ideologies, such as *democratic socialism* and *libertarianism*, challenge much of the existing social and political order. Democratic socialists do not accept the capitalist system or what they consider to be the inordinate power of the big corporations. Socialists want to remove most of the major economic decisions on investments, wages, and prices from the private sector and place them in the hands of government. Libertarians seek to establish an economic system free of governmental interference and regulation and to dismantle most of the existing welfare state programs. These ideologies challenge many of the existing arrangements in our political system.

Exotic as socialism or libertarianism may seem to most Americans, these ideologies and movements operate within the framework of our democratic system. Democratic socialists and libertarians believe in peaceful change and accept the rules of the game. They frequently enter candidates in elections, although they rarely win and only then at the state and local levels. But because their ideas challenge the dominant ideologies of our time, it is important to understand their criticisms and their prescriptions for the future, just as it is important to understand beliefs that are more widely held.

Liberalism

One influential American ideology is **liberalism**. Liberalism begins with the assumption that individuals are, in the main, rational beings capable of overcoming obstacles to progress without resorting to violence. The roots of liberalism can be traced to the great English philosopher John Locke (1632–1704). Locke, who believed in the natural goodness of man, developed the **contract theory** of the state. According to Locke's theory, the state gains its legitimacy from the consent of the governed and is formed primarily to protect individuals' rights to life, liberty, and property. Locke's ideas of limited government, resting on the consent of the governed, became the textbook of the American Revolution. Locke was an inspiration to Thomas Jefferson, one of the most important early American liberal thinkers.

Classic Liberalism: Thomas Jefferson and Andrew Jackson

Contemporary American liberalism is vastly different from what was known in the nineteenth century as **classical liberalism** (see Table 4.1). Liberals of that time, going back

---

liberalism

An ideology that regards the individual as a rational being capable of overcoming obstacles to a better world, and supports changes in the political and economic status quo.

contract theory

Theory holding that the state gains its legitimacy from the consent of the governed and is formed primarily to protect the rights of individuals to life, liberty, and property.

classical liberalism

A view, dating from the nineteenth century, that government should play a minimal role in society and should permit maximum economic freedom for the individual.

TABLE 4.1

Key Ideas of American Ideologies

Different forms of liberalism and conservatism have defined much of the ideological debate in American politics; other ideologies challenged and influenced mainstream ideas.

IDEOLOGY	KEY IDEAS AND POLICIES
LIBERALISM	
CLASSICAL LIBERALISM	Minimal government; protection of property rights
POPULISM	Democratization of government; economic reforms
PROGRESSIVISM	Social programs to cope with problems caused by industrialization; public limits on private corporate power
CONTEMPORARY LIBERALISM	The positive state; faith in solving problems collectively through government; programs to provide for the economic well-being of the nation, including the basic material needs of each individual; tolerance of various lifestyles
NEOLIBERALISM	Creation, not redistribution, of wealth; free trade; reform of entitlement programs; a strong but economical defense
CONSERVATISM	
EARLY AMERICAN CONSERVATISM	Sanctity of private property; distrust of unchecked popular rule; duty of government to promote a healthy economic environment and a virtuous citizenry
INDUSTRIAL AGE CONSERVATISM	Laissez-faire economics; individualism; social Darwinism
CONTEMPORARY CONSERVATISM	Reduced spending on social programs; revamping tax policies to encourage economic growth; strong military defense; little positive action to redress racial and gender discrimination; duty of government to promote a virtuous citizenry
NEOCONSERVATISM	Skepticism of government's ability to solve social and economic problems; acceptance of a modest welfare state; opposition to racial and gender quotas to redress discrimination; creation, not redistribution, of wealth; assertive foreign policy
CHALLENGES TO THE STATUS QUO	
NEW RIGHT	Critical of big government, big corporations; distrustful of national media; social ills seen as the product of liberal policies; radical steps needed to return the nation to traditional cultural values
DEMOCRATIC SOCIALISM	Public ownership of basic industries, banks, agricultural enterprises, and communications systems; wage and price controls; redistribution of wealth to achieve true economic equality; expanded welfare programs
LIBERTARIANISM	Minimal government; protection of property rights and freedom of individuals; no governmental regulation of the economy; noninterventionist foreign policy; drastic reduction in defense spending

to Thomas Jefferson and Andrew Jackson, believed that a government that governed least governed best. Those nineteenth-century liberals felt that government should step out of the way so that the new entrepreneurs of the young Republic—the small business owners and farmers—could have an opportunity to compete in the economic system. Jefferson shared Locke's view that government must treat property rights with particular care. Jefferson had high praise for Adam Smith's *Wealth of Nations* (1776), the bible of capitalism. In his first inaugural address, Jefferson stated:

> A wise and frugal government, which shall restrain men from injuring one an-
> other, shall leave them otherwise free to regulate their own pursuits of industry
> and improvement and shall not take from the mouth of labor the bread it has
> earned. This is the sum of good government.[2]

President Andrew Jackson's struggle against the wealth and power of a national bank (see Chapter 2) was a classic example of the nineteenth-century liberal creed in action. Jackson also opposed extensive government expenditures on roads and canals. He believed that such expenditures "would make the federal government a partner with business in the financial prosperity of the upper class."[3] Speaking for the liberal reformers of his day, Jackson declared that a strong central government "is calculated to raise around the administration a moneyed aristocracy dangerous to the liberties of the country."[4]

Like Jefferson, Jackson believed that liberty was the absence of government interference with the rights of all citizens to enjoy the fruits of their labor and prosperity.

Populism and Progressivism: The Repudiation of Classic Liberalism

In the latter part of the nineteenth century, liberal attitudes toward government began to change. In the decades following the Civil War, American farmers, the backbone of support for Jeffersonian and Jacksonian liberalism, suffered through a perpetual economic crisis. Agricultural prices fell and interest rates rose. The target of liberal reform became the railroads and the banks, not the government. Out of this turmoil evolved a new liberal movement, known as populism. The populists, who formed their own political party in the 1880s, called for further democratization of government through the secret ballot, direct election of senators, and voter initiatives and referenda. They also advocated fundamental economic reforms that would strengthen government's role, including nationalization of the railroads and the telegraph, a graduated income tax, free coinage of

---

[2]Quoted in Walter E. Volkomer, ed., *The Liberal Tradition in American Thought* (New York: Capricorn Books, 1969), p. 104.
[3]Robert V. Remini, *Andrew Jackson and the Course of American Freedom, 1822–1832*, vol. 2 (New York: Harper & Row, 1981), p. 116.
[4]Ibid., p. 33.

silver, and a vastly expanded supply of paper money. The Populist party did not supplant either of the two major parties, but its ideas, particularly with the nomination of William Jennings Bryan as the Democratic presidential candidate in 1896, profoundly affected the Democratic party in the twentieth century.

In urban America, among the middle classes, there was also a growing movement for social and economic reform, known as **progressivism**. Progressives supported government programs to ease the problems of industrialization, including worker's compensation, a ban on child labor, regulation of corporations, and a minimum wage.

Progressives achieved their major successes during the presidential administrations of Theodore Roosevelt (1901–1909) and Woodrow Wilson (1913–1921). During Roosevelt's years, Congress passed the Hepburn Act, which regulated the railroads, and the Pure Food and Drug Act and the Meat Inspection Act, which eliminated many of the unhealthy practices of food and drug industries. Woodrow Wilson signed into law bills regulating the banking industry, restricting unfair business competition, and establishing an eight-hour day for railroad workers. The populist and progressive belief that government could remedy the economic ills of the nation by limiting the power and wealth of private corporations and banks had a profound effect on American liberalism. The rise of populism and progressivism signaled a decline in the faith of liberalism in laissez-faire (minimal government regulation of economic affairs) and began a new era of belief in the power and virtues of a strong central government.

progressivism

An urban reform movement of the late nineteenth and early twentieth centuries that called for direct primaries, restrictions on corporations, and improved public services. Influential in the administrations of Theodore Roosevelt and Woodrow Wilson.

Woodrow Wilson on his daily ride in the outskirts of Washington. *(Library of Congress)*

Wilson felt that Jefferson would have understood the need for more activist government. He said:

> If Jefferson were living in our day, he would see what we see: that the individual is caught in a great confused nexus of all sorts of complicated circumstances, and that to let him alone is to leave him helpless.[5]

Contemporary Liberalism: The Welfare State and Beyond

The administration of President Franklin D. Roosevelt (1933–1945) took the concerns of the populists and progressives a step further. Roosevelt's New Deal program reflected the change in the constituency of liberalism. In contrast to the nineteenth-century liberal, who addressed the needs of the entrepreneurial class, New Deal liberals were concerned about the farmers, the unemployed, and the labor union movement. Carrying on the populist and progressive tradition, liberals no longer saw government as a threat to liberty or as the inevitable partner of the rich and powerful. In a complex industrial age, particularly one racked by the Great Depression of the 1930s, liberals believed that government action should ensure the economic well-being of the nation and should provide basic material guarantees (food, shelter, health care, and education) for every individual. The New Deal included programs to ensure protection for the unemployed, pensions for the elderly, and guaranteed prices for the farmers. It symbolized the idea of the positive or interventionist state, which became the hallmark of contemporary liberalism.

In the 1960s, President Lyndon Johnson's Great Society moved beyond the New Deal. Civil rights laws protected the rights of minorities, Medicare and Medicaid laws provided health insurance for the elderly and the poor, and funds aided impoverished elementary and secondary school districts. In the 1970s, liberals proposed a broad range of programs to protect the environment, to assist consumers, and to expand welfare benefits through the food stamp program.

Liberals today believe that a strong central government is necessary to protect individuals from the inequities of a modern industrial and technological society, and that the growth of government has enhanced, not diminished, individual freedom. Although the positive state is central in the contemporary liberal creed, liberals do not believe that government should displace private enterprise. Most liberals are capitalists, if not forthrightly so. In fact, many argue that American capitalism has survived because government has humanized the industrial order, and that Franklin Roosevelt's New Deal saved capitalism from repudiation during the 1930s. Liberals argue that the positive state cushions the inequalities of power and wealth that arise in any capitalist system. They see government as correcting the injustices of the marketplace, not supplanting it. Liberals recognize that in any society there will be some inequalities of wealth and income; but

http://www.self-gov .org/lp-quiz.shtml

The World's Smallest Political Quiz is a tool designed to assess one's political ideology. The quiz was created by a libertarian organization. Does that make it too biased, or is it useful? Visit the above site and decide for yourself.

[5]Quoted in Arthur A. Ekrich, Jr., *Progressivism in America* (New York: New Viewpoints, 1974), p. 170.

they feel that government must intervene to redress the most excessive inequalities. Thus, in debates over tax laws, liberals frequently support shifting more of the burden to people in the upper income brackets.

Franklin D. Roosevelt. *(Library of Congress)*

The idea of a benevolent government that offers services to the disadvantaged (unemployment insurance) as well as to the middle class (Social Security) has been for generations the centerpiece of American liberalism. Liberal ideas fueled the administrations of Presidents Franklin Roosevelt, Harry Truman, John Kennedy, and Lyndon Johnson. Johnson, for one, saw the United States as "an endless cornucopia." His Great Society began a virtual torrent of new government programs: rent supplements for the poor, scholarships for college students, aid to the arts and humanities, higher pensions for government workers and veterans, aid to children with disabilities, and a massive food stamp program. These programs assisted the poor and the disadvantaged as well as many in the middle- and upper-income brackets.

But in the 1970s and early 1980s the growth rate of the economy declined while the demand for government services continued. Unlike his predecessors, President Carter (1977–1981) did not offer a new set of governmental programs and benefits. Hampered by the problems of inflation and an energy shortage, Carter could offer few initiatives. His administration stirred little enthusiasm among liberals.

industrial policy

Proposals for partnership in economic decision making among government officials, corporate leaders, union officials, and public interest groups.

Liberals remain wedded to the idea of affirmative government. In the early 1980s, some began to discuss the idea of an industrial policy. Championed by liberal economic thinkers such as Robert Reich and Felix Rohatyn, an **industrial policy** involves a partnership in economic decision making among government officials, labor unions, and public interest groups. President Bill Clinton (1993–2001) endorsed this approach in a slightly modified form in his 1992 election campaign, and later named Reich secretary of labor.

But in matters involving national security and personal morality, liberals seek to restrict the role of government. This philosophy became more pronounced in the 1970s and 1980s. Liberals extend broad tolerance to different lifestyles and dispute government efforts to impose a single standard of religious practice or sexual morality.

Consequently, liberals are at the forefront of opposition to constitutional amendments that might sanction prayer in schools or limit the rights of women to obtain an abortion.

Since the Vietnam War, liberals have backed away from an interventionist, military-oriented foreign policy. In January 1991 most Congressional liberals voted against authorizing President Bush to use military force in the Persian Gulf and preferred the continuation of economic sanctions against Iraq. Liberals are also critical of large defense budgets and, with the end of the Cold War, advocate deep cuts in military spending.

In general, liberals favor government programs and budgeting priorities that put domestic social programs before those of the Pentagon. Their belief in a strong activist government concentrates primarily on domestic issues (see Table 4.2).

Who are the liberals? They are usually found in the Democratic party, although the Democrats do harbor some conservatives and the Republicans a handful of liberals. The association of liberals with Democrats is in part due to the fact that the constituency of the Democratic party—minorities, the labor movement, feminists, the poor—supports a wide range of liberal welfare programs. **Americans for Democratic Action** (ADA) is the best-known pressure group for contemporary liberalism. Founded in 1947, ADA presidents have included Senators Hubert Humphrey (D-MN)* and George McGovern

Americans for Democratic Action

The best-known pressure group for contemporary liberalism.

* "D-MN" is a journalistic designation used for members of the U.S. Senate and House of Representative: "D" or "R" indicates political party, followed by the member's home state.

TABLE 4.2

Milestones in American Liberalism

1690	John Locke's *Second Treatise on Government* published.
1776	Adam Smith's *Wealth of Nations,* Thomas Paine's *Common Sense,* and the Declaration of Independence published.
1832	President Andrew Jackson vetoes a bill to recharter the Bank of the United States.
1892	First Populist party convention held.
1896	William Jennings Bryan wins Democratic presidential nomination; the Democratic party adopts much of the Populist program.
1909	Herbert Croly's *Promise of American Life p*ublished; a group of African American leaders, including W. E. B. DuBois, meets at Niagara Falls, Canada, and inaugurates the modern civil rights movement.
1913–1916	President Woodrow Wilson steers his New Freedom program through Congress.
1933–1936	President Franklin Roosevelt's New Deal reforms inaugurate the modern welfare state.
1954	The Supreme Court declares racial segregation unconstitutional in *Brown v. Board of Education of Topeka.*
1964	Congress passes the landmark Civil Rights Act of 1964.
1965	President Lyndon Johnson successfully pushes his Great Society programs through Congress.

(D-SD), both one-time nominees of the Democratic party for president. Headquartered in Washington, D.C., the ADA is an advocate of legislation designed to reduce economic inequality and defense spending and to protect consumers. It opposes laws that encroach on civil rights and civil liberties. Each year it rates members of Congress on a broad spectrum of liberal issues.

Neoliberalism: Adjusting Liberalism to the Twenty-First Century

During the administrations of Franklin Roosevelt, Harry Truman, and John Kennedy, liberalism focused on economic issues and emphasized government's obligation to assist those on the lower end of the income scale. In recent decades liberalism has shifted its focus somewhat and reached into social and foreign policy issues. However, it did so at a political cost. The strong association of liberalism with the civil rights movement hurt liberals among southerners who identified with the old white-dominated political order and among northern white ethnics living in urban enclaves who also felt threatened by African American advancement. Many voters also associated liberalism with controversial Supreme Court decisions legalizing abortion and banning school prayer. After the Vietnam War, liberals were highly critical of American military intervention and the level of defense spending, alienating some voters who considered them "soft" on defense. Although liberal candidates were quite successful in congressional and state elections, such negative associations dogged them at the presidential level.

neoliberalism

A pragmatic form of liberalism that emphasizes such beliefs as the promotion of wealth rather than its redistribution, and the reform of military practices rather than the simple reduction of military spending.

Stunned by these successive presidential defeats, a group of young journalists and elected officials attempted to sharpen and modernize the focus of contemporary liberalism. The leader of the movement was Charles Peters, the editor of the *Washington Monthly* (see Table 4.3), who adopted the label "neoliberal." **Neoliberalism** calls for a shift in the emphasis of liberalism from the redistribution of wealth to the promotion of wealth, for a far less critical attitude toward American capitalism, and for policies that promote greater government and business cooperation.

Neoliberals do not repudiate the New Deal and Great Society legacies; they simply feel that the emphasis of liberal reform should be different. They argue that liberals must confront public distrust of government. As a writer for the *Washington Monthly* put it, "any time a liberal politician says the word 'program,' most voters hear 'bureaucracy' and right away get turned off." [6]

Neoliberals direct their attention not to the expansion of government services, but to their effective delivery. Neoliberals criticize government unions and the size and costs of the government bureaucracy. Neoliberals also call for reform of entitlement spending programs such as Social Security that go to people who already are well

[6]Paul Glastris, "The Phillips Curve," *Washington Monthly*, June 1990, p. 54.

TABLE 4.3

A Guide to Contemporary Political Ideas and Leaders

American ideologies are expressed through a variety of journals, writers, and political leaders.

IDEOLOGY	MAJOR JOURNAL	LEADING SPOKESPERSON	POLITICAL LEADERS
Liberalism	*New Republic*	Andrew Sullivan	Edward Kennedy
Neoliberalism	*Washington Monthly*	Charles Peters	Bill Bradley
Conservatism	*National Review*	William F. Buckley, Jr.	Newt Gingrich
Neoconservatism	*Weekly Standard*	William Kristol	William J. Bennett
Paleoconservatism	*Chronicles*	Paul Gottfried	Pat Buchanan
New Right	*Conservative Digest*	Ralph Reed	Alan Keyes
Democratic Socialism	*Dissent*	Michael Walzer	Bernard Sanders
Libertarianism	*Reason*	Mary Ruwart	Harry Browne

protected by private pensions and their own investments. The neoliberals criticize civil service and military retirement benefits for being far more generous than those in the private sector. They believe the increases in spending for these programs should be geared not to the cost of living but to the rate of real growth in the economy.

Traditional liberals take issue with the neoliberal emphasis on government efficiency. They emphasize older liberal issues, such as the problem of personal income inequality that has became more pronounced in recent decades. Traditional liberals would like to increase the top income tax rate, which is currently 39.6 percent. They unapologetically champion the cause of affirmative government and the positive state. Arthur Schlesinger, Jr., a prominent liberal spokesperson for over a generation, argues for greater government investment in research and development and in education; in the rehabilitation of our bridges, dams, and highways; and in the protection against toxic waste, acid rain, and the greenhouse effect. "The markets," writes Schlesinger, "will solve none of these problems."[7]

Some traditional liberals feel that Michael Dukakis's emphasis on competency not ideology during the 1988 presidential campaign was in fact a neoliberal theme that failed to ignite the electorate. By contrast, Bill Clinton in 1992 and 1996 and Al Gore in 2000 were able to blend older, more populist ideas, such as raising taxes for the rich, with neoliberal themes, such as a partnership between government and business.

---

[7]Arthur Schlesinger, Jr., "The Liberal Opportunity," in *The American Prospect,* Spring 1990, p. 15.

Conservatism

In contrast to liberalism's confidence in the capacity of individuals to overcome obstacles collectively, political **conservatism** reflects doubt and distrust. Conservatism emphasizes the value of tradition and established practices as guides for the future. It finds its origins in the writings of Edmund Burke (1729–1797), whose most famous work, *Reflections on the Revolution in France* (1790), is considered the first major statement of conservative principles. A leading figure in the British Parliament, Burke was appalled by the excesses of the French Revolution and by its rejection of tradition. Burke was suspicious of any generation's claim that it could remake society, believing that the experience of past generations was the most reliable guide to good government. Customs, traditions, and laws embodied the wisdom of the past and should not be carelessly discarded. Thus, argued Burke, people should act with deliberation, seeking change only when necessary. Burke believed that society grew slowly and with purpose; therefore, the past gave continuity to present and future generations. Burke was suspicious of the general public and its capacity to appreciate tradition and custom. He believed in government by the propertied class. People were not equal in ability or talent, according to Burke, and should not be so considered when it came to the governing of society. In Burke's view, a natural inequality among people meant that a ruling class of ability and property must control government.

Early American Conservatism: John Adams

It was difficult to make Burkean conservatism relevant to the American experience, which had no landed aristocracy, no established church, and no royal tradition. American conservatism, although influenced by Burke, found its own voice in John Adams, the second president of the United States, who lived from 1735 to 1826. Like Burke, Adams was repelled by the excesses of the French Revolution, particularly its executions and confiscation of property. Adams agreed with Burke unreservedly about the sanctity of private property (see Table 4.1). But unlike Burke, Adams did not associate property rights with a landed aristocracy. Adams believed that property should be widely held and that a propertied class would produce a natural aristocracy of talent. Although Adams was one of the architects of the American Revolution and a passionate defender of the right of every individual to life, liberty, and property, he distrusted unchecked democratic rule as much as he did excessive power in the hands of the aristocracy. Unlimited rule of the people led to clamor for dictatorship. Adams rejected the Jeffersonian notion of the natural goodness of humankind; he felt that people were neither totally innocent nor totally depraved. Laws and government, in Adams's view, were needed to promote public virtue and to curb private greed. By public virtue Adams meant "a positive passion for the public good, the public interest, honor, power, and glory established in the minds of the people."[8] A properly balanced government could serve to suppress the evils of ambition, selfishness, self-indulgence, and corruption.

John Adams found this balance in the American Constitution. A popularly elected House would represent the people, an indirectly elected Senate would protect the rights of property, and the president would represent the whole. Thus the poor could not confiscate the property of the rich, and the rich would not be able to exploit the poor. Society would retain its balance, and liberty would be safeguarded from both the excesses of democracy and the abuses of an aristocracy. After Adams had appointed John Marshall, a conservative Federalist, to the Supreme Court in 1801, Adams looked to the judicial branch as the ultimate guarantor of property rights against any attempts by legislatures to compromise them.

In the 1820s, long after he had left the presidency, Adams joined with other American conservatives, including Chief Justice Marshall and Senator Daniel Webster, in opposing the elimination of property qualifications for voting. These conservatives considered *universal suffrage* (and in that era they debated only universal *white manhood suffrage*) a threat to the Republic. Men without property lacked the independence, judgment, and virtue to be voting members of a free republic.[9]

Chancellor James Kent of New York, one of the most famous legal scholars and jurists of the early nineteenth century, argued that "there is a tendency in the majority to tyrannize over the minority and trample down their rights; and in the indolent and profligate to cast the whole burden of society upon the industrious and virtuous."[10] The victory of Jacksonian democracy in the states during the 1820s brought an end to antidemocratic conservatism. Conservatives seemed to realize the finality of their defeat on that issue and concentrated in the latter part of the nineteenth century on a defense of property rights and the system of economic laissez-faire.

Conservatism and the Industrial Age: Herbert Spencer and William Graham Sumner

Industrialization following the Civil War brought a major change in American conservatism. Although conservatives of the early Republic fervently believed in property rights, the belief that government should play a limited role in the economy did not necessarily follow. Conservatives such as John Adams, John Marshall, and Alexander Hamilton supported a strong central government to defend the propertied classes from the encroachments of the more radical state governments. They defended the Bank of the United States against the attacks of the Jefferson-Jackson liberals.

[8]Quoted in James M. Burns, *The Vineyard of Liberty* (New York: Knopf, 1982), p. 225.
[9]Clinton Rossiter, *Conservatism in America,* 2d ed., rev. (Cambridge, MA: Harvard University Press, 1982), p. 118.
[10]Quoted in Jay Sigler, ed., *The Conservative Tradition in American Thought* (New York: Capricorn Books, 1969), p. 118.

laissez-faire economics

French for "leave things alone"; the view in economics that government should not interfere in the workings of the economy.

social Darwinism

A set of ideas applying Charles Darwin's theory of biological evolution to society and holding that social relationships occur within a struggle for survival in which only the fittest survive.

But as America industrialized, conservatives embraced **laissez-faire economics** —an economic system that operated free of government control. Burke and Adams regarded the state as essential to the promotion of public virtue and the protection of property, but in the Industrial Age the state became the object of conservative scorn. In stressing individualism, economic growth, and the limited role of government, conservatives seemed closer to Jefferson and Jackson in this regard than to Burke and Adams.

Herbert Spencer (1820–1903), an English social scientist, and William Graham Sumner (1840–1910), an American sociologist, developed the theory of economic individualism that became the keystone of late-nineteenth-century and early-twentieth-century conservatism. The theory was popularly known as **social Darwinism**. Sumner stated the case in a somewhat extreme form. People, Sumner argued, should be free to compete with each other for survival. From this economic competition, the fit will survive and the weak will perish. The result will be the betterment of humankind through the survival of superior individuals. Sumner opposed governmental aid to the needy as inconsistent with his views on social and economic evolution. Government was inefficient by nature, Sumner argued, and should be limited to fundamental concerns. Sumner wrote, "At bottom there are two chief things with which government has to deal. They are, the property of men and the honor of women. These it has to defend against crime."[11]

Although these views were far too extreme even for the nineteenth century, Spencer and Sumner made a great impact on conservative thinking. Conservatives of the Industrial Age did not emphasize the individual's obligation to the state or the state's obligation to promote public virtue; instead, the emphasis was almost entirely on the individual. If people worked hard, they argued, people could become successful, and economic growth would ensue. The government need only stand out of the way. Many business leaders were attracted to this philosophy, although it did not prevent them from helping themselves to governmental favors (tariff protection or direct subsidies) when the occasion arose. These business leaders invoked conservatism to justify opposition to antitrust laws, bills regulating hours and wages, and a progressive income tax.

In short, conservatism became the ideology of America's business class. As long as most Americans shared somewhat in the growth of the American economy, they were willing to accept most of the tenets of conservatism. From the end of Reconstruction to the New Deal, Americans elected presidents (with the exceptions of Theodore Roosevelt and Woodrow Wilson) who reflected those values.

Contemporary Conservatism: A Response to the Welfare State

The Great Depression ended America's romance with conservatism. It brought about the election of Franklin Roosevelt and the beginning of the New Deal, with its numerous

---

[11]Quoted in Rossiter, *Conservatism in America*, p. 138.

welfare state programs. The general popular acceptance of these programs placed American conservatism on the defensive for the next several generations. From 1933–1981, conservatism could be better measured by what it was against than what it was for. Conservatives opposed most major liberal domestic reforms, from the Social Security Bill of 1935 to the Medicare Bill of 1965.

Conservatism since the 1980s has taken on a more positive cast, with an agenda of its own—reducing social spending, reshaping the tax code, and rebuilding national defense. In economic matters, conservatives draw on many of the ideas of nineteenth-century individualism. Conservatism still remains at its core a defense of economic individualism against the growth of the welfare state. Conservatives oppose any increase in the role of the federal government over the general direction of the economy, and contend that a vibrant private-sector economy can best create jobs for the poor, immigrants, and minorities. Welfare state programs, conservatives argue, only create a permanent class of the poor who are dependent on the state and have no genuine incentives to enter the working world.

Although many conservatives opposed the major civil rights laws of the 1960s on the grounds that they represented a serious encroachment on states' rights, most now accept these laws as a permanent part of our political landscape. But they do challenge the idea of quotas and other affirmative-action policies as a means of enforcing civil rights laws in the areas of jobs, educational opportunities, and access to federal contracts. They argue that civil rights should mean equality of treatment and not equality of results.

On social and cultural issues conservatives remain close to Burkean ideals. Contemporary conservatives believe that the state must promote virtue and social responsibility and take appropriate measures to improve the moral climate of society. They support constitutional amendments restricting abortion and permitting prayers in public schools. They oppose the concept of civil rights for homosexuals in jobs, the military, and housing. Speaking as a modern-day Burkean, conservative philosopher and syndicated columnist George Will wrote, "Traditional conservatism has not been, and proper conservatism cannot be, merely a defense of industrialism and individualist 'free market' economics. Conservatism is about the cultivation and conservation of certain values or it is nothing."[12]

As conservative causes have gained broader public support, conservatives no longer invoke the suspicion of the masses, as they did in John Adams's day (see Table 4.4). Nor do they talk very much about the independence of the judicial branch as a check on the excesses of legislative power. In fact, conservatives have been particularly critical of Supreme Court decisions outlawing prayers in school and legalizing abortion.[13]

---

[12]George Will, *Statecraft as Soulcraft: What Government Does* (New York: Simon & Schuster, 1983), pp. 119–120.

[13]*Engel v. Vitale*, 370 U.S. 421 (1962); *Roe v. Wade*, 410 U.S. 113 (1973); *Wallace v. Jaffree*, 472 U.S. 38 (1985).

They support efforts to have such decisions overturned by constitutional amendment or weakened by legislative action. Direct democracy, so feared by the conservatives of the eighteenth and nineteenth centuries, has become an important tool of contemporary conservatives. Conservatives have successfully employed the popular referendum (a device that permits people to vote on policy questions as well as for candidates) in California and Massachusetts as a check on the power of state legislatures to tax their own citizens.

Some conservative causes have generated intense (although not broad) rank-and-file support. In part because of conservative support for reduced taxes, prayer in school, and restrictions on abortion, conservatism has been transformed from an elitist philosophy of the propertied class to a more populist cause of the working and middle classes.

Who are the conservatives? In most cases their political home is in the Republican party. Ronald Reagan was the first president since the Great Depression to identify himself openly with conservatism and conservative causes. Previous Republican presidents—Eisenhower, Nixon, and Ford—were men of the center who shunned ideology and ideological labels. Perhaps the best-known conservative journal is *National Review*,

TABLE 4.4

Milestones in American Conservatism

1790	Edmund Burke's *Reflections on the French Revolution* published; Alexander Hamilton, first U.S. Treasury secretary, introduces a report recommending a national bank.
1883	William Graham Sumner's *What Social Classes Owe to Each Other* published.
1890	Herbert Spencer's *Social Statics* published.
1905	Supreme Court in *Lochner v. New York* strikes down New York law limiting working hours of bakers as a violation of freedom of contract under the Fourteenth Amendment.
1920	Warren Harding elected president, marking the beginning of a new era of conservative dominance lasting until 1932.
1955	*National Review* founded, marking the beginning of the intellectual revitalization of post–World War II conservatism.
1964	Barry Goldwater receives the Republican presidential nomination, beginning the conservative ascendancy in the party.
1981	President Ronald Reagan begins his program of tax reductions, domestic spending cuts, and defense buildup.
1994	Newt Gingrich and his "Contract with America" sweep the Republican Party into the majority in both chambers of Congress for the first time in 40 years.
2000	George W. Bush and Dick Cheney win the electoral vote and embark on an agenda of tax cuts, defense spending, and environmental deregulation.

founded by William Buckley, himself one of the most prominent spokespersons for modern conservatism.

Neoconservatism versus Paleoconservatism: Conservative Splits at the turn of the Century

neoconservatism

A belief, associated with many former liberal intellectuals, that contemporary liberalism has transformed the modest New Deal welfare state into an intrusive paternalistic state.

In the 1970s a number of leading American intellectuals, many of them longtime liberals, became openly critical of the drift of contemporary liberalism; thus began the ideology labeled **neoconservatism** in the popular press. Neoconservatives feel that liberals have overestimated the ability of government to solve social problems such as industrial pollution, economic inequality, and racial discrimination. They argue that liberals have gone beyond the initial New Deal concept that government need only provide a "safety net" for the subsistence needs for society's victims—the unemployed, the disabled Americans, and the elderly. Contemporary liberalism, the neoconservatives claim, transformed the New Deal's modest welfare state into a more intrusive paternalistic state. Neoconservatives disagree with such liberal ideas as the use of racial or gender quotas as a means of assuring fairness in hiring, promotion, or acceptance to professional schools. They also reject the idea of forced school busing as a means of achieving racial balance in enrollments. They consider these ideas elitist liberal schemes not supported by the vast majority of Americans.

Neoconservatives feel that liberals no longer speak for the "average person" but rather for a "new class" of relatively affluent reformers—lawyers, social workers, educators, city planners—with careers in the expanding public sector. This liberal new class intends "to propel the nation from that modified version of capitalism we call 'the welfare state' toward an economic system so regulated in detail as to fulfill many of the traditional anticapitalist aspirations of the left."[14]

Neoconservatives also argue that liberals emphasize policies (such as higher taxes on the upper middle class) that were aimed not at creating wealth but only at redistributing it. Skeptical about government's ability to erase economic inequalities, neoconservatives stress policies such as lower taxes on large incomes and less regulation of business to promote economic growth. Such growth, they feel, would more likely broaden economic opportunity and create greater social stability. Likewise, they are suspicious of policies that polarize one class or group against another: racial busing that pits the white working-class communities in the large cities against the poor African American community, and gender and racial quotas that place the interests of women and minorities against those of white males.

In short, neoconservatives feel that modern liberals have promised too much to too many groups, and that a government that promises too much cannot deliver and be-

http://adaction.org /voting.html

Are your congressional Representatives and Senators generally liberal, or are they mostly conservative? Americans for Democratic Action is an organization that attempts to answer that question by assigning each legislator a "Liberal Quotient" score based on their voting record.

---

[14]Irving Kristol, *Reflections of a Neoconservative: Looking Back, Looking Ahead* (New York: Basic Books, 1953), p. 212.

comes "overloaded." As a result, they argue, government loses its authority and cannot govern effectively. But neoconservatives differ from traditional conservatives in that neoconservatives support, in principle and practice, a modest welfare state (Social Security, unemployment insurance, and Medicare). In fact, neoconservatives argue that a properly constructed welfare state strengthens citizens' loyalty to the existing capitalist system and is thus a stabilizing force.

Neoconservatives have engendered some resentment among many members of the Old Right, now dubbed paleoconservatives (*paleo* from the Greek meaning "ancient"). They decry the neoconservative accommodation to the welfare state and remain hostile to government efforts to establish social and economic equality. The paleoconservatives believe that religious traditions embodied in the church and family should be the basis of a stable and ordered society. The welfare state philosophy of the New Deal and Great Society is, according to them, an effort to create a secular moral order. By defending the New Deal legacy, the paleoconservatives charge the neoconservatives with defending not only a misguided political idea but a religious heresy.

The sudden collapse of communism in 1989 opened up new fissures in contemporary conservatism. With the unraveling of the Soviet Union, some paleoconservative leaders such as journalist Patrick Buchanan, who challenged President George Bush in the 1992 primaries, sounded older conservative themes of isolationism and America first. Neoconservatives, in turn, strongly supported continued American leadership in world affairs.

Yet, the neoconservative belief in a limited form of welfarism has influenced a new generation of conservative political leaders. Representative Newt Gingrich (R-GA) and former Housing and Urban Development Secretary Jack Kemp developed a new conservative "empowerment" agenda to assist the poor with an emphasis upon anti-bureaucratic, market-oriented programs. George W. Bush (2001–) followed this lead with a presidential campaign that promised "compassionate conservativism."

Neoconservatism has emerged as an influential intellectual and political force. Its ideas have influenced the Reagan administration and both Bush administrations, and have brought about a more respectful hearing for conservatism in general among academics and intellectuals.

Ideological Challenges to the Status Quo

Not all American ideologies fit comfortably under the rubrics *liberal* and *conservative*. Some challenge dominant opinion and propose policies that are outside today's mainstream. Yet the fact that they represent a minority point of view does not make them unimportant. The history of American political thought is full of examples of "extreme" ideas that gained acceptability and entered the mainstream.

The New Right: Populist Conservatism

New Right

A political movement, led by Christian evangelicals, that supports the re-establishment of traditional moral values, the abolition of abortion and pornography, and the legalization of school prayer.

In the late 1970s and 1980s a new political movement combined the elements of traditional conservatism and the populist belief that government was run by narrow, selfish interests. Known as the **New Right**, it included Christian evangelicals, anti-abortionists, and anti-gun control advocates. It also included many members of the working and middle class who were alienated from contemporary liberalism and who never felt comfortable with pro-business conservatism (see Table 4.1).

The New Right feels that permissive liberal values are responsible for a broad range of social ills, including high levels of premarital sex, adultery, abortion, income tax cheating, excessive personal and government debt, and the expectation of large numbers of middle-class and wealthy people (farmers, businesspeople, and bankers) of receiving government subsidies.

The movement may be conservative only in the sense that its cultural values are traditional, because the New Right, unlike most conservative movements, does not defend established institutions. The New Right believes that the major institutions of contemporary America—the bureaucracy, the media, the managerial hierarchies of the unions and corporations—should not be defended but exposed.

In the late 1980s and early 1990s, New Right political organizations atrophied. The end of the Cold War removed communism as a powerful political issue. The retirement of President Ronald Reagan and a series of sex scandals that implicated evangelical television ministers Jim Bakker and Jimmy Swaggart disheartened the movement. The Reverend Jerry Falwell disbanded his Moral Majority organization; Pat Robertson's 1988 presidential campaign gained little support, and his Christian Broadcasting Network focused more on entertainment than politics. Nor did the New Right political leaders consider Yale-educated George Bush someone whose heart was genuinely with them. But George W. Bush's appointment of religious conservatives to his cabinet, such as Attorney General John Ashcroft, and his creation of Centers for Faith-Based and Community Initiatives, may indicate something of a revival for the New Right in the new millennium.

Democratic Socialism: A Radical Challenge to American Capitalism

democratic socialism

An economic system in which the major industries are owned by a democratically elected government responsible for planning and directing the economy.

Democratic socialism is an economic system in which the basic industries, banks, agricultural systems, and communication networks are owned and controlled by the government at either the local or national level. While a private sector of the economy may continue to exist under socialism, major industries and corporations would be owned by the state, and thus the government would be responsible for planning and directing the economy. Key decisions concerning investments, prices, and wages would be placed in the hands of public institutions. What separates democratic socialists from communists, who also believe in the principle of public ownership, is that democratic socialists reject the idea of violent revolution. Instead, democratic socialists advocate the adoption of socialism through peaceful and constitutional means; they support the basic democratic rights embodied in our Constitution.

Economic equality is an essential idea in socialism. Socialists argue that capitalism in America, despite its success in creating wealth, has failed to solve the fundamental problem of poverty. Equality of opportunity is not enough, socialists argue. A genuinely democratic society must produce equality of results. Socialists wish to replace a society based on competition with a society based on cooperation. The socialist ideal sees individuals motivated not by profit and personal gain, but by a sense of social responsibility.

In short, democratic socialism requires:

1. Government ownership and control of the major industries, utilities, and transportation systems
2. A limit on individual wealth and property
3. A welfare system that guarantees all persons decent health care, an education, and adequate food and shelter
4. Extensive governmental regulation of the economy

Democratic socialism was a powerful force in Western Europe throughout the twentieth century. But in the United States socialism and social democratic parties have had little or no success. In the early years of the twentieth century, the Socialist party, headed by Eugene V. Debs and later by Norman Thomas, gained some influence and support. During the Great Depression the millions of unemployed provided the socialists with a major opportunity. In 1932, their last significant showing in a presidential election, Norman Thomas gained about two percent of the popular vote. But the election of Franklin Roosevelt and acceptance of his New Deal welfare measures stole much of the socialists' thunder. Irving Howe, co-chair of the Democratic Socialists of America, admitted in 1984 that "the Socialist Party fell apart because it could not come to terms with Roosevelt."[15]

The Democratic Socialists of America, the successor to the Socialist party of Debs and Thomas, no longer expects to galvanize broad mass support behind its banners. Instead, it operates within a number of liberal organizations, including the Democratic party, to influence their ideas and direction.

The issues that faced the socialist movement in the pre–New Deal days were relatively simple and dramatic: the elderly needed a guaranteed pension; the unions needed government guarantees of their rights to organize and bargain; the unemployed needed some form of protection. The New Deal established programs to deal with these issues, and

---

[15]"Voices from the Left: A Conversation Between Michael Harrington and Irving Howe," *The New York Times Magazine*, June 17, 1984, p. 28.

the subsequent questions of their financing and administration were no longer dramatic. What, then, is the social democratic program in the post–New Deal, post-welfare state era?

Full employment, guaranteed by the government, has become a major demand of contemporary socialists. This requires a reduction of the work week from 40 to 35 hours so that more people can work fewer hours, with the government compensating workers with tax credits for any wages they lose by a reduction of their hours. Socialists call for a massive public works program for rebuilding America's *infrastructure* (roads, bridges, sewage systems) in order to create millions of new jobs for the currently unemployed. Because full employment can stimulate inflation, the socialists would also employ controls on wages, prices, incomes, rents, and dividends.

Sensitive to the issue that socialism spawns bureaucracy and centralization, American socialists support a system of public ownership characterized by worker-owned or community-controlled businesses and factories. Nevertheless, Americans remain resistant to the idea of socialism, associating it with either the authoritarian communism that plagued Eastern Europe or, in its democratic form, with the sluggish economy that characterized pre-Thatcherite Great Britain. In the present era, socialism presents more of an intellectual challenge to American capitalism than a serious political threat. Nonetheless, in 1990 longtime socialist Bernard Sanders, not running under the Democratic banner, was elected to the House of Representatives from Vermont. He was the first independent socialist elected to Congress in over half a century. In 2000 he was returned to Congress for his sixth consecutive term, winning over 70 percent of the votes.

Libertarianism: A Revival of Classical Liberalism

Although the Libertarian party remains on the fringe of American politics, its ideas have stimulated considerable interest. The intellectual roots of libertarianism can be traced to the classical liberal movement of the eighteenth and nineteenth centuries and the ideas of Thomas Jefferson and Andrew Jackson. In the 2000 presidential election, the Libertarian party candidate, Harry Browne, polled over 380,000 votes.

libertarianism

A belief that the state should regulate neither the economic nor the moral life of its citizens.

Like classical liberalism, **libertarianism** holds that the state must be kept extremely small. The essential role of government should be only the protection of human rights:

1. The right to life, by which libertarians mean protection against the use of force by others
2. The right to liberty, meaning the freedoms of speech, press, and assembly and protection against any government restrictions on ideas, books, films, or other means of communication

3. The right to property; libertarians support legislation that protects the property rights of individuals against confiscation, robbery, trespass, libel, fraud, and copyright violations.[16]

Libertarians also oppose the interference of government in the private lives of citizens. They seek, for example, the repeal of all laws that involve so-called victimless crimes (prostitution, pornography, gambling). They seek an unfettered, free-market economy and oppose laws regulating the price of milk as well as those that prohibit the use of marijuana. Unlike the liberals, who support laws expanding the role of government in the economy, and the New Right, which supports legislation outlawing abortion and pornography, the libertarians oppose with equal fervor laws that regulate either the moral or the economic life of individuals.

Libertarians favor nonintervention in the affairs of other nations. They believe that military alliances and arms aid only lead to war, and that wars and war preparation bring about a vast increase in the power of government. One leading libertarian theorist argues that the United States should revoke all its military and political commitments to other countries.[17]

Libertarians call for a drastic reduction in the defense budget and a defense policy designed solely to defend the territory of the United States. Accordingly, the military draft is considered a form of involuntary servitude. Because proponents of the Libertarian movement and the Libertarian party have no immediate prospect of coming into power, their positions remain free of the need to compromise. In the 2000 campaign, candidate Harry Browne called for the elimination of government controlled Social Security, the repeal of all gun laws and all income taxes, an end to the War on Drugs, and international isolationism.

Although the Libertarian party remains a minor party, its ideas have influenced both major parties. The Republican party has taken a much more aggressive stand against the social programs of the 1960s and 1970s. It has also championed the reduction of income tax rates and the deregulation of business and industry. The Democratic party has supported broader freedom from government interference in the areas of abortion, school prayer, and gay rights. Nevertheless, Americans have generally been reluctant to follow radical or revolutionary movements. Perhaps they perceive libertarianism as an interesting criticism, but they are not yet prepared to accept its far-reaching solutions.

---

[16]John Hospers, "What Libertarianism Is," in Tibor Machan, ed., *The Libertarian Alternative: Essays in Social and Political Philosophy* (Chicago: Nelson-Hall, 1974), p. 13.
[17]Murray Rothbard, *For a New Liberty: The Libertarian Manifesto*, rev. ed. (New York: Collier, 1978), p. 291.

SUMMARY

1. People do not simply dispute over issues that reflect their own self-interest. They also disagree, at times sharply, about what constitutes a good society. Since the American and the French revolutions, disputes between liberals and conservatives have occupied center stage in the Western democracies and in the United States in particular. But liberalism and conservatism have often changed colors and even exchanged attitudes.

2. Nineteenth-century liberals Thomas Jefferson and Andrew Jackson equated the idea of a powerful state with the protection of the wealthy merchant classes. But liberalism changed in the Industrial Age. Deeply affected by the Populist and Progressive movements, liberalism saw government as an important vehicle for the protection of the many from the exploitation of the few. Liberals and neoliberals today still regard governmental programs and intervention as the key to solving our economic problems. But in matters of personal morality, liberals hark back to an earlier age. Their opposition to governmental interference in matters of abortion and school prayer is reminiscent of Jefferson's concerns.

3. Conservatives in the early days of the American republic were the supporters of a strong government. They believed that only a government of a talented and propertied elite could preserve the sacred rights of all people. As the voting franchise extended to more and more people, conservatives lost their faith in central government and focused on the rights of property, independent of the state, and rights of individuals to be free of governmental interference. But by their opposition to abortion, pornography, and gay rights, conservatives remain true in matters of moral and social policy to the old Burkean belief that the state can promote social virtue. The central controversy between liberals and conservatives today is not over whether government should be strong or weak, but *when* it should be strong or weak.

4. The New Right, libertarianism, and democratic socialism advocate fundamental alterations in the status quo. The New Right wants to use government to curb the power of the big banks, the media, the unions, and the big corporations. Their programs may not be welfarist in that they oppose most social programs, but by their opposition to people in positions of power and influence, their tone and temperament are clearly populist.

5. Social democrats, by contrast, focus on the good of the whole society and envision a system under which all people will be equal economically and

politically. They support a broad program of governmental control that includes ownership of the major corporations and industries. Unlike the libertarians, who see the state as the greatest threat to human liberty, the social democrats see the state as the greatest hope for human equality.

6. Libertarians, in their opposition to the very idea of big government, hark back to the nineteenth-century liberals. They are opposed to government interference in the setting of agricultural price supports as well as in the prohibition of so-called illegal drugs. They believe that government should exist primarily to defend the rights to life, liberty, and property, and to defend the homeland from attack.

KEY TERMS

liberalism (106)

contract theory (106)

classical liberalism (106)

progressivism (109)

industrial policy (111)

Americans for Democratic Action (112)

neoliberalism (113)

conservatism (115)

laissez-faire economics (117)

social Darwinism (117)

neoconservatism (120)

New Right (122)

democratic socialism (122)

libertarianism (124)

READINGS FOR FURTHER STUDY

A broad overview of political ideologies can be found in Roy C. Macridis, *Contemporary Political Ideologies*, 2d ed. (Boston: Little, Brown, 1983).

Both Walter E. Volkomer, ed., *The Liberal Tradition in American Thought* (New York: Capricorn Books, 1969) and Jay Sigler, ed., *The Conservative Tradition in American Thought* (New York: Capricorn Books, 1969) provide a valuable collection of important historical readings.

Alpheus T. Mason and Gordon E. Baker, *Free Government in the Making,* 4th ed. (New York: Oxford University Press, 1985) supplements readings on American political thought with helpful essays.

Readers interested in exploring socialist thought should consult Michael Harrington, *Socialism* (New York: Saturday Review Press, 1970).

Those interested in a greater understanding of libertarianism should see Murray Rothbard, *For a New Liberty: The Libertarian Manifesto*, rev. ed. (New York: Collier, 1978).

For a discussion of neoliberal and neoconservative thought, consult Charles Peters and Phillip Keisling, eds., *The Neoliberal Movement* (Lanham, MD: Madison Books, 1985) and Irving Kristol, *Reflections of a Neoconservative* (New York: Basic Books, 1983).

For an overview of the impact of the contemporary ideological debate on American politics, see E. J. Dionne, Jr., *Why Americans Hate Politics* (New York: Simon & Schuster, 1991).

CHAPTER 5

Public Opinion and Political Participation

A/P World Wide

Chapter Objectives

This chapter examines what the American people actually think about politics, how they come to think what they do, and how they translate their thoughts into politically relevant actions. Chapter 4 described the major patterns of American political beliefs in philosophical and historical terms. In this chapter we concern ourselves with the extent to which the general public actually subscribes to those beliefs, which leads into an examination of how people learn to think about politics. What are the influences that encourage people to become Democrats, independents, or Republicans, as well as determine their opinions on political issues? These topics are discussed in the sections on political socialization. The chapter concludes with a discussion of how political beliefs are translated into political actions, ranging from voting to protest demonstrations and civil disobedience.

Public Opinion: What Americans Think About Politics

What Americans *think* about politics is important because it determines, in part, how they act politically. The diverse but predominantly moderate character of Americans' political views and the relatively modest intensity with which most people advance their views set the tone for the whole political process. To understand how people think about politics is to understand an essential element of the environment within which the political process functions.

The Character of Public Opinion

public opinion

The array of beliefs and attitudes that people hold about political and related affairs.

Public opinion may sound like a simple and stable concept, but in reality it is actually complex and ever changing. **Public opinion** is a combination of the views, attitudes, and ideas held by individuals in a community. There is no single public opinion; there is, rather, a wide variety of viewpoints. Different publics or groups of people think differently about political questions. Some people hold very sophisticated views about politics; others do not. Some people devote their entire lives to politics; others hardly ever think about politics.

Certain facets of public opinion are remarkably constant. Love of country and pride in the nation's accomplishments, for instance, are attitudes that are almost always present and widely shared. Other facets of public opinion are *dynamic*, fluctuating considerably in response to social, political, and economic events. Some opinions are held *intensely*; others seem to be little more than *casual preferences*. An opinion that is intensely held is more likely to influence what a person thinks about political candidates and how that person might get involved politically.

The politically sophisticated and the general public observe the same political world. However, much of the public sees it, to borrow an expression from the Bible, "through a glass darkly." Politicians and political commentators can argue at length about what they see as the major political issues of the time, but much of this seems to pass by most of the public. As explained in the following sections, a substantial share of the American public does not care much about politics, knows relatively little about it, and does not think about it in very sophisticated terms. Still, few would admit that public opinion is unimportant. Indeed, political analysts and politicians are very concerned about what the public thinks.

How Much Americans Care and Know About Politics

The first public opinion pollsters assumed that the public cared and was reasonably well-informed about politics; however, they were startled to find that many Americans cared little and knew less about what went on in the political arena. More recent surveys have done little to contradict these early findings, or show any recent increase in public interest and information—a surprising finding given the rising level of education and the proliferation of the media, particularly television news, over the last few decades.

This is not to say that the public as a whole is essentially uninterested in politics; indeed, a substantial number of people indicate a considerable degree of interest. For example, in 1998 one survey found that 27 percent of the public said that they followed government and public affairs "most of the time," 37 percent only "some of the time," 25 percent "only now and then," and 12 percent "hardly at all."[1] These results fall

---

[1] The National Election Studies, Center for Political Studies, University of Michigan. Electronic resources from the NEW World Wide Web site www.umich.edu/nes. Ann Arbor, MI: University of Michigan, Center for Political Studies [producer and distributor], 1995–2000.

short of the democratic ideal of a keenly interested electorate, but are reasonably reassuring in that most people do seem to be at least somewhat interested in politics.

But the meaningfulness of such expressions of interest is called into question by the public's level of information about politics. In a 1998 survey, 34 percent of Americans did not know that the Republican party held a majority of the seats in Congress. A 1999 study found that 24 percent of Americans could not name the country that the United States gained its independence from following the Revolutionary War.[2]

What Americans Hold in Common

On many fundamental political matters, the vast majority of Americans are in substantial agreement. First of all, Americans are proud of their country and emotionally attached to it and its symbols. In a 1999 poll, 65 percent of Americans said they were either extremely patriotic or very patriotic; only 5 percent said they were not especially patriotic.[3] Studies consistently show that the percentages of people expressing enthusiasm and pride for their country are, in fact, higher in the United States than in any other country.

Americans are also positive about their country's political, social, and economic institutions. When asked how much confidence they had in their country's public and private institutions, Americans consistently responded more favorably than citizens from four other European democracies (Figure 5.1). Although some Americans are critical of their nation's institutions, what is most striking is that Americans are clearly less critical than people in other countries. Even for institutions that are sometimes singled out as objects of public disdain in the United States, such as the media, labor unions, and Congress, Americans consistently have more confidence in them than do their European counterparts.[4]

Why are Americans generally so proud of their country and positive about its institutions? One reason is that they have been taught all their lives to think of America as the best (see the section on political socialization, pp., 141–149). But the roots of American pride run deeper than that. Americans also take pride in their country because they are generally raised to hold certain basic values, and to believe that the United States, among all nations, is particularly dedicated to the fulfillment of those values. The Declaration of Independence, discussed in Chapter 1, exemplifies these values.

> WE hold these Truths to be self-evident, that all Men are created equal, that
> they are endowed by their Creator with certain unalienable Rights, that among
> these are *Life, Liberty, and the Pursuit of Happiness*. That to secure these rights,

---

[2]American National Election Studies, 1998, and Steve Crabtree, "Americans Are Widely Patriotic, but Many Think Founding Fathers Would Frown on Modern America," The Gallup Organization, July 1999, www.gallup.com/poll/releases/pr990702.asp (24 August 2001).
[3]Ibid.
[4]Laurence Parisot, "Attitudes About the Media," *Public Opinion* (January–February 1988): 18.

FIGURE 5.1

Confidence in Public Institutions: A Comparative Perspective

Americans consistently express greater confidence in their country's political, social, and economic institutions than do citizens of other democratic countries.

SOURCE: Humphrey Taylor, "Confidence in Leadership of Nation's Institutions Slips a Little But Remains Relatively High," Harris Poll Library, February 2001, http://www.harrisinteractive.com/harris_poll/index.asp?PID=219 (31 October 2001) and European Commission, Eurobarometer Report Number 55, October 2001, http://europa.eu.int/comm/dg10/epo/eb /eb55/eb55.html (31 October 2001).

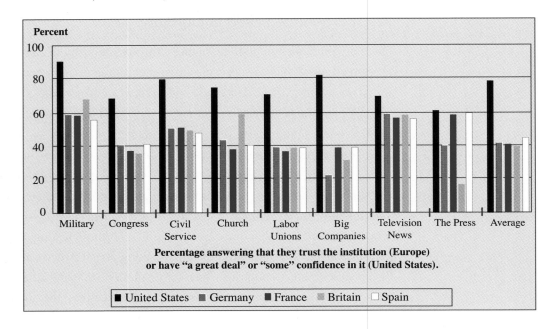

Governments are instituted among Men, deriving their just Powers from the *Consent of the Governed*. [italics added]

To these three basic values of democracy—equality, freedom, and consent of the governed—can be added most Americans' commitment to capitalism and the free enterprise system.

- *Equality*. Surveys suggest that roughly 80 percent of Americans genuinely believe in equality and that, whether or not they really think people are equal, more than 90 percent believe that the government should treat everyone as if they were equal.[5]
- *Freedom*. Americans believe in their capacity to do what is best for themselves. Hence, they think that individuals should be free to act as they please, with minimal government interference, as long as they do not

---

[5]ABC News/*Washington Post* Poll, Survey 77.

Politics and Ideas
Textbooks and Children's Ideas About American Politics

American students typically spend a dozen or more years of their lives poring over textbooks of various sorts. Some of these books have little to do with politics: math books, chemistry books, foreign language books. But many of them deal directly or indirectly with topics related to politics: social studies books, history books, American government books, economics books, and sociology books.

Because students spend so much time reading them, textbooks seem likely to significantly affect how students think about politics. Further, the books may be particularly influential because of the way students are likely to approach them. Students treat the material in textbooks as information they need to know, rather than as information to be read critically or thought about afterward in depth. Almost as soon as the material is known, it starts to be forgotten. As the specific facts fade, what tends to be remembered is a general impression, a color and tone and feeling that can persist for years.

The influence of textbooks brings up some of the most important and difficult issues of political socialization.[a] Much of political socialization occurs not in sudden and dramatic jumps from ignorance to knowledge or from ambivalence to passion, but through a slow, steady gain and loss of political information and impressions. The content of school textbooks is determined by a combination of scholarly, economic, and political factors. The final product is shaped by the scholars who write the book, the editors and publishers who mold the book to help it sell, and the more or

less politically accountable officials who pick the books to be used. But who should decide which textbooks American children should read? Are not school boards democratic institutions? And, more generally, who should decide what children will be taught? How democratic do we want the education process to be?

Earlier textbooks often presented children with an idealized picture of American history, society, and politics ("sugarcoating," some scholars have called it), but recently there has been more sentiment toward giving students the "unvarnished truth." For example, by the 1990s textbooks became more multicultural—featuring stories and descriptions of ethnic and racial minorities and women.[b] However, is there such a thing as "unvarnished truth," or are there just different perspectives? Is there a "best" way to present America's diverse cultural history? And, again, who should decide?

Teaching children to think critically about their country, as newer texts tend to do, is certainly an admirable goal, but it can run counter to the goal of political socialization necessary to promote good citizenship. How does a society create in its children the appropriate balance of respect and skepticism for its basic values? To put it differently, every society wants to instill in its youth favorable feelings towards its values and institutions, but where is the line between socialization and brainwashing?

---

[a] Frances FitzGerald, *America Revised* (New York: Random House Vintage Books, 1980).
[b] Jesus Garcia, "The Changing Image of Ethnic Groups in Textbooks," *Phi Delta Kappa* 75 (1993): 29–35.

interfere with other people's freedom. Surveys have long shown a strong commitment to freedom of speech, press, religion, and association.[6] For example, 81 percent of Americans responding to a 2000 poll indicated that the First Amendment protection for freedom of speech is a good thing in America today.[7] On the other hand, when rights come into conflict, Americans are faced with tough choices regarding which freedoms to support. The issue of school prayer often pits those who favor free exercise of religion against those who oppose the establishment of religion. In a recent poll, 72 percent of Americans said prayer should be allowed in public schools, even though the Supreme Court has consistently found such prayer unconstitutional.[8]

- *Consent of the governed.* Americans see their acceptance of government as voluntary. About 86 percent of Americans believe that periodic elections make the government "pay attention to what the people think." While only 40 percent responded that they trust the government most or all of the time, only 1 percent of Americans said they never trust the government.[9] Americans also believe firmly in the idea that the majority (more than half) of the people should rule in political affairs. At the same time, however, they believe that majorities should not possess unlimited power and that the rights of a minority (less than half) of the people should be protected against the whims of the majority.

- *Capitalism and the free enterprise system.* Americans believe in the value of hard work, in private property, in economic competition, and in profit. In contrast to some other societies, most Americans tend to view hard work as a virtue and laziness as a vice—tenets of the so-called Protestant ethic. They see private property as an essential element of economic progress. They believe that competition brings out the best in people and that the most successful competitors deserve the greatest rewards. Americans' preference for freedom over equality manifests itself in the economic as well as the political sphere. This particular combination of values fits well with a free-market, entrepreneurial economy. Americans like the idea of a fair competition in which everybody starts out equally, but in which they all have the freedom to pursue their self-interest and thus end up unequally well-off according to how well they have pursued their self-interest. A series of Gallup polls taken between 1994 and 2000

---

[6]Herbert McClosky and Alida Brill, *Dimensions of Tolerance: What Americans Believe About Civil Liberties* (New York: Russell Sage Foundation, 1983), pp. 48–135.
[7]Rasmussen Research, Portrait of America, July 2000, http://www.portraitofamerica.com/html/home.html.
[8]Ibid.
[9]American National Election Studies, 1998.

indicates that a consistent majority of Americans believes the government "is trying to do too many things that should be left to individuals and businesses." In 2000, 74 percent of Americans indicated that they were in favor of a cut in federal taxes.[10] The survey also found 87 percent of respondents saying that private property was as important to a good society as freedom. Thus, Americans have little interest in moving toward a communist or socialist system.

Although Americans are proud of their country and its system of government, and although they believe in the fundamental values on which it rests, they are not beyond finding fault with it. In fact, since the 1960s the American political system has struggled with a widespread undercurrent of dissatisfaction with the way in which the system is working, fired by the urban disorders of the 1960s, the Vietnam War, the Watergate scandal, and the nation's ongoing economic problems. Between 1964 and 1994 the percentage of Americans who said they trusted the government to do what was right all or most of the time fell from 76 percent to 21 percent, and the percentage who said that public officials care what "people like me" think declined from 62 percent to 22 percent. This sense of alienation may have started to turn around in the 1990s, however, as the trust in government number rose to 40 percent and the percent who believed government cared about what they think rose to 25 percent by 1998. Such mood changes may not be entirely unrelated to Americans' pocketbooks. In 1993, 68 percent of Americans were at least moderately worried about their personal economic situation. By January of 2000, however, a majority of Americans were only a little worried or not at all worried.[11]

Where Americans Differ

Citizens of the United States manifest considerable agreement on the general principles of democracy just described, but

Richard M. Nixon, who appeared on nationwide television to resign his position following the Watergate scandal. *(Library of Congress)*

---

[10]The Gallup Organization, 2001.
[11]American National Election Studies, 1998, and The Gallup Organization, 2000.

consensus is far from complete. The American people differ on the implications of these general principles when applied to particular cases. They also differ in their political ideologies.

The Meaning of Equality   Although Americans profess a belief in equality in the abstract, just what this means and to whom it applies are matters for disagreement. First, as discussed in Chapter 3, does equality mean equality of opportunity or equality of result? That is, should everybody have an equal chance to pursue an education and earn a high income, or should everybody get the same education and earn the same income? Americans seem to lean away from equality of result. Only 22 percent believe the government should see to it that every person has a job and good standard of living.[12]

Second, just which "men" are equal? Some Americans do not believe that men and women are equal. According to a 2000 survey, 9 percent think that "women's place is in the home rather than business, industry, or government."[13] A substantial percentage of Americans do not regard African Americans and whites as equals. In a 1990 survey, 78 percent of whites thought that African Americans were more likely to prefer living on welfare than whites; 62 percent thought African Americans less likely to be hardworking; 56 percent thought African Americans more prone to violence; and 53 percent thought African Americans less intelligent. African Americans see this sense of racial inequality from a different perspective. In a 2001 poll, 38 percent of whites, but only 9 percent of African Americans, believe that the two races are treated equally in this country. Additionally, 85 percent of whites believed that African American children have the same chance as white children to get a good education, whereas only 52 percent of African Americans share this view.[14]

Limits of Freedom   Although Americans believe in freedom as a general principle, they do see it as having definite limits. More than 95 percent endorse the principle of freedom of expression in the abstract, but percentages drop sharply with the possibility that "bad" or "dangerous" ideas will be expressed.[15] For many Americans, freedom of expression does not extend to speaking, writing, or teaching when the ideas are unpopular ones—antireligious, racist, or communist.[16] Further, some Americans do not agree that people should be able to express their views any way they want. The Supreme Court's decisions in 1989 and 1990 upholding the rights of protesters to burn the American flag set off a bitter national debate. A constitutional amendment to criminalize the act has been introduced in Congress every session since.

---

[12]American National Election Studies, 2001.

[13]American National Election Study, 1988.

[14]The Gallup Organization, *Black-White Relations in the United States,* 2001 Update, 2001.

[15]For perhaps the most thorough analysis of the gap between support for freedom of speech in the abstract and support for it in particular situations, see McClosky and Brill, *Dimensions of Tolerance,* pp. 48–58.

[16]National Opinion Research Center, General Social Survey, 1988.

Majority Rule Versus Minority Rights   The American people's adherence to the ideals of majority rule and minority rights sometimes loses something in the translation to everyday political questions. Slightly more than half of the respondents in one survey held that only people who were well informed about issues should be allowed to vote in elections in which questions relating to "tax-supported undertakings" are at issue, and four out of five held that only taxpayers should be allowed to do so.[17] The idea that any citizen should be able to grow up to be president is endorsed in the abstract but rejected by some in practice. One out of eight Americans would not vote for a qualified woman for president, and one out of six white Americans would not vote for a qualified African American for president.[18] In 1999, seven percent of Americans would not vote for a qualified woman for president and four percent would not vote for a qualified African American.[19]

Free Enterprise in Practice   As enamored of the free enterprise system as Americans are, their affection for it still has some limits. While 63 percent of Americans have a "great deal" or "quite a lot" of confidence in small business, only 28 percent feel the same way about big business.[20] And, although Americans are against government regulation of business in the abstract, they actually support its current level or favor increasing it in many particular instances. A majority of Americans believe the government should do more to prevent big business mergers.[21] A particular concern as America has faced tougher economic competition from abroad has been business's focus on short-term profits rather than long-term growth and prosperity.[22]

Political Ideology   Perhaps the most important matter on which Americans differ is political ideology. American politics is often portrayed as a controversy between liberals and conservatives. As discussed in Chapter 4, with the rise of neoconservatism, neoliberalism, the populist conservatism of the New Right, and the return to classical liberal principles in libertarianism, particularly in recent years, the reality has become much more complicated. Commentators have also distinguished among the different dimensions of liberalism and conservatism: economic, social, and cultural. Such debates have certainly occupied the attention of the intellectual elites, but what is striking is how far removed they are from the concerns of most Americans. Even the most basic notions of liberalism and conservatism meet with limited recognition. Only about half of U.S. citizens recognize the terms liberalism and conservatism and have some general sense of what they mean.[23] In a 2000 national survey, 27 percent of the respondents declined to

---

[17]James W. Prothro and Charles M. Grigg, "Fundamental Principles of Democracy," *Journal of Politics* 22 (1960): 276–294.
[18]National Opinion Research Center, General Social Survey, 1988.
[19]The Gallup Organization, 1999.
[20]The Gallup Organization, 1997.
[21]The Gallup Organization, 2000.
[22]Seymour Martin Lipset and William Schneider, *The Confidence Gap* (New York: Free Press, 1983), pp. 166–168.
[23]Eric R. A. N. Smith, *The Unchanging American Voter* (Berkeley: University of California Press, 1989), pp. 56–58.

place themselves on a liberal–conservative scale when asked to do so because they said they did not know or had not thought that much about it.[24] Studies of people's answers to questions raising liberal–conservative issues have long shown little consistency between answers, suggesting that many people do not think about politics in ideologically coherent terms.[25] Such findings are important because, first of all, they suggest that a good share of the population does not really have a grasp on the debate between liberals and conservatives. Second, the findings raise questions about the meaningfulness of the American public's responses to questions about their political ideology. When people are unsure what they are being asked, a safe response is often in the middle.

Figure 5.2 shows how over the last two decades more Americans have characterized themselves as conservatives than as moderates or liberals. This trend peaked in 1994, when 36 percent of Americans identified themselves as conservative and only 14 percent as liberal. The years since then have shown a small reversal, yet still 10 percent

---

[24]American National Election Studies, 2001.

[25]The path-breaking study on attitude consistency in particular and mass political ideology more generally is Philip Converse's "The Nature of Belief Systems in Mass Publics," in David Apter (ed.), *Ideology and Discontent* (New York: Free Press, 1964). For perhaps the best overview of the long and complicated series of challenges and counter-challenges to Converse's work over the last 25 years, see Smith, *The Unchanging American Voter*.

FIGURE 5.2

Americans Rate Themselves on the Liberal–Conservative Scale, 1972–2000

While the number of Americans identifying themselves as conservatives has remained higher than the number identifying themselves as liberals over the last 30 years, a majority of Americans do not identify with either label.

SOURCE: National Election Studies, 2001.

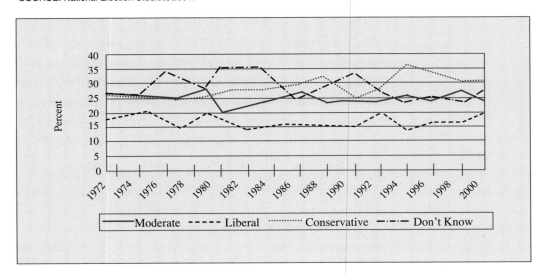

more Americans said they were conservative than liberal in 2000. When given the opportunity to clarify the degree of their ideology, however, Americans reveal that their ideological beliefs are, for the most part, mild. Both liberals and conservatives were more likely to indicate that they were slightly ideological than moderately or extremely so. In fact, no more than 3 percent of respondents in any of the survey years indicated that they were "extremely liberal" or "extremely conservative."

What these findings really mean is difficult to interpret without some sense of what the American public means when it uses the words liberal and conservative. Different people appear to mean different things by them. A national election survey in 1988 asked people what they had in mind when they said that someone's political views were liberal or conservative. Setting aside the substantial number of people who said they did not know, as mentioned earlier, the most common responses described liberals as people who are open to change and new ideas, for government action to help solve social problems, allied with working people, inclined to spend government money, and somewhat rash. In contrast, conservatives were viewed as resistant to change, for free enterprise solutions, allied with big business and the rich, against government spending, and cautious.[26]

And what about the people who don't think in terms of, or even recognize, liberal and conservative labels? Political scientists have tried to plumb political thinking to get at the mental images of these people. What they have found does not paint an encouraging portrait. Many Americans seem to respond to political issues on an essentially individual basis, without any broad or overarching political philosophy to guide them. Instead, their responses are shaped by their sense of identification with one or another political party or group, by their feelings about whether "it's good times" or "it's hard times," or by their feelings about a particular candidate or public figure.[27]

However, there may be an important qualification: The level of coherence in public thinking may be at least partially dependent on how politicians handle issues in campaign and policy-making discussions. When candidates and public figures address the public on issues, the public does seem to respond by becoming more conscious of and concerned about those issues. For example, in the relatively placid 1950s, candidates and parties did little to bring issue differences to the attention of the public, and the public showed little awareness of issues or coherence in its thinking about them. But from the mid-1960s into the 1970s, candidates began to discuss compelling issues such as the Vietnam War and urban disorder, and the public seemed to respond with increased awareness and coherence.[28]

---

[26]American National Election Survey, 1988.

[27]Angus Campbell, Philip E. Converse, Warren E. Miller, and Donald E. Stokes, *The American Voter* (New York: Wiley, 1960); Norman H. Nie, Sidney Verba, and John R. Petrocik, *The Changing American Voter,* enlarged ed. (Cambridge, MA: Harvard University Press, 1979).

[28]Nie, Verba, and Petrocik, *The Changing American Voter.*

Politics and Economics
Economic Status and Ideology

Conventional wisdom has it that political ideology is closely tied to economic status, with the less well-off holding liberal beliefs and the better-off aligning themselves with a conservative view point. But how well does this relationship hold up in America? Figure 5A shows the relationship between the respondent's professed political ideology and the income of the respondent's family. The poorest Americans are the least likely group to identify themselves as liberal. These citizens are more moderate and conservative than they are liberal. It is only in the second and third groups that the number of liberals is the second most populous group. In the other three categories, liberals are clearly the smallest contingent. Conservative views outnumber the others in every income category, and there does seem to be some support for the claim that wealthier individuals are more likely to be conservative. Additionally, the higher income groups are more likely to express an

ideological identity: 97 percent of the wealthiest group identified with one of the three categories, but only 58 percent of the poorest group did. One striking feature of these data is the relative weakness of the ideological differences between the income groups. More than 23 percent of the poorest Americans describe themselves as conservative. In the wealthiest group, 15 percent describe themselves as liberal. Surprisingly, then, not everybody who pays through taxes for liberal government programs opposes them, and not everybody who might benefit from them supports them. Clearly, economic standing alone does not determine the ideological views of the American public.

What other factors might determine how liberal or conservative a person is? How do you think the neoliberal and neoconservative viewpoints discussed in Chapter 4 might relate to economic status?

More recent research has called into question the degree and meaningfulness of the changes observed in the 1960s and 1970s, suggesting that they may result from changes in the way questions were asked and that much of the research into this area may be fatally flawed. It may be that the public's level of sophistication about politics has always been low and that it has changed little over the last 40 years. Whatever apparent increases in liberal-conservative thinking there have been may result from the public merely parroting the heightened liberal-conservative rhetoric of candidates without really understanding it.[29]

The political beliefs of the American public establish patterns that help to shape politics. The general agreement on principles such as freedom and majority rule defines the boundaries within which the game of American politics is played. These limits help to blunt any potential for political instability or violence. Commitments to ideas such as

---

[29]The best summary of, and most substantial contribution to, this recent research is Smith, *The Unchanging American Voter.* On the role of political rhetoric, see especially pp. 45–104.

Economic Status and Ideology, *continued*

FIGURE 5A

Political Ideology and Income

Poor people tend to be less conservative and rich people tend to be more conservative, but all income levels have substantial numbers of conservatives, and some rich people are liberal.

SOURCE: American National Election Study, 2001.

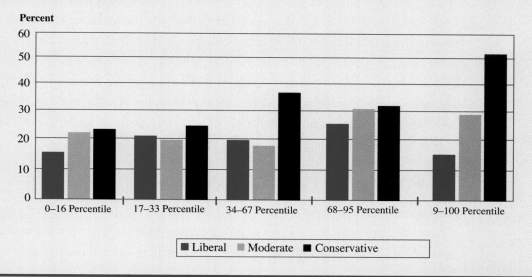

equal opportunity tend to define the basic objectives of the political system. The relatively low level of ideological thinking provides political leaders with room to maneuver and thereby fosters political stability.

Nevertheless, differences in ideological perspective result in fundamental conflicts that the political process must resolve. For instance, how actively should the government promote the interests of disadvantaged or oppressed groups? Where should the government strike the balance between promoting social change and maintaining social stability? How the public thinks about politics defines, in part, some of the most fundamental principles and problems of American democracy.

The Sources of Public Opinion: Political Socialization

Given the importance of public opinion, it is useful to comprehend why the public thinks as it does about politics. The origins of public opinion lie in history and philosophy, as discussed in Chapter 4. But knowing where ideas come from does not explain how people come to hold certain beliefs; understanding that phenomenon requires a discussion of political socialization.

political socialization

The process by which citizens acquire politically relevant knowledge, beliefs, attitudes, and patterns of behavior.

Political socialization is the process by which citizens come to think what they do about politics. Through political socialization, citizens internalize, or incorporate into their own thinking, beliefs, feelings, and evaluations (judgments on whether something is good or bad) about the political world in which they live. Think of the tremendous range of knowledge, feelings, and evaluations that people have about politics, and think of the many sources from which they all come; political socialization is obviously a long and complicated process.

Most of what people think and feel about politics has been learned from somebody else. But to leave it at that would deny the dynamic nature of the process and ultimately the possibility of any political change. That is, if all people simply stuck with what they have been taught about politics, nobody would ever think of anything new, and nothing would ever change. Clearly, then, some people break away from rigid adherence to old ideas and put thoughts together in new ways. But even those people start somewhere, building upon what already exists. Thus, political socialization is important to both stability and change in American politics.

The Processes of Political Socialization

How do people learn about politics? Psychologists say that people tend to repeat behavior patterns that are rewarded and not to repeat patterns that are not rewarded or that are punished. Much of what people know about politics they learn through explicit teaching. Information is presented to them, and they are either rewarded for learning it (by a higher grade or the praise of teachers or parents, for example) or punished for not learning it (by a lower grade or the criticism of teachers or parents). The mechanisms of learning are really the domain of psychology. Listed below are some of the basic processes that political scientists have identified as important in political socialization.

- *Social learning theory*. People experience subtle rewards and punishments from the psychological attachments they form to particular people around them, some of whom admire, others of whom they dislike. Because people like to have favorable images of themselves, they may attempt to boost their self-images by acting like people they admire, or by avoiding the behavior of those they do not like. Thus, a little boy may parrot his mother's views about the president, or a rebellious teenager may criticize a candidate that her disliked father holds dear.
- *Transfer theory*. People may carry over attitudes developed in a narrower setting, such as the family or school, to the broader political setting. A boy who dislikes his father may rebel against political authority more generally.

- *Cognitive development theory*. What people can learn about politics depends on the stage of their mental development. Some things can be learned only early in life, while others can be learned only later on. An adult immigrant newly arrived in America may never develop the deep emotional attachment to the nation felt by a person who has grown up in this country from birth. By contrast, a first grader lacks the intellectual capacity to master the intricacies of federalism.[30]

These different theories of how people learn about politics are not competing, but complementary. Social learning sometimes occurs through explicit teaching. The possibilities of transference, social learning, and explicit teaching probably all vary, depending on the intellectual development of the learner. Political socialization is too complex to be accounted for by any one theory or explanation.

The Agents of Political Socialization

agents of socialization

A "teacher" in the process of political socialization, for example, the family, the school, a peer group, or the mass media.

Agents are the people and institutions from which we learn. A person growing up in the United States learns about politics from many teachers. A comprehensive list would be too long to include here, but it is possible to identify a few of the most important agents. (Another important agent, the mass media, is discussed in the next section.)

- *The Family*. Under almost any realistic theory of political socialization, the family is uniquely situated to be a potent agent. The young individual who, according to developmental theory, is most vulnerable to socialization, spends much time with the family. Thus, the family has the first chance at influencing political development. Psychological attachments are often strong and therefore conducive to the transference of attitudes toward authority, which influences attitudes and behavior relating to participation and partisanship. Although much learning takes place in the family, how much of that learning is political is difficult to pinpoint and varies from family to family. Politics is not of paramount interest to most Americans, and thus is not usually at the top of the typical family's agenda for discussion. As such, it is not surprising that children sometimes grow up to be politically different from their parents. Research indicates that the transmission of political attitudes from parents to their children is substantial only when the attitudes relate to topics that regularly come up for discussion in the family.[31]

---

[30]Robert D. Hess and Judith V. Torney, *The Development of Political Attitudes in Children* (Garden City, NY: Doubleday/Anchor Books, 1967), pp. 24–26, offers a good overview of various psychological theories of socialization.

[31]M. Kent Jennings and Richard Niemi, *Generations and Politics* (Princeton, NJ: Princeton University Press, 1981), pp. 76–114.

Student studying for classes. *(AP Wide World)*

- *The School.* The school is also a prime agent of political socialization. Education can be related to many political orientations—political participation, political knowledgeability, and political tolerance, among others. Certainly the school is the primary explicit teacher of information about politics and government. A good share of the learning fades away, as every student well knows, unless it is periodically reinforced by additional education, exposure to the media, political discussion, or repeated use.

  However, schools involve more than just the presentation of facts; they are complex and diverse bundles of experiences and impressions. Students encounter teachers, books, authority figures and role models (such as principals and coaches), and their fellow students or peers. Some of the people students encounter may be very much like themselves, and some may be different. Meeting students of different races or religions in the school setting often provides children with their first real encounter with social diversity. Students may involve themselves in low-level political activities: class and club elections, student government, protests against school policies, and so on. They acquire not just facts but subtle impressions about the way things are and the way things ought to be. They develop feelings about social and political involvement and what they can hope to accomplish through the political process.[32]

---

[32]David C. Bricker, *Classroom Life as Civic Education* (New York: Teachers College Press, 1989), is one recent discussion of some of these issues.

- *Peer Groups*. Peer groups are groups of people, roughly equal in social position, who interact with one another. Students who go to school together, people who work together in an office or factory or bowl on the same team, the neighbors on the block—all are peer groups. Social pressures on group members to conform can be quite powerful. Group members adopt "proper" attitudes and behavior because they seek the boost to their self-image that comes with the approval of others or because they fear that nonconformity will lead to ostracism. Because other things are usually more important, peer groups do not always set norms relating to politics. However, when they do, the political consequences can be significant.[33]

The Development of Political Self

How does political learning actually take place? How do politically blank infants develop into full-blown political beings? Probably the first political thought to blossom in the mind of a small child in the United States is a psychological attachment to America. This is by no means a sense of what America is, just a feeling of belonging to it. In families where partisanship is important, a primitive sense of "I'm a Republican" or "I'm a Democrat" may appear. A sense of external authority above the authority of the parents that must be obeyed also emerges. This is most often attached to two specific figures: the president and the police officer. The president is the focal point of the American political system; thus, it is not surprising that this focused attention influences even very small children. The police officer gains attention as a less remote figure of considerable authority who moves about in a child's world. Perhaps the most striking feature of these early images is their positive character. Small children tend to idealize political authorities, attributing to them all possible virtues.[34]

As children grow, their political orientations evolve. In school they begin to acquire substantial new knowledge pertinent to politics. Much of this they soon forget, but some of it becomes part of their lasting store of information. Their conceptions of politics become less personal and more institutional. For example, the president is important not so much as a person but as a position. Idealization of political authority fades to realism: Public figures have flaws, they make mistakes, and people criticize them. Once in school, where teachers may try to minimize classroom conflict by downplaying partisan differences, children tend to become less partisan.

As partisanship declines, the ability to deal with the political world on a more abstract level increases. Children develop intellectually and morally to the extent that they can begin to look at politics in a more sophisticated and structured way. The critical age at which political thinking really starts to blossom seems to be about 12. Within a

[33] Theodore M.. Newcomb, "Persistence and Regression of Changed Attitudes: Long-Range Studies," *Journal of Social Issues* 19 (1963): 3–14.
[34] Fred I. Greenstein, *Children and Politics* (New Haven, CT: Yale University Press, 1965).

Contemporary Controversies
Public Opinion and Terrorism:
American Government in the Eyes of the World

Nathan Brink, 3, of Klamath Falls, Oregon, wears his father's fire-fighter helmet as he watches the September 11 parade in remembrance of the victims of the September 11, 2001 terrorist attacks. *(AP Wide World)*

As soon as the first wave of terrorist attacks hit the United States on September 11, 2001, Americans and governments and citizens throughout the world began to react to the unfolding events. Many of these reactions were captured in opinion polls conducted by the news media and by independent polling agencies. Although reactions were initially quite uniform, cleavages soon began to emerge around the world.

A vast majority of Americans supported the government's initial responses. The president's approval ratings (in response to the question "Do you approve or disapprove of the way George W. Bush is handling his job as president?") initially jumped from 51 percent just prior to September 11th to 86 percent a few days later. This figure rose to 90 percent in the following weeks, and remained there for longer than any previous president since The Gallup Organization started measuring approval ratings in the 1940s. Throughout the weeks that followed, Americans also indicated strong support for Congress (84%), military action in Afghanistan (88%), and the use of ground troops (80%). When it came to the next steps, however, diversity of opinion—a hallmark of democracy—began to return to American politics. Although support for the government's overall actions was high, about half of the nation (49%) believed that the government's repeated warnings about the possibility of further terrorist attacks didn't help but "just scared people." When political leaders began to speculate about the need to restrict personal freedoms, such as personal privacy, in order to prevent future acts of terror, 60 percent of Americans opposed "making it easier for legal authorities to read mail, e-mail, or tap phones without the person's knowledge."

Around the world reactions have been even more varied. Although countries almost universally condemned

Public Opinion and Terrorism:
American Government in the Eyes of the World, *continued*

the terrorist attacks against the United States, opinions were wide ranging regarding America's military response. In the weeks following the September 11th attacks and the October 7th launch of a military response, America's closest traditional allies tended to be the most supportive. British Prime Minister Tony Blair made his nation's support evident, and the British people followed suit. Ninety-three percent favored arresting anyone found to be aiding terrorists and 70 percent believed the U.S. and its allies should "be prepared to take military action" against nations harboring the terrorists responsible for the attacks. Britons were wary, however, of the consequences of such actions—78 percent believed any military response would create a wider conflict between "the Western world and the Islamic world."

The people of many other nations were deeply split over support for the military response. The Russians, a newly acquired and still cautious ally, expressed confidence in the Bush administration's ability to "handle the situation," but only 42 percent approved of the military strikes against Afghanistan. The Russian people themselves had experienced first-hand the misery of a protracted Afghan war in the 1980s, and many (60%) believed the actions of the United States would threaten Russian security. Some (54%) blamed terrorism and the Taliban regime for the military conflict, but others (30%) held American leadership and American society responsible. One of the main concerns expressed in the Russian press and elsewhere was that the United States was engaging in actions that would not solve the prob-

lem of terrorism, and was doing so without providing evidence of al Qaeda's guilt to the rest of the world.

Finally, the citizens of several nations stood opposed to nearly all American military efforts, some believing the United States should have pursued a diplomatic solution and others asserting that America's foreign policy and global capitalism were merely reaping what they had sown. Although the official government response of nations such as Egypt and Pakistan, for example, was initially supportive of American strikes against Afghanistan, the people of these countries demonstrated opposition through anti-American street protests and peace vigils. Why such a reaction? One factor is that many nations in the Middle East and Asia have large Muslim populations, who expressed concerns that an attack on one Muslim nation could spread to others. This was the case in Turkey, where 80 percent of Turkish citizens opposed an American military response.

How did you react to the initial attacks on America? What policy approaches have you approved of and disapproved of since then? Are the world's citizens right to criticize American foreign policy, or are their perspectives too limited by the information they receive? Is there such a thing as an objective, or "correct," view of politics?

SOURCE: The Gallup Organization, "Reactions to the Attacks on America and U.S.-Led Response," October 9, 2001, http://www.gallup.com/poll/releases/pr010914f .asp (4 November 2001); The Gallup Organization, "Attack on America: Key Trends and Indicators," October 23, 2001, http://www.gallup.com/poll/releases /pr010926c.asp (30 October 2001); CNN.Com, "World Reacts to War on Terror," http://www.cnn.com/ (3 November 2001); and World Press Review, "After September 11: A New Worldview," http://www.worldpress.org/specials/wtc/front .htm (3 November 2001).

couple of years, children's thinking becomes nearly as abstract and sophisticated as that of adults. Also, with increasing exposure to the sometimes unattractive facets of political life, realism often fades into cynicism. By the late teens, most individuals have established a political identity.

Political socialization does not end at the age of 21, however; learning about politics continues through adulthood. As people age, their needs and concerns evolve from, for example, their own education to their children's education to, in later life, their own health care. People's social environment changes, as their family role shifts from child to parent to grandparent, as the school years recede into the past, and as peer groups switch from fellow students to fellow workers to fellow retirees. Broader social change affects political learning too, as large-scale social transformations such as the civil rights movement and the women's movement alter the expectations that people have of themselves and of society. Major unresolved issues revolve around how much childhood socialization persists into adulthood, and how much adult political learning is constrained by what has been learned as a child.[35]

Diversity in Socialization

Socialization is not an identical process for all Americans. American society includes many subsocieties, with their own distinctive political subcultures or shared patterns of political attitudes and behavior—many of which are racially and ethnically based. African Americans constitute the largest distinctive subculture. Although African Americans and white Americans view many issues similarly, significant divisions exist, particularly with regard to equality and the government. For example, 83 percent of whites believe that equal housing opportunities exist for African Americans, but only 48 percent of African Americans hold this view. While 66 percent of African Americans believe they are treated less fairly by the police, only 35 percent of whites believe this is true.[36] The Latino and Asian subcultures are harder to characterize, partly because neither is not a single subculture, but rather a collection of them. The rapidly growing Latino subculture encompasses the Mexican-oriented culture of the Southwest, as well as the Cuban-oriented culture of south Florida and the Puerto Rican culture of New York City and other large cities. Similarly, the Asian subculture includes the long-established Chinese communities of San Francisco, Los Angeles, and New York City, and the more recently established communities of immigrants from Vietnam and other southeast Asian countries.

The different regions of the United States, to some degree, also constitute distinctive subcultures with unique patterns of political thought and behavior. The South is perhaps the most distinct from the others, owing to the continuing legacy of slavery and

---

[35]Roberta S. Sigel, ed., *Political Learning in Adulthood* (Chicago: University of Chicago Press, 1989) provides a good overview of adult political socialization and recent research on the topic.
[36]The Gallup Oganization, *Black-White Relations in the United States,* 2001 Update.

subsequent racial strife, as well as its more rural, agricultural subculture. Earlier studies of socialization found children in the South to differ from those in the North, but these differences seem to be fading.

In fact, the general trend seems to be away from clear-cut differentiation and toward greater homogeneity. Some attribute this trend to the "nationalization" of American culture and politics, which tends to blur regional differences. Americans in all parts of the country eat the same fast food and buy the same national-brand products. Most important politically, they read the same wire-service news stories and national news magazines and watch the same network news broadcasts. As a result, public opinion in the United States is becoming more and more uniform from region to region.

One other aspect of diversity in political socialization involves gender differences. Much of the early research on political socialization portrayed females as less political than males, and traced those differences back to the childhood years.[37] But the changing social and economic role of women from the eighteenth century to today is both a cause and a result of changes in the political interest, competence, and involvement of women.[38] The move toward more equal roles for men and women fostered by the feminist movement is likely to manifest itself in, and benefit from, less political difference between young males and females.

http://www.gallup
.com/

Keep your finger on the pulse of American public opinion with the latest polls from the Gallup Organization.

Political Participation

So far we have examined what Americans think about politics and why they think what they do. The next step in our discussion is to focus on what Americans *do* about what they think. In other words, how is public opinion translated into political participation? Of course, putting it in those terms suggests that political participation stems exclusively from political considerations such as concern about issues and ideology. But such considerations are only part of the story.

Motives for Political Participation

The conventional image of political participation is that of concerned citizens trying to advance their views by engaging in political activity. This is no doubt an accurate picture for some people. However, substantial numbers of people who are relatively unconcerned about politics nevertheless participate, and substantial numbers of people who are concerned about politics do not participate. Obviously, other factors must also motivate political participation.

---

[37]See, for example, Fred L. Greenstein, "Sex-Related Political Differences in Childhood," *Journal of Politics* 23 (1961): 353–371.
[38]Ethel Klein, *Gender Politics* (Cambridge, MA: Harvard University Press, 1984), pp. 117–119.

political efficacy

A person's sense of being able to accomplish something politically. An important determinant of political participation.

sense of duty

A motivating factor, felt by some citizens, to get involved in politics.

party identification

Psychological attachment that a citizen may feel toward a particular political party.

Some participation is sparked by *political motivations*. **Political efficacy** is a person's sense of being able to accomplish something politically. It involves judgments both about one's own competence in the political arena (sometimes called *internal efficacy*) and about the responsiveness of the political system to one's efforts (*external efficacy*). People with a very strong sense of efficacy are more likely to be politically active than those with a weak sense of efficacy. Other citizens are motivated to become involved by a **sense of duty**. They may care less about the issues or be put off by politics, but they have been socialized to think that good citizens get involved in politics. People with a strong sense of duty are more likely to participate politically than those without it.

Party identification, the psychological attachment that many Americans feel toward a particular political party, also provides a strong impetus to political action. The highest rates of political activity are observed among people with a strong commitment to one or another of the political parties. A person who strongly supports programs advocated by the Democratic party, for example, will probably work to promote a Democratic victory. Yet someone who sees little difference between the parties and who cares little about issues may not even vote.

Other factors spurring people on to political involvement are essentially nonpolitical or *social motivations*. Many people engage in political activity for its social rewards: meeting people, making friends, and developing new relationships. People low in self-esteem or lacking in confidence may attempt to bolster their self-image by taking on the social opportunities and challenges that political activity offers. In other cases, concern about an issue may initially mobilize a citizen into political involvement, but even when the concern fades away, the social connection keeps the person going.[39] This is not to say that political activity so inspired is of no political consequence; the labor, the money, or the vote of such a person counts the same as that of the most ideological partisan. Rather, the point is that not all political action can be understood simply in terms of political motives.

Forms of Participation

Any American who wants to become politically involved has a broad range of options, from merely glancing at the TV news occasionally all the way to running for president of the United States. Some of these forms of participation are the focus of other chapters in this book. Participation related to campaigns and elections will be discussed in greater detail in Chapter 8. Much political activity occurs within the framework of interest groups and political parties. These facets of participation will be examined more closely in Chapter 7. The rest of this section focuses on some of the most important other ways in which Americans can participate politically.

---

[39]Samuel J. Eldersveld, *Political Parties: A Behavioral Analysis* (Chicago: Rand McNally, 1964), pp. 290–292.

Following Politics   Just paying attention to politics constitutes a simple form of political participation. For many Americans politics is, if nothing more, an entertaining spectator sport. As noted earlier in this chapter, about three-fourths of Americans say they
follow government and public affairs "most" or "some" of the time. How active their
pursuit of public affairs is suggested by this statistic: 66 percent of the American people
say they read a newspaper "just about every day," and a slightly higher percentage (71
percent) say that they regularly watch the nightly network news broadcasts.[40]

Contacting Public Officials   One of the most direct ways to convey a political message
is to deliver it straight to a politician or governmental authority. Not many Americans do
this very often. One recent study found that only 30 percent of Americans had phoned or
sent a letter or a telegram to a public official in the last four years.[41] So where does all that
mail to public officials come from? First, an occasional letter from even a small proportion of a large number of constituents can generate a lot of mail, as the caseworker in almost any congressional office can confirm. Beyond that, it appears that a small group of
letter writers writes a large number of letters. Another study estimated that two-thirds of
all mail to public officials comes from just 3 percent of the population.[42]

Direct face-to-face contact with members of Congress and other public officials
is harder to assess. One estimate is that about 20 percent of Americans directly contact
public officials about an issue or problem.[43] Another standard strategy for contacting
public officials is the petition, a right protected by the First Amendment. A petition is a
written statement requesting that the government follow some course of action, circulated among and signed by a group of citizens. More than half (55 percent) of Americans
claim that they have signed petitions, although only 10 percent claimed to have circulated them.[44]

Protests within and Beyond the Law   Abstract theories of representative democracy
and, indeed, the original Constitution itself focus on the election of representatives as
the principal means of communication between citizens and government. But the First
Amendment to the Constitution, in its guarantees of freedom of speech, assembly, and
petition, reminds us of other forms of political expression. These guarantees reflect a
political tradition in which political protest sometimes assumes an important role and
embody the view that at least some such actions are legitimate.

Political protest can assume many different forms, some of which are discussed
below.

---

[40]Ornstein, Kohut, and McCarthy, p. 133.
[41]Ibid.
[42]Philip E. Converse, Aage R. Clausen, and Warren E. Miller, "Electoral Myth and Reality: The 1964 Election," *American Political Science Review* 59 (Tune 1965): 321–336.
[43]Sidney Verba and Norman Nie, *Political Participation in America: Political Democracy and Social Equality* (New York: Harper & Row, 1972), p. 31.
[44]Ornstein, Kohut, and McCarthy, p. 133

- *Marches and rallies*. Marches and demonstrations have a long-standing tradition in American politics. Perhaps the most famous example was the great march on Washington in August of 1963. This landmark event in the civil rights movement, which brought more than 250,000 peaceful demonstrators to the Mall, culminated with Dr. Martin Luther King's historic "I have a dream" speech from the steps of the Lincoln Memorial. The Vietnam War brought numerous marchers to Washington in the late 1960s and early 1970s. In the 1980s and 1990s, the abortion issue drew many pro-choice and pro-life marchers to the streets of the nation's capital and some state capitals, as has the issue of gay rights.

- *Boycotts*. Boycotts, the refusal of citizens to buy a particular product or use certain service, are another important tool of protest. In the late 1950s, the refusal of African Americans in the South to ride in the rear of buses exerted economic pressure on municipalities and attracted public attention to their cause. Some 15 percent of the American people say that they have participated in a boycott.[45]

- *Picketing*. Groups of protesters trudging back and forth or huddled around a fire in an empty metal barrel, angry placards in hand, are a common sight on the American political scene. One of the most frequent uses of picketing in the late 1980s was by the anti-abortion movement, which picketed doctors' offices and clinics in which abortions were being performed.

Protest demonstrations are one of the most visible, though certainly not the most common, forms of political participation in America. Accurate estimates of the extent of protest are notoriously difficult to obtain because people are sometimes reluctant to admit their participation to researchers. A study spanning a four-year period in the mid-1980s found that 6 percent of Americans claimed that they had participated in at least one public demonstration over that period.

Estimates of participation are even more difficult when it comes to actions that involve violence and crime.

- *Political violence*. On some occasions, American citizens have engaged in violent outbursts with political connotations. At the very founding of the United States, Massachusetts farmers led by Daniel Shays forced the closing of local and state courts before the rebellion was forcibly put down by the state militia. The antidraft riots of the Civil War, the urban ghetto riots of the 1960s, and the antiwar violence of the Vietnam War era resulted in widespread personal injury and destruction of property for

---

[45]Ornstein, Kohut, and McCarthy, p. 133.

political ends. In the last few years, perhaps the most visible recurring instances of political violence have involved anti-abortion protesters forcibly blocking and even burning abortion clinics. An even more dramatic event occurred in the spring of 1992: the large-scale riot in Los Angeles, which followed the announcement of not guilty verdicts in the cases of four police officers accused of brutally beating a young African American motorist, Rodney King. The riot resulted in the destruction of more than $500 million in property and the loss of more than 90 lives.

- *Politically motivated crimes.* Although riots and other violent outbursts have at least the appearance of spontaneity, other politically relevant acts are clearly premeditated criminal violence. The civil rights movement in particular has spawned a number of violent reactions: the death of four African American children in a fire-bombed church, the murder of three young civil rights workers—Goodman, Chaney, and Schwerner—in Mississippi in 1963, and the assassination of Dr. Martin Luther King in Memphis in 1968.

civil disobedience

A form of political protest in which advocates of a cause deliberately break a law as a means of asserting its illegitimacy or drawing attention to their cause.

passive resistance

A form of civil disobedience in which protesters do not actively oppose government attempts to control them, but rather refuse to cooperate by doing nothing—for example, by going limp when police try to pick them up or insisting on being carried to a police van rather than walking.

Many types of political protest are perfectly legal, particularly as long as they do not endanger the well-being of others. Peaceful marches and demonstrations certainly fall into this category. Others are clearly illegal: Most people would probably agree that rioting and assassination fall into the latter category because they destroy both life and property. Nevertheless, the line between legitimate and illegitimate political protest is sometimes hard to define. Further, some acts of political protest, even if illegal, are undertaken on the basis of a moral justification. These are acts of **civil disobedience**—deliberate violations of the law as a means of asserting the illegitimacy of the law or calling attention to a higher moral principle. Civil rights activists in the South in the 1950s and 1960s organized sit-ins at lunch counters and other facilities designated for whites only with the explicit intention of being arrested. They saw such action as a way of calling attention to unjust laws and more generally to their unjust treatment. A related strategy is the practice of **passive resistance**, in which protesters do not actively oppose government, but rather refuse to cooperate by doing nothing. For example, protesters may not struggle with angry white citizens or police, but simple lie down in the face of attack or arrest and force the police to drag them off to the police van and jail. In recent years, anti-abortion activists have adopted some of these tactics in their efforts to shut down abortion clinics.

Dr. Martin Luther King, Jr., provided a good explanation of the moral legitimacy of an illegal action in a famous letter that he wrote from a Birmingham jail:

> I submit that an individual who breaks a law that conscience tells him is unjust, and willingly accepts the penalty by staying in jail to arouse the conscience of the community over its injustice is in reality expressing the very highest respect for law.

Civil disobedience is thus characterized by a moral justification, a willingness to accept whatever penalty the action incurs, and, some would add as a critical element, an intention to avoid physical harm to others. Only a small proportion of Americans, two percent, say that they have themselves broken the law in a protest for a political or social cause.[46] However, civil disobedience is widely recognized as an acceptable strategy in extreme circumstances: When asked whether people should obey the law without exception, or whether there are exceptional occasions on which people should follow their consciences even if it means breaking the law, 40 percent of a national sample supported obeying the law, whereas 52 percent opted for following one's conscience.[47]

Differences in Participation

What determines the forms of political participation in which citizens tend to engage? In probably the most thorough study yet done of political participation in America, Sidney Verba and Norman Nie identified six categories of citizen participation and determined the kinds of people who fell into each.[48]

1. *Inactives.* These people, comprising about 22 percent of the population, take virtually no part in political life. Lower-status social and economic groups, African Americans, women, the youngest, the oldest, and the least concerned about politics are particularly likely to fall into this category.

2. *Voting specialists.* About 21 percent of the population do little more politically than vote regularly. This group is distinctive primarily in its strong sense of partisanship. It seems that some inactives get firmly attached to a party and that connection is enough to bring them to the polls at most elections.

3. *Parochial participants.* About 4 percent of the population contacts public officials when they have a particular personal problem and seek governmental assistance in solving it. Such activity is more common among lower-status groups, Catholics, and urban dwellers than among higher-status, Protestant, and rural citizens. Such people show little partisan or ideological involvement, but they can sometimes make a difference in what government does.

4. *Communalists.* Another 20 percent of the population have little involvement in electoral politics apart from voting, but they do engage in group and community activities with the aim of solving social problems. This group is highly involved in politics, but decidedly nonpartisan and non-

http://www.fec.gov /votregis/vr.htm

Are you registered to vote? You can register using the Federal Election Commission's National Mail Voter Registration Form at the above Web site.

---

[46]Ornstein, Kohut, and McCarthy, p. 133.

[47]National Opinion Research Center, General Social Surveys, 1983–1987.

[48]Verba and Nie, *Political Participation in America*, pp. 56–81. If a particular characteristic is not mentioned, the group is about average for that characteristic.

conflictual in its orientation. This group is very much an upper-status group socially and economically, predominantly white, Protestant, and more small-town and rural than urban.

5. *Campaigners.* In sharp contrast to the preceding group, this 15 percent of the population engages in little group activity but much campaign activity. This pattern stems in part from a highly partisan and more conflictual orientation to politics. The group tends to be of higher status, but African Americans and Catholics are also campaigners, as are urban and suburban dwellers.

6. *Complete activists.* About 11 percent of the population do it all: voting, contacting, group activities, and campaigning. This is a group highly attuned to politics, predominantly upper-status and middle-aged.

What difference does it make that different groups tend to participate in different ways? Public officials are bombarded with messages from the public and people claiming to represent the public. Public officials have preconceptions and make judgments about the forms of political participation they need to be most attentive to. Because different kinds of people tend to participate in numerous ways, officials get varying impressions of public opinion depending on the forms of participation to which they pay attention. A senator who focuses on constituency service by reading all the mail from parochial participants will get a different sense of the public's mind than one who hobnobs with campaign workers and financial supporters. The people staging a sit-in in front of a congressional representative's district office have very different things on their minds from those who pulled the lever in the voting booth a couple of Novembers earlier. For politicians assessing public opinion, the medium of participation in large measure determines the message. What is distinctive about political participation in America becomes clearer when compared with participation in other countries (see Figure 5.3).

The Impact of Political Participation

Does political activity really make any difference? The stereotypical notion of democracy is that the people's wishes become the law of the land. However, the democratic process cannot be that simple. On some issues, many people do not know what they want. Even if they do, they may not be moved to express their preferences via the political process. Politicians, whether they are presidents, Senate or House members, or Supreme Court justices, may be attentive to what the "public" wants, but such preferences are rarely the only factors they take into account. First of all, our nation is comprised of many publics, not just one. Further, constitutional constraints, legal constraints, budgetary constraints, foreign policy constraints on domestic policy, and domestic policy constraints on foreign policy also impact the decisions government officials can make.

FIGURE 5.3

Differences in Participation: A Comparative Perspective

As in most democracies, voting is the predominant form of participation in the United States, even if it is not as common as in some other democracies. Americans are particularly inclined to try to solve community problems by joining or working through groups. They also get involved in political campaign activities, but they tend not to use contact with public officials as a way of resolving difficulties in their personal matters.

SOURCE: Sidney Verba, Norman H. Nie, and Jae-on Kim, *Participation and Political Equality: A Seven-Nation Comparison* (Cambridge, England: Cambridge University Press, 1978), pp. 58–59.

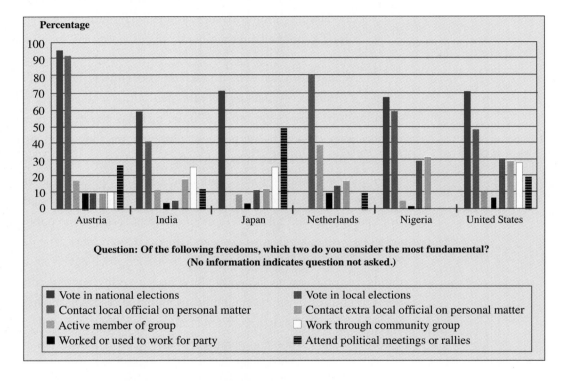

Question: Of the following freedoms, which two do you consider the most fundamental?
(No information indicates question not asked.)

■ Vote in national elections	■ Vote in local elections
■ Contact local official on personal matter	■ Contact extra local official on personal matter
■ Active member of group	☐ Work through community group
■ Worked or used to work for party	▤ Attend political meetings or rallies

Little wonder, then, that most studies of the relationship between public opinion and public policy have found the connection to be a relatively loose one.[49] Public opinion is usually sufficiently amorphous, officials' perceptions of it sufficiently cloudy, and more tangible pressures sufficiently strong enough that officials are not severely constrained by public opinion. But when there is a clearly expressed body of opinion on a salient issue, the relationship between public opinion and public policy can be substantial.[50] For example, growing public concern over drugs in the late 1980s led politicians to move antidrug legislation to the top of the agenda. In 1989, the much-publicized

---

[49]Perhaps the most famous study is Warren E. Miller and Donald E. Stokes, "Constituency Influence in Congress," *American Political Science Review* 57 (1963): 45–56.

[50]Benjamin L. Page and Robert Y. Shapiro, "Effects of Public Opinion on Policy," *American Political Science Review* 77 (1983): 175–190, show how changes in public policy between 1935 and 1979 in the United States related to changes in public opinion, particularly when there were large and enduring changes in public opinion on salient issues.

oil spill from the tanker Exxon Valdez into Prince William Sound on the Alaska coast re-energized the flagging environmental movement and sparked a flurry of environmental legislation in the early 1990s. After a series of energy crises in early 2001, 21 percent of Americans in a nationwide poll mentioned energy as the most important problem facing the country.[51] In the wake of recent terrorist attacks, 46 percent of Americans in an October 2001 poll indicated that terrorism was the most important problem.[52]

A Rationality of Political Participation

rational actor model

A perspective that looks at politics as a system in which individuals and organizations pursue their self-interests, defined in terms of costs and benefits, and choose to do those things that give them the greatest benefit at the least cost.

Does it make sense to participate politically? Forty-five years ago, Anthony Downs pioneered a new field of political analysis in an important and influential book called *An Economic Theory of Democracy*.[53] He examined political activity in terms of the so-called **rational actor model**. In this model, a citizen rationally weighs the costs and the benefits of participating. If the benefits exceed the costs, the citizen participates; if not, the citizen does not. Focusing on voting, Downs pointed out that getting registered, keeping informed, and going to the polls all take a substantial amount of time. The benefits, by contrast, are actually quite low. What politicians from one party or the other actually do after an election may not be very different from what their opponents would have done. Even more important, one individual's vote is very unlikely to determine whether his or her favored candidate wins. These factors make the expected benefit of voting relatively small.

A similar analysis could be made of most other individual political actions. The costs weighed against the low probability of any benefit make individual political actions appear to be of dubious rationality. One possible exception is what Verba and Nie call "parochial participation." With a narrow personal objective and the expenditure of a fair amount of effort directed toward a particular decision maker, the individual may stand a fair chance of achieving success.[54] Collective activities may also be more effective. Joining together allows costs to be shared and resources to be pooled. All other things being equal, many citizens will probably be more influential than one.

Finally, even political protest may prove to be a rational strategy. Minority and dissident groups often lack political clout because they lack resources and thus cannot afford the costs of participation. One political scientist has called this the "problem of the powerless."[55] A rational strategy for such people is to attract the attention of those with resources and draw them into the cause. A minimal expenditure of resources is required to engage in unusual or dramatic activities, such as sit-ins and demonstrations, that call public attention to the plight of the protesters. Such activities constitute, to borrow one apt description, the use of "protest as a political resource."[56]

---

[51]The Gallup Organization, 2001.
[52]The Gallup Organization, 2001.
[53]New York: Harper & Row, 1957.
[54]Verba and Nie, *Political Participation in America,* pp. 104–106.
[55]James Q. Wilson, "The Strategy of Protest: Problems of Negro Civic Action," *Journal of Conflict Resolution* 3 (September 1961): 291.
[56]Michael Lipsky, "Protest as a Political Resource," *American Political Science Review* 62 (1968): 1144.

SUMMARY

1. Public opinion is complicated because our nation consists of not one public, but many, and because opinion varies over time and in intensity and sophistication. Americans differ widely in their interest in and sophistication about politics; most of them have relatively little day-to-day concern, knowledge, or real understanding about what goes on in the political world. Americans do agree on certain basic values. However, they disagree about exactly what many of these values mean in particular circumstances and about political ideology.

2. Political socialization is the process by which young Americans are taught about political life in the United States. Through various processes of socialization, young people acquire the information and the ability to reason about politics. The values that they draw on as political actors are learned from their parents, schools, peers, and the mass media.

3. Americans involve themselves in politics in many ways for a variety of reasons. Involvement can range from simply following politics and voting to intense immersion in campaigns, community activities, or more dramatic forms of participation such as protest marches, sit-ins, and demonstrations. But the impact of participation on policy is often weak, and much political participation is hard to justify in purely rational terms.

KEY TERMS

public opinion (130)   party identification (150)

political socialization (142)   civil disobedience (153)

agents of socialization (143)   passive resistance (153)

political efficacy (150)   rational actor model (157)

sense of duty (150)

READING FOR FURTHER STUDY

Classic works on public opinion include Walter Lippmann's *Public Opinion* (New York: Macmillan, 1960) and one of the first major reports on survey research into public opinion, *Voting: A Study of Opinion Formation in a Presidential Campaign*, by Bernard R. Berelson, Paul F. Lazarsfeld, and William N. McPhee (Chicago: University of Chicago Press, 1954).

Paul Abramson's *Political Attitudes in America* (San Francisco: Freeman, 1983) provides a more recent overview.

Perhaps the major contributor to our understanding of basic American political values is Herbert McClosky, who has written (with Alida Brill) *Dimensions of Tolerance* (New York: Russell Sage, 1983) and (with John Zaller) *The American Ethos* (Cambridge, MA: Harvard University Press, 1984).

Although oriented more toward comparative than American politics, *Political Socialization*, 2d ed. (Boston: Little, Brown, 1977), by Richard E. Dawson, Kenneth Prewitt, and Karen S. Dawson, provides a good overview of the topic of political socialization.

A broader treatment can be found in Ronald Berkman and Laura W. Kitch, *Politics in the Media Age* (New York: McGraw-Hill, 1986).

Perhaps the best overall empirical study of political participation in all its facets is *Political Participation in America: Political Democracy and Social Equality* (New York: Harper & Row, 1972), by Sidney Verba and Norman Nie.

CHAPTER 6

Politics and the Media

A/P World Wide

Chapter Objectives

Most of the chapters in this book focus on political institutions and leaders and the things they do. This chapter focuses on part of American corporate life called the "mass media." Of special interest are journalists: people who gather, write, edit, report, and produce the news that people read in the newspapers, hear on the radio, watch on television, and browse on the Internet.

Of course, nobody votes for journalists. They are not public officials. They do not make laws. They do not work for the government. So why do the mass media rate a chapter in a book on American government? The mass media have a chapter all to themselves because newspapers, radio, television, and the Internet matter politically. In carving out a specific guarantee for freedom of the press, the First Amendment of the Constitution gives a strong hint that the news media are supposed to matter. They are the means by which much political information and many political ideas reach the American people. They are often the forums for clashes between ideologies. In short, they help to define political reality for the nation. Understanding the business of print and electronic journalism is now a necessary part of understanding American government.

journalists

People who gather, write, and report the news for newspapers, magazines, radio, television, and the Internet.

The job of the White House Press Secretary is to move information in two directions—from the president to the people and from the people to the president. Ari Fleischer, President George W. Bush's press secretary, regularly stands before the White House press corps (a select group of respected **journalists**) to describe the president's actions and answer questions. He is also, though, responsible for informing and updating the executive branch of the government on the news stories being reported in the press. Few in the White House, on Capitol Hill, or in any statehouse or city hall, are unconcerned about or uninterested in the news business. All want to know what has become news and how others have reacted to the news.

mass media
___
Instruments such as newspapers, magazines, radio, television, and the Internet that provide the means for communicating with large numbers of people in a short period of time.

Political leaders since George Washington's time have known that access to knowledge and control of communication matter in a democracy. Essential to both today are the **mass media**: newspapers, magazines, radio, television, and the Internet. The word *media* in this context refers to the *means* of communication with large numbers of people. In recent years this has also meant taking a leading role in the development of new media, such as cable and satellite television and web site and streaming video communication via the Internet. The media now offer the American people rapid access to large amounts of news about public affairs, making it possible for Americans to be the best-informed nation on earth. Indeed, the distribution of news and opinion is som important that the press occupies a special place in the constitutional system.

The "Fifth Branch"

fifth branch
___
Refers to the press in its role as a check on public officials, after the other four branches (Congress, the president, the Supreme Court, and the bureaucracy).

The press is sometimes called the **fifth branch** of government, after Congress, the president, the Supreme Court, and the bureaucracy. This classification reflects the fact that the mass media can serve as additional checks on the powers of public officials through discovery and coverage of news and commentary on events. However, because the media are mainly businesses that exist to make money, it is essential first to know something about these commercial enterprises. Like government, the news media have changed greatly over the course of two centuries.

The Dynamics of an Industry

Newspapers have been part of American culture since early colonial days. In an era during which news could travel only as fast as the fastest horse, these were four-page weeklies, with type painstakingly set by hand. It was through the medium of these early papers that news about skirmishes with the British at Lexington and Concord and copies of the Declaration of Independence circulated up and down the eastern seaboard in 1775 and 1776. Publication of *The Federalist Papers* and much of the rest of the debate over ratification of the Constitution, discussed in Chapter 2, took place in the press.

Telegraphy, larger and faster presses, lower unit production costs, and improved literacy made possible the rapid growth of newspapers in the nineteenth century. The "penny press" (named for its price) became the main contact for many Americans with events around the nation and the world. No doubt the intensity of feeling about slavery and secession, North and South, on the eve of the Civil War was due in part to the pervasiveness of the press. Growth of the industry later opened the door to increased political influence of publishers and editors such as Joseph Pulitzer and William Randolph Hearst.

Yet eighteenth- and nineteenth-century newspapers were distant cousins in size arid circulation to today's computer-composed, mass-produced daily papers that frequently fill 100 pages or more and contain news and photographs transmitted by fax and satellite. As Table 6.1 suggests, print journalism has experienced changes brought about by advances in technology; altered life-styles; competition from television, radio, and the Internet; and other economic forces.

Magazines are another form of print journalism that became popular in the nineteenth century. Counting scholarly journals, over 13,000 periodicals other than newspapers are published in the United States, more than double the number available in 1950. While most are small or have little to do with public affairs, political news and opinion are the main content of many. Mass circulation news weeklies include *Time, Newsweek,* and *U.S. News and World Report.* Others, such as *Washington Monthly, The New Republic,* and *National Review,* described in Chapter 4, are journals of opinion and are targeted at different political audiences.

The year 1920 marks the beginning of radio as a mass medium. Within a decade, as Table 6.2 shows, radios were common household appliances. Not far behind was television. Its astonishing growth since 1950 now permits almost all households to be served by at least several stations. Thanks to cable and satellite systems, many homes now have more than 100 stations from which to choose.

TABLE 6.1

American Daily Newspapers in the Twentieth Century

Daily newspaper circulation since 1980 has decreased even as the population has increased. Roughly half of American households seem cut off from regular access to a daily print newspaper. Also, the decline among dailies has been greater for afternoon than morning papers.

SOURCES: Bureau of the Census, Statistical Abstract of the United States; Editor & Publisher Co.

YEAR	NUMBER OF DAILY PAPERS	CIRCULATION	CIRCULATION AS PERCENT OF NUMBER OF HOUSEHOLDS*
1900	2226	15,102,000	95
1920	2042	27,791,000	114
1930	1942	39,589,000	132
1940	1878	41,132,000	118
1950	1772	53,829,000	124
1960	1763	58,882,000	112
1970	1748	62,108,000	99
1980	1745	62,200,000	77
1990	1625	62,005,000	67
2000	1480	55,800,000	53

*A "household" is the Census Bureau's term for a living unit.

TABLE 6.2

Growth of Radio and Television in the United States

Nearly half of all American households owned a radio set by 1930, enabling Franklin Roosevelt to become the first "media president." World War II delayed the commercial development of television; TV sets are now as common in homes as refrigerators. The average number of television sets in American homes is 2.4.

SOURCES: Bureau of the Census, Statistical Abstract of the United States; Federal Communications Commission.

	(A) RADIO		
YEAR	NUMBER OF AM STATIONS	NUMBER OF FM STATIONS	HOUSEHOLDS WITH AT LEAST ONE RADIO SET (%)
1922	30	0	0.2
1930	618	0	46.0
1940	847	3	82.0
1950	2144	753	94.0
1960	3483	906	95.0
1970	4288	2542	99.0
1980	4689	4546	99.9
1990	4977	5694	99.9
2000	4783	5766	99.9

	(B) TELEVISION	
YEAR	TV STATIONS*	HOUSEHOLDS WITH AT LEAST ONE TV SET (%)
1950	104	9
1960	626	87
1970	881	95
1980	1132	98
1990	1446	98
2000	1585	98

*Includes commercial and educational stations on VHF and UHF channels.

Beginning in the 1970s, cable services developed, transmitting not over the air like ordinary television stations but by satellite directly to cable companies in hundreds of cities and towns. Over the last thirty years cable, digital satellite, and other subscription services have drastically changed the way Americans view television. Rather than offering only local stations and a few large networks for free, pay television now provides access to hundreds of stations broadcast from around the world and serves interests ranging from the very broad to the quite narrow. Today, over 95 million televisions are equipped with some type of paid premium service, or an average of nearly one per household.

In recent years, the growth of cable has produced several new networks devoted exclusively to news. CNN, MSNBC, CNBC, and Fox News have become worldwide sources for news. Many world leaders, including American presidents, have been known to tune in to these stations, especially when following critical events as they unfold at almost any point on the globe. For example, millions of Americans, and many political leaders, watched the coverage on these networks nearly around the clock on September 11, 2001 in a search for answers regarding terrorist attacks on the World Trade Center and Pentagon. Government agencies sometimes find cable news a more accurate source of timely information than their own official sources. That so many leaders might rely on the same source at the same time could have a major impact in the management of international crises and in other situations calling for rapid decision making.

The impact of cable and satellite television continues to be felt. The proliferation of channels is the major reason (along with widespread use of VCRs and DVD players) that the share of the viewing audience claimed by the major broadcast networks (NBC, ABC, CBS, and Fox) has declined steadily. By 2001, cable network news had surpassed the broadcast networks, claiming nearly 60 percent of the total news audience.

As a result of the phenomenal growth of the video industry, television has largely displaced radio as a major source of news. Except for a few all-news stations, the radio industry invests little in national news reporting beyond providing a headline service interspersed in music and talk shows. Indeed, television has surpassed the newspaper as the primary source of national news for most Americans, although newspapers remain the main source for local news.

The average American spends 66 minutes a day with some form of news media. Thirty-one of those minutes are spent watching television news, 18 are reading the newspaper, and 17 are spent listening to the radio. In addition to these traditional sources, 20 percent of Americans go online at least once a week to get news. Of course, when topics beyond just the news are considered, television is the clear winner. The average American watches over 4 hours of television per day. Over 98 percent of households have at least one television and 93.5 percent of Americans view television on at least a weekly basis.[1]

About eight in ten Americans report that they get at least some news on a daily basis. Fifty-five percent of Americans watch television news daily, 41 percent read a daily newspaper and/or listen to the radio, and 16 percent get daily news online. One might expect that the 9/11 attack and the war on terrorism would have transformed Americans' attentiveness to international politics. Changes, however, have been modest.

---

[1]The Pew Research Center for the People and the Press, "Internet News Takes Off," 8 June 1998, http://people-press.org/reports/display .php3?ReportID=88 (28 June 2002) and U.S. Census Bureau, *Statistical Abstract of the United States*, 2000.

In 2002, 65 percent of Americans said they follow international news either "very closely" or "somewhat closely," up slightly from 59 percent in 2000.[2]

Just as television overtook radio, the Internet may someday surpass television as Americans' primary news source. In 2000, 51 percent of households reported having computers and over 41 percent had Internet access. Roughly one-third of Americans reported accessing news online on at least a weekly basis. With continuing technological advancement in communications, the number of individuals accessing news via cell phones, Pads, and other digital devices seems destined to increase in the future.[3]

Easy access to information and entertainment, however, does not guarantee attentiveness to public affairs. While young Americans from 1941 to 1975 knew as much about issues and followed major news events as closely as did their elders, this is no longer the case. Younger people are now far less attentive to public affairs. Even though someone who is 21 years old is more likely than someone who is 50 years old to have used a computer, to have gone to college, or currently to be reading a book, the younger individual is likely to be substantially less aware of current events and public figures. As Table 6.3 suggests, one implication of such differences is that Americans in different age groups may be consuming different types of news. Older Americans are the most likely to be aware of events reported on televised news, while younger Americans are more likely to be aware of news reported online.

The Constitutional Basis of the Press

It is not by chance that the media count politically. The Constitution confers on journalists explicit recognition and protection: "Congress shall make no law . . . ," the First Amendment declares, "abridging the freedom of . . . the press," a restraint that has applied to state and local governments as well since 1931.[4] As explained in Chapter 3, aside from obscenity and libel, prevailing interpretations of the Constitution by the Supreme Court tolerate almost no restrictions on the content of what editors decide to publish. "A free press is indispensable to the workings of our democratic society," Justice Felix Frankfurter (1939–1962) once declared. The point to remember is that the Constitution creates the *opportunity* for the press to play an active role in public affairs. What the role actually becomes, however, is left up to reporters, editors, and publishers—and to their readers and viewers.

Protection of the press from most governmental restraints is necessary because its involvement with "the workings of our democratic society" guarantees conflict between journalists and government. "Politics and media are inseparable," veteran CBS

---

[2]The Pew Research Center for the People and the Press, "Public's News Habits Little Changed by September 11," 9 June 2002, http://people-press.org/reports/display.php3?ReportID=156 (28 June 2002).
[3]The Pew Research Center for the People and the Press, "Internet Sapping Broadcast News Audience," 11 June 2000, http://people-press .org/reports/display.php3?ReportID=36 (13 September 2002) and U.S. Census Bureau, *Statistical Abstract of the United States*, 2001.
[4]*Near* v. *Minnesota*, 283 U.S. 697 (1931).

TABLE 6.3
News Consumption "Yesterday"

Younger Americans read newspapers and watch news on television less than older Americans. Younger Americans also "consume" such news far less regularly than they did a few decades ago. In the category of Internet news usage, however, younger Americans seem to be leading the way.

SOURCES: The Age of Indifference: A Study of Young Americans and How They View the News. (Washington, DC: Times Mirror Center for The People & The Press, 1990), p. 20; The Pew Research Center for the People and the Press, "Internet Sapping Broadcast News Audience," 11 June 2000, http://people-press.org/reports/display.php3?ReportID=36 (13 September 2002); and U.S. Census Bureau, Statistical Abstract of the United States, 2001.

	1965	1990	2000
Read a Newspaper Yesterday			
All respondents 21 and older	71%	44%	46%
Under 35*	67	30	29
35–49**	73	44	43
50+	74	55	58
Watched TV News Yesterday			
All respondents 21 and older	55%	53%	55%
Under 35*	52	41	44
35–49**	52	49	51
50+	62	67	67
Online at Least Once a Week for News			
All respondents 21 and older			33%
Under 30			46
31–49			37
50+			20

*For the year 2000, the age range for this category is under 30.
**For the year 2000, the age range for this category is 30–49.

correspondent Walter Cronkite observed. "It is only the politicians and the media that are incompatible."[5] The First Amendment anticipates a common failing: the tendency to attempt to silence those who criticize or disagree. In personal relations the tendency may only be annoying, but in political relations between leaders and citizens it can prove deadly to democracy.

The Federal Communications Commission

While the news media enjoy constitutionally protected freedom, some of the media are freer than others. This is because electronic journalism operates under legal restraints that do not (and could not constitutionally) apply to print journalism.

---

[5]James F. Fixx, ed., *The Mass Media and Politics* (New York: Arno Press, 1972), p. ix.

With the development of radio early in the twentieth century, the nation faced a choice. Table 6.4 shows how the political implications of the new medium, soon followed by television, became apparent. The new medium could be left to grow almost unregulated, like newspapers, or it could be operated mainly by government, as is done now in most places in the world (France and Great Britain, for example) even where some privately owned stations are permitted. Because of the ideological preference for free enterprise, however, public ownership in the United States was never a serious possibility. Because of the potential for chaos on the airwaves, complete freedom for broadcasters was unacceptable as well. Congress chose a middle route of private ownership under government supervision.

Initial regulation was in the hands of the Department of Commerce, but Congress created the Federal Radio Commission in 1927 with the power to issue station licenses, allocate frequencies, and fix transmitting power. Present regulation of all wired and wireless communication, including transmission via satellite, is the responsibility of the **Federal Communications Commission (FCC)**, established in 1934 as the successor to the Radio Commission. The FCC has broad rule-making authority, which it has employed to require radio and television stations to operate "in the public interest." For instance, stations are limited in the number of commercials that may be broadcast per hour, a certain amount of time must be set aside for public service and public affairs programming, and obscenity and "filthy words" are prohibited.[6] The justification for such governmental intrusion has been that frequencies (and therefore the number of stations) are finite and that the airwaves are public property.[7]

Today, the FCC is composed of five commissioners appointed by the president and confirmed by the Senate for seven-year terms. Since the 1970s the FCC has moved toward less regulation of radio and television, adopting the view that the marketplace and not the commissioners should dictate development of the industry, with the commission confining itself to licensing stations, assigning frequencies, and policing their use. But among the regulations, two have been very significant for news reporting.

The Equal-Time Rule

The **equal-time rule**, from section 315 of the Communications Act of 1934, requires stations to give or sell time to one political candidate if the station has given or sold time to another candidate for the same office. The time must not only be equal in length but must also be at a similar time of the day. A station cannot give a candidate for school board five minutes of airtime at 8:00 A.M. and then relegate an opponent to 2:30 A.M.

Federal Communications Commission (FCC)
An agency of the national government that regulates the telecommunications industry in the United States, including the licensing and operation of all radio and television stations.

equal-time rule
A provision of the Communications Act of 1934 that requires radio and television stations to give or sell equivalent time to one political candidate if the station has given or sold time to another candidate for that office.

[6]*Federal Communications Commission v. Pacifica Foundation*, 438 U.S. 726 (1976).
[7]*Red Lion Broadcasting Co. v. Federal Communications Commission*, 395 U.S. 367 (1969).

TABLE 6.4

Radio, Television, the Internet, and Politics: Milestones

Commercial radio has been part of American culture since the 1920s. Television became widespread after World War II ended in 1945. The Internet emerged as an important news source in the 1990s. All three media are politically important today.

1920	KDKA in Pittsburgh announces election results in the presidential race between Harding and Cox.
1923	President Calvin Coolidge's opening address to Congress is broadcast by a series of stations, linked by telephone lines, as far west as Dallas.
1927	Congress establishes the Federal Radio Commission, assuring private ownership of the broadcast industry, with government regulation.
1928	General Electric Co. and the Radio Corporation of American begin experimental television transmissions.
1933	President Franklin Roosevelt delivers his first "fireside chat" to Americans via radio.
1934	Congress establishes the Federal Communications Commission, replacing the Federal Radio Commission.
1939	NBC begins limited regular television programming.
1940	The Democratic and Republican conventions are televised.
1943	The FCC requires NBC to sell its second ("blue") network, which becomes ABC.
1947	President Harry Truman's State of the Union message is the first complete presidential address transmitted on television.
1948	President Truman is the first to sit in the White House and watch his opponent nominated on television.
1951	The Supreme Court rules that movies qualify for First Amendment protection.
1952	Richard Nixon's "Checkers speech" on television helps to convince Eisenhower to keep him as his running mate; the Republican party makes first use of TV commercials in a presidential campaign.
1960	Candidates John Kennedy and Richard Nixon meet in the first televised debate between presidential candidates.
1961	President John Kennedy institutionalizes "live" televised White House press conferences.
1963	Evening network news programs expand from 15 to 30 minutes.
1964	Television networks call the results of the presidential election between President Johnson and Senator Goldwater before the polls have closed on the West Coast.
1965	The networks provide regular coverage of the Vietnam fighting on the evening news; first regular transmission of television signals via satellite begins.
1979	U.S. House of Representatives approves live television coverage of its sessions (now carried on C-SPAN, a cable channel).
1980	Cable News Network (CNN), a 24-hour all-news cable-only service, begins operation.
1984	TV networks cease "gavel-to-gavel" coverage of presidential nominating conventions.
1986	U.S. Senate approves television coverage of its sessions.
1987	The FCC repeals the fairness doctrine.
1991	Live media coverage of the Persian Gulf War allows Americans a view of the conflict as it unfolds.
1996	Congress passes Communications Decency Act to regulate Internet content (later held unconstitutional, in part, by the Court).
2000	Over 112 million American adults have access to the Internet either at home or at work.

Politics and Ideas
Media Monopolies?

America today teems with information. As Tables 6.1 and 6.2 suggest, print and electronic media are within easy reach of almost everyone. Multiple outlets as depicted in Figure 6A, however, do not themselves assure diversity of news and opinion. Indeed, *concentration* is the word that best applies to the mass media today. This economic reality raises questions about the role of the media in a democratic political system.

Most newspapers and radio and television stations rely on relatively few sources of national and international news. Wire services such as the Associated Press and United Press International are indispensable for daily newspapers and for locally produced newscasts. They are often the only sources for news of statewide interest. Only the largest newspapers will maintain reporters in Washington, the state capital, and abroad as independent sources. The largest television audiences belong to the more than 700 commercial stations affiliated with one of the four major broadcast networks: ABC, CBS, Fox, and NBC. Public television stations, funded by private contributions, state appropriations, and since 1967 the federally chartered and congressionally supported Corporation for Public Broadcasting, divide a much smaller audience. Network programming typically accounts for about 65 percent of a local station's airtime, with much of the rest consisting of reruns of discontinued network shows.

Among newspapers, competition for reporting news and setting advertising rates has all but disappeared in many sections of the nation. Today, only a dozen or so American cities have separately owned and fully competitive daily newspapers, compared to 502 cities in 1923.

Chain ownership is fast dominating the newspaper and television business. Locally owned newspapers and television stations may soon be a thing of the past. Media mergers over the past two decades mean that today just nine corporations control over half of the broadcast media in America.[a] In 2001, the 10 largest media companies earned revenues totaling over 98 billion dollars—an amount greater than the next 90 largest companies combined.[b] This consolidation trend is not

FIGURE 6A

Channels Receivable Per TV Household

In 2000 some 69 percent of American households with television sets could receive more than 26 channels.

SOURCES: A.C. Nielson Co. and Pew Research Center for the People & the Press.

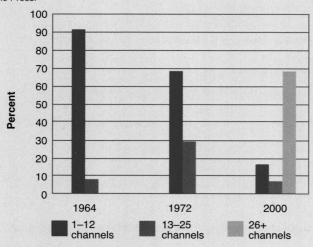

[a]Paul Wellstone, "Growing Media Consolidation Must Be Examined to Preserve Our Democracy," *Federal Communications Law Journal*, 52 (2000): 551–554.
[b]"100 Leading Media Companies," *Advertising Age*, 19 August 2002.

Media Monopolies?, *continued*

limited to traditional media. Even the Internet has not escaped the move toward mega-media corporations. Between 1999 and 2001 the number of companies controlling 60 percent of online time shrank from 110 down to only 14.[c] Some media corporations own several outlets of the same type—newspapers *or* television stations. Many stress cross-media ownership, combining newspapers, radio, television, cable, and Internet services. AOL Time Warner, for example, owns hundreds of online services (America Online, Netscape Communications), book and magazine publishing companies (Time-Life Books, Sports Illustrated), and cable and broadcast television stations (HBO, CNN, WB). Disney owns the ABC network, 10 television stations, 28 radio stations, and 11 cable channels, among its many ventures.[d]

Aside from antitrust restraints, which apply to all businesses, additional limitations on media concentrations come in the form of regulations issues by the Federal Communications Commission. The most significant of these limitations include rules that prevent a single company's stations from reaching more than 35 percent of viewers and prevent a single company from owning more than one of the four major networks, a rule limiting the number of television stations a company can own across the country, and rules limiting the number of media sources (radio, TV, and newspaper) a company can own in a single market.[e]

Alongside these restrictions is the growth of satellite technology and cable television, the former now serving14 percent of American households and the latter 66 percent.[f] Satellites decrease the cost of transmitting news over vast distances and increase a local station's news sources. Aside from one of the four major networks, a station may have a contract with CNN, may receive "feeds" direct from government agencies, and may exchange stories with other local stations. For viewers, cable television at first glance means greater choice, yet many of the cable channels are themselves owned by the media conglomerates.

If concentrations in ownership are easy to measure, their effects are not. One view argues that an information conglomerate's "most powerful influence . . . is the power to appoint media leaders" such as editors, producers, and publishers.[g] To what degree does the economic reality of media corporations tend to decrease the diversity of news and opinion Americans read, see, and hear? Does concentration of ownership increase the political power of these corporations?

[c]Press Release, Jupiter Media Metrix, 4 June 2001.\
[d]"Who Owns What," *Columbia Journalism Review,* http://www.cjr.org/owners/ (17 September 2002).
[e]Yochi J. Dreazen, "FCC Will Simultaneously Review All of Its Media-Ownership Rules," *Wall Street Journal,* 18 June 2002, http://online.wsj.com/article _email/0,,SB1024337625179502320,00.html (18 September 2002).

[f]The Pew Research Center for the People and the Press, "Public's News Habits Little Changed by September 11," 9 June 2002, http://people-press.org/reports /display.php3?ReportID=156 (16 September 2002).
[g]Ben H. Bagdikian, *The Media Monopoly*, 6th ed. (Boston: Beacon Press, 2000).

During the 1980 and 1984 presidential campaigns, for example, television stations had to cease showing old movies starring Ronald Reagan. That would have amounted to free time, which could have been demanded in equal quantities by his Democratic opponents, Jimmy Carter and Walter Mondale. In 1984 the FCC decided that the rule does not apply to televised debates among candidates, thus allowing a station to invite some candidates and not others. This ruling allowed networks to invite only Al Gore and George W. Bush to the 2000 presidential debates, despite protestations by excluded third party candidates.

The Fairness Doctrine

fairness doctrine

A regulation of the Federal Communications Commission that required radio and television stations to devote some airtime to a balanced discussion of public issues. Abolished in 1987.

The **fairness doctrine** was an FCC regulation that applied throughout the year, not just during political campaigns. Stations had to devote a "reasonable" percentage of airtime to a discussion of public issues and had to assure fair coverage for each side. If a station presented only one side of an issue, advocates for the other side had a legal right to be heard. If, in the discussion of an issue, the honor or integrity of a person or group was attacked, the station had to notify the person or group and supply both a transcript of the attack and an opportunity to respond on the air. Moreover, if a station endorsed a candidate for public office, the same requirements for notice and reply applied. It was to avoid conflict with the fairness doctrine that the television networks, for example, routinely allowed a "Democratic response" following an address by a Republican president, a practice that has survived the demise of the doctrine itself. For a time, public broadcasting stations were treated differently and prohibited by law from editorializing at all on the air, a restriction the Supreme Court voided in 1984.[8]

Given the trend toward deregulation of the broadcast industry, it was not surprising that the FCC repealed the fairness doctrine in 1987. The FCC concluded that the doctrine was unconstitutional and that expansion of cable television had largely undercut the original rationale for treating radio and television stations differently from newspapers. Most communities now have access to more television channels than newspapers, meaning that the potential for competition among viewpoints is now greater in electronic than print journalism. That being said, access to more channels does not necessarily mean access to media owned by a wider variety of individuals or companies. As "Politics and Economics: Media Monopolies?" indicates, fewer regulations on media ownership can have a dampening effect on competition.

Regulating the Internet

While the FCC is responsible for regulating interstate and international communication within the U.S., its jurisdiction does not extend to global communications

---

[8]*Federal Communications Commission v. League of Women Voters*, 468 U.S. 364 (1984).

such as the Internet. As the Internet becomes an increasingly important force in mass media, the federal government will face challenges in its attempt to regulate Internet content. Efforts to crack down on Internet fraud have been handled by the Federal Trade Commission and have met with some degree of success. The Supreme Court, though, has found that the First Amendment protects nearly all non-fraudulent commercial and private uses of this medium. In 1996 Congress passed the Communications Decency Act in an attempt to limit postings of obscene and offensive materials on web sites. As discussed in Chapter 3, the Court held that this and subsequent congressional efforts have been overbroad limitations on protected speech. Since efforts to restrict offensive materials have been unsuccessful, any regulation of news content seems highly unlikely to pass constitutional muster. For now, almost anything goes on the Internet.

Politics and the Press

Understanding why the press matters politically requires a look at several roles the media play in American politics. The media serve as *vehicles* of direct communication, as *gatekeepers* of political knowledge and attitudes, as *spotlights* on issues, and as *talent scouts* in campaigns.

Direct Communication: The Media as Vehicles

With heavy doses of entertainment and information in abundance, the mass media understandably have real significance for politics and government in the United States. Radio, television, and the Internet have become *vehicles,* making it possible for a president or other national political leader to speak simultaneously and directly to virtually everyone in the land. "No mighty king, no ambitious emperor, no pope, no prophet ever dreamt of such an awesome pulpit, so potent a magic wand," observed CBS veteran news director Fred W. Friendly.[9] Former Senator J. William Fulbright (D-AR) even claimed that television had changed the constitutional system by doing "as much to expand the powers of the president as would a constitutional amendment formally abolishing the co-equality of the three branches of government."[10]

Among recent presidents, Ronald Reagan and Bill Clinton have appeared the most comfortable communicating directly with the American people via television. Regardless of preferences, circumstances often force presidents into the national spotlight. During his first several months in office, George W. Bush gave relatively few nationally televised addresses, preferring to communicate less formally, or through his

[9]Quoted in Newton Minnow et al., *Presidential Television* (New York: Basic Books, 1973), p. vii.
[10]U.S. Congress. Senate. Committee on Commerce. Subcommittee on Communication. *Hearings on S.J. Res. 209.* 91st Cong. 2d Sess. 1970, p. 15.

Press Secretary, Ari Fleischer. After the 9/11 tragedy, however, Bush was compelled to deliver a series of difficult televised addresses. By many accounts, this tragedy turned a reluctant speechmaker into a formidable public communicator.

Political Knowledge and Attitudes: The Media as Gatekeepers

As *gatekeepers,* editors and journalists in newsrooms across the land decide in large measure what the American people will know about. Just because the media report a lot of news, however, does not mean that Americans are always eager to receive it or, when they are, successful at remembering most of what they read or see.[11] It was shown in Chapter 5 that many Americans do not know very much about their political leaders and what they do or how the American political system works. In part, this is because most of the time spent watching television, reading newspapers, or browsing the Internet is not spent watching or reading the news. About half of Americans report that they follow national news closely only "when something important or interesting is happening."[12]

Even when people pay attention to the news, they do not retain large amounts of specific information for very long. Given the number of events and situations that are televised, written about, and talked about, one day's news is overtaken by the next.

The mass media also influence political attitudes—what people think about their political leaders and institutions. Of course, the formation of political attitudes is complex, stretching from childhood to old age, but the media are part of this process. News stories contribute to emotions and impressions that can matter politically, apart from whatever facts are transferred from the tube or page to the brain. Feelings of outrage, sadness, pride, trust, or distrust can linger long after the specific content of a news story has been forgotten.

It makes a difference, then, how journalists keep watch over public life, in pointing to shortcomings, corruption, failures, and successes. One study of network television news coverage of the White House found that stories reflecting favorably on the president and his policies were outnumbered by those that reflected unfavorably on the administration. The author suggested that this fact accounts for the difficulty recent presidents have had in maintaining their popularity past the initial "honeymoon" stage.[13] President Clinton was an amazing exception to this rule, leaving office after eight years with an approval rating higher than when he started. This was not due to favorable news stories (indeed, a vast number of stories centered on the scandals that led to his impeachment), but to a favorable economy. Americans consistently gave high marks to Clinton's job performance, but low

---

[11]Charles Atkin, "A Conceptual Model for Information Seeking, Avoiding, and Processing," in *New Models for Mass Communication Research,* ed. Peter Clarke (Beverly Hills, CA: Sage, 1973), pp. 205–242.

[12]The Pew Research Center for the People and the Press, "Internet Sapping Broadcast News Audience," 11 June 2000, http://people-press.org/reports/display.php3?ReportID=36 (13 September 2002).

[13]Fred Smoller, "The Six O'Clock Presidency," *Presidential Studies Quarterly* 26 (1986): 42–44.

marks to the president "as a person."[14] The media were initially critical of George W. Bush's job performance, but rallied around him after the 9/11 attack, possibly in response to a perceived need for national unity.

Issue Making and Issue Reporting: The Media as Spotlights

Just as the media can act as gatekeepers, they can be *spotlights* as well. Sometimes journalists talk about their work as if television, newspapers, and the Internet were mirrors of society. That would mean that life in its many varieties and experiences would be reflected in the programs people watch and the articles they read. Most of the humdrum of daily living, however, goes unnoticed and unreported by the media.

Wife and husband read different newspapers that cover the Clinton/Lewinsky scandal. (*AP Wide World*)

Indeed, many people watch television to escape, not relive, such humdrum. Rather than thinking of the media as "mirroring" society, it is probably more helpful to think about the media as spotlighting or highlighting parts of it.

The media help to identify and define the issues people regard as important. Moreover, prominent coverage of a topic such as drunk driving day after day may heighten the importance people assign to it, just as an absence of coverage can lead people to believe that a problem such as hunger is no longer serious.

When news stories and "op-ed" pieces highlight events and conditions, government officials and other politicians will frequently regard them as important too. Extensive video footage of drug sales on street corners in broad daylight, for instance, is almost certain to produce some kind of response from the mayor or police chief. More media attention then results because officials are now considering the problem and deciding what action, if any, to take. Journalists and government officials will sometimes collaborate to "manufacture" an issue. For example, the staff of a congressional committee might share information with reporters about waste and cost overruns in the military. The

[14]The Gallup Organization, "Clinton Leaves Office With Mixed Public Reaction," 12 January 2001, http://www.gallup.com/poll/releases/pr010112.asp (14 September 2002).

Contemporary Controversies
Confidentiality of News Sources and Information

Government cannot constitutionally prevent reporters from publishing news, but protection of a reporter's news sources and information remains uncertain. The success of much investigative journalism depends on the willingness of people with information to share it with journalists. For a variety of reasons, however, these news sources do not want their identities revealed. Some may fear embarrassment or the loss of a job; in the case of disclosure of criminal wrongdoing, they may be concerned about their physical safety. With no assurance of confidentiality, news sources might dry up, resulting in a loss of news to the public. Moreover, without some legal protection, officials could harass reporters they did not like by hauling them into court. Where it becomes apparent that reporters possess information, such as the names of witnesses, that law enforcement agents do not have, many people believe that journalists should have to testify just like ordinary citizens. Moreover, they say,

because government officials rely on the press for a favorable public image, abuses would rarely, if ever, occur. Besides, sources do not disappear simply because the assurance of confidentiality is not absolute. In 1972 the Supreme Court ruled 5 to 4 in *Branzburg v. Hayes*[a] that the First Amendment does not protect the identity of a reporter's sources, but half the states have enacted **shield laws** that give varying degrees of protection to news sources. Some protect only a journalist's sources, while others protect undisclosed information too. Congress has not passed a shield law for federal investigations.

The Supreme Court has also ruled in a case from Stanford University that the First Amendment does not shield newspaper offices from police searches, even when the newspaper, broadcast station, or its

[a]408 U.S. 665 (1972).

---

shield laws

Statutes that protect the identity of journalists' news sources or their knowledge of criminal acts.

priming

Occurs when the news media, especially television, set the terms by which the public judges its leaders.

objective is to generate widespread feeling that new policies are needed to cope with a recently "discovered" problem.[15]

Especially when the news is not favorable, journalists may run afoul of officials. When investigating a story on local corruption, for instance, reporters will need "inside" sources to provide information and insight. These sources understandably will not want their names made public. Yet if the story leads to arrests by the police, witnesses will have to be called. Should reporters nonetheless be allowed to protect the identity of their sources? This is the question probed in "Contemporary Controversies: Confidentiality of News Sources and Information."

Spotlighting issues may affect political attitudes by **priming** the public. Priming occurs when the news media, especially television, set the terms by which the

---

[15]Fay Lomax Cook et al., "Media and Agenda Setting: Effects on the Public, Interest Group Leaders, Policy Makers, and Policy," *Public Opinion Quarterly* 47 (1983): 32–33.

Confidentiality of News Sources and Information, continued

staff is not accused of wrongdoing.[b] Following violent demonstrations on the campus, the *Stanford Daily* published photographs of the clash. Police concluded that the newspaper's files might contain other evidence to help identify rioters and searched the premises. In reaction to the Stanford case, Congress passed the Privacy Protection Act of 1980, which prohibits unannounced searches of news media offices and those of authors and researchers by federal, state, and local police departments. There are three exceptions: when a reporter may have committed a crime, when the desired information is classified or otherwise related to national defense, or when someone's physical safety is at risk. The 1980 act has not ended newsroom searches but has reduced their frequency.[c]

More recently, news leaks regarding the War on Terrorism have led government officials to seek out the informant on their own, rather than going after the journalists. On June 19, 2002 CNN first reported that the National Security Agency had intercepted conversations regarding an imminent terrorist attack prior to September 11, 2001. Since the intelligence community had only shared this classified information with a limited number of individuals—namely the Senate Intelligence Committee—the FBI investigation focused on the senators rather than the news media.[d]

Whether in shielding the identity of sources or investigatory material, should journalists have legal protection denied to other citizens? Should government officials be held to different standards? How might threats to national security change your views?

[b]*Zurcher* v. *Stanford Daily*, 436 U.S. 547(1978).
[c]Jane E. Kirtlet, "Dealing with Newsroom Searches," National Association of Broadcasters InfoPalt, October/November 1988.

[d]Kate Snow, "FBI Seeks Senators' Records in 9/11 Leak Probe," *CNN.com*, 24 August 2002.

public judges its leaders. The way in which the media present an issue, such as protecting the environment, can make it appear to be the business of a particular official, such as the president. If viewers and readers then regard the problem as important—as they probably will if it appears to be a problem of presidential magnitude—they are then likely to judge officials according to how well they think the latter have responded to the challenge.[16] So the media do not tell the people what to think. Rather, American media are significant because they tell the people what (and whom) to think about.

Candidates and Campaigns: The Media as Talent Scouts

Just as every aspiring singer and shortstop wants to be noticed and taken seriously, candidates for political office want "good press." Political parties have historically been

[16]Shanto Iyengar and Donald R. Kinder, *News That Matters* (Chicago: University of Chicago Press, 1987), pp. 98–111.

intermediaries, or linkages, between governors and the governed. To a degree, the two major parties still perform these functions. But as parties have weakened, the media have come to occupy an ever-larger political role in campaigns, partially displacing the parties themselves.

Today voters receive more political information from the media than from parties. More voters can see a presidential candidate simultaneously in a single appearance on television than during a three-week whistle-stop train tour of the nation 75 years ago. Good reporting can help voters understand a candidate's stand on the issues.

All too often, however, the media treat campaigns as if they were little more than horse races. News stories identify "serious" contenders and "front-runners," those whose campaigns have "momentum," as well as those who have "peaked too soon" or are "has-beens." For example, candidates want to do well at the start, with their early successes featured in the news.[17] Sometimes this means getting more votes than any of the other candidates, or it may mean getting more votes than journalists expected. News accounts may then affect outcomes in later primaries because they affect the support that flows toward or away from a candidate. On the other side, especially in state and local races where turnouts are usually lower than in national elections, a lack of media attention will leave voters in the dark about who the candidates are and where they stand on the issues.

Moreover, given the legal constraints on campaign gifts and spending, news stories that place candidates in a favorable light can add up to free advertising. Particularly for campaigns run on a financial shoestring, journalists are indispensable in bringing candidates' views and personalities to the attention of the electorate. Without such "free publicity," for example, third party candidates Pat Buchanan (Reform Party) and Ralph Nader (Green Party) would not have been able to reach as many potential voters. This "free" media attention, however, comes at a price. When candidates have to rely on journalists to present their message they often find themselves at the mercy of the journalists' perspective. Once most mainstream media outlets decided Buchanan and Nader were not serious contenders for the presidency, they devoted significantly less attention to these candidates, possibly reducing public support for these presidential hopefuls.

Believability

Whether functioning as vehicles, gatekeepers, spotlights, or talent scouts, many news media receive respectable marks from the public for "believability"—whether people are inclined to accept what they read and see as true. Believability thus makes news reporting more important politically. Polls done a half-century ago indicated that about one person in three at the time thought the news media were inaccurate. A survey performed in 1986 yielded similar figures,[18] but by 2000, 45 percent of those polled said they thought the

---

[17]Richard Joslyn, *Mass Media and Elections* (Reading, MA: Addison-Wesley, 1984), p.215.
[18]*The People and the Press* (Los Angeles: Times Mirror, Inc., 1986), p. 20.

FIGURE 6.1

Believability Ratings for Selected Mass Media

In a 2002 survey, respondents were asked to rate the believability of selected mass media organizations on a four-point scale. They were told that a 4 meant "you can believe all or most of what they say" and 1 meant "you can believe almost nothing of what they say." The graph shows the degree of believability (score of 3) and the high believability (score of 4). Percentages shown in the graph are based on total responses of 1, 2, 3, and 4, and exclude responses of "never heard of" and "can't rate."

SOURCE: The Pew Research Center for the People and the Press, "News Media's Improved Image Proves Short-Lived," 4 August 2002, http://people-press.org/reports/print.php3?PageID=631 (14 September 2002).

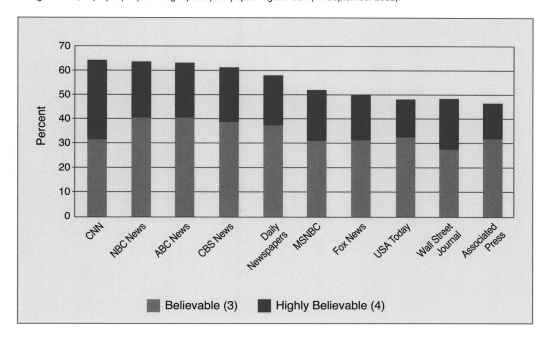

media's news stories were often inaccurate.[19] With reference to *particular* news sources, the believability scores are very high, as Figure 6.1 indicates. Also high are believability ratings, shown in Figure 6.2, for specific television journalists. Yet nearly two in three Americans see the press as influenced by powerful people and organizations.[20]

Tools of the Trade: Politicians and the "Fifth Branch"

If politicians need the mass media, the media also need candidates and officials. The relationship between the two is *symbiotic:* It is advantageous to both, with each contributing

---

[19]The Pew Research Center for the People and the Press, "News Media's Improved Image Proves Short-Lived," 4 August 2002, http://people-press.org/reports/print.php3?PageID=631 (14 September 2002).
[20]*The People and the Press; Part 5* (Los Angeles: Times Mirror, Inc., 1989), p. 13.

FIGURE 6.2

Believability Ratings for Selected Television Journalists

In a 2002 survey, respondents were asked to rate the believability of individual television journalists, using the same four-point scale applied to the ratings in Figure 6.1. In this study, only Secretary of State Colin Powell received higher believability ratings than all of the news organizations and journalists. President George W. Bush was believable to about as many Americans as the top news organizations, but to fewer Americans than the top television journalists. Vice-President Dick Cheney was only believable to a little more than half of the Americans surveyed.

SOURCE: The Pew Research Center for the People and the Press, "News Media's Improved Image Proves Short-Lived," 4 August 2002, http://people-press.org/reports/print.php3?PageID=631 (14 September 2002).

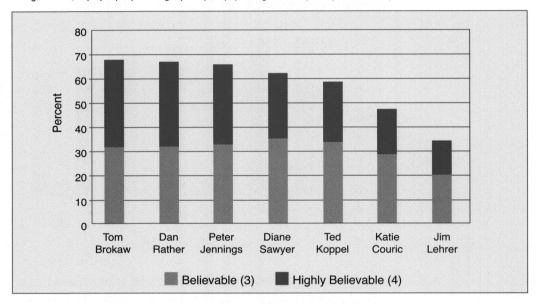

something to the needs of the other. In dealing with the media, politicians have several tools that they can use to their own advantage, for journalists compete with each other for page space and airtime. "What producers and reporters want more than anything else," admitted Fred Friendly, "is to get on the air."[21]

Access

Journalists rely on candidates and officials for access to news and news sources. Access in turn promotes their stature and advancement in the profession. For example, reporters assigned to cover the White House who are usually among the first to learn what is happening, who are called on at presidential news conferences, or who have their telephone calls returned are envied by their peers and valued by their employers.

---

[21]"The New Face of TV News," *Time*, February 25, 1980.

leak

The deliberate release of information by an official to a journalist for a specific purpose.

exclusive

An interview that an official or other individual grants to one or more journalists that provides information not generally made available to all media.

news release

A story written by a press agent for distribution to the media.

press conference

A meeting of journalists and an official or other person at which the latter answers the questions posed by the former.

news briefing

An announcement or explanation of policy by an official.

backgrounders

News briefings in which reporters may not reveal the identity of the source of their information.

Access sometimes takes the form of being the recipient of a **leak**. A leak is rarely accidental. It is a deliberate release of information by an official to a reporter for a specific purpose. Besides doing the journalist a favor, the official may be trying to embarrass a supervisor, impress the journalist, expose bad management or corruption, provide damaging details to discredit a policy, or test the political waters for a new idea. Leaks can spring from the pettiest personal motives or from the loftiest patriotic sentiments. They counterbalance an agency's tight control of information. In 1986, for instance, the *Washington Post* angered high officials in the Defense Department by revealing the location, number, cost, and test flight routine of the Air Force's hitherto super-secret stealth bomber, even the existence of which the government would not acknowledge. The story made it clear that this was information the *Post* had acquired from persons involved with the project.[22]

The source of a leak is only rarely revealed. By contrast, the **exclusive** is an acknowledged interview that an official grants to one or more journalists. The subject may be the first lady, the president, or the chief justice of the United States. Such people consent to interviews infrequently. Being scarce, interviews are therefore marks of status and recognition every reporter covets. Yet both leaks and exclusives sometimes create ethical and legal dilemmas for journalists. Consider the examples in "Contemporary Controversies: Confidentiality of News Sources and Information."

Public Announcements

In contrast to leaks and exclusives, news releases, press conferences, and news briefings are aimed at all interested reporters. These devices make news by virtue of their happening. Written by an official's press secretary, the **news release** is a ready-made story distributed for the purpose of attracting media attention to some event or situation. The **press conference** and **news briefing** are similar. In the first, an official or a candidate stands before reporters, cameras, and microphones and answers questions. With his quick wit and disarming smile, President John Kennedy (1961–1963) was the first to make the televised White House press conference a regular event. It was a forum in which he excelled.

In a briefing, an official makes an announcement or attempts to explain a policy. In international hostage situations, for instance, much of the news originates with regular briefings given reporters at the State Department. **Backgrounders** are like briefings, except that reporters may not cite the source. They permit officials to make statements without having their names attached to what is reported. Each form of public announcement attempts to create a newsworthy event that qualifies for press coverage. Officials may achieve much the same result by agreeing to appear on Sunday interview shows

---

[22]*Washington Post,* August 22, 1986, p. Al. For a discussion of leaks prior to the American raid on Lybia in 1986, see David C. Martin and John Walcott, *Best Laid Plans: The Inside Story of America's War Against Terrorism* (New York: Harper & Row, 1988), pp. 269–271.

such as *Face the Nation* and *Meet the Press*. Often statements made on these programs generate front-page stories in Monday's newspapers.

Other Media Events

Like news releases, letters can make news. Rather than simply letting it be known that a senator is concerned about, say, unfair trade restrictions abroad, the senator writes a letter to the secretary of commerce and releases a copy to the press. Reporters might have trouble writing a story about a vague concern, but a letter is concrete. Moreover, as an event, it is something to report.

visual

An image or series of images representing news in action. A visual depiction of a political act, such as campaigning, may carry more impact than words alone.

Designed for television, the **visual** features someone's appearance at an appropriate location. For a state legislator who wants to launch a campaign against potholes, merely complaining may go unheard. But if she stands in a pothole (after alerting camera crews, of course), she will be hard to miss. Television reporters do their own visuals. When a story breaks at the White House, network correspondents take turns doing their "stand-ups" with the lovely mansion as a backdrop.

photo opportunities

Events scheduled to give newspaper reporters and television crews a chance to photograph someone.

Important for newspapers but more especially for television, **photo opportunities** are events staged not so much for the purpose of dramatizing an issue as for creating visible activity. They show an official or candidate *doing something,* providing footage for the evening news or a good shot for tomorrow's front page. When a foreign leader comes to Washington to confer with the president, little may be released about what is actually discussed. Instead, viewers will see the two chatting informally over coffee, taking a stroll in the Rose Garden on the White House grounds, or tossing horseshoes at Camp David.

A Right to Know?

All of these "tools of the trade" involve officials providing news of one kind or another to the media. There are plenty of other occasions, however, when reporters want information but can find no one to provide it. "A free press and a purposeful government are destined always to be involved in a war of sorts," observes one former White House aide.[23] Although the Constitution protects the reporter's right to print news, there is not an equal right in all situations to acquire it. The press "is free to do battle against secrecy and deception in government," Justice Stewart once said, "but the press cannot expect from the Constitution any guarantee that it will succeed."[24]

For instance, how much access should journalists have to ongoing military operations? Traditionally, journalists have witnessed most American military operations, even if for security reasons dispatches might be delayed or censored. The Vietnam

---

[23]Douglass Cater, *Power in Washington* (New York: Random House, 1964), p. 235.
[24]Potter Stewart, "Or of the Press," *Hastings Law Journal* 26 (1975): 634.

War ushered in the first major television coverage of day-to-day combat, with evening news shows displaying in vivid color battle scenes that had occurred within 24 hours of airtime. In contrast with World War II, there was virtually no government-imposed restriction on what could be shown. As a result, some people believe that daily scenes of battlefield carnage, combined with questioning by journalists of war aims, gradually undermined American resolve to continue the fighting.[25]

Although the exact role television played in changing public attitudes about the war will probably never be known, the Vietnam experience has prompted officials in the Defense Department to rethink the custom of open media access to combat areas. No such free access exists in authoritarian countries, and even democracies such as Israel and Great Britain permit only limited access. Tighter controls, the argument goes, reduce the need for outright censorship and avoid unfavorable coverage as well as the inconvenience of having reporters underfoot. Taking a cue from other nations, and the negativity surrounding the Vietnam conflict, the American military took a very limiting stance on reporter access during the Grenada and Panama invasions of the 1980s and the Gulf War in 1991. During the American government's "War on Terrorism," which began in late 2001, the Defense Department has taken a somewhat more inclusive position on media access. The military has allowed a select number of journalists to accompany fighting units in "embedded" positions. In other words, the reporters have observed the conflict directly, alongside troops and with all of the related dangers. While this approach has led to some excellent, up-close coverage, some worry that the Defense Department may be extending an open invitation in certain situations only so that the decision to restrict access elsewhere won't be questioned. When actions are committed in secret, without press coverage, Americans are prevented from forming objective opinions. As Michael Gelter, ombudsman of the *Washington Post*, has remarked, "we don't know what we don't know."[26]

Are the Media Biased?

Politicians, including most American presidents, have long complained about news coverage. Are the media biased? Most Americans apparently think so. No less than 59 percent of the public report believing the media are "politically biased in their reporting."[27] Some bias is probably unavoidable in reporting the news. The bias is both *personal* and *structural*. It results from the political attitudes of reporters and editors as well as from the nature of the news-reporting business itself.

---

[25]Edward J. Epstein, *Between Fact and Fiction: The Problems of Journalism* (New York: Random House/Vintage Books, 1975), pp. 210–232.

[26]"Press Coverage and the War on Terrorism: Assessing the Media and the Government," Brookings/Harvard Forum transcript, 9 January 2002, http://www.brook.edu/dybdocroot/comm/transcripts/20020109.htm (15 September 2002).

[27]The Pew Research Center for the People and the Press, "News Media's Improved Image Proves Short-Lived," 4 August 2002, http://people-press.org/reports/print.php3?PageID=631 (14 September 2002).

The Journalists

Vice-President Spiro Agnew (1969–1973) once publicly accused the news media of controlling news. "A small group of men, numbering perhaps no more than a dozen anchormen, commentators, and executive producers," argued Agnew, "settle upon the film and commentary that is to reach the public. They decide what 40 to 50 million Americans will learn of the day's events in the nation and the world."[28]

Of course, news is influenced by the people who write it. Reporters and commentators are not value-free machines that simply grind out a product. Their attitudes and outlooks are bound to affect what Americans read and see, even if journalists make every effort to be accurate. Who are the journalists staffing the major newspapers and network news bureaus? Generally, they tend to come from small towns, largely in the Midwest, rather than the cities and suburban communities of the Northeast or the West. Many of them went to state colleges, not to Ivy League or other highly selective private institutions. They probably majored in journalism or English, rather than in philosophy, economics, or political science. Few have been politically active in the sense of strongly identifying with and working for a party and its candidates.

Yet when they vote, journalists overwhelmingly favor Democratic or otherwise liberal candidates. Moreover, they tend to be suspicious of most politicians, whether Democratic or Republican, liberal or conservative. As one scholar has concluded, journalists distrust politicians because politicians have to compromise. Compromise "tends not to involve the clear and snappy opposition of right and wrong that is the stuff of television drama." There is a journalistic idea "of the individual good citizen, independent of special interests and party loyalties, making up his own mind about the measures and candidates that will best promote the public good."[29]

Suspicion of politicians in turn leads to suspicion of "the establishment," the people in power. In a campaign, the underdog may be more appealing than the supposed front-runner. And with numerous exposés to their credit that have uncovered corruption and shady deals by public officials, it is only natural that journalists see themselves as a permanent "loyal opposition" or "watchdog" apart from the competition between the ins and the outs of the two-party system. Surely the important role of newspaper sleuths in uncovering and probing the Watergate scandal during the early 1970s has only strengthened this perception. Without a watchful press, President Richard Nixon (1969–1974) and "all the president's men" would probably have survived the impeachment controversy that led to his resignation in August 1974.[30] Yet the press collectively was far less vigilant in the late 1980s in reporting the growing insolvency of the savings and loan

---

[28]*Collected Speeches of Spiro Agnew* (New York: Audubon Books, 1971), p. 89.

[29]Austin Ranney, "The Cook Lectures: Politics in the Television Age," *Law Quadrangle Notes* 26 (1982): 19. See also Austin Ranney, *Channels of Power* (New York: Basic Books, 1983), pp. 55–63.

[30]Carl Bernstein and Bob Woodward, *All the President's Men* (New York: Simon and Schuster, 1974).

industry. Whether because the subject was so complex, involved so many people and institutions, or seemingly lacked drama and interest, journalists initially ignored the topic all the while Congress, the executive, and the regulatory agencies allowed the problem to fester. Finding a more gossipy, attention-grabbing story, the media devoted a great deal of attention to the extra-marital scandals of the Clinton presidency during the 1990s.

Other forces tend to compensate for a liberal bias, to the extent it exists in the national press. Editorial endorsements from the "front office" usually go to conservatives, and reporters in towns and small cities may have a more conservative outlook too. (Still, the more liberal urban papers have larger circulations.) Moreover, reactions of advertisers, viewers, readers, and officials have to be considered. Editors and producers, for example, may want to curry favor with sponsors by avoiding subjects or ideas that sponsors might find offensive. In addition, the media mergers that have occurred over the past two decades mean that a large number of media outlets are owned by a small number of mega-corporations—a trend that may be leading to more favorable coverage of big business and more conservative coverage generally. Another concern is that because journalists rely on officials for access to information, journalists may become "lap dogs" by placing favorable slants on stories they write. Conservative officials and causes may therefore get more balanced treatment than they would otherwise receive. Some critics say that these considerations mean that certain issues may be neglected altogether or covered only in a shallow fashion. The result is that people are poorly informed by a bland style of reporting that succeeds only because it is marginally acceptable to most and offensive to only a few. Still, a tradition of journalistic professionalism argues strongly for both *depth* and *evenhandedness* in news coverage.

Deciding What Becomes News

agenda setting

The process by which the news media select and focus on a small number of stories from a large number of possibilities. Doing so shapes, in part, Americans' opinions about what is important.

Since literally thousands of events occur in the world every day, space and time constraints mean that most of them go unreported. Selecting what becomes news—the process of **agenda setting**—is especially critical in television. Approximately 22 minutes are available for news during a 30-minute news show, allowing for 10 to 15 stories at most. This means that even the major stories are usually allotted only 2 to 3 minutes each. The news reported last evening on television could easily fit on the front page of this morning's newspaper. If a "big story" is in the news, other stories are crowded out. Once cut, these would-be stories may never have a second chance to appear. Expanded coverage is possible only on more lengthy programs such as the "The News Hour with Jim Lehrer" on public television.

What factors seem to guide this inevitable selection? Some events seem destined to become news: natural disasters and political "turning points" such as elections, revolutions, and military invasions. Other events or circumstances will become news if they happen to appeal to the people responsible for selecting stories or if they have a high interest among the reading and viewing audience. Still others qualify as news because they are "scoops"—attention-getting stories made public by a single newspaper or station. A day's delay might give the competition the chance to claim a scoop as its own. Aside from scoops, there seems to be substantial agreement among the networks on what constitutes the most newsworthy events. One study found that two of three major networks carried the same lead story on the evening news 91 percent of the time, and in only 7 percent of the programs did two run the same lead story without the third network placing it somewhere in the program.[31]

Even economics plays a part in news selection. Especially for television, operating costs are high. For every story viewers see, there is not only a reporter but also a camera operator, a technician, and a producer involved directly on the scene. Equipment is expensive to move and set up, and circuits for satellite linkages and coaxial lines must be reserved and paid for. Network news editors, therefore, do not casually send reporters, crews, and equipment to all potentially newsworthy locations.

This is one reason that about half the network news stories originate from, or focus on, Washington. Washington is not only the capital and therefore the location of many stories reporters deem important, but staff, equipment, and circuits are already there. This makes reporting Washington-based stories relatively easy and cost-efficient. Within Washington, however, news coverage is not equally dispersed. About half the stories deal primarily with the "golden triangle" of the White House and the departments of defense and state. Reporters and technicians assigned just to cover the White House number more than 200. Congress receives somewhat less coverage, with the Senate drawing more attention than the House. Regulatory agencies and the Supreme Court receive the least. Moreover, two-thirds of the stories on the presidency, but only half of those on Congress, are accompanied by film or videotape. Presidential stories typically run more than twice the length of those on Congress and tend to come earlier in the broadcast.[32] Of course, these figures are dependent on the relative levels of congressional and White House initiative, as well as the number of international crises, and are therefore subject to some variation from year to year. Campaign reporting by the four broadcast networks tilts even more sharply toward the presidency.

What accounts for this disparate treatment? It is partly a function of the stories journalists think are most important. Also, the executive branch, though many times larger than Congress, is more easily personified. One can associate the president or the secretaries of state and defense with policies in a way that is not as conveniently done in Congress with its 100 senators and 435 representatives. Moreover, much congressional

---

[31]Joe Foote and Michael Steele, "Degree of Conformity in Lead Stories in Early Evening Network TV Newscasts," *Journalism Quarterly* 63 (1986): 21.

[32]Lynda Kaid and Joe Foote, "How Network Television Coverage of the President and Congress Compare," *Journalism Quarterly* 62 (1985): 59.

time is consumed with deliberation. This is often not as dramatic to report as an initial proposal to Congress that originated in the White House or an executive decision based on legislation Congress has passed. Imbalance in coverage between presidential and congressional races on the networks is largely explained by the difficulty ABC, CBS, Fox, and NBC have in interesting viewers (and therefore in holding their audiences) in one state in House and Senate races in another state. The solution for the networks is obvious: ignore most of the congressional races most of the time.

Television coverage of Congress is technically easier now that both the House (since 1979) and Senate (since 1986) permit television cameras in their chambers, and so coverage of the legislative process has increased, especially on locally produced newscasts. Aside from interviews with individual legislators, networks and local stations can pick up statements from floor debates to include on news programs. This is an opportunity that has not gone unnoticed, as some members have learned to "play" to the cameras, even before a virtually empty room. Indeed, continuous television in Congress now means that floor debate sometimes resembles a video equivalent of the telephone answering machine. Even in the momentous debate in the House and Senate in January 1991 over the use of force in the Persian Gulf crisis, most members with something to say filed into their respective chamber at the designated time, made a speech that was recorded for posterity, and then returned to their offices or homes to watch their colleagues do the same—on television.

Yet, just because something *can be* considered newsworthy is not necessarily reason enough why it *should* become news. Journalistic ethics play a role too. To what extent, for instance, should journalists probe the private lives of officials and candidates? This was the question posed when the *Miami Herald* published reports in 1987 accusing Democratic presidential front-runner Gary Hart of improprieties in spending a weekend with a woman who was not his wife. When made aware of additional damaging information in the possession of the *Washington Post* a few days later, candidate Hart announced his withdrawal from the race.[33] The media's success with Hart laid the groundwork for their approach to the Monica Lewinsky scandal during the Clinton Administration. Issues that would have been deemed "off limits" in a previous generation made their way, for good or ill, into prime time news coverage. Some people argue that the lives of candidates should be like a "fish bowl" or an open book." Others say that one's personal life should not be the public's business unless it reflects on a candidate's qualifications to be president or to hold another public office.

framing

The way in which the media presents a story, consisting of angle, tone, and point of view.

Deciding How the News Appears

Journalists describe or portray events in different ways, with different emphases. This process of shaping stories is sometimes called **framing**. In one of the televised debates in

---

[33]Paul Taylor, "Hart to Withdraw from Presidential Campaign," the *Washington Post*, May 8, 1987, p. Al. Hart later re-entered the race and competed in some of the 1988 primaries before withdrawing again.

1976 between President Gerald Ford (1974–1977) and challenger Jimmy Carter (1977–1981), for example, Ford slipped up by saying that Poland was not under Soviet domination. In surveys immediately after the debate, viewers were almost evenly divided when asked which candidate had done the better job. But over the next 24 hours, as news reports about the debate emphasized Ford's blunder, reaction shifted dramatically in Carter's favor. Some people later admitted to changing their minds, saying that the news stories about the debate led them to conclude that their initial judgments (favoring Ford) must have been wrong. The "newsworthy" part of the debate had become Ford's blooper.[34]

Today candidates are reluctant to leave interpretation of events solely to journalists. In all three debates in the 2000 presidential campaign between Vice-President Al Gore and Texas Governor George W. Bush, for example, the candidates had hardly uttered their closing statements when the "spin doctors" went to work. Viewers were presented with ample "post-debate quarterbacking" from office-holders and campaign officials from each party who crowded around the press to provide instant analysis of what "really happened." Unlike the usual press conference, however, there were more interviewees than interviewers. Do the spin doctors make a difference? Unless one candidate commits a major blunder, as Ford did in 1976, most viewers will probably not be greatly swayed by post-debate commentary. Still, it probably shapes the opinions of some, and neither campaign wants to leave the other free to provide an unanswered interpretation of events.

More than print journalism, television news reporting calls for *intepretation* of events, rather than a bare statement of what happened. This is also the case with stories on programs such as "60 Minutes." Because of the need to hold a viewing audience to a particular channel, television news is purposely designed to be gripping and dramatic. An executive producer of the NBC nightly news once made this point a requirement for his staff:

> Every news story should, without any sacrifice of probity or responsibility, display
> the attributes of fiction, of drama. It should have structure and conflict, problem and
> denouement, rising action and falling action, a beginning, a middle, and an end.
> These are not only the essentials of drama; they are the essentials of narrative.[35]

What if an event lacks the elements of fiction, drama, or conflict? The item might be passed over entirely or, if reported, given the added drama it needs. Reporting the news may well mean molding it too. The irony is that politicians often succeed by managing conflict and reconciling differences among groups. Journalists succeed by capitalizing on conflict and magnifying those differences.[36]

---

[34]Frederick T. Steeper, "Public Responses to Gerald Ford's Statements on Eastern Europe in the Second Debate," in *The Presidential Debates: Media, Electoral, and Policy Perspectives*, ed. George F. Bishop et al. (New York: Praeger, 1978), pp. 81–101.
[35]Reuven Frank, quoted in Edward Jay Epstein, *News from Nowhere* (New York: Random House/Vintage Books, 1973), pp. 4–5.
[36]Herber Schmertz, "The Media and the Presidency," *Presidential Studies Quarterly* 26 (1986): 21.

Because news reporting is a business, stations sell time on news programs just as they do during weekend football games and afternoon soap operas. Newspapers sell space. Understandably, media executives are acutely conscious of circulation figures and **Nielsen ratings**. Such numbers largely determine commercial revenue and therefore profits. Economic considerations understandably dictate that the media attract as many viewers and readers as possible.

Nielsen ratings

Surveys conducted by the A.C. Nielsen Company to measure the size of television audiences.

The Impact of the Visual

Television's unique quality is its capacity to transmit images into virtually every home in the land simultaneously. Thus, television gives a special meaning to the old saying that a picture is worth a thousand words. A news article about a plane crash will not have the same effect as color videotape of the same scene. Consider, for example, the emotionally moving nature of the photographs and video of the World Trade Center collapse. The tragedy seems all the more real and near because it is on television.

The *visual* also becomes a factor in the selection of stories and in the way those stories will be presented. Television news editors prefer stories that can be easily visualized. Similarly, they prefer to cover the parts of a story that display movement. Televised reports on political campaigns, for instance, typically emphasize what candidates are *doing* more than what they are *saying*. Instead of the issues that divide candidates, viewers may get an eyeful of colorful rallies, parades, flagwaving, and handshaking. One may see a lot of activity without necessarily *learning* very much about a candidate or the substance of the campaign. Sometimes, knowledge voters glean about the candidates is more likely to have come from the candidates' own advertisements than from news reports on their campaigns.

Likewise, television's preference for action shapes the way candidates conduct their campaigns. Appearances must be timed so that coverage can make the evening news. A prepared statement on grain subsidies or interest rates will not draw nearly the attention generated by a ride on a tractor across a wheat field or a visit to the home of a farmer whose house and farm are about to be foreclosed. Including such visuals in newscasts is far easier today than it was a generation ago because of the miniaturization of cameras and other devices that have largely replaced bulkier and more cumbersome equipment. Because television favors images over words, candidates learn to include "sound bites" in their speeches—one or two catchy sentences or phrases designed for the brief coverage television provides. With the advent of streaming video on the Internet, viewers can now watch these sound bites over and over at their own leisure when visiting media web sites. Such use further enhances the value of a good sound bite—and the cost of an embarrassing one.

In politics, television has clearly benefited some political leaders more than others. One of the earliest examples of television's impact occurred in 1960 when

President George W. Bush with Jay Leno during an appearance on "The Tonight Show with Jay Leno." *(AP Wide World)*

Senator John Kennedy (D-MA) debated Vice-President Richard Nixon (1953–1961) in the first televised debate between presidential candidates. While transcripts of the debates show plainly how the candidates differed on some of the issues, many viewers were struck more by what they saw than by what they heard. Nixon went into the debate widely perceived as the "candidate of experience" even though he and Kennedy had entered Congress in the same year. While Kennedy had served in the Senate as well as the House, many thought that he was inexperienced and maybe just a little too youthful and immature for the presidency. The September debate, the first of four that fall, shook both sets of preconceptions. Perhaps the perfect television candidate, Kennedy seemed mature, firm, vigorous, and at ease. Nixon appeared drooped, tired, nervous, even haggard. In short, Kennedy *looked* presidential and thus achieved on television in an instant what it would have otherwise taken weeks of campaigning to accomplish.

The televised debates in the 2000 election likely helped one candidate and hurt the other due largely to their inability to meet with viewers' and the media's preconceived expectations and the impact of the visual. Vice President Gore, assumed to be the more practiced and qualified statesperson, did not dominate his opponent the way many had predicted he would. On the other hand, Governor Bush, depicted in the media as an inexperienced leader with a poor grasp on foreign policy, held his own. Gore's visual image reinforced descriptions of him as stiff and wooden. Bush's expressive face allowed viewers to develop a sense of being personally connected with the candidate. Thus, even though the content of the debates resulted in a draw at best for Bush, the fact that he performed better than many in the media had predicted and provided viewers with a more human visual image led to a boost in his poll numbers following each debate."[37] While reactions to a debate do not necessarily translate into votes, a televised debate presents an opportunity for voters to sense which candidate they would rather see as the nation's leader during the next four years. As voters form impressions of candidates, few doubt that the visual component of television plays an important role.

A Public Trust

If bias exists in news reporting, does this mean that journalists have somehow betrayed a trust? Are journalists worthy of the protections accorded them by the First Amendment? Were Americans of President Washington's time alive today, they would probably confess that they expected bias in the news. The press then, as well as throughout the nineteenth century, was far more biased, inaccurate, partisan, and vitriolic than almost any newspaper widely available today.

The First Amendment does not assume a bias-free press any more than the Constitution assumes pure and ambition-free politicians. Recall the constitutional system of checks and balances discussed in Chapter 1. At the heart of this arrangement, the media amount to another kind of check and balance. Just as the Constitution allows ambition to counter ambition, so the First Amendment allows one opinion to combat another, one claim of truth, perspective, and opinion to compete with another. In this way, the media best serve democratic politics.

---

[37]The Gallup Organization, "Major Turning Points in 2000 Election: Primary Season, Party Conventions, and Debates," 7 November 2000, http://www.gallup.com/poll/releases/pr001107c.asp (16 September 2002).

SUMMARY

1. The media today are characterized by less diversity in ownership and in the production of news. While Americans have access to more television channels than ever before, most national news originates from several networks and major newspapers. Moreover, the number of daily newspapers is declining. The First Amendment makes possible an important role for the media by prohibiting most restrictions on what is published. The electronic media, however, are subject to special kinds of regulations that do not apply to the print media. That being said, a constitutional method of regulating new media sources such as the Internet has proven more elusive.

2. The mass media—newspapers, magazines, radio, television, and the Internet—are vital links between citizens and their government. As observers of the political arena, the media serve as vehicles, gatekeepers, spotlights, and talent scouts.

3. The relationship between politics and media is symbiotic. While officials need the media, individual reporters depend on candidates and officeholders for access to news sources and newsmakers.

4. Bias in journalism may result from the political views of the people who report, publish, and broadcast the news and from the structure of the news media. Half of network news stories focus on Washington, and of these about half deal mainly with the executive branch. The visual nature of television not only influences which events will be deemed newsworthy but also influences the ways political campaigns are conducted and the ways officials attempt to gain publicity.

KEY TERMS

journalists (161)

mass media (162)

fifth branch (162)

Federal Communications
  Commission (FCC) (168)

equal-time rule (168)

fairness doctrine (172)

shield laws (176)

priming (176)

leak (181)

exclusive (181)

news release (181)

press conference (181)

news briefing (181)

backgrounders (181)

visual (182)

photo opportunity (182)

agenda setting (185)

framing (187)

Nielsen ratings (189)

READINGS FOR FURTHER STUDY

Two good, up-to-date texts that approach the topic of American politics through the lens of the mass media are David L. Paletz's *The Media in American Politics: Contents and Consequences*, 2nd ed. (New York: Longman, 2002) and Hoyt Purvis's *Media, Politics, and Government* (Fort Worth: Harcourt, 2001).

Two of the leading contemporary researchers in the field of politics and the media are Doris Graber and Shanto Iyengar. Graber's recent works include *Processing Politics: Learning from Television in the Internet Age* (Chicago: University of Chicago Press,

2001) and the edited volume *Media Power in Politics*, 4th ed. (Washington, DC: CQ Press, 2000). Iyengar has written *News That Matters: Television and American Opinion* (Chicago: University of Chicago Press, 1989) with Donald R. Kinder and Benjamin I. Page and edited *Do the Media Govern?: Politicians, Voters, and Reporters in America* (Thousand Oaks, CA: Sage, 1997) with Richard Reeves.

The Boys on the Bus (New York: Ballantine, 1990) by Timothy Crouse is a classic case study of journalists in the 1972 presidential contest.

A more recent look at journalists is provided by Beth J. Harpaz's *The Girls in the Van* (New York: St. Martin's Press, 2001), which follows Hillary Clinton's 2000 Senate campaign.

For details on legal regulation of both print and electronic journalism, see T. Barton Carter, Marc A. Franklin, and Jay B. Wright's *The First Amendment and the Fourth Estate: The Law of Mass Media*, 8th ed. (Mineola, NY: Foundation Press, 2000) and *The First Amendment and the Fifth Estate: Regulation of Electronic Mass Media*, 5th ed. (Mineola, NY: Foundation Press, 1999).

Michael Parenti's *Inventing Reality: The Politics of News Media*, 2nd ed. (New York: St. Martin's Press, 1993) argues that journalism is the tool of established economic and political interests in the United States.

Ben H. Bagdikian's *The Media Monopoly*, 6th ed. (Boston: Beacon Press, 2000) addresses some of the problems associated with media consolidation.

The Power of the Press: The Birth of American Political Reporting by Thomas C. Leonard (New York: Oxford University Press, 2000) is a study of the rise of political journalism in the nineteenth century.

Finally, in *Democracy and the News* (New York: Oxford University Press, 2003) Herbert J. Gans explores the relationship between democracy and the news media in light of new media developments such as cable and satellite television and the Internet.

CHAPTER 7

Interest Groups and Political Parties

A/P World Wide

Chapter Objectives

People get involved in politics not just as individuals but also in groups. This chapter examines the uniquely important role that two kinds of groups, interest groups and political parties, play in the American political system. The first part of the chapter focuses on interest groups, their activities, and the reasons behind differences in their effectiveness. This discussion sets the stage for an examination of some of the major interest groups on the American political scene today, and an evaluation of the role that interest groups play. The second part of the chapter focuses on parties, which differ from interest groups in that political parties run candidates for public office. By trying to elect members to office, the party serves a variety of important political functions—for example, channeling and clarifying political consensus and conflict, training political leaders, and organizing elections and government. The American parties form a loosely organized two-party system—a system that is in transition. Are the parties in trouble? What does the future hold for them? These questions are considered in this chapter.

Interest Groups in American Politics

Interest groups are associations of people who hold common views and who work together to influence what government does. Their interest is in a position, benefit, or advantage (such as favorable treatment under the tax laws) that they want to protect and perhaps enlarge. Interest groups look out for their members' political interests by campaigning for policies that promote their goals and by opposing policies that work against those goals. The American Federation of Labor-Congress of Industrial Organizations (AFL-CIO), one of the largest groups of unionized labor in the nation, obviously seeks to win favorable wage and job benefits from companies employing its members, but it also exists to ensure that government protects its unionizing activities and adopts policies on issues such as trade, interest rates, and education that promote the well-being of its members.

Interest groups have been a prominent feature of American politics since the earliest years of the Republic. During the thick of the public debate over the adoption of a new constitution in 1787, James Madison wrote in *Federalist* No. 10 about the divisions he saw as naturally developing in a society:

> A zeal for different opinions concerning religion, concerning government, and many other points. . . . have, in turn, divided mankind into parties, inflamed them with mutual animosity, and rendered them much more disposed to vex and oppress each other than to cooperate for the common good. . . . The regulation of these various and interfering interests forms the principal task of modern legislation and involves the spirit of party and faction in the necessary and ordinary operations of government.

Compared to other countries, interest groups in the United States play a particularly prominent role in political life. Chapter 5 reported Verba and Nie's finding that roughly 30 percent of Americans (communalists and complete activists) engage in group activities and that joining and working through groups to solve community problems is more common in the United States than in other democracies. It is not surprising, therefore, that scholars studying the American social and political system have focused on interest groups as a uniquely important element in American life. As noted in "Politics and Ideas: Pluralism and Elitism" on p. 198, many see these groups as the basic building blocks of American political life. Perhaps the dominant view is of America as a **pluralist democracy**: American society is made up of many different groups, each looking to secure its members' interests. The principal task of government is therefore one of managing the interplay of group interests.

Why American society and politics should be so group-conscious is hard to say. Probably the best explanation is that America is the coming together of so many diverse groups—the "**melting pot**" of different races, nationalities, religions, cultures, and languages—that the variety itself constantly calls attention to the existence and the activities of groups. Beyond being one of the most universally identified features of American politics and society, interest groups are also among the most controversial. Interest groups have long been praised as one of the most important contributors to the success of American democracy. Yet, particularly as they have become more visible, sophisticated in their tactics, and powerful, interest groups are now sometimes condemned as one of the greatest threats to the continuing viability of the American political system. These are concerns we will return to later.

pluralist democracy

A system in which the people rule and have their interests protected through the interaction of many different social, political, and economic groups, and in which the principal task of government is to manage group conflict and cooperation.

melting pot

Characterization of America as the coming together of a wide variety of racial, ethnic, and religious groups.

Characteristics of Interest Groups

A stunning variety of organizations fits under the general definition of interest group. The different forms and features that interest groups assume can have an impact on a group's political effectiveness. Of course, no determinant of effectiveness is absolute. A group's influence must be measured relative to the groups with which it contends. Several major characteristics distinguish interest groups and affect their influence.

One of the most obvious characteristics is size. Interest groups vary dramatically in size. All other things being equal, the bigger the group, the more effective it is likely to be. Large groups can mobilize more members, raise more money to support lobbying activities and favored political candidates, and swing more votes in an election. Although, as will be seen shortly, being large is not an unequivocal advantage for an interest group, given a democracy's reliance on plurality and majority decision making, being large is generally better than being small. Sometimes, when an interest group is large or a number of interest groups band together in a common cause, the result is referred to as a **movement**, as in the civil rights movement, the environmental movement, or the feminist movement.

Interest groups vary in membership procedures. Some groups enroll members formally, as when labor unions ask workers to join and pay dues. Other groups rest on a more informal notion of membership in which people just think of themselves as belonging. People may never go to church but nevertheless think of themselves as Catholics. Even this informal sense of membership can vary: Some groups evoke in their membership a very strong sense of identification with the group, whereas others do so only weakly. For still other groups, membership is not even a choice of the individual involved—people belong by the fact of having a particular characteristic. African

movement

An effort to attain an end through an organized set of actions and individuals.

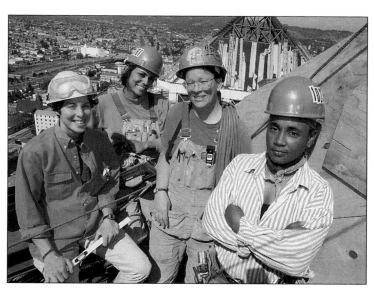

(AP Wide World)

Politics and Ideas
Pluralism and Elitism

Pluralism is one of the fundamental ideas of American politics. But it is hard to appreciate this unique American contribution to political thought without understanding a little about the political perspective with which it so sharply contrasts. Elitism holds that power in a society is concentrated in the hands of a small group of powerful people, a ruling class. This "elite" is often seen as exercising its power in ways that work to its own benefit and to the disadvantage of those whom it rules, the "masses." Other commentators portray elites as more benevolent, using their power to improve the lot of the less fortunate and to promote democratic values. The major American contributor to elitist theory was C. Wright Mills.[a] He saw real power in the United States as concentrated in the hands of the highest political, military, and corporate leaders. Mills did not argue for malevolent conspiracy. Rather, he saw the leaders of these institutions as coming from similar backgrounds, sometimes trading positions, interacting with one another, and therefore tending to hold similar values. Foremost among them was a belief in a strong and stable society.

Pluralism, in contrast, sees power as dispersed among many different centers of power, the leaders of various groups that make up society: labor organizations, professional associations, veterans, industries, and the like. Sometimes these centers of power are in agreement, but other times they are not. In any case, collective action is difficult without a reasonable amount of consensus among the groups about what should be done. This need for consensus compels politics to be moderate and stable. For example, laws passed since the early 1970s to reduce harmful automobile emissions were not imposed on the nation by a single small elite. The laws do not represent a "perfect" solution, but rather a compromise among many groups: environmentalists, health care specialists, the elderly, automobile manufacturers and dealers, labor unions, and petroleum companies.

What evidence of a power elite do you see in American society? Who is in it? To what ends does it use its power? What evidence do you see of pluralism in American society? What are the dominant groups? How do they use their power?

[a] *The Power Elite* (Oxford: Oxford University Press, 1956).

Americans and women are often identified as important interest groups, but most African Americans and most women belong to no race- or gender-based organization. They may not even think of themselves as belonging to some large group. Rather, they are labeled as a member of the group simply because they possess a particular biological characteristic. Generally speaking, the stronger the bonds of the individual members to the group, the more effective the group will be.[1]

Groups also differ in how well they are organized, and the success of an interest group in advancing its interests depends in some measure on this criteria. A strong net-

[1] The ideas in this section and the next are drawn in part from the seminal discussion of group influences in politics in Angus Campbell, Philip E. Converse, Warren E. Miller, and Donald E. Stokes, *The American Voter* (New York: Wiley, 1960), pp. 295–332.

work of communication and control can amplify the power of one group, whereas poor internal organization and an inability to coordinate common efforts can dissipate the influence of another. Groups also differ in how democratic they are. Some groups are run as virtual autocracies, with the leadership exerting almost dictatorial control over the group, and others are very democratic. The relationship between how democratic a group is and its effectiveness is an uncertain one. Groups run democratically may benefit from the additional commitment that broad membership participation engenders, as long as members can reach substantial consensus in the group. But when a lack of consensus hinders decision making, the group may suffer from a lack of common purpose. Conversely, groups run by narrow elites may benefit from singleness of purpose but suffer a lack of support if members feel estranged from the leadership.

How connected a group is to politics can also affect its influence. Some interest groups have little if any connection to politics. They are generally not concerned with political issues or involved in political activity. The town bowling league rarely has anything to do with politics. Indeed, it would probably suffer as an organization if it became embroiled in partisan political struggles. Its political significance lies in its potential to become politically active should its interests somehow be threatened in the political arena. Legislation to outlaw bowling as an immoral pastime would undoubtedly inspire it to take up the cudgels of politics. However, under normal circumstances it stands completely aside from the political fray. Other interest groups exist solely to pursue political ends. A political action committee, which we will say more about later, exists in most cases solely for the purpose of channeling money to political candidates sympathetic to the interests of the group. Between these two extremes reside many organizations that are involved in politics to a greater or lesser degree. The more closely a group is tied to political issues, personalities, and organizations, the more likely it is to be effective politically.

Finally, groups differ in terms of their adherence to the essentially mainstream views of society. Some groups pursue a course outside the American mainstream—for example, the American Nazi party leans to the right of it and the Communist party to the left of it. Where a group stands in relation to the consensus of American politics has considerable effect on how influential it will be. The most passionate, best-organized interest group in the country will make little headway if it pursues policies that are far off the beaten track of American politics. Groups that argue for complete nationalization of health care, for example, are likely to make less headway than those that argue for modest reform in the current system.

What Interest Groups Do

Interest groups engage in a broad range of activities to protect and advance the well-being of their members. Foremost among these activities is the attempt to influence public opinion. Many interest groups try to create public support or sympathy for their political goals. The major channel for accomplishing this is the mass media. When a group's political interests are threatened, representatives of the group use the media to make the group's views known. Interviews on radio and television news broadcasts, quotations in newspaper and magazine articles, letters to the editor, and essays for newspaper op-ed pages are all tools of influence for interest groups. In recent years interest groups have developed the use of an individual (as opposed to mass) medium to influence public opinion. This is the **direct mail** method, in which modern computer technology is used to generate thousands of personally addressed letters soliciting support and financial contributions from potentially sympathetic citizens.

Interest groups, of course, are involved in the electoral process through the votes their members cast. More important, interest group members can work in the campaigns of their favored candidates. In recent years interest groups have been deeply involved in the financing of political campaigns, usually through **political action committees** or PACs. PACs are organizations devoted to channeling money from members of interest groups to political candidates sympathetic to the groups' policy preferences. By law, PACs must register with the Federal Election Commission (FEC), have at least 50 contributors, and make contributions to at least five candidates for federal office. No contributor can give any one PAC more than $5,000, and no PAC can give any one candidate more than $5,000 per election. Individuals are limited in their total contributions to candidates and committees to $25,000, but there is no limit on how much PACs may raise or give in total. Nor is there any limit on the total amount that a candidate can accept from different PACs. In addition to making direct contributions to candidates, PACs may also spend as much money as they want on independent activities in behalf of one or more candidates, usually purchasing advertising in the broadcast or print media.

PACs blossomed as a result of the **Federal Election Campaign Act of 1974**, which was an attempt to prevent the misuse of campaign funds brought to light in the Watergate scandal. A few PACs existed previously, but the 1974 act, by setting limits of $1,000 on individual contributions and $5,000 on group contributions, made group contributions more attractive and led to a proliferation of PACs. From 1974 to 2000, the number of PACs increased from 100 to about 4,500 (see Figure 7.1). During the same period the amount of money contributed to federal candidates by PACs rose from about $10 million to over $260 million. PACs have become a controversial issue in American politics, with many questioning whether the post-Watergate reforms have not been a cure that is worse than the disease.

Lobbying, the attempt to influence the shape of legislation emanating from the U.S. Congress and other political decision-making bodies, has traditionally been a mainstay of interest group activity. Lobbying involves more than just hobnobbing with legislators; in many cases, lobbyists are a major source of reliable information for the

---

direct mail

Contacting citizens by mail, rather than through personal contact or the mass media.

political action committee (PAC)

Political organization set up to channel campaign money from a group to political candidates sympathetic to the group's political views.

Federal Election Campaign Act of 1974

Law passed in 1974 and amended several times that regulates campaign financing. It requires full disclosure of sources and uses of campaign funds and limits contributions to political candidates.

lobbying

Attempting to influence legislation under consideration, particularly through personal contact by group representatives.

FIGURE 7.1

The Proliferation of PACs, 1977–1997

The number of political action committees has soared since the post-Watergate campaign reforms made them the preferred vehicle for channeling money from interest group members to political candidates.

SOURCE: Federal Election Commission, 2001.

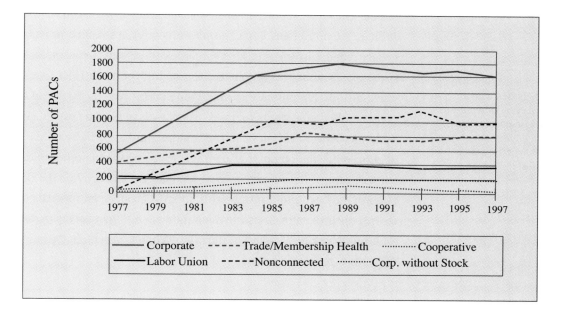

legislature. Lobbyists provide published materials and advisory letters and testify before congressional committees. They sometimes become deeply involved in the actual process of writing legislation by collaborating with members of Congress and their staffs on the drafting of bills or amendments. In some cases, they may even draft legislation themselves and pass it on to a senator or representative willing to introduce it on the floor. Modern lobbyists are a far cry from the shady figures of folklore. Some are among the most highly paid, respected, and influential figures in Washington.

The idea of lobbying extends beyond the corridors and offices of Capitol Hill. The effect of a law depends not just on how the legislation is written but also on how it is translated into action. Therefore, interest group representatives keep close watch on the rules and regulations set by the many agencies of the executive branch of government and the various independent regulatory commissions. When group interests appear to be threatened, representatives swing into action: They publicize the potential threat, mobilize group and public opinion, meet with agency officials, and ask legislators sympathetic to the "true intent" of the original legislation to intercede with the erring bureaucrats. Interest group representatives are so closely involved with legislators and

iron triangle

The combination of interest group representatives, legislators, and government administrators seen as extremely influential in determining the outcome of political decisions.

administrators in the making and implementation of public policy that the threesome has come to be called the **iron triangle** of American politics.

Traditionally, the American judiciary has been seen as isolated from external political pressures. However, a more realistic appraisal is that the courts, like the other branches of government, are susceptible to the influence of interest groups in several ways. First, interest groups can affect the selection of judges who sit on state and federal benches. Most prominently, when the president nominates a candidate to fill a vacancy on the Supreme Court, interest groups line up to express their views to the Senate Judiciary Committee. For example, pro- and anti-abortion rights groups and women's groups angered by Anita Hill's charges of sexual harassment lobbied vigorously after Clarence Thomas was nominated for the high court in 1991 (see Chapter 12). Second, interest groups can play a role in the judicial process as parties in cases brought before the courts, either as litigants themselves or in **class action suits**. Class action suits allow litigation to be initiated on behalf of a large number of individuals without any formal connection other than their sharing a grievance against another party. Third, interest groups can encourage individuals to bring legal action and provide the financial, legal, and moral support they need to do so. Fourth, interest groups can formally make their views known to the courts even in cases in which they are not themselves parties. This is done by filing an **amicus curiae** ("friend of the court") **brief**, in which a group offers "friendly" advice about how to decide a case.

class action suit

Legal action initiated on behalf of a large number of individuals without any common interest other than their grievance against the person or institution being sued.

amicus curiae brief

Latin for "friend of the court." Persons, government agencies, or groups that are not parties to a case but nonetheless have an interest in its outcome can make their views known by filing an amicus curiae brief with the court.

Major Interest Groups

Americans belong to a myriad of interest groups. As noted, some are members of more than one group. *The Encyclopedia of Associations*, which confines itself to formal organizations, lists over 23,000 different groups. There is even a lobby for lobbyists: the American League of Lobbyists. Taking into account all the uncounted formal groups and the multitude of informal groups, there are tens of thousands more. Interest groups can be categorized by their characteristics, goals, tactics, and degrees of success. Major groups usually fit into economic, social, religious, ideological, or issue categories. Table 7.1 summarizes the major concerns of different types of interest groups and gives examples of each type of group.

Economic Groups   Interest groups frequently form around economic issues. In *Federalist* No. 10, Madison said, "The most common and durable source of factions has been the various and unequal distribution of property." The various ways in which people gain their livelihood lead to great diversity in the array of groups that form.

Business groups are among the most powerful of all interest groups. Perhaps business's most prominent advocate is the Chamber of Commerce of the United States, which pursues efforts to influence government on a broad front. It engages in extensive

TABLE 7.1

Types of Major Interest Groups

The table includes only a few of the thousands of groups that exist. In addition, note that a group may be of more than one type; this occurs when economic groups, for example, make statements about social and ideological questions.

TYPE	CONCERNS	EXAMPLES
ECONOMIC	Business, labor, agriculture, and professions	National Association of Manufacturers; American Federation of State, County, and Municipal Employees; American Bar Association; American Farm Bureau Federation
SOCIAL	Gender, race, and ethnic discrimination; economic advancement	National Organization for Women; National Association for the Advancement of Colored People; Mexican-American Legal Defense and Educational Fund; American Indian Movement
RELIGIOUS	Religious freedom; values reflected in public policy	U.S. Catholic Conference; National Council of Churches; American Jewish Committee; Mennonite Central Committee
IDEOLOGICAL	Political impact of specific public policies	Americans for Democratic Action; People for the American Way; Heritage Foundation; National Committee for an Effective Congress
SINGLE-ISSUE	Narrow agenda; limited political goals	Environmental Defense Fund; National Right-to-Life Committee; National Abortion Rights Action League
PUBLIC INTEREST	Broadly-defined consumer and general welfare goals	Common Cause; Public Citizen; Consumers Union of the United States; Equal Justice Foundation; League of Women Voters

grass-roots lobbying

Attempting to influence members of Congress by encouraging citizens in the home district or state to contact their legislators.

grass-roots lobbying by encouraging its members across the country to contact their elected officials about issues of concern. However, its effectiveness is sometimes diminished, due to the fact that the breadth of its membership makes it difficult for it to take stands that are satisfactory to all its members.

Mother and son hold hands as they march in a walk sponsored by the Washtenaw County chapter of the Million Mom March. *(AP Wide World)*

Business interests combine into other, larger organizations based on their special concerns. Large manufacturing companies, for example, have come together in the National Association of Manufacturers. A vast array of industry-wide trade associations, such as the American Iron and Steel Institute and the American Gas Association, represent more particular interests. At the other end of the spectrum are small businesses—the hundreds of thousands of small manufacturing concerns, neighborhood TV repair shops, and "mom and pop" grocery stores. The National Federation of Independent Business is one of the best-known small–business-oriented groups. Particular professions are represented by important organizations such as the American Medical Association (the leading organization of doctors), the National Association of Realtors, and the American Bar Association. Business groups do not always speak with one voice, however, because political issues sometimes pit one business interest against another. For example, in the late 1990s and early 2000s, many software companies found themselves at odds with industry giant Microsoft when the latter fought against federally-imposed antitrust actions.

When people think of labor as an interest group, they usually think first of its more visible side, labor as organized into unions. Individual unions themselves function as independent interest groups. The International Ladies Garment Workers Union, the Teamsters, and the American Federation of State, County, and Municipal Employees are just a few of the many unions recognized as politically active. The American Federation of Labor-Congress of Industrial Organizations (AFL-CIO) is an umbrella organization of unions with a total membership of approximately 13.2 million that spearheads political activity on behalf of organized labor. Organized labor was once seen as a monolithic mainstay of the Democratic coalition, but in recent years its influence has diminished, primarily because the share of the labor force belonging to unions has dropped considerably in the last 50 years.

Labor has another, less visible but numerically much larger side than the unionized contingent. The majority of American working people do not belong to unions. In fact, workers in the new high-technology industries are much less likely to be unionized than workers in the old smokestack industries they are supplanting. The nonunion workers' lack of organization limits their political influence. Although some of their interests are advanced by their more organized counterparts, their opportunities for political representation are often limited to the actions of their individual members.

Farmers have long been a potent force in American politics. Even today agriculture is a huge industry. Long-standing organized groups include the American Farm Bureau Federation and the National Grange. They lobby furiously as Congress, once every five years, revises the rules governing agricultural subsidies. But dwindling numbers and hard economic times have conspired to reduce the political power of the agricultural interests. In 1930 more than 25 percent of all Americans lived on farms; by the 1990s that number had fallen to less than 2 percent. Such pressures have spawned several more radical and aggressive farm groups, such as the National Farmers Organization (NFO) and the American Agricultural Movement (AAM). The heyday of the farm lobby is over, but agriculture remains a sector that cannot be ignored.

Social Groups Birth, not choice, determines membership in some interest groups. One of these groups, women, composes one of the largest potential interest groups in the United States. Slightly more than half of the American population are women, but relatively few belong to politically relevant women's organizations. The most prominent organization is the National Organization for Women (NOW), which presses for economic and political equality of women and, particularly, freedom of choice on abortion. NOW has only about 500,000 actual members, about one out of every 285 American women. Within such a group, the sense of identification can run strong, although the feminist consciousness does not seem to run strong in the female population as a whole.

The women's movement is closely tied to politics in that many of its goals relate to political issues. Ties have also been strengthened by the increasing number of female candidates running for public office. For many years the legitimacy of female involvement in politics was impugned by the old saying that "a woman's place is in the home," but recently women have increasingly been accepted as worthy participants in the American political process. Perhaps the best indication of change is the growing number of women who have been elected to public office in the past 30 years (see Figure 7.2). The nomination of the first major party female candidate for president or vice-president occurred in 1984, when Geraldine Ferraro was the Democratic candidate for vice-president. After the 2000 elections there were 60 women in the House of Representatives and 13 in the Senate. The percentage of female state legislators increased to 22.4 percent, more than five times what it was in 1969.

The first African-American woman to serve in the U.S. House of Representatives. (*AP Wide World*)

Certainly the most prominent of all biologically based interest groups in recent American history is the African American population. Whereas African Americans constitute only about one-tenth of the American population, they gain considerable influence from two sources: their strong sense of group identification, and the close ties between the group and the world of politics. Shut out from the social and economic establishment, African Americans had little recourse but to pursue advancement through the political system, which in itself has given their cause a special political legitimacy. Further, forceful African American leaders such as Dr. Martin Luther King, Jr., and the Reverend Jesse Jackson have not hesitated to spur African Americans to political action. The National Association for the Advancement of Colored People (NAACP) remains perhaps the most visible African American interest organization. Although only a small percentage of African Americans (less than two percent) belong to it, with a membership of about 400,000 it is the most widely recognized formal African American organization in America.

Although the United States is far from a total resolution of its racial problems, the African American civil rights movement has over the long term met with considerable success. This success is at least partly due to the fact that the movement's goals are not an attack on fundamental values but, rather, a push for broader realization of traditional American social, political, and economic equality. In recent years, a major effort has been aimed at encouraging African-Americans to use their hard-won right to vote and get more African Americans elected to public office. All told, the United States now has more than 8,800 elected African American officials[2] (see Figure 7.2). The number of African Americans in the House of Representatives has risen from 17 in 1981 to 38 in 2001.

Another prominent ethnic group is the Latino segment of the American population—primarily Mexican-Americans, Cuban-Americans, and Puerto Ricans. Although Latinos in the United States currently number about 20 million, they confront a situation similar to what African Americans faced 30 years ago. Like African Americans, Latinos lag in educational level and are only now developing a strong sense of collective political

---

[2]Statistical Abstract of the United States, 1990, pp. 257, 260.

FIGURE 7.2

Female, African American, and Latino National and State Legislators, 1969–1999

The increasing numbers of women, African Americans, and Latinos elected to public offices such as the U.S. Senate and House and state legislatures in the last 30 years demonstrates how the political process has opened up to members of these groups.

SOURCES: Statistical Abstract of the United States, 2000; Center for the American Woman and Politics (CAWP) 2001; *Vital Statistics on American Politics*, 4th ed., 1999–2000.

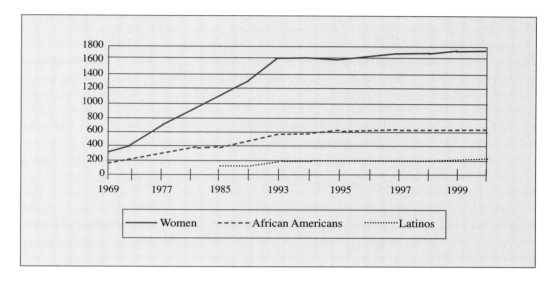

identity. Fewer Latino-Americans are registered to vote (only 35 percent of the 23 million Latinos of voting age), and those who are registered do not always vote (27 percent, compared to the national average of 54 percent in 1996). Those who cast ballots do not necessarily vote for Latino candidates. Latinos lack a cohesive national organization on the order of the NAACP. As a result, there are fewer elected Latino leaders (see Figure 7.2). Outside the Southwest and a few big cities, Latinos are seldom recognized as a significant political bloc. However, the Latino people have considerable political potential. They are concentrated in a number of big states that can be critical to victory in a presidential election. Partly because of this fact, the number of Latinos in the House jumped from 6 to 19 between 1981 and 2001.

Religious Groups   Although the Constitution provides for separation of church and state, the religious freedom the Constitution also guarantees inevitably results in the existence of religious groups that are active on a wide variety of political issues. This involvement has engendered some controversy. The **Christian Right**, as fundamentalist groups are often called, has worked for a constitutional amendment to allow prayer in the public schools, tax credits for private school tuition, and the teaching of creationism

Christian Right

Conservative, religiously-based groups that involve themselves in the political process.

in public schools, and against the teaching of anything but abstinence in sex education and laws favoring the rights of women and homosexuals.

The religious right loomed as a major factor in American politics through the early 1980s, but its visibility receded in the late 1980s after revelations of sexual and financial misconduct by such well-known figures as Jim and Tammy Bakker and Jimmy Swaggart. However, since then conservative Christians have been working quietly but diligently around the country to elect their adherents to state and local offices and have virtually taken over the Republican party organization in several states. Perhaps the most prominent organization spearheading this activity is television evangelist Pat Robertson's Christian Coalition. The Christian Right was credited with playing an important role both in the election of a Republican Congressional majority in 1994 and the election of George W. Bush in 2000. Other more socially liberal denominations such as the United Church of Christ—in effect, an emerging "Christian Left"—have involved themselves in controversies over arms control, human rights abroad, and U.S. policy in central America, among others.

But no issue in recent years has drawn religious groups more into the political fray than abortion. The Catholic church and the Christian Right have both worked hard to make abortion a political issue through support of sympathetic candidates and demonstrations outside abortion clinics. A particularly dramatic example by the Roman Catholic church was its use of the threat of excommunication against Catholics who tolerate or even support abortion.

Ideological Groups   Some groups pursue an explicitly political agenda almost exclusively. When that agenda is broad, the group is characterized as an ideological one. Such groups typically have a clear philosophy of governmental action and evaluate public policy proposals in those terms. Perhaps the best example is the Americans for Democratic Action (ADA), a relatively small group with about 85,000 members that has long espoused a liberal perspective on American politics. It has thus become a beacon to those on the American left and an enemy to those on the right. The ADA is perhaps best known for the ratings of members of the House and the Senate, which it publishes every year as a way of calling attention to individual legislators' fidelity to liberal values.

Single-Issue Groups   In contrast to the broad political agenda of ideological groups, single-issue groups have narrower agendas and more limited political goals. By far the most visible of all the narrow single-issue groups has been the anti-abortion or right-to-life movement. Groups such as the National Right-to-Life Committee have been single-minded in their attempts to ban abortion. These groups regard the issue of abortion as the overriding issue of contemporary politics—a so-called litmus test of whether a candidate should be supported. The uncompromising position of anti-abortion groups has spawned some similarly uncompromising reactions from single-interest abortion rights groups. The most prominent among these groups is the National Abortion and Reproductive Rights Action League, which claims some 250,000 members.

Single-issue groups are a controversial political phenomenon. Advocates contend that there are indeed some overriding moral issues that people should rightly pursue to the exclusion of everything else. Others see single-issue groups as a threat to democracy because they refuse the compromise that helps to make a democratic system work.

Public Interest Groups   With so many interest groups vying for advantage in the political arena, it sometimes seems that everybody's political interests get served but the public's as a whole. Thus, organizations have formed to represent broad-based notions of the public's interest. These groups focus on issues such as product safety and the effectiveness of government regulation of public utilities and industry. Perhaps the most prominent such group is Common Cause, the self-styled "citizens' lobby" founded in 1970. It has taken on a broad range of issues, including that of campaign financing.

Perspectives on Interest Groups

Given the visibility and the pervasiveness of interest groups in American democracy, it is not surprising that they evoke strong reactions from both the general public and political experts. Some citizens view interest groups in highly positive terms, seeing them as essential elements of a successful democracy. Others take a dimmer view, finding them to be perpetual and inevitable dangers to the common good.

Interest Groups as the Foundation of Democracy

Classical democratic theory demands that citizens be interested in politics, informed about politics, rational in their political judgments, and active in the political process. As Chapter 5 made clear, many people fall short of these expectations. The question is how American democracy can continue to function and even prosper in the face of this disparity.

Some observers see interest groups as the answer. As noted earlier, the United States is a pluralist society. Most Americans belong to at least one formal group as well as to a number of other groups. The leaders of these various interest groups act on behalf of their members to protect and advance their causes. Because there are so many groups, sheer force of competition prevents any single group or handful of groups from dominating the others. Thus, every member of society has his or her interests protected without having to be politically active. Democracy functions through representation—not just formal representation via elected officials, but representation of individual citizens by the leaders of the interest groups.

Further, because most Americans belong to several groups, political disputes seldom run along the same lines. To illustrate, one woman may be a white Catholic homemaker, whereas her neighbor is a white Protestant public school teacher. The two will probably agree about property taxes and the Equal Rights Amendment but disagree about tuition tax credits for parents with children in private schools. Political scientists call this tendency for different coalitions to form on different issues **cross-cutting cleavage**, and see it as a brake on polarizing conflict in society. These two elements, competition between interest groups and cross-cutting cleavages, contribute to an equitable and stable society. Indeed, some scholars laud the pluralistic character of American society as an essential factor in the success of its democratic system.[3]

Not surprisingly, critics have found flaws in this flattering portrait of American politics. Not every citizen belongs in any meaningful way to a significant interest group, and group leaders do not necessarily represent the best interests of all the group members. In fact, the structure of some interest groups may be very undemocratic. Also, pure competition cannot exist among all the interest groups in a society. Some groups are big and powerful and can dominate; others are small and weak and can be dominated. With what, after all, does a small and powerless interest group have to bargain? It is very hard for a group to enter into negotiations with nothing and emerge with something. Thus, "pluralist democracy" may in reality turn out to be **interest group elitism**. The elites within interest groups pursue their own interests rather than their members' interests, and the elite interest groups—the biggest and most powerful groups—pursue their interests at the expense of the small and powerless groups.

Interest Groups Versus the Public Interest

Interest groups are most widely reviled when they are seen as using the political process to achieve selfish objectives. A manufacturing group that resists regulation by the Consumer Product Safety Commission may claim that it is only defending the public's right to buy whatever it wants at the lowest possible price. The public may perceive the group instead as demanding the right to make money by producing shoddy and unsafe goods. This kind of spectacle is no doubt one of the greatest frustrations of democratic government, and has caused many people to favor tighter regulation of lobbying and other interest group activities. But what is the "common good"? Who gets to define it? Should the common good never be impaired in the slightest, even to do a great good for a small number? Does a common good exist, in fact, apart from the outcome of the democratic process that defines it?

Interest group obstructionism of the majority may seem indefensible until it is our own interests that the majority is about to trample on. A person might protest loudly when import quotas on automobiles make imported cars more expensive and push up prices of domestic models. Yet that same person would probably think differently if he or she worked in a Detroit auto assembly plant or owned a Ford dealership. The real quarrel of

---

cross-cutting cleavage

The overlapping of interest group memberships from individual to individual. The result is that the society rarely finds the same people lined up on opposite sides on all the issues, and is thus protected against political polarization.

interest group elitism

The idea that the leaders of interest groups may act in ways that promote their own interests rather than the interests of the broader membership of the group.

---

[3]The leading advocate of this point of view is Robert A. Dahl. See, for example, his classic book *Who Governs?* (New Haven, CT: Yale University Press, 1961).

those who decry interest group activities may not be with interest groups themselves, but with the political processes that strike the balance between majority and minority interests.

Interest Group Gridlock

Pluralist theory envisions a myriad of interests doing battle in the political arena and the government emerging with policies that, although probably not ideal for any, are acceptable to all. But what if no consensus can be reached? Critics charge that a pluralistic system can arrive at a virtual state of paralysis, in which an overabundance of interest groups develops, each refusing to compromise. One commentator has called this situation interest group gridlock, analogous to the traffic gridlock that often develops in large cities.[4] In an analogy to the clogged arteries that threaten many people's health, another commentator has characterized these stalemates as "demosclerosis"—a state in which the political process is so clogged by the piling up of numerous permanent commitments to interest groups that the government lacks the resources to deal with new problems that arise.[5] Interest group gridlock and demosclerosis may be stark warnings of the dangers of pluralism run amok. The hope of democracy is that good "traffic regulation" by public officials and a more moderate diet for interest groups can help to smooth the way for the successful development of public policy.

Political Parties

political party

Group that seeks to influence public policy by placing its own members in positions of governmental authority.

A **political party** is an organization that seeks to influence public policy by putting its own members into positions of governmental authority. In the United States and other democratic nations, in which most important public officials are chosen by popular election, this means placing a party member's name on the ballot, identifying the candidate as a member of that party, and then working to elect the party member to the office. Parties and interest groups are alike in that their members may share common political views or objectives and may engage in collective political activities. They differ in that interest groups do not run their own candidates for public office. Further, there are many interest groups, each with narrower agendas, but there are just two major parties, each with a broader agenda.

What Parties Do

socialization functions

With reference to political parties, the ways in which parties, by seeking to win elections, help to socialize voters into politics and form public opinion.

In the pursuit of elective office, parties can perform several important functions that help to bring order to the electoral process and coherence to government. First, by making themselves visible actors on the stage of politics and trying to gain public support, parties accomplish several important **socialization functions**. Because people tend to

---

[4]Robert J. Samuelson, "Interest Group Gridlock," *National Journal* (September 25, 1982): 1642.
[5]Jonathan Rauch, "Demosclerosis," *National Journal* (September 5, 1992): 1998–2003.

identify with political parties, parties provide a psychological hook that pulls people into the world of politics. Parties also help to structure people's perceptions of politics. They provide important cues to citizens as they perceive and try to make sense of the political world around them. Parties educate citizens about politics and mobilize them into political action. In their attempts to attract voters to their causes, parties tell voters about what is going on in politics, how it affects them, and why they should get involved. Finally, whereas candidates and issues come and go from one election to the next, parties tend to persist. By providing relatively fixed reference points in a changing political scene, parties help people keep their political bearings and thus help to maintain political and social stability.

Winning elective office requires getting votes. Given the wide range of voters' interests, a single issue will probably not appeal to enough voters to win. The party, therefore, must put together a package of positions on a variety of issues that will attract sufficient numbers of voters. In doing so, parties accomplish four important **electoral functions**. The first is to integrate interests. It is unlikely that any one candidate will offer everything that every voter seeks; however, candidates who satisfy needs common to large numbers of voters will receive their support. Second, the set of alternatives voters can pick from is simplified. Because substantial numbers of voters find their views reflected by one or the other of the coalition candidates, fewer candidates are needed on the ballot. Third, the parties complement the legally established process for choosing public officials. By setting up procedures for determining who will represent a party in a campaign and for supporting these candidates in the election, parties fill important gaps in the selection process. Finally, parties are a prime means of recruiting and training political leaders. Parties provide many people with an entry into politics and opportunities to develop their political skills.

Once a political party achieves electoral victory, it confronts the task of governing. By trying to achieve what they have proposed during the campaign, parties accomplish two important **governmental functions**. First, they organize government and give coherence to governmental policy. Because the founders saw centralized political power as a threat to individual freedom, the Constitution dispersed power to avoid the tyranny of the majority. Power was broken up by function in the separation of powers and by geography in the federal system. Experience soon showed, however, that this fragmentation of power led to a lack of coordination, stagnation, and even paralysis in government. Political parties evolved as a new source of coordination in the political system. With like-minded individuals pursuing common objectives dispersed throughout the executive, legislative, and judicial branches of both the national and state governments, coherence and coordination were restored to policymaking.[6]

electoral functions

With reference to political parties, the ways in which parties, by seeking to win elections, help to bring order to campaigns and elections.

governmental functions

With reference to political parties, the ways in which parties, by seeking to win elections, help to organize the government, give coherence to public policy, and make government responsible to the people.

---

[6]V. O. Key, *Politics, Parties, and Pressure Groups*, 5th ed. (New York: Crowell, 1964), p. 656.

Second, parties help make government responsible to the people. Because parties are stable features on the American political scene, the electorate can reward a party that does a good job of governing and punish a party that does not. Thus, even though the public is not in a position to supervise every detail of governmental action, parties allow the public to exert some degree of oversight and control over what the government does.

Basic Characteristics of the American Party System

Political parties exist under almost every form of government. However, the particular shape a party system assumes varies from one country to another. In the United States, the party system is characterized by having just two major parties, and a loose relationship between the national, state, and local parties and the three components that make up the party: the formal party organization, the party in the electorate, and the party in the government.

A Two-Party System

plurality election

Election in which a candidate wins simply by getting more votes than any other candidate, even if it is less than a majority of the votes.

majority election

Election in which a candidate wins by getting more than one-half of the votes cast.

runoff election

An election pitting the leading candidates of a previous election against each other when the previous election has not produced a clear-cut winner.

From its beginnings, the United States has had a two-party system. Never have there been more than two large and enduring political organizations at the same time. Party fortunes, of course, have ebbed and flowed. At some times, minor parties have flourished. At other times, some people have feared that one party would rule the nation unchallenged. But always the minor parties have always faded, the party with the overwhelming majority has faltered, or the opposition party has rebounded.

Why does this pattern consistently recur? One theory is based on the old saying that "there are two political parties because there are two sides to every question." This explanation sounds good, but many political questions have more than two sides. Also, unless there are fewer sides to political questions in the United States than in other countries, every country should have a two-party system, and many of them do not.

Another old adage may come closer to the truth: "There are two political parties because there are two sides to every office—inside and outside." In the American system, where most offices are contested on an individual basis (i.e., one person wins a single office such as mayor or governor or congressional representative), winning usually requires simply getting more votes than anybody else. This is called **plurality election**. Plurality elections contrast with **majority elections**, in which the victor must receive more than half of all the votes. A **runoff election** is required under a system of majority elections if more than two candidates run and none gets a majority. With plurality or majority elections, most electoral contests in the United States have a single winner and

Politics and Economics
Economic Status and Party Identification

Traditional wisdom portrays the Democrats as the party of the economically less well-off and the Republicans as the party of the more economically successful. How well does this image square with current reality? Figure 7A shows the relationship between party identification and family income in 1998. Interestingly, about ten percent of Americans at every income level identify themselves as purely Independent—not leaning toward the Democrats *or* the Republicans. Apart from this fact, the trends anticipated by the traditional image of the parties do appear. Far more of the poorest people are Democrats than Republicans, and considerably more of the wealthiest people are Republicans than Democrats. However, a significant number of the poorest people are Republicans, and an even larger

number of the wealthiest people are Democrat. Thus, economic status has some effect, but party choice in the United States is not made on the basis of economic self-interest alone.

Why is the Democratic party traditionally associated with the less well-off and the Republican party with the better-off? Why does party affiliation not divide more clearly along economic lines—that is, why are some poorer people Republicans and some richer people Democrats?

SOURCE: American National Education Studies, 1998.

FIGURE 7A
Party Identification by Income, 1998

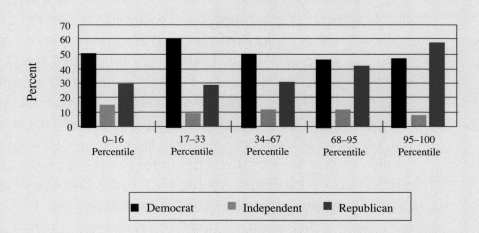

one or more losers—one "in" and one or more "outs." Because the only way for an outsider to displace an insider is to win more votes, the natural tendency is for political organizations to form around those in power and those out of power.

An alternative electoral system is **proportional representation**, whereby offices such as seats in a legislature are awarded in proportion to the percentage of votes a party receives. Proportional representation may encourage the growth of more than two parties because a party may place third or fourth in an election and still win seats. Proportional representation is relatively rare in the United States, but it is more common in other countries, such as France and Italy.

The plurality election system is not the only reason the United States has a two-party system. Undoubtedly other factors enter in as well, including the predominantly centrist distribution of opinion, the impact of history, and the absence of consistently intense ethnic and religious divisions that might lead to chronic political fragmentation. However, the electoral system has certainly played a significant role in shaping the basic structure of the American party system.

This discussion of the two-party system should not obscure the fact that **third parties** do have a place in the American political system. As shown in Figure 7.3, third parties have existed for a long time. Although most third parties have been little more than temporary vehicles for a particular candidate or issue, they nevertheless have played an important role in influencing the actions of the major parties. They have raised issues that the major parties were eventually forced to address. For example, the abolitionist parties of the mid-nineteenth century forced slavery onto the agendas of the major political parties. Persistent advocacy of egalitarian ideas such as female suffrage; government regulation of big business; Social Security; and low-cost health care by the Populists, Progressives, and Socialists laid the groundwork for much of the New Freedom of Woodrow Wilson, the New Deal of Franklin Roosevelt, and the Great Society of Lyndon Johnson.

In a few cases, the presence of third parties in the field has tipped the balance from one of the major parties to the other. In 1912, in the middle of a long period of Republican dominance, former President Theodore Roosevelt's Bull Moose party garnered 27 percent of the popular vote and 88 electoral votes, siphoning off enough votes from the Republican incumbent William Howard Taft to give the Democrat Woodrow Wilson the victory. (This was, by the way, the only time in American history that a third party actually outpolled one of the major parties in a presidential election.) In 1968 American Independent candidate George Wallace won 14 percent of the popular vote and 46 electoral votes, probably drawing off enough votes from Democrat Hubert Humphrey to give Republican Richard Nixon the victory.

In 1992, independent presidential candidate Ross Perot, running under the banner of his United We Stand movement, garnered 19 percent of the popular vote, making his the most successful third-party movement in recent American history. Because Perot

---

proportional representation

A system for allocating seats in a legislative body in which the number of seats a party gets of the total is based on the percentage of votes that the party receives in an election.

third party

In the American political context, a minor party attracting only a small share of the electorate's vote—a party other than the two major parties that have dominated politics through most of American history.

FIGURE 7.3

American Political Parties Since 1789

The chart indicates the years parties either ran presidential candidates or held national conventions. The life span for many political parties can only be approximated because parties existed at the state or local level before they ran candidates in presidential elections, and continued to exist at local levels after they ceased running presidential candidates. For example, in the year 2000, 16 parties running a candidate for president in at least one state, but only seven candidates were on the ballot in all or nearly all of the states: George W. Bush (Republican), Al Gore (Democrat), Ralph Nader (Green), Pat Buchanan (Reform), Harry Browne (Libertarian), John Hagelin (Natural Law), and Howard Phillips (Constitution).

SOURCES: *Congressional Quarterly's Guide to the U.S. Elections,* 2d ed. (Washington, DC: Congressional Quarter y, 1985), p. 224; *Congressional Quarterly Weekly Report,* November 5, 1988, p. 3184; Federal Election Commission, "1992 Official Presidential General Election Results," Press Release of January 14, 1993; Federal Election Commission Web site http://www.fec.gov/.

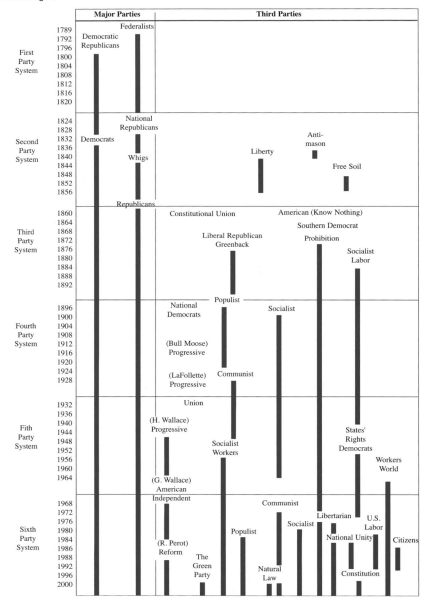

seemed to draw votes almost equally from Bush and Clinton, it is unlikely that he changed the outcome of the election. However, Perot participated in the three presidential debates and was instrumental in making deficit reduction and economic revival major issues in the campaign. Perot ran again in 1996, but only managed to gain about half of the total vote he had earned in 1992. In 2000, Pat Buchanan ran on the Reform Party ticket and Ralph Nader ran as a Green Party candidate. The two combined to garner over 3.3 million votes in a very tight election. Since Nader, who generated about 2.9 million of those votes, was a decidedly liberal candidate, some have suggested that he cost Gore the election.

Consumer Advocate Ralph Nader speaks at a news conference in Washington. *(AP Wide World)*

Such conclusions, however, overlook the fact that many Nader voters were disenchanted with the two-party system and might not have voted at all if Bush and Gore were the only choices available.

A Complex Party Structure

An American political party is not a single organization, but a broad family of related formal organizations and informal groupings. It is complex, not in the sense that it is particularly hard to understand, but in that it is made up of many different parts. Perhaps the most useful way to think about all these parts and the relationships between them is to imagine the party as being divided along two dimensions: a vertical dimension corresponding to the levels of government in the United States, and a horizontal dimension corresponding to the different components that make up a party.

Parties and the Levels of Government: National, State, and Local Because party organizations tend to grow up and operate around institutions of government, it is only natural that their structure tends to parallel that of government. One of the most important divisions of government in the United States is the federal system. Just as the American government is divided into national, state, and local institutions, so also are parties divided into national, state, and local organizations and groupings. As in the government, the relationship among the levels is not a strictly hierarchical one; each level retains some level of independence and autonomy from the others.

http://rnc.org /gopinfo/platform Republican platform

http://democrats .org/issues /platform /platform.html Democratic platform

Both major political parties draft statements of beliefs, called platforms, every presidential election year. You can find the most recent democrat and republican platforms at the above Web sites.

formal party organization

The official structure of a political party, including people who officially belong to it, its elected and appointed officers, and committees. One of the three components or sectors of a political party.

national convention

The quadrennial meeting of an American political party that focuses on the upcoming presidential election.

platform

A broad statement of the philosophy and program under which a party's candidates run for election.

national committee

The body responsible for guiding political party organization on an ongoing basis.

political machine

Political organization that recruits and controls its membership through the use of its governmental authority to give benefits (jobs, contracts, etc.) to its supporters and deny them to its opponents.

state committee

The body responsible for guiding a state political party organization on an ongoing basis.

Parties and Their Components: Formal, Electoral, and Governmental   Even at any one level of government, a political party is not just a single organization. Rather, it has at least three distinguishable sectors or components: the formal party organization, the party in the electorate, and the party in the government.[7] The **formal party organization** is the party narrowly construed, and what most people would think of if asked to define political party. It consists of the people who actually work for the party as leaders or followers, professionals or volunteers, and members of committees or attenders of meetings.

The formal structure of American parties parallels the structure of federalism. Power is vested at both the national and state levels. Ultimate authority lies with the party's **national convention**, which meets prior to the presidential election every four years. Because political parties exist to contest elections, most of what the convention does is related to the upcoming presidential campaign: writing a **platform** (a statement of the party's proposed program) and selecting the party's candidates for president and vice-president. These activities are discussed in more detail in Chapter 8.

Some of the convention's activities have a more strictly organizational slant. The convention is the ultimate authority in setting the party's rules, and it formally designates the **national committee**, the permanent body that oversees the party's affairs on an ongoing basis. Each state's members on the national committee are usually picked by state party organizations in conventions or primaries; The national committee in turn formally elects the party chairperson. The national chairperson supervises the work of the headquarters staff, a role that has become more significant in recent years, for reasons to be seen shortly.

State and local parties for years were the bedrock of the American party system, often due to the influence of state and local "political machines." A **political machine** is a political organization that recruits and controls its membership through the use of its governmental authority to bestow benefits on its supporters and withhold them from its opponents. This patronage includes benefits such as government jobs, government contracts, and "favors." To gain benefits, people had to support the machine by voting for its candidates and campaigning for the machine. The great urban political machines, in large part, have faded from the American political scene, although the use of public power to perpetuate partisan dominance lives on in many municipalities and some states.

The structure of the state and local parties is in many respects similar to that of the national parties, with state party conventions and **state committees**, usually made up of representatives from the state's counties or congressional districts. The party typically elects a state chairperson, who is in charge of the day-to-day operations of the party.

---

[7]This distinction is another legacy of V. O. Key, Jr., originated in his *Politics, Parties, and Pressure Groups,* 5th ed. (New York: Crowell, 1964). It has now been widely adopted by students of the American party system. See, for example, Frank J. Sorauf and Paul Allen Beck, *Party Politics in America,* 6th ed. (Glenview, IL: Scott, Foresman, 1988).

Underlying the statewide party organization is a hierarchy of county, city, ward (or district), and precinct committees and chairpersons. In some locales this organization constitutes a formidable political force, while elsewhere the structure is moribund, with many of the positions not even filled.

There is more to a party than just its formal organization. A party includes, not in any formal sense, but psychologically and socially, the citizens out in the electorate who support it. This party in the electorate can be looked at in two different ways. At the individual level, the defining component of the connection of an individual to a party is party identification, "a psychological identification" or "sense of individual attachment to a party," independent of "legal recognition or even without a consistent [voting] record of party support."[8] Appropriate to the definition, party identification has typically been measured simply by asking people whether they think of themselves as Republicans, Democrats, Independents, etc., and following up with questions about strength of feeling. Thus, the party in the electorate is really defined by people who claim to think of themselves as belonging to the party. Figure 7.4 shows how the distribution of party identification has varied over the last 50 years.

Individuals who identify with a party relate to it not just as individuals, but also as members of the various groups to which they belong. Parties, in other words, can be seen as coalitions of the various social, economic, regional, and religious groups. The Democratic party has traditionally been seen as the party of the working class, the rural and southern constituents, and Catholics, whereas the Republican party has been seen as the party of the middle and upper classes, big businesses, and Protestants. Thus, the party in the electorate also includes also these groups that are thought of as belonging to the party's **coalition**.

Finally, there is the **party in the government**. Once a party's candidates are elected, the elected officials (at least in theory) need to organize themselves and work together to implement the policies on the basis of which they campaigned. Thus, the party in government consists of the elected candidates of a party—presidents, governors, mayors, senators, members of the House, state legislators, city council members—as well as the organizations these officials establish and the leaders that they designate to help them carry out their work. The most visible of these are the legislative party meetings (caucuses, as the Democrats call them, and conferences, as the Republicans call them), the congressional campaign committees, and the majority and minority leaders and whips. But the party in government also includes the less visible and informal "executive party" created by presidents and governors who tend to appoint members of their own party to administrative positions, and even the shadowy "judicial party" suggested by patterns of party-oriented bloc voting in some courts.[9]

coalition

A subgroup of a party, based on common social, economic, and religious characteristics.

party in the government

One of the three components or sectors of a political party, the party as embodied in those of its members who have been elected or appointed to public office, the organizations they establish, and the leaders they choose to help them carry out their work.

---

[8]Campbell, et al., *The American Voter,* pp. 121–122.
[9]Sorauf and Beck, pp. 396–446.

FIGURE 7.4

Party Identification of the American Electorate, 1952–1998

The Democratic party held a substantial edge in party identification from the 1950s into the 1970s, but this was eroded by Republican resurgence beginning in the 1980s.

SOURCE: American National Election Studies, 1998, Center for Political Studies, University of Michigan.

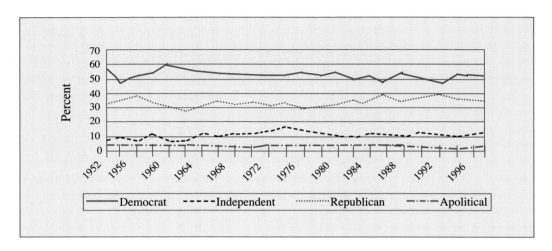

American Political Parties: Past, Present, and Future

The health of the American party system has been one of the most talked-about political subjects over the last 25 years. To understand the current state of the American party system and what its future may be, it is necessary to understand a little about the history of the American party system.

Parties Past

party system

Period during which the pattern of support for political parties based on a particular set of important political issues remains reasonable stable.

Political parties emerged early in the history of the American republic and have existed ever since. American history up through 1968 can be divided into five major **party systems**[10] (see Figure 7.3 on p. 216). The first party system (1789–1824), which developed from the pre-revolutionary alignment of parties paralleling the British system of the period (conservative Tories and progressive Whigs), pitted Federalists against Antifederalists. The two parties disagreed primarily on whether the new government should be relatively centralized and elite (the Federalist view) or decentralized and democratic (the Antifederalist view). The Federalist party faded away after 1800, but the Democratic Republicans, as the Anti-Federalists came to be called, continued on to gov-

---

[10]Walter Dean Burnham, "Party Systems and the Political Process," in *The American Party Systems,* eds. William Nisbet Chambers and Walter Dean Burnham (New York: Oxford University Press, 1967), p. 289.

ern through a period of comparatively little national political conflict between 1815 and 1825, called the Era of Good Feelings.

By the mid-1820s the weak framework of the Democratic Republican party began to fall apart. Andrew Jackson emerged from this factional conflict as the founder of the Democratic party, which continues as an active party today, making it the oldest party in the world. The Democrats confronted a new Whig party in the second party system (1824–1860). The Democrats were the party of lower-class rural and urban "working people" and old-fashioned machine politics, whereas the Whigs were the party of business and political reform. Slavery destroyed the Whig-Democratic party alignment; through the 1850s both parties split into northern and southern branches over the issue that would soon tear apart the nation as well.

Beginning in 1860, under the third party system (1860–1896), former Whigs, led by Abraham Lincoln of Illinois, combined with some progressive remnants of the northern Democrats to form the new Republican party, built on opposition to slavery, but also on the idea of government as a promoter of commerce. The Democratic party receded into the Confederacy during the Civil War. After the war and the restoration of the union, the Democrats reemerged on the national scene to compete vigorously with the Republicans for the favor of business. The pro-business tilt of the third party system fostered progressive and populist sentiment for more regulation of big business and protection of common people's interests.

These sentiments, fired by a series of disastrous recessions and depressions, came to a head in the election of 1896, when the populist Democrat William Jennings Bryan challenged the candidate of the business establishment, Republican William McKinley. The failure of the populist challenge marked the beginning of the fourth party system (1896–1932), throughout which the Republicans dominated the national political scene and allowed the capitalist system free reign. Only when former Republican president Teddy Roosevelt's progressive Bull Moose party split Republican ranks were the Democrats able to put their candidate, Woodrow Wilson, into the White House from 1912 to 1920.

The onset of the Great Depression in 1929, in part the result of the lack of restraint placed on the free enterprise system, drove Republican president Herbert Hoover from office. Franklin Delano Roosevelt swept into the White House in 1932 on a flood tide of national discontent and despair. In a bold effort to use the power of the federal government to end the depression and restore economic prosperity, he ushered in a new era of governmental involvement in economic affairs and government responsibility for ensuring the people's basic well-being. He also initiated a period of Democratic dominance that constituted the fifth party system (1932–1968).

In each of these years—1824, 1860, 1896, 1932—a new party system evolved from an old one in a relatively short period of turmoil and change called "realignment."

realignment

A major change in the pattern of support for political parties and the important issues on which that pattern of support is based.

dealignment

Period during which the partisan ties of the public diminish and the party system breaks down.

Realignment occurs when a reasonably stable pattern of party support based on a particular set of important political issues is replaced by a new pattern of party support based on a new set of issues. Because realignments are such landmark events in the American party system, scholars have devoted much effort to determining when and why they occur. They have identified a number of significant changes that seem to accompany realignment, most notable of which is a period before each realignment in which the old party structure seems to fall apart, or **dealign**. Why do realignments occur? As the preceding discussion suggests, the single most important factor may be the emergence of some new issue that cuts across the existing party lines and divides the electorate in some new way—for example, slavery in the third party system and the Great Depression and the role of the federal government in the economy in the fifth party system. Also, quite clearly, realignments have tended to come at approximately 36 year intervals.

Parties Present

Beginning in the mid-1960s, the fifth party system began to falter. This was most evident in the woes of the Democratic party, whose long-standing dominance began to unravel. Consistent with the pattern of a major partisan shift every 36 years, the Democratic party, which had won the White House in every election over the 36 years from 1932 to 1968 except 1952 and 1956—seven of nine elections—lost the 1968 election, and over the next 20 years would win only one of five more. The only bright spot for the Democrats was that they did mostly manage to hold on to their majorities in the House and Senate throughout the period, the one exception being the Republican's majority in the Senate from 1981 to 1987, primarily as a result of the Reagan victory in 1980.

That exception alone was sufficient to set political analysts abuzz. Dealignment was clearly underway. But while some saw realignment into a new Republican majority as in the offing, others worried that the party system was confronting an even more fundamental crisis—the possibility of complete collapse.

Certainly, beginning in the 1960s, both parties were beset by signs of deterioration. At the national level, the national party headquarters, the national chairperson, and the national committee seemed increasingly irrelevant to the course of American politics and, specifically, political campaigns. Their principal function seemed to be to organize the national party convention once every four years. The title of a study published in 1964 seemed to sum up their plight: *Politics Without Power: The National Party Committees?*[11]

The party in the electorate, the mass base of the political parties, also showed signs of weakening. Through the early 1960s more than 75 percent of the American people said that they identified strongly or weakly with one or the other of the parties and less than 25

---

[11]Cornelius P. Cotter and Bernard C. Hennessy (New York: Atherton, 1964).

percent described themselves as independents. But beginning about 1964 attachments to parties started to weaken substantially. By the late 1970s only about 60 percent said that they identified with a party, and more than a third said they were independents. Not only were people were less likely to identify with the parties, voters were also less likely to see the parties in favorable terms and to vote according to their party identification.

Trouble loomed as well for the other aspect of the party in the electorate, the party coalitions. The coalitions that had supported the major parties, particularly the Democratic coalition, seemed to be coming apart. At its peak in the Johnson landslide, the Democratic party had expanded to encompass not just the Roosevelt New Deal coalition of the working class, unions, the poor, urban residents, citizens of the South, Catholics, Jews, and liberals, but also African Americans. The Republican party was left as the party of the upper class, big business, and people residing in the suburbs. But clearly through the 1970s and peaking in 1980, the Democratic coalition fell into disarray, as working class people, Catholics and some Jews, and white Southerners were drawn away in the Reagan landslide, leaving the Democratic party looking more and more like the party of liberals and African Americans—two groups too small for the party to have much of a future as a winning coalition.

The parties in government also suffered their own difficulties through the 1970s and 1980s as party discipline and coordination seemed to deteriorate. Party discipline seemed to sag in the Congress, as members less dependent on the party for help in getting reelected increasingly broke party ranks when local needs or special interest groups dictated.[12] Party coordination between the executive and the legislature suffered as presidents and members of their own party in Congress were often at odds on legislation.

decline

The idea that the American political parties are collapsing and may, perhaps, eventually disappear.

What caused the parties to go into **decline**? A number of governmental, electoral, and socialization changes seem to have contributed to the deteriorating condition of American political parties since the mid-1960s. As noted earlier, patronage was one of the traditional reservoirs of party strength. It provided party leaders with bargaining chips to use in the game of politics. But reformers intent on reducing the power of the bosses and increasing the competence and integrity of public employees pushed for the establishment of a system of civil service. As more public jobs fell under civil service, politicians found themselves with fewer "goodies" to give out and thus were less able to marshal political support.

Another governmental change that hurt the parties was the rise of the public welfare system. The parties of earlier years built support by serving as a kind of informal welfare system for their supporters. A faithful party member in financial trouble could seek help in the form of money, food, or shelter from the neighborhood party

---

[12]William J. Keefe, *Parties, Politics, and Public Policy in America* (Hinsdale, MN: Dryden Press, 1976), pp. 139–140; Barbara Sinclair Deckard, "Political Upheaval and Congressional Voting: The Effects of the 1960s on Voting Patterns in the House of Representatives," *Journal of Politics* 38 (1976): 326–345.

**http://www.pirg
.org/**

What issues affect
the public in your
state? The Public
Interest Research
Groups' Web site is a
good starting point
for answering this
question.

caucus

A meeting of mem-
bers of a political
party. The members
of a party in a legisla-
ture are also referred
to as a party caucus.
Parties in some
states use caucuses
to select delegates to
the national conven-
tions, which nominate
presidential candi-
dates.

organization. People came to owe the party. With the rise of the modern welfare system, the government itself formally began to ensure a minimal level of well-being among cit- izens. Consequently, the party lost its exclusive role as a source of help and its ability to put people in its debt.

Electoral changes played an important part in hurting the parties, as well. In ear- lier years political parties were an essential part of the electoral apparatus of the United States. To get a message to the electorate, a candidate needed an army of workers to fan out over the constituency, buttonholing passersby, knocking on doors, handing out party literature, and twisting arms. Modern technology provides less labor-intensive alterna- tives. Nowadays, with a string of appearances on television news programs and in cam- paign advertisements, a candidate can make more frequent and seemingly more "personal" contact with far more voters than could an army of party workers on the streets. Computerized direct mailing techniques can yield large sums of money, which can be used to buy more television time and send out more mail, which can generate more money, and so on. Simply put, candidates no longer need to rely as much on par- ties and party workers to serve as their intermediaries with the public.

Parties have also traditionally been important sources of campaign funds for their candidates. Today, however, members of Congress benefit from the support of the PACs, and presidential candidates can rely on public financing. Access to these new sources of money has made candidates less dependent on parties for help and, conse- quently, has contributed to the weakening of the parties. Also, in an earlier era parties tightly controlled the process by which candidates for public office were selected. Party leaders got together in party **caucuses** (meetings) or conventions to pick the party's can- didates. However, political reformers fought to open up the nomination process to repre- sent a broader cross section of the population, leading to selection of convention delegates by open conventions or primary elections.

Parties long existed as standing armies of campaign workers, ready to step into political battle on behalf of the party candidates. Now more and more candidates are relying not on the party machinery but on their own personal organizations for cam- paign assistance. Although candidates obviously want to capitalize on their party's name, many run without the aid of the party machinery. Once in office, they are likely to feel little obligation to help the party. Single-issue groups also pose a challenge to the existing party system by threatening to siphon off precious campaign resources and public support. The anti-abortion movement is perhaps the most prominent recent example.

Finally, most people acquire their sense of party identification through social- ization by their parents. But the process of transmission has appeared to break down in recent years. Between the 1950s and the 1970s the percentage of young people adopting the same party as their parents dropped by about 15 percent. Expansion of the Vietnam

War tarnished both parties, the Republican party was scarred by the Watergate scandal, and the Democratic party suffered from the economically difficult Carter years. Party disenchantment in one generation sows party disenchantment in the next. Thus, it is not hard to understand why the ranks of the party faithful dwindled and the ranks of the independents swelled.

Many of these changes were viewed with concern; analysts were not clear as to whether what was occurring was dealignment leading toward realignment, or dealignment leading toward collapse. The deeper concern was that the functioning of our democratic system might be impaired by the weakening or disappearance of political parties. Think of all the valuable functions parties perform and then think about what might happen if the parties were not around to perform them.

Just as the idea that the parties were dead or dying began to gain widespread currency, a new group of commentators rose to argue that the parties were making a comeback. Led by Xandra Kayden and Eddie Mahe, Jr.'s *The Party Goes On: The Persistence of the Two-Party System in the United States*,[13] a number of new studies found evidence of the parties in **resurgence**. The major center of revitalization in the formal party organizations has been in the national party organizations, particularly the national party headquarters supervised by the national chairperson and operated on a day-to-day basis by an increasingly professional, sophisticated, and well-paid staff. These staff employ modern computerized systems to gather and analyze polling results, conduct direct mail campaigns, and raise money.

Although the American public has not flooded back to embrace the political parties, the trend against them has at least been arrested and perhaps slightly reversed. There is also some evidence that the party coalitions are reforming along somewhat different lines. The Democratic party has suffered from the loss of the white South and some working-class Catholic and union support, but it has gained a new constituency in female voters. The Republican party has gained substantially among working-class whites and in the South.

There is little concrete evidence that party discipline within the legislature or coordination between the president and his party in the legislature has improved. Indeed the budget crisis of 1990 suggested that such coordination has not occurred, as evidenced by both the majority of congress members who broke with their leaders and the Republicans with their president, in order to defeat the budget deal worked out between the congressional leadership and the White House.

The primary reason for party resurgence is that the parties, instead of standing on the sidelines and allowing themselves to be kept out of the game, have at last recognized the changing environment of the American political system and adjusted their activities

resurgence

The idea that American political parties, following a period of decline from the 1960s to the early 1980s, are now making a comeback, gaining in organizational, electoral, and governmental strength.

---

[13]New York: Basic Books, 1985.

accordingly. For example, they have recognized that modern political campaigns depend less on armies of party volunteers tramping from door to door and more on money and the media. Thus, they have moved to become a major source of political money, in effect not fighting the PACs but joining them. They have seen how candidates must rely on a modern media campaign and have moved to provide candidates with the training and production services that they need to conduct such campaigns. They know that candidates want to use polling results and direct mail, so they share polling results and direct mail strategies and technologies.

Parties Future

Realignment, dealignment, resurgence—it is hard enough to say where the American party system is now, much less where it is going. The Democrats' victory in the 1992 presidential election did not make the task any easier. Certainly some sort of realignment took place in the transition from the fifth party system's clear Democratic dominance, to what seemed to be a sixth party system starting in 1968 of divided government, Republican domination of the presidency, and Democratic domination of Congress. Was 1992 a return to Democratic dominance? Events since 1992 suggest that, despite Clinton's victory in 1992, we are still very much in the era of divided government. United Democratic governance lasted only until the 1994 midterm elections, when the Republican party won majorities in both the House and Senate. Clinton won reelection in 1996, and his last six years in office were a continuation of the dealignment era's divided government pattern, although this time with a Democratic president and Republican Congress. At first, the 2000 election looked to be another opportunity for realignment, as the Republicans gained unified control of the government for the first time since the Eisenhower administration. But George W. Bush's opportunity to lead a united Congress was even shorter-lived than Clinton's had been. After the election, the Senate stood evenly divided, with 50 Democrats and 50 Republicans. The Republicans maintained a procedural majority since Vice President Dick Cheney, in his role as President of the Senate, could break any tie votes. In May 2001, however, Jim Jeffords, a third-term senator from Vermont, left the Republican party. This action provided Democrats with a 50–49 majority and returned the nation to divided party government.

Is the recent resurgence of the parties just the last gasp of a dying system? Some critics think it is, and that the two-party system is really on its last legs.[14] However, the parties' comeback probably represents a broader and more permanent change. Through much of American history, political parties were decentralized because political power in the United States was decentralized. But political power has become more centralized, and parties, although slow to react, have now adapted to that new reality with

---

[14]Theodore Lowi, "The Party Crasher," *The New York Times Magazine* (August 23, 1992): 28–33.

stronger central party organizations. It makes little sense to think that parties will move again toward decentralization unless the government does—and that does not appear to be in the offing. Similarly, the resurgence of the national party organizations occurred in response to the rise of the modern media campaign and the increased demand for campaign money. It would make sense to think that the organizations would again wither away only if the media and money somehow became less important, and there is no sign that such changes are on the immediate horizon.

Of course, this analysis does not take into account the myriad of other factors that might change and affect the parties, either strengthening or weakening them. The recent episode of decline and resurgence, though, does teach us something about parties that is useful when contemplating their future: The parties have demonstrated an ability to adapt to changing circumstances, not always quickly, not always entirely successfully, but eventually and sufficiently. Unforeseen social and political changes involving circumstances hardly envisioned in this chapter may occur and lay the parties low again, but past experience suggests that parties—perhaps not exactly as we know them today, but parties nevertheless—will adapt again.

SUMMARY

1. Groups are an essential element in the functioning of the American democratic system. A group's political effectiveness depends on its size, the strength of its members' identification, its proximity to politics, its internal organization, and its closeness to the broader societal consensus.

2. Interest groups engage in a wide array of politically relevant activities. They press their views on their own membership, the general public, and the political elites of the legislative, executive, and judicial branches. One of their most potent weapons of late has been the political action committee (PAC).

3. Some of the major group participants in the American political process are based on different interests. There are economically-based groups, such as the Chamber of Commerce of the United States and the AFL-CIO; socially based groups, such as the National Organization for Women (NOW) and the National Association for the Advancement of Colored People (NAACP); ideological groups, such as the liberal Americans for Democratic Action; single-issue groups, such as the right-to-life and pro-choice movements; and public interest groups, such as Common Cause, the "citizens' lobby."

4. The role that interest groups play in a democratic society is as controversial as it is pervasive. Pluralistic theory sees interest groups as working to overcome the deficiencies of individual citizens and to perpetuate a functioning democracy. Other perspectives see interest groups as failing to serve their own members' interests, the public interest, or both.

5. In a democracy, political parties try to influence public policy by backing members as candidates in elections to public offices. In the course of getting their members elected to public office, political parties perform a number of important functions for the system of government: socializing citizens, pulling together the diverse interests contending in a society, simplifying the alternatives confronting the voters, structuring campaigns and elections, recruiting and training political leaders, and organizing and coordinating government.

6. The American party system is a two-party system, probably due primarily to the plurality election system commonly used in the United States and the generally centrist distribution of political beliefs in America. The parties are characterized by a relatively loose relationship among their component parts, divided into national, state, and local at one level and into formal party organization, the party in the electorate, and the party in the government at another level.

KEY TERMS

pluralist democracy (196)

melting pot (196)

movement (197)

direct mail (200)

political action committee (PAC) (200)

Federal Election Campaign Act
  of 1974 (200)

lobbying (200)

iron triangle (202)

class action suit (202)

amicus curiae brief (202)

grass-roots lobbying (203)

Christian Right (207)

cross-cutting cleavage (210)

interest group elitism (210)

political party (211)

socialization functions (211)

electoral functions (212)

governmental functions (212)

plurality election (213)

majority election (213)

runoff election (213)

proportional representation (215)

third party (215)

formal party organization (218)

national convention (218)

platform (218)

national committee (218)

political machine (218)

state committee (218)

coalition (219)

party in the government (219)

party system (220)

realignment (222)

dealignment (222)

decline (223)

caucus (224)

resurgence (225)

READINGS FOR FURTHER STUDY

James Madison's *Federalist* No. 10 remains mandatory reading for anyone interested in exploring the role of groups in American political life.

A more modern, yet classic, study is *The Governmental Process* (New York: Knopf, 1951) by David Truman.

For a fascinating, if highly critical, account of the interest groups' most potent tool, the political action committee, see Elizabeth Drew's *Politics and Money* (New York: Macmillan, 1983).

Interest groups are important elements in the pluralist perspective on American democracy. Robert A. Dahl sets out that perspective most clearly in *Who Governs?* (New Haven, CT: Yale University Press, 1961).

As a central feature of American politics, parties are one of the most written-about of all American political institutions. V. O. Key, Jr., provides a classic description of the role that parties play in the American political system in *Politics, Parties, and Pressure Groups*, 5th ed. (New York: Crowell, 1964).

James L. Sundquist's *Dynamics of the Party System* (Washington, DC: Brookings Institution, 1973) offers a historical perspective on the parties, centering around the notion of realignment.

Good overviews of the causes and consequences of the decline in American political parties are Everett Carll Ladd, *Where Have All the Voters Gone?* 2d ed. (New York: Norton, 1982) and Martin P. Wattenberg, *The Decline of American Political Parties* (Cambridge, MA: Harvard University Press, 1984).

The best accounts of the parties in resurgence are Xandra Kayden and Eddie Mahe, Jr., *The Party Goes On: The Persistence of the Two-Party System in the United States* (New York: Basic Books, 1985), and Paul S. Herrnson, *Party Campaigning in the 1980s* (Cambridge, MA: Harvard University Press, 1988).

CHAPTER 8

Campaigns and Elections

A/P World Wide

Chapter Objectives

In a campaign and the election that concludes it, all the actors in the political process come into vigorous interplay. Parties begin selecting and promoting candidates. Interest groups mobilize their forces to ensure that their interests will be remembered.

The mass media put politics more clearly and consistently at center stage. As a result, the public, whose interest in political affairs is generally limited, now turns its attention to the candidates vying for public office. This chapter examines the process from the perspectives of the two principal types of players in the drama: voters and candidates. For voters, the basic questions are whether to vote and how to vote. Candidates, whether presidential or congressional, must devise strategies that will bring voters to the polls and attract their votes. They must pull together the financial resources and organization needed for a credible campaign, obtain the nomination of their party, and compete against the other party's candidate in the general election campaign.

The Voter's Perspective: To Vote or Not to Vote

As discussed in Chapter 5, politics is not usually a matter of concern to most citizens. Their interest is most aroused around Election Day, when they begin to take note of the campaign, think about going to the polls to cast their ballots, and sometimes engage in activities related to the campaign. Many begin to follow it on television or in newspapers and talk about it with family and friends; some try to influence the way in which someone else will vote. A somewhat smaller number wear buttons, display stickers or signs on their cars or houses, and attend campaign meetings, rallies, speeches, or dinners. A few actually work for or give money to a candidate or party. But even with these other kinds of campaign-related activities, voting remains the most frequent act of political participation and the most meaningful act as well. In a representative democracy, voting forges the essential link between the citizens and their government. In the end, then, it comes down to two basic decisions: whether to vote and how to vote.

Voting Requirements and Eligibility

Not everyone is in a position to decide to vote. Some people are excluded by law. In fact, for more than 100 years after the founding of the United States, a majority of the American people were not eligible to vote. The states during that period controlled who could or could not vote, and they typically limited the electorate to white males over the age of 21. Since then the United States has made great strides in eliminating restrictions on voting.

Racial barriers to voting began to fall first. The Fifteenth Amendment (1870) outlawed denying the right of citizens to vote on grounds of "race, color, or previous condition of servitude." Nevertheless, after the Civil War the South created a new system of inferior status for African Americans, which came to be called "Jim Crow." Jim Crow included several elements limiting African American voting. One element was the white primary. As discussed in Chapter 3, in the one-party South of the post-Reconstruction era, winning the Democratic primary was equivalent to an election because the general election was nearly always a rout of the disfavored Republicans. The Democratic party routinely excluded African Americans from its primaries, which effectively barred them from any meaningful role in the electoral process. The white primary was struck down by the Supreme Court in *Smith v. Allwright* in 1944.

Another element of Jim Crow was the **poll tax**, which stipulated that in order to vote, citizens had to pay a tax. This tax was often enforced cumulatively, meaning that people had to pay the tax for every previous election in which they had not voted. Because African Americans had not been able to vote in many previous elections, they confronted large cumulated poll taxes that they could not pay. Thus they were excluded from voting. Poll taxes were prohibited in federal elections by the **Twenty-fourth Amendment** and in state elections by the Supreme Court's decision in *Harper v. Virginia Board of Elections*, both in 1964.

A third element of Jim Crow was the literacy test. In order to vote, a person had to demonstrate the ability to read. Many African Americans at that time were illiterate, so they were thereby excluded. This requirement was prohibited by the **Voting Rights Act of 1965**, which waived literacy tests for anyone with a sixth-grade education. The Voting Rights Act of 1965 and a subsequent amendment in 1982 took other important steps to protect African American voting rights, as discussed in Chapter 3.

While African American participation declined under Jim Crow, political pressures to grant **female suffrage**, the right of women to vote, increased. This movement, stirred to life in the early nineteenth century, achieved its first major success when the

poll tax

A tax on voting, applied discriminatorily to blacks under "Jim Crow" in the post–Civil War South.

Twenty-fourth Amendment

Adopted in 1964, this amendment forbids the use of poll taxes in federal elections. Since 1966 the Court has applied this proscription to state elections as well.

Voting Rights Act of 1965

Major legislation designed to overcome racial barriers to voting, primarily in the southern states. Extended in 1982 for 25 years.

female suffrage

The right of women to vote, bestowed nationally by the Nineteenth Amendment in 1920.

Nineteenth Amendment

Constitutional amendment of 1920 giving women the right to vote.

Twenty-sixth Amendment

Constitutional amendment adopted in 1971 that fixed the minimum voting age at 18 years.

residence requirements

State laws designed to limit the eligible electorate by requiring citizens to have been a resident of the voting district for a fixed period of time prior to an election.

Voting Rights Act of 1970

A law to further ensure voting rights, it limited residence requirements to 30 days for presidential elections.

register

To place one's name on the list of citizens eligible to vote.

territory of Wyoming granted suffrage to women in 1869. Activists first coalesced into two competing organizations with somewhat different styles—the more militant National Woman Suffrage Association led by Susan B. Anthony, and the more conservative American Woman Suffrage Association led by Lucy Stone. The two groups joined forces in 1890. Final success was not achieved on the national level until 1920, when the states ratified the **Nineteenth Amendment**, which gave women the right to vote.

The last major broadening of the electorate occurred in 1971, when the **Twenty-sixth Amendment** reduced the voting age from 21 to 18. In the midst of the Vietnam War, the argument that people old enough to die for their country ought to be able to vote in their country's elections was very persuasive. In addition, both Republicans and Democrats hoped to capitalize on the large bloc of new voters. In combination with the coming of age of the post-World War II baby boom generation, the lowering of the voting age produced one of the greatest expansions of the electorate in American history.

The laws of the United States still exclude from voting people who are not citizens of this country. In most states, people who have been convicted of a felony or who are confined in prisons and mental institutions cannot vote. Most jurisdictions also typically exclude citizens who have not resided within their boundaries for a minimum amount of time. This law is intended to ensure that citizens are reasonably permanent residents of the community. Impediments to voting imposed by lengthy **residence requirements** were weakened substantially by the **Voting Rights Act of 1970**, which mandated that states require no more than 30 days' residency to establish eligibility to vote in presidential elections. Today the 30-day rule is standard for all elections.

Beyond meeting the basic qualifications, potential voters in most places in the United States are required to **register**—that is, to enter their names on the local government's list of those eligible to vote in a particular area, usually by visiting a government office. This requirement poses enough of an inconvenience that many people do not bother. Recent studies have shown, in fact, that the registration requirement may reduce electoral participation by as much as 10 to 15 percent.[1] Because registration reduces voting, it has long been the target of political reformers. Some places now permit registration by mail or via the Internet, and a few allow citizens to register on Election Day, even at the same time and place as they vote. Such arrangements seem to make a difference. In 1980 voter turnout in states with Election Day registration was 13 percent higher than the national average.[2]

Recognizing the important role played by registration laws, Congress passed the National Voter Registration Act of 1993, also known as the "Motor Voter" law since it

---

[1]Steven Rosenstone and Raymond Wolfinger, "The Effect of Registration Laws on Voter Turnout," *American Political Science Review* 72 (1978): 22–45; G. Bingham Powell, Jr., "American Voter Turnout in Comparative Perspective," *American Political Science Review* 80 (1986): 35.
[2]David P. Glass, Peverill Squire, and Raymond E. Wolfinger, "Voter Turnout: An International Comparison," *Public Opinion* (December 1983–January 1984): 49–55.

Politics and Economics
Turnout, Choice, and Economic Status

Economic status influences voter turnout. For example, as Figure 8A shows, in 1996 the higher a citizen's income, the more likely the citizen was to vote. The same pattern has been observed in many previous elections. This pattern emerges in part because higher income encourages many of the factors that promote voting, particularly education, political interest, and efficacy.

Voting choice is also influenced by economic status. As Figure 8B shows, in 1996 the higher a citizen's income, the more likely the citizen was to vote for Bob Dole. This tendency of higher income people to favor Republican candidates has also been observed in many previous elections. It results primarily because higher-income people tend to identify with the Republican party, as discussed in Chapter 7, and because Republican identifiers tend to vote for Republican candidates.

These two factors combine to hurt Democratic candidates and help Republican candidates. Democratic candidates have a greater following among lower-income people, but those people turn out to vote less often. Republican candidates have a greater following among higher-income people, who vote more often. This is one reason why the Republicans, even as the minority party, have been so successful in getting their candidates elected to public office.

What other reasons are there for the Republicans' success in winning elections, even though they have been in the minority for so long?

Figures 8A and 8B
The higher income of a voter's family, the more likely that citizen is to vote.

SOURCE: American National Election Studies, 1998.

required voter registration to be made available at the state Departments of Motor Vehicles. Over 15 million Americans registered to vote via their state motor vehicle agency in 1997–98. Partly as a result of this new law, registration rates climbed to over 70 percent in 1998, the highest level in a congressional election year since 1970. It is important to note that this piece of legislation passed during a period of unified Democratic government. Many prior proposals had failed primarily because of Republican opposition. The historical pattern has been for Republicans to oppose such measures and for Democrats to support them. The Democrats generally emphasize the virtues of higher turnout, whereas the Republicans worry about opening the door to fraud.[3]

---

[3]Federal Election Commission, *The Impact of the National Voter Registration Act on the Administration of Elections for Federal Office, 1997–1998,* http://www.fec.gov/pages/9798NVRAexec.htm (26 August 2001).

Turnout, Choice, and Economic Status, *continued*

FIGURE 8A

Voting Turnout by Family Income, 1996

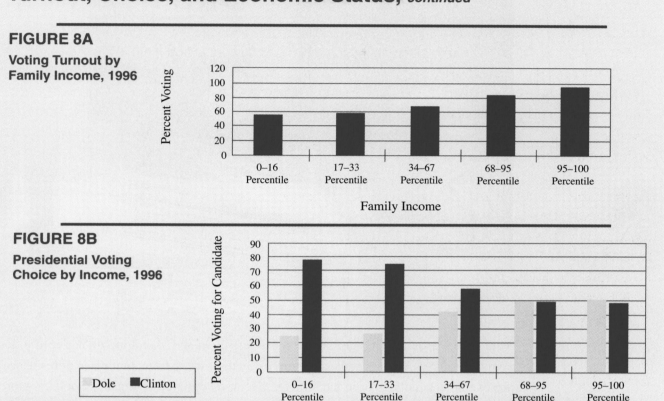

FIGURE 8B

Presidential Voting Choice by Income, 1996

Dole   ■Clinton

Who Votes?

Voting turnout varies with people's social characteristics and psychological and political attitudes, as well as with the circumstances of voting. Voting participation used to vary dramatically across a wide variety of social groupings in the United States. Whites were much more likely to vote than African Americans, men were more likely to vote than women, and so on. In recent years there has been a general convergence in the voting rates among various groups of citizens. This is due partly to the success of the long struggle to ensure equal access to the voting booth. Just as significant, the broader trend toward social and economic equality has tended to promote political equality.

Two social characteristics show the strongest relation to voting turnout: age and education. (A third important factor is discussed in "Politics and Economics: Turnout, Choice, and Economic Status.") The older a person is, the more likely that person is to

Poll worker explains to a woman how to use one of the new voting machines.
(AP Wide World)

vote. One reason is that older people move less often and, therefore, do not need to re-register as often. Young people are more likely to be away from their place of residence, for example, at college or in the military. Because voting by absentee ballot takes more forethought and is more difficult than voting in person, young people are more likely to be discouraged from voting. They are also more preoccupied with getting a start in life than with relatively remote political concerns. As people grow older, they have more time and inclination to participate in politics and consequently build a habit of voting.

The more educated a person is, the more likely he or she is to vote. About half of the eligible voters with a grade-school education or less voted in 1996, whereas almost 90 percent of those with a college degree or graduate-school education voted. Education plays such a big role because it stimulates political interest and provides the information that people need to be effective participants in the political process. Differences in education have undoubtedly contributed to voting differences between social groups in the past. African Americans and women voted less often than white males in part because they did not enjoy the benefits of education that white males did. With the recent expansion of educational opportunities for minorities and women, levels of voting for these groups have approached those for white males.

Psychological influences play a role as well. Not surprisingly, the greater a person's interest in politics, the more likely the person is to vote. The more a citizen thinks he or she can accomplish politically (i.e., the more political efficacy he or she has), the greater the likelihood the person will vote. Partisanship is a powerful motivating force. The stronger a person's attachment to a political party, the more inclined that person will be to vote. However, some psychological factors thought to have a major impact on turnout really do not. Conservatives and liberals are only slightly more likely to vote than moderates, probably because they tend to be more interested and partisan. Surprisingly, despite much attention in the late 1960s and early 1970s, trust—defined as reliance on the integrity of public officials—has little effect. In 2000, just over 51 percent of the voting age population cast a ballot for president. In the 1998 midterm elections, only 36 percent of the voting age population turned out to vote nationwide.

Finally, primarily as a result of differences in psychological factors, turnout varies substantially across the different types of elections. In elections that the public finds interesting and important, so-called **high-stimulus elections**, turnout is usually relatively high; in less interesting, **low-stimulus elections** it is usually low.[4] Presidential elections are generally higher-stimulus than congressional elections, and general elections are usually higher-stimulus than the primary elections that precede them. Turnout in recent presidential elections has averaged between 50 and 55 percent, while turnout in congressional elections has run between 35 and 40 percent. Voting rates in presidential general elections also typically far exceed the turnout rates of 30 percent and less observed in primary elections.

Declining Turnout

Although presidential voting remained over the 50 percent mark in 2000, this level remains part of a troubling long-term trend toward lower voter turnout in the United States, as shown in Figure 8.1. After an explosion in the early nineteenth century, owing to the expansion of the electorate discussed earlier in this chapter, voter turnout by the 1990s had fallen to one of its lowest points in the last 150 years and had sagged substantially since its post–World War II peak in 1960. Although the long-term trend in turnout is striking, it is not necessarily ominous. The greatest part of the decline took place in the late-nineteenth and early-twentieth centuries. Some theorists attribute this to growing disaffection from the political system,[5] but other factors were probably involved. The widespread imposition of voter registration systems lowered turnout, both by excluding fraudulent votes and by discouraging some honest ones.[6] Moreover, Jim Crow laws in the South wiped out the gains made among African American voters in the years after the Civil War.

high-stimulus election

Election that the public finds interesting and important.

low-stimulus election

Election that the public finds uninteresting or unimportant.

[4]Angus Campbell, "Surge and Decline: A Study of Electoral Change," in *Elections and the Political Order,* eds. Angus Campbell, Philip E. Converse, Warren E. Miller, and Donald E. Stokes (New York: Wiley, 1966), p. 41.
[5]Walter Dean Burnham, "The Changing Shape of the American Political Universe," *American Political Science Review* 59 (1965): 7–28.
[6]Philip E. Converse, "Change in the American Electorate," in *The Human Meaning of Social Change,* eds. Angus Campbell and Philip E. Converse (New York: Russell Sage Foundation, 1972), pp. 281–286.

FIGURE 8.1

Turnout in Presidential and Congressional Elections, 1790–2000

Since the end of the nineteenth century, the long-term historical trend has been downward. Turnout in midterm congressional elections is lower than in presidential elections.

SOURCES: Harold W. Stanley and Richard G. Niemi, *Vital Statistics on American Politics* (Washington, DC: CQ Press, 1990), p. 78; Federal Election Commission, "55.9 Percent Turnout in 1992 Presidential Election Highest Since 1968," Press Release of January 14, 1993.

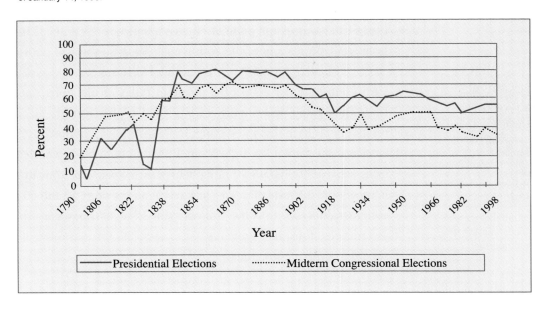

The Nineteenth Amendment, which enlarged the electorate by giving women the right to vote, temporarily reduced turnout. Many women had never voted before and did not immediately begin to exercise the right. As women, particularly younger women, got used to the newly opened political world, turnout climbed steadily through the 1930s. World War II disrupted voting interest, but it bounced back in the 1950s. Demographic and institutional changes reduced voter turnout in the 1960s and 1970s. The maturation of the postwar baby boom and the reduction of the voting age from 21 to 18 added millions of new voters, but because younger citizens are not as likely to vote as older people, this drove turnout down.

Yet many observers still believe that deep-seated psychological inclinations account for some of the contemporary decrease. Some blame political alienation or distrust. They argue that the American people are discouraged by what they see going on in politics and are therefore increasingly inclined not to vote. However, as noted earlier, trust does not seem to have much effect on voting, so an increase in distrust does not necessarily imply a decrease in voting. In fact, many of the new voters in 2000 seemed to be motivated more by the emergence of a national campaign by the Green Party than anything else. On the other hand, decreasing partisanship and external political efficacy clearly relate to voting turnout.[7] Young people are less partisan, and less partisan people are less likely to vote. It may therefore be that weakening partisanship is due to the influx of young people into the electorate, resulting in a decline in voting.

Some commentators view the long-term decline in voter turnout with alarm. The success of democracy, they argue, depends on the enthusiastic participation of its citizens; thus, declining electoral involvement is not a good sign. However, other commentators believe that less than total participation may be desirable because it can give a democracy room for compromise and flexibility.[8] Nonvoting may not imply a lack of trust or support for the political system but is perhaps a passive nonvote of confidence. In other words, staying home on Election Day may just be a way of saying that everything is all right.

The Voter's Perspective: How to Vote

Just as various political, social, and psychological factors contribute to citizens' decisions about whether to exercise their voting rights, different elements help determine for whom they cast their ballots. Analysts have identified three major factors that seem to influence how people vote: parties, candidates, and issues.

Parties

For many years, affiliation with a political party was regarded as the mainstay of voting decisions in the United States. For some people, all that mattered was that a candidate belonged to "their" party. However, voter allegiance was not the only impact of strong party affiliation. In many instances party identification colored the way in which a voter looked at the pivotal elements of a presidential election. Party continues to play an important role in American electoral behavior. A national campaign by the Green Party in the 2000 presidential race complicated the situation, but how people voted still bore a strong relationship to their sense of partisanship. Thus 85 percent of Democrats reported voting for the candidate of their party, while only 10 percent crossed party lines to vote for Bush (3 percent voted for Nader). Moreover, 91 percent of Republicans voted for the candidate of their party, while only 7 percent defected to Gore (1 percent voted for Nader). As might be expected, Green Party candidate Ralph Nader's greatest strength came from independents, among whom he captured 9 percent.[9]

Yet, as established in Chapter 7, there can be little doubt that party has weakened as a reference point for many American voters in recent years. As party has become less

[7]Paul Abramson, *Political Attitudes in America* (San Francisco: Freeman, 1983), pp. 291–306.
[8]This argument is most often associated with Bernard Berelson, *Voting* (Chicago: University of Chicago Press, 1954), pp. 305–323.
[9]The Gallup Organization, 2001.

Contemporary Controversies
Campaign and Electoral Reform: A Comparative Perspective

Opponents of campaign and electoral reform often contend that changing the current system will upset the finely tuned balance of the American political system and impair the functioning of democracy. Proponents point, however, to other countries with different systems that work just fine.

One criticism of American presidential campaigns is that they go on too long, close to two years counting the run-up to the primaries and then the general election campaign. And congressional campaigns, in a sense, never stop: as soon as congressmen take office in January, they must begin to look to the next election "only" 22 months away. Clearly other nations, particularly those with parliamentary systems, accomplish the process much more quickly. The best example is Great Britain, where the span from the announcement of an election to the new government's taking office is little more than a month.

Another area of comparison is in campaign finance. The United States has partial public funding of presidential campaigns and no public funding of congressional campaigns. Acceptance of public funding binds presidential candidates to some limits, but there are no limits on what congressional candidates can spend.

Even the effort to limit presidential spending, though, can be partially circumvented by a wealthy or well-funded candidate, such as George W. Bush in the 2000 election cycle, who declines public funds. Britain, Israel, and Japan have no public funding whatsoever. Britain and Japan do impose limits on spending while Israel does not. Denmark, France, Italy, and Germany all have public funding, based either on strength in the previous election or a reimbursement according to strength in the current election.

A third point of comparison is in the use of television in campaigns. Of the eight countries just mentioned, the United States is the only one that does not provide free television time to candidates for public office (apart from debates between candidates, which broadcasters cover, at their discretion, as news events). Most of the countries above provide free and equal time in proportion to the parties' strength in the previous election.

Do other countries' successes with shorter campaigns and different arrangements for campaign finance and television use mean that such reforms would work well in the United States? What differences between the United States and these other countries might make the impact of of such reforms differ?

important to voters, it has become a less important determinant of their voting decisions, which has left more room for candidate characteristics and issues to have an influence.

Candidates

Opinions about the candidates themselves play a powerful role in influencing how voters ultimately vote. Because partisanship is fairly stable, assessments of the candidates are major contributors to changes in presidential voting from one election to the next.[10] Voters seem to put the greatest weight on three factors:

- *Experience*. The public shows a marked preference for someone with substantial political experience. Hence, the public leans very much toward incumbent presidents, vice-presidents, senators, and governors from large states. The only recent presidents without substantial national political experience prior to taking office were Dwight Eisenhower (1953–1961), who had extensive military experience, and Jimmy Carter (1977–1981), the governor of a smaller state, Georgia. Although Bill Clinton (1993–2001) was the governor of a small southern state, he had been active on the national scene for many years as a leader in the National Governors' Association and the Democratic Leadership Council.

- *Leadership*. The public is partial toward candidates who seem able to take command of a situation, who do not wallow in pessimism or indecision, and who act when the time is right. President Carter suffered in the 1980 campaign because, in the face of economic problems and the Iranian hostage crisis, he was not seen as taking decisive and effective action. Twelve years later in 1992 George Bush was hurt by the widespread public perception that he had no plan for addressing the economic problems besieging the country.

- *Personal qualities*. At the same time that voters want someone who will be a strong leader, they are also inclined to want an attractive and "nice" person in the White House. Eisenhower, Kennedy (1961–1963), and Reagan (1981–1989) all benefited from attractive personalities. Bill Clinton's campaign in 1992 mounted a major effort to offset early perceptions of him as dishonest and untrustworthy—"Slick Willy"—with an image-rebuilding effort that campaign insiders dubbed the "Manhattan Project" after the World War II program to develop the atomic bomb.[11] Not only did Clinton overcome negative public perception to win the election in 1992 and reelection in 1996, but when he left office in January 2001, despite eight years of investigation which ultimately led to his impeachment, 65 percent of the American public approved of the way he handled his job as president.[12]

Candidate factors proved to be a major issue in the 2000 presidential campaign; the Republicans attacked Al Gore's involvement in a fundraising scandal and his stiff

[10]Donald Stokes, "Some Dynamic Elements of Contests for the Presidency," *American Political Science Review* 60 (1966): 19–28.
[11]"Manhattan Project, 1992," *Newsweek* special election edition (November/December 1992): 40–56.
[12]The Gallup Organization, 2001.

personality. The Democrats responded with attacks on George W. Bush's past indiscretions, including a 1976 drunk driving arrest.

Issues

Today more than ever, issues seem to drive the public toward a particular electoral choice. Even observers who have previously minimized the importance of issues now concede that issues can make a difference when the public knows and cares about them and when the candidates differentiate themselves on them. Single-issue groups, described in Chapter 7, play a big role in emphasizing particular concerns. Opponents of gun control or abortion, for example, can "target" an official for defeat. But even without the participation of single-issue groups, social issues such as crime control and foreign policy issues such as nuclear arms reduction usually receive considerable attention in a campaign.

More often, though, the voter's focus is on economic issues. Year in and year out, the mainspring issue driving most electoral decisions seems to be the economy. Even the earliest voting studies that discovered issues to be relatively unimportant found that bread-and-butter economic issues did make a difference. Personal economic well-being seems to influence how Americans vote. Figure 8.2 relates the percentage of the popular vote for president received by the incumbent party to an indicator of how much a citizen's disposable income had increased during the election year. Clearly, the better off people are during an election year, the more likely they are to vote for the party holding the White House. Some political commentators pointed to Ronald Reagan's celebrated question near the end of his 1980 election debate with Jimmy Carter—"Are you better off now than you were four years ago?"—as the symbolic turning point of that campaign. The statistical evidence suggests that the Reagan campaign may have been right in emphasizing the role of the economy. The same is true for the 1992 presidential election; exit polls showed Bush running far ahead of Clinton (62 percent to 24 percent) among voters who thought their family's financial situation had improved over the preceding four years, and the two candidates dead even (at 41 percent each) among those who thought things had stayed the same. But Clinton outpolled Bush 61 percent to 14 percent among those felt they were worse off and, fortunately for Clinton, those voters outnumbered by a margin of four to three voters who felt they were better off—enough to give Clinton the victory. Clinton benefited from an economic upturn during his first administration, and the fact that a majority of Americans in the fall of 1996 believed that national economic conditions were improving helped him retain office. However, although an even higher percentage of Americans thought the economy was getting better in fall 2000, Al Gore was unable to translate his connection to the incumbent Democratic administration into electoral victory.[13]

---

[13]The Gallup Organization, 2001.

Figure 8.2

The Economy and Presidential Voting

The better the economy, the better the candidate of the incumbent party does in the presidential election. The diagonal line shows the basic trend in the relationship—that is how much on average voting is related to improvements in the economy.

SOURCE: Updated from Edward Tufte, *Political Control of the Economy* (Princeton, NJ: Princeton University Press, 1978), p. 123.

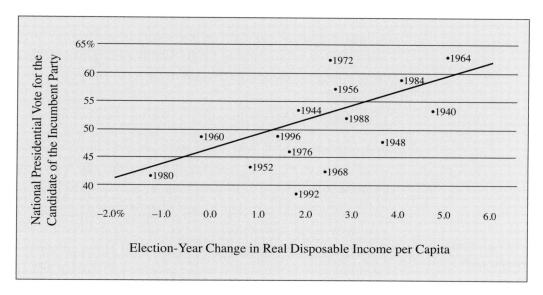

This is not to say that economics is the only issue that sways voters. Other issues have some impact. No doubt the candidates' differences on abortion, health care, and foreign policy influenced some voters to opt for Bush or Gore in 2000. However, 2000 was a year in which the economy again dominated the campaign and likely played a role in the very tight electoral outcome.

In talking about parties, candidates, and issues separately, this discussion runs the risk of oversimplification. In reality, the relation among parties, issues, and candidates as influences on the vote is complex. Voters may take a position on an issue because it is the position of their party; or, they may choose their party on the basis of its position on issues. Voters may tend to prefer certain candidates because they are the candidates of their party and reject other candidates because they are candidates of the other parry; or, they may judge a party according to how much they like its candidates. Finally, voters may like candidates because they agree with their positions on certain issues; or, voters may adopt certain positions on issues because they like the candidates who advocate them. Thus, voter decision-making is based on the interplay of a number of factors, and not just on those factors alone.

The Candidate's Perspective: Running for President

While voters need to decide whether and how to vote, candidates confront a more complicated set of choices. Their basic decisions include whether to run and how to attract enough votes to win. To achieve the latter, they must make scores of strategic decisions. Contemporary presidential candidates must carve out a clear position as a serious contender early on; raise large amounts of money; choose the right campaign consultant; decide which issues to raise; select the primaries and caucuses on which to concentrate; garner enough delegates in the national convention to secure the nomination; choose a running mate; and win states with enough electoral votes to win the electoral college. These tasks are compounded by the fact that a candidate must also outmaneuver opponents who are working equally hard to attract voters.

Who Runs for President?

In American political folklore, anyone can grow up to be president, whether they have humble beginnings, like Abraham Lincoln, or high social and economic status, like Franklin Roosevelt. But is such folklore actually true? In fact, the Constitution lays down few requirements: The person must be a natural-born citizen of the United States, a resident of the United States for at least 14 years, and at least 35 years of age. The **Twenty-second Amendment** (1951), ratified in the aftermath of Franklin Roosevelt's unprecedented four elections to the presidency, imposes one more restriction: An individual cannot be elected to the presidency more than twice, or more than once if the individual has completed more than two years of another president's term.

Twenty-second Amendment

Ratified in 1951, this amendment restricts the president to two terms in office.

Despite the relatively small set of formal qualifications, however, evidence suggests that the path to power is fairly steep and narrow. The key to attaining the highest political office in the United States is to have held other reasonably high political offices. Consider the 20 individuals who have run under the banner of the major parties for the presidency in the last 14 elections. Seven of them had been governor of their state; eight had previously served as vice-president; ten had served in the U.S. Senate. Only one, Dwight Eisenhower, had never held an elective office. However, the best assurance of being elected president is to already *be* president. In the 28 elections in which an incumbent president sought reelection, the incumbent was successful in 19, or 68 percent of the time. This statistic probably stems in part from the incumbent president's unique ability to manipulate events in his favor and the high visibility and name recognition a president enjoys.

What other qualities put an individual in line to be considered for the highest office in the land? Recent history suggests several qualities are prevalent. For one, the presidency has so far been a white male preserve. In addition, most presidents in recent times have been from at least reasonably well-off Protestant backgrounds, and have been reasonably well-educated. Not until 1960, with the election of John F. Kennedy, did a Catholic become president. No Jew has ever been elected president, and Joe Lieberman became the first Jewish vice-presidential candidate of a major party in 2000.

In this age of media politics, an attractive image is clearly an important asset. But perhaps the most important quality of all is determination. Securing a major party's presidential nomination nowadays typically takes months, even years, of grinding work. In some cases candidates start campaigning in January of the year before the presidential election year and continue nonstop for almost the next two years. Presidential hopeful Gary Hart vividly illustrated the kind of ordeal that a modem presidential candidate has to endure when he revealed that some mornings during his 1984 campaign he would awaken in a strange hotel room and have to reach for the phone book in order to remember what city he was in.

The Media Campaign

The primary determinant of the shape of the modern political campaign is the mass media. Candidates used to be concerned primarily with mobilizing the party organization behind their efforts. Now their principal concern is mobilizing the media, particularly television, to bring their name and "image" before the public. Such efforts assume three principal forms. The first form is the expenditure of most of the campaign treasury on political advertisements. Precious paid television time is generally devoted to short advertisements that focus on simple images and issues, rather than longer speeches that focus on in-depth discussions of public policy. Campaign debates waged in 1-minute, 30-second, and even 15-second spots have drawn considerable criticism for oversimplifying campaign issues. Ross Perot's 1992 and 1996 campaigns defied traditional practice by spending millions of dollars on half-hour blocks devoted to detailed discussions of economic problems and solutions—and defied conventional wisdom by drawing large viewing audiences.

A second way candidates bring their name before the media is to structure traditional campaign events, such as speeches, rallies, and news conferences, in order to get media attention. These activities, once the core of the traditional political campaign, are now used mainly as "media events," or opportunities to attract coverage by the news media.

A third strategy is for candidates to try to get as much free television time as possible on regular news and interview broadcasts. Extended nationally televised appearances on the nightly network news broadcasts, traditional news interview programs such as "Nightline," and, more recently, "softer" interview shows such as "Larry King Live" and "Oprah," are the candidate's dream—but these coveted appearances are hard to come by.

Democratic presidential candidate Vice-President Al Gore on the "Oprah Winfrey" show. *(AP Wide World)*

media consultant

An expert hired by a political candidate to give advice on the use of the mass media, particularly television and direct mail, in a campaign for public office.

The bread and butter of free television time comes in two forms: the "sound bite" on the national network news broadcasts and the daily stream of interviews on local TV stations as candidates travel around the country. Sound bites are short taped excerpts from statements that a candidate makes. Candidates hope to get at least one sound bite on the network news broadcasts every night during the course of the campaign, and thus attempt to say things in ways that are "sound biteable" to the TV crews covering them.

Another major development of recent years has been the rise of the professional **media consultant**. In the past candidates tended to rely on party leaders or a personal coterie to plan and execute their campaign strategy. The current trend, however, is toward reliance on professional campaign consultants. Such individuals, while certainly oriented more toward one party or philosophy than another, make themselves available for hire to candidates able to pay for their services. One of the best known and most successful media consultants in recent years is James Carville, who led Bill Clinton's media campaign in 1992 and then served as Senior Political Advisor to President Clinton.

The media typically concentrate not on the issues of the campaign, but on the strategies, tactics, and likely outcome of the campaign. Politicians and commentators call such a focus the horse race. Poll results are tracked throughout the campaign to see who is in the lead and to test the potential effect of various moves by the candidates. Some critics have argued that the emphasis placed on the polls in the mass media serves to make polls the makers, rather than the measurers, of public opinion. Polling results

Contemporary Controversies
An Election Gone Wrong?

The Constitution charges the American states with the responsibility of regulating the time, place, and manner of elections. Traditionally, this has meant that each state establishes its own rules and designs its own ballots. Since the presidential election is combined with state and local races, county election boards often end up designing ballots of their own, following state guidelines. Typically this is not an issue of concern, but controversy arose on November 7, 2000 when one county's choice of ballot seemed to determine the outcome of an extremely close presidential election.

Palm Beach County, Florida voters were confronted with a "butterfly ballot" (so called because the pages on either side of the center punch card resemble wings) that listed presidential candidate names alternately on both the left and right sides of the holes. The Republican Party candidates were listed first on the left side and the Democratic Party candidates second, but in between the two the Reform Party candidates were listed on the *right* side. Many voters claimed to be confused as a result of this ballot—a claim that

seemed well-supported by the election results. In Palm Beach County, 5,330 voters punched holes for both Al Gore and Pat Buchanan. Did some, or even most, of these voters intend to select Al Gore? We will never know for certain, but after careful analysis of the Florida vote, it seems possible that this ballot irregularity cost Al Gore the presidency.

A study commissioned by *USA Today* and several other papers concluded that George W. Bush still would have been victorious even if a hand recount of all the Florida votes had taken place. But the study also noted that a majority of Florida voters probably intended to vote for Al Gore. In an election so close as the presidential race in 2000, a poorly designed ballot in a single county can have an enormous effect.

Should the federal government regulate ballots? Should it provide suggested guidelines to the states? What standards are needed to guarantee a fair and accurate election?

showing a candidate doing better than expected tend to increase that candidate's credibility and thereby contribute to further gains in the polls. Polling results showing a candidate lagging far behind may lead the public to write off that candidate as a wasted vote. Also, a poor showing in the polls can cause potential contributors to cut the flow of money to a candidate. Politicians, particularly those trailing in the polls, like to say that "the only poll that counts is the one on Election Day." Yet preelection polls may encourage shifts in opinion that are translated into shifts in voting on Election Day. In 1992 interest in the election was heightened as public opinion polls showed the race between Bush and Clinton tightening in the last two weeks of the campaign, only to have the drama diminish as the apparent Bush surge fell back in the last few days before the voting. In 2000, the race was tight right down to the wire; opinion polls during the last two weeks before the election consistently found the race too close to call. In this case the polls were right. The election turned out to be one of the tightest in recent history, with only a few hundred votes separating Bush and Gore in some key states.

exit poll

A poll of voters taken as they leave the polling place, usually conducted by the media to get an advance indication of voting trends and facilitate analysis of the reasons behind the outcome of the election.

In recent years, the media and the polls have become controversial even on Election Day itself. Modem sampling techniques and **exit polls** (interviews with voters leaving the polls) often enable analysts to predict the winner long before polls everywhere have closed. For example, in 1988 CBS and ABC projected George Bush as the victor over Michael Dukakis at 9:20 P.M. Eastern Standard Time, well before many voters in western states had voted. Do early predictions about who is winning or losing dissuade those who have not yet voted from doing so, create a "bandwagon" effect for the projected winner, or incur sympathy votes for the projected loser? The evidence on these questions is mixed, but there are some signs that early projections do reduce turnout. In the 2000 election, the media caused an even bigger uproar, by first declaring Al Gore the winner of Florida's 25 electoral votes, then retracting and declaring Bush the winner of both Florida and the national election, and then finally admitting that the race was too close to call. In its race to break an important story, the news media risked its credibility with the public.

As the media have come more and more to shape the modern presidential campaign, and as dissatisfaction with modern campaigns has grown, the media have become the object of blame for the problems and the target of reform. As reasonable and laudable as the proposed media reforms sound, many of them collide with the First Amendment principles of freedom of the press and speech, potentially infringing on broadcasters' rights as journalists and candidates' rights to express themselves freely. Below are some of the specific proposals that have been advanced in recent years.

- Requiring broadcasters to give more free time to candidates, thus reducing the candidates' need for money to spend on advertising.
- Establishing rules for political advertising on television. Broadcasters and candidates might be forced to present only spots of one minute or more, and any unfair or negative elements could be prohibited.
- Conditioning federal campaign funding for presidential candidates on their agreement to participate in at least four televised debates.
- Challenging television news organizations to devote more time to the substance of the campaign and less to the horse race.
- Prohibiting television news organizations from projecting winners before all polls have closed. An alternative is a uniform national poll-closing time.

Campaign Finance

Financing campaigns has always been an issue for presidential candidates. The rate at which modern media-based, jet-borne, poll-addicted campaigns consume money has made the problem even greater. The Federal Election Commission (FEC) reports that in congressional races alone candidates spent over $1 billion in the 2000 election cycle. With the demands for more money have come growing public concern and increased legislative action to prevent political money from tainting the electoral and governmental processes.

Federal Election Campaign Act

Law passed in 1971 and amended several times that regulates campaign financing. It requires full disclosure of sources and uses of campaign funds and limits contributions to political candidates.

In 1971 Congress passed the **Federal Election Campaign Act** (FECA). The unfolding of the Watergate scandal in 1974 and other subsequent developments have led to amendments to FECA. Current campaign finance law requires full disclosure of the sources and uses of campaign funds on the theory that requiring candidates to disclose where their money came from will encourage them to behave more ethically. Candidates must thus file a complete accounting of where they get their money and how they spend it with the FCC.

The law bans direct contributions to candidates by corporations and labor unions, although such organizations can set up political action committees (PACs) through which their employees or members can contribute. (For more on PACs, see Chapter 7.) The law also places limits on campaign contributions. Currently individuals may give up to $1,000 per candidate in each primary and general election, but the total for each federal election year may not exceed $25,000. An individual cannot give more than $5,000 to a PAC per election per year, and a PAC cannot give more than $5,000 to one candidate in a federal election. However, there are no limits on the total a PAC can contribute to all federal candidates, or on the total a candidate can receive from all PACs. National party committees can also spend about 6 cents per member of the voting population on the presidential election campaign.

Presidential Election Campaign Fund

Pool of money available to presidential candidates for campaign expenses, that is collected by a $3 checkoff on the federal income tax form.

The Revenue Act of 1971 created a system of public financing for presidential campaigns. Every taxpayer has the option of earmarking $1 of federal income tax for the **Presidential Election Campaign Fund**. This earmark has since been raised to $3. The money generated is distributed directly to presidential candidates according to specific formulas that tie amounts that can be spent to the rate of inflation. Before the party conventions, candidates are eligible for federal matching funds. To receive these funds, candidates must raise at least $5,000 in each of at least 20 states. Contributions are limited to $250 per contributor. Once a candidate has qualified, the federal government will match all individual contributions up to a specified amount if the candidate agrees to hold total spending under a limit. After the party conventions, major-party candidates who give up the right to accept any contributions from the public whatsoever can opt for federal financing of their campaigns, up to limits set by the law. Since the Revenue Act of 1971

Contemporary Controversies
Low Voter Turnout: A Comparative Perspective

The public debate about low voter turnout in the United States and what to do about it takes place against an international backdrop that offers some unflattering comparisons. As Figure 8C shows, the United States ranks near the bottom of democratic countries in the percentage of its voting-age population that actually votes.

All kinds of explanations relating to distrust of government and lack of confidence in American political institutions have been offered to account for the low rate of turnout in the United States. But the evidence shows that these factors have little impact and that, in any case, trust and confidence in government are higher in the United States than in many other countries.

Turnout is lower in the United States than elsewhere primarily because there are more obstacles and fewer incentives to vote than elsewhere. The primary obstacle is, of course, the American system of voter registration. In fact, in many other democratic countries, registration is automatic. In Germany, Italy, and Sweden, for example, citizens who move are required to report their new address to the government. Once they do this, their voting rights are automatically cancelled at their old polling place and reinstated at their new one. Other countries (for example, Australia, Belgium, Greece, and Spain) have given people an incentive to vote by establishing penalties for nonvoting that, even if rarely enforced, seem to boost turnout by 10%. Perhaps the most effective sanctions are found in Italy. Italian citizens who fail to vote have "DID NOT VOTE" stamped on their identification papers, which can be a significant embarrassment and disadvantage in dealing with government officials.[a]

Despite such evidence, solutions to low voter turnout may take time to materialize. The American government took steps to address the registration concern with passage of the National Voter Registration Act in 1993. Although this effort to simplify the process resulted in higher registration rates, voter turnout in the 2000 presidential election barely topped 51 percent.

Voting is the defining act of a democracy. While such problems as fraud cannot be ignored, the United States might take a lesson from many of its sister democracies: low turnout is not an intractable given, but a problem that can be addressed by reducing obstacles and increasing incentives.

[a] David Glass, Peverill Squire, and Raymond Wolfinger, "Voter Turnout: An International Comparison," *Public Opinion,* December 1983, pp. 49–55.

Low Voter Turnout: A Comparative Perspective, *continued*

Figure 8C
Percentage of Voting-Age Population That Votes in Twenty-One Western Countries

The United States ranks near the bottom of democratic countries in the percentage of the voting-age population that actually votes, primarily because it places more obstacles in front of, and offers fewer incentives to, voters.

SOURCE: International Institute for Democracy and Electoral Assistance, "Voter Turnout: A Global Survey," http://www.idea.int/voter_turnout/voter_turnout.html (22 October 2001).

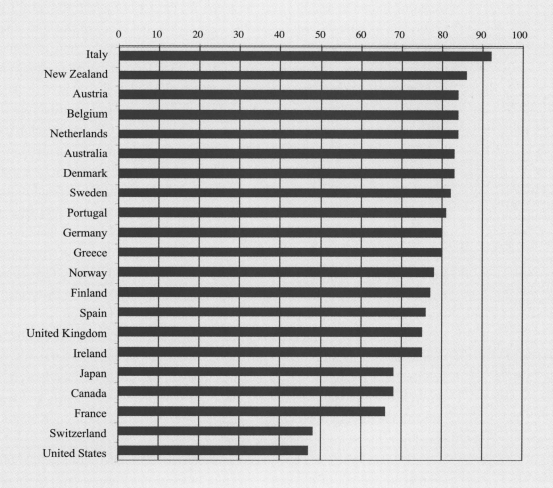

was passed, all major-party presidential candidates have opted for federal funding—until 2000, when George W. Bush decided to forego this option. In 2000, over $57 million was distributed in matching funds through the Presidential Election Campaign Fund.

Individual, PAC, and party contributions, as well as federal funds, are not the only money that can be spent on a candidate's behalf. Independent of the official campaign, individuals and PACs can spend as much as they want on behalf of a presidential candidate on such things as their own political advertisements and direct mail. Also, candidates willing to forgo federal funding can spend as much of their own money as they want. In 1992 independent candidate Ross Perot was estimated to have spent at least $60 million of his own money in his bid to win the White House. Candidates who do opt for federal funding are limited to spending $50,000 of their own money.

The problems with PACs have led many recent candidates to reject financial support from them. Many critics now call for the abolition of PACs, or for tighter controls on them, but these actions would raise serious questions of freedom of speech. As a result, PACs may be a permanent fixture of American politics; how candidates manage their relationships with them, however, is another, less predictable matter. Proposals for PAC reform include increasing the amounts that individuals can give to candidates (for example, to $5,000) and restoring tax deductions for political contributions.

The major loophole in the controls on money that can be spent on a candidate's behalf was a seemingly innocuous amendment to the campaign finance laws passed by Congress in 1979—the so-called **soft money** loophole. The tight controls on party spending imposed by the FECA laws in the early 1970s had the effect of drastically reducing the money that the national party could give to state and local parties to help pay for grass-roots activities supporting the presidential campaign—handing out buttons and bumper stickers, for example. In 1979 Congress moved to solve this problem by allowing the national parties to raise and spend money, without any restrictions, for state and local parties, routine operating expenses, and "party-building" activities, as long as the expenditures were not directly related to any federal campaign.

The parties soon began to exploit this exception to the hilt. Within the law, they moved to solicit unlimited contributions from individuals, corporations, and unions. Within the law, they cleverly spent the money in ways that technically were not directly associated with federal candidates, but clearly helped the candidates and freed up other party funds to help them. Under the new law, parties have to report virtually nothing about how the money is raised or spent.

Many critics, led by such organizations as Common Cause, see the soft money exception an evasion of the entire structure of campaign finance law. These organizations have prodded the FEC to scrutinize more closely whether state and local expenditures are too closely tied to federal candidates, and to rewrite the rules governing the raising and spending of soft money. The FEC has been slow to make changes, but one reform that

http://www.open secrets.org

Where does all the money for a political campaign come from? Find out who contributes to your favorite (or least favorite!) candidates at the Center for Responsive Politics.

soft money

A category of campaign money created by an amendment to the campaign finance laws in 1979. The national parties are allowed to raise and spend money, essentially without restriction, for state and local parties, routine operating expenses, and party-building activities, as long as the expenditures are not directly related to any federal campaign.

stands some chance of being implemented is fuller disclosure of the sources and uses of soft money—partly because the parties have already begun to do this on a limited, voluntary basis in an attempt to head off more restrictive reforms. Some would like to see the 1979 amendment that opened the soft money loophole repealed, but such repeal seems unlikely given that so many of the legislators voting on the issue benefit from the soft money system.

Getting Nominated

The modern-day orientation toward the media, supported by unending efforts to raise money, is superimposed over the traditional political events that in the heyday of political parties were the central mechanisms by which candidates were selected: primaries, caucuses, and conventions.

The most visible part of the presidential nominating process in recent years has been the long string of primary elections and party caucuses, running from the Iowa caucuses and the New Hampshire primary in early February, to the big primaries in such populous states as California and New York in March, to the latecomers like New Jersey and Montana in June. **Primary elections** are intraparty elections in which a political party selects the candidates it will run for office in the final interparty **general election**. Primary elections differ from state to state in terms of who is allowed to vote. In an **open primary**, any voter regardless of party affiliation can participate in the selection of the party's candidates. In a **closed primary**, only voters registered as members of the party can participate in the selection process for that party. Some states express their presidential preferences in **caucuses**, or small party meetings. Caucuses typically include discussion before voting, thus giving them a more deliberative character than the simple voting of a primary election.

The earliest presidential primaries and caucuses are the most important because they quickly sort out the field into contenders and also-rans. Most important in this respect is the New Hampshire primary, which provides the first real electoral test of the candidates' popular appeal. Candidates in the earliest contests run not so much against one another as against the expectations that the press and polls have created about how they should fare. After the early contests shape the field, the political battles move out onto a broader plain.

The protracted series of primaries and caucuses leading up to the party conventions seems excessive to many observers. The crucial early events, which set the tone for the rest of the campaign, take place in relatively small and unrepresentative states. Some see this as a good thing: A long primary season with many of the early events centered in small states keeps the political process open by giving less well known candidates with limited resources a chance to break into the political arena. Others see this as a disadvantage. They say the American political process is served less well by the election of

primary election

Preliminary election in which a party picks delegates to a party convention or its candidates for public office.

general election

Election to choose the candidates who will hold public office. General elections occur in November, following primary elections held during the spring and summer.

open primary

A primary election in which any voter, regardless of party affiliation, can participate.

closed primary

A primary election in which only the members of the party holding the election are allowed to participate.

caucus

A meeting of members of a political party (the members of a party in a legislature are also referred to as a *party caucus*). Parties in some states use caucuses to select delegates to the national conventions, which nominate presidential candidates.

obscure outsiders than by that of better-known insiders who understand how to make the system work as soon as they take office.

One reform proposal suggests that the primary process be compressed in time and broadened in representation by instituting either a one-day national primary or a series of regional primaries. Advocates argue that such moves would speed up the nominating process and give the citizens of every state, not just those with early delegate selection procedures, the opportunity to play a meaningful role in the selection of presidential candidates. The one-day national primary strikes many as a radical change, giving only the best-known and most prosperous candidates a real chance at the nomination. A reasonable compromise between the current fragmented system and a single national primary has been proposed—a series of **regional primaries** in different areas of the country, perhaps spaced two weeks apart over two months. Lesser-known candidates would then have the opportunity to build from small beginnings in their home regions.

The state caucuses and primaries culminate in the selection of delegates to the national **party conventions** held in July and August of the presidential election year. It is here that the party nominees are finally selected. In the past, the outcome of the nominating contest was often in doubt, as delegates wrangled over disputes about rules, credentials, and party platforms and as decisions were made in "smoke-filled rooms" by party elites. But in recent years conventions have become more sedate. The publicity surrounding the selection of delegates has made the convention process almost perfunctory. The parties have tried hard to settle differences in advance of or off of the convention floor, lest public bickering paint an inharmonious picture of the party on television screens across the country. As the parties have tried to control and exploit media coverage of their conventions, the "news value" of these political events has declined and the television networks have given them less coverage.

One of the most important strategic decisions a presidential candidate must make by the end of the convention is selection of a vice-presidential running mate. Much political folk wisdom revolves around this choice, particularly the need to **balance the ticket** geographically or ideologically. The idea is to pick a running mate who differs from the presidential candidate in a way that makes the ticket attractive to a broader range of voters. Thus, southern outsider Jimmy Carter picked northern insider Walter Mondale in 1976, western outsider Ronald Reagan picked eastern insider George Bush in 1980, and eastern liberal Michael Dukakis picked southern conservative Lloyd Bentsen in 1988. Bill Clinton broke with this practice in 1992 when he chose Al Gore, a moderate white southern male like himself, as his running mate. In 2000, Al Gore attempted to purify a candidacy tainted by connection to campaign finance scandals and chose Joe Lieberman, a Senator whose ethical standards were above reproach. George W. Bush, perceived by some as being an intellectual lightweight, chose the more cerebral Dick Cheney to balance his ticket.

---

regional primary

A primary election held across an entire geographic area (for example, the South or the West) rather than within a single state.

party convention

Regularly scheduled general meeting of a political party, held for the purpose of ratifying party policies and deciding on party candidates.

balance the ticket

A political party's effort to appeal to a wider cross-section of voters by providing regional or ideological balance in its nominations for president and vice-president.

The vice-presidency has long been the object of political scorn. Nevertheless, the offer of the vice-presidential nomination is something that few politicians would sneer at. The amenities that go with the job are first-class, and recent presidents have gone to special lengths to see that their seconds have meaningful work. Perhaps most important is the fact mentioned earlier: The vice-presidency is the most direct stepping-stone to the White House. Of the 44 people who have served as vice-president, 14 have gone on to become president. No other job in the world gives its holder better odds of becoming president. However, the ascent typically comes by death of the president rather than election. Since 1800, only two incumbent vice-presidents have gone on to win a presidential election: Martin Van Buren in 1836 and George Bush in 1988.

The Electoral College

electoral college

Institution established by the Constitution for electing the president and vice-president. Electors chosen by the voters actually elect the president and vice-president. Each state has a number of electors equal to the total number of its senators and representatives, while the District of Columbia (under the terms of the Twenty-third Amendment) has three electors.

Twenty-third Amendment

Constitutional amendment adopted in 1961 granting the District of Columbia three electors in the electoral college.

The main factor driving strategic decisions in the general election is the electoral college. The election of the president of the United States is an indirect process: Citizens' votes elect *electors* and those electors, constituted as the **electoral college**, elect the president. Each state gets a number of electors equal to the combined number of its representatives in the Senate and House. Thus, every state gets at least three electors, with additional electors depending on the size of its population. The District of Columbia currently gets three electors under the terms of the **Twenty-third Amendment** (1961). (Table 8.1 shows the number of electoral votes for each state.) The electoral college has 538 in all, with 270 needed to win the presidency. There is no constitutional requirement about how states choose their electors; such choices are left to the discretion of each state's legislature. All but two of the states have chosen to award all their electoral votes to the candidate (actually the slate of electors for that candidate) who wins a plurality in the state. The exceptions are Maine and Nebraska, which award two electoral votes to the statewide winner and the rest of their electoral votes by congressional district.

The members of the electoral college never actually meet in one place. Electors from each state meet in their state capitals to cast their ballots on or about December 15 of the election year. The results are sent to the U.S. Senate, and the president of the Senate (who is, of course, the vice-president of the United States) presides over the counting of the results in the presence of the Senate and House of Representatives. A presidential candidate who has a majority (more than 50 percent) of the electoral votes is elected outright. If no candidate has a majority, the House of Representatives, with each state delegation casting a single vote, elects a president by majority from among the top three contenders. If no president can be elected by this process, the vice-president becomes acting president. A vice-presidential candidate who has a majority is elected outright. If no candidate has a majority, the Senate picks the vice-president from the top two contenders by majority vote of individual members. In the days following the 2000 election, Gore found himself with 267 electoral votes and George W. Bush had

TABLE 8.1

Electoral Votes, 2000 Presidential Election

STATE	BUSH	GORE	STATE	BUSH	GORE
AK	3		MS	7	
AL	9		MT	3	
AR	6		NC	14	
AZ	8		ND	3	
CA		54	NE	5	
CO	8		NH	4	
CT		8	NJ		15
DC		2*	NM		5
DE		3	NV	4	
FL	25		NY		33
GA	13		OH	21	
HI		4	OK	8	
IA		7	OR		7
ID	4		PA		23
IL		22	RI		4
IN	12		SC	8	
KS	6		SD	3	
KY	8		TX	32	
LA	9		UT	5	
MA		12	VA	13	
MD		10	VT		3
ME		4	WA		11
MI		18	WI		11
MN		18	WV	5	
MO	11		WY	3	

*The District of Columbia has 3 electoral votes, but one elector abstained, giving Gore one fewer electoral vote than he would have had otherwise.

246—with disputed Florida returns still in question. The need for the House of Representatives to decide the outcome was averted when the Supreme Court ruled against additional recounts and Bush was declared the winner in Florida, allowing him to clear the threshold with 271 electoral votes.

The electoral college has been, perhaps, the most prominent target of the advocates of electoral reform. Because a state's representation is determined by the number of senators as well as the number of representatives, small states are represented out of proportion to their populations. Electors are chosen state by state by plurality election, so a winner's advantage and a loser's disadvantage, no matter how slim, are magnified in the extreme. The greatest gains can be made at the smallest cost with narrow victories in big states, so candidates often focus their efforts almost entirely in the larger states. Further, persons chosen as electors for a particular presidential ticket are under no effective legal obligation actually to cast their ballots for that ticket (the **faithless elector** problem).

Worst of all to some people is the prospect of a popular-minority president, a president who gets fewer popular votes than the opponent, but still wins the presidency. This has happened four times in American history. In 1824 Andrew Jackson received more votes than John Quincy Adams, but the House chose Adams as president. In 1888 popular-vote winner Grover Cleveland lost to Benjamin Harrison. In 1876 the Democratic candidate Samuel J. Tilden outpolled Republican Rutherford B. Hayes, but a Republican-controlled commission appointed to settle a dispute over the electoral votes of three southern states awarded them—and thus the White House—to Hayes. And the 2000 presidential contest provides the most recent occurrence, when Gore received 50,992,335 popular votes to George W. Bush's 50,455,156, making Gore the popular-vote winner but electoral-vote loser.

To repair all these alleged defects, reformers have come up with a variety of changes. The most sweeping proposal is to do away with the electoral college entirely and to replace it with **direct popular election** of the president and vice-president. Thus, whichever candidate received the largest percentage of the national popular vote total would win the White House. Such a process solves all the problems cited so far. But critics of direct national election see it as jeopardizing the delicate balance of the American political system. Simple plurality election would mean that presidents could be elected with the support of far less than half the people. Instituting a requirement of a majority or 40 percent of the votes to be elected might often mean a runoff election. That, in turn, would encourage more candidates to run in the first-round election. The result might be the end of the two-party, middle-of-the-road approach that has so long characterized American politics. Critics of the popular election can easily point to one of the electoral college's greatest virtues: with only the four exceptions cited, it always produces a clear-cut winner.

Seeing problems with both the current electoral college and direct popular election, moderate reformers propose to steer a course somewhere between the two. One idea for reducing the impact of the statewide winner-take-all system with the resultant candidate emphasis on big states is to move to a winner-take-all system on the level of congressional districts, as Maine and Nebraska have done. This would reduce the tendency of large blocs of votes to be awarded on the basis of narrow popular-vote margins. Solutions to the faithless elector problem propose requiring electors to vote for the presidential candidate under whose banner they were elected, or to do away with electors completely and simply tally up electoral votes.

faithless elector

A person chosen to vote for particular presidential and vice-presidential candidates in the electoral college who nevertheless votes for different presidential and vice-presidential candidates.

direct popular election

Selection of officials on the basis of those receiving the largest number of votes cast. The term sometimes refers to a proposal to choose the president and vice-president on this basis rather than through the electoral college.

http://uselection atlas.org/

Look at maps, examine party success over time, and compare vote totals for every presidential election at Dave Leip's Atlas of U.S. Presidential Elections.

Another call for reform focuses on the problems generated by a president who is compelled to spend the last half of a first term running for a second term. Critics of the current law, which limits a president to two full four-year terms, contend that single-term presidents do not have enough time to master the job and that first-term presidents who aspire to a second term are diverted from their duties by their efforts to get re-elected. Defenders of the status quo argue that the limitation of two four-year terms gives good presidents plenty of time to achieve their objectives and allows the public ample opportunity to vote out poor presidents. A president limited to a single term, they say, would become an instant lame duck. A compromise would be to allow the president one longer term, for example, a term of six years.[14]

Campaign Strategies

Presidential campaigns must pay careful attention to several strategic problems. One such problem is that of image. Most candidates seek to fix an image of themselves in the public mind. For an incumbent, the choice is usually an easy one: to exploit as much as possible the resources of the presidency. Presidents often try to look fully occupied with governing the country and thus too busy to engage in partisan politics. For opponents the choices are more difficult. Should the challenger go on the attack against the incumbent president, or instead play the role of the statesman? If the president is popular, the electorate may take the former as an attack on the country; however, the latter course is likely to attract little attention. Neither of these does the challenger much good.

How much focus to place on issues is another strategic problem. Should the candidate present specific proposals regarding national problems or instead project a broad and necessarily fuzzy vision of the future? The American people continually decry candidates who do not take clear positions on issues because they deny voters a choice. But it is sobering to note that the two candidates in postwar history who gave the public the clearest choices, the conservative Barry Goldwater in 1964 and the liberal George McGovern in 1972, went down in two of the biggest defeats in American electoral history.

Nowhere are the questions of images and issues raised more directly and dramatically than in presidential debates. For an incumbent, a debate is close to a no-win proposition. It gives publicity to the opponent, puts the challenger on an equal footing with the president, and risks embarrassment either by an inadvertent slip or by an aggressive challenger. Only the desire not to appear intimidated keeps a president from opting out of debates completely. As a result, incumbents usually want as few debates and as much structure as possible. For a nonincumbent, a debate represents perhaps the best strategic opportunity of the campaign. It provides the greatest media exposure, "presidential" standing, a chance to flush the president (if the incumbent is the oppo-

---

[14]Tom Wicker, "Six Years for the President?" *The New York Times Magazine* (June 26, 1983): 16.

nent) out of the Rose Garden, and an opportunity to display one's intellectual, political, and rhetorical wares.

The 1992 debates provided a case study on many of these issues. George Bush, as an incumbent tied to a weak economy facing an experienced and articulate debater in Bill Clinton, initially tried to avoid debates as long as possible. But Clinton's taunts that Bush was afraid to debate (accompanied by Clinton supporters dressed in chicken suits haunting Bush campaign appearances) and Clinton's persistent lead in the polls forced Bush campaign advisors to go with a heavy debate schedule as one of their few hopes of turning the election around.

In the debates, Clinton appeared presidential and Bush failed to deliver either a negative knockout punch or a positive vision of his plans for a second term. In fact, many saw Bush's fumbling response in the second debate to a young woman's question about how the bad economy had affected him personally as a clear sign that he was not going to be able to turn the election around. Bill Clinton, who followed up with a more articulate and sensitive response to that question, and Ross Perot, who scored overall with his homespun rhetoric and humorous one-liners, emerged as the overall winners.

The questions of campaign strategy are numerous and complex. The most vexing fact, though, is that strategy is always at the mercy of events. An unforeseen event can make a candidate look like a hero or a fool. A serious economic dislocation, a negative

President Bush, left, talks with independent candidate Ross Perot as Democratic candidate Bill Clinton stands aside at their debate in 1992. *(AP Wide World)*

revelation about an associate, an outbreak of violence halfway around the world—any of these things can make one candidate look inept and another candidate look "presidential." Because incumbent presidents have the power to take action rather than just talk about events, they generally gain some advantage in such circumstances. But if events prove to be intractable, incumbent presidents can suffer badly. Jimmy Carter's futile struggle to free the hostages from the American embassy in Tehran, Iran, during the 1980 campaign, and George Bush's poor economic record in 1992 stand as recent examples. Sometimes there is little anyone, even the president of the United States, can do to overcome events.

The Candidate's Perspective: Running for Congress

Running for Congress is much like running for president, except, of course, the stage is smaller—a state (for the Senate) or a congressional district (for the House) instead of the entire country. The basic strategic elements are the same: the problem of getting money; the two-phase contest of getting the nomination and then winning the election; the impact of party, candidate appeal, and issues; the growing importance of the media; the long hours on the campaign trail; and so on. However, different aspects tend to be particularly problematic.

Campaign Finance

Like presidential campaigns, House and Senate elections have become big-money enterprises. Candidates need money for television advertising, direct mail operations to get their messages across and raise more money, polling to see how their messages are playing, and expensive media consultants. According to Federal Election Commission statistics, candidates for the House and Senate in 2000 spent more than $1 billion on their contests. This figure represents a 36 percent increase in spending over the 1997–98 election cycle.

Although public financing is an important resource for presidential elections, congressional campaigns continue to operate without it. This leaves as the primary resources for most congressional campaigns money donated or spent by individuals, parties, and PACs. Recent congressional elections have seen widespread efforts by candidates and parties to get around the restrictions imposed by federal campaign finance laws. Foremost among such efforts were the increasing use of independent PAC expenditures to avoid the legal limits on direct contributions to candidates and the use of soft money by parties.

A key question is whether this money actually helps a candidate. Research suggests that it helps challengers more than officeholders. The more money a challenger spends, the more likely he or she is to defeat the incumbent. Such a tendency is probably due to the fact that money can be used to buy the name recognition and visibility necessary to offset the advantages of incumbency. Incumbents who spend a lot of money, however, do not fare as well as those who spend less. This is probably because incumbents tend to spend a lot of money only when they find themselves facing a serious challenge.[15]

As in presidential campaigns, financing is a frequent target for reform in congressional campaigns. The focuses for reform are similar in some respects—for example, too much PAC money, particularly for incumbents, and too much soft money. However, the problems for congressional elections are exacerbated by the lack of public financing of congressional campaigns. This makes congressional candidates much more dependent than presidential candidates on problematic sources of funds. Thus, the most significant campaign reform in congressional campaigns would be to institute public funding. Congress has struggled repeatedly over the last several years to institute this reform, but so far it has been unable to arrive at any plan agreeable to both Democrats and Republicans. Many Democrats and Republicans now say they want public financing; the bone of contention lies over whether spending limits should be imposed. Democrats want limits because they fear the wealth and fund-raising potential of some Republican candidates. Republicans, on the other hand, oppose limits because they think outspending the firmly entrenched Democratic incumbents is the only way to dislodge them.

Incumbency

Incumbency is even more of an asset to members of Congress than it is to presidents. In 2000 more than 97 percent of all representatives who ran for reelection won—down slightly from the 98 percent who retained their seats in the 1998 election. In the Senate, incumbency is also an important advantage, although the retention rates are rarely as high. In 2000 the success rate for incumbent senators was well over 80 percent.

safe seats

Congressional districts in which the division of voters between the parties is so lopsided as to virtually ensure one party of victory.

The main reason for the difference between the House and Senate return rates is that about five out of six congressional districts are **safe seats**. That is, House districts tend to be homogeneous, and the division of party affiliation within them is lopsided enough that one or the other party is virtually assured of victory. Because senators represent states, their "districts" are often more heterogeneous, with a more even division between the parties. For both representatives and senators, incumbents are usually much better known than their challengers.[16]

As described in Chapter 9, incumbents in Congress continually boost themselves by taking credit for every beneficial activity the federal government undertakes in their states and districts. Incumbents also generally have a much easier time raising campaign funds. For example, in recent elections, more than 80 percent of all PAC money contributed to House campaigns went to incumbents. In addition, members of Congress are in a good position to use the resources of their offices to get reelected. One

[15]Gary Jacobson, *Money in Congressional Elections* (New Haven, CT: Yale University Press, 1980), p. 49.
[16]Edie N. Goldenberg and Michael W. Traugott, *Campaigning for Congress* (Washington, DC: Congressional Quarterly, 1984), p. 136.

**franking
privilege**

A congressional
benefit that permits
members to send out
official mail using
their signature rather
than postage.

term limits

Laws restricting the
number of terms an
elected representative
may serve. The Court
has struck down state
efforts to limit terms
for federal offices,
but allowed state
laws that limit terms
for elected officials at
the state level.

of the most valuable resources they have is the **franking privilege**, the right to send out official mail without any postage. Senators and representatives frequently use this privilege to send out newsletters extolling their activities on behalf of the district, or questionnaires soliciting the public's opinion on current issues. In almost every case, the name and face of the legislator are prominently displayed. Another valuable resource is staff. Most members of Congress use much of their staff's time to perform constituency services, mostly running interference through the Washington bureaucracy for constituents with problems. Needless to say, the hope is that the satisfied home voters will remember the favor on Election Day.

Critics charge that the high rates of reelection for incumbents have led to legislative stagnation and unresponsiveness. One solution that has attracted broad attention in recent years, and particularly in the 1992 campaign, is **term limits**, restricting the number of terms a person can serve in the House or Senate (for example, to 12 years). Term limits were on the ballot in 14 states in 1992 and won in all 14. In 1995 the Supreme Court held that these restrictions were unconstitutional at the federal level, although limitations on state level officials now exist in over 20 states.[17] Another solution is to reduce the advantages that come with a seat in the House or Senate, in particular to limit the amount of mail members of Congress may send at public expense under their franking privilege. A series of revisions to the franking privilege in the late 1990s require members of Congress to deduct franking costs from their official budgets, though there is no restriction on the amount of their budgets they can use for mailings.

Parties, Candidates, and Issues

After incumbency, the single most important determinant of voting in congressional races is party. Both party and incumbency provide "low-cost" information cues to people facing a voting decision. The candidate's party is supplied on the ballot. The incumbent's name and generally positive reputation are known. Either may be used with little time and effort in information gathering—and either one may be substituted for the other.[18]

Earlier discussion indicated that the issues themselves usually do not play a major role in presidential campaigns. The same is even more true of congressional campaigns. The major problem is information, or rather a lack of it. If, as in many contests, voters do not even recognize the names of the candidates, they obviously know even less about the candidates' positions and voting records on the issues.[19] Of course, the impact of issues can soar when differences between the candidates are sharp and well publicized on matters of importance. The only issue that consistently achieves salience with

---

[17]*U.S. Term Limits, Inc. v. Thornton*, 514 U.S. 779 (1995).
[18]Barbara Hinckley, *Congressional Elections* (Washington, DC: Congressional Quarterly, 1981), p. 68.
[19]Thomas Mann and Raymond Wolfinger, "Candidates and Parties in Congressional Elections," *American Political Science Review* 74 (1980): 629.

the public is the economy. In both presidential and midterm election years, the better the economy is doing, the better the congressional candidates of the president's party do.[20]

The other major factor in congressional voting, as in presidential voting, is the candidates themselves. Candidates for the House rest their appeal on such general qualities as trust and competence, and voters seem to respond most favorably to them.[21] Senate candidates, in contrast, are evaluated in more specific terms of experience and ability, qualities that are closer to those by which presidential candidates are judged.[22] This difference in factors affecting voting decisions between House and Senate candidates is probably due to the fact that Senate candidates are generally better known than House candidates. Negative campaigning is as much a trend and an issue for congressional campaigns as it is for presidential ones.

The success of the congressional candidates from each party may be affected by the popularity of their party's president or presidential candidate. In the years when congressional elections coincide with a presidential election, a presidential candidate whose popularity appears to give a boost to his party's candidates for the House and Senate is said to have coattails. Ronald Reagan was said to have coattails in 1980 because his appeal seemed to help Republican congressional candidates to do better than had been expected. In contrast, in 1988 George Bush was said to have no coattails because his party picked up no seats. In two of the last three presidential elections, the winning candidate's party actually lost seats in Congress—an effect known as negative coattails. In midterm elections, the Congressional vote is often interpreted as a referendum on how the president is doing. Historically, the president's party has tended to lose congressional seats in midterm elections. A gain or a small loss for the president's party is interpreted as an endorsement of the president and a big loss as a repudiation. In the 1998 midterm elections President Clinton's Democratic party gained five seats.

---

[20]Edward Tufte, *Political Control of the Economy* (Princeton, NJ: Princeton University Press, 1978), pp. 113, 120.
[21]Richard Fenno, *Home Style: House Members in Their Districts* (Boston: Little, Brown, 1978), pp. 54-61.
[22]Hinckley, *Congressional Elections*, pp. 79–82.

SUMMARY

1. The American voter confronts two fundamental decisions on Election Day: whether or not to vote and, if so, how to vote. Qualifications for voting and registration in most states define the boundaries of the electorate. Beyond that, voting turnout varies substantially with social characteristics and psychological outlook toward politics.

2. The voter's decision about how to vote is similarly influenced by a broad range of factors. Throughout much of American history, partisanship has

established a baseline in the division of the vote, but in recent years opinions about candidates and issues have caused voters to break from party lines.

3. Presidential candidates confront a challenge that is difficult in both strategic and physical terms. Strategically, a candidate for president confronts two separate contests: the intraparty race for the nomination and the interparty race for the White House. Physically, the candidate faces a grueling journey that begins not long after one presidential election and ends in elation or disappointment on election night four years later.

4. Congressional candidates confront a similar range of problems in getting elected. Money is an even greater problem because public financing has not yet come to congressional campaigns. Private contributions, particularly from PACs, remain a major source of political lifeblood. Because congressional elections are generally less visible than presidential campaigns, personalities and issues usually count for less and party and incumbency for more.

KEY TERMS

poll tax (232)

Twenty-fourth Amendment (232)

Voting Rights Act of 1965 (232)

female suffrage (232)

Nineteenth Amendment (233)

Twenty-sixth Amendment (233)

residence requirements (233)

Voting Rights Act of 1970 (233)

register (233)

high-stimulus election (237)

low-stimulus election (237)

Twenty-second Amendment (244)

media consultant (246)

exit poll (248)

Federal Election Campaign Act (249)

Presidential Election Campaign
    Fund (249)

soft money (252)

primary election (253)

general election (253)

open primary (253)

closed primary (253)

caucus (253)

regional primary (254)

party convention (254)

balance the ticket (254)

electoral college (255)

Twenty-third Amendment (255)

faithless elector (257)

direct popular election (257)

safe seats (261)

franking privilege (262)

term limits (262)

READINGS FOR FURTHER STUDY

The voter's side of campaigns and elections is explored in two major works on voting, the classic *The American Voter* by Angus Campbell, Philip E. Converse, Warren E. Miller, and Donald E. Stokes (New York: Wiley, 1960), and the more recent *The Changing American Voter*, rev. ed., by Norman Nie, Sidney Verba, and John Petrocik (Cambridge, MA: Harvard University Press, 1979). The former is based on surveys from the 1950s, and the latter updates and in some cases challenges the earlier study with surveys from the 1960s and 1970s.

An excellent study of voting turnout is Raymond Wolfinger and Steven Rosenstone, *Who Votes?* (New Haven, CT: Yale University Press, 1980).

The literature on presidential campaigns and elections is rich indeed: Virtually every election spawns at least one substantial account of what "really" went on. Most notable is the "Making of the President" series by Theodore H. White, particularly the classic *The Making of the President 1960* (New York: Atheneum, 1961).

Herbert E. Alexander is a leading authority on the important topic of campaign finance; his *Financing Politics: Money, Elections, and Political Reform*, 2d ed. (Washington, DC: Congressional Quarterly, 1980), provides a good overview.

Congress

A/P World Wide

Chapter Objectives

Thanks to the Constitution, Congress is the chief lawmaking body in the land. Because it is the branch of government established in Article I of the Constitution, Congress is sometimes called the "first branch." Of the three branches, Congress is also called the "people's branch" because its members are the public officials who seem most immediately responsive to changes in the public's moods and opinions. Congress is also the branch of the national government in which the political ideas of Americans are most visibly represented. Few legislative bodies possess greater authority over the lives, property, and happiness of a nation. Congress makes, or at least ratifies, fundamental decisions about national policy—for instance, whether the United States will have a military draft. Congress determines the fraction of every person's income the government will collect as taxes and the purposes for which that money will be spent. Key to understanding the first branch are the 535 individuals who serve in Congress: 435 as members of the House of Representatives and 100 as members of the Senate. Knowing who they are, what their job is like, what forces influence what they do, and how Congress is organized helps to explain how laws are passed.

---

necessary and proper clause

Also called the "elastic clause," Article I, Section 8, of the Constitution. This is the source of "implied powers" for the national government, as explained in *McCulloch v. Maryland* [17 U.S. (4 Wheaton) 316 (1819)].

The Constitutional Powers of Congress

The very first words of the Constitution declare that "all legislative powers herein granted shall be vested in a Congress which shall consist of a Senate and a House of Representatives." What are those powers? As summarized in Table 9.1, Congress may levy taxes, borrow and spend money, regulate foreign and interstate commerce, coin money, declare war, maintain the armed services, and establish federal courts inferior to the Supreme Court, to name but a few. Perhaps the most important grant of power is in the **necessary and proper clause**, which authorizes Congress to "make all laws which are necessary and proper for carrying into execution the foregoing powers and all other powers vested by this Constitution in the government."

TABLE 9.1
The Constitutional Powers of Congress

Article I of the Constitution grants many powers to Congress. In most cases, both houses must act, but in a few instances the Constitution specifies that one house or the other has a special role.

RESPONSIBILITIES OF BOTH HOUSE AND SENATE	RESPONSIBILITIES OF SENATE ONLY	RESPONSIBILITIES OF HOUSE ONLY
Levy taxes	Try impeachments	Bring impeachments
Borrow and spend money	Ratify treaties	Originate tax bills
Regulate commerce	Confirm all federal judges, ambassadors, cabinet members, and other officials	
Regulate currency		
Establish postal system		
Provide for patents and copyrights		
Establish federal courts below Supreme Court		
Declare war		
Maintain armed forces		
Govern the nation's capital		
Oversee national property		
Make laws "necessary and proper" to carry out above powers		

In *McCulloch v. Maryland*,[1] Chief Justice Marshall, speaking for the Supreme Court, found ample power in this clause for Congress to use all appropriate means to achieve its enumerated goals. In this case, discussed in Chapter 2, the Court supported the congressional power to create a national bank, even though this explicit power was not mentioned in the Constitution. Marshall made it clear that the necessary and proper clause added implied powers to those enumerated in the Constitution. With few exceptions, the powers of Congress have been construed broadly ever since. That being said, the current Supreme Court has demonstrated a greater willingness than its recent predecessors to rein in congressional power. Even with these occasional setbacks, though, the powers granted by the necessary and proper clause remain vast.[2]

But the Constitution does impose some constraints. First, the enumeration of specific powers limits what Congress can do to those powers and others implied from them.

---

[1] 17 U.S. (4 Wheaton) 316 (1819).
[2] For example, *United States v. Lopez*, 514 U.S. 549 (1995) and *United States v. Morrison*, 529 U.S. 598 (2000).

bill of attainder

A law that punishes an individual and bypasses the procedural safeguards of the legal process. Prohibited by the Constitution.

ex post facto law

A law that makes an act a crime after it was committed or increases the punishment for a crime already committed. Prohibited by the Constitution.

checks and balances

The system of separate institutions sharing some powers that the Constitution mandates for the national government. The purpose is to keep power divided among the three branches; legislative, executive, and judicial.

Seventeenth Amendment

Ratified in 1913, it provides for the direct popular election of United States

Second, Article I, Section 9, contains eight specific limitations, including a ban on **bills of attainder** (legislative acts that declare an individual guilty and mete out punishment without a trial) and **ex post facto laws** (laws that make an act a crime after it was committed or increase the punishment for a crime already committed). As described in Chapter 3, the Bill of Rights places a set of personal liberties beyond the reach of Congress. For example, Congress cannot establish a state religion or abolish jury trials in criminal cases without violating the First and Sixth Amendments. But in the area of economic and social policy, Congress is given a wide berth; for example, Congress can decide whether to regulate certain industries or to continue price supports for certain farm commodities.

The Constitution requires Congress to share many of its powers. This is the principle of **checks and balances** discussed in Chapter 1. The Senate ratifies treaties, but the president or his advisers negotiate them. Congress may pass laws, but the president can veto them (and can be overruled by a two-thirds vote in each house), and the Supreme Court can declare them unconstitutional. In foreign policy the president and Congress battle for control. Although Congress can declare war, the president commands the armed forces and can send them anywhere on the globe.

Congress also shares power within itself, for it is divided into two chambers—the Senate and the House of Representatives. The House, according to one of the Founders, George Mason, "was to be the grand depository of the Democratic principles of government." Each state was granted representation in the House according to its proportion of the national population, and members were selected by direct election. In 1964 the Supreme Court, in *Wesberry v. Sanders*,[3] took the principle a step further, requiring that each congressional district within the states be apportioned on the basis of equal population.

The delegates to the Constitutional Convention assumed that the House, being the most democratic of our institutions, would also be the most impulsive. Thus the Senate was meant to constrain the excesses of popular government. As Madison put it, "The use of the Senate is to consist in its proceeding with more coolness, with more system, and with more vision than the popular branch."[4]

Apportioned two for each state, senators were originally elected by the state legislatures with the expectation that they would be more conservative and partial to entrenched economic interests. With direct election of senators required in 1913 by the **Seventeenth Amendment**, the Senate also became subject to the mass electorate, and the distinction the Founders considered to be so important faded away.

Yet differences between the House and the Senate remain, as Table 9.2 indicates. Almost all members of the House represent only part of a state, whereas each senator represents an entire state. Although the Constitution assigns both equal weight in writing

[3]376 U.S. 1 (1964).
[4]Quoted in Roger J. Davidson and Walter J. Oleszek, *Congress and Its Members,* 3d ed. (Washington, DC: Congressional Quarterly, 1990), p. 23.

TABLE 9.2

Differences Between the House and the Senate

Although the House and the Senate are alike in many ways, differences give each a special character. In addition, the Constitution assigns to the Senate particular confirmation and treaty-ratifying powers and to the House the right to originate tax bills.

SENATE	HOUSE OF REPRESENTATIVES
Senators represent entire states, with each state differing in population from other states	Members represent only part of a state (unless a state is assigned only one representative); House districts are equal in population
Senate contains 100 members	House contains 435 members
Senators serve six-year terms	Representatives serve two-year terms
Floor debate important in shaping outcome of legislation	Committee work important in shaping outcome of legislation
Unlimited debate	Limited debate
Riders (nongermane amendments) permitted	Riders prohibited
More prestige, media coverage, and visibility	Less prestige, media coverage, and visibility
Larger staffs for each senator, with size determined by population of state and distance from Washington	Smaller staffs of equal size for each member
Casework less important	Casework more important
Fewer committees	More committees
Source of many presidential aspirants	Few presidential aspirants
Vice-president is presiding officer	House elects presiding officer (Speaker); Rules Committee important

laws, it commands unique duties to each. The Senate has the sole power to try impeachments, to confirm presidential nominations, and to ratify treaties. The House must originate tax bills (and by custom appropriation bills as well) and bring impeachments. Although neither chamber has ever consistently dominated the other, the prestige of a senator is greater than that of a House member. The reasons are obvious; there are fewer senators, and their terms are three times longer (six years versus two years). Representatives frequently give up their House seats to run for the Senate, but the reverse is seldom done.

The Members of Congress

The powers the Constitution bestows on Congress present the opportunity for congressional action and influence on national policy. Much of what Congress actually does, however, is not specified in the Constitution but is largely a product of the values and interests of the 535 members who sit in the House and the Senate.

Who Are They?

The constitutional requirements for membership in Congress are simple. A House member must be 25 years old, a U.S. citizen for seven years, and a resident of the state (not the district) he or she represents. A senator must be 30 years of age, a U.S. citizen for nine years, and a resident of the state he or she represents. Although these requirements open the door to most of the adult population of the country, in practice the people who eventually go to Congress do not represent a cross section of the adult population. Members of Congress are predominantly white and upper–middle-class. In the One-Hundred Seventh Congress (2001–2003) the vast majority were lawyers or people who came from banking or business.[5] Some members—such as Tom Osborne (R-NE), a former football coach, and both Steve Largent and J.C. Watts, former football players who are now Republican Representatives from Oklahoma—have cashed in on their celebrity status to gain election to Congress.

From its beginnings Congress was predominantly a men's club. The percentage of women serving in Congress in 1991 (5.8 percent) was only slightly higher than the percentage serving in 1953 (3 percent). Dubbed "the year of the woman," the 1992 election brought 24 new women to the House and four new women to the Senate. In the One-Hundred Seventh Congress, women make up 14 percent of the House and 13 percent of the Senate. These percentages are likely to continue to grow in the coming years as more women are elected to state legislatures, a common launching ground for a congressional race.

African Americans were barely represented in Congress a generation ago. Between 1900 and 1928 there were no African Americans in Congress, and until the passage of the Voting Rights Act of 1965 there were no African Americans representing the South. Judicial interpretation of the Voting Rights Act has required that minorities be given maximum opportunity to elect their own to Congress. Consequently, in the 1992 election 13 new African Americans and six new Latinos won election to the House. In the One-Hundred Seventh Congress there are 38 African Americans in the House and none in the Senate. African Americans still constitute only 9 percent of Congress, although they comprise 12.9 percent of our population. Table 9.3 profiles members of Congress by age, gender, and ethnicity.

How Do They See Their Role?

The great eighteenth-century English political thinker Edmund Burke felt that an elected representative should seek to represent not his constituents' views but his own conscience and the broad interests of the nation. "Your representative owes you," said Burke, "not his industry only, but his judgment; and he betrays, instead of serving you,

---

[5]*Congressional Quarterly Weekly Report,* November 7, 1992, pp. 8–9.

TABLE 9.3
Profile of the One-Hundred Seventh Congress (2001–2003)

SOURCE: Congressional Research Service, Membership of the 107th Congress: A Profile, 2001.

	SENATE	HOUSE
Average Age	59	53
Men/Women	87/13	374/61
African Americans	0	38
Latinos	0	19
Asians and Pacific Islanders	2	5
American Indians	1	1

trustee role

The concept that legislators should vote on the basis of their consciences and the broad interests of the nation and not simply on the views of their constituents.

delegate role

A concept of legislative work as simply voting the desires of one's constituents, regardless of one's own personal views.

politico style

A manner of representation in which members of Congress attempt to strike a balance between the interests of their constituents and the dictates of their own judgment and conscience.

if he sacrifices it to your opinion."[6] Such an understanding is known as the **trustee role**. Those who see themselves as simply voting their constituents' desires perform the **delegate role**. Most legislators combine both roles into what is known as the **politico style** of representation. These members consider both their constituents' opinions and their own view of the national interest in making up their mind. The weight assigned to each varies with the issue involved. On bread-and-butter questions, such as public works and farm supports, members are more likely to follow their constituents' views than on moral questions such as abortion or school prayer.

How Long Do They Stay?

In the early years, few members considered an actual career in Congress. Washington in the 1800s was a provincial, mosquito-ridden town, and most members lived in boardinghouses. Until after the Civil War it was not uncommon for half the members of the House to be first-timers. Nor was it unusual for a representative or senator to resign in midterm to pursue a more lucrative profession. Few served longer than two terms.

Toward the end of the nineteenth century, more members began to see service in Congress as a career. As the role of the national government expanded, the business of Congress seemed more urgent and exciting. Between 1850 and 1950 the average tenure for both senators and representatives increased, and the percentage of first-term members declined. In the 1970s those trends began to flatten. Fewer members seemed interested in a lengthy congressional career, and the number of House members with 20 or more years' service decreased by half.

---

[6]David J. Vogler, *The Politics of Congress*, 4th ed. (Boston: Allyn & Bacon, 1983), p. 76.

How Much Do They Do?

Today's legislators work almost 11 hours a day when Congress is in session, which adds up to approximately 300 working days a year. The business of Congress has expanded in both volume and complexity. No longer does Congress have the luxury to ruminate over the two or three issues of the day. In the Sixteenth Congress, when James Monroe (1817–1825) was president, 480 bills were introduced. In the One-Hundred Sixth Congress (1999–2000), 10,840 measures were introduced, and they were longer and more intricate and involved practically every area of our economic and social life.

Legislators' schedules are "long, fragmented, and unpredictable." On any particular day they may breakfast with a reporter; attend several committee hearings; meet with constituents, lobbyists, or officials on legislative issues; discuss pending legislation with other members or staff; and attend floor debate. Evenings are often consumed with meetings, receptions, and fund-raisers. Most of this is crammed into four working days so that members may return home for a weekend of campaigning. A 1987 survey of members showed that one-half had no personal time and one-third had no time for family.[7]

What Do They Do?

The imperative of getting reelected motivates most members of Congress; therefore, they must cultivate the support and the trust of their constituents. How they do that is described by Richard Fenno as a member's *home-style*, which involves: (1) the members' allocation of time and resources to their district; (2) their personal style; and (3) their explanation of their Washington activities. Sophisticated use of the **franking privilege** (free postage for official business) has become an increasingly effective method of members for keeping their constituents informed. In 1990 the cost of the congressional frank exceeded $100 million. Computerized mailing lists allow incumbents to target their messages to particular constituencies.

A recent phenomenon is satellite-feed videotapes, whereby members can send prepackaged statements directly to a local television channel. Both parties have high-tech studios on Capitol Hill. For example, in the Hart Office Building the Senate Republicans have studios, film-editing rooms, and dishes on the roof so that Senators can do call-in shows or interviews for local cable channels.[8] With an advanced copy of the president's State of the Union Address, members can send their taped reaction to the speech to local television stations in time for the eleven o'clock news.

Members use a variety of methods to gain recognition and build support back home. They fight hard to see to it that their state or district gets its share of the governmental pie. Known as *pork barrel politics*, the process involves gaining federal funds for sewage plants, housing units, and dams.

franking privilege

A congressional benefit that permits members to send out official mail using their signature rather than postage.

---

[7]Hedrick Smith, *The Power Game: How Washington Works* (New York: Ballantine Books, 1989), p. 108; Davidson and Oleszek, pp. 124–227.
[8]Ibid., pp. 130–131.

As eager as legislators are to denounce the size of the federal budget, they are far more anxious to secure a new federal office building, a bridge, or a hospital in their own district. But one cannot denounce Congress for such hypocrisy, because it is shared by the public at large. Constituents expect their representatives in Washington both to cut the budget and to gain them a slice of the pork.

Beyond legislative work, members also are expected to serve as an **ombudsman** or go-between who intervenes with the federal bureaucracy on behalf of individual constituents. Such intervention is called **casework**, and may include helping a student who requests information on a government scholarship program, a soldier interested in an early discharge, or someone with a tax or immigration problem. Such matters are usually handled by the staff through phone calls to the appropriate agency. If the case is difficult or involves influential people in the state or district, a member will deal with it personally.

How Do They See Each Other?

Legislative norms are the standards or unwritten rules of acceptable behavior in Congress. Some of these norms operate differently in each chamber, and time has altered others. First among the most important norms is **reciprocity**. Members are expected to extend support to other members in the expectation that the favor will be returned. An urban representative may support a farm bill in exchange for a rural member's vote for the food stamp program. This practice is known as **logrolling**. Among the general public it is considered vaguely disreputable, but members consider such conduct perfectly acceptable.

During the recent years of large deficits and budget cutbacks, legislation often requires that sacrifices rather than rewards be shared. In a form of negative logrolling, members will accept across-the-board reductions that limit all programs or benefits. If members can claim that everyone is taking their lumps, they can more easily avoid blame.[9]

Second, since political conflict is inherent in Congress, members are expected to extend as much *personal courtesy* to each other as is possible. On the floor of Congress, colleagues refer to each other as "the gentleman from . . ." or "the gentlewoman from . . . ." Members who engage in personal attacks on their colleagues are frequently rebuked.

Historically, because of the Senate's smaller size, its members have gotten to know each other better than those in the House. This tendency has changed somewhat in recent years. The necessity of dealing with larger staffs, media demands, and frequent traveling have made it difficult for senators to establish close friendships. The Senate's clubbiness and sense of esprit have consequently declined.[10]

---

ombudsman

A person who intervenes with the bureaucracy on behalf of individual citizens.

casework

The congressional task of handling requests by constituents for information or assistance with the federal bureaucracy.

legislative norms

The unwritten rules of acceptable behavior in Congress.

reciprocity (or logrolling)

A practice whereby two or more members of Congress exchange support for legislation important to each other.

---

[9]R. Kent Weaver, "The Politics of Blame Avoidance," *The Brookings Review* 5 (Spring 1987): 43–47.
[10]Barbara Sinclair, *The Transformation of the U.S. Senate* (Baltimore, MD: Johns Hopkins University Press, 1989), pp. 98–100.

Third, members are expected to *specialize* in one or two subjects, usually matters within their assigned committee. This gives Congress a degree of expertise on complex issues ranging from arms control to acid rain. Specialization also makes a legislator's job manageable, allowing members to allocate their time and energy more efficiently. The degree of specialization is greater in the House than the Senate. Large staffs do an enormous amount of legwork, enabling a Senator to become knowledgeable on a broad range of issues.[11]

In the 1950s, when Congress was dominated by older, conservative, and generally southern members, junior members were expected to serve a period of apprenticeship. They were expected to work hard, stay out of floor debates, and defer to their seniors; in brief, they were to be seen and not heard. Today a more independent and outspoken membership rarely observes such deference. The liberal members elected in the 1960s and 1970s and the conservatives elected in the 1980s and 1990s have been too independent and impatient. In the House, new members who recognize the need for some period of apprenticeship see it as months, not years. Junior senators feel no obligation to serve an apprenticeship, and senior members no longer expect it of them.

The Structure of Congress

Congress contains a complex network of party organizations, committees, subcommittees, and supporting agencies. Understanding each part of this network is important to comprehending the whole.

Party Leadership: The House

Speaker of the House

The presiding officer of the House of Representatives, selected by the majority party.

The **Speaker of the House** is the presiding officer of the House of Representatives. The position, established by the Constitution (Article I, Section 2) is, according to the Presidential Succession Act of 1947, next in line to succeed the president after the vice-president. Although formally elected by the entire House membership, the Speaker is nominated by the majority party, all of whose members routinely vote for him. When the president and the Speaker are of the same party, the Speaker is expected to mobilize support for the president's program in the House and to represent House opinion to the president, seeing to it that unnecessary clashes are avoided.

The Speaker's power once rivaled that of the president, and toward the end of the nineteenth century, he was frequently referred to as a czar. The office reached its pinnacle under Speaker Joseph Cannon (R-IL) (1903–1911). Cannon had the power to make committee assignments and appoint and remove committee chairpersons. His impact on national policy was unmistakable. A staunch reactionary, Cannon helped to stifle

[11]Andy Plattner, "The Lure of the Senate: Influence and Prestige," *Congressional Quarterly Weekly Report,* May 25, 1985, pp. 991–998.

much of President Theodore Roosevelt's (1901–1909) reform program on child labor, lower tariffs, and banking. In the 1910–1911 session of Congress a rising tide of progressivism (see Chapter 4) swept the House, and a revolt arose against Cannon in particular and the powers of the Speaker in general. The Speaker lost the power to make committee assignments and appoint committee chairpersons, and for some years after the revolt, the Speaker once again became a figurehead.

In 1975 the House Democrats increased the substantive power of the Speaker considerably. The Speaker became the chair of the party's *Steering and Policy Committee*, with the power to nominate all Democratic members of the Rules Committee, which clears major legislation going to the House floor. During his brief tenure as Speaker (1987–1989), Jim Wright (D-TX) aggressively exploited the new powers of the office to speed his legislative priorities through the House. He exerted tight control of scheduling and used the **Rules Committee** to restrict the amendments offered on the House floor. Wright referred pieces of major legislation to multiple committees with strict deadlines for consideration, a device known as "multiple referrals." He oversaw the passage of major trade legislation, a farm credit bill, and catastrophic health insurance. Wright resigned from the House in 1989 under fire for ethics violations. Yet, in two years he had transformed the office from a consensus builder to an agenda setter.[12]

The **majority leader** is the Speaker's chief deputy and the second most powerful figure in the majority party. Elected by the party caucus, the formal organization of House Democrats and House Republicans, the majority leader is his party's leader on the floor of the House, its chief spokesperson, and defender of the party's record from partisan attacks. He assists the Speaker in scheduling legislation and deciding party strategy in floor debates. Owing to his influence with the Speaker, the majority leader can help colleagues schedule legislation for floor consideration. When the president is of the same party, the majority leader confers regularly with him and frequently works to advance his programs. Denny Hastert (R-IL), the Speaker for the One-Hundred Seventh Congress, has held this position since 1999.

The leader of the loyal opposition in the House is the **minority leader**, a post filled in the One-Hundred Seventh Congress by Dick Gephardt (D-MT). Being the leader of a minority can be dispiriting, since one's party does not control the committee agenda and frequently loses votes on the floor.

The **party whip** acts as an assistant majority or minority leader. Whips are chosen by the party caucus. Although they have little independent power, they serve their party leadership by encouraging party discipline and floor attendance during important votes. This makes the whips the heart of the party communication system. They poll members on crucial legislation and, when possible, pressure uncommitted members to follow the party line. They have the major responsibility of ensuring that the necessary

Rules Committee

Powerful House committee that clears most important bills for floor consideration and decides the rule under which bills should be considered. Also, the committee of a party convention that recommends changes in the way a party conducts its affairs.

majority leader (House)

Leader and chief spokesperson for the majority party in the House.

minority leader (House)

Leader and chief spokesperson for the minority party in the House.

party whip

Member of each party's leadership responsible for party discipline and attendance for key votes.

---

[12]Roger H. Davidson, "The New Centralization on Capitol Hill," *Review of Politics* 50 (1988): 358–359.

members are present during important votes. The House Majority Whip's office is a large intelligence-gathering organization that includes a chief deputy whip, seven deputy whips, more than 30 at-large whips, and more than 20 assistant whips.

The major arm of the Republican caucus, known as the **Conference**, is the House Policy Committee. This is a 46-member committee composed of the Speaker, the majority leader, the whips, the chairs of five major committees, the congressional campaign committee chair, the chair of the conference, the conference vice-chair, the conference secretary, the leadership chair, 11 regionally elected members, six class representatives, and 15 members appointed by the Speaker.

Conference

The Republican leadership committee in the House.

Dick Gephardt. *(AP Wide World)*

Committee chairs, who once received their position by reason of seniority, are now selected by a secret-ballot vote by the caucus prior to each Congress. On rare occasions the caucus has defied the principle of seniority. In 1975 the caucus rejected three committee chairs, in 1985 it rejected one, and in 1991 it rejected two. By this action, it sent a message to all committee heads that their behavior would be closely monitored.

The Democratic caucus, which has been in the minority since 1995, elects Democratic leadership, approves committee assignments, and enforces party rules and discipline. It is composed of a number of task forces that report on important current policy issues. In the One-Hundred Seventh Congress, the Democratic Caucus has 14 task forces, covering topics such as campaign finance reform, energy, and education.

Party Leadership: The Senate

president pro tempore

The presiding officer of the Senate in the absence of the vice-president. A largely honorific post, usually given to the senior majority party member.

Because the Senate has fewer members, party organization in the Senate is not as elaborate as it is in the House. Moreover, a tradition of independence cuts against attempts to regiment the membership along party lines. The *president of the Senate* and chief presiding officer is the vice-president of the United States. But their role is entirely ceremonial. It involves presiding over Senate sessions, which rarely occurs and voting only to break a tie, which happens infrequently. In addition to the vice-resident, the Constitution also provides for a **president pro tempore** who may preside over the Senate in the absence of the vice-president. An important exception to this general rule occurred in early

Vice-President Dick Cheney. (*AP Wide World*)

majority leader (Senate)

Leader and chief spokesperson for the majority party in the Senate.

minority leader (Senate)

Leader and chief spokesperson for the minority party in the Senate.

2001, when Vice-President Dick Cheney cast tie-breaking votes multiple times in a Senate that was evenly divided between the parties. In practice, the task of presiding over the Senate debates is given to a dozen or so junior senators in the majority party who serve about a half-hour each day. Since 1945 the post of president pro tempore has been regarded as largely honorific and given to the senior majority party member. The **majority leader** is the leader of the majority party in the Senate, elected at the beginning of each session. The **minority leader**, who leads the minority party, is also elected by party colleagues. But the majority leader is the dominant figure. As the floor leader, the majority leader is recognized first in debate, influences who will be recognized, and controls the scheduling of bills for floor consideration. Like the House Speaker, the majority leader may influence committee assignments of new senators and of other senators seeking to gain more desirable committee positions.

The Senate is far more difficult to lead than the House. Its 100 members, elected for six years, have a strong sense of independence and expect more deference to their wishes from the leadership than do House members. Only by a vote of 60 members can debate be terminated, and most routine Senate business is conducted by unanimous consent. Much of the majority leader's time is spent accommodating the hectic schedules of the individual senators. Rising constituent demands involve more service and visits to home states. The need for aggressive self-promotion and perpetual campaigning requires much from senators. Not only must they make frequent home visits, but they must engage in a constant round of media appearances, speeches, and fund-raising activities. Former Majority Leader Robert Byrd (D-WV) once explained his role as "a traffic cop, babysitter, welfare worker, minister, lawyer, umpire, referee, punching bag, target, lightning rod [and] . . . the cement that holds his party group together."[13] Thus, an effective majority leader must be a consummate diplomat, nurturing inflated egos, accommodating individual agendas, and smoothing ruffled feathers in order to pass important legislation.

The function of the party leader goes beyond managing the business of the Senate. The party leader is also a media personality and spokesperson for the party. Senator Tom Daschle (D-SD) has carried that burden since the summer of 2001, when the Democrats regained the majority in the Senate. Daschle is considered a master of the brief, pithy comment that is so effective on the evening news.

The whip system in the Senate is smaller and less institutionalized than in the House. The *Senate whips* basically serve the floor leaders as vote counters and are not major power brokers. Both the Senate majority and minority whips are elected by their caucus on a secret ballot prior to the beginning of each new Congress.

The Committee System

Contemporary lawmaking involves an understanding of numerous complex subjects. Members of Congress cannot be expected to master the details of the hundreds of bills that come before them. Through the committee system, they can gain specialized knowledge of particular areas of policy and legislation.

There are three classes of committees. **Standing committees** (19 in the House and 16 in the Senate) are at the center of the congressional process. They alone can approve legislation and send it to the House or Senate floor for consideration. **Joint committees** are permanent committees made up of members from both houses. **Special or select committees** are created periodically to study particular problems or new areas of legislation not covered by the standing committees.

The concept of seniority, or privileges based on length of service, permeates Congress and is essential to understanding the committee system. **Congressional seniority** is based on length of continuous service in Congress. Seniority can affect committee assignments, the amount of office space a member is granted, and even the deference shown a member during floor debate. Committee seniority is determined by the years of continuous service on a particular committee. The committee chair is usually the member of the majority party with the longest consecutive service on the committee. A member who switches committees must start at the bottom of the committee ladder. This

---

standing committees

The permanent committees of Congress that alone can approve legislation and send it to the floor of the House or Senate.

joint committees

Permanent committees of Congress made up of members from both houses.

special or select committees

Committees of Congress created periodically to study particular problems or new areas of legislation.

Congressional seniority

Based on a members' length of continuous service in the Congress, it can affect committee assignments, the amount of office space granted, and even the deference shown a member during floor debate.

---

[13]Quoted in Samuel C. Patterson, "Party Leadership in the U.S. Senate," *Legislative Studies Quarterly* 14 (1989): 409.

Politics and Ideas
Contrasting Approaches to Foreign Policy:
Idealism, Realism, and Isolationism

American foreign policy is a complex mixture of domestic pressures and geopolitical interests and ideas. Over the course of this century several fundamental ideas about foreign policy have emerged and have found articulate spokespersons and advocates.

One of those ideas is the concept of *realism*, which accepts conflict as a permanent part of international policies. Realists believe that foreign policy can, at best, limit conflict, not eliminate it. Peace and national self-interest from the realist view is best assured by constructing a stable balance of power. Since not all conflicts threaten the balance of power, realists support a policy of limits: a nation should only commit itself to those struggles in which vital interests are at stake and in which it has the means to prevail. President Theodore Roosevelt (1901–1909) was one of the earliest exponents of realism.

Roosevelt asserted America's primary interest in the Caribbean, where he could exclude the European powers without dragging the country into a major war. In 1903, he promoted Panama's rebellion from Columbia and then acquired the Canal Zone from Panama. In 1905, he placed the finances of Santo Domingo under American control to prevent any European country from assuming authority over that beleaguered country. Critics argued that such realism had only short-term benefits, brought America few friends, and encouraged the belief that military threats could solve all problems.

The idealist approach to foreign policy begins with the assumption that human nature is basically good and that wars and other forms of conflict are not the normal conditions of mankind. Political *idealism* holds that the goal of American foreign policy should be to promote the principles of universal peace, human rights, and democracy. President Woodrow Wilson (1913–1921) is the American political leader most closely identified with this school of thought. In the years 1914–1916, Wilson sent American troops to Mexico, Haiti, and the Dominican Republic, not as Roosevelt had to stave off European intervention, but to establish democratic governments.

After war broke out in Europe in 1914, Roosevelt, then a private citizen, urged American intervention to pre-

adherence to seniority has been challenged and revised in recent years. In 1995, a newly-elected Republican majority disregarded seniority in making many of its committee leadership selections.

　　　Members consider desirable committee assignments crucial to their reelection. After each congressional election, freshman representatives and senators scramble to gain assignments suitable to their political fortunes and interests. Incumbents maneuver to gain more prestigious assignments. Assignments are first handled by a committee on committees in each house by each party, approved by the party caucuses (Democrats

Contrasting Approaches to Foreign Policy: Idealism, Realism, and Isolationism, *continued*

vent Germany from dominating Europe and thus upsetting the balance of power on that continent. Wilson was reluctant to intervene until Germany began unrestricted submarine warfare against American merchant ships. Then he justified involvement upon the most lofty ideals. In asking Congress for a declaration of war, Wilson claimed that America would fight for "the ultimate peace of the world and the the liberation of its peoples . . . the world must be made safe for democracy." When World War I ended, Wilson insisted upon a peace settlement, known as the Fourteen Points, which would require a global peacekeeping entity (the League of Nations), arms limitations, open diplomacy, and the self determination of nations. The eventual treaty, signed in Versailles in 1919, embodied few of these principles except for the League of Nations and was rejected by the United States Senate.

In twenty years Europe was embroiled in another war. Critics argued that Wilson's efforts at peace making did not end European habits of power politics, hostile alliances, and imperialist politics. Such moralistic policies, they contended, only lead to futile crusades and endless wars.

The doctrine of *isolationism* has deep roots in American history, going back to George Washington's admonition in his Farewell Address. According to the isolationist credo, America should be a beacon light of liberty for all humanity, but not attempt to impose its way of life on other societies. America would only be contaminated by its involvement in the power struggles of the world. One of the leading spokespersons for isolationism prior to World War II was former President Herbert Hoover (1929–1933). Hoover saw no clear moral choice between Imperialist Britain and Communist Russia on one side and Nazi Germany and Fascist Italy on the other. Hoover feared that permanent involvement in the affairs of the world would so enlarge the role of the government and the military in the life of a nation as to constitute a threat to our liberty. Most Americans spurned Hoover's advice, believing that America must play a continual role in the international community.

Do you see the influences of realism, idealism, or isolationism in contemporary foreign policy?

only), and then, in what is always a formality, approved again by the full Senate and House. Several criteria govern these assignments. For example, House Democrats rarely allow any member serving on what they call the "exclusive" committees (Ways and Means, Rules, and Appropriations) to serve on any other standing committee. Both Republicans and Democrats in the Senate agree that no member will receive two major committee assignments until every member has received one. Almost every senator now has the opportunity to serve on one of the four most prestigious committees (Appropriations, Armed Services, Finance, and Foreign Relations).

**http://thomas.loc
.gov**

You can search
through the full text
of federal legislation
and track bills
through the legis-
lative process at
THOMAS — a serv-
ice of the Library
of Congress.

Members concerned primarily with reelection seek to join committees whose work has a direct impact on their constituents. A representative or senator from an area with considerable defense installations and large military contracts will probably seek membership on the Armed Services Committee, which handles the defense budget. Westerners are attracted to the House Resources and Senate Energy and Natural Resources committees, whose jurisdictions include mining, government lands, immigration, and environmental laws. Members from states that produce crops heavily dependent on government support programs (wheat, peanuts, tobacco, and sugar) seek membership on the agriculture committees. Those interested in influencing national policy seek membership on committees that consider broad public issues such as education, foreign policy, and civil rights. Some members, as they become more senior and more entrenched at home, seek to expand their influence within their respective chambers. They are drawn to committees that decide matters of importance to practically every member, such as the tax-writing committees (Senate Finance and House Ways and Means), the spending committees (Appropriations and Budget), and, in the House, the scheduling committee (Rules).

Members cannot passively wait for their assignments. They must make their preferences known, urge senior members from their own states to lobby for them, personally meet with the chair or ranking minority member of the committee, and cultivate the support of the party leadership. Election results are barely known in November when senators and representatives descend on Washington to compete for the choicest committee seats. Committee assignments, one of the few benefits the congressional leadership can control, are employed when possible to promote party loyalty and responsibility. At one time, committee chairs gained their position by sheer dint of seniority and ran their committees like feudal baronies. They appointed subcommittee chairs, abolished or created subcommittees, decided whether or not to call committee meetings, and hired staff. Although the chairs still retain many of these powers (influencing the agenda, hiring staff, controlling committee funds), they are no longer the autocrats of yesteryear.

The reforms of the 1970s limited and defined the chairs' power. In the House they lost the power to prevent committees from meeting, to designate subcommittee chairs, and to refer legislation to subcommittees. In the Senate chairs no longer control all staff appointments, and consequently they have lost their influence over this important group of experts. Chairs do not want to appear to be obstructing legislation strongly supported by a majority of the caucus for fear of losing their positions. But chairs still hold considerable power, although it is far from absolute. To get things done, they must use all their diplomatic and legislative skills. Former House Rules Committee Chairman Joe Moakley (D-MA) put it this way: "The days of snarling chairmen who look through junior members are long gone. To survive, you have to be gracious even when you say no."[14] Nor can chairs exercise their authority behind closed doors. The Legislative Reorganization Act of 1970 opened up the committee process, which had previously

---

[14]*Congressional Quarterly Weekly Report*, December 8, 1990, p. 406.

been conducted away from the direct scrutiny of the public and the media (as well as the lobbyists). Open committee hearings are now required in most cases, and committee roll-call votes are available to the public.

Subcommittees

Most of the standing congressional committees are divided into subcommittees. In the One-Hundred Seventh Congress there were 88 subcommittees in the House and 68 in the Senate. House committee chairs previously controlled their subcommittees by packing them with members who would follow their lead. Under such circumstances, subcommittees would rarely report to the full committee legislation that the chair opposed. When the era of the autocratic chair came to an end, however, the trend in the House toward "subcommittee government" began.

In 1973 the House Democratic caucus adopted a subcommittee "bill of rights." Democrats on every committee were given the authority to select subcommittee chairs, establish subcommittee jurisdiction, and provide the budgets for running the sub-committees. It required that all committees with more than 20 members be required to establish at least four subcommittees, ending the Ways and Means Committee's unique practice of operating without subcommittees. Subcommittee chairs and the ranking minority members were allowed to hire staff to work directly for them on their subcommittee.

Subcommittees assumed greater independence, conducting legislative hearings once held primarily by the full committee. Whereas only 30 percent of the legislative hearings in the early 1950s were conducted by subcommittees, by the mid-1970s the figure had risen to 90 percent. Subcommittees were also drafting more legislation and frequently gaining full committee approval. Subcommittee chairs were replacing committee chairs as the managers of legislation on the floor.

This movement toward subcommittee government is less prevalent in the Senate, where subcommittees primarily hold hearings and key votes are taken in the full committee. Yet in the Senate Commerce, Judiciary, and Labor committees, subcommittees have gained greater autonomy.[15]

The more democratic subcommittee government came with a cost. As more members exercised initiative and fewer could deliver the votes and call the shots, the committee system became increasingly unwieldy. With additional centers of power in Congress, party leaders had a far more difficult time building coalitions and constructing compromises.

Congressional Staff and Agencies

One hundred years ago senators and members of Congress performed their duties with only a few clerks, paid from members' own personal funds. By the 1990s over 14,000

---

[15]Lawrence Dodd and Bruce Oppenheimer, "The House in Transition: Change and Consolidation," *Congress Reconsidered,* 2d ed. (Washington, DC: Congressional Quarterly, 1981), p. 42; Davidson and Oleszek, *Congress and Its Members,* p. 230.

people were employed on Capitol Hill as personal staff to representatives and senators or as committee staff, all paid from public funds. This burgeoning congressional bureaucracy reflects the complexity of modern government. The issues have grown more intricate, the congressional work load has expanded, and Congress has felt the need to match the expertise of the executive branch. A typical congressional office will include a **legislative assistant (LA)** to analyze bills, draft laws, write speeches, and prepare position papers, and an **administrative assistant (AA)** to act as the legislator's alter ego in dealing with colleagues, constituents, and lobbyists. In addition, most legislators have offices in their home states or districts to provide efficient constituent service and a personal touch. Who are these staff people? They are relatively young (average age slightly under 40), well educated (close to half have postgraduate or professional degrees), and predominantly male (over 70 percent). In an earlier time they may have been political operatives or cronies of the legislator, but today they are bright university graduates. The experience of being a staffer can be both exhilarating and precarious. Staffers are frequently in the center of dramatic legislative battles, but they have no civil service protection and can be fired by their representative or senator without cause or notice.

Unlike the personal staffers, whose job it is to serve the member and his or her political interest, the *committee staffers* are responsible for developing the legislation that comes from the committees. They are appointed by the committee chair, subcommittee chair, or ranking minority party member. They organize hearings, conduct research, assist in the drafting of legislation, and prepare the reports that accompany bills sent out of committee. The chief committee aides—those most familiar with the details of a particular bill—may accompany the committee chair when the bill is debated on the floor. Because a member's time is stretched thin, staffers may act as stand-ins for the legislators themselves, negotiating with lobbyists, executive branch officials, and even other legislators to gain support for a particular bill. Like the rest of the congressional bureaucracy, the congressional committee staffs grew from about 400 in 1947 to over 2,500 in 1999—an increase of over 600 percent.

Has this expansion of staff solved the congressional need for more information? Some argue that members have become too dependent upon committee staff. Frequently, staffers are the only ones who understand increasingly complex legislation such as the Clean Air Act of 1990. Others argue that more staff generate more legislation, diluting a member's ability to concentrate on what is important. Has the Congress simply transferred its dependency for information from the executive branch to its own staff?[16]

In addition to staff, three agencies provide Congress with research and analysis of policy options:

legislative assistant (LA)

A congressional aide who analyzes bills, drafts laws, writes speeches, and prepares position papers.

administrative assistant (AA)

Top aide to a member of Congress who frequently acts on behalf of the legislator in dealing with staff, colleagues, constituents, and lobbyists.

---

[16]Michael L. Mezey, "The Legislature, the Executive, and Public Policy: The Futile Quest for Congressional Power," in James A. Thurber, ed., *Divided Democracy* (Washington, DC: Congressional Quarterly, 1991), p. 107.

1. The **Congressional Research Service** (CRS) serves the entire Congress—members, committees, and aides. On request, it conducts legal research and policy analysis and digests and summarizes legislation. Congress created the CRS to remedy the dearth of information at Congress's disposal as compared to the information resources long available to the president.
2. The **General Accounting Office** (GAO), known as the watchdog agency, reports to Congress on the efficiency and performance of federal programs. With over 3,200 employees, its task is to determine whether a program is achieving the objectives that Congress has prescribed.
3. The **Congressional Budget Office** (CBO) provides essential analysis of the economy and the federal budget for Congress. Specifically, it provides an assessment of the inflationary impact of major bills, projects the five-year costs of proposed legislation, and forecasts economic trends. The CBO gives Congress an independent base of economic and budgetary expertise to challenge the economic assumptions behind the president's budget.

Congressional Procedures: How a Bill Becomes a Law

Ultimately, Congress impacts American government because it is the chief lawmaking body. Presidents, parties, and interest groups may propose a host of programs, but unless Congress acts favorably, each proposal remains an idea, not a law. The legislative process in Congress is an obstacle course (see Figure 9.1). A bill can be stalled or defeated at various points along the way, and most are. Of the nearly 9,000 bills introduced in the One-Hundred Sixth Congress, only 580 eventually became law.

Committee to Floor Debate

The objective of guiding a bill through Congress is to have both houses pass the bill in identical form. Only then can it go to the president for signing. At the initial stage of the legislative process, only a member of the House or the Senate may introduce a bill, although the proposal frequently originates in the executive branch, an interest group, or a member's staff. Once a bill is introduced, it is sent to the appropriate committee; should a committee refuse to consider the bill, it is consigned to an early death. If the bill is considered, it is usually assigned to a subcommittee for study, and the process begins. The subcommittee may then hold hearings inviting government officials and other experts to testify. These hearings serve not only to obtain information but also to test public opinion, build support for the measure, or perhaps delay ultimate consideration. Except in the case

http://www.access
.gpo.gov/congress
/cong013.html

Every year the U.S. Congress passes hundreds of laws. Where do they end up? In the United States Code, an extensive resource that is updated annually and accessible at the above Web site.

FIGURE 9.1

How a Bill Becomes a Law

At each step along the way a bill can be stymied, making this journey a genuine obstacle course.

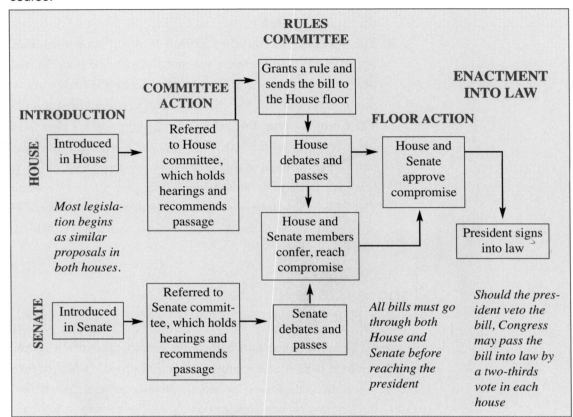

mark-up

The process in which a legislative committee sets the precise language and amendments of a bill.

Union Calendar

The House schedule for the consideration of tax and appropriation bills.

of national security matters, most hearings are open to the public. When the hearings are complete, the bill is **marked up**. This is the process whereby the subcommittee decides on the bill's precise language and on amendments. Like hearings, most mark-up sessions are open to the public.

The bill, if approved by the subcommittee, then goes to the full committee for consideration. If the full committee approves the bill (it may mark up the bill or add its own amendments), it sends the bill to its respective chamber for consideration. Bills voted out of committee are often accompanied by an extensive report that explains the bill's purpose, the committee amendments, its effect on existing law, and its probable costs.

Floor Debate: The House

Bills finally reported out of committee are listed on one of the House calendars. Tax and appropriation bills are placed on the **Union Calendar**. Non-money bills go to the

House Calendar

The legislative schedule in the House of Representatives for non-money bills.

Private Calendar

The schedule for House bills that concerns personal rather than general legislative matters.

Consent Calendar

The House calendar of business for noncontroversial measures.

closed rule

An order from the House Rules Committee that prohibits amendments to a bill under consideration on the House floor.

open rule

An order from the House Rules Committee whereby amendments to a bill are permitted on the floor.

modified rule

An order from the House Rules Committee allowing a limited number of amendments to a bill during floor consideration.

Committee of the Whole

A parliamentary device used by the House of Representatives to facilitate floor consideration of a bill. When the House dissolves itself into the Committee of the Whole, it can suspend formal rules and consider a bill with a quorum of 100 rather than the usual 218.

House Calendar. Private bills, such as one that granted citizenship to an 111-year-old Albanian woman so that she could vote in a free election before she died, are placed on the **Private Calendar**. Noncontroversial measures, such as one declaring National Dairy Goat Awareness Week, are placed on the **Consent Calendar**.

The Speaker and the majority leader determine when bills are called off the calendar and placed on the House floor. Bills on the Consent Calendar and the Private Calendar are brought directly to the floor usually by unanimous consent and passed with little debate. The Speaker may also bring other minor bills directly to the floor by a suspension of the rules. Under this procedure, which requires a two-thirds vote of the House, debate is limited to 40 minutes, and no amendments are allowed. Other matters are considered privileged and can be brought to the House floor at almost any time. But most major bills must take the route from the committee to the House floor via the Rules Committee. The Rules Committee decides the amount of time the House will spend debating a bill and dictates the amending process. The committee may send a bill to the floor with a **closed rule**, prohibiting all amendments except those from the committee that reported the bill; an **open rule**, permitting any amendments from the floor; or a **modified rule**, allowing a limited number of amendments. Tax bills reported out of the Ways and Means Committee are usually given the privilege of a closed rule. The Republicans on the Rules Committee are appointed by the Speaker, and the committee is thus an arm of the leadership.

When floor debate begins, the Speaker has a member of the Rules Committee from each party explain the rule under which the bill will be debated and voted on. Usually the Rules Committee specifies from one to two hours of debate, but it will grant controversial bills of particular importance up to 10 hours. Debate begins with a statement from the floor manager of the bill, by custom the chairperson of the committee or subcommittee that reported the bill. The floor manager has the responsibility of guiding the bill to passage. Frequently debate is conducted in the **Committee of the Whole**. This device allows the House to conduct business more quickly by relaxing the formal rules by allowing a quorum of only 100, instead of the usual 218. But the full House must approve decisions made by the Committee of the Whole before they are official.

After general debate covering the pros and cons of the bill, the amending process begins. Here the fate of a bill may be decided. Opponents of the bill may try to amend it beyond recognition or else add objectionable provisions destined to kill it. The House rules require that amendments be germane to the bill under consideration. Amendments are debated no more than 10 minutes—five minutes for the sponsors and five for the opponents.

An electronic voting system, installed in 1973, makes time-consuming roll-call votes unnecessary. Members may insert a plastic card into one of 40 voting machines and vote "yes," "no," or "present" (abstaining). The vote is recorded on an electronic display board on the wall of the chamber, and the process takes about 15 minutes.

Politics and Ideas
Two Ideologues Leave the Senate

Ideologues can rarely be called great architects of legislation, although they can have an important effect on a legislative body. Consider two recent members of the Senate, Jesse Helms and Paul Wellstone. Standing at opposite ends of the political spectrum, Senator Paul Wellstone (D-MN) and Senator Jesse Helms (R-NC) were ideologues—people for whom it is more important to defend principles than to resolve differences. Helms served in the Senate for 30 years, retiring in 2002, and Wellstone served from 1991 until his life was cut short in a plane crash on October 25, 2002.

Helms, a major spokesperson of the New Right, advocated a hard-line foreign policy, wanted to see prayer allowed in public school, and opposed legalized abortion. He used all his parliamentary acumen to influence the foreign policy of the executive branch and to force his Senate colleagues to take public positions on issues they would rather avoid. As the ranking minority member of the Foreign

Relations Committee, Helms has blocked or delayed the nominations of foreign policy officials whose views he did not share. By simply threatening a filibuster, Helms could cajole the Senate leadership, pressed with a busy agenda, not to bring up the nomination of an official he opposed. In 1985 Helms held up several dozen diplomatic appointments until he received assurances from the Reagan administration that they would find positions for six diplomats who supported Helms' conservative views.

Helms consistently sought roll-call votes on anti-abortion and school prayer laws, in spite of clear evidence that they had no chance of enactment. None of this endeared him to the Senate, which places a premium on cooperation and collegiality. It did, however, score points with the thousands of people across the country who contributed to his campaign. In his 1996 reelection campaign, Senator Helms raised over $14 million from direct mail and out-of-state conservative contributions.[a]

Executive Calendar

One of two registers of business in the U.S. Senate that contains presidential nominations and treaties.

riders

Provisions, usually attached to appropriation bills, that "ride" into law on the backs of necessary pieces of legislation. The president would have to veto an entire bill in order to kill the amendment.

Members are alerted to floor votes by a series of bells that ring through the halls and offices of Congress.

Floor Debate: The Senate

The Senate, being smaller, has a more flexible set of procedures. First, the Senate has only two calendars: an **Executive Calendar** for presidential nominations and treaties and a Calendar of General Orders for all other legislation. Second, there is no equivalent of the House Rules Committee. Thus the Senate imposes no time limits on general debate, no five-minute rule on amendments, and no restrictions on the number of amendments. In addition, amendments need not be germane to the bill under consideration.

Non-germane amendments, called **riders**, allow a proposal to bypass a hostile Senate committee that otherwise would have considered and probably killed it. The rider must then only survive the conference committee if the complete bill passes the Senate.

Two Ideologues Leave the Senate, *continued*

While sharing few, if any, of Jesse Helms' views, liberal Senator Paul Wellstone employed some of the same techniques. Before his election in 1990, Wellstone made no secret of the fact that he "despised" Helms, but once he joined Helms in the Senate, he quickly learned to employ his colleague's obstructive techniques.[b] Employing the filibuster, forcing roll-call votes, and attaching excessive amendments to bills were important parts of Wellstone's arsenal in his fight against legislation he viewed as anti-labor or anti-liberal. Such aggressive tactics, and a willingness to stand virtually alone at times on the far left, have earned Wellstone the admiration of progressives nationwide, but the scorn of some members of his own chamber—Democrats and Republicans alike. In March 2001, for example, Wellstone pushed through an amendment to the McCain-Feingold Campaign Finance Reform bill that placed limits on some television campaign advertisements. Although Wellstone argued that he was closing a loophole, his approach created a bill that could no longer muster majority support, leading to criticism from both sides of the aisle.

Both Helms and Wellstone paid a price for their obstructionism, as creating enemies sometimes led to a lack of support for the measures they proposed themselves. Frequent threat or use of the filibuster by ideologues such as Helms and Wellstone makes the work of the Senate more difficult and the schedule less controllable. These maverick senators were more interested as using the Senate as a platform for their ideas than in forging coalitions and compromises. But senators are reluctant to alter the rules in order to make the Senate run more efficiently. Do Senators such as Helms and Wellstone raise important issues, or do they merely obstruct the business of Congress?

[a]Center for Responsive Politics, "Money in Politics Data," http://www.opensecrets.org/1996os/index/S8NC00015.htm (23 October 2001).
[b]Brad Wetzler, "Peace, Love, and Grandstanding," *George*, March 1999, pp. 108–113, 126.

unanimous consent agreement

A common mechanism used by the Senate leadership to limit Senate debate.

filibuster

Continuing debate designed to prevent consideration of a particular bill; a technique used in the Senate.

Riders are also used to force the president to accept a program that would be vetoed were it to reach him as a separate piece of legislation. This is done by attaching the rider to necessary legislation, such as a general appropriations bill, that the president will feel compelled to sign. One may wonder how, with such permissive rules, the Senate ever accomplishes anything. The answer is that through the mechanism of **unanimous consent agreements**, terms of Senate debates are limited. These agreements, usually secured by the majority leader in cooperation with the minority leader, are carefully negotiated to accommodate the desires of senators who wish to speak or offer amendments.

The best-known technique for forestalling the work of the Senate is the **filibuster**—a continuing debate designed to prevent passage of a bill. A filibuster can be conducted by a single senator or a group of senators. The filibuster is essentially a political device to stop a bill that the minority does not have the votes to defeat, to win concessions on a bill, or to arouse public opposition to it. Defenders argue that the filibuster protects minority rights and requires the Senate to consider not only the extent of

cloture

Rule 22 of the Senate in which discussion on a piece of legislation can be suspended after no more than 30 hours of debate by a vote of 60 members.

opposition but its depth and intensity as well. Critics claim that the filibuster thwarts majority will and allows a small minority to exercise disproportionate influence on a bill or even to defeat it altogether. Until 1917 the Senate had no way of ending debate except through unanimous consent. At that time the Senate adopted Rule 22, a **cloture** (debate-ending) rule that allowed two-thirds of the senators present to end debate. In 1975 the rule was amended so that 60 members (or three-fifths of the membership) can shut off debate. Once cloture is invoked, the Senate can continue consideration of the bill for only 30 additional hours. Prior to the 1970s a filibuster was a rare event, used primarily by southern Democrats to block civil rights legislation. Now it is almost commonplace and occurs on a wide range of issues. Cloture votes, which numbered six in the Ninetieth Congress (1967–1969), rose to 56 in the One-Hundred Sixth. Owing to the time constraints on a busy Senate (more committee meetings, more recorded votes, more bills considered), even the threat to delay business by a filibuster can force a concession on a bill. (See "Politics and Ideas: Two Ideologues in the Senate," above.)

The Conference Committee: Resolving Senate-House Differences

House-Senate Conference Committee

A joint committee designed to reconcile differences between the House and Senate versions of a bill.

Rarely do the Senate and House pass bills in identical form. If one house makes only minor changes in a bill passed by the other, the chamber that initially passed the bill will usually agree to the changes and send the bill on to the president for signature. But when there are major differences over a bill, a **House-Senate Conference Committee** must reconcile them. The conferees are named by the House Speaker and the Senate presiding officers on the recommendation of the chairperson of the committee that reported the bill. The majority from each delegation must be from the majority party in that chamber. Each chamber has one vote in the conference, which is determined by a vote of the majority of its delegation. When the conference finishes its job, it sends the conference report or compromise bill back to the House and Senate for approval. Approval of the conference report by both houses constitutes final approval of the bill. Numerous traps await a bill before it gets to the president's desk. Bills must pass the Senate and the House within the two-year time period that makes up a particular Congress; otherwise, the bill must start through the obstacle course anew with the next Congress. It can be buried in committee or by the House Rules Committee, stifled by a Senate filibuster, or caught in a conference committee deadlock. Sponsors of a bill must know congressional procedure, be sensitive to key personalities such as the Speaker or the important committee chairs, and must at each crucial point weave a majority coalition for the bill.

Congress and the Political System

The legislative process alone does not explain why some bills become law and others do not. Congress is also part of the broader political system. Everything it does affects citizens as well as one or more interest groups and governmental agencies. These different constituencies labor mightily to influence congressional decisions.

Lobbies

As the range of government programs, subsidies, and entitlements has grown, so has the number of interest groups with a stake in them. The result has been the proliferation of lobbies and lobbyists, as described in Chapter 7. Critics feel that lobbies distort the political process and give particular groups inordinate influence over legislation.

distributive policies

Programs such as water reclamation projects that provide considerable benefits for a few people and relatively small costs for many. They usually provoke little opposition.

Lobbyists are most successful in affecting **distributive policies** (special interest subsidies such as water reclamation projects, farm price supports, and new post offices). These programs usually provoke little opposition because they are perceived as providing considerable benefits at little relative cost. As a result, the entire Congress rarely pays close attention to such questions. Lobbyists can then concentrate their efforts on a key subcommittee or committee, simplifying its task. Open committee sessions allow lobbyists to monitor congressional action quite carefully. Rather than waiting outside a closed door while a committee mark-up session is going on, a lobbyist may be right in the committee room suggesting precise legislative language or a compromise amendment.

redistributive policies

Programs such as tariffs or tax reforms that produce considerable benefits to some segments of society but high costs to others.

Lobbies have the most difficulty affecting **redistributive policies**, those that produce benefits to some segments of society at substantive cost to others. These include broad budget decisions that place social programs against defense spending or proposals for tax reform. Such issues are frequently resolved on the floor of Congress, not in committee. Because they usually involve conflicts among interest groups, the result is often a compromise, with no single lobby getting exactly what it wants.

Contemporary lobbying must go beyond working the halls of Congress; moving legislation often requires affecting public opinion. Therefore, lobbyists must employ the techniques of mass marketing: targeted mailings, television advertising, and slick public relations campaigns. The National Rifle Association can generate millions of telegrams in 24 hours opposing a gun control measure; the retirees' lobby swamped former Speaker Wright in one day with over 15 million postcards and letters warning against tampering with the cost-of-living formula for Social Security.[17] Much of the increase in lobbying is a result of the weakened power of the committee chairs and the decentralization of power in Congress. Now that there are more committee members and staffers to be persuaded, more lobbyists are required to do the job.

The Bureaucracy

Interest groups are not the only lobbying forces in Congress. The bureaucracy itself exercises considerable influence on the congressional process. Together with interest

---

[17]Smith, *The Power Game*, p. 383.

FIGURE 9.2

The "Iron Triangle" and Veteran's Policy

The triangular relationship among congressional committees, bureaucratic agencies, and interest groups indicates how relatively few people can determine public policy on some questions. The relationship does not mean that the groups are always in agreement, but it does mean that the dominant opinion represented will usually have the largest say in setting veterans' policy. Sometimes the components in the triangle are more numerous. A proposed change in educational benefits, for example, would involve higher education lobbies and other committees and agencies. A change in job-training policy for veterans would involve the Labor Department as well as the labor committees in Congress.

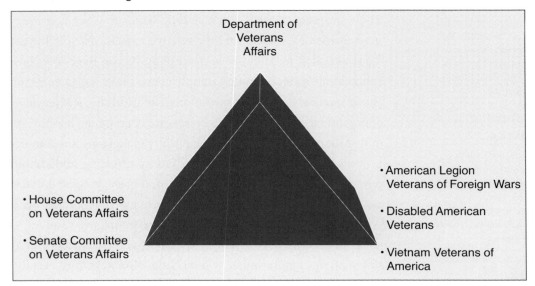

iron triangle

The combination of interest group representatives, legislators, and government administrators seen as extremely influential in determining the outcome of political decisions.

groups and congressional committees, bureaucratic agencies often develop informal partnerships called *subgovernments* or **iron triangles**. Each group scratches the back of the other. The agency gets its budget from the committee and political support from the interest group. The interest group gets favorable legislation from the committee and sympathetic treatment from the agency. The congressional committee members get campaign reelection support from the interest group and conscientious constituency service from the bureaucracy. These subgovernments have special influence over distributive policy.

The veterans' programs provide an example of such interplay. In this case, the subgovernment includes the veterans' groups, the veterans' committees of Congress, and the Department of Veterans Affairs (see Figure 9.2). Together these pieces of the subgovernment conspire to protect veterans' programs from the budget-cutter's scalpel. Veterans' benefits are usually not matters at the top of the president's agenda, nor are they issues that excite broad congressional interest. They are, in fact, typical of the type of distributive policies that are shaped by subgovernments.

To function effectively an iron triangle requires that the participants be shielded from the glare of publicity. Over the past two decades the environment has changed and the effectiveness of these subgovernments has declined. The media are more aggressive in covering Congress, the number of lobbies with competing interests in legislation has increased, new public interest lobbies watch for special interest favoritism, and no committee has exclusive control over such broad issues as energy, foreign trade, and the environment. In a period of tight budgets fewer issues can be classified as distributive, providing benefits to a few without significant and visible costs to the many.[18]

What Role for a Changing Congress?

Largely through its own efforts, Congress democratized its rules and opened up its procedures. The seniority system is no longer sacred. Committee chairs do not control their committees. Committee sessions are now accessible to the public. Junior members can make an immediate impact, often serving as subcommittee chairs. And the creation of the Congressional Budget Office, plus the addition of more professional staffers, has put Congress in the position to challenge the expertise of the executive branch.

Many people welcome the resurgence of congressional will as a necessary corrective to the presidential excesses that produced the Vietnam War and the Watergate scandal. They argue that the openness of Congress is essential to a democratic society. But other observers question whether Congress has gone too far in its reassertion of power and independence. Congress cannot control inflation, negotiate arms agreements, or solve our trade deficit. Congressional leaders feel that the American government functions best under the leadership of the president. Only the president, they argue, can define national objectives that can arouse a majority of citizens. The historic statements of national policy, so the argument goes, were presidential not congressional: the Monroe Doctrine, the Emancipation Proclamation, the War on Poverty. Although Congress cannot lead, it does have an important role to play. It provides more citizen access to policymaking and offsets the impersonality of the bureaucracy. In a larger sense, Congress brings the parochialism of Main Street, the suburban kaffeeklatsch, and the union hall to Washington's corridors of power. The many and often confusing voices with which Congress speaks are the clatter of the democratic process.

---

[18]Morris P. Fiorina, *Congress: Keystone of the Washington Establishment,* 2d ed. (New Haven, CT: Yale University Press, 1989), pp. 122–123.

SUMMARY

1. Since 1819 the Supreme Court has granted Congress great leeway in legislating on social and economic matters. Both houses have equal weight in writing laws. But the Senate, owing to its longer member terms, its special responsibilities (ratifying treaties and confirming presidential appointments), and its smaller size, seems to command somewhat greater prestige.

2. The task of members of Congress has many dimensions: mastering fields of legislation, bringing back a share of federal benefits for their state or district, meeting the needs of individual constituents, learning the norms and rules of their respective chambers, and voting on a wide variety of legislative questions. It is a demanding, complex, full-time job.

3. Power in the contemporary Congress is no longer the exclusive prerogative of a few senior members. In the House much of the power has flowed to the subcommittees. Individual senators have become increasingly assertive. Junior members feel little obligation to serve a period of apprenticeship. Congress as a result is both more democratic and more unwieldy.

4. Leadership in Congress is based largely on persuasion and ability. Autocratic leaders are increasingly rare. The influence of the caucus requires that most congressional leaders be sensitive to the concerns of the rank-and-file members.

5. Before a bill can become a law, it must pass through a complete obstacle course. At each crucial point, successful sponsors must weave a majority coalition for their bill.

6. Congress, although influenced by presidential leadership, is not the president's rubber stamp and initiates much legislation on its own.

KEY TERMS

necessary and proper clause (267)

bill of attainder (269)

ex post facto law (269)

checks and balances (269)

Seventeenth Amendment (269)

trustee role (272)

delegate role (272)

politico style (272)

franking privilege (273)

ombudsman (274)

casework (274)

legislative norms (274)

reciprocity (274)

logrolling (274)

Speaker of the House (275)

Rules Committee (276)

majority leader (House) (276)

minority leader (House) (276)

party whip (276)

Conference (277)

president pro tempore (277)

majority leader (Senate) (278)

minority leader (Senate) (278)

standing committees (279)

joint committees (279)

special or select committees (279)

Congressional seniority (279)

legislative assistant (LA) (284)

administrative assistant (AA) (284)

mark-up (286)

Union Calendar (286)

House Calendar (287)

Private Calendar (287)

Consent Calendar (287)

closed rule (287)

open rule (287)

modified rule (287)

Committee of the Whole (287)

Executive Calendar (288)

rider (288)

unanimous consent agreement (289)

filibuster (289)

cloture (290)

House-Senate Conference
    Committee (290)

distributive policies (291)

redistributive policies (291)

iron triangle (292)

READINGS FOR FURTHER STUDY

For a comprehensive overview of Congress, consult Roger H. Davidson and Walter J. Oleszek, *Congress and Its Members*, 8th ed. (Washington, DC: Congressional Quarterly, 2002), and Morris P. Fiorina, *Congress: Keystone of the Washington Establishment*, 2d ed. (New Haven, CT: Yale University Press, 1989).

A collection of highly readable essays on the problems of the contemporary Congress can be found in Lawrence C. Dodd and Bruce I. Oppenheimer, eds., *Congress Reconsidered*, 7th ed. (Washington, DC: Congressional Quarterly, 1989).

Up-to-date information and lively accounts of individual senators and representatives are available in Michael Barone and Grant Ujifusa, *Almanac of American Politics* (Washington, DC: National Journal), published every two years.

A valuable collection of data appears in Norman J. Ornstein, Thomas E. Mann, and Michael J. Malbin, *Vital Statistics on Congress*, 1999–2000 ed. (Washington, DC: Congressional Quarterly, 1999).

CHAPTER 10

The Presidency

A/P World Wide

Chapter Objectives

The American presidency is an awe-inspiring and complex office. Its demands are numerous and often contradictory. The president is expected to be honest and trustworthy, yet tough if not ruthless; to be a moral leader who is above politics as well as a political operator who can achieve results; to control government spending and taxes and yet provide extensive governmental services; and to preserve American honor against international threats and yet keep the peace. When the president extends his power, he is chastised for being imperial; when he fails to offer decisive leadership, he is considered weak and ineffective.

Even the most powerful American presidents have rarely been able to dictate the political agenda. They have had to lead, and leadership in a democratic society requires an ability to persuade without being tiresome, a capacity to administer without getting lost in details, and a sense of when to compromise and when to stand one's ground. The office is a complex mixture of authority and constraints, too subtle to capture in any one theoretical model. Some presidents have mastered the office, and some have been mastered by it.

Commentators on the presidency in the 1950s and 1960s stressed its great powers and the capacity of its occupant to accomplish great things. Franklin D. Roosevelt (1933–1945) was the model—a president who dominated Congress, shepherded through an ambitious reform agenda, centralized decision making in his own hands, fully exercised his powers as commander-in-chief, and inspired the nation with his speeches. Roosevelt's presidency influenced many to regard the office in heroic terms.

The fall from political grace of Lyndon Johnson (1963–1969) over Vietnam and Richard Nixon (1969–1974) over Watergate led later scholars of the office to warn against the dangers of an imperial presidency. Responding to the mood of the general public, Congress in the mid-1970s passed a series of laws constraining the president's power to impound funds, to authorize covert intelligence activities, to send troops into combat, to sell arms abroad, and to proclaim national emergencies. The two presidents of that period, Gerald Ford (1974–1977) and Jimmy Carter (1977–1981), thus besieged, appeared to be weak. Ford, upon leaving office, talked about an "imperiled presidency." Although weakened by the Iran-contra affair toward the end of his term, President Ronald Reagan (1981–1989) restored some personal power to the office, but not its institutional authority. George Bush (1989–1993), who was unable to exert the mastery over domestic and economic policy that he had shown in the Desert Storm operation, was defeated for reelection. Bill Clinton (1993–2001), although elected twice, tarnished the image of the presidency when his difficulties with marital fidelity and misleading testimony led him to become only the second president to be impeached by the House of Representatives.

The President and Symbolic Leadership

chief of state

The role the president plays as the ceremonial head of the nation. It can also make the president a symbol of national unity during times of crisis.

head of government

The chief executive officer of a government. The president is the head of government in the United States.

America has no purely symbolic head of state. Unlike most Western democracies, America does not separate the ceremonial **chief of state** from the actual **head of government**. We have no constitutional monarch, as in Great Britain, the Netherlands, and Sweden, and no ribbon-cutting ceremonial president, as in Germany, Italy, and Israel. The American president is both monarch and prime minister, reigning as well as ruling.

As the head of state, the president in a single week may meet with the winners of the high school Voice of Democracy essay contest, honor the teacher of the year, and prepare a humorous speech for the Washington Gridiron Club. Although a president usually spends no more than one or two hours a week on such activities, they are not as trivial as they may sound. Such ceremonies are important to a nation's morale, its sense of unity, and its recognition of common values.

The ceremonial presidency also has a political dimension. Because the president is our only symbolic head of state, the office carries with it a considerable fund of public goodwill and support. Presidents, no matter how narrow their election victory, find that in the weeks and months after assuming office they are the object of public adoration. According to opinion polls, their approval rating is rarely as high again.

During this honeymoon period some presidents have successfully translated public goodwill into notable political victories. Franklin Roosevelt, in his first hundred days, persuaded Congress to pass the bulk of his economic recovery program. Lyndon Johnson, soon after succeeding John Kennedy (1961–1963), pushed through Congress the far-reaching Civil Rights Act of 1964 (see Chapter 3). Ronald Reagan, in the months following his first inauguration, won major victories on budget and tax issues.

In times of international crisis the public will often rally to support the office. When the nation perceives itself to be threatened or to have been wronged, the president is the symbol of unity. After the Japanese attack on Pearl Harbor in 1941, Franklin Roosevelt's popularity rose 12 percent. After the Korean War broke out in 1950, Harry Truman's (1945–1953) rose 9 percent. Even after the ill-fated Bay of Pigs invasion in Cuba in 1961, John Kennedy's support increased 12 percent. After the hostages were seized in Iran in 1979, Jimmy Carter's popularity increased a dramatic 31 percent. And immediately after hostilities commenced in the Gulf War in 1991, George Bush's approval rating soared to 89 percent.

But the fusion of symbolic and political authority in this office can result in a distorted public image of what its occupant can achieve. Just as the public will rally to the president in a time of crisis, so will people frequently blame him when events turn sour. Presidential popularity is often directly related to whether the news is good or bad. In other words, given the symbolic nature of the office, the public may both credit and blame a president for events over which he has little control.

Since the presidency has both symbolic and substantive power, a paradox is built into the office. The president is expected to be both the symbol of national unity and the intensely political leader of the executive branch. Inevitably, the president must promote solutions to problems that will alienate some faction of the public, and symbolic leadership will be sacrificed by the need for substantive leadership. The result is that presidential popularity frequently will decline from the time he enters office to the time he leaves.

Dwight Eisenhower (1953–1961), Ronald Reagan (1981–1989), and Bill Clinton (1993–2001) were exceptions to the rule; they seemed to be able to reconcile the two roles. All three completed two full terms and left office as popular as they entered (see Table 10.1). Eisenhower avoided taking on issues that he knew would cost him

TABLE 10.1

Public Approval Ratings of Presidents Roosevelt to Clinton

Public approval ratings usually vary widely during a president's time in office. Sometimes they reflect the president's handling of events. At other times, they reflect public frustration over events largely out of a president's control.

SOURCE: Gallup Opinion Index, August 1986, January 1989; *Facts on File*, December 21, 1992.

	BEGINNING OF TERM	END OF TERM	HIGH	LOW	AVERAGE
FRANKLIN ROOSEVELT*	-	-	84	54	75
HARRY TRUMAN	87	31	87	23	43
DWIGHT EISENHOWER	68	59	79	49	65
JOHN KENNEDY	72	58	83	56	71
LYNDON JOHNSON	79	49	80	35	55
RICHARD NIXON	59	24	68	24	49
GERALD FORD	71	53	71	37	47
JIMMY CARTER	66	34	75	21	47
RONALD REAGAN	51	63	68	35	52
GEORGE BUSH	51	49	89	32	61
BILL CLINTON	58	65	73	37	55

*Polls taken 1938–1943 only.

Politics and Ideas
A "New Kind of War"—The Ongoing War on Terrorism

When President George W. Bush (2001–) spoke to New York leaders in the wake of the September 11th attacks, he stated "my resolve is steady and strong about winning this war that has been declared on America. It's a new kind of war. And I understand it's a new kind of war. And this government will adjust." These comments acknowledge the need for adaptation in light of a significant change. America has officially declared war five times, and has been involved in numerous military conflicts, but the ongoing war on terrorism represents the first time that our nation has embarked on a war with a concept rather than a nation. What is a war on terrorism and where does the authority to conduct such a war reside?

Article I, Section 8 of the U.S. Constitution states in part that "The Congress shall have Power. . . . To declare War . . . and make Rules concerning Captures on Land and Water." On the other hand, Article II of the Constitution begins by vesting the executive power in the president. While it is widely agreed that the Framers of the Constitution intended to provide the president with the authority to repel sudden attacks, but also intended to reserve for Congress the power to move the nation from a state of peace to a state of war, there is a large gray area in the middle and the distinction between presidential and congressional powers has proved difficult to maintain in practice.

Examples of congressional action in response to the terrorist attacks consist of a joint resolution authorizing the president to use military force, the Air Transportation Safety and System Stabilization Act, which, in part, provided economic subsidies for the struggling airline industry, and the Patriot Act, which authorized law enforcement agencies to develop a number of new tools for combating and preventing future terrorist attacks.

support, such as civil rights, and jealously protected his political goodwill. Reagan took controversial positions, but his reassuring personality and rhetorical skills generated much public trust. Clinton was often mired in personal scandal, but the public was largely able to separate their disapproval of the president's personal life from their enthusiasm for his leadership skills and success in guiding the economy. All three were fortunate in avoiding protracted and unresolved military conflicts and in presiding over a period of general prosperity. The latter, above all, may be the key to presidential popularity.

The President and the Constitution

To understand the presidency, one must start with the Constitution. As with members of Congress, discussed in Chapter 9, the Constitution is specific with regard to who may be president.

A "New Kind of War"—The Ongoing War on Terrorism, *continued*

Presidential actions taken by President Bush have included the creation of the new executive post Office of Homeland Security, securing the diplomatic and military support of other world leaders, and, in coordination with his national Security Council, directing the military actions of Operation Enduring Freedom. Other actions have been taken by executive branch agencies that receive funding and authority from Congress and are, ultimately, under the direction of the president and his appointees. When the Federal Aviation Administration, for example, greatly expanded its Federal Air Marshal program, it did so with the approval of its parent agency, the Department of Transportation, and the funding of Congress.

In addition to granting powers, the Constitution also limits governmental power by placing many individual liberties off limits from government control. Even though most Americans have welcomed increased security measures to, for example, decrease the risk of further anthrax contamination, it is unlikely that many Americans would willingly sacrifice all their freedoms just to decrease threats to their security. Fortunately, the Constitution and its Amendments, through such guarantees as free speech, free press, due process, and equal protection assure us that we will not have to make such choices.

What else makes the war on terrorism a "new kind of war"? Is our Constitution equipped to handle such a war, or are changes necessary? When faced with a decision between maintaining fundamental freedoms for all Americans and increasing security to reduce the risk of future terrorist attacks, what criteria should we employ? Who in American government should make these decisions, and how do we know when they are making the right choices?

SOURCE: George W. Bush, "President Pledges Assistance for New York in Phone Call with Pataki, Giuliani," 13 September 2001, http://www.whitehouse.gov/news/releases/2001/09/20010913-4.html (4 November 2001).

natural-born citizen

A person actually born in the United States.

naturalized citizen

A person born in another country who becomes a citizen of the United States by a procedure set by Congress.

Only **natural-born citizens**, not **naturalized citizens**, qualify. Article II is the only place in which the Constitution distinguishes between one kind of citizenship and another. (A natural-born citizen is one who has American citizenship by birth, although it is unclear whether a person born abroad of American parents qualifies as natural-born within the meaning of the Constitution. A naturalized citizen is an alien who has become a citizen by virtue of a procedure established by Congress.) Moreover, a president must be 35 years of age or older and a resident of the United States for at least 14 years.

Unlike representatives, who serve terms of two years, and senators, who serve terms of six, presidents have four-year terms. Although the Constitution in 1787 placed no limit on the number of terms a president could serve, George Washington's preference for a maximum of two terms set a tradition that remained unbroken until Franklin Roosevelt ran for his third term in 1940 and was then elected to a fourth term in 1944.

Twenty-second Amendment

Ratified in 1951; limits the president to two terms in office.

Mainly in response to Roosevelt's multiple terms, the **Twenty-second Amendment** (1951) banned any future president from being elected president "more than twice." This amendment prohibits not only a third successive term but also an additional term even if a gap exists between the first two.

Executive Power

The Constitution confers many powers on the Congress, but few substantive powers on the president. Indeed, Article I, which establishes Congress, is more than two times the length of Article II, which creates the presidency. Section 1 of Article II declares, "The executive Power shall be vested in a President of the United States." What do these words define? Does the phrase *executive Power* give the president an inherent authority to meet emergencies in the absence of any specific constitutional or legislative mandate?

stewardship theory

An expansive theory of presidential power, put forth by Theodore Roosevelt, that holds that the president can undertake any act as long as it is not prohibited by a specific provision of the Constitution or statutory law.

Presidents have interpreted this power differently throughout history. At one extreme, President William Howard Taft (1909–1913) construed his powers narrowly. Taft claimed, "The president can exercise no power which cannot be fairly and reasonably traced to some specific grant of constitutional or legislative power." By contrast, President Theodore Roosevelt (1901–1909), Taft's predecessor, argued that the president could "do anything that the needs of the nation demanded unless such action was forbidden by the Constitution or by the laws."[1] Roosevelt's broad interpretation of the office became known as the **stewardship theory**, and Taft's narrow interpretation as the **constitutional theory**.

constitutional theory

The concept, associated with President William Howard Taft, that the president cannot exercise any power unless it is based on a specific constitutional provision or legislative grant.

Between these somewhat extreme views is the more balanced approach of Supreme Court Justice Robert H. Jackson, put forth in the steel seizure case (see Chapter 12): "When the President acts in absence of either a congressional grant or denial of authority . . . there is a zone of twilight in which he and Congress may have concurrent authority." Jackson implied that the Court would decide such constitutional boundary disputes on the basis of "the imperatives of events and contemporary imponderables rather than on abstract theories of law."[2]

Justice Jackson was close to the mark. Presidents since George Washington (1789–1797) have all possessed nearly identical formal constitutional powers, yet some have been far more influential than others. The reason comes from the *plasticity* of the presidency—the tendency of the office to be molded according to the energy and personality of its occupant in combination with the needs and challenges of the day.

The Power of Appointment

Section 2 of Article II states that the president "shall nominate, and by and with the Advice and Consent of the Senate, shall appoint Ambassadors, other public Ministers

---

[1] Quoted in Christopher H. Pyle and Richard M. Pious, *The President, Congress, and the Constitution* (New York: Free Press, 1984), pp. 68, 70.
[2] Ibid., p. 130.

and Consuls, Judges of the Supreme Court, and all other Officers of the United States."
For positions that require confirmation, the Senate generally allows the president to select people with whom he feels comfortable personally and ideologically. The Senate restricts itself in most cases to the personal qualifications of the nominee and to any
possible conflicts of interest.

The president's power to appoint affects the judicial branch as well, because he
appoints Supreme Court justices and all federal judges. These judges serve until they retire or, in rare circumstances, are impeached. Franklin Roosevelt's nine appointments to
the Supreme Court changed its character for a generation, and Ronald Reagan's three
appointments and George Bush's two gave the Court a decidedly conservative cast in
the 1990s (see Chapter 12).

The Removal Power

The Supreme Court in *Myers v. United States*[3] declared that the president's power to remove non–civil service appointees was unrestricted and beyond the reach of Congress.
But later the Court ruled in *Humphrey's Executor v. United States*[4] that President
Roosevelt could not fire a member of the Federal Trade Commission (FTC), an independent regulatory commission, because of policy differences. The FTC Act specified
that the president could only remove a commissioner for "inefficiency, neglect of duty,
or malfeasance in office." The Court ruled that the president's removal powers applied
only to "purely executive offices." The FTC (and by inference all independent regulatory commissions) was a "quasi-legislative" and "quasi-judicial" agency, according to
the Court, and the president's removal authority did not apply. (These commissions are
discussed in greater detail in Chapter 11.)

Presidents cannot dismiss career civil servants except for cause (misconduct, inefficiency, incompetence, or criminal conduct). They can, however, subject to the procedures of the civil service laws, transfer or demote them. Presidents can also work
through the budgetary process to reduce or eliminate funding for a particular agency,
thus eliminating numerous jobs.

The Power to Pardon

Article II, Section 2, gives the president the exclusive power to grant "Reprieves and
Pardons for Offenses against the United States, except in Cases of Impeachment." The
power includes the president's right to grant a full pardon, a conditional pardon,
clemency for a class of people (amnesty), a commutation or reduction of a sentence, and

---

[3]272 U.S. 52 (1926).
[4]295 U.S. 602 (1935).

the remission of fines. This power is limited to violations of federal laws and does not apply to state or local laws.

The use of this power rarely gains headlines, but it did in 1974, 1992, and 2001. On September 8, 1974, President Ford granted a complete pardon to former President Richard Nixon for any misdeeds that he may have committed during his presidency, which, of course, embraced the Watergate affair. Many criticized Ford's action as improper because formal charges had yet to be brought against Nixon. Without the benefit of trial, many argued, the full facts in Nixon's case and in the whole Watergate affair were unlikely to be uncovered. Others thought that Ford spared the country the unpleasant and disruptive sight of a former president placed on trial. On Christmas Eve 1992, President Bush pardoned former Secretary of Defense Caspar Weinberger and five others involved in the Iran-contra affair. The special prosecutor in the case, Lawrence E. Walsh, called the pardons a "cover-up" of misdeeds. Bush argued that Walsh's prosecutions did not represent legitimate law enforcement but were "the criminalization of policy differences." Just prior to leaving office on January 20, 2001, Clinton pardoned billionaire Mark Rich, who had been living in Switzerland since 1983 to avoid federal charges of tax evasion and other misdeeds. After the public learned that Rich's ex-wife donated about $1 million to the Democratic Party, the House Committee on Government Reform began an investigation of the pardon. Notwithstanding the merits of their decisions, Ford, Bush, and Clinton were acting within their constitutional powers. The courts had established that a presidential pardon may be granted prior to a conviction or even an indictment.[5]

The President and the Executive Branch

In order to formulate and implement policy, the president must appoint a considerable number of senior officials to whom he will turn for support and assistance. Who are these people? They include cabinet secretaries, undersecretaries, and the administrators and deputies of the various independent agencies, all of whom require Senate confirmation. These officials, plus about 60 senior White House aides whom the president can appoint without Senate confirmation, make up **the administration**—the people who direct government policy on the president's behalf.

The Cabinet

Despite its prestige, the president's Cabinet (see Table 10.2) is not a collective high-level decision-making body. Because ours is not a parliamentary government, the president is not obligated to share responsibility with the Cabinet. Its officers serve at the president's discretion, and he is under no obligation to consult with them individually or collectively.

the administration

The president plus senior officials such as Cabinet officials, undersecretaries, and the administrators and deputies of the various independent agencies.

[5]Louis Fisher, *The Politics of Shared Power: Congress and the Executive,* 2d ed. (Washington, DC: Congressional Quarterly, 1987), p. 11.

TABLE 10.2

The Cabinet, 2001

The Cabinet is composed of the heads of the 14 executive departments and certain other officials in the executive branch to whom the president has accorded Cabinet rank. The vice-president also participates in meetings of the Cabinet, and from time to time the president may invite others to participate in the discussion of particular subjects.

SOURCE: *Facts on File*, January 28, 1993, p. 44.

Secretary of Commerce	Secretary of Health and Human Services	Secretary of Veterans Affairs
Secretary of Treasury	Secretary of Housing and Urban Development	Director of the Office of Management and Budget
Secretary of Defense	Secretary of Transportation	Administrator, Environmental Protection Agency
Secretary of Labor	Secretary of Energy	Vice-President
Secretary of Interior	Secretary of Education	U.S. Trade Representative
Secretary of Agriculture	Director of the National Drug Control Policy	Attorney General
Secretary of State		

Yet individual officers can have great significance for the president. As will be discussed in Chapter 11, they serve as the president's arm in controlling the massive federal bureaucracy and in imposing his political priorities upon it. The Cabinet also provides a mechanism for bringing into the administration people who represent different social, economic, and political constituencies. Often presidents will make appointments from constituent groups who did not support him but whose support he needs.

After several years in office, presidents become more concerned with controlling the bureaucracy than with decorating their Cabinet with people whose value is more symbolic than substantive. Thus, they look for Cabinet officers who may be less well known but will be more loyal.

The selection of the right Cabinet is a difficult problem. Few Cabinet officers, whatever their temperament or background, can serve simply as the president's loyal agent. They must also represent to the president the perspective of their department and the *constituent groups* it serves. For example, the secretary of labor should have a good working relationship with organized labor; the secretary of the interior should have a solid relationship with the developers or the environmentalists, preferably both; and the secretary of agriculture must have a good rapport with farmers and the agribusiness community.

inner Cabinet

Cabinet officers whose departments handle issues of broad national importance. Included are the secretaries of state, defense, and the Treasury, and the attorney general.

outer Cabinet

Cabinet officers whose departments deal with sharply defined programs and are subject to considerable pressure from client groups.

Not all Cabinet officers are created equal. The Cabinet is often divided into an **inner Cabinet** and an **outer Cabinet**.[6] The inner group consists of secretaries of state, defense, and the Treasury as well as the attorney general. These people handle issues of broad importance: national security, the economy, and the administration of justice. Of necessity, they have a direct and close working relationship with the president. The outer group is made up of the remaining members: the secretaries of agriculture, commerce, education, energy, health and human services, housing and urban development, interior, labor, transportation, and veterans affairs. These officers deal with sharply defined programs and are subject to considerable pressure from client groups. Only when a crucial issue arises will they gain frequent access to the president, and such instances are the exception. This lack of access by members of the outer Cabinet often leads to a sense of isolation from the president, gravitation toward the constituent interests served by their departments, and a strained relationship with the White House staff.

To avoid such problems, President Reagan established the Economic Policy Council and the Domestic Policy Council, chaired, respectively, by the Treasury secretary and the attorney general. The councils consisted of relevant Cabinet officers and senior White House aides. They were designed to coordinate policy and to keep members of the outer Cabinet in close contact with the president and his thinking. When these councils met to make a crucial policy decision, the president himself would chair the meeting. Satisfied with this arrangement, President George H.W. Bush kept the same system when he entered office.

From the president's perspective, the ideal Cabinet member should be clearly in charge of his or her department, sensitive to the department's constituency, able to distinguish between the president's interest and those of that constituency, and able to work well with Congress. Obviously, the job requires well-developed administrative and political skills. President Clinton was anxious to have a cabinet that "looked like America." Thus, out of 16 cabinet rank positions, Clinton appointed five women, four blacks, and two Hispanics. However, his cabinet included a higher percentage of millionaires than did President Bush's cabinet. President George W. Bush indicated his priorities by affording cabinet-level status to the Director of the Office of Management and Budget, the Director of the National Drug Control Policy, and the U.S. Trade Representative. After the September 2001 terrorist attacks, Bush created the post of Office of Homeland Security, which he named Pennsylvania Governor Tom Ridge to head.

The White House Staff

Prior to the presidency of Franklin Roosevelt, White House aides played no role in policy. They were clerks—managers of files, appointments, and correspondence. Cabinet

---

[6]Thomas E. Cronin, *The State of the Presidency,* 2d ed. (Boston: Little, Brown, 1980), pp. 253–296.

officers were the president's primary source of advice and counsel. Today the president's closest confidants are rarely his Cabinet members, who spend much of their time managing their departments. Presidents now rely heavily on their White House staff. They select for senior White House positions people with whom they are comfortable and with whom they share a common background and political perspective. The loyalty of these people is not to a political party, an ideology, or their own political careers but to the president, first and last.

Responsibilities of senior White House aides involve the following tasks:

- Giving the president broad-gauged advice not influenced by a departmental or interest group perspective
- Setting legislative strategy
- Keeping check on the bureaucracy
- Reviewing the performance of Cabinet and sub-Cabinet officials
- Planning the president's time
- Saying no for the president to people who want something that he cannot give

Presidents manage the White House to suit their own personalities. Eisenhower and Nixon preferred a formalistic system and a highly structured staff. Eisenhower, who had spent most of his adult life in the military, was comfortable with a clear chain of command. At the opposite end of the spectrum was the competitive style of Franklin Roosevelt. Roosevelt had no rigid chain of command and was, in fact, his own chief of staff. He insisted on surrounding himself with strong-minded generalists who had divergent points of view and who could work on a variety of problems.

Although the elder President Bush appointed a chief of staff, John Sununu, Bush's style was closer to Roosevelt's than Nixon's. Bush relied upon a process known as **multiple advocacy**, which was designed to allow the president to hear all sides of an issue. White House aides would stage policy debates for the president's benefit. Dubbed "scheduled train wrecks," these debates would involve senior officials with sharply differing views on such issues as clean air proposals. President Bush, who relished these debates, would take notes, interrupt with questions, and afterward solicit the views of others in the administration or Congress. With his passion for secrecy and surprise, Bush would often conceal his final decision from everyone until he was ready for a public announcement.

The Executive Office of the President

Across a small side street from the White House is an imposing Victorian building that houses part of the **Executive Office of the President (EOP)**. The EOP was created in 1939 as the managerial arm of the modern presidency when a presidential commission ut-

multiple advocacy

A system of advising the president in which all sides of an issue are presented to him.

Executive Office of the President (EOP)

Created in 1939 to serve as the managerial arm of the presidency, it includes such agencies as the National Security Council, the Office of Management and Budget, and the Council of Economic Advisers.

tered its famous recommendation, "The president needs help." In its early years the EOP consisted of six administrative assistants and three advisory bodies—the National Resources Planning Board, the Liaison Office for Personnel Management, and the Office of Government Reports—all of which are now defunct.

The structure of the EOP reflects the dominant issues of the time. In the 1940s its agencies, such as the Office of Defense Mobilization, mirrored concerns with war and defense planning. In the 1960s and 1970s the EOP agencies (Cost of Living Council, Council on Environmental Quality, Energy Resources Council) paralleled the national concern with the problems of energy, the environment, and inflation.

During the Reagan years the EOP was pared back. One of its permanent agencies, the **Office of Management and Budget (OMB)**, became one of its most important. Created in 1921 as the Bureau of the Budget and renamed the Office of Management and Budget in 1970, the OMB has three major responsibilities:

1. Helping the president to develop the annual budget he submits to Congress
2. Serving as a clearinghouse for legislative proposals submitted to the president by the various departments, and assuring that all such proposals are consistent with presidential objectives
3. Monitoring the implementation of the president's programs and making sure they are administered efficiently

Presidents usually employ the OMB to suit their own needs. Because the Nixon administration was interested in controlling the bureaucracy and in mobilizing the executive branch to support its programs, the OMB had the primary responsibility of supervising administration programs in some detail. Under Ford and Carter the OMB played a relatively minor role.

During the Reagan and elder Bush administrations it enjoyed a significant comeback. Richard Darman, Bush's OMB director, was a powerful member of Bush's administration, shaping the contours of the budget and negotiating budget and tax policy with Congress. As long as budgetary politics dominate a president's agenda, the OMB will remain a vital arm of the presidency.

The **National Security Council (NSC)**, established by the National Security Act of 1947, is an essential part of the EOP. It is designed to provide the president with advice and policy coordination on questions of national security. Its members are the president, the vice-president, the secretary of state, the secretary of defense, and other officials the president may wish to add. As with the OMB, presidents use the NSC to suit their own styles.

Truman and Eisenhower employed the NSC to coordinate policy but not to formulate it. Both relied on strong secretaries of state for policy advice. Under President

Office of Management and Budget (OMB)

An agency in the Executive Office of the President that provides the president with budgetary information and advice and is responsible for compiling the president's annual budget proposal to Congress.

National Security Council (NSC)

Designed to provide the president with advice and policy coordination on questions of national security. Its members include the president, the vice-president, the secretaries of state and defense, and any other officials the president may add.

Politics and Ideas
A Six-Year Term for Presidents?

In 1913, the Senate passed a resolution favoring a single six-year term for the president. Earlier presidents had advocated it as well. Although the idea has never been adopted, it continues to arouse interest. Is is a good idea? People who favor the proposal argue that it would free the president of reelection concerns and allow him to rise above partisan politics. A president could escape the lure of political expediency. Had not President Nixon been so concerned with reelection, some speculate, the Watergate affair might not have happened.

But should a president be above politics, unconcerned for his own reelection? Some commentators say no. The prospect of an election concentrates the mind of a political leader on issues of importance to the general public. In a democracy this should not be a fault. A concern for reelection would prevent presidents from becoming too isolated from the mood of the country. Besides, a single six-year term would make a president a "lame duck" from the very first day in the White House.

Another argument for the proposal maintains that presidents are rarely effective over two terms. Once reelected to a second term, particularly if by a wide margin, presidents can become intoxicated with their own power and overreach their authority. Four modern presidents made such miscalculations early in their second term. Franklin Roosevelt introduced his court-packing scheme to Congress; Lyndon Johnson began escalating American involvement in Vietnam; Richard Nixon engaged in a cover-up of the Watergate affair; and Ronald Reagan became entangled in the Iran-contra affair.

Another argument against the idea came from Woodrow Wilson, who maintained that six years is too long for an ineffective president and too short for an outstanding one. Would a single six-year term allow a president to act like a statesman, or would it contribute to his isolation from the public? Do limits on presidential terms (including the Twenty-second Amendment limiting presidents to two terms) thwart democracy, or do they protect us from potential usurpers of power?

Kennedy the council itself fell into disuse and was rarely convened. Instead Kennedy relied on the NSC staff headed by the national security adviser to provide him with information and expertise.

When President Nixon appointed Dr. Henry Kissinger to be his national security adviser in 1969, the role of the NSC grew substantially. With Nixon's encouragement, Kissinger and his staff not only dominated policy-making but became deeply involved in the actual conduct of foreign policy, shutting the State Department out of Nixon's major diplomatic initiatives. Kissinger conducted the negotiations that led to Nixon's historic visit to China, the Vietnam armistice, and the SALT I treaty.

The NSC's involvement in the foreign policy operations reached its height during the Iran-contra affair. Congressional restrictions had barred direct aid to the

Nicaraguan contras, fighting to overturn the pro-Soviet Sandinista government. Frustrated by the restrictions, President Reagan authorized the NSC staff to seek contra assistance from friendly governments such as Israel and Saudi Arabia. Marine Lt. Col. Oliver North, a senior NSC staffer, supervised this effort as well as those of private domestic groups seeking to provide funds for the contras. The president also authorized the NSC to oversee the secret sale of arms to Iran to encourage the release of our hostages. Without the president's apparent knowledge, part of the profits of that sale were diverted to contras. The affair seriously diminished Reagan's public support and resulted in extensive congressional investigations and lengthy criminal trials.

A presidential commission to examine the Iran-contra affair was appointed by Reagan and headed by former Texas Senator John Tower. The Tower Commission recommended that the NSC "focus on advice and management, not implementation and execution." President Bush's NSC adviser Brent Scowcroft, a member of the Tower Commission, appeared to follow this advice and kept the NSC out of covert operations. Under Scowcroft the NSC functioned as an honest broker, coordinating advice from the bureaucracy and providing the president with policy options. When George W. Bush appointed Condoleezza Rice to be his National Security Advisor, she became both the first woman and first African American to hold this post.

The **Council of Economic Advisers (CEA)**, established by the Employment Act of 1946, is another permanent part of the EOP. Consisting of three members and a small staff, its chairperson, usually a prominent academic economist, is the predominant figure. The CEA's primary task is to analyze economic issues, make economic forecasts, and prepare the president's annual Economic Report to Congress. The CEA can be an important source of economic advice for the president, but it must share economic policy-making with the OMB, the Treasury Department, and the Federal Reserve Board.

The effectiveness of the CEA depends largely on the ability of the chair to gain the president's confidence and to translate obscure economic jargon into language the president can readily understand. President Reagan had little interest in the intricacies of economic policy; he let the CEA wither on the vine, and even considered its abolition. George H. W. Bush, who had a fascination with details, frequently consulted with the CEA and let its chair become a major player in his administration.[7] Clinton, who had promised in his campaign to focus on economic issues "like a laser," established a new National Economic Council to coordinate overall economic policy. It would have a status similar to the National Security Council. The chair of the CEA would now have to compete with yet another source of economic policy-making.

The **Office of Policy Development (OPD)**, formed in 1981 from domestic policy staff within the White House, focuses on the formulation, coordination, and imple-

Council of Economic Advisers (CEA)

Established by the Employment Act of 1946 as a part of the Executive Office of the President, it consists of a chairperson, usually a prominent academic economist, and two other members who have the primary task of analyzing economic issues for the president.

Office of Policy Development (OPD)

Created in 1981 as part of the Executive Office of the President, it focuses on the formulation, coordination, and implementation of domestic and economic policy. Provides staff support for the Economic and Domestic Policy Councils.

---

[7]Paul Strobin, "In the Loop," *National Journal* (March 24, 1990): 715–718.

mentation of economic and domestic policy. The OPD also provides staff support to two Cabinet councils, the Economic Policy Council and the Domestic Policy Council.

The Vice-President

Until 1941 vice-presidents merely served in the ceremonial role as president and chief presiding officer of the Senate and had little influence on decisions in the White House. The office was a frequent target of ridicule and disdain, even by its occupants. The first vice-president, John Adams, called it "the most insignificant office that ever the invention of man contrived or his imagination conceived."

Later vice-presidents continued to find the job deeply frustrating. Harry Truman was not even aware of the existence of the secret atomic bomb project when he succeeded to the presidency upon Roosevelt's death. Richard Nixon, Eisenhower's vice-president for two terms, served as partisan "hit man," making attacks on the Democrats that Eisenhower felt were beneath the dignity of the president to do himself. This same demeaning task Nixon later assigned to his own vice-president, Spiro Agnew. Lyndon Johnson, who had been the powerful Senate majority leader, was given largely ceremonial responsibilities as John Kennedy's vice-president. Johnson, a proud and sensitive man, felt humiliated in the job and considered himself merely a spectator in the Kennedy administration.

The experience of Walter Mondale as Jimmy Carter's vice-president has given fresh hope that the office can become a vital part of the executive branch. Mondale served as President Carter's intimate adviser. He had an office in the White House West Wing, close to the president, and was given access to all important meetings and policy papers. Mondale had a private lunch every Monday with Carter so that he could give the president confidential and candid advice. By all accounts, Mondale was involved in all major policy decisions. The Carter-Mondale arrangement converted the vice-presidency from an office without a role into that of a senior policy adviser to the president.

Twenty-fifth Amendment

Ratified in 1967, provides the mechanism for the vice-president to assume the presidency in the event of a presidential disability and the selection of a replacement for the vice-president should that office become vacant.

Presidential Succession

Should a president be impeached and convicted, resign, or die in office, the vice-president automatically becomes president and fills the remainder of the term. Should a president become disabled and unable to fulfill his duties, the **Twenty-fifth Amendment**, ratified in 1967, provided a mechanism whereby the vice-president could serve as an acting president. The president can declare himself disabled and can authorize the vice-president to assume his job. Alternatively, the vice-president and a majority of the Cabinet can declare that the president is disabled, in which case the vice-president also assumes the job. The president may claim at any time, however, that his disability is over and resume the office. Should the vice-president and a majority of the Cabinet disagree, the issue goes to Congress. If both houses decide by a two-thirds vote that the president is unfit to resume his duties, the vice-president continues as acting president.

The Twenty-fifth Amendment also established a mechanism to fill a vacancy in the vice-presidency. During our nation's history, six vice-presidents have died in office, two have resigned, and nine have succeeded to the presidency—in each case leaving the office vacant. The amendment now eliminates the possibility that the vacancy will stand for long. The president is authorized in the event of a vacancy to nominate a vice-president, subject to confirmation by both houses of Congress. This procedure was first used in October 1973 when Spiro Agnew resigned because of allegations of misconduct and President Nixon selected Gerald Ford as vice-president.

In the unlikely event of a simultaneous double vacancy in the presidency and the vice-presidency, the **Presidential Succession Act of 1947** applies. It establishes the following line of succession: (1) the Speaker of the House; (2) the president pro tempore of the Senate; (3) the Cabinet secretaries in the chronological order of the establishment of their departments, beginning with the secretary of state and ending with the secretary of veterans affairs.

The President and Congress: Foreign Policy

In foreign policy the Constitution divides formal power between the president and Congress. But the president does maintain the initiative. He negotiates treaties, mediates disputes, and proclaims friendship with new governments or works covertly to undermine them. Congress may reject these initiatives by refusing to ratify treaties, discouraging foreign arms sales, or outlawing covert activities. But when the president puts his prestige on the line, as President Bush did in securing support for his Gulf War policy, he generally prevails. Why is that? Congress fears eroding presidential influence in international negotiations, a fear presidents use to their own advantage. But Congress also lacks access to classified information and often defers to executive expertise. The reality is that Congress can influence foreign relations, but only the president can conduct them; thus the extent of Congress's influence is subject to the ebb and flow of history.

During the period from Pearl Harbor (1941) to the end of the Vietnam War (1973), the president dominated foreign policy, and congressional rebukes were rare and ineffective. The unpopularity of the Vietnam War, however, produced a subsequent public disdain of future military involvements and with it an end to the era of presidential domination. The president still had the leading role in foreign policy, but he no longer controlled the play.

Over President Nixon's veto in 1973, Congress passed the War Powers Resolution, requiring congressional approval after 60 days of any presidential decision to send troops into combat. In 1974 Congress passed the Hughes-Ryan amendment, requiring congressional notification of covert operations conducted by the CIA. Emboldened by its

Presidential Succession Act of 1947

Established the line of presidential succession after the vice-president as follows: the Speaker of the House, the president pro tempore of the Senate, and the Cabinet secretaries in the order of the establishment of their departments.

http://www.white house.gov/

Find out about presidential history and current executive policy agendas at the official White House Web site.

newfound authority, Congress actually banned covert action in Angola from 1978 to 1983 and during the 1980s limited covert aid to the Nicaraguan contras. Presidential leadership in foreign policy now requires considerable skill and subtlety. Congress can be very independent unless a president carefully consults it and develops strong public support for his policies.

Negotiating Treaties

By the terms of Article II of the Constitution, the president negotiates and signs treaties, subject to a vote of approval by two-thirds of the Senate. During the course of our history the vast majority of treaties have been approved by the Senate. But the most notable defeat came in 1919, when the Senate refused to ratify the Treaty of Versailles, which formally ended World War I and would have brought the United States into the League of Nations. This defeat provided a profound object lesson for future presidents.

President Woodrow Wilson (1913–1921), who negotiated the Versailles treaty, did not include a single senator from either party in the negotiating delegation, nor did he provide the Senate with information on the progress of the negotiations. In shutting the Senate out of the negotiating process, Wilson failed to build broad bipartisan support for the treaty.

Presidents Franklin Roosevelt and Harry Truman were careful to avoid Wilson's mistake and included both democratic and republican members of the Senate Foreign Relations Committee in the negotiations for the United Nations Treaty (1945) and the North Atlantic Treaty Organization (1949). During the decade that followed World War II, the Senate ratified without reservations or significant opposition mutual security treaties with over 40 nations. Since then the Senate has become more jealous of its prerogatives; approval of important treaties is now rarely routine and often requires presidential concessions.

Executive Agreements

executive agreements

Agreements between heads of state that, unlike treaties, do not require approval by the Senate. There are no clear legal distinctions between the substance of a treaty and that of an executive agreement.

Presidents can avoid the political brambles of Senate ratification by entering into **executive agreements** with foreign governments. These agreements do not require Senate approval. Theoretically, a treaty involves a legal relationship between nations, whereas an executive agreement is merely an understanding between heads of state. In practice, however, no distinction can be observed, and the Supreme Court has provided no clear guidelines.

In the early years of the Republic, executive agreements involved relatively minor matters, such as the settlement of claims American citizens had against foreign governments. Beginning with Franklin Roosevelt, however, executive agreements became a serious tool of foreign policy. In September 1940 Roosevelt agreed to trade 50 American destroyers to Great Britain in exchange for leases of naval bases on British territory in Newfoundland and the Caribbean. Toward the end of World War II Roosevelt concluded a secret executive agreement with Joseph Stalin granting the Soviet Union territory and rights in the western Pacific previously belonging to China and Japan. In exchange Stalin agreed to enter the war against Japan.

Such secret agreements, unusual even in wartime, have now become almost commonplace. Of the 4359 agreements in force in 1972, almost 400 were classified and kept from Congress. Many involved commitments and informal alliances with other nations such as Spain, Laos, and Ethiopia.

To remedy what Congress considered an abuse of executive power, it passed the **Case Act** (1972), which placed some restrictions on the use of executive agreements, particularly secret ones. The Case Act requires that the secretary of state submit to the Senate the final text of any executive agreement. Should the agreement concern sensitive national security matters, it can be submitted in private to the Senate Foreign Relations Committee and the House Foreign Affairs Committee. The Case Act is largely symbolic and does not give Congress the power to alter or reject executive agreements. Moreover, compliance with the act is not easy to obtain. A 1976 Senate study disclosed that the executive branch had delayed submitting a number of executive agreements by almost a year and avoided submitting others by renaming them "arrangements."[8]

Case Act

Requires the secretary of state to submit to the Senate the final text of any executive agreement. Allows agreements concerning sensitive national security matters to be submitted privately to the Senate Foreign Relations and House Foreign Affairs committees.

The President and Congress: The War Power

The war power is also divided in the constitution. The formal power to declare war is given to Congress (Article I, Section 8: "The Congress shall have the power . . . To declare war"), and thus the power to *initiate war* rests with it alone. But the framers of the Constitution were careful to leave the president with some independent war-making authority. At the urging of James Madison and Elbridge Gerry, the Constitutional Convention changed the original phrase from "make war" to "declare war." In changing this language, the framers intended to leave the president with the power to *repel sudden attacks on the United States, its territories, its possessions, or its armed forces*. The **commander-in-chief clause** (Article II, Section 2) was not designed to alter this relationship nor to grant the president additional war-making powers. The clause simply established the principle of civilian control over the military. The president was to be, in Alexander Hamilton's words, "the first general and admiral."

commander-in-chief clause

Article II, Section 2 of the U.S. Constitution. This clause names the president as the civilian head of U.S. military forces.

The Mexican and Civil Wars

Presidents have used the power to control the armed forces in order to manipulate Congress and preempt the war power itself. In 1846, for example, President James Polk

[8]Thomas M. Franck and Edward Weisband, *Foreign Policy by Congress* (New York: Oxford University Press, 1979), p. 142.

(1845–1849) ordered troops into the territory disputed by the United States and Mexico and set the stage for the Mexican War. The troops occupied high ground overlooking a Mexican village and aimed their artillery on the town square. The Mexican government, feeling threatened by the maneuver, responded militarily. Congress, at Polk's request, passed a declaration of war. Several years later the House of Representatives, feeling deceived by Polk's maneuver, passed a resolution that condemned him for a war "unnecessarily and unconstitutionally begun."

When Abraham Lincoln became president (1861–1865), he used the war power in a manner more consistent with the original understanding of the framers. After the attack on Fort Sumter (1861), which began the Civil War, Lincoln announced a blockade of the southern ports, increased the size of the army and navy, instructed the Treasury Department to spend $2 million to purchase military supplies, and in certain areas suspended the writ of *habeas corpus* (a judicial safeguard against unlawful imprisonment). None of these steps had been authorized by Congress, which was not in session. On July 4, 1861, Congress, back in session, ratified all of Lincoln's actions except the suspension of the writ of *habeas corpus* and the naval blockade. The Supreme Court in the Prize Cases[9] declared that Lincoln was within his constitutional powers "in suppressing an insurrection."

The Two World Wars

Twice in the twentieth century (1917 and 1941) Congress formally declared war and delegated vast discretionary powers to the president. During World War I Congress granted President Wilson almost dictatorial control over the economy. This included the power to seize mines and factories, fix prices, license the distribution of foodstuffs, and take over railroads and telephone lines. Although Wilson did not exercise all this authority, he did assume unprecedented control over prices, consumption, and industrial production.

Congress granted Franklin Roosevelt similar authority during World War II, but Roosevelt, who had a broad and expansive view of the office, asserted wartime powers independent of Congress.

The most dramatic and controversial of Roosevelt's actions came early in World War II. On February 19, 1942, Roosevelt decreed that 112,000 persons of Japanese descent living in the Pacific Coast region (70,000 of whom were American citizens) be removed from their homes, stripped of their jobs and property, and sent to detention camps. Concern about sabotage was the justification, although there was no evidence of its likelihood. Yet many of these people remained in the camps for the duration of the war. Congress later passed a law embodying the president's order and in effect ratifying it. In *Korematsu v. United States*[10] the Supreme Court upheld the exclusion program as within the combined

---

[9]67 U.S. (2 Black) 635 (1863).
[10]323 U.S. 214 (1944).

war powers of Congress and the president. The entire case, repudiated by a government commission years later and the subject of renewed litigation in the 1980s, serves as a reminder of how difficult it is in time of war to maintain democratic standards and values.

The Cold War

Only when America became a global power after World War II did presidents assert independent war-making powers, in the context of the Cold War with the Soviet Union. The most dramatic example came in June 1950, when President Truman, on his own independent authority, ordered American ground, air, and naval forces to aid the government of South Korea against an invasion of North Korean forces. Truman declined to ask Congress for a resolution authorizing this decision and simply cited his powers as commander-in-chief. Because the Korean invasion did not involve a sudden attack on American troops, citizens, or territory, Truman's unilateral action fell outside the framers' original understanding of the war power. Although Congress later implicitly ratified the decision by voting military appropriations for the war, Truman had nevertheless initiated American's involvement in a war that lasted three years and cost 30,000 American lives.

During the next two decades presidential war-making authority grew, nurtured by a new political consensus. Unlike the Americans of the eighteenth and nineteenth centuries, who believed in having no permanent military alliances, limited international interests, and a small standing army, Americans of the mid–twentieth century concluded that only through collective security and armed strength could war be prevented. Given this political climate, presidents felt emboldened to establish overseas bases, station troops abroad, and even send them into combat—all on the presidents' own authority. Congress did little to object.

In 1955 President Eisenhower requested from Congress a joint resolution authorizing him to use military force to protect Taiwan from a possible invasion by the People's Republic of China. The resolution stated that the president had the authority "to employ the Armed Forces as he deems neces-

President Eisenhower. *(AP Wide World)*

sary" to defend Taiwan. This undated check to the president to make war on his own terms passed Congress overwhelmingly. The comments of House Speaker Sam Rayburn (D-TX) reflected the measure of congressional acquiescence to presidential authority in those Cold War years. "If the President had done what is proposed here without consulting Congress," Rayburn acknowledged, "he would have had no criticism from me."[11]

The Vietnam Trauma

Gulf of Tonkin Resolution

A congressional resolution passed in 1964 granting President Johnson the authority to undertake military activities in Southeast Asia.

As hundreds of thousands of American troops entered the Vietnam War in the mid-1960s, presidential control of the war-making authority continued to go unchallenged. An alleged attack on two American destroyers by North Vietnamese patrol boats off their coastal waters triggered action from President Lyndon Johnson, who sought broad authority from Congress. At Johnson's request, Congress passed the **Gulf of Tonkin Resolution** (1964), which stated:

> The United States is, therefore, prepared, *as the president determines*, to take all necessary steps including the use of armed forces to assist any member or protocol state of the Southeast Asia Collective Defense Treaty requesting assistance in defense of its freedom.

The resolution passed unanimously in the House and, with only two dissenting votes in the Senate, recognized the president's claim to unilateral war-making authority.

As the Vietnam War lost public support, Congress sought to regain its constitutional authority largely through its control of spending power. But the task was arduous and the results ambiguous. In 1970, Congress, fearing an extension of the war, barred the use of funds to "finance the introduction of the ground troops into Laos or Thailand." President Nixon circumvented the law, however, by ordering continued aerial bombing and paramilitary activities in Laos. After he authorized an invasion of Cambodia that year, Congress responded by prohibiting the use of funds for ground combat troops in that beleaguered country. Although Nixon eventually withdrew the ground troops from Cambodia, he continued the bombing.

The Paris Peace Accords (1973) ended direct American combat involvement in Vietnam but not the bombing of Cambodia and Laos. Thus, the war continued—but with very little congressional support. Finally, in June 1973, Congress was able to use its power of the purse to control the power of the sword. President Nixon, weakened and distracted by the Watergate scandal, signed an appropriation bill that prohibited the further use of funds for all combat activities in Indochina as of August 15, 1973. However,

---

[11]*Congressional Record* (January 25, 1955): 672.

the bill was signed only after American combat activities against the North Vietnamese had ended—and nine years after Congress had passed the Gulf of Tonkin Resolution.

The War Powers Resolution

Chastened by the Vietnam experience and anxious to recapture its war-making authority, Congress passed the War Powers Resolution in the fall of 1973 over President Nixon's veto. The resolution specified that the president could not commit troops to combat beyond 60 days unless authorized by Congress. It also stipulated that before introducing troops into combat, the president had to consult with Congress in every possible instance.

The War Powers Resolution was criticized by both hawks and doves. Senator Barry Goldwater (R-AZ) argued that the 60-day cut off provision was an unconstitutional interference with the president's powers as commander-in-chief. Senator Thomas Eagleton (D-MO) claimed that the resolution placed no defined limits on when a president could take the country to war without prior congressional approval. So far the resolution has had little effect on presidential behavior, confirming neither the fears of its critics nor the hopes of its sponsors.

For years supporters of the resolution were concerned about the failure of presidents to abide fully by its provisions were the Congress to challenge the president. The effectiveness of the resolution depends on how seriously Congress takes its responsibilities. Congress was not tested until January 12, 1991, when it granted President Bush the power, as authorized under the War Powers Resolution, to begin military operations to enforce the United Nations Security Council Resolutions demanding Saddam Hussein's military withdrawal from Kuwait.

As long as American foreign policy requires global political commitments and a powerful mobile military, any limits on the president's role as commander-in-chief will be difficult for Congress to impose. The era of American isolation and neutrality has long passed, and along with it a small standing army. Contemporary presidents shape a large defense budget, select major weapons systems, control access to classified information, and send large carrier task forces around the globe. Thus, congressional attempts to reassert its authority meet with mixed results.

The President and Congress: Domestic Policy

In domestic policy as well as foreign, the relationship between the president and Congress is rarely easy and never a predetermined fact. A president's capacity to push his legislative program through Congress is a strong indication of his power, and often determines his historical impact on the office. Few presidents have been able to dominate Congress, and those who have only for short periods. Presidents with an ambitious domestic agenda and aspirations beyond maintaining the status quo have a particular need for congressional support. Getting such support requires great skill, a sense of what the public will support, and a capacity to persuade 535 independent-minded senators and representatives. What are the political ingredients that enable presidents to be successful leaders of Congress? Recent experience suggests several.[12]

Legislative Skills

A President Must Know the Legislative Environment   One of Franklin Roosevelt's advisers once explained that a president must understand who influences whom, who the key players are on an issue, and what a group wants that others can be persuaded either to accept or to tolerate. Lyndon Johnson made it his business to know as much as he could about the key members of Congress. By contrast, Jimmy Carter, whose legislative performance was less than spectacular, was unfamiliar with the ways of Washington and held himself aloof from the congressional leadership.

A President Needs a Good Sense of Timing   He must know when to lead and when to pause. For example, wars often deplete the national energy for reform, and Congress itself can reflect such a national mood. Postwar presidents Warren Harding (World War I), Truman (World War II), and Eisenhower (Korea) were unable to get much reform legislation from Congress. Harding and Eisenhower did not even try, but Truman did and found the going very difficult.

Presidents Must Establish Their Priorities and Know Where to Concentrate Their Energies   No president will get everything he asks from Congress; therefore, he must put forward programs that are not only important, but that also have a chance of success. Early successes may build a reputation for political mastery that can be translated into future legislative victories. Ronald Reagan focused on the budget and taxes in his first year and achieved astonishing success.

Presidents Must Have a High-Quality Legislative Liaison Office   Presidents cannot personally keep in touch with all members of Congress. An effective liaison office gives members more access to the White House, if not to the president himself. It also provides the president with vital intelligence: how many votes he has for a particular bill; which members need to be persuaded; and what particular favors he can grant dissenters to sway their votes. The liaison office can build crucial loyalty and support for the president and his policies.

---

[12]The following discussion derives from Reo M. Christenson, "Presidential Leadership of Congress," in *Rethinking the Presidency,* ed. Thomas E. Cronin (Boston: Little, Brown, 1982), pp. 255–271.

Presidents Must Consult with Party Leaders, in the Opposition as well as in Their Own Party, When They Are Developing a Major Policy Initiative   A president needs to have a strong working relationship with those who can tell him the mood of Congress. Jimmy Carter failed to consult with the appropriate congressional leaders when he unveiled his energy program in 1977. To the surprise of very few, Congress extensively revised and rewrote it.

Wise Presidents Remember Jefferson's Advice: Great Innovations Should Not and Cannot be Forced upon Slender Majorities   Major innovations require broad bipartisan support or else they will fail. Truman worked closely with leading senior Republicans in Congress in order to gain support for the United Nations treaty, the Marshall Plan (economic rehabilitation aid to Western Europe after World War II), and the North Atlantic Treaty Organization. Presidents Kennedy and Johnson, in building a consensus for their civil rights program, cultivated Republican leaders in both houses. President Reagan's strong working relationship with conservative southern Democrats in the House (known as "Boll Weevils") was essential to his legislative success in 1981 and 1982. Clinton failed to heed this advice early in his first term when he presented Congress, and its slim Democratic majority, with a sweeping plan for health care reform. Rejection of this plan forced Clinton to be more cautious later in his administration.

The Presidential Veto

The president has a number of constitutional and statutory powers that he can use in his dealings with Congress, but none is more important than the veto. According to Article I, Section 7, the president may veto a congressional bill within ten days after it reaches his desk. He then returns the bill to the congressional chamber of origin with a message explaining his reasons and perhaps suggesting changes that could make the bill acceptable. Congress may override the veto by a two-thirds majority of each house of Congress. The bill then becomes a law without presidential approval. Should Congress announce its adjournment during the ten-day period, the president may employ a pocket veto by simply killing the bill without a formal message and without the need of returning it to Congress. Congress cannot override a pocket veto. Presidents cannot veto constitutional amendments, but they can veto joint resolutions, which are formal expressions of congressional opinion and have the force of law. Table 10.3 summarizes presidential vetoes and overrides since Franklin Roosevelt.

The president, unlike a number of state governors, does not possess an *item veto*, which allows an executive to veto sections of a bill and sign the remaining portion. President Reagan, for one, was a vocal supporter of the item veto, the implementation of which would require a constitutional amendment. Under certain conditions, the president

TABLE 10.3

Presidential Vetoes and Overrides

The veto remains one of the president's most significant constitutional powers. Yet the president does not possess authority for an item veto—the power to reject part of a bill; the president must accept or reject the entire bill.

SOURCE: *Congressional Quarterly Weekly Report,* January 7, 1989, p. 7; *Congressional Quarterly Weekly Report,* December 19, 1992, p. 3925.

	TOTAL VETOES	POCKET VETOES	VETOES OVERRIDDEN
FRANKLIN ROOSEVELT (1933–1945)	633	261	9
HARRY TRUMAN (1945–1953)	250	70	12
DWIGHT EISENHOWER (1953–1961)	181	108	2
JOHN KENNEDY (1961–1963)	21	9	—
LYNDON JOHNSON (1963–1969)	30	14	—
RICHARD NIXON (1969–1974)	43	19	5
GERALD FORD (1974–1977)	66	16	12
JIMMY CARTER (1977–1981)	31	18	2
RONALD REAGAN (1981–1989)	78	39	9
GEORGE BUSH (1989–1993)	46	5	1
BILL CLINTON (1993–2001)	37	1	2

can refuse to spend part of an appropriations bill. Occasionally, a president may sign a bill and at the same time note that certain provisions are unconstitutional and cannot be enforced. The president's authority to do this has yet to be tested in court, however. As discussed in Chapter 9, a common congressional technique for avoiding a veto is to attach amendments (riders) to an appropriations bill. Frequently, the president cannot afford to veto such a bill without having the government run out of money. During the Vietnam War, Congress attached such riders to defense bills restricting the president's authority. President Nixon, in need of the appropriations to continue funding the war, was forced to accept these riders, which he otherwise surely would have vetoed. In April 1996 Congress passed the Line Item Veto Act in an effort to allow the president the authority for item vetos. After President Clinton first used this authority in early 1997, several members of Congress who had voted against the bill challenged the constitutionality of the law in court. In 1998, the Supreme Court held that the law violated the presentiment clause of Article I of the Constitution. Thus, the president's line item veto authority was short-lived.[13]

---

[13]*Clinton v. City of New York,* 524 U.S. 417 (1998).

Executive Privilege

Control over policy requires control over information. Thus, since George Washington's time, presidents have claimed that personal communications with their advisers were immune from congressional or judicial scrutiny. Presidents have argued that they need the protection of confidentiality to ensure that they will receive frank and candid advice. The right of the president to refuse information requested by Congress and the courts is called executive privilege.

During the Watergate affair President Nixon attempted to enlarge the power of executive privilege. Nixon asserted that it included the authority to withhold from Congress and the courts information in the possession of any employee of the executive branch. In 1973 Nixon maintained that even the papers and tapes of conversations under subpoena by the Watergate special prosecutor were protected by executive privilege. Nixon's lawyer maintained that a president's claim of executive privilege was absolute and not subject to review by the courts or Congress. This broad definition suffered a setback from the Supreme Court in *United States v. Nixon*[14] when it ruled that although the president did enjoy a right to executive privilege, the privilege was not absolute. The Court concluded that the need for the tapes and papers as evidence in the Watergate trial outweighed the president's claim of confidentiality and ordered Nixon to produce the tapes and papers.

In the criminal trial of Admiral John Poindexter, the District Court Judge Harold H. Greene ordered President Reagan to turn over his personal diaries to the court. Judge Greene read the diaries in camera (in his private chambers), weighing the former president's claim of executive privilege against Poindexter's assertion that he could not get a fair trial without access to them. After reviewing 100 diary entries, judge Greene declared that the diaries furnished "no new insights" into the Iran-contra affair and concluded that Reagan's claim of executive privilege outweighed Poindexter's need for the material.[15]

United States v. Nixon and the Poindexter case addressed only the president's right to withhold information from the courts and not his right to withhold information from Congress. Since the Watergate scandal Congress has become more assertive against such claims and suspicious that they were used to cover up maladministration, if not corruption. In 1982 there were, in fact, charges of collusion between top officials of the Environmental Protection Agency (EPA) and corporations cited for allegedly dumping toxic waste. When EPA director Anne Burford refused to hand over to a House subcommittee documents relating to the enforcement of the toxic waste program, the House voted her in contempt of Congress.

President Reagan, claiming executive privilege for Burford, had the justice Department challenge the contempt citation in federal court. The federal judge of the

---

[14]418 U.S. 683 (1974).
[15]*The New York Times*, March 22, 1990. p. Al.

case, reluctant to enter into this unchartered area of law, urged both sides to settle their differences out of court. The judge stated, "When constitutional disputes arise concerning the respective powers of the legislative and executive branches, judicial intervention should be delayed until all possibilities for settlement have been exhausted."[16] As a result of the political controversies that developed around the toxic waste program, Burford resigned, and President Reagan released all the documents to the relevant congressional committees. Presidents have to consider whether the assertion of a particular claim of executive privilege outweighs the political costs of withholding the information. In the matter of Anne Burford, President Reagan felt that the costs of asserting the privilege were too high.

Impeachment

In the struggle between the president and Congress, presidential impeachment and removal from office is the ultimate congressional weapon. Article II, Section 4 of the Constitution states: "The President, Vice-President and all Civil Officers of the United States shall be removed from Office on Impeachment for, and Conviction of, Treason, Bribery, or other high Crimes and Misdemeanors."

The actual impeachment resembles a criminal indictment in which the House acts as the grand jury. The investigation is done by the House Judiciary Committee, which votes its recommendation whether to impeach to the full House. The House can vote to impeach by a simple majority. The question of guilt or innocence is then determined by a trial, conducted by the Senate. The chief justice of the United States serves as the presiding judge over the proceedings involving the president or the vice-president, and a vote of two-thirds of the Senate is required for conviction and removal.

President Andrew Johnson (1865–1869) was impeached in 1868 by an overwhelming majority in the House, but escaped conviction in the Senate by one vote. More than a century later, in 1974, President Richard Nixon faced a serious threat of impeachment. After eight months of hearings, the House Judiciary Committee voted three articles of impeachment, charging Nixon with (1) obstruction of justice for encouraging perjury, destruction of evidence, and interfering with investigations by the FBI; (2) abuse of power for authorizing the FBI and IRS to harass his political opponents; and (3) contempt of Congress for refusal to comply with congressional subpoenas for tapes and papers relevant to the impeachment investigation. Before the House had an opportunity to vote on the Judiciary Committee report, Nixon resigned the presidency.

The Nixon experience helped to clarify the question of what is an impeachable offense. Treason and bribery are clear offenses, and Nixon was charged with neither. But what constitutes a "high crime and misdemeanor"? The framers, especially

---

[16]*Congressional Quarterly Weekly Report*, February 12, 1983, p. 334.

Politics and Economics
The President and Economic Policy-Making

Nowhere is the gap greater between what the public expects and what the president can do than in economic policy. Accustomed to general prosperity, the American public demands full employment, stable prices, and an increased standard of living. Presidents who fail to provide all of these things usually do not get reelected. Herbert Hoover, Gerald Ford, Jimmy Carter, and George H. W. Bush—all defeated incumbents—stand as examples: Hoover presided over the Great Depression; Ford served during a period of high unemployment; Carter contended with double-digit inflation; and Bush served during a recession and a slow recovery.

How much blame presidents should share for such conditions is unclear. They act under severe constraints, and it may seem unfair that they must take responsibility for things they cannot control. What are some of these constraints? First, the president can propose a budget and tax plan, but the Congress must approve them. The president must deal with a complex congressional budgeting process and the powerful special interests that influence Congress. Often the budget the president does finally get from Congress does not resemble the one he requested (see Chapter 14). Second, the president's budget must be prepared 16 months before its enactment; during that period the economy can change dramatically. Third, the president must share power with the Federal Reserve Board, which sets interest rates and controls the supply of money in the economy. Fourth, much of the budget (approximately 75 percent) is controlled by legislation that is supported by powerful interests and hard to change—Social Security payments, Medicare, Medicaid, military pensions, and farm support subsidies, to name a few. The interest on the national debt, another legal obligation, now consumes about 12 percent of the budget.

Alexander Hamilton and James Madison, believed that the phrase included the abuse of political power. By including the abuse of power in the articles of impeachment, the House Judiciary Committee accepted the view of Madison and Hamilton that high crimes and misdemeanors involve "the violation of some public trust." Nixon's attempt to use the FBI and the IRS against his political enemies was considered by the committee a threat to political order and therefore an impeachable offense.

The Clinton Impeachment

Of course, the most recent case of presidential impeachment came in December 1998, when the House of Representatives passed two articles of impeachment against President Bill Clinton. The story of Clinton's impeachment begins in 1994, when an Independent Counsel was assigned the task of investigating a Clinton real estate investment known as Whitewater. Although the Whitewater investigation never led to charges against Clinton,

The President and Economic Policy-Making, *continued*

In addition to the problems of budget making, the president must contend with the economy itself, which is complex and unpredictable. The cycles of inflation and recession frequently elude economists' crystal balls. In addition, America is part of the international economic system and affected by events beyond the president's reach. The sharp increase in oil prices by the Organization of Petroleum Exporting Countries (OPEC) contributed to the high inflation of the 1970s.

Over the past two decades, Japan, Western Europe, and South Korea have emerged as major economic powers, providing steep competition for key American industries such as steel, automobiles, textiles, and electronics. In the 1980s America became dependent on Japanese purchases of government bonds to assist in financing its deficits, and upon Japanese investments in the private sector to help in sustaining its economic growth. Changes in the behavior and economic fortunes of countries such as Japan can have a significant impact on our economy. The downturn in several Asian economies in the late 1990s, for example, created significant fluctuations in the American stock market.

Over the past two decades presidents have devoted increased time and energy to economic policy. Their economic advisers have become major players in the administration. The role of the OMB Director in providing the president with budgetary advice and negotiating the budget with Congress has grown. The Treasury secretary, who must advise the president on international economic policy and the supervision of the savings and loan industry, is usually a close confidant of the president. The president must also develop a good working relationship with the chairman of the Federal Reserve Board. Whether or not the economic conditions that prevail during his administration are the results of the president's policy, the public will hold him accountable.

Independent Counsel Kenneth Starr asked for and received authority to investigate additional leads on potential misdeeds that had turned up during the course of the Whitewater investigation. At the same time, Clinton was being sued by Paula Jones, a former Arkansas state worker, for sexual harassment. In January 1998, Clinton gave a deposition in that case in which he was asked questions about a number of possible improprieties, among them an affair with former White House intern Monica Lewinsky. At about the same time, Kenneth Starr, acting on a tip from Lewinsky's former friend Linda Tripp, sought authority to extend his investigation to cover possible wrongdoings (perjury, obstruction of justice) regarding the Lewinsky affair. In August 1998, President Clinton testified before a grand jury about his relationship with Lewinsky and allegations of his efforts to cover up that relationship. In his testimony, Clinton admitted that the relationship had been inappropriate. As a result, Starr issued a several-thousand-page report to Congress in September 1998, which recommended impeachment based on inconsistencies between Clinton's January and August testimonies. In November and

Senators sworn in for President Clinton's impeachment trial. *(AP Wide World)*

early December, the House wrestled with the gravity of the president's wrongdoing. Had he just been misleading and immoral, as the Democrats claimed; or did Clinton's actions constitute the kind of "high crimes and misdemeanors" that the Constitution outlined as impeachable offenses, as the Republicans claimed? Ultimately, a Republican-lead House of Representatives that voted almost entirely along party lines voted to approve one article of impeachment that charged the president with lying under oath, and another that charged him with obstruction of justice. This action created the need for an impeachment trial in the Senate in early 1999, where two-thirds of the Senate could vote to convict and remove the president from office. By the time the final vote was taken on February 12, Congress, the president, and the American people were all weary of the issue. In the final tally, the Senate rejected both articles of impeachment. Ten different Republicans voted against either one or both of the articles, but not a single Democrat voted in favor of either. Was this impeachment the pursuit of justice against a president who was acting above the law, or a mere partisan attack? The debate still goes on.

The President and the Media

Presidents and the media are usually involved in a love-hate relationship that resembles a bad marriage. They need each other, yet they have difficulty living together. Practically every president has complained about the press. George Washington charged that the unfavorable stories about his administration were "outrages of common decency." President Thomas Jefferson, a champion of a free press, stated that "even the least informed of the people have learned that nothing in a newspaper is to be believed." Richard Nixon, who suffered serious criticism of his Vietnam policy, had a considerable number of Washington reporters on his "enemies list." Ronald Reagan during the Iran-contra affair, claimed that reporters were circling the White House like "sharks." George Bush championed this slogan during his unsuccessful 1992 reelection campaign, "Annoy the media. Reelect Bush/Quayle." The media found virtually nothing off-limits during the Clinton administration, as discussion of his possible sexual improprieties became a frequent story in the national news.

Such conflict is built into the relationship. Chief executives are advocates of their own administration and want to see it portrayed favorably. They also feel the responsibility of suppressing information that, in their eyes, could damage national security. Presidents, therefore, are inclined to control the content and timing of information about their administration. Reporters, in contrast, want to get their hands on as much interesting and relevant information as possible, regardless of its sensitivity. Many a president has had his day ruined by seeing material from a highly classified document cited in the morning papers.

Editors want stories that sell newspapers or improve television ratings. Trivial stories, such as Nancy Reagan's purchase of expensive china for the White House or Hillary Clinton's changing hairstyles, will often receive more attention than a complex and important one.

As much as presidents may grouse about the media, they are not above using it for their own purposes. Michael Deaver, a senior aide to President Reagan, spent much of his time constructing effective visual backgrounds for presidential stories on the nightly news.

Phases of the Relationship

The relationship between the president and the media can go through a series of phases. The first is cooperation, and occurs in the early honeymoon stage of an administration. Presidents in this phase woo the media, grant numerous interviews, have nationally syndicated columnists for dinner, may visit influential reporters in their homes, and see to it that a reporter's calls to the White House are returned. During this time, stories frequently appear about what a fresh breath of air his administration has brought to Washington.

The second phase begins after the administration has settled in, begun to develop some internal conflicts, seen some sensitive information leak, suffered through its first crisis, and received its first series of negative stories. It is at this point that the relationship turns to one of conflict. Presidents will try more vigorously to control leaks,

http://www.lib.msu
.edu/vincent/presi
dents/index.htm

Listen to recorded
speeches by every
U.S. president since
Benjamin Harrison
at the Vincent Voice
Library.

may deny critical reporters access to top officials, and favor those writers who support the administration. After enjoying a honeymoon with the press and beginning to see stories critical of his leadership, President Kennedy said he was "reading more and enjoying it less."

The third phase can be described as detachment. The president becomes less accessible to the press. He holds fewer press conferences, and he appears largely before sympathetic audiences. In the final months of his administration, Lyndon Johnson, under constant attack for his Vietnam policy, spoke primarily at military installations. Besieged by negative stories during the Iran-contra affair, President Reagan went months without holding a news conference. Clinton did the same in the wake of the Monica Lewinsky scandal. In this phase the media become more aggressive in seeking out stories. Their sources may be largely from those outside the White House or from disgruntled former officials. Consequently, the stories may grow more negative. By the end of a presidential term, the relationship has exhausted itself.[17]

The Imperial President Versus the Imperial Media

Both the president and the media have powerful weapons at their disposal in dealing with each other. The president can decide what format to use in presenting his case to the public—a prime-time news conference, a fireside chat, or an off-the-record briefing. He can orchestrate his public appearances for the maximum visual effect. He can leak information to those reporters he favors and withhold it from those he disdains.

The media, in turn, can do extensive investigative reporting and take advantage of leakers in the administration who want to undercut a particular presidential policy. Reporters can pressure the president to release information through the Freedom of Information Act, and barrage him with persistent questions at press conferences. They can portray presidential scandals as dramatic, and initiate "who-done-its," as was done in Watergate, Iran-contra, and Whitewater, whetting the public appetite for more information and placing the administration on the defensive.

The contest is usually a standoff. No president has been able to manage the press, and the media cannot make or break a president. The vast majority of American newspapers opposed Franklin Roosevelt and endorsed his opponents. Many Washington reporters had slight regard for Ronald Reagan's ability or wisdom. Yet such media opinions had little or no effect upon the ultimate judgment of the American people.

---

[17]Michael Baruch Grossman and Martha Joynt Kumar, *Portraying the President: The White House and the News Media* (Baltimore, MD: Johns Hopkins University Press, 1981), ch. 11.

SUMMARY

1. Because the president is the ceremonial head of state as well as the actual governmental leader, the office of the presidency has strong symbolic power. The president can use this power to rally the country behind him in time of crisis. But the power and visibility of the office can also mean that the public will hold the president responsible for events over which he may have no control.

2. The actual nature of the "executive Power" that the Constitution grants to the president is not clear, and presidents have given it different interpretations. The general contours of the specific powers of appointment, removal, and pardon, however, are quite clear and leave little room for ambiguity.

3. Although the president has the complete power to appoint all his top advisers, he must be careful to appoint those who will both carry out his policies and run their department effectively.

4. In foreign policy, the Constitution divides power between the president and Congress. The president retains the initiative, but Congress can limit his options—and in the period since Vietnam it has. For the president to lead in foreign policy, he cannot simply impose his will; he must persuade both the public and Congress to accept his leadership.

5. In domestic policy the task of presidential leadership is even more difficult. The president must be able to develop a close working relationship with Congress and have a clear sense of his priorities and the public mood.

6. Conflict is inherent in the relationship between the president and the media. The president wants the media to portray his administration favorably, and the media are anxious for news that gains public attention regardless of how the president and his administration are characterized.

KEY TERMS

chief of state (298)

head of government (298)

natural-born citizen (301)

naturalized citizen (301)

Twenty-second Amendment (302)

stewardship theory (302)

constitutional theory (302)

the administration (304)

inner Cabinet (306)

outer Cabinet (306)

multiple advocacy (307)

Executive Office of the President
  (EOP) (307)

Office of Management and Budget
  (OMB) (308)

National Security Council (NSC) (308)

Council of Economic Advisers (CEA) (310)

Office of Policy Development (OPD) (310)

Twenty-fifth Amendment (311)

Presidential Succession Act of 1947 (312)

executive agreements (313)

Case Act (314)

commander-in-chief clause (314)

Gulf of Tonkin Resolution (317)

READINGS FOR FURTHER STUDY

For a broad overview of the presidency consult Norman C. Thomas, Joseph A. Pika, and Richard A. Watson, *The Politics of the Presidency*, 3d ed. (Washington, DC: Congressional Quarterly Press, 1993), and George C. Edwards III and Stephen J. Wayne, *Presidential Leadership: Politics and Policy Making*, 2d ed. (New York: St. Martin's Press, 1990).

An important collection of documents concerning the constitutional powers of the office is Christopher H. Pyle and Richard M. Pious, *The President, Congress, and the Constitution* (New York: Free Press, 1984).

A highly readable collection of essays on the contemporary presidency can be found in Michael Nelson, ed., *The Presidency and the Political System*, 3d ed. (Washington, DC: Congressional Quarterly Press, 1990).

A useful general reference is Leonard W. Levy and Louis Fisher, eds., *Encyclopedia of the American Presidency*, 4 vols. (New York: Simon & Schuster, 1993).

CHAPTER 11

Bureaucracies

A/P World Wide

Chapter Objectives

This chapter examines the work of the federal bureaucracy and its employees, who are called bureaucrats. Although bureaucrats have been favorite targets of criticism over the past several decades, the bureaucracy occupies an important place in American government. Congress and the president may attract more media attention; however, without bureaucrats, ideas might be discussed, speeches might be delivered, elections might be held, Congress might debate, presidents might sign bills, but nothing would actually happen. Ultimately, space stations are built, toxic waste dumps are cleaned up, and Social Security checks are delivered to the elderly because of the work of bureaucrats. This chapter describes who bureaucrats are and what they do, the major organizational types of bureaucracies, and the means the nation has adopted to ensure competence in the bureaucracy. The chapter also examines the problem of bureaucratic responsibility. As reflected in conflicts among interest groups, Congress, and the president, Americans do not always agree on what bureaucrats should do. Consequently, deciding to whom bureaucrats should be answerable is central to understanding bureaucrats and their place in the political system. Finally, the chapter explores how government regulations as issued by bureaucratic agencies illustrate the changing policy agenda and conflict over the appropriate role of government.

Bureaucracies as the Fourth Branch of Government

The Constitution contains specific articles on the legislature, the executive, and the judiciary, but the document only alludes to bureaucracy in several short phrases. Compared to 1789, Congress is now larger, the president has much greater staff help, and the number of courts and judges has increased. But the truly explosive growth in government has occurred in the development and evolution of bureaucracies. The result has been a U.S. government that employs about 3 million civilians and spends $1.9 trillion annually.

Bureaucracies: Translating Ideas into Action

Once an idea becomes public policy, that is, once Congress and the president agree to an idea and it becomes law, somebody must carry that idea into action. Bureaucracies exist because translating ideas into action always requires an organization of people and resources devoted to that task. For example, debate over the Social Security program is really a dispute over ideas and their attendant costs. Congress and the president decide whether the payroll tax should be cut or increased and whether benefit checks should be linked to increases in the cost of living, but they cannot translate those decisions into action. Implementation is left to bureaucrats, in the cases just mentioned to employees of the Internal Revenue Service and the Social Security Administration.

Most Americans do not really ponder the intricacies of administering the huge Social Security program. Someone must determine who is eligible for Social Security, and the exact amount of money each person will receive every month. The logistical demands inherent in the idea of a Social Security system inevitably require a group of people to administer the program on a day-to-day basis. Without bureaucrats, grandmothers and elderly uncles would simply not get their Social Security checks.

A **bureaucracy** is an organization that exists to accomplish certain goals. It consists of a group of people, hired because of specific duties they can perform and arranged in a hierarchy—an order based on rank in which each member is responsible to a person at the next higher level. The goals or objectives of a bureaucracy are called **public purposes**. Max Weber, the great German sociologist, identified bureaucracy as a unique form of decision-making authority. For Weber, a division of labor, hierarchy, expertise, and impersonal rules characterize an "ideal-type" bureaucracy.[1] These ideal characteristics distinguish bureaucracy as a unique form of social organization designed to make decisions and get things done.

Who Are the Bureaucrats?

The term **bureaucrat** in American government generally refers to any individual who works in the executive branch of government. The Social Security Administration, for example, is comprised of some 65,000 employees who translate the idea of Social Security into action. Among these individuals are computer programmers and technicians, information officers, clerks, policy researchers, receptionists, and hearing officers—all of whom in some way contribute to the execution of the Social Security idea.

Figure 11.1 shows a schematic organization of the United States government. It does not display actual patterns of authority or the real size (in numbers of people or dollars spent) of various units. But the chart does provide a general outline of the branches of government. In terms of numbers of people employed and dollars spent, the

---

bureaucracy

An organization that exists to accomplish certain goals. It consists of a group of people hired because of specific duties they can perform, and is arranged in a hierarchy. The goals or objectives of a bureaucracy are called *public purpose*s.

public purpose

A goal or objective of a bureaucracy.

bureaucrat

Individuals working in the executive branch of government who have received their positions on the basis of some type of appointment.

---

[1] A more extended discussion can be found in H. H. Gerth and C. Wright Mills, eds., *From Max Weben Essays in Sociology* (New York: Oxford University Press, 1958), pp. 196–198.

FIGURE 11.1

The Government of the United States

The fourth branch is comprised of executive departments, independent establishments, and government corporations. Although the president appears to be in command of the executive departments and other agencies, his actual control is measured by the degree of influence he is able to have on their decisions and programs. Most bureaucrats have civil service status and cannot be dismissed at the president's discretion. Only a relatively few administrative heads serve "at the pleasure of the president."

SOURCE: Updated from *U.S. Government Manual*, 2001/2002, p. 22.

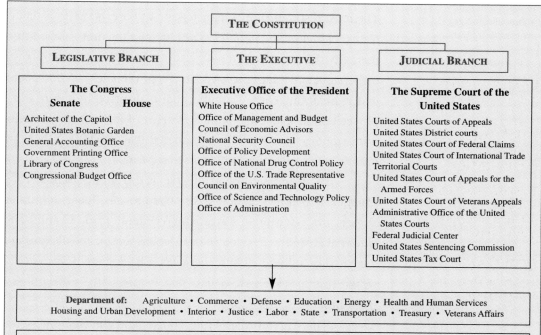

THE CONSTITUTION

LEGISLATIVE BRANCH　　　**THE EXECUTIVE**　　　**JUDICIAL BRANCH**

The Congress
Senate　　　**House**

Architect of the Capitol
United States Botanic Garden
General Accounting Office
Government Printing Office
Library of Congress
Congressional Budget Office

Executive Office of the President

White House Office
Office of Management and Budget
Council of Economic Advisors
National Security Council
Office of Policy Development
Office of National Drug Control Policy
Office of the U.S. Trade Representative
Council on Environmental Quality
Office of Science and Technology Policy
Office of Administration

The Supreme Court of the United States

United States Courts of Appeals
United States District courts
United States Court of Federal Claims
United States Court of International Trade
Territorial Courts
United States Court of Appeals for the Armed Forces
United States Court of Veterans Appeals
Administrative Office of the United States Courts
Federal Judicial Center
United States Sentencing Commission
United States Tax Court

Department of: Agriculture • Commerce • Defense • Education • Energy • Health and Human Services • Housing and Urban Development • Interior • Justice • Labor • State • Transportation • Treasury • Veterans Affairs

Independent Establishments and Government Corporations

African Development Foundation
Central Intelligence Agency
U.S. Commission on Civil Rights
Commodity Futures Trading Commission
Consumer Product Safety Commission
Corporation for National and Community Service
Defense Nuclear Facilities Safety Board
Environmental Protection Agency
Equal Opportunity Commission
Export-Import Bank of the U.S.
Farm Credit Administration
Federal Communication Commission
Federal Deposit Insurance Corporation
Federal Election Commission
Federal Emergency Management Agency
Federal Housing Finance Board
Federal Labor Relations Authority
Federal Maritime Commission
Federal Mediation and Conciliation Service

Federal Mine Safety and Health Review Commission
Federal Reserve System
Federal Retirement Thrift Investment Board
Federal Trade Commission
General Services Administration
Inter-American Foundation
Merit Systems Protection Board
National Aeronautics and Space Administration
National Archives and Records Administration
National Capital Planning Commission
National Credit Union Administration
National Foundation on the Arts and the Humanities
National Labor Relations Board
National Mediation Board
National Railroad Passenger Corporation (Amtrak)
National Science Foundation

National Transportation Safety Board
Nuclear Regulatory Commission
Occupational Safety and Health Review Commission
Office of Government Ethics
Office of Personnel Management
Overseas Private Investment Corporation
Peace Corps
Pension Benefit Guaranty Corporation
Postal Rate Commission
Railroad Retirement Board
Securities and Exchange Commission
Selective Service System
Small Business Administration
Social Security Administration
Tennessee Valley Authority
Trade and Development Agency
U.S. Agency for International Development
U.S. International Trade Commission
Office of Special Counsel
U.S. Postal Service

executive branch is the largest. It includes the president and his Executive Office staff, as well as bureaucracies such as executive departments (Department of Defense), independent establishments (National Aeronautics and Space Administration), and government corporations (U.S. Postal Service). Because the president and his staff are politically separate in many ways from executive departments, independent agencies, and government corporations, these latter units are sometimes called a **fourth branch** of government.[2]

fourth branch

Viewed as separate from the presidency, the collection of executive departments, independent establishments, and government corporations.

Distinguishing Characteristics of Bureaucracies

The most distinguishing characteristic of bureaucracies is that only they are responsible for executing public policies. The bureaucratic units in the fourth branch are also fundamentally different from the other three branches in size, diversity of purpose, physical dispersion, and relative anonymity. Approximately 65,000 people work in the legislative and judicial branches, a number that is dwarfed by the nearly 2.7 million civilian employees in the executive branch. As part of his cost-cutting efforts at the start of his administration, President Clinton ordered that 100,000 of these positions in the executive branch be eliminated over a four-year period.

Bureaucracies are as diverse as the public purposes of government. Getting astronauts into orbit (National Aeronautics and Space Administration), protecting consumers from deceptive advertising (Federal Trade Commission), and collecting taxes (Internal Revenue Service in the Department of the Treasury) are each public services executed by individual bureaucracies. The degree of diversity among bureaucratic units in the fourth branch is so vast that it makes the other three branches appear almost monolithic in comparison.

The Capitol, the White House, and the Supreme Court Building are familiar Washington landmarks. However, the bureaucracy has no such single physical symbol. Rather, individual bureaucracies are dispersed throughout the Washington area. Some are housed in highly visible and well-known places, such as the Pentagon or the J. Edgar Hoover FBI Building. But discovering where most bureaucracies are located requires initiative and enterprise. Indeed, 86 percent of bureaucrats work outside Washington in thousands of regional and field offices throughout the nation.

Most bureaucracies usually carry on their work with little sustained public awareness. The president performs his tasks in what seems like a fishbowl. Congress receives enormous media attention, and major Supreme Court decisions are given extensive news coverage as well. However, except for some highly visible Cabinet secretaries, most bureaucrats work relatively anonymously. Their names and exactly what they do are unknown to most citizens.

---

[2]For an example of use of the phrase, see Kenneth J. Meier, *Politics and the Bureaucracy: Policymaking in the Fourth Branch of Government,* 3d ed. (Pacific Grove, CA: Brooks/Cole, 1993).

Aerial view of the pentagon. *(AP Wide World)*

In the early decades of the nineteenth century only several thousand people worked for the executive branch. That number grew to about a quarter of a million by the beginning of the twentieth century. Executive branch employment expanded rapidly during the New Deal decade of the 1930s and reached its highest point ever at almost 4 million by the end of World War II. For several decades, the number of civilians working in the executive branch remained fairly stable, at about 3 million people. Over the past several years, it has declined slightly, to about 2.7 million.

Many government employees do not fit into the stereotypical view of bureaucrats as clerks and office workers. Practically every occupation is performed by someone working for the federal government. Executive branch employees include engineers, accountants, investigators, biologists, mathematicians, librarians, and veterinarians. Many blue-collar occupations are represented as well. The range of jobs in the federal service suggests the wide variety of public purposes. Generalizations about bureaucrats and bureaucracy, therefore, almost always refer in fact to *some* bureaucrats, or *some* bureaucracies, or a *portion* of the federal service.

Executive Branch Organization: Types of Bureaucracies

Individual bureaucracies are generally created in response to specific political pressures in a particular area of public policy. A mix of diverse demands and expectations in the political struggle to define the public purposes government ought to pursue produces an array of organizational types of bureaucracies.[3] In terms of size and visibility, five types are particularly important: the Executive Office of the President, executive departments, independent agencies, independent regulatory commissions, and government corporations.

The Executive Office of the President

The president has a variety of personal and institutional staff advisers, comprising organizations such as the Office of Management and Budget, the National Security Council, and the Council of Economic Advisers. Beyond the economic and foreign policy advice they offer, Executive Office units are resources the president can use in his attempts to influence other bureaucracies in the executive branch.

Executive Departments

As a group, the executive departments are generally the largest and most visible bureaucracies in the national government. The heads of these departments comprise the president's **Cabinet**, a source of collective advice that the president may or may not seek as he sees fit. Cabinet status is naturally conferred on organizations whose governmental purposes, such as national defense, are crucial by any standard. Beyond the groups that carry out these crucial activities, just what organizations deserve Cabinet status is a political question.

> For example, following President Reagan's endorsement of the idea, Congress in 1988 gave Cabinet status to the Veterans Administration. Creation of the Department of Veterans Affairs reflected the considerable political clout of veterans' groups in their demand for representation in the Cabinet. As recognition of the high place environmental issues have on the nation's policy agenda, President Clinton early in his administration pushed for legislation to elevate the Environmental Protection Agency to Cabinet status. The absence of departments of science and consumer affairs suggests the crucial role that political support plays in awarding public purposes a place in the Cabinet. President George W. Bush's early effort to create five Centers for Faith-Based Community Initiatives within existing cabinet departments is a signal of his priorities for the nation.

> Table 11.1 shows that executive departments differ in their dates of creation, number of employees, and amounts of money they spend. Each department has a unique organizational history, and the dates of creation listed in the table mark either the beginning of Cabinet status or significant organizational change. For example, the Department of Defense was created in 1949 following the consolidation of the departments of the Army, Navy, and Air Force into the National Military Establishment in 1947. But the nation had a Department of War (the army) beginning in 1789.

Cabinet

Political institution comprised mainly of executive department heads who collectively serve as a source of advice for the president.

[3]Harold Seidman, *Politics, Position, and Power: The Dynamics of Federal Organization*, 3d ed. (New York: Oxford University Press, 1980), p. 321.

TABLE 11.1

The Executive Departments

Executive departments vary widely in terms of employees and budgets. But expenditures are not always related to size of staff, as the numbers for the Departments of Defense and Health and Human Services show.

SOURCE: Office of Management and Budget, *Budget of the United States Government*, Fiscal Year 2002. Data on employees are estimates for fiscal 2001. Employee data (full-time equivalent) are rounded. Expenditure data are 2001 estimates.

DEPARTMENT	DATE OF CREATION	EMPLOYEES	EXPENDITURES (IN BILLIONS)
Defense	1949*	641,000**	$295.1
Veterans Affairs	1988	2205,900	47.5
Treasury	1789	148,400	389.8
Justice	1870	129,100	21.5
Agriculture	1862	97,900	72.6
Interior	1849	69,900	9.5
Transportation	1966	65,000	61.0
Health and Human Services	1979	63,500	436.4
Commerce***	1913	39,700	5.2
State	1789	27,700	8.1
Labor	1913	17,700	39.2
Energy	1977	16,400	17.4
Housing and Urban Development	1965	10,300	24.6
Education	1979	4,700	40.3

*The War Department, predecessor of the Defense Department, was created in 1789.
**Number includes civilian employees only.
***A Department of Commerce and Labor existed between 1903 and 1913.

In terms of number of employees, as Table 11.1 shows, the Department of Defense overwhelms all the others. With about 640,000 civilian employees (the additional 1.8 million military personnel are not included in the table), the Defense Department alone accounts for almost one-fourth of the total number of civilians working for the national government. Health and Human Services, largely because of the huge Social Security program, accounts for the largest single chunk of money that the government spends.

Executive departments have presidentially appointed secretaries and assistant secretaries who provide direction. But these departments are really organizational "umbrellas" or "holding companies" within which a variety of smaller bureaucratic units are located. For example, the Federal Bureau of Investigation (FBI) is a unit within the

Department of Justice. The Federal Aviation Agency (FAA), which is responsible for the safety of airports and airliners, is located within the Department of Transportation. The National Institutes of Health (NIH), overseeing what is probably the largest life sciences research program in the world, is an agency within the Department of Health and Human Services. The NIH has as its public purpose the satisfaction of one of the most persistent public expectations of the twenty-first century, namely, that government discover the causes and cures of disease. Although it is only part of a Cabinet department, the NIH itself spends more money than the Department of State and employs more people than the Department of Education.

Independent Agencies

independent agency

A type of bureaucratic unit organizationally located outside of an executive department and generally headed by a single individual.

A third major type of bureaucratic unit is the **independent agency**. Among the best examples of such agencies are the National Aeronautics and Space Administration (NASA) and the Peace Corps. These units are called independent because they are located outside executive departments. The president can hire and fire their heads, and the amount of money these agencies spend must go through the regular appropriations process whereby the president and Congress make final expenditure decisions.

The determination of whether an agency shall be placed inside or outside an executive department is strongly influenced by political considerations. Some group may want an agency serving its purposes to be more highly visible, be unfettered by Cabinet control, or have more direct access to the president. Agencies can also be granted independent status because of the judgment that no executive department would be an appropriate home for the agency. For example, NASA was established as an independent unit to avoid the inter-military service rivalry that marred the early space program and to give the nation's space program a nonmilitary cast.

Independent Regulatory Commissions

independent regulatory commission

A type of bureaucratic unit organizationally located outside of an executive department, headed by a group of individuals called a commission, and charged with regulating a specific industry or economic practice.

A fourth type of unit is the **independent regulatory commission**. As the title suggests, such units are headed by commissions (comprised of usually 5 to 11 people) rather than single individuals. The commission device was justified on the grounds that a group of experts in a particular field of economic activity, relatively insulated from partisan political considerations, could make reasonable and fair judgments on the basis of their technical knowledge.[4] The Interstate Commerce Commission, created in 1887, served as an organizational model for subsequent regulatory efforts.

Like independent agencies, independent regulatory commissions lie outside executive departments. However, the independence of the commissions has greater signif-

---

[4]For a more detailed assessment of the commission form, see Marver H. Bernstein, *Regulating Business by Independent Commission* (Princeton, NJ: Princeton University Press, 1966), pp. 23–30.

icance, for they have a special status that insulates them to some degree from control by the president. The terms of the commissioners are fixed, so the president may appoint new commissioners only when vacancies occur. Often their terms are longer than the president's. In addition, the Supreme Court has ruled that commissioners can be removed by the president only for causes specified in statutory law governing the commission. Because the commissions are not purely "executive" agencies, the president's controls over them are more limited.[5]

Government Corporations

government corporation

A type of bureaucratic unit that offers some service for which the benefiting individual or institution must pay directly.

A fifth type of bureaucratic unit is the **government corporation**. Examples of government corporations include the U.S. Postal Service, the National Railroad Passenger Corporation (Amtrak), the Federal Deposit Insurance Corporation, and the Resolution Trust Corporation, an agency Congress established in 1989 to take over the finances of failed savings and loan institutions. Government corporations provide services, such as delivering mail, offering insurance, or producing electric power, that are also provided by private corporations. In the provision of these services, government corporations generally produce much of their own revenue. For example, people must pay a specific fee to the U.S. Postal Service to deliver letters and packages.

Historically, certain types of essentially commercial enterprises have been judged to be of sufficient public importance to merit substantial government involvement. A system of delivering mail to every corner of the nation and beyond at a reasonable price is such an enterprise. Compared to other public bureaucracies, such corporations have been granted a degree of financial and operational flexibility because of the essentially commercial character of their work. And because they generally rely on user fees, they are not tied to the regular appropriations process as are other types of bureaucracies.[6]

The Search for Competence in the Civil Service

In assessing bureaucrats and their role, two questions are particularly important. First, how can the nation ensure that bureaucrats are competent? Second, to whom are bureaucrats responsive in the political system? The issue of responsiveness has become particularly important as government has grown over the last half-century; but concern over competence is as old as the Republic itself.

President Washington stressed the importance of "fitness of character" in appointments to high office. His ideal appointees tended to be educated members of the upper classes who looked on government as a high calling. When the Jeffersonians took control from the Federalists after the election of 1800, many moderate Federalists

---

[5]*Humphrey's Executor v. United States*, 295 U.S. 602 (1934).
[6]See Seidman, *Politics, Position, and Power*, pp. 265–276.

remained on the job. This era has been called one of "government by gentlemen," because the "business of governing was prestigious, and it was anointed with high moral imperatives of integrity and honor."[7]

The Spoils System

spoils system

The practice of making appointments to government jobs on the basis of party loyalty and support in election campaigns.

The early period of integrity and honor is not nearly as widely known as the famous, or infamous, **spoils system**, the practice of making appointments to government jobs on the basis of party loyalty and support in election campaigns. The term spoils system comes from a statement made by Senator William F. Marcy of New York during a Senate debate over a presidential appointment in 1832: "They see nothing wrong in the rule that to the victor belong the spoils of the enemy."[8]

The beginning of the spoils system is traditionally associated with the presidency of Andrew Jackson (1829–1837), which began a period of "government by the common man," a reaction against the elitism of government service in earlier decades.[9] The spoils system led to wholesale changes in government personnel after presidential elections. Government posts were openly bargained for and traded. Presidents spent much of their time not pondering great affairs of state but dealing with people whose needs were much more simple—they wanted government jobs. The result was a view of government as an employment agency and a perception, continuing even today, of government and politics as a corrupt and dirty business.

President Andrew Jackson. *(Library of Congress)*

In an irony of history, the single most important contributor to the demise of the spoils system was an individual who sorely wished to take advantage of it. Charles Guiteau asked President James Garfield (1881) for an appointment as consul to Paris. When he did not receive a government job, Guiteau shot the president, who died several months later. In galvanizing public opinion, an assassin's bullet accomplished what for so long eluded reasoned debate.

---

[7]Frederick C. Mosher, *Democracy and the Public Service,* 2d ed. (New York: Oxford University Press, 1982), pp. 58, 60.
[8]U.S. Civil Service Commission, *Biography of an Ideal: A History of the Federal Civil Service* (Washington, DC: Government Printing Office, 1973), pp. 16–17.
[9]Mosher, *Democracy and the Public Service,* pp. 64–66.

The Pendleton Act and the Merit Principle

Pendleton Act

Legislation passed in 1883 that created a Civil Service Commission charged with the task of using merit, rather than partisan political connections, as a condition of government employment.

Hatch Act

Legislation that prohibits civil servants from participating in partisan political activity.

President Garfield's assassination, combined with public reaction against scandals and corruption in the preceding Grant and Hayes administrations, led to the passage of the single most significant piece of legislation affecting public service. The **Pendleton Act** of 1883 established a Civil Service Commission whose task was to introduce the concept of merit as a condition of government employment. Merit was to be determined by competitive examinations that tested an individual's ability to perform the job in question. Expertise replaced partisan political connections as the criterion of selection. In the beginning the Pendleton Act covered only about ten percent of all government positions. However, as a result of a variety of executive and legislative actions over the past century, the vast majority of government jobs are now filled on the basis of merit. This emphasis on merit has been so strong that in 1939 Congress enacted the **Hatch Act**, which banned civil servants from participation in partisan political activity.

People become government employees through a variety of avenues. The military services have their own system of recruitment. Similarly, other agencies, such as the Postal Service, the FBI, and the State Department's Foreign Service, each have their own separate systems of hiring and merit. However, most government jobs are covered by the civil service system administered by the Office of Personnel Management. This agency has assumed most of the functions of the Civil Service Commission, which was abolished in 1978. For many positions, particularly at lower levels, competitive examinations are required. But for others, individuals are rated on the basis of their experience and qualifications.

Clerical and administrative personnel within the competitive service are classified in a "general schedule" (GS) divided into 15 "grades," with stages within each grade. Specific grades are based on the experience and qualifications of individuals, as well as the job responsibilities they are assigned. Lower grades are assigned to individuals who perform clerical, secretarial, or administrative support tasks. College graduates generally begin at grade 5 or above, whereas grades 13, 14, and 15 are "midlevel management positions."[10] Individuals with higher-level positions beyond GS-15 are generally in the Senior Executive Service discussed below. Presidential appointments are in a separate Executive Schedule.

The Civil Service Reform Act of 1978

As a candidate for the presidency, Jimmy Carter made reform of the federal bureaucracy one of his campaign themes. Among the most significant pieces of legislation enacted

---

[10]Many individuals who were formerly in grades 16, 17, and 18 (which have been abolished) are now members of the Senior Executive Service. See Meier, *Politics and the Bureaucracy*, pp. 34–36.

Civil Service Reform Act of 1978

Legislation designed to improve the level of performance of civil servants by creating incentives for high-quality work, protecting whistle-blowers, and making it easier to fire inadequate employees.

Senior Executive Service (SES)

Created by the Civil Service Reform Act of 1978, a class of civil servants comprised of individuals drawn from the highest grades who might be given bonuses, transferred among agencies, or demoted, all depending on the quality of their work.

Office of Personnel Management (OPM)

Created in 1981 as part of the Executive Office of the President, it focuses on the formulation, coordination, and implementation of domestic and economic policy. Provides staff support for the Economic and Domestic Policy Councils.

Merit Systems Protection Board

An agency charged with protecting individual employees against violations of the merit principle or actions taken against whistle-blowers.

during his term was the **Civil Service Reform Act of 1978**, the most far-reaching attempt to change the civil service since the Pendleton Act. The act was intended to defend the merit principle and to provide incentives for high-quality work. It established a system of merit pay for mid-level managers and provided protections for whistle-blowers, individuals in the bureaucracy who report waste or fraud. The act also created the **Senior Executive Service (SES)**, a group of about 8000 high-level civil servants who might be given bonuses, transferred among agencies, or demoted, all depending on their performance.[11]

President Carter established the **Office of Personnel Management (OPM)** as the government's principal personnel agency with ultimate responsibility for hiring and maintaining the highest-quality work force. He also redesignated the Civil Service Commission as the **Merit Systems Protection Board**, charged with protecting individual employees against violations of the merit principle or actions taken against whistle-blowers.

The 1978 reform has not lived up to its promise, however. In the decade following passage of the act, the merit pay system was hobbled by a lack of adequate funds and perceptions of inequity in merit pay awards.[12] Hopes that the SES would become a prestigious and respected group of senior civil servants were not fulfilled. SES members expressed dissatisfaction with their political superiors, their compensation, and the generally unfavorable public perceptions of the federal civil service.[13] Some change in these attitudes started to occur by the 1990s. For example, senior civil servants generally expressed satisfaction with their salaries after a generous pay raise in 1991.[14] The brief history of the 1978 act nonetheless shows that efforts to reform the civil service system are at once difficult and durable.

The Search for Bureaucratic Responsiveness: The Political Environment of Bureaucracies

Who determines what bureaucrats do is a matter of critical importance in any discussion of bureaucracy. Because the political system is one of dispersed power, the work of bureaucrats is shaped by a variety of individuals and institutions, including the president, Congress, the courts, and pressure groups. Both the president and Congress can point to specific clauses in the Constitution that give each a claim to control over the bureaucracy. Conflict about who ought to control the bureaucracy is therefore inevitable.

[11]Patricia W. Ingraham and David H. Rosenbloom, "Symposium on the Civil Service Reform Act of 1978: An Evaluation," *Policy Studies Journal* 17 (1988–1989): 311–312, provide a more complete list of the act's goals. The symposium contains a series of articles assessing the act from various perspectives (pp. 311–447).
[12]U.S. General Accounting Office, *Pay for Performance* (Washington, DC: Government Printing Office, 1989), p. 12.
[13]U.S. General Accounting Office, *The Public Services: Issues Affecting Its Quality, Effectiveness, Integrity, and Stewardship* (Washington, DC: Government Printing Office, 1989), p. 34.
[14]U.S. General Accounting Office, Senior Executive Service: *Opinions About the Federal Work Environment* (Washington, DC: Government Printing Office, 1992), p. 4.

The President

As the title "chief executive" suggests, the individual most responsible for the performance and actions of bureaucrats in the executive branch is the president of the United States. The Constitution charges the president with the responsibility to "take care that the Laws be faithfully executed." In addition, the Constitution authorizes the president to make appointments to head departments and allows him to "require the opinion, in writing, of the principal officer in each of the executive Departments, upon any subject relating to the Duties of their respective Offices."

Despite such constitutional authority, incoming presidents have discovered that they have to work hard to achieve bureaucratic responsiveness to their demands and requests.[15] The relationship sometimes resembles more a struggle among contestants than the easy downward flow of power suggested by neat organization charts.

Presidential control of bureaucracy is difficult for a variety of reasons. First, the sheer size and diversity of the executive branch means that close presidential control and direction of every bureaucrat is a literal impossibility.[16] Much of the work of government has a dynamic of its own, and each day, without direct presidential attention, the assigned tasks must be accomplished.

Second, as specialists in some area of public policy, bureaucrats tend to be committed to their own work rather than to the person of the president. Such commitment is strengthened by the fact that they usually hold relatively permanent positions, whereas presidents are in office for a much shorter period of time. Perhaps most important, bureaucrats, taking advantage of the dispersion of power in the political system, can make alliances with other groups and institutions. Congress, its committees, and political interest groups are among the main sources of power bureaucrats can tap in their struggles with the president.

Bureaucrats can delay, take no action, or offer alternatives in response to a presidential request. But presidents determined to get action have at their disposal a variety of tools to make bureaucrats responsive. First, the president has the power to make some 3,000 appointments to the departments and agencies. These individuals, who include Cabinet secretaries, assistant secretaries, and the heads of independent agencies, are the people the president depends on to carry forward his programs in the executive branch. President Reagan, for example, skillfully used his appointments to help shape his public policy goals. President Bill Clinton won the presidency with the promise of new public policies to produce jobs and higher growth in a lagging economy. Meeting that promise depends in some measure on the people he has chosen to fill important executive branch posts in the Clinton administration.

---

[15]For a concise history of presidential efforts to get control of bureaucracy, see Francis E. Rourke, "Responsiveness and Neutral Competence in American Bureaucracy," *Public Administration Review* 52 (November–December, 1992): 539–546.

[16]Herbert Kaufman, "Fear of Bureaucracy: A Raging Pandemic," *Public Administration Review* 41 (January–February 1980): 3–4.

Second, presidents can use the budget process to propose cuts or increases in the financing of specific bureaucracies. Although the president cannot independently determine expenditures, his proposals can significantly affect the size of bureaucratic budgets. For example, in his budget proposals President George W. Bush is the single most important individual shaping Defense Department spending and proposals to shift resources to new civilian technologies. Finally, subject to congressional approval, the president can reorganize agencies to make them more compliant to his wishes. Using this power, the president can abolish agencies, create new ones, and rearrange lines of responsibility among existing agencies.

Congress

The president's most powerful competitor in the effort to ensure bureaucratic responsiveness is Congress. According to the Constitution, presidential appointments shall be made "by and with the Advice and Consent of the Senate." The document also grants to Congress taxing powers to provide for "the general welfare of the United States." And the Constitution grants what is probably the most potent power of Congress over bureaucracy by stating that "no money shall be drawn from the Treasury, but in Consequence of Appropriations made by Law." Like the president and his staff, Congress cannot hope to oversee consistently and in any detailed fashion the daily operations of every bureaucratic unit. However, a Congress determined to make a difference can substantially shape bureaucratic behavior.

First, Congress has the ultimate responsibility for the creation and abolition of agencies. Second, the Senate must confirm presidential appointments, particularly those at the highest bureaucratic levels. Although presidents generally get approval for their appointees, the Senate occasionally exercises its constitutional right to reject nominees. And the possibility of Senate rejection no doubt eliminates some candidates from consideration at the outset. Third, congressional power to enact a budget means that Congress may substantially shape both the amount and the purpose of money bureaucrats spend. Finally, pursuant to its constitutional authority to enact laws, Congress can use its power to investigate bureaucratic behavior. In hearings before its committees, Congress can question bureaucrats about allegations of abuse of the purpose of specific legislation.

Congress engages in efforts to control bureaucracies partly because of self-interest. Members' reelection frequently depends on what bureaucrats do and how they do it. Indeed, one observer argues that the growth of big government and the expansion of bureaucratic involvement in the lives of citizens are in no small measure the responsibility of Congress itself. According to this view, members of Congress find electoral profit in "pork-barreling" and "casework" activities.[17] Pork-barreling refers to the attempt by mem-

---

[17]Morris P. Fiorina, *Congress: Keystone of the Washington Establishment,* 2d ed. (New Haven, CT: Yale University Press, 1989), pp. 40–47 and 85–94.

bers of Congress to get as many federal dollars and projects to flow into their districts as possible. Casework refers to services to individual constituents who are having difficulties with government agencies, ranging from a lost Social Security check to getting a passport.

The Case of the Legislative Veto

legislative veto

Congressional power to halt an executive initiative by a vote of one or both houses or by a congressional committee. In 1983 the Supreme Court ruled the legislative veto unconstitutional.

As society has become increasingly technological and interdependent, Congress has delegated more generous discretionary authority to the president and executive agencies to grapple with the technical and complicated issues confronting government. To temper executive discretion, Congress also provided for a **legislative veto**. Under this provision, a vote by one or both houses of Congress—or even by a congressional committee in some instances—can halt an executive initiative, bypassing the president in the process. In this way, rather than initially specifying what could be done, Congress reserved for itself the right to react to what had been done. Congress has written legislative veto power into many laws, among which are statutes governing the rulemaking powers of regulatory agencies. In one of its best-known exercises of legislative veto power, Congress invalidated a proposed agency regulation that would have required used-car dealers to give potential buyers more extensive information about the cars. Critics of legislative veto power charged that the provision allowed Congress to interfere with executive prerogatives. In 1983, in *Immigration and Naturalization Service v. Chadha*,[18] the Supreme Court declared the legislative veto unconstitutional because it violated the separation of powers mandated by the Constitution.

However, the Court's ruling did not settle the matter, for "[t]he decision has been eroded by open defiance and subtle evasion."[19] The legislative veto power continues to be written into some statutes. In addition, informal arrangements provide that agencies will not take certain actions without consulting Congress. For example, NASA and the House Appropriations Committee have agreed that they will not exceed spending ceilings on NASA programs without informal committee approval. The legislative veto continues because bureaucrats need to exercise some discretion as they administer federal programs, but Congress needs to place limits on that discretion without always resorting to the cumbersome process of enacting laws. The continuing use of the legislative veto is the practical result of these realities.

Interest Groups

Bureaucracies are engaged in day-to-day execution of public purposes; thus, political interest groups understandably try to shape what bureaucrats do. Practically every

[18]462 U.S. 919 (1983).

[19]Louis Fisher, *Constitutional Dialogues: Interpretation as a Political Process* (Princeton, NJ: Princeton University Press, 1988), p. 225. This discussion of the persistence of the legislative veto draws on Fisher's analysis, pp. 226–228. See also Fisher's *Constitutional Conflicts Between Congress and the President* (Lawrence, KS: University Press of Kansas, 1991), pp. 146–152.

bureaucratic unit has the strong support of some group. In some cases, groups have what amounts to a proprietary interest in specific departments and agencies. Veterans' groups consider the Department of Veterans Affairs "theirs," and farmers view the Department of Agriculture in much the same way. In other cases, groups compete as they press their claims on the same agency. The Environmental Protection Agency (EPA) is consistently in the middle of a cross fire of conflicting demands from environmental groups, who charge that the EPA is not enforcing environmental laws vigorously enough, and industrial groups, who argue that the EPA is enforcing such laws too vigorously. Debate over public purposes naturally extends to the work of bureaucracies.

Groups can make direct appeals to the bureaucrats themselves, for example, by commenting on proposed regulations. But groups can also make claims on bureaucracies through other institutions, such as the mass media, the courts, and Congress. Groups can use press conferences or advertising campaigns to influence bureaucratic decisions. Or, they can ask the courts to order bureaucracies to halt "unfavorable" actions or begin "favorable" actions. But most of all, groups can try to influence Congress to use its substantial powers to bring about the kind of bureaucratic activity that groups see as favorable to their own interests.

One of the most familiar models of decision making in American government is the **iron triangle**, comprised of interest groups, relevant congressional committees, and one or more executive branch agencies (see Chapter 9, Figure 9.2, for an example of the iron triangle and veterans' policy). Iron triangles characterize the decision-making process for many areas of public policy. One triangle, for example, consists of the Defense Department, congressional armed services committees, and corporate contractors who manufacture weapons systems.

Each of the sides of these triangles depends on and can support the other two, because the triangles are held together by large doses of mutual self-interest. The development of a new aircraft or the continued production of an older one, for example, is a decision heavy with political and economic significance. Congressional appropriations for production not only satisfy units in the Department of Defense but also please aircraft companies, their suppliers and contractors, unions, and local communities, all of which benefit when government money is spent. Defense cuts strain these relationships. Attempts to cancel development of a new plane or to shift the contract for production to another company (and perhaps a different section of the country) are sure to provoke resistance from those who have the most to lose.

The Courts

The courts play a more passive role in the political environment of bureaucracies. However, in a variety of ways, courts can significantly shape what bureaucrats do. First, the courts can determine the constitutionality of some congressional or presidential action and, therefore,

iron triangle

The combination of interest group representatives, legislators, and government administrators seen as extremely influential in determining the outcome of political decisions.

can affect the work of bureaucrats. More than a half-century ago, the Supreme Court ruled that Congress had unconstitutionally delegated its own powers to the National Recovery Administration, a New Deal agency created to help relieve the economic crisis in the Great Depression.[20] Although the Court since the New Deal has generally allowed Congress to determine the matter of delegation, controversial subjects such as the legislative veto and claims of executive privilege have been tested in the courts in recent years.

Second, the courts attempt to ensure procedural fairness in the efforts of bureaucratic units to promulgate rules and regulations. If the courts determine that a group has not been given adequate notice or the right to comment, the rule may be struck down. Third, in discerning congressional intent behind legislation that is either vague or ambiguous, the courts can decide what bureaucracies can or cannot do. For example, if Congress in statutory law bans the use of public funds in "programs where abortion is a method of family planning," can the Department of Health and Human Services (HHS) issue rules that forbid medical personnel in federally funded clinics from even *discussing* with patients abortion as an option? Although President Clinton later lifted the ban, in 1991 the Supreme Court in *Rust v. Sullivan* upheld the HHS regulations banning such discussion as a plausible interpretation of the congressional statute.[21] When Congress is not precise in what a bureaucracy should or can do in a specific instance, the courts ultimately decide the legitimacy of bureaucratic action.

Finally, as another example of judicial power over bureaucracies, the courts can determine whether rules issued by regulatory agencies are reasonable in light of available evidence. The courts must wait for cases to come to them, but judges can powerfully shape the work of bureaucrats.

Bureaucrats and Government Regulation

Because of the great diversity among public purposes, bureaucrats engage in a wide range of activities, from doing research on AIDS to collecting taxes to building space stations. Issuing rules and regulations that affect a large number of individuals and companies throughout the nation has been the most controversial activity of bureaucrats over the past several decades. Regulations have produced sharp debate because of the costs and behavior changes they impose on the people affected. A review of regulatory policy illustrates the role of bureaucrats in public policy and the intensely political environment that shapes their work.

Regulation in Perspective

The Environmental Protection Agency has the Herculean task of producing regulations required by the Clean Air Act Amendments that Congress enacted in 1990. For example,

---

[20]*Schecter Poultry Corp. v. United States,* 295 U.S. 495 (1935).
[21]59 U.S.L.W. 4451.

in the effort to limit the release of ozone-depleting chlorofluorocarbons (CFCs) into the atmosphere, Congress required the EPA to produce regulations on the servicing of motor vehicle air conditioners. The EPA rules are highly detailed and technical, and provide an illustration of the role of bureaucrats in translating ideas into action—in this instance producing specific requirements that will change behavior to protect the ozone layer.[22]

Evidence of regulations in a wide range of policy areas is all around us. Electricity used in millions of homes may be produced by nuclear power plants regulated by the Nuclear Regulatory Commission. Radio and television stations are regulated by the Federal Communications Commission. The Food and Drug Administration certifies the safety of prescription drugs. The EPA sets detailed standards for safe drinking water. The physical safety of workplaces is regulated by the Occupational Health and Safety Administration. Baby cribs and toys are subject to regulation by the Consumer Product Safety Commission.

Government regulations touch people's lives at the most basic levels. For example, more than 300 federal regulations shape what goes into a pizza and how it may be sold.[23] Ingredients must meet specified nutritional requirements to pass federal inspection. Regulations similarly affect other common foods. The hamburger, an American staple, is shaped by 41,000 federal and state regulations.[24] Few people who eat pizza or hamburgers are aware of or give much thought to the dense network of rules that surrounds their meals. For those who produce and market pizza and hamburgers, however, these regulations are a constant reminder of the pervasiveness of government in even the ordinary activities of life. Such rules are intended to protect consumers from unsafe products and to try to ensure nutritional, high-quality meals.

One of the continuing issues in regulatory policy debate is whether regulatory agencies go beyond congressional intent in their creation of rules. Congress has delegated much authority to these agencies due to the fact that members of Congress have neither the time nor the expertise to draft such rules. How to place limits on experts without crippling their expertise is an ongoing issue in the relationship between legislators and policymakers.

regulations

Rules devised by government agencies that shape the actions of individuals and groups in order to achieve purposes mandated by law.

Regulatory Agencies and Types of Regulations

Regulations are rules devised by government to shape the actions of individuals and groups to achieve purposes mandated by law.[25] With the increase in public expectations and the general expansion of government activity, rules and regulations cover practi-

---

[22]57 *Federal Register* 31242 (July 14, 1992).

[23]"A Pizza with the Works—Including 310 Regulations," *U.S. News & World Report* (May 31, 1982): 55, 25.

[24]"Your Hamburger: 41,000 Regulations," *U.S. News & World Report* (February 11, 1980): 64.

[25]This definition draws on Kenneth J. Meier, *Regulation: Politics, Bureaucracy, and Economics* (New York: St. Martin's Press, 1985), pp. 1–2.

economic regulation

Type of regulation in which a government agency issues rules that shape the structure of some industry, such as limiting entrance into the broadcast industry, or banning or encouraging certain business practices.

social regulation

Type of regulation in which a government agency issues rules designed to achieve noneconomic policy goals, such as fair treatment in employment, clean air, or safe workplaces.

quasi-legislative

A function of regulatory agencies in which they can make rules that, like legislation, apply to whole classes of people.

quasi-judicial

A function of regulatory agencies in which, like a court, they can make decisions in individual cases.

administrative law judge

An officer with relatively independent status in a regulatory agency who presides over and makes findings in judicial proceedings in which the agency's actions in individual cases are at issue.

cally every commercial activity and achieve a variety of policy goals. More than 100 agencies have regulatory powers.

The distinction between economic regulation and social regulation is useful in understanding the regulatory goals of government. In **economic regulation**, a government agency issues rules that shape the structure of some industry or ban or encourage certain business practices. For example, the Federal Trade Commission is charged with limiting monopolistic practices. In **social regulation**, agencies issue rules that are designed to achieve social goals, such as fair treatment in employment, clean air, or safe workplaces.[26] For example, the Equal Employment Opportunity Commission is charged with limiting employment discrimination. The consequence is the enhancement of the political and social status of some groups, such as women and African Americans.

Regulatory agencies perform both **quasi-legislative** and **quasi-judicial** functions. In their quasi-legislative roles, agencies issue rules that, like legislation, apply to whole classes of people. For example, rules of the Securities and Exchange Commission (SEC) against stock market trading on the basis of insider information apply to all individuals and firms in the securities industry. As quasi-judicial bodies, agencies, like courts, can make decisions in individual cases. Because of action by the SEC, for instance, "junk bond" trader Michael Milken agreed in 1990 to pay $600 million in fines and compensation to investors for securities law violations.

As another example, consumers or competitors can complain to the Federal Trade Commission that a company is engaged in deceptive advertising. The commission can investigate the charge with an **administrative law judge**, who hears the case in what amounts to a trial proceeding. Administrative law judges were mandated by the Administrative Procedure Act of 1946 as part of a general effort to provide procedural protections for individuals and groups in agency proceedings. Administrative law judges hold an insulated status in agencies to protect their judicial function, and their findings in particular cases can be appealed to the commission and, if necessary, to the federal courts.

Table 11.2 lists selected regulatory agencies, their dates of creation, and their purposes. Major government initiatives to regulate the economy first occurred in the decades around the beginning of the twentieth century. As industrialization proceeded in the late nineteenth century, the relationships between the buyers and sellers of goods and services became increasingly national in scope. The growth of corporations and nationalization of the economy brought a variety of unsavory practices, such as price gouging, and structures, such as monopolies, to the marketplace. Such iniquities led to demands that government remedy the imbalance between producers and purchasers. These problems frequently crossed state lines; in many instances, redress involved the national government.

---

[26]See *Federal Regulatory Directory,* 6th ed. (Washington, DC: Congressional Quarterly, 1990), pp. 2, 5–13.

TABLE 11.2

Selected Regulatory Agencies

Establishment of regulatory agencies has come in waves or groups, as Congress has responded to persistent political demands. The first wave occurred around the turn of the twentieth century and dealt with the unprecedented size and impact of major industrial corporations, and with the problems encountered by the buyers and sellers of goods and services. The second, in the 1930s, sprang from the economic dislocation caused by the Great Depression. The third, in the 1960s and 1970s, came in response to demands to remedy inequalities and to protect the environment and the workplace.

SOURCE: Statements of purpose taken, with some modifications, from *U.S. Government Manual,* 1992/93 (Washington, DC: GPO, 1992).

AGENCY	DATE OF CREATION	PURPOSE
Interstate Commerce Commission (ICC)	1887	To regulate interstate surface transportation, including trains, trucks, buses, and water carriers
Federal Trade Commission (FTC)	1914	To protect economic competition against monopoly or restraints on trade, and to protect against unfair or deceptive trade practices
Food and Drug Administration (FDA)	1930*	To protect the health of citizens against impure and unsafe foods, drugs, cosmetics, and other potential hazards
Federal Communications Commission (FCC)	1934	To regulate interstate and foreign communications by radio, television, wire, satellite, and cable
Securities and Exchange Commission (SEC)	1934	To provide protection for investors and to ensure that securities markets are fair and honest and, when necessary, to provide the means to enforce securities laws through sanctions
National Labor Relations Board (NLRB)	1935	To safeguard employees' rights to organize, determine through elections whether workers want unions as their bargaining representatives, and prevent and remedy unfair labor practices
Equal Employment Opportunity Commission (EEOC)	1964	To eliminate discrimination in employment on the basis of race, color, religion, sex, national origin, disability, or age
Occupational Safety and Health Administration (OSHA)	1970	To develop, promulgate, and enforce occupational safety and health standards
Environmental Protection Agency (EPA)	1970	To control and abate pollution in the areas of air, water, solid waste, pesticides, radiation, and toxic substances
Consumer Product Safety Commission (CPSC)	1972	To protect the public against unreasonable risks of injury from consumer products, to develop consumer product safety standards, and to promote product safety and research
Nuclear Regulatory Commission (NRC)	1974**	To license and regulate the civilian use of nuclear energy to protect public health and safety and the environment
Federal Energy Regulatory Commission (FERC)	1977***	To set rates and charges for the transportation and sale of natural gas and oil by pipeline and for the transmission and sale of electricity and the licensing of hydroelectric power projects

*Assumed functions placed in the Department of Agriculture in 1906.
**Assumed many of the functions given to the Atomic Energy Commission in 1946.
***Assumed many of the functions of the Federal Power Commission created in 1920.

Establishment of regulatory agencies has come in waves or groups, as Congress has responded to persistent political demands. The first wave occurred around the turn of the twentieth century and dealt with the unprecedented size and impact of major industrial corporations and with the problems encountered by the buyers and sellers of goods and services. The second, in the 1930s, sprang from the economic dislocation caused by the Great Depression. The third, in the 1960s and 1970s, came in response to demands to remedy inequalities and to protect the environment and the workplace.

In 1887 Congress created the Interstate Commerce Commission to regulate the railroads. The commission device was justified on the grounds that a group of technical experts in a particular field of economic activity, who were relatively insulated from partisan political considerations, could make reasonable and fair judgments. New industries and new demands for regulation came in the twentieth century, and the Interstate Commerce Commission served as a model for subsequent regulatory efforts. Other enactments followed, such as the Sherman Anti-Trust Act (1890) and the Federal Trade Commission Act (1914), which tried to limit the growing economic power of trusts and large corporations. The goal of regulation was to establish government as a counterweight to the concentration of economic power in a small number of businesses.

Another kind of regulation tried to protect consumers of specific products. In the ideal free market, companies compete with each other to sell products at the lowest price to consumers who make their purchase choices based on full information about the relative merits of the products. However, in the real world consumers either do not have access to such information or do not take the trouble to get it. Regulation of consumer products means that government action compensates for such market failures. Largely in response to publicity about unsavory practices in particular industries, Congress enacted the Pure Food and Drug Act (1906) and the Meat Inspection Act (1907) to protect unwary consumers. Such regulation continues, as contemporary rules on pizza and hamburgers suggest.

The next period of new regulatory activity occurred during the explosion of government initiatives during the New Deal of the 1930s. Regulation increased as part of the general response of government to the Great Depression. The drive for active government brought entire industries under federal regulation. Among the regulatory agencies created were the Securities and Exchange Commission for financial exchange markets, the Federal Communications Commission for electronic communications, and the Civil Aeronautics Board for the airline industry.[27] In the effort to combat unfair labor practices, the National Labor Relations Board was established to regulate employer-employee relationships in businesses in interstate commerce.

---

[27]To deregulate and allow the operation of market incentives in the airline industry, the Civil Aeronautics Board has since been abolished.

Until the past generation most government regulations had predominantly economic goals. The objects of regulation were relationships among businesses, rates, business practices, and entry into an industry. However, in the 1960s and 1970s new regulatory efforts went beyond economic concerns to encompass such social goals as affirmative action, worker safety, environmental protection, and consumer product safety. Among the regulatory agencies established were the Equal Employment Opportunity Commission to fight discrimination in the workplace, the Environmental Protection Agency to limit environmental pollution, the Occupational Safety and Health Administration to promote worker safety, and the Consumer Product Safety Commission to protect consumers from unsafe products. Social regulation has been the lightning rod drawing most of the conflict over regulation since the 1960s.

The Regulatory Process

slip law

The written text of an act of Congress.

U.S. Statutes-at-Large

Chronological compilation, by year, of slip laws passed in each session of Congress.

U.S. Code

Compilation of laws currently in effect, classified by subject matter, such as transportation or labor.

Federal Register

A daily government publication that contains proposed and final regulations, presidential proclamations, and executive orders.

Code of Federal Regulations (CFR)

Compilation of U.S. administrative rules currently in effect, classified by agency and subject matter.

Regulatory agencies make rules that can have real consequences easily discernible to most people. For example, almost everyone has had the experience of struggling to open a "childproof" aspirin bottle. Yet almost no one thinks about the circuitous route such regulations travel before they touch us. Figure 11.2 shows where regulations come from. All regulations ultimately have their roots in the Constitution, which grants Congress the power to pass laws and to establish agencies to accomplish specific purposes. Each act of Congress is published in the form of a **slip law**, which is the written text of the legislation. Depending on the subject matter, slip laws can range from a single page to several hundred pages in length. The slip laws passed by each session of Congress are bound together to form a volume of *U.S. Statutes-at-Large*. Laws currently in effect are classified by subject matter, such as transportation, labor, or public health and welfare, in the *U.S. Code*, a collection of dozens of volumes periodically revised to reflect changes in legislation.

Once established, agencies must abide by stringent procedural requirements in their promulgation of rules and regulations. To provide adequate notice and opportunity for hearing, under the provisions of the Administrative Procedure Act of 1946 agencies must publish proposed rules to allow anyone affected to comment on them. Such rules appear in the *Federal Register*, a daily government publication that also contains presidential proclamations and executive orders. The *Federal Register* on any given day may be several hundred pages in length, a fact that suggests the complexity and scope of the federal regulatory effort. All rules and regulations currently in effect are compiled by agency and subject matter in the *Code of Federal Regulations (CFR)*, a collection of almost 200 volumes revised annually on a staggered basis. The regulations are arranged topically in the *CFR* just as statutes are arranged topically in the *U.S. Code*.

Regulations setting acceptable contaminant levels in drinking water traversed this process, as did those requiring childproof aspirin bottles to prevent accidental

FIGURE 11.2

Where Regulations Come From

Regulatory authority lies in the Constitution, which authorizes Congress to enact and the president to approve the creation of departments and programs. A new piece of legislation appears first as a slip law and then in *U.S. Statutes-at-Large* and the *U.S. Code.* Established by such legislation, agencies issue and enforce regulations. These in turn appear in the *Federal Register* and later in the *Code of Federal Regulations.* Regulations may be contested in the courts.

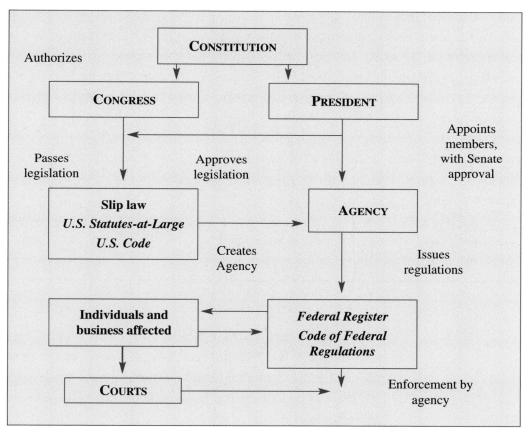

poisoning. In 1972 Congress enacted the Consumer Product Safety Act, which gave wide-ranging powers on consumer safety to the Consumer Product Safety Commission (CPSC). The act entered the *U.S. Statutes-at-Large* and the *U.S. Code.*[28] By publishing proposed rules in the *Federal Register,* receiving comment, and then issuing final rules, the commission establishes safety standards that a large number of consumer products must meet. The standards are compiled in the *Code of Federal Regulations.*

---

[28]The act transferred responsibility for poison prevention packaging from the EPA and HEW to the new commission.

Politics and Economics
Regulation and Cost-Benefit Analysis

Regulations obviously cost money. Regulatory agencies require buildings, people, and sometimes sophisticated equipment and research capabilities, all of which must be funded by tax dollars. Agency rules can also require that other people spend money. The protection of workers may require that companies make expensive physical alterations in the workplace. Environmental quality standards may require that manufacturing plants install special equipment to reduce air emissions. Companies may be forced to spend scarce research and development dollars to meet mandated consumer product safety standards. One of the most durable and volatile issues in regulatory policy debate is whether these costs are worth the effort.

Cost-benefit analysis is one of the techniques used to assess the impact of regulations. In theory, cost-benefit analysis should enable government officials to determine whether regulations are worth their costs. The technique can take complicated mathematical forms. In general, the costs of a regulation are tallied and then compared with the benefits the regulation is designed to gain. For example, are the benefits of the lives saved from cleaner air worth the costs of EPA enforcement activities and air scrubbers used in manufacturing plants? The matter is complicated by the fact that progressively higher standards may require geometrically higher costs. For example, cleaning the air of 90 percent of its particulate matter may be equal to or less than the cost of cleaning the next 5 percent.

Efforts to make cost-benefit analyses an integral part of rule-making have been controversial. In 1981 President Reagan issued an executive order requiring

---

The congressional act that established the CPSC is only 27 pages in length, but an entire volume of the *Code of Federal Regulations*, which is more than 600 pages long, is devoted to the commission and its rules. Among the detailed safety standards in the CFR are 21 pages on poison prevention packaging requirements, including rules on aspirin bottles.

Agencies themselves may go through a complicated internal sequence of steps before they issue a rule.[29] A variety of groups and individuals within the agency, including lawyers, technicians, scientists, and economists, shape the proposed regulation. The proposed rule is then reviewed by the Office of Management and Budget, after which it appears as a proposal in the *Federal Register*. After a period for public comment to take public reaction into account, the regulation is published as a final rule in the *Federal Register*. The process may not end here, for affected parties, such as a trade association, might contest the rule in the courts or try to get Congress to change the enabling statute.

---

[29]For example, see Gary C. Bryner, *Bureaucratic Discretion: Law and Policy in Federal Regulatory Agencies* (New York: Pergamon, 1987), pp. 98–105.

Regulation and Cost-Benefit Analysis, *continued*

that agencies assessing proposed or existing regulations be guided by an analysis of costs and benefits. According to the order, agencies can make rules only if "the potential benefits to society for the regulation outweigh the potential costs to society." Agencies proposing major rules—rules having an impact of $100 million or more on the economy—must submit to the Office of Management and Budget a regulatory impact analysis before the rule goes into effect. Critics in Congress charged that the OMB used its powers of reviewing regulatory costs and benefits to delay or weaken proposed rules designed to enhance worker or consumer safety or to meet environmental goals. In the Bush administration, the White House Council on Competitiveness, headed by Vice-President Dan Quayle, assumed the role of regulatory watchdog as it diluted rules it judged to be too costly.

The OMB and the Competitiveness Council were strongly supported by those who wanted to keep in check what they saw as unreasonably costly regulations. But the sharp criticism of the limits these agencies placed on regulations illustrates the political debate that can swirl around cost-benefit analysis.

The existence of the debate indicates that cost-benefit analysis does not offer easy answers for public officials. Efforts to tally costs and benefits can become mired in questions such as how much a life is worth or how the benefit of a smog-less day can be calculated. Political interests are highly resistant to conclusions that do not support their positions, regardless of how mathematically sound they appear. Acknowledging the limitations of cost-benefit analysis, what questions can be asked about any proposed rule to assess its worth?

Because regulators make choices, their work is naturally and continually shaped by the political demands of groups affected by those choices.

The Ebb and Flow of Regulatory Debate

Regulations have been a controversial political issue because they symbolize government interference in the daily lives of individuals and businesses. Some economic regulation, in fact, actually benefited the regulated industries by limiting competition and supporting the prices of services. In the name of economic efficiency and increased competition, some industries have been deregulated. For example, as part of the general effort to lighten the regulatory burden, the Civil Aeronautics Board, which sets airline routes and rates, was eliminated in 1985. Congressional enactments have also limited the regulatory role of the Interstate Commerce Commission in the interstate trucking, railroad, and busing industries.

In response to criticism of regulation, recent presidents have made regulatory reform a policy objective. Emphasizing the view that regulatory costs threaten economic

deregulation

Process of reducing
the number and
scope of government
regulations.

productivity,[30] President Reagan in particular made **deregulation** a major theme in his call to "roll back" the growth of government. He created a presidential task force on regulatory relief and appointed to regulatory agencies people who shared his interest in reducing the impact of regulations. The budgets of regulatory agencies were cut, and many new proposed regulations were suspended. The Office of Management and Budget assumed an active role in assessing the costs and benefits of new rules. However, as the box "Politics and Economics: Regulations and Cost-Benefit Analysis" suggests, OMB review of regulations has been controversial.

As the 1980s wore on, critics saw deregulatory efforts as attempts to strip government of its power to pursue worthy economic and social goals.[31] A turning point came early in the decade in the battle between Congress and President Reagan over the EPA. In 1980 Congress gave to the EPA the task of cleaning up toxic waste dumps with money drawn from a "superfund" financed by a tax on chemicals. Within a short time critics charged that the EPA was being too responsive to the interests of the chemical companies and was not vigorously enforcing the toxic waste law. The House of Representatives cited the head of the EPA (a Reagan appointee) for contempt of Congress for refusing to make available agency documents. Six congressional committees began investigations amid intense criticism that the agency reflected Reagan administration neglect of environmental concerns. To contain the political damage, the White House made sweeping changes in the agency's leadership and released the requested documents. The struggle uncovered the deep political support for strong governmental action in environmental protection.

By the mid-1980s, regulation as a volatile political issue temporarily receded, and renewed receptivity to government regulation became more evident. In 1986 Congress broadened environmental regulations on drinking water and toxic wastes.[32] Later in the decade some critics argued that the financial disaster of the collapse of savings and loan institutions could have been avoided had the regulatory atmosphere not been so lax.[33] However, as a lagging economy dogged his presidency, in his 1992 State of the Union address President Bush called for a "moratorium on any new federal regulations that could hinder growth." Predictably, the moratorium drew fire from consumer and environmental groups and support from those charging that regulations pose a costly burden. The scope of regulatory activity was an issue in the 1992 presidential campaign, and Bill Clinton's victory promised, as a contrast to the Bush moratorium, greater receptivity in the White House to consumer and environmental regulations.

---

[30]For a critique of regulation, see Murray L. Weidenbaum, *The Future of Business Regulation: Private Action and Public Demand* (New York: AMACOM, 1979).

[31]See Susan J. Tolchin and Martin Tolchin, *Dismantling America: The Rush to Deregulate* (Boston: Houghton Mifflin, 1983).

[32]Michael E. Kraft, "Environmental Gridlock: Searching for Consensus in Congress," in Norman J. Vig and Michael E. Kraft, eds., *Environmental Policy in the 1990s* (Washington, DC: Congressional Quarterly, 1990), pp. 110–111.

[33]Jeff Gerth, "Regulators Say 80's Budget Cuts May Cost U.S. Billions in 1990's," *The New York Times*, December 19, 1989, pp. A1, B10.

However, a knotty task that the Clinton administration confronted was making regulation more vigorous to protect the environment, workers, and consumers without limiting job growth and economic productivity.[34] By adopting many tenets of a market-driven approach to public management, known as "reinventing government," the Clinton administration was largely able to succeed in its objectives.[35]

Regulatory bureaucrats caught in the middle of the cross fire of conflict surrounding regulation are really at the center of a debate over the appropriate role of government. The attempt to ban unsafe toys may be hailed by consumer groups but criticized by manufacturers. Environmentalists want to protect endangered species and wilderness areas, but loggers fear a loss of jobs. Handicapped citizens promote efforts to make buildings more accessible, but corporations and universities have worried about the high financial costs of providing such accessibility. Health groups vigorously support efforts to regulate cigarette advertising, but the tobacco industry views such regulation as a threat. Businesses cite the high financial burden of some worker safety requirements, but labor unions see efforts to limit such rules as increasing physical risks to workers. The contests over changes in regulatory efforts are more than differences over financial costs. The intensity of the debate may ebb and flow, but conflict over regulations springs from disagreement over what government should do, who should benefit from government action, and whether compromises among competing goals can be achieved.

Bureaucracies: Targets and Mirrors of Conflict

For much of the past generation, bureaucrats have been the target of biting criticism from elected officials, candidates for public office, and private citizens. Like lightning rods, bureaucrats have drawn criticism aimed at government in general.

red tape

Bureaucratic rules and procedures that seem to complicate and delay needed action unnecessarily.

Four charges summarize the criticism. First, bureaucrats waste or defraud precious public resources. Second, they wrap much of their work in what appears to be endless amounts of **red tape**, which can be defined as "unnecessary" procedural requirements that impede needed action. Third, bureaucrats do work that either duplicates or conflicts with the work of other bureaucrats. Fourth, and perhaps the most important, they play an independent and "political" role in public policy—that is, through their use of discretion, unelected bureaucrats make choices that either directly counter or go beyond the wishes of elected politicians.

Every large organization has individuals who work diligently and conscientiously and others whose work is either haphazard or detrimental to the goals of the organization.

---

[34]For a discussion of the debate over regulations in the campaign, see Gerald F. Seib and Bob Davis, "Bush and Clinton Joust Over How to Regulate U.S. Business Activity," *Wall Street Journal,* September 23, 1992, pp. A1, A6.
[35]David Osborne and Ted Gaebler, *Reinventing Government* (Reading, MA: Addison-Wesley, 1992).

Given the size of the national government, it is inevitable that waste and fraud exist. But there is no agreement on their extent. The national government spends huge amounts of time and money trying to limit waste and ensure integrity of work. The battle is always being fought.[36]

http://63.240.14.150

Which bureaucracies are involved in regulating your education? What about the food you eat or the place in which you live? You can search federal agencies by topic at the above location.

The criticism of red tape can be more accurately leveled at groups in the political system generally rather than at individual bureaucrats. One observer has argued that "one person's red tape may be another's treasured safeguard."[37] That is, what appears to be red tape is really the result of conflicting expectations on the parts of different groups in the political system. For example, advocates of nuclear power may decry the long bureaucratic process of hearings, certifications, and licensing procedures that accompanies the construction of a nuclear power plant. Yet environmentalists and some local residents may see such procedures as absolutely essential to public health and safety. Perhaps red tape is more a reflection of the attempt to satisfy political values in our society, such as consideration of different points of view, than it is an effort by bureaucrats to paralyze action.[38]

Similarly, charges that bureaucrats engage in work that duplicates or conflicts with the work of other bureaucrats in large measure can be explained by outside expectations. For example, in granting college funds to veterans, the Department of Veterans Affairs (DVA) may be duplicating the educational programs of the Department of Education. Yet the political expectation that the DVA serve veterans encourages that agency to assume educational functions of its own. Similarly, the Agriculture Department represents the economic demands of tobacco farmers, while Health and Human Services represents the demands of health groups. The conflicting demands of different groups in society are largely reflected in conflict among different groups of bureaucrats.

The most serious criticism of bureaucrats, however, is that even though they are unelected, they independently make choices affecting public policy and in the process play an unintended political role. However, three qualifications need to be made about their political role. First, in executing policy purposes, bureaucrats obviously strive to achieve their institution's goals. For example, an administrator at the NIH may stress the importance of additional funding for cancer research; defense analysts may call for the construction of a new weapons system. Executing policy is their work, and bureaucrats, not surprisingly, want the most favorable environment possible in which that work can proceed.

Second, bureaucrats cannot always exercise discretion in translating ideas into action. The Internal Revenue Service, for example, cannot decide to tax certain income groups at rates higher or lower than those prescribed by law. The greater the specificity of the idea written into law, the lower the degree of discretion bureaucrats have in translating that idea into action.

---

[36]See the discussion in Herbert Kaufman, *Red Tape: Its Origins, Uses, and Abuses* (Washington, DC: Brookings Institution, 1977), pp. 50–54.
[37]Ibid., p. 4.
[38]Ibid.

Third, if the law is vague or ambiguous, bureaucratic discretion is inevitable. In much legislation, Congress cannot possibly provide for every contingency or circumstance. Such detailed decisions fall to bureaucrats. For example, the Social Security Administration (SSA), in administering benefits to disabled Americans, must determine just what constitutes disability in individual cases. Depending on how rigorous that determination is, the SSA, in effect, can make public policy toward citizens with disabilities.[39]

In many areas of public policy, different groups and institutions have conflicting ideas on what government ought to do; they are interested in bureaucracy because they want to get their ideas translated into action. In large measure, the issue of bureaucratic responsiveness centers on the determination of whose ideas ought to be translated into action. In an enlightening and provocative statement, a civil servant in the EPA declared during a controversy over environmental policy: "I signed an oath of office, and it was not to the president. It was to the American people."[40] The statement implies that control over the bureaucracy comes to those who can successfully claim to determine what "the American people" want. The search for that determination, like the struggle to control bureaucracy, lies at the heart of political conflict.

---

[39]See, for example, Susan Gluck Mezey, *No Longer Disabled: The Federal Courts and the Politics of Social Security Disability* (Westport, CT: Greenwood, 1988).
[40]Hugh B. Kaufman, quoted in Cass Peterson, "A Nagging Voice from E.P.A. Depths Now Singing from the Catbird Seat," the *Washington Post,* February 14, 1983, p. A9.

SUMMARY

1. The principal task of bureaucracy is the translation of policy ideas into action. Bureaucrats are people appointed to positions in the executive branch. Individuals responsible for executing public policies work relatively anonymously in bureaucracies. Compared to the other branches of government, bureaucracies are much larger, more diverse in purpose, and physically disperse. The 2.7 million government employees work in a great variety of occupations.

2. Executive Office units advise and serve the president. The executive departments generally contain a large number of smaller bureaucratic units. Independent agencies are placed outside the executive departments, generally in response to political demands for greater visibility. More insulated from presidential control than other bureaucracies, independent regulatory agencies monitor various sectors of the economy. Government corporations are public bodies engaged in essentially commercial enterprises.

3. Government service was seen as a high calling in the early decades of the Republic. In the spoils system, government jobs were rewards for political service. The Pendleton Act of 1883 established the merit principle as the basis for government employment. The Civil Service Reform Act of 1978 attempted to protect the merit system and rid the system of abuses, but its success has been questioned.

4. The president can shape bureaucracies by exercising his appointment, budget proposal, and reorganization powers. Congress can contest the president in the struggle to control bureaucracy through its statutory, budget, confirmation, and investigative powers. In iron triangles, interest groups can work with members of Congress to make claims on bureaucracies. The courts can shape the work of bureaucracies by declaring laws unconstitutional, ensuring procedural fairness, interpreting statutes, and judging the reasonableness of agency actions.

5. Regulation is a major policy of government that affects practically everyone in some way. Economic regulation centers on specific industries, and social regulation tries to achieve a variety of social goals. Major regulatory initiatives were made in the late nineteenth and early twentieth centuries, during the New Deal, and in the 1960s and 1970s. Regulatory agencies issue rules pursuant to powers they receive from congressional enactments. Debate over the regulatory role of government ebbs and flows with the debate over the appropriate role of government and who should bear the costs of government action.

6. Bureaucracies have been targets of sharp criticism over the past generation. Depending on the amount of discretion Congress allows in law, bureaucrats can potentially make policy. The issue of bureaucratic responsiveness centers principally on determining whose policy ideas should be implemented.

KEY TERMS

bureaucracy (332)	spoils system (340)
public purpose (332)	Pendleton Act (341)
bureaucrat (332)	Hatch Act (341)
fourth branch (334)	Civil Service Reform Act of 1978 (342)
Cabinet (336)	Senior Executive Service (SES) (342)
independent agency (338)	Office of Personnel Management (OPM) (342)
independent regulatory commission (338)	
government corporation (339)	Merit Systems Protection Board (342)

legislative veto (345)

iron triangle (346)

regulations (348)

economic regulation (349)

social regulation (349)

quasi-legislative (349)

quasi-judicial (349)

administrative law judge (349)

slip law (352)

U.S. Statutes-at-Large (352)

U.S. Code (352)

Federal Register (352)

Code of Federal Regulations (CFR) (352)

deregulation (356)

red tape (357)

READINGS FOR FURTHER STUDY

The United States Government Manual (Washington, DC: Government Printing Office) is a basic reference work that contains a history, relevant congressional enactments, and an organization chart for each bureaucratic unit.

James W. Feslerand and Donald F. Kettl, *The Politics of the Administrative Process* (Chatham, NJ: Chatham House, 1991) is a comprehensive and erudite review of bureaucracies in the policy process.

A classic work on the obstacles to the implementation of policies is Jeffrey L. Pressman and Aaron B. Wildavsky, *Implementation*, 3d ed. (Berkeley: University of California Press, 1984).

A fascinating history and analysis of the public service in light of political culture can be found in Frederick C. Mosher, *Democracy and the Public Service*, 2d ed. (New York: Oxford University Press, 1982).

An interesting analysis of bureaucracy and democratic theory can be found in Douglas Yates, *Bureaucratic Democracy: The Search for Democracy and Efficiency in American Government* (Cambridge, MA: Harvard University Press, 1982).

William T. Gormley, Jr., *Taming the Bureaucracy: Muscles, Prayers, and Other Strategies* (Princeton, NJ: Princeton University Press, 1989), reviews and analyzes efforts to control bureaucracy.

Richard A. Harris and Sidney Milkus, *The Politics of Regulatory Change: A Tale of Two Agencies* (New York: Oxford University Press, 1989), examines the Federal Trade Commission and the Environmental Protection Agency within the context of regulatory politics in the 1970s and 1980s.

A. Lee Fritschler's *Smoking and Politics: Policymaking and the Federal Bureaucracy*, 4th ed. (Englewood Cliffs, NJ: Prentice-Hall, 1989) is an illuminating analysis of the Federal Trade Commission's attempt to regulate cigarette advertising.

CHAPTER 12

The Supreme Court and the American Judiciary

A/P World Wide

Chapter Objectives

One of the distinguishing characteristics of American government is the major role the Supreme Court and other courts play in governing the nation. Because of the importance of the issues that confront American judges, their decisions weigh heavily in shaping the liberties, fortunes, and quality of life of many citizens. Chief among courts is the United States Supreme Court, the third branch of government. The Supreme Court enjoys prominence because of the Constitution and because Americans have been reluctant to place their fate entirely in the hands of elected officials and popular majorities. The Court, therefore, sits as an institution primarily responsible for interpreting the law of the land. Yet because the Court appears antidemocratic in a government that strives to be democratic, Americans have also been wary of giving judges too much power. Explaining what judges do, discerning the Supreme Court's place in American government, and exploring how the Court decides cases are the objectives of this chapter.

The National Court System

A look at almost any recent term of the Supreme Court turns up decisions on subjects as varied as presidential powers, crime, taxation, religious freedom, and racial and sexual equality. The fact that the Supreme Court confronts important issues makes the Court similar to other major political institutions in Washington. Yet three factors distinguish the Supreme Court and other courts from the rest of the national government:

1. The judiciary operates only in the context of cases.
2. The cases develop in a strictly prescribed fashion.
3. Judges rely heavily on reason in justifying what they do.

case

A controversy to be decided by a court.

criminal case

Judicial proceedings the government begins against individuals following commission of a crime.

crime

A public wrong; an offense, such as murder, against society at large—even though it may have been committed against only a single individual.

civil case

Noncriminal legal action, such as divorces or attempts to recover damages following an automobile accident.

state courts

Courts of the 50 states, as opposed to the federal or national courts.

federal courts

The courts of the United States, as distinguished from the courts of the 50 states.

jurisdiction

Authority of a court or other agency to act.

The judiciary is distinctive because it is the part of government that speaks the language of the fundamental values of the political system.

Cases: Raw Material for the Judiciary

The judiciary acts by deciding cases. A **case** is a dispute handled by a court. Like most disputes, there are at least two opposing parties. A case may pit one individual against another, a government agency against an individual, a corporation against the government, and so forth. Cases are criminal or civil. **Criminal cases** result when the government begins legal action against someone following commission of a **crime**. A crime is a public wrong. That is, it is an offense, such as murder, against society at large—even though it may have been committed against only a single individual. **Civil cases** encompass all noncriminal legal actions and commonly include attempts to redress a private wrong or to settle a private dispute. Divorces and recovery of damages following an automobile accident, for example, present civil law questions. They involve efforts by one party to enforce a right or to be compensated for harm caused by another.

By deciding cases, courts, like other governmental institutions, attempt to resolve conflicts peacefully. It is only a slight exaggeration to say that disputes that bring a regiment of soldiers into the streets of some countries summon a battalion of lawyers into the courtrooms of America.

Fifty-One Judicial Systems

Topped by the Supreme Court, the national court system contains both state courts and federal courts. The latter in turn consist of district courts, courts of appeals, and a few special courts.

References to **state courts** and **federal courts** can be confusing to anyone not familiar with the political features of American federalism (see Chapter 2). Concisely put, each state has its own system of courts, and the national government has its own system of courts (see Figures 12.1 and 12.2). The national courts are usually referred to, somewhat misleadingly, as "federal courts."

The two types of courts hear different kinds of cases. Almost all divorce and personal injury cases, for example, are heard in state courts, as are violations of state criminal laws. Antitrust actions and violations of federal criminal laws, by contrast, are adjudicated in federal courts. Someone charged with robbing a corner grocery will be tried in state court; someone charged with robbing a post office will be tried in federal court. The dual system of courts means that almost everyone in any of the 50 states is simultaneously within the jurisdiction, or reach, of two judicial systems, one state and the other federal. **Jurisdiction** refers to the authority a court has to entertain a case. The term has two basic dimensions: who and what. The first identifies the parties who may take a case into a particular court. The second refers to the subject matter the parties can raise in their case.

FIGURE 12.1

The United States Court System

Almost all cases the Supreme Court decides each year are part of its appellate jurisdiction. These cases begin in the state and federal courts.

SOURCE: Administrative Office of the United States Courts.

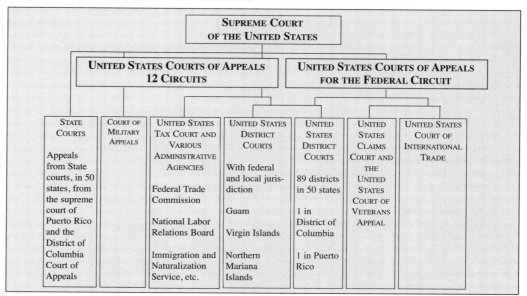

Still, state and federal courts have at least two important points in common. First, the U.S. Constitution binds all American courts. Second, the U.S. Supreme Court may decide cases that originate in both systems. Because the Supreme Court hears only a tiny fraction of all the cases looked at by judges each year across the land, however, the quality of justice in the nation depends largely on what these other courts and judges do. The Supreme Court weighs heavily in American politics not because it can literally oversee what every other court does, but because these other courts consider the Supreme Court's decisions binding on questions of national law and policy.

State and Local Courts

State and local courts are organized according to the laws and constitutions of the 50 states. The resulting variety only serves to make them interesting, not insignificant. They handle the great bulk of legal business: Excluding minor traffic violations, the total number of cases filed each year in state courts exceeds 34 million. Felony criminal cases alone total over 1 million. Most crimes committed each year are violations of state laws and are tried in state courts, as are most disputes over estates, contracts, and property. As will be explained, a relative few are ever candidates for review by the U.S. Supreme Court. Most Americans, then, who go to court go to state courts and only state courts.

FIGURE 12.2

Typical Organization of State Courts

Each state has its own system of state courts. No system is exactly like another, but all are organized in a hierarchy similar to that pictured here. All states have courts of limited jurisdiction, courts of general jurisdiction, and a court of last resort. In Texas and Oklahoma, there are two separate courts of last resort—one for criminal appeals and one for all other types of cases. Most, but not all, states have at least one intermediate appellate court. In the 12 states that have no intermediate court, cases move on appeal from courts of general jurisdiction to the court of last resort.

SOURCE: National Center for State Courts.

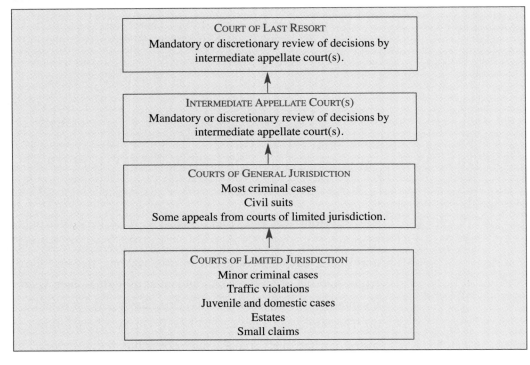

http://www.ncscon
line.org/index.html
The vast majority of court cases take place in our nation's state court system. Find out about your state's court system through the National Center for State Courts at the above location.

courts of limited jurisdiction

The lowest-level court in a state's judicial system, hearing particular kinds of cases involving small claims, traffic violations, and minor criminal infractions.

courts of general jurisdiction

The basic unit of a court system, receiving appeals from courts of limited jurisdiction and serving as trial courts for serious criminal offenses and civil suits involving substantial amounts of money.

The judicial systems of most states are divided into four levels (see Figure 12.2). At the bottom are **courts of limited jurisdiction**, which hear cases in villages, towns, and cities involving small claims, traffic violations, domestic matters, juvenile affairs, and minor criminal offenses. Such courts are variously labeled municipal court, county court, magistrate's court, traffic court, or recorder's court. Usually such cases are decided by a judge sitting without a jury. On the next tier are **courts of general jurisdiction**; usually one such court is located in each county. These courts receive appeals from the bottom tier and serve as trial courts for serious criminal offenses and civil suits involving substantial amounts of money. Again, the names vary from state to state: superior court, county court, or court of common pleas. Above these courts in many states,

intermediate appellate courts

Courts between courts of general jurisdiction and the court of last resort. In the federal court system, the courts of appeals are intermediate appellate courts.

court of last resort

The highest court within a particular judicial system, such as a state supreme court, to which a litigant may appeal a case.

Missouri Plan

Method of selecting state judges, involving appointment from a list of recommended nominees and a later retention vote by the electorate.

especially the more populous, are one or more **intermediate appellate courts**, which are labeled superior court or court of appeals, and that accept appeals from the courts of general jurisdiction. At the top is a **court of last resort**, usually called the supreme court. Most states have only one "supreme court," but Texas and Oklahoma have two, with one specifically designated to hear appeals in criminal cases. (In New York the highest court is called the Court of Appeals, and a supreme court is a court of general jurisdiction.)

Unlike federal judges, who are appointed for life and removable only by impeachment, most state judges are elected. In some states judges run in nonpartisan elections or in partisan elections just as legislative candidates do. In other states the governor appoints judges from a list of nominees provided by a panel of lawyers and other citizens. The latter method is called the **Missouri Plan**, after the state that pioneered its use. Following initial election or appointment, judges may then be subject to retention votes every 5 or 10 years. That is, instead of running for reelection like other officeholders, judges have their names placed on a ballot alongside the question, "Shall judge X be continued in office for another term?" A negative vote creates a vacancy, and a new election is held or a new appointment is made. At present 19 states use a single method for selecting judges, and in the remaining states judges are selected by one of two (or even three) methods, depending on the court involved.

Whether chosen by election or the Missouri Plan, the people can unseat state judges at the polls. Critics say that this possibility undercuts judicial independence, making judges too dependent on the voters and perhaps afraid to render unpopular decisions. Others reply that the people should retain control over all public officials, even judges. Experience shows that judges elected on partisan ballots are more likely than those chosen on nonpartisan ballots or under an appointment/retention plan to be turned out of office by the voters.

United States District Courts

United States district courts

Trial courts in the federal court system in which almost all federal cases begin; courts of general jurisdiction.

Of all federal courts, the Constitution only provides for the Supreme Court. Article III left the creation of other ("inferior") courts to the discretion of Congress. Plausibly, Congress could have permitted the existing state courts to handle national business, but chose instead in the judiciary Act of 1789 to organize a separate court system for the nation as a whole.

Almost all federal cases (over 310,000 annually, excluding bankruptcy filings) begin in the 94 **United States district courts**, staffed by 655 judges. There are 89 district courts in the 50 states, plus one each in the District of Columbia, Guam, Puerto Rico, the Virgin Islands, and the Northern Mariana Islands. Each state has at least one district court, and no district crosses a state line. Some states have two or three districts, and the populous states of California, New York, and Texas have four each (see Figure 12.3).

The jurisdiction of district courts extends to cases that arise under the Constitution, laws, and treaties of the United States, as well as admiralty and maritime cases. Questions of state law (such as liability in an automobile accident) may get into district court through diversity jurisdiction. This occurs when the parties to a case are citizens of different states and when the amount at issue is greater than $50,000. As a way of reducing the volume of cases in the district courts, Congress has considered repealing diversity jurisdiction altogether. Should this happen, cases now qualifying for diversity jurisdiction would be decided by state courts, entirely outside the federal court system.

United States Courts of Appeals

United States courts of appeals

Intermediate appellate courts in the federal court system, just below the Supreme Court.

Thirteen **United States courts of appeals**, staffed by 167 judges, occupy a middle position in the hierarchy of the federal judiciary. Twelve of these courts have a regional jurisdiction or circuit, as Figure 12.3 shows.

Although district judges sit individually in most cases, appeals judges normally sit in panels of three. In special situations cases are heard en banc, with most of a cir-

FIGURE 12.3

Geographic Boundaries of U.S. Courts of Appeals and U.S. District Courts

The map shows how the 94 U.S. district courts and 13 U.S. courts of appeals exist with the court systems of the 50 states and the District of Columbia.

SOURCE: Administrative Office of the United States Courts.

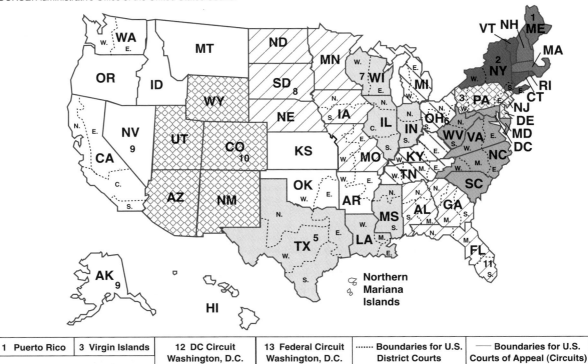

| 1 Puerto Rico | 3 Virgin Islands | 12 DC Circuit Washington, D.C. | 13 Federal Circuit Washington, D.C. | ······ Boundaries for U.S. District Courts | —— Boundaries for U.S. Courts of Appeal (Circuits) |

cuit's bench sitting at once. Cases in the courts of appeals number more than 54,000 annually. Most are appeals come from disappointed parties in the district courts and the Tax Court (see Figure 12.1). Under exceptional circumstances, cases may go from district courts directly to the Supreme Court, bypassing a court of appeals. Another large source of work for the appeals courts comes in the form of reviewing rulings of various administrative and regulatory agencies of the national government, such as the Federal Communications Commission, the Federal Trade Commission, and the National Labor Relations Board. The Court of Appeals for the District of Columbia Circuit hears more of these agency cases than any of the other appeals courts, making this court one of the most influential in the land.

The thirteenth appeals court is the newest and, unlike the other 12, has both a different and a national jurisdiction. The Court of Appeals for the Federal Circuit accepts appeals in patent cases from any district court, as well as all appeals from the Claims Court, the Court of International Trade, and the Court of Veterans Appeals. For most litigants, the courts of appeals are the courts of last resort in the federal judicial system, due to the fact that the Supreme Court accepts relatively few cases.

Special Courts

Congress has created other tribunals to hear particular kinds of cases in which considerable specialization and expertise are desirable. Into this category fall the following:

1. The **Claims Court** hears suits involving monetary damages against the U.S. government.
2. The **Court of International Trade** adjudicates controversies concerning the classification and valuation of imported merchandise.
3. The **Tax Court** decides disputes between taxpayers and the Internal Revenue Service.
4. The **Court of Veterans Appeals** reviews decisions on benefits and entitlements from the Board of Veterans Appeals in the Department of Veterans Affairs. The newest special court, it heard its first case in 1990.
5. The **Court of Military Appeals** reviews judgments handed down by courts-martial in the several branches of the armed forces.

These courts rarely make the headlines, but they are quite important. In the first four, millions of dollars may ride on the outcome of decisions. The lives and liberties of hundreds of thousands of American citizens are in the care of the fifth.

The Supreme Court of the United States

It is from these courts, state and federal, that the nine justices of the Supreme Court receive almost all the cases they decide each term. At present, some 7,000 new cases

appellate jurisdiction

Includes cases a court receives from lower courts. The appellate jurisdiction of the U.S. Supreme Court is defined by Congress.

federal question

An issue that involves the interpretation of the Constitution or a statute or a treaty of the United States.

rule of four

Procedure of the U.S. Supreme Court by which the affirmative votes of four justices are needed to accept a case for decision.

original jurisdiction

Authority of a court over cases that begin in that court. Courts of general jurisdiction have original jurisdiction over most criminal offenses. The original jurisdiction of the U.S. Supreme Court is very small.

Eleventh Amendment

The first reversal of a Supreme Court decision [*Chisholm v. Georgia*, 2 U.S. (2 Dallas) 419 (1793)] by constitutional amendment. The amendment denied federal courts jurisdiction in suits against a state brought by citizens of another state or a foreign country.

appear annually on their docket, joining about 800 carried over from the previous term. All but a handful invoke the Court's **appellate jurisdiction**. Defined by Congress, this is the authority the Court has to review decisions of the federal courts, as well as decisions of the highest state courts that raise **federal questions** (matters involving the interpretation of the Constitution, a statute, or a treaty of the United States). Today, almost all cases reach the Supreme Court on a writ of certiorari (Latin for "to be informed"). Except for a few cases involving the Voting Rights Act, review by the Supreme Court is plainly discretionary, not obligatory. It takes a minimum of four justices (one short of a majority) to agree to accept a case for review. This **rule of four** allows the Court not only to limit the number of cases it decides, but to engage or avoid particular issues.

A very few cases each term are candidates for the Court's **original jurisdiction**, meaning that the case begins or originates with the Court. Indeed, the number of "original" cases the Court decided between 1789 and 2000 totaled only about 200. The Supreme Court's original jurisdiction is spelled out in Article III of the Constitution and includes four kinds of disputes:

1. *Cases between one of the states and the U.S. government.* For example, in *United States v. Maine*,[1] the justices ruled that the national government—not the states—had control of oil deposits more than three miles offshore.

2. *Cases between two or more states.* In 1967 Michigan and Ohio each claimed the same piece of mineral-rich territory in Lake Erie; and in a series of cases, Arizona and California have battled each other over water resources.[2]

3. *Cases involving foreign ambassadors, ministers, or consuls.* The framers wanted cases that could involve the nation's relations with other countries to be heard initially by the highest court.

4. *Cases begun by a state against a citizen of another state or against another country.* The **Eleventh Amendment**, however, requires suits initiated *against* a state by a citizen of another state or of a foreign country to begin in the courts of that state. The Eleventh Amendment came about because of a 1793 decision by the Supreme Court that a citizen of South Carolina could sue the state of Georgia in the federal courts.[3]

Only controversies between states qualify today exclusively as original cases in the Supreme Court. The justices have been content for Congress to grant concurrent original jurisdiction to the U.S. District Courts for cases in the other three categories. As

---

[1]420 U.S. 515 (1975).
[2]*Michigan v. Ohio*, 386 U.S. 1029 (1967); *Arizona v. California*, 460 U.S. 605 (1983).
[3]*Chisholm v. Georgia*, 2 U.S. (2 Dallas) 419 (1793).

such, although one of these cases *could* begin in the Supreme Court, in almost every instance the case will begin in a district court—unless it involves a dispute between two states of the Union.

The Supreme Court is headed administratively by the chief justice of the United States (the position has been filled since 1986 by William H. Rehnquist). Through the years, the Court has usually been known by the name of the chief justice (the Marshall Court, for example), but the chief's vote in cases counts no more than the vote of any of the eight associate justices. The chief justice also presides over the judicial Conference of the United States, which is composed of representatives of the lower federal courts and makes recommendations to those courts as well as to Congress with regard to staffing needs and operating efficiency.

Federal Judicial Selection

The Constitution gives the president power to appoint federal judges, subject to confirmation by a majority vote of the Senate. In practice, a president rarely personally knows any of the district or appeals judges he appoints. Judges on the district, appeals, and Supreme Court benches serve "during good behavior," a provision of the Constitution that effectively ensures lifetime tenure, with removal only by impeachment. In contrast to presidents and members of Congress, the Constitution spells out no qualifications, such as age or citizenship, for any federal judge. Federal judges do not even have to be lawyers, although since 1789 each has had legal training of some kind. Today, it would be unthinkable for the Senate to approve a nominee who is not a law school graduate and a member of the bar.

Presidents overwhelmingly appoint members of their own political parry to the federal bench (during the past 100 years, only in the Taft, Hoover, and Ford administrations has the figure dropped below 90 percent). The choices for the district courts are usually made by officials in the Justice Department working with political leaders from the state in which the appointment is to be made. A state's U.S. senators (one or both)—particularly if they are of the same party as the president—traditionally play a prominent role in the selection. There is some truth in the wisecrack that a federal judge is a lawyer who knows a senator. In contrast, appointment of appeals judges reflects more national and less local influence, with the attorney general and other officials in the Justice Department having a large say in the selection. District judges are obvious choices for appeals posts, because they have observable judicial "track records."

Under present policy of the Senate judiciary Committee, a "blue slip" (indicating disapproval) from a home-state senator is sufficient to block a judicial nominee outright if the administration fails to consult with home-state senators before naming a candidate. This is an example of **senatorial courtesy**, the practice that allows home-state senators considerable control over the fate of presidential nominees. If a senator

http://www.supreme courtus.gov

You can read the latest Supreme Court opinions, find biographical sketches of the current justices, and even see the Court's upcoming calendar at the Supreme Court Web site above.

senatorial courtesy

Custom in the Senate to reject a nominee for federal office who is unacceptable to a senator from the nominee's state when the senator and president are of the same party.

submits a blue slip after having been consulted, the committee considers the senator's objections but does not always reject the nominee.

An additional screening role is played by the Committee on the Federal Judiciary of the American Bar Association, the largest organization of lawyers in the country. Before the president sends a nominee's name to the Senate, the attorney general submits the name to the ABA committee for review. This committee then finds the candidate "well-qualified," "qualified," or "not qualified." Only occasionally will a president nominate someone the committee considers not qualified, and some are nonetheless confirmed by the Senate when he does. The ABA's participation in the review process is significant because it means that a private organization in effect shares the confirmation role the Constitution assigns to the Senate. The committee's screening attracts the most attention when the president nominates an individual to the Supreme Court.

In contrast to the other federal courts, vacancies on the Supreme Court occur relatively infrequently. Including the six original seats George Washington (1789–1797) filled, 108 persons have served on the Court through 2001. Supreme Court nominations are far more likely to personally occupy a president's time and attention. Such focus is not simply because the Supreme Court decides important questions, but also because, once appointed, justices tend to stay on the Court a long time—usually far longer than the president who named them remains in the White House. Five considerations most often are at work as presidents make up their minds about who to appoint:

1. *Professional qualifications.* How respected is the nominee?
2. *Acceptability to the Senate.* Will he or she be confirmed?
3. *Ideological fit.* Will the nominee support the president's program?
4. *Personal friendship.* Does the president want an old friend on the Court?
5. *Region, race, religion, gender, and other background factors.* Does a particular group need "representation" on the Court?

Since Washington's time, presidents have wanted a Court supportive of their administration; yet they are not always successful in picking "right-thinking" justices. President Dwight Eisenhower (1953–1961) once remarked that appointing Earl Warren (1953–1969) as chief justice was "the biggest damnfool mistake I ever made" after Warren turned out to be more liberal than Ike had supposed. President Richard Nixon (1969–1974) hardly approved of Justice Harry A. Blackmun's (1970–1994) authorship of the 1973 abortion decision,[4] and Presidents Ronald Reagan and George Bush were disappointed when three of their appointees (Justices Sandra O'Connor [1981–], Anthony Kennedy [1988–], and David Souter [1990–]) voted against administration positions on school prayer.[5]

---

[4]*Roe v. Wade,* 410 U.S. 113 (1973).
[5]*Lee v. Weisman,* 60 U.S.L.W. 4723 (1992); Marcia Coyle, "The Court Confounds Observers," *National Law Journal,* July 13, 1992, p. 1.

Particular background factors have frequently been important in aiding or hurting one's chances to become a Supreme Court justice. Most presidents have taken geographical region into account. Moreover, religion, race, and gender have sometimes been important considerations as well. Even so, Supreme Court justices have hardly been representative of American society. Of the 108 justices who sat through 2001, all but 18 were Protestant males of Anglo-Saxon origin. Justice Antonin Scalia (1986–) is the Court's first Italian-American member. Justice Thurgood Marshall (1967–1991) was the first African American member of the Court, and Justice O'Connor is its first female member. Clarence Thomas became the second African American to serve in 1991, and Ruth Bader Ginsburg became the second woman in 1993. Most of the 108 have come from economically comfortable and civic-minded families. All have been lawyers or have held law degrees. About one-third graduated from the most prestigious colleges and universities in the United States. Most have been active in public affairs or have held political office, but some, including justice Byron White (1962–1993), had no prior judicial experience. Moreover, Chief Justice Rehnquist is only the third chief justice (out of a total of 16 since 1789) to have been "elevated" directly from associate justice. All other chief justices were nominated from outside the Court.

Whatever a president's motivations, the Senate must still vote to confirm the nominee. Such approval has been forthcoming most of the time, but on 26 occasions the Senate has not given it. In this century, four presidents—Herbert Hoover (1929–1933), Lyndon Johnson (1963–1969), Richard Nixon (1969–1974), and Ronald Reagan (1981–1989)—have had their choices blocked by the Senate. Nixon, in fact, struck out twice in succession before the Senate handily confirmed Judge Harry Blackmun, his third nominee for the same vacancy. When Reagan picked judge Robert Bork to succeed retiring justice Lewis Powell (1971–1987), the Senate said no. Reagan's second choice, Judge Douglas Ginsburg, withdrew his name from consideration after acknowledging disclosures that he had smoked marijuana as a student in the 1960s and as a member of the Harvard law faculty in the 1970s. Powell's seat remained vacant until early 1988 when the Senate confirmed Reagan's third choice, Judge Anthony M. Kennedy.

The Clarence Thomas Affair

President Bush's nomination of Judge Clarence Thomas after justice Thurgood Marshall retired in 1991 barely eked out enough votes in the Senate. Although Marshall had long been hailed as a tenacious advocate of civil liberties and civil rights, Democrats claimed that Thomas would threaten both, particularly in abortion and affirmative action cases.

Objection to Thomas's constitutional values led to a 7–7 split when members of the Judiciary Committee voted on September 27. Thus, the nomination went to the Senate floor without a recommendation to confirm or reject. Still, press accounts

Professor Anita F. Hill. *(AP Wide World)*

predicted that Thomas would be confirmed easily in a vote scheduled for October 8.

Events, however, suddenly took an unexpected turn. A "leak" to the press during the weekend of October 5 quickly placed the nomination in doubt. Several weeks before the committee's vote, Professor Anita F. Hill of the University of Oklahoma School of Law had notified the committee's staff, in confidence, that Thomas had sexually harassed her from 1981 to 1983, during the time she was his assistant—first at the Department of Education and later at the Equal Employment Opportunity Commission (EEOC). At least some members of the committee were aware of Hill's accusations prior to their vote on September 27. Thanks to the leak of Hill's charges, virtually the entire nation knew about them.

To proceed with the vote on schedule now seemed hasty at best. Senators were themselves on trial for failing to take sexual harassment seriously. Accordingly, they sent the nomination back to the Judiciary Committee. What followed was a marathon television spectacle that left few satisfied: 28 hours of additional hearings marked by lurid details, bitter charges and countercharges, and equally bitter denials and counterdenials. Thomas told the committee that he was the victim of a "high-tech lynching for uppity blacks." Likened by some to a morality play or a psychodrama, the acrimonious hearings drew a larger viewing audience than the National League and American League play-offs going on at the same time.

The charges were grave and were potentially fatal for the nomination. Thomas, after all, had headed the agency responsible for enforcing the law against sexual harassment. Moreover, the charges undercut his principal strength. Because he lacked a record of legal scholarship or extensive judicial service, the case for his nomination had rested all along on character—precisely what Hill had called into question.

Unlike the baseball play-offs, however, the hearings concluded in a draw. There was no clear-cut victory in the court of public opinion for either Thomas or Hill. Although polls showed that more people seemed to believe Thomas's denials than Hill's accusations, polls also revealed that substantial doubts remained about the nominee. On October 15, such doubts helped to make the Senate's vote to confirm, 52 to 48, one of the closest on record for a successful Supreme Court nominee. Not since the controversy over membership in the Ku Klux Klan enveloped justice Hugo Black (1937–1971)—shortly *after* his confirmation in 1937—had a justice begun his tenure under a cloud of such suspicion.

Clarence's Supreme Court confirmation battle had an important "spillover" effect: Anita Hill's accusations against Thomas made many people more conscious of sexual harassment. By mid-1992, the EEOC (ironically, the agency Thomas once headed) reported that sexual harassment complaints filed in the first half of the fiscal year had increased by more than 50 percent, compared to the same period in the previous year.[6] Moreover, sexual harassment as a political issue galvanized both voters and candidates in the 1992 election.

What Courts Do

In the process of deciding cases, the Supreme Court and other courts perform several functions, including constitutional interpretation, statutory interpretation, fact determination, clarification of the boundaries of political authority, education and value application, and legitimation. Not all courts perform each function in every case, and some courts do more of one than another. As will be noted, fact determination is largely, though not exclusively, the province of trial courts. Appellate courts are heavily engaged in constitutional and statutory interpretation.

Constitutional Interpretation

American government is constitutional government—government according to basic institutions, procedures, and values inscribed in a written document. The Constitution of the United States is not without ambiguity, however. Because some of its provisions are not clear, and because the framers could not possibly have anticipated all contemporary issues, the document invites interpretation. This need for interpretation in turn guarantees disagreement over what the correct interpretation should be.

judicial review

The authority of courts to set aside a legislative act as being in violation of the Constitution.

Interpretation involves the power of **judicial review**, first formally declared by the United States Supreme Court in the 1803 case of *Marbury v. Madison*.[7] Judicial review provides a court with the authority to set aside decisions made by elected representatives of the people, if the court concludes that a law violates the Constitution. Judicial review allows contending political groups to continue their political skirmishes in the context of

---

[6]Jane Gross, "Suffering in Silence No More: Fighting Sexual Harassment," *The New York Times,* July 13, 1992, p. Al.
[7]The *Marbury* case and the concept of judicial review are discussed in Chapter 1.

cases built around opposing interpretations of particular clauses of the Constitution. Groups that have not prevailed in executive offices or legislative chambers often resort to the courts. Whether the question involves education, immigration, or criminal justice, one side seeks to persuade the constitutional umpire that the other has broken the rules.

Statutory Interpretation

Many cases require courts to interpret statutes passed by Congress or state legislatures. In a typical term, about half the cases the Supreme Court decides involve the meaning the justices give to words the legislators have written. At first glance this task seems avoidable. Why are legislators not able to say exactly what they mean? Sometimes legislators expect judges to fill in the blanks, so to speak. Legislators will write laws that set up certain standards for judges to apply; or, as a way of avoiding controversy, legislators will deliberately choose language that is vague. In addition, ambiguities can arise that the people who wrote the law simply did not anticipate. Judges will often try to discover the **legislative intent** of a law by trying to figure out what the legislators who wrote the law would have wanted.

legislative intent

A legislature's understanding of the meaning of a law and what it is designed to accomplish.

One of the first pages in this book refers to a copyright. The holder of the copyright has exclusive use and control of the work for a specified period of time. In this century, copyrights have been extended to motion pictures and television programs. When Congress last rewrote the Copyright Act in 1976, provision was made for "fair use." "Fair use" allows one legally to make copies of protected material "for purposes such as criticism, comment, news reporting, teaching . . . scholarship, or research," all without violating the copyright or paying a fee to the holder of the copyright. Is in-home video-taping of television programs an example of "fair use," or an infringement of copyright? Congress decreed only that certain factors are to be taken into account in deciding whether something amounts to "fair use," leaving the task of adding precision to judges. With fuzzy guidance, different courts arrived at different conclusions. In the end, the Supreme Court announced that in-home videotaping of copyrighted materials was "fair use" within the meaning of the statute.[8]

Fact Determination

Often the meaning of statutes and constitutional passages may be clear, and cases turn on the facts instead. Through fact determination, judges select from competing testimony and evidence which facts they accept as true and which they reject as false. This task is inescapable because the judicial process in the United States is adversarial. That is, cases pit one side against the other. Each side attempts to build the stronger argument to persuade

---

[8]*Sony Corporation v. Universal City Studios*, 464 U.S. 417 (1984).

trial court

A court of limited or general jurisdiction in which the disputed facts of a case are heard and decided.

the judge or jury to accept its version of the truth. Fact discretion is perhaps most visible in a **trial court**, the arena in which the issues and merits of a case are heard for the first time. In the federal court system, trial courts are the district courts. In state courts systems, trials occur in both the courts of limited and general jurisdiction (see Figures 12.1 and 12.2).

Clarification of the Boundaries of Political Authority

As explained in Chapter 1, the Constitution mandates separation of powers—the division of political functions among the three branches of government. It is not obvious, however, where the legitimate power of one branch stops and another's begins. Courts sometimes try to resolve this built-in tension. In 1952, for example, President Harry Truman (1945–1953) directed the secretary of commerce to seize and operate the nation's steel mills. Labor disputes in the steel industry threatened the supply of war materials needed for American troops in the Korean conflict. Truman based his actions not on any statutory authority, but on the president's responsibility for national security as commander-in-chief of the armed forces. Voting 6 to 3, the Supreme Court held that Truman had exceeded his powers under the Constitution. Although Congress might provide for such a takeover of industries by statute, Congress had not done so. Furthermore, the Court found nothing in the Constitution authorizing the president to act on his own.[9]

Education and Value Application

In deciding cases, judges teach and apply values. Even an ordinary criminal trial involves a judgment on what kinds of behavior are acceptable and unacceptable, on the part of both the suspect and the police. One of the hallmarks of constitutional government, after all, is that limits apply not just to the governed but to the governors as well. The constitutions and statutes of the state and national governments all represent value choices that define the kind of nation its citizens expect to enjoy. Judicial opinions give judges an opportunity to articulate those values.

Harry Truman. *(Library of Congress)*

[9]*Youngstown v. Sawyer,* 343 U.S. 579 (1952).

Of course, no one pretends that judicial opinions are widely read by the general public. However, they are read and studied by journalists, scholars, and other opinion leaders, who in turn inform the public and help shape the attitudes Americans have about the courts and the issues judges confront.

Legitimation

Because of the powers of judicial review, courts are expected to make sure that actions of public officials conform to the Constitution and statutes. In the great majority of cases, judges uphold the challenged laws or policies, thus placing a "seal of approval" on what others have done. Securing legitimacy may be crucial when a policy emerges from a long and loud national debate. Winners look to the judiciary for support, losers look to the judiciary for redress. Both typically see the courts as offering "the final word." During the civil rights movement of the 1960s, for example (see Chapter 3), Congress took the bold and controversial step of banning racial discrimination in restaurants, hotels, theaters, and other privately owned places of public accommodation. During debate on the bill in 1963 and 1964, opponents argued that the ban would be an unjustified intrusion into the right of owners of businesses to run their enterprises as they wished. The Supreme Court's decision upholding the constitutionality of the law virtually ended the controversy. Within a matter of months, most public agitation over the legitimacy of the new policy simply ceased.[10] A ruling can, however, inflame an issue, not soothe it. On occasion it may appear that the judges have thrust a broom handle into a hornet's nest, as the abortion controversy illustrates.

The Supreme Court at Work

Cases decided by the Supreme Court move through five distinct stages: petition for review, briefs on the merits, oral argument, conference and decision, and assignment and writing of opinions.

Petition for Review

briefs

Documents filed with a court containing the argument of the parties to a case.

Litigants who lose in lower courts begin climbing the steep slope toward the Supreme Court when their lawyers file documents called **briefs** with the Court's clerk. In these petitions for review, the opposing parties attempt to convince the justices that the issues the case raises are so important (or unimportant) that they deserve (or do not deserve) the Court's attention. As discussed previously, the Court will not accept a case unless a minimum of four justices agrees that the case warrants review.

---

[10]*Heart of Atlanta Motel v. United States*, 379 U.S. 274 (1964).

FIGURE 12.4

Caseload in the U.S. Supreme Court, 1950–1999

Figure 12.4 shows the number of cases on the docket of the Supreme Court in each of six years and the number of cases decided with full opinion. The justices decide other cases summarily each term. The number of summary decisions each term sometimes equals the number of cases decided with full opinion. The volume of cases has grown more than sixfold since 1950, while the number of cases decided has varied only modestly. Indeed, since 1988 when 171 decisions were issued, the Court has been deciding fewer cases, a trend aided by the virtual elimination of the Court's obligatory appellate jurisdiction in 1988. Almost all of each year's cases come from the lower federal courts and the state supreme courts. Only a handful, at most, of original cases appears each term. A minimum of four justices must agree to hear a case.

SOURCE: Administrative Office of the United States Courts.

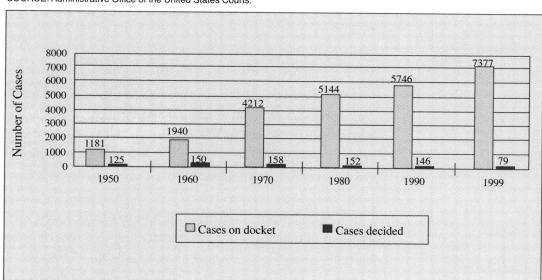

From the thousands of cases on its docket each term, the justices will typically decide no more than 150 with full opinion, in accordance with the procedure laid out below. Other cases may be decided "summarily" without opinion by a directive affirming or reversing the lower court. Except for cases carried over into the following year's term, the justices deny review in all other cases. The result is that the lower court's decision stands (see Figure 12.4).

What factors seem to guide the Court in selecting cases for decision? Although the justices rarely explain their reasons for rejecting cases, chances for review by the nation's highest court are significantly increased if one or more of the following is present:

- The United States is a party to the case and requests Supreme Court review.
- The case presents a question that has been decided differently by different courts of appeals.
- The case involves an issue some of the justices are eager to resolve.
- A lower court has made a decision clearly at odds with established Supreme Court interpretation of a law or constitutional provision.
- The Court's work load permits accepting another case for decision.
- The case presents an issue of overriding importance to the nation.

Even if a case fits into one of the categories listed, the Supreme Court will not necessarily grant review. Because the Court's docket contains thousands of cases each term, a litigant's chances of having a case heard by the justices are usually very long. Claims that someone will "take this all the way to the Supreme Court" are therefore more threat than promise.

Briefs on the Merits

Once the Court has placed a case on its "decision calendar," attorneys for the opposing sides file a second round of briefs. This time the arguments focus on the decision the justices should make, not on whether they should accept the case. Briefs of opposing counsel are supplemented by **amici curiae** briefs. Submitted by "friends of the court," these documents come from interest groups and others who are not parties to the case, but who have a stake in its outcome.

One lawyer whose briefs the justices routinely read with extra care is the **Solicitor General of the United States**—the third-ranking official in the Justice Department and the government's lawyer before the Supreme Court. In cases in which the government has lost in a lower court, the "S.G." decides whether the United States will petition the Supreme Court for review. If so, the solicitor general is responsible for both written briefs and oral argument supporting the government's position. The job is important because the United States is a party in about half the cases that confront the justices.

Oral Argument

The most public part of the Court's work is **oral argument**. On about 40 days (always Mondays, Tuesdays, and Wednesdays), starting in October and concluding in late April, opposing lawyers face the justices. Cases are routinely allotted one hour, with each side receiving 30 minutes. A spontaneous event, oral argument gives each justice an opportunity to ask questions about the case. Sometimes questioning from the bench is lively and intense; at other times the justices may barely seem interested. At all times they

amicus curiae

Latin for "friend of the court." Refers to persons, government agencies, or groups that are not parties to a case but nonetheless have an interest in its outcome. They make their views known by filing an *amicus curiae brief* with the court hearing the case.

Solicitor General of the United States

The lawyer for the United States in the Supreme Court; decides which cases the government will appeal to the Supreme Court.

oral argument

Stage in the decision-making process of a court, during which opposing counsel verbally present their views to the court.

The Supreme Court and the American Judiciary 381

rock back and forth in their leather swivel chairs, occasionally pass notes and whisper among themselves, and send pages on errands for documents and law books. The justices attach great importance to the oral argument step of the decision-making procedure. Whether such arguments change many minds, however, is a question only the justices can answer.

An appearance before the Supreme Court can be intimidating even for the most seasoned advocates. Standing at the small lectern before the raised bench, an attorney can feel very lonely. Heightening the tension are the time limits, which the Court rigidly enforces. When five minutes remain, the marshal flicks a switch that turns on a white light at the lectern. A red light signals that time is up. The chief justice may allow counsel to complete a sentence or to answer a question, but Chief justice Charles Evans Hughes (1910–1916, 1930–1941) is said to have cut off one attorney in the middle of the word *if*.

Conference and Decision

On Wednesday afternoons, after argument has finished at 3 o'clock, and all day on Fridays, the justices convene in a small room adjacent to the chief justice's chambers to discuss the cases they have heard that week. They also act on petitions for review. The importance of oral argument may be enhanced because the spoken words are fresh on the justices' minds when they take up a case in conference. The usual practice is for the chief justice to lay out his views first, followed by each associate justice, starting with the most senior. By the time all have had their say, each justice's position is often clear. If not, a vote is taken. These votes, recorded by each justice in a leather-bound docket book, are tentative. The decision does not become final until it is announced in court, weeks or even months later.

In contrast to the openness of oral argument, the conferences are closed. No pages or law clerks are present in the room, only the justices. If something is needed, the most junior justice acts as messenger and goes to the door. What happens inside the room is very secret. In fact, the Court has the best secrecy record in Washington. Leaks, as prevalent in the nation's capital as the summer humidity, are so rare at the Court that they make headlines when they occur. Confidentiality is crucial, not just because it gives the justices freedom to talk and maneuver amid the most controversial issues of the day, but also because political and economic fortunes often hang in the balance.

Assignment and Writing of Opinions

opinion of the Court

Statement representing the views of a majority of the judges of a court.

On Saturday or early in the week after the standard two-week session of oral argument, the chief justice circulates an assignment list to the justices. If part of the majority, the chief justice makes the opinion assignment in a particular case. If not, the task falls to the senior associate justice in the majority. The goal is an **opinion of the Court**, which

**concurring
opinion**
_____
A statement issued
separately by a judge
voting with the
majority.

**dissenting
opinion**
_____
A statement issued by
a judge explaining his
or her disagreement
with the majority
position.

*United States
Reports*
_____
The officially pub-
lished decisions of
the United States
Supreme Court.

is an explanation and justification of the decision agreed to by at least a bare majority of the justices. Between assignment of the opinion and announcement of the decision in open court, vigorous give-and-take routinely goes on among the justices. The justice writing an opinion has a draft printed in the Court's own print shop, done in strictest secrecy. Copies circulate among the other justices. Those in the majority will insist on changes. It is not unusual for an opinion to go through a dozen or more rewrites. Each opinion of the Court therefore represents the consensus of the majority, not merely the views of its author. Justices in the majority may write one or more **concurring opinions** when they reject the majority's reasoning while accepting its result; or, they simply may have other thoughts to add.

In only about a third of the cases each term do all nine justices agree on the result. For the rest, justices in the minority typically write one or more **dissenting opinions**. These help to explain what divides the Court, and are written for the express purpose of undercutting the logic and/or exposing the folly that dissenting justices find in the majority viewpoint.

Majority, concurring, and dissenting opinions are later collected and published as the *United States Reports*. This is the official record of the Court's work; it currently comprises over 500 volumes.

Law Clerks

Assisting the justices are law clerks, recent law school graduates who typically serve a justice for a year. The justices use their clerks in a variety of ways: to do research, summarize certiorari petitions, and write and critique drafts of opinions. Justice Blackmun confessed that his clerks managed to entice him to an Orioles baseball game at least once a term! Diversions aside, a clerk's day is long and includes evenings and weekends. Nonetheless, the opportunities for close association with the justices can be rewarding. Of the justices on the Court in 2001, three (William Rehnquist, John Stevens, and Stephen Breyer) were former clerks.

The Supreme Court and American Government: An Assessment

Early in our nation's history, the justices assumed a prominent role in governing the nation. However, this role has never been free from controversy. For most of its history the Court has seen itself as the guardian of preferred values. Years ago, for instance, the justices routinely censored social and economic legislation that they thought interfered unduly with property rights. In the years since President Roosevelt (1933–1945) confronted the justices in the "court-packing" fight of 1937 (see "Politics and Economics: The

Supreme Court and Economic Policy"), the Court's decisions have emphasized civil liberties and civil rights instead. Now about half the cases each term involve a provision of the Bill of Rights or the Fourteenth Amendment.

Judicial Review and Democracy

As explained in Chapter 1 and as noted earlier in this chapter, the authority to interpret the Constitution carries with it the power of judicial review. Some critics assert that judicial review is antidemocratic because judges invalidate decisions made by elected representatives of the people. Moreover, they say that judicial review encourages citizens to rely on judges and not the political process to protect their rights. Without judicial review, elected officials would have to give more thought to the constitutionality of their actions. Besides, critics maintain, individual rights survive in nations like Great Britain, where judges exercise no judicial review at all.

Others reply that the very idea of a written constitution means that a majority is not always supposed to get what it wants. Democracy American-style stresses not just majority rule but minority rights. Judicial review is but one of several constitutional features designed to control government power. Although citizens' control over their leaders through election is the primary check on government, judicial review can be an additional safeguard. Whatever the experience in other countries, enforcement of limits on government in this country seems to require the existence of institutions—like the federal courts—that are not directly accountable to the people.

Influences on Supreme Court Decision Making

What are some of the major factors that shape the Supreme Court's decisions? In the face of Chief Justice Marshall's broad self-denial that "courts are the mere instruments of the law, and can will nothing,"[11] political leaders have long recognized that justices do not make decisions in a vacuum. Surely, "judicial decisions are not babies brought by constitutional storks."[12] Individual and institutional forces, as well as legal and extralegal factors, affect what the Court does.[13]

Foremost perhaps are the justices' own *political ideas*. A jurist adamantly opposed to capital punishment, for example, will be more inclined than one who is not to regard the death penalty as one of the "cruel and unusual punishments" prohibited by the Eighth Amendment. A justice who does not place high value on the free exchange of views will probably not be a strong defender of the First Amendment's guarantee of free

---

[11]*Osborn v. Bank of the United States*, 22 U.S. (9 Wheaton) 738, 866 (1824).
[12]Max Lerner, quoted in Henry J. Abraham, *The Judicial Process*, 5th ed. (New York: Oxford University Press, 1986), p. 348.
[13]Tracey E. George and Lee Epstein, "On the Nature of Supreme Court Decision Making," *American Political Science Review* 86 (1992): 323.

Politics and Economics
The Supreme Court and Economic Policy

Although Supreme Court decisions today may affect the economy, just as they affect American life in other ways, between the years 1890 and 1937 the justices (and lower court judges too) played a far more active role in economic affairs. Then judges routinely reviewed the constitutionality of many kinds of social and economic laws that are now accepted without question.

In the decades after the Civil War, Congress and state legislatures passed hundreds of laws regulating working conditions, prices, wages and hours, and health standards in an effort to cope with the harmful effects of growth and industrialization. Opponents of such legislation advanced the arguments of laissez-faire economics, claiming that government regulation of business and economy should be kept to a minimum. Soon justices of the Supreme Court decided that freedom from economic regulation was a constitutionally protected liberty. This did not mean that the Court turned aside all legislative attempts to improve the life of working people, but it did mean that the justices had what amounted to the last word on which regulatory policies were acceptable and which were not. For example, *Lochner v. New York* struck down a law that set a maximum number of working hours for bakery employees, and *Hammer v. Dagenhart* invalidated a congressional act banning interstate shipment of goods manufactured with child labor. The Court's role as economic censor came under sharp attack when laissez-faire economics faced the realities of the Great Depression in the 1930s. As states and the national government responded with policies to deal with eco-

nomic dislocation, the Court proved to be a stumbling block. In 1935 and 1936 the justices invalidated 10 acts of Congress, cutting the heart out of President Roosevelt's New Deal program of economic recovery.

After his landslide reelection in 1936, Roosevelt proposed legislation (dubbed by its enemies the "court-packing plan") that would permit him to appoint one additional justice for every sitting justice over the age of 70, up to a total bench size of 15. Under the guise of aiding the justices with their work, the plan was actually a ploy to create seats for new justices who would support the president's programs. The plan never became law, but one or more justices quickly changed their positions in economic regulation cases to give the president the majority he needed. Tagged "the switch in time that saved nine," in *National Labor Relations Board v. Jones & Laughlin Steel Corporation* the Court upheld by a vote of 5 to 4, the far-reaching Wagner Labor Act of 1935, which created the National Labor Relations Board and guaranteed to unions the right of collective bargaining. The law remains the foundation of American labor policy. Thanks to changed views and a series of retirements and new justices, the Court soon made it clear that it was retreating from its old role as economic censor. Since that time the Court has by and large left economic policy-making to the president, Congress, and the states.

Recently, however, the Court has hinted that limits may still exist to a state's regulatory powers over property owners. Does the Constitution require the Court to keep its hands off economic policy?

speech. Indeed, research indicates that judicial decisions of most justices reflect a generally consistent ideological position.[14]

Role perception,[15] akin to but different from political ideas, is another factor that affects decision making. What does being a justice mean to an individual named to the Supreme Court? Some justices have been *result-oriented*—that is, they see their task as one of writing certain political ideas into their decisions. Other justices are *process-oriented*; they are hesitant to interfere with majority rule. Although they are prepared to apply the constitutional brakes to runaway legislatures, they are less inclined to do so than their result-oriented colleagues. Instead, they believe that judges should allow maximum discretion to the people's elected representatives.

Jurists most eager to apply judicial review are **judicial activists**. Those most reluctant to do so are **judicial restraintists**. Yet, even by practicing judicial restraint the Court makes policy. Judicial restraint results in upholding the judgment made by some other part of the political system. By affirming someone else's judgment, the Court is legitimating it and making the original judgment the Court's own. When the Court upholds the validity of a search of someone's home by police, for example, it is accepting the police officer's understanding of the Fourth Amendment (see Chapter 3).

Whether an activist or restraintist, no justice today writes on a blank slate. Although a new case is rarely identical to one the Court has decided in years gone by, prior decisions in similar cases called **precedents** may point the way to the decision the Court should render. When courts adhere to legal principles established in prior cases, they are following the doctrine of **stare decisis** (Latin for "let the decision stand"). Stare decisis does not mean that the Supreme Court must rule as it ruled 100 years ago, or even 10 years ago, but it does result in the reluctance of justices to overrule decisions that are already "on the books." They do so only when a legal principle seems plainly wrong or when public necessity dictates a change.

The power of precedent was an acknowledged factor in 1992 when five justices rejected the Bush administration's request to overrule the 1973 landmark decision *Roe v. Wade*,[16] which created a constitutionally protected right to abortion. Three of the five (Justices O'Connor, Kennedy, and Souter) indicated that they would not have sided with the majority position in *Roe* had they been on the Court in 1973. Nineteen years later, however, they believed that the Court should not turn back the clock.[17] In 2000, the Court upheld the judicially-created requirement of Miranda warnings, even though

---

judicial activists

Judges who are least hesitant to invoke judicial review to strike down an act of Congress or of a state legislature.

judicial restraintists

Judges who are reluctant to invoke judicial review to strike down an act of Congress or of a state legislature.

precedents

Prior decisions of courts; cited as authority by other courts.

stare decisis

A legal doctrine that suggests courts should follow precedent as a general rule, breaking with previously legal principles only on rare occasions.

---

[14]David W. Rhode and Harold J. Spaeth, "Ideology, Strategy, and Supreme Court Decisions: William Rehnquist as Chief Justice," *Judicature* 72 (1989): 247; Harold J. Spaeth and Stuart H. Teger, "Activism and Restraint: A Cloak for the Justices' Policy Preferences," in Stephen C. Halpern and Charles M. Lamb, eds., *Supreme Court Activism and Restraint* (Lexington, MA: Lexington Books, 1982), pp. 277–301.

[15]Harold J. Spaeth, *Supreme Court Policy Making* (San Francisco: Freeman, 1979), pp. 109–139; Mark W. Cannon and David M. O'Brien, eds., *Views from the Bench* (Chatham, NJ: Chatham House, 1985), pp. 253–302.

[16]410 U.S. 113 (1973).

[17]*Planned Parenthood of Southeastern Pennsylvania v. Casey,* 60 U.S.L.W. 4795 (1992).

several of the justices had elsewhere opposed the judicial activist stance taken in the Miranda decision.[18]

The Court's own decision-making process, described earlier in this chapter, also shapes its decisions. Briefs and oral argument inform the justices and define the issues the case presents. Briefs and arguments may even supply the reasoning the Court uses in justifying its decision. Articles in *law reviews*, the scholarly journals law schools publish, may also be of influence. Justices, like everyone else, are sensitive to evaluations of their work by others, and they pay attention to suggestions for evolution in the law that find their way into print. Moreover, because all justices participate in each case, *collegial interaction* becomes a factor. Discussion in conference and persuasive comment by one justice on an opinion drafted by another contribute to the form a decision eventually takes, and sometimes cause a justice to change positions in a case.[19]

Finally, justices are aware of *public opinion*. Although Justice John Stevens (1975–) may be correct in asserting that "it is the business of judges to be indifferent to unpopularity,"[20] nevertheless, public attitudes count in judicial decisions in at least two ways. First, public attitudes may influence the meaning justices give certain provisions in the Constitution. In the case of capital punishment, for example, most states reenacted death penalty laws after the Supreme Court set rigorous new standards for capital punishment in 1972 (see Chapter 3).[21] State legislatures, in effect, were telling the Court that they did not think capital punishment was "cruel and unusual" but instead was a form of punishment the American people accepted. These new laws probably made it easier for some justices to decide in 1976 that capital punishment is not cruel and unusual.[22] Second, courts matter in American government ultimately because their decisions are accepted and applied, if grudgingly, by the rest of the political system. Thus, public reaction to judicial decisions may affect compliance with them.

Checks on Judicial Power

Supreme Court justices and other federal judges enjoy substantial independence from outside political control. Thanks to the Constitution, they never face the voters in an election and may not have their salaries decreased by Congress. Yet, although the Court is a potent institution in American government, it does not enjoy unlimited power. Through *constitutional amendment*, Congress and the states may correct the Supreme Court's interpretation of the Constitution. Admittedly, amending the Constitution is not easy, but the justices have been reversed by amendment four times. The Eleventh Amendment (restricting federal court jurisdiction over the states) overturned *Chisholm*

---

[18]*Dickerson v. United States,* 530 U.S. 428 (2000), and *Miranda v. Arizona,* 384 U.S. 436 (1966).
[19]Walter F. Murphy, *Elements of Judicial Strategy* (Chicago: University of Chicago Press, 1964), ch. 3.
[20]"Reflections on the Removal of Sitting Judges," *Stetson Law Review* 13 (1984): 215, 217.
[21]*Furman v. Georgia,* 408 U.S. 238 (1972).
[22]*Gregg v. Georgia,* 428 U.S. 153 (1976).

v. Georgia. The Fourteenth Amendment (granting both national and state citizenship to all persons born or naturalized in the United States) countered the infamous *Dred Scott* decision, which had held that the Constitution did not intend for African Americans to be citizens. The Sixteenth Amendment (allowing for a national tax on incomes) reversed *Pollock v. Farmers' Loan and Trust Co*. And the Twenty-sixth Amendment (establishing a nationwide voting age of 18) set aside *Oregon v. Mitchell*.[23]

Similarly, *statutory amendment* allows Congress to correct the Court's interpretation of a statute. Although passing a law is easier than amending the Constitution, however, it still is not an easy task, as Chapter 9 made clear.

Impeachment of justices by Congress may be only a "scarecrow," as President Thomas Jefferson (1801–1809) once said, but it is a weapon available in extraordinary situations. On grounds of misconduct, Congress has removed seven judges of lower federal courts through impeachment, including U.S. district judges Walter Nixon of Mississippi and Alcee Hastings of Florida in 1989. However, a Supreme Court justice has never been removed. In fact, the Senate has held no impeachment trial for a justice since the Jefferson administration attempted to have Supreme Court Justice Samuel Chase (1796–1811) removed in 1805. The House of Representatives might have begun impeachment proceedings against Justice Abe Fortas (1965–1969) after certain improprieties came to light, but Fortas resigned.[24] Five other federal judges have either been acquitted by the Senate or have had charges against them dismissed before a Senate trial began.

Congress may attack the Court by *withdrawing jurisdiction* to hear certain types of cases. Because Article III grants appellate jurisdiction to the Supreme Court "with such exceptions, and under such regulations as the Congress shall make," opponents of particular judicial doctrines can try to prevent certain types of cases from reaching the Court altogether. Such extreme measures are frequently threatened but only very rarely carried out. Congress may also *change the size* of the Court, which was the heart of President Franklin Roosevelt's "court-packing" proposal in 1937. Although the plan failed, the Court changed its interpretation of the Constitution to uphold the president's New Deal program (see "Politics and Economics: The Supreme Court and Economic Policy" on page 384).

Appointment of new justices by the president can place new ideas as well as new personalities on the bench. *Senate confirmation*, however, may limit the range of a president's choices. But judicial vacancies occur irregularly as well as infrequently. For example, President Nixon was able to name four justices between 1969 and 1971, whereas President Carter (1977–1981) was able to name none.

To be effective, Supreme Court decisions require *compliance*. Judges possess very little power to actually coerce obedience. Therefore, courts depend on others to

---

[23]2 U.S. (2 Dallas) 419 (1793); 60 U.S. (19 Howard) 393 (1857); 158 U.S. 601 (1895); 400 U.S. 112 (1970).

[24]Bruce Allen Murphy, *Fortas: The Rise and Ruin of a Supreme Court Justice* (New York: William Morrow, 1988).

obey and to carry out their decisions. An absence of widespread compliance with the Supreme Court's school integration decision of 1954[25] (see Chapter 3) meant that for nearly a decade the decision went largely unenforced. Reaction to this decision was a reminder that the Supreme Court needs the support of both state and federal courts as well as other agencies of government to carry out its judgments. Hostile reaction to the 1954 school decision highlighted an additional check: *litigation*. African American families were sometimes afraid to initiate legal action against local officials who continued to disregard the Supreme Court's decision. Without a case, no court could act. Unlike legislators, who may introduce bills, judges do not initiate the cases they decide.

As cases bring issues old and new to the Court each term, the justices play a part in American government. For more than 200 years the Supreme Court has conducted a dialogue with the people that reflects the public's historic attraction to, and suspicion of, majority rule. "The people have seemed to feel that the Supreme Court," wrote Justice Robert H. Jackson (1941–1954), "whatever its defects, is still the most detached, dispassionate, and trustworthy custodian that our system affords for the translation of abstract into concrete constitutional commands."[26] The justices are the keepers of American constitutional morality. That truth is both a source of and limit on their power.

---

[25]*Brown v. Board of Education*, 347 U.S. 483 (1954).
[26]*The Supreme Court in the American System of Government* (Cambridge, MA: Harvard University Press, 1955), p. 23.

SUMMARY

1. As the highest court in the land, the Supreme Court of the United States annually confronts a variety of important political issues that appear in the form of cases. The system of courts in the United States consists of the federal courts and the courts of the 50 states. Major federal courts include the district courts and the courts of appeals, in addition to the Supreme Court. Supreme Court justices and all federal judges are appointed by the president and confirmed by a majority of the Senate.

2. In deciding cases, the Supreme Court and other American courts engage in constitutional and statutory interpretation, fact determination, clarification of the boundaries of political authority, education and value application, and legitimation.

3. Cases decided by the Supreme Court proceed through five major stages: petition for review, briefs on the merits, oral argument, conference and decision, and assignment and writing of the opinion of the Court.

4. The decisions of the Supreme Court are the products of several factors, and have been a source of controversy during most of American history. Although the Court enjoys considerable political independence from Congress and the president, external checks on judicial power, do exist.

KEY TERMS

case (364)

criminal case (364)

crime (364)

civil case (364)

state courts (364)

federal courts (364)

jurisdiction (364)

courts of limited jurisdiction (366)

courts of general jurisdiction (366)

intermediate appellate courts (367)

court of last resort (367)

Missouri Plan (367)

United States district courts (367)

United States courts of appeals (368)

appellate jurisdiction (370)

federal question (370)

rule of four (370)

original jurisdiction (370)

Eleventh Amendment (370)

senatorial courtesy (371)

judicial review (375)

legislative intent (376)

trial court (377)

briefs (378)

amicus curiae (380)

Solicitor General of the United States (380)

oral argument (380)

opinion of the Court (381)

concurring opinion (382)

dissenting opinion (382)

United States Reports (382)

judicial activists (385)

judicial restraintists (385)

precedents (385)

stare decisis (385)

READINGS FOR FURTHER STUDY

A helpful survey of the role of the Court during much of the nation's history is Robert G. McCloskey, *The American Supreme Court* (Chicago: University of Chicago Press, 1960).

Henry J. Abraham, *Justices and Presidents*, 3d ed. (New York: Oxford University Press, 1992), is the standard work on appointment of Supreme Court justices.

Behind Bakke: Affirmative Action and the Supreme Court, by Bernard Schwartz (New York: New York University Press, 1988), takes a close look at how the Court reached its decision in a single case.

David M. O'Brien's *Storm Center: The Supreme Court in American Politics*, 3d ed. (New York: Norton, 1993), explores the broader political environment in which the Supreme Court operates.

Important decisions of the Supreme Court interpreting the Constitution are readily found in edited form in casebooks such as Alpheus T. Mason and D. Grier Stephenson, Jr., *American Constitutional Law*, 10th ed. (Englewood Cliffs, NJ: Prentice-Hall, 1993).

Guide to the U.S. Supreme Court, 2d ed. (Washington, DC: Congressional Quarterly, Inc., 1990) contains information on almost all aspects of the Court's work.

Articles about the Court, past and present, appear in the *Journal of Supreme Court History*, published by the Supreme Court Historical Society.

CHAPTER 13

Government and Public Policy

A/P World Wide

Chapter Objectives

Public policy is collectively what governments do. This chapter will address, first, what public policy is and how it is related to the political process. Second, we will learn to think about public policies so that what appears to be a chaotic mass of procedures, institutions, and personalities is more understandable. Finally, given the fact that government does so many different things, this chapter attempts to differentiate among different kinds of public policies.

Public Policy in the Political Process

public policy

Whatever governments choose to do or not to do.

Public policy can be defined in a variety of ways, but the simplest is: "public policy is whatever governments choose to do or not to do."[1] Financing cancer research, providing a Social Security system, cutting or raising taxes, initiating or halting development of a new weapons system, and attempting to clean up toxic waste dumps are all examples of public policies. This chapter will introduce the process of public policy; the following three chapters will address economic, domestic, and foreign policies, respectively.

Conflict over the Ends of Government

Government is always subject to conflicting demands, due to the great differences among citizens in economic status, occupations, and political ideas. Different groups

[1]Thomas R. Dye, *Understanding Public Policy,* 10th ed. (Englewood Cliffs, NJ: Prentice-Hall, 2001), p. 2.

will likely press for public policies in their own interest, regardless of the effect those policies might have on other groups. The use of rules, procedures, representatives, and institutions is important to such groups only toward the end of achieving public policies favorable to them.

The results of public policy mirror conflicts in demands. No governmental action can affect all citizens in exactly the same way. Whatever government does will have varying consequences for different groups. For example, placing limits on Medicare spending will provide some relief to taxpayers by reducing pressure for higher taxes, but those same limits will place economic strains on hospitals and other health-care providers. Increasing the money supply to reduce interest rates will help first-time home buyers by making mortgages easier to afford, but will hurt senior citizens who depend on higher interest rates to bolster their investment income. Differences in demands and in the consequences of government action create political conflict. At issue in public policy debate is which groups shall win and which shall lose in the effort to shape government actions to their own interest.

Perspectives on Policymaking

The nature of politics and policy is such that a variety of models or explanations has been offered as accurate or desirable portrayals of public policymaking. Among the most familiar is the **systems model**, which holds that policy is the product of an interlocking relationship between the political system and its social, cultural, and economic environment.[2] From its environment the political system receives "inputs" in the form of demands and supports. Through its decision-making process the political system then converts demands into "outputs," which are authoritative or official decisions. These decisions may in turn affect the environment and shape new inputs into the system. For example, demands that government reduce the burden of regulations may result in government decisions to eliminate some regulations. But these decisions may penalize people who benefited under the old regulations, and those people may then clamor for reinstatement. As another illustration, a court decision that weakens the constitutional claim to the right to have an abortion may shift much of the political battle over abortion to state legislatures.

Other models view policymaking from different perspectives. The **bureaucratic model** posits the crucial role of bureaucracies and the commitment and expertise they can provide in making policy. Some models use ideological frameworks with an economic focus to explain how policies are or should be make. The **Marxism model** holds that public policy decisions in non-Marxist regimes reflect the interests of the

---

systems model

A model of policymaking that holds that policy is the product of an interlocking relationship between institutions of government and its social, economic, and political environment.

bureaucratic model

A model of policymaking that holds that bureaucracies play a crucial role in making policy because of their commitment and the expertise they can provide.

Marxism model

A model of policymaking that holds that public policy decisions in non-Marxist regimes reflect the interests of the ruling economic class at the expense of workers.

---

[2]For a comprehensive statement of the systems model, see David Easton, *A Systems Analysis of Political Life* (Chicago: University of Chicago Press, 1979).

TABLE 13.1

Selected Perspectives on Policymaking

Given the complexity of making policy and the sharp conflicts that can drive policy debate, a variety of models, interpretations, and approaches have been offered as portraits of how policy is or should be made.

I. Models of the Policymaking Process	
Systems model	Policy is the product of an interlocking relationship between institutions of government and its surrounding social, economic, and political environment.
Bureaucratic model	Because of their commitment and the expertise they can provide, bureaucracies play a crucial role in making policy.
Marxism model	Public policy decisions reflect the interest of the ruling class at the expense of workers.
Free market capitalism model	The natural forces of supply and demand are allowed to work in the marketplace, and government plays only a limited role in shaping those forces.

II. Interpretations of Who Makes Public Policy	
Elitism	Public policy decisions are made by a relatively small group of individuals acting in their own self-interest rather than the interest of all citizens.
Pluralism	Public policy decisions are the result of struggle among contesting groups, with the various interests among the masses reflected and represented in the policy process.

III. Approaches to How Public Policy Is Made	
Rational-comprehensive approach	Decision makers should identify problems, rank the values they wish to achieve, consider various policy alternatives that can attain these values, assess the cost and benefits of each alternative, and select and implement the policy strategy that can best achieve the stated values with the highest benefits and lowest costs. Critics of the model argue that information in the real world of policymaking is limited and uncertain and that the clash of interests in the policy process makes any ranking of values impossible.
Incrementalism	Since present decisions are only marginally different from past decisions, policymakers focus on proposed marginal changes in existing policies. A capacity to achieve agreement among contesting interests defines a good public policy. Critics of the model argue that the tie to past policies reduces the possibility of new policy approaches and that the sensitivity to political power and the emphasis on agreement risk the exclusion of interests without political power.

free market capitalism model

A model of policymaking that posits a limited role for government so that the natural forces of supply and demand are allowed to prevail in the marketplace.

ruling economic class at the expense of the workers. The **free market capitalism model** sees a limited role for government in which the natural forces of supply and demand are allowed to prevail in the marketplace. Other models might be discussed as well; the interplay of interests and passions that drives policy debate and the rich complexity of making public policy have produced numerous models of policymaking.

Two of the most useful perspectives are elitism and pluralism. They are particularly helpful in understanding the maze of public policy because they address a fundamental question about which there has been much debate: *Who* makes public policy decisions?

FIGURE 13.1

The Systems Model of Policymaking

The systems model describes policymaking in terms of the relationship between a political system and its environment. "Inputs" (demands and supports) are converted into "outputs" (policy decisions). By affecting the environment of the political system, these outputs may generate new inputs.

SOURCE: James E. Anderson, *Public Policymaking,* 4th ed. (Boston: Houghton Mifflin, 2000), p. 18.

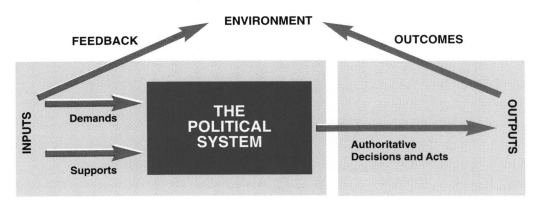

elitism

A model of policymaking that holds that public policy decisions are made by a relatively small group of individuals acting in their own self-interest rather than in the interest of the mass of citizens.

pluralism

A model of policymaking that holds that public policy decisions are the result of struggles among contesting groups that reflect the various interest among citizens.

Elitism holds that public policy decisions are made by a relatively small group of individuals acting in their own self-interest.[3] The theory takes a variety of forms, depending on who is included in the elite. Some elements of the mass media, big business, and the military have been variously portrayed as comprising the elite. According to the model, on issues of importance to them, members of the elite make public policy judgments in the interest of the elite rather than in the interest of the mass of citizens.

Pluralism holds that public policy decisions are the result of struggle among contesting groups rather than a single elite.[4] The groups represent various interests in society and press for decisions responsive to those interests. Policy is determined not by a single set of values as in elitism but by a contest of conflicting values held by various groups. Even though the number of participants in the making of public policy is small, they reflect and convey the broad range of positions held by the mass of citizens. Competing elites with different values ensure democratic responsiveness. In the pluralist view, government is a broker among groups, seeking to satisfy as many as possible. Conflicts among groups produce a balance so that no single group dominates. This is sometimes called the *countervailing theory of pressure politics.*

---

[3]For a classic statement on elitism, see C. Wright Mills, *The Power Elite,* 2nd ed. (New York: Oxford University Press, 2000).
[4]An analysis of pluralism that helped set the terms of the debate with elitism is Robert Dahl, *Who Governs? Democracy and Power in an American City* (New Haven, CT: Yale University Press, 1961).

rational-comprehensive model

A model of decision making that holds that policymakers should identify problems, consider various policy alternatives and their costs and benefits, and select and implement the policy strategy with the highest benefits and the lowest costs.

incrementalism

A model of decision making that holds that new policies should differ only marginally from existing policies.

A second issue is how decisions are made.[5] Two contrasting perspectives are the rational-comprehensive approach and incrementalism. The **rational-comprehensive model** involves a sequence of steps for "rational" decisions. Decision makers identify problems, rank the values they wish to achieve, consider various policy alternatives that can attain these values, assess the costs and benefits of each alternative, and select and implement the policy strategy that can best achieve the stated values with the highest benefits and lowest costs. This model has been criticized for imposing unrealistic demands on people making policy decisions. Critics argue that information in the real world of policymaking is limited and uncertain, and the clash of interests makes impossible any ranking of values.

Incrementalism is an alternative model that takes these criticisms into account. In the view of critics, the tie to past policies reduces the possibility of new policy past decisions. Policymakers do not begin with a clean slate but rather focus on proposed marginal changes in existing policies. Deciding on budgets is an example. Rather than creating an entirely new budget each year, budget makers focus on proposed marginal changes from the previous year's budget.

By highlighting marginal changes in existing policies, incrementalism poses lower information demands. In addition, incrementalism holds that a capacity to achieve agreement among contesting interests defines good public policy. This definition of good policy is in sharp contrast to the rational-comprehensive emphasis on the search for costs and benefits of alternative policy approaches.[6]

Incrementalism has been criticized for being too conservative in its implications. In the view of critics, the tie to past policies reduces the possibility of new policy approaches. In addition, the sensitivity to political power and the emphasis on agreement in the model risk the exclusion of interests without power. In the effort to be realistic and pragmatic, incrementalism neglects some interests in the search for the appropriate purposes of government.

Despite these criticisms, incrementalism does raise important questions in public policy. Under what circumstances is the political system capable of *fundamental* rather than incremental changes in policy? What does it take to make a substantial break with the past? Change in the number of people insured by the Social Security system and increases in taxes to pay for the program have been incremental over the past half-century, as Figure 13.2 shows. But the decision to establish the system in 1935 was a fundamental break with the past. Decisions to create new agencies (or abolish existing ones) or to initiate new programs (or terminate current ones) are fundamental rather than incremental. The circumstances allowing such decisions can be the threat of crisis or substantial

---

[5]For a review of different analytical approaches to decision making, see James W. Fesler and Donald F. Kettl, *The Politics of the Administrative Process* (Chatham, NJ: Chatham House, 1996).

[6]The classic argument for incrementalism and its comparison to the rational-comprehensive approach is Charles Lindblom, "The Science of 'Muddling Through,'" *Public Administration Review* 19 (1959): 79–88.

FIGURE 13.2

Incrementalism and Social Security Tax Rates

The creation of the Social Security program in 1935 was a fundamental change in government policy. Once Social Security was established, changes in the rates of taxes to pay for the program occurred in incremental steps over time. Short of an emergency of the magnitude of the Great Depression, it is unlikely that there will be any drastic and abrupt changes in the program. Rather, adjustments will come gradually.

SOURCE: Data from *Social Security Bulletin, Annual Statistical Supplement, 2001*, p. 87.

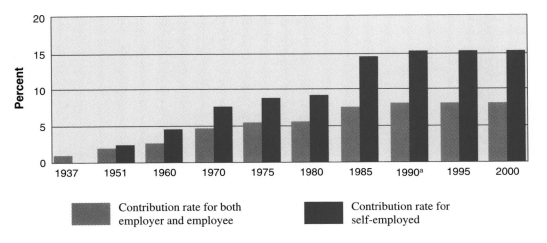

[a]The tax rates of 7.65 percent for employees and employers, and 15.3 percent for the self-employed, will remain in effect for future years unless Congress and the president decide to change Social Security tax rate policy.

changes in technology, in social or economic values, or in the alignment of political power. The model of incrementalism may be as important for the questions it raises about policy as it is for the explanations it offers.[7]

Whether looking at incrementalism or another policymaking model, it is well to remember that models are learning tools. By abstracting from reality, they try to explain why things happen as they do. The utility of a model lies in increasing our understanding of reality. Yet no single model describes completely a complex political system. Thinking of events in terms of two or three models may be a better way to think about how policy is made and about who is influential in shaping policy.

Stages in the Policy Process

In the real world of politics and conflict, the making of public policy frequently appears to be full of chaos. Groups demand or oppose, members of Congress respond or criti-

---

[7]For a review of the criticisms of the rational-comprehensive approach and incrementalism, see Amitai Etzioni, "Mixed-Scanning: A 'Third' Approach to Decision-Making," *Public Administration Review* 27 (1967): 385–392.

cize, presidents agree or refuse, judges rule or defer, bureaucrats proceed or halt, and the mass media report or ignore. The making of public policy is not like a play where all the actors follow a predetermined script. Rather, in the making of policy, a group leader or a congressional representative may say and do things without knowing how others will respond or whether they will respond at all. In the efforts to shape policy, hope, uncertainty, and chance all play a role. Consequently, the policy process may seem to be a confusing clash of ideas, events, and personalities.

Public policy analysts try to break down the process of making policy into definable stages to order and make sense out of what appears to be chaotic.[8] Figure 13.3 portrays the stages in the evolution of public policies. In the real world, policies do not evolve in such neatly defined and apparently simple steps. Participants in the process make demands, offer responses, and make decisions without consciously following some analytical framework. Nonetheless, identification of these stages helps to make the evolution of public policies and the role of government procedures and institutions in the process more understandable.

As Figure 13.3 shows, there are five stages in the evolution of policies.

1. A problem or issue must somehow get on the agenda of government.
2. Specific proposals to do something about the problem are discussed.
3. Government officials adopt a policy by choosing some specific strategy for action from among the proposals discussed.
4. Bureaucrats implement or translate into action the adopted proposal.
5. The policy is evaluated to determine whether or not it succeeded in solving or ameliorating the originally defined problem.

1. Getting Issues on the Agenda of Government

The **policy agenda** of government is comprised of the list of issues that engage the attention of elected officials. Obviously, governments cannot simultaneously deal with every conceivable problem. Like individuals, governments must make choices on which matters will get their attention at particular times. Issues get on the policy agenda in a variety of ways. No single explanation can capture the rich complexity of the process.[9]

Factors that contribute to moving some particular issue onto the government agenda include technological change, the demands of politically emerging groups, the evolution of social values, the threats of crisis or war, changing economic conditions, and the political will of a strong leader. Sometimes the mass media can create issues by focusing attention on particular concerns. For example, the Watergate affair, which resulted in the resignation of President Richard Nixon, became a matter of nearly constant public discussion between 1972 and 1974 as the press revealed wrongdoing. More

http://www.moving ideas.org/

Moving Ideas is an online magazine for students, journalists, activists, and legislators interested in keeping up with current topics in public policy. See whether any of the stories captures your interest at the site above.

policy agenda

The public issues that engage the attention of elected officials.

---

[8]James E. Anderson, *Public Policymaking,* 5th ed. (Boston: Houghton Mifflin, 203), pp. 30–31.
[9]See John W. Kingdon, *Agendas, Alternatives, and Public Policies,* 2nd ed. (New York: Addison-Wesley, 1995).

FIGURE 13.3

Stages in the Policy Process

Although policies do not always develop in the neatly defined steps outlined below, an awareness of what happens in each step helps us understand the process that occurs as government attempts to solve problems and accomplish goals. Any number and combination of persons and events can bring concerns to the attention of political leaders (step 1). Policymakers in the executive and legislative branches then study the range of choices open to them to meet those concerns (step 2). A variety of public officials may be involved in selecting a course of action or in deciding to do nothing at all (step 3). The policy then becomes the responsibility of bureaucrats to administer (step 4). Finally, evaluation occurs. Does the plan work? Is it worth its costs (step 5)? The evaluation may become a factor in encouraging further policymaking by government.

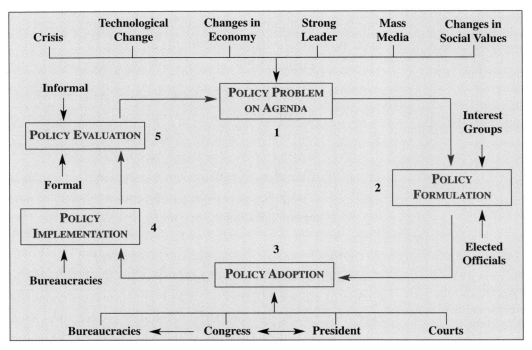

recently, the Clinton Impeachment and the 9/11 tragedy and subsequent war on terrorism have been events that have played major roles in the government's agenda.

Further, the issues on the policy agenda are always changing. Those that get resolved or lose relevance in a changing society are simply no longer discussed. For example, slavery was the most bitterly divisive issue of the nineteenth century, yet one consequence of the Civil War was that slavery is no longer a matter of public debate. Some issues in their demise simply give rise to other issues. Slavery is no longer an issue, but the economic and social status of African Americans is a matter of continuing policy debate and discussion.

Different sets of issues have dominated policy discussion at different times. The severe economic problems of the Great Depression of the 1930s moved government officials to spend much of their efforts on programs to deal with high unemployment, bank failures, and factory closings. During the 1960s poverty, hunger, and despair in urban ghettos were targets of major policy initiatives before the war in Vietnam intervened. In the 1970s concern about the quality of the nation's physical environment emerged as a major policy issue. The Arab oil embargo of that decade also put a sudden end to cheap energy; consequently, the competition between the search for new energy sources and the quest for environmental quality dominated the agenda of those years.

Thus far in the twenty-first century, two issues seem to be overwhelming and affecting practically all others on the policy agenda: the use of money as a public resource, and the role of the United States in the international arena. Domestically, how much the government should spend (and on what), how much and whom government should tax, the impact of budget deficits and surpluses on the economy, and how far the reach of the federal government (as opposed to that of states and private parties) should extend in such areas as Social Security, welfare, and health care are the questions that drive most policy debate. In foreign affairs, how to respond to terrorism, whether and how to take unilateral military action in a world of increasing multinational organization, and the ethical responsibilities of superpower status are the concerns driving policy. The policy agenda of government is like a kaleidoscope: the turn of decades results in constantly shifting patterns of issue concerns.

2. Formulating Policy Proposals

Once an issue gets on the agenda of government, public debate centers on specific proposals on what government ought to do and how it should do it.[10] To say that government ought to "do something" about budget deficits, the needs of children in poverty, toxic wastes, or drug abuse is only a beginning. To achieve results requires a specific **policy strategy,** some specific course of action designed to deal with the originally defined problem.

If the budget deficit is a problem, should we increase taxes, decrease spending, or press for a balanced budget amendment? If the needs of children in poverty are a problem, should we increase family assistance payments, track down absent fathers, or build orphanages? If toxic wastes are a problem, should we ban or control the use of certain chemicals that produce such wastes, or should we tax the use of chemicals to pay for the cleanup of toxic waste sites? If drug abuse is a problem, should we open more treatment centers, or eradicate drug producing crops around the world, or legalize the use of drugs? Of course, several policy strategies to deal with a problem might be pursued simultaneously, but the relative emphasis on one or another strategy can provoke intense controversy.

http://www.naspaa .org/students /careers/service.sap

Interested in an internship or career in public policy? The National Association of Schools of Public Affairs and Administration offers these suggestions and starting points for you.

policy strategy

A specific course of action designed to deal with a public problem.

---

[10]For a discussion of the contributions and limits of knowledge in efforts to resolve policy problems, see Peter deLeon, *Advice and Consent: The Development of the Policy Sciences* (New York: Russell Sage, 1988).

Questions of what government should do, who should benefit, and who should bear the costs of such action comprise the raw material of policy debate. Groups with different ideological beliefs are likely to propose different solutions to policy problems. To reduce budget deficits, for example, conservatives are likely to propose cuts in social welfare spending and liberals are likely to propose cuts in defense spending. The groups that benefit under one proposal will suffer under the other. The demands of interest groups, debates in Congress, requests by bureaucracies, conflicts between political parties and candidates, presidential speeches, and reporting in the mass media all focus on the question of what government ought to do in some specific policy area.

3. Adopting Policy Proposals

Although an issue can get on the policy agenda and various policy strategies can be debated and discussed, nothing happens until **policy adoption** of a proposal by institutions of government. At some point a formal, authoritative decision must be made on the action government will take to address a particular concern. Ultimately, the institutions of government exist to make such formal, authoritative decisions.

Formal adoption occurs in several ways. A bill passed by both houses of Congress and duly signed by the president is an example of formal adoption. For example, if growing budget deficits are deemed an important issue on the policy agenda, one specific strategy to deal with the problem might be a tax bill designed to raise revenue. If both houses can agree on a bill and if the president concurs on the wisdom and necessity of the measure, the resulting law is the formal adoption of a strategy for action. Similarly, decisions by the Supreme Court and the declaration of regulations by bureaucracies are also illustrations of adoption in the making of policy. If the Court requires busing to eliminate racially segregated schools, it is, by making an authoritative, formal decision, in effect adopting a strategy for action. If a regulatory agency requires the installation of air bags in automobiles, it, too, is adopting a strategy for action.

Adopting some policy strategy does not end the debate, however. The losers (both inside and outside the government) in the adoption process may retreat to other units in the political system and seek to have the decision changed or revised. A tax law may become an issue in a subsequent electoral campaign, or a regulatory decision on air bags may end up in the courts. Alternatively, those who have lost may simply wait for another day, when events or changing times or different officials will allow their position another hearing. In the short run, few issues are resolved by the adoption of some particular strategy for action. Rather, the discussion usually continues as revisions are proposed or as the consequences of the adopted strategy become matters of debate. The wheel of policymaking turns endlessly. Moreover, failure to adopt a policy proposal is policymaking too. It represents a formal, authoritative decision to leave policy where it was before the debate began, with the effect that taxes do not go up or air bags are not required.

---

policy adoption

A formal, authoritative decision, such as the enactment of legislation, made by institutions of government to address an issue on the policy agenda.

4. Implementing Policies

Policy debate is really debate over *ideas*. For example, Congress and the president may decide that sending retired persons monthly checks funded by people currently employed is a good idea and formally adopt a strategy. However, that idea or strategy for action must be *implemented* before anything happens. A bureaucracy must be charged with the task of actually getting the right checks to the right people. Bureaucracies play the central role in this step in the policy process, for they are ultimately responsible for **policy implementation**, or translating policy ideas into action. The difficulties and obstacles that frequently accompany the implementation process are suggested by the expressive (if lengthy) subtitle of a classic book: "How Great Expectations in Washington Are Dashed in Oakland; Or, Why It's Amazing that Federal Programs Work at All, This Being a Saga of the Economic Development Administration as Told by Two Sympathetic Observers Who Seek to Build Morals on a Foundation of Ruined Hopes."[11] Clearly, implementation is neither automatic nor predictable.[12]

Given the vast differences among policy ideas, not every policy can be implemented in exactly the same way. Different bureaucracies have very different problems in their implementation tasks. For example, getting astronauts to the moon and back was a clear task with a sharply defined end, and once the task was accomplished, the implementation process ended. By contrast, collecting taxes and funding medical care for the elderly are ongoing programs that are never completed. Moreover, Congress and the president give some bureaucracies very little discretion in implementing policy ideas, while they give other bureaucracies vague, broad mandates. The Social Security Administration has no freedom in determining whom among the elderly should get how much each month, but the Consumer Product Safety Commission has flexibility in determining which consumer products will become subject to new regulations.

Continuing debate frequently accompanies the implementation process. In the judgment of the opponents of some particular policy strategy, a bureaucracy may outrun, or even contradict, the intent of Congress. For example, efforts in Congress to invalidate regulations of the Federal Trade Commission by legislative veto were attempts to put controls on the agency. Alternatively, a bureaucracy may not be vigorous enough in discharging its task. For example, in 2001, some members of Congress charged the Environmental Protection Agency with being too vigorous in enforcement of prohibitions in rural areas, but far too lax in enforcing violations in places with greater political clout, like the metro Washington D.C. area.[13] Or a bureaucracy can be caught in the same crossfire of conflicting demands that were present in the debate before a strategy was formally adopted. On

---

policy implementation

The translation of policy ideas into action.

---

[11]Jeffrey L. Pressman and Aaron B. Wildavsky, *Implementation,* 3rd ed. (Berkeley: University of California Press, 1984).

[12]On the heightened attention that policy analysts have given to implementation over the last two decades, see Dennis Palumbo, *Public Policy in America: Government in Action,* 2nd ed. (Stamford, CT: Thomson, 1997).

[13]EPA Criticized for Selective Enforcement, *Environment and Climate News,* September 2001.

Politics and Ideas
The Road to a New Cabinet Department

America's response to the 9/11 terrorist attack illustrates both the speed with which public policy can be enacted and the hurdles that must be overcome in the public policy process. On September 20th, 2001—just nine days after the tragedy—President George W. Bush announced that he would be establishing an Office of Homeland Security, headed by Pennsylvania Governor Tom Ridge, in an effort to prevent future terrorist attacks on the United States. Although the office was established quickly via an executive order on October 8, 2001, the president's goal of making the office a cabinet level department would require a much longer route. The first step of the policy process, getting the issue on the policy agenda, was certainly the easiest. Domestic security was in the forefront of every government official's mind in the Autumn of 2001.

President Bush delivered the second stage, developing a policy strategy, during his address. He proposed

a course of action to address the problem of terrorism. Specifically, he suggested a cabinet level office designed to prevent future terrorist attacks, reduce American vulnerability, and help in recovery efforts for attacks that do occur.[a] In this case, strategy development occurred very quickly; this speed was a result of the gravity of the problem the policy addressed.

Policy adoption became a sticking point for homeland security. Although President Bush was able to swiftly establish an executive office without the need of additional approval, creation of a full-blown cabinet department requires a congressional act. Thus, on June 24, 2002 Representative Dick Armey (R-TX) introduced the Homeland Security Act of 2002 in the House of Representatives. Although the Republican-led House of Representatives voted to approve the bill

---

[a]The Department of Homeland Security, http://www.whitehouse.gov/deptofhomeland/ (23 September 2002).

---

pollution control policy, for example, the EPA can be in the middle of conflict between environmentalists and business interests fearful of the costs of environmental regulations. In any case, the implementation step in policy is frequently a continuation of the political struggle that surrounds an issue from the time it first gets on the policy agenda.

5. *Evaluating Policies*

The final analytical stage in the evolution of policies is evaluation.[14] This step logically follows from the others because of the reasonable expectation that we ought to know whether a particular policy strategy "worked." Determining whether the formally adopted, implemented strategy in fact ameliorated or solved the originally defined problem is the

---

[14]See Pressman and Wildavsky, *Implementation*, for a discussion of the relationship between evaluation and implementation, pp. 181–205.

The Road to a New Cabinet Department, *continued*

just one month later (quick adoption by congressional standards), the Democratic majority in the Senate voiced reservations about the extent of the proposed department's powers. Senator Robert Byrd (D-WV) cautioned that "Congress must never act recklessly," as he and others voiced concerns about civil service employee protections in light of the bill's proposed merger of 22 federal agencies into a single department.[b] Eventual adoption would depend on the ability of Congress and the president to reach a compromise.

Policy implementation will involve a large-scale restructuring of existing offices and agencies, affecting over 170,000 federal employees. Even though an executive office was already in place, coordinating and organizing such a large number of workers into four newly created divisions will take a considerable

[b]"Democrats urged to Act on Homeland Security Bill," 18 September 2002, http://www.cnn.com/2002/ALLPOLITICS/09/18/homeland.security.ap/index.html (23 September 2002).

amount of time. Initial stages of policy implementation tend to be measured in months, but completion of large scale policy changes can sometimes take years.

The final stage of the process, policy evaluation, started to take place as soon as President Bush announced his intentions. From the moment his speech ended, journalists, politicians, and policy analysts have been assessing success and failure. In addition to formal evaluation, such as the annual appropriations process in Congress, informal evaluation of Homeland Security is likely to occur every time American security is threatened. Although policies are tested constantly, only time can tell of ultimate success or failure.

The speed of the public policy process varies. What aspects seem too fast? Too slow? Which perspective on policymaking, discussed earlier in this chapter, provides the best description of efforts to create a Department of Homeland Security?

policy evaluation

The act of determining whether a formally adopted and implemented policy ameliorated or solved a public problem.

goal of **policy evaluation**. However, the expectation that policy strategies ought to be evaluated definitively is more easily stated than actually met.

Formal evaluation of policies has received increased attention since the late 1960s. As the national government attempted to do more policymaking, criticism surfaced that government did not deliver on its promises. Consequently, demands for policy evaluation intensified. The techniques of such formal evaluation range from simple before-and-after studies to more sophisticated controlled experiments. Do special education programs (new curricular efforts, charter schools, the expenditure of additional funds, etc.) in fact improve learning skills among disadvantaged children? Do rehabilitation programs (employment training, special counseling, etc.) in fact reduce the likelihood that individuals released from prison will commit crimes again? In a controlled experiment, do individuals who receive a guaranteed income behave any differently from another group of individuals who do not?

Such questions are legitimate, but formal evaluation efforts almost never give unequivocal answers that end debate over the policy. In fact, debate frequently swirls about evaluation results, especially if the answers do not coincide with the expectations of the people who want the policy to work. Unfavorable results can almost always be explained away by citing inadequate research instruments, insufficient time to assess the policy, or inaccurate interpretations of the findings.[15] For example, people who want school vouchers to work might criticize negative findings on vouchers because the study was based on too short a time span. Evaluation results are more likely to continue rather than end policy debate.

Not every government policy goes through a formal evaluation procedure. There may not only be insufficient time and money but analytical difficulties as well. For example, are nuclear weapons policies preventing nuclear war? The answer may be that they are for now, but if such a war should occur, the assertion would obviously be proved wrong, with dire consequences few wish to even contemplate. In this instance the policy relies on hope rather than on unattainable evaluation results. Or, in the absence of a cure for cancer or AIDS, is the nation's medical research policy working? No reasonable person would suggest that cancer or AIDS research should be halted because individuals continue to die of the disease. Again, hope for success sustains the policy. Yet the very existence of some policies constitutes almost a definition of success. The Social Security program, for example, is working as long as the checks are regularly sent out.

Although most policies are not evaluated formally, they are often appraised *informally* during the process of implementation. Some informal assessments of government programs include congressional budget and authorization hearings, the sharp policy conflicts between opposing candidates in electoral campaigns, presidential speeches to set the nation's policy priorities, and the eternal demands of interest groups. Ultimately, most evaluation of government policies is the product of the endless interplay of political passions at the root of all political conflict.

The Purposes and Presence of the National Government

Readers of newspapers and viewers of television newscasts are told almost daily of a bewildering array of national government actions: The Air Force presses to keep a new bomber program alive. NASA announces plans for a staffed mission to Mars. The Nuclear Regulatory Commission publishes a new set of rules on certification procedures for the operation of nuclear power plants. The Supreme Court hands down yet another decision on the constitutionality of abortion regulations. Congress continues to wrestle with budget deficits. The president's budget director defends a plan to cut the in-

---

[15]See, for example, Dye, *Understanding Public Policy.*

heritance tax. This blizzard of activity reflects the pervasiveness of the national government as well as the complexity and scope of its work.

Views of Public Policy

foreign policy

A nation's collective decisions about relations with other nations.

domestic policy

A category of public policy that is comprised of policy decisions about matters affecting individuals within a political system.

No single set of categories can adequately capture everything government does. However, some divisions among policies can help make the scope of government activity more comprehensible. The identification of policy categories defines patterns of government action to clarify what government does and how it goes about its work.

Perhaps the most common set of policy categories is **foreign policy**, decisions about relations with other nations, and **domestic policy**, decisions about matters affecting citizens within the United States. Some foreign policies can have important domestic consequences. For example, international trade policy with Japan can affect the prices of cars in the United States. In general, however, public officials make foreign policy decisions in ways different from those used in social welfare policies. The president is less constrained by other officials and groups in the international arena than he is in seeking changes in the Social Security system. Interest groups tend to be less concerned about foreign policies than about domestic policies, which affect them more immediately and directly.[16] Domestic policy can be further subdivided into functional areas, such as education, health, transportation, energy, and environment.

Politics and Economic Self-Interest

The presence or absence of *economic self-interest* can also be a useful criterion for differentiating policies. Economic self-interest plays little or no role in the disposition of issues such as abortion, the legal drinking age, and the draft. In each of these cases money would not resolve the conflict. Some people, for example, vehemently believe that abortion is an undeniable evil, while others see abortion as an inalienable right of women. Proponents of abortion argue that women should be able to decide not to have children for economic as well as personal reasons. However, money concerns are not paramount in this debate.

Another category includes government actions on matters in which money plays a central role. For example, debates over taxes and budget deficits are essentially economic questions. Who shall pay government, and who shall receive how much out of it? Which states shall receive more than others in federal grants? Which groups shall bear the brunt of cuts in social welfare spending? Does inflation merit more government action and attention than unemployment?

Finally, in some policy debates economic self-interest and assertions of principle are mixed. Money plays an important but not exclusive role in these issues. Policies on civilian nuclear power, civil rights, and pornography are examples. Electric power

---

[16]See, for example, Aaron Wildavsky, "The Two Presidencies," *Trans-Action*, December 1966, pp. 7–14.

companies have an economic interest in favorable governmental policies on nuclear plant construction. Similarly, groups like women, African Americans, and Americans with disabilities see active civil rights policies on hiring and promotion as favorable to their economic self-interest. But assertions of principle also play an important role in the debates. The opponents of civilian nuclear power see nuclear power plants as a threat to public health and the quality of the environment. Civil rights advocates see the enhanced status of certain groups as a matter of right and justice. Finally, while the producers and sellers of pornography assert the principle of freedom of speech, their opponents see the defense of pornography (from which money is made) as a defense of economic self-interest.

Categories of National Government Policies

No single set of categories can adequately capture everything government does. However, even though overlaps occur, some divisions among policies can help make the scope of government activity more comprehensible. Over time the national government has taken on new functions and responsibilities in response to crises, changing technologies, citizen demands, and political pressures. Six substantive categories can help to bring some order to the scope of national government policies.

Foreign and Defense Policies   The oldest functions of the national government are to conduct relationships with foreign nations, such as trade negotiations with Mexico and Canada, and to maintain national security against threats from other nations, using physical force if necessary, such as the use of troops in the war in the Persian Gulf in 1991, or in the War on Terrorism beginning in late 2001.

Social Welfare   In terms of the amount of money the national government spends, the growth of social welfare activities was the most significant policy change in the role of government in the twentieth century. Like a huge check processor, the national government takes money from taxpayers or borrows it, and disburses cash or in-kind benefits such as food stamps to millions of people who qualify because of old age, disability, unemployment, or poverty.

Protection of Legal and Constitutional Rights   The protection of legal and constitutional rights has been one of the principal sets of national government activities over the past generation. Supreme Court justices, presidents, and members of Congress have all brought to bear, to varying degrees, the power and influence of the national government to protect the rights of a variety of groups, such as political, religious, and ethnic minorities; Americans with disabilities; and people accused of crimes.

Promotion of Science and Technology   Basic research, new technologies, and changing public expectations have drawn the national government into efforts to achieve certain public policy goals with the help of science and technology. Examples of such policies include the civilian space program, continuing research efforts on diseases such as AIDS and cancer, the use of stem cells in research, therapeutic cloning, and the development of new civilian technologies to help the nation become more competitive in the world economy of the twenty-first century.

Regulation　Regulations are among the tools government uses to shape sectors of the economy. However, because their purposes go beyond economic goals, regulations can be considered a specific category of policy. As the chapter on bureaucracies indicated, government regulations are designed to structure relationships in specific industries, such as broadcasting and the marketing of securities, or to ensure social objectives, such as clean air and worker safety.[17]

Economic Policies　Given a national budget that now exceeds $2 trillion, what the national government does (or does not do) in its spending, taxing, and borrowing policies has enormous consequences for the economy. Spending on education and on transportation and communication networks will shape the kind of economy the nation has in coming decades. Tax laws that eliminate or create tax deductions and tax credits influence investment decisions made by individuals and corporations. Large deficits can

[17]For a discussion of the purposes of regulation, see *Federal Regulatory Directory,* 10th ed. (Washington, DC: CQ Press, 2001).

The activities of the New York Stock Exchange and all securities trading are regulated by the Securities Exchange Commission. *(AP Wide World)*

encourage higher interest rates, just as higher government spending can reduce unemployment rates. Through its control of the money supply, the Federal Reserve can also affect interest and unemployment rates and private investment decisions. Government efforts to shape the economy through its spending, taxing, borrowing, and money supply decisions comprise a major part of the policy agenda.

SUMMARY

1. Public policy is whatever government chooses to do or not to do. Ultimately, political activity springs from conflict within society over what government ought to do and for whom or to whom it ought to do it. The elitism and pluralism models offer different explanations of who should make public policy decisions. The rational-comprehensive approach and incrementalism raise fundamental questions about how decisions are made.

2. Definable stages of policymaking are getting issues onto the agenda of government, formulating policy proposals, formally adopting policy, implementing policy, and evaluating policy.

3. Public policies can be distinguished from one another in a variety of ways. Economic self-interest is a useful criterion in distinguishing among policies. Six substantive categories differentiate national government policies: foreign and defense policies, social welfare, protection of legal and constitutional rights, promotion of science and technology, regulation, and economic policies.

KEY TERMS

public policy (391)   incrementalism (395)
systems model (392)   policy agenda (397)
bureaucratic model (392)   policy strategy (399)
Marxism model (392)   policy adoption (400)
free market capitalism model (393)   policy implementation (401)
elitism (394)   policy evaluation (403)
pluralism (394)   foreign policy (405)
rational-comprehensive model (395)   domestic policy (405)

READINGS FOR FURTHER STUDY

A good overview of public policy analysis and the stages of the public policy process can be found in James E. Anderson, *Public Policymaking*, 5th ed. (Boston: Houghton Mifflin, 2003).

John Kingdon's *Agendas, Alternatives, and Public Policies*, 2nd ed. (New York: Addison-Wesley, 1995) is an interesting discussion of the changing shape of the public policy agenda.

An excellent account of policymaking, and an attempt to explain the apparent contradictions involved in the process, is Deborah A. Stone's *Policy Paradox: The Art of Political Decision Making*, revised ed. (New York: Norton, 2001).

The theories behind public policy are addressed in *Theories of the Policy Process: Theoretical Lenses on Public Policy* (Boulder, CO: Westview Press, 1999) by Paul A. Sabatier, ed.

The causes for the rise and fall of public policies over time are explored in Frank R. Baumgartner and Bryan D. Jones, eds. *Policy Dynamics* (Chicago: University of Chicago Press, 2002).

Two quarterly journals of the Policy Studies Organization, the *Policy Studies Journal* and the *Review of Policy Research*, are sources of current scholarship on the field of policy analysis and on specific policy areas.

CHAPTER 14

Public Policy and Economics

A/P World Wide

Chapter Objectives

Economic issues are typically high on the political agenda because they affect so many people and often lead to sharp conflicts that the political process must resolve. This chapter defines fiscal and monetary policy, elements of economic policy, and outlines the tenets of three major schools of thought about what economic policy should be: Keynesian economics, monetarist economics, and supply-side economics. Given the importance of national budget policy in the 1990s and 2000s, the chapter then pays special attention to spending choices in fiscal policy by surveying major categories of spending and addressing the issue of the deficit and why government expenditures are so hard to control. The chapter concludes with a review of how budget decisions are made and a discussion of the eternal search, driven by the persistence of high deficits, for better procedures in deciding how money will be spent.

Government and Economic Policy

economic policy

The decisions a government makes that affect the production, distribution, and consumption of goods; the provision of services; the flow of income; and the distribution of wealth.

Some of the sharpest conflicts in a society are economic—who gains and who loses, who gives and who receives, who has and who has not. These issues affect the lives and well-being of millions of Americans. Further, with the development of an increasingly interdependent world economy, these issues affect billions of people around the world as well.

In its broadest sense, **economic policy** refers to the decisions a government makes that affect the production, distribution, and consumption of goods; the provision of services; the flow of income; and the accumulation of wealth. In a complex and interdependent modern economy such as that of the United States, virtually everything the government does has economic consequences. For example, President Kennedy's 1961 declaration to put a man on the moon by 1970 set off an explosion of research in metallurgy, electronics, and computers during the 1960s. This research in turn sparked the growth of new high-tech industries and the introduction of consumer goods such as the personal computer.

Nevertheless, the term *economic policy* is usually confined to decisions government makes with the explicit intention of influencing the economy. These decisions inevitably address fundamental questions about the role that government should play in the economy and society and, indeed, about the kind of economy and society the United States should be.

Basic Issues of Economic Policy

Economic questions have been part of American politics since the earliest days of the Republic. As Chapter 1 explained, unpopular British tax policies helped to spark the drive for independence before 1776. Barriers to trade and threats to creditors contributed to the call for a new and stronger national government in 1787. Political conflicts today over taxes, deficits, surpluses, the national debt, trade, and alternative strategies for ensuring prosperity demonstrate the durability of economic issues on the nation's policy agenda. Current controversies illustrate five important economic issues that have recurred as themes through American history, from the beginning to the present.

First, *should government involve itself in economic affairs at all?* As discussed in Chapter 4, one long-standing philosophical view is that the government should stay out of economics and business. Known as **laissez-faire** (French for "leave things alone"), this idea maintains that completely free economic competition among individuals, each pursuing his or her own self-interest, will work naturally to the benefit of all.[1] Under laissez-faire, most economic regulations, such as regulation of the securities business, simply would not exist. This view contrasts starkly with **socialism**, which holds that people will be best off if economic decision making is completely under the control of the government and if government owns and operates most of the major industries. Although Americans have always favored laissez-faire much more than socialism, they divide over just where to strike the balance between the two.

Second, even if government does involve itself in economic affairs, *should it try to stabilize the economy, or should it remain neutral?* Over the course of American history the economy has gone through periodic booms and busts. When the economy goes into a slump—a **recession** when the slump is relatively minor and short-lived, a **depression** when it is serious and sustained—or when it accelerates too quickly, some people

laissez-faire

French for "leave things alone"; the view in economics that government should not interfere in the workings of the economy.

socialism

The view in economics that economic decision making should be completely under the control of political authority.

recession

A minor and relatively short period of economic decline.

depression

A period of serious and sustained economic decline.

---

[1]Eighteenth-century English economist Adam Smith called this idea the "invisible hand" in his classic *Wealth of Nations*.

A migrant worker reclining during the Great Depression. *(Library of Congress)*

argue that the government should not interfere but should rather allow the economy to correct itself in time. Others want the government to moderate the trend. Before the arrival of the New Deal during the Great Depression of the 1930s, the view that government should remain neutral prevailed. Since then the judgment that government should take an active role in stabilizing the economy has been dominant. Today, the increasingly global nature of the American economy means that foreign as well as domestic policies are a part of this active governmental role.

Third, if government is to maintain economic stability, *which policies will achieve that goal*? Some economists believe that government should adjust its spending and taxing decisions when the economy needs to accelerate or to slow down. Others think the government should try to shape general economic activity by adjusting the money supply and interest rates to influence the willingness of individuals and companies to borrow money.

Fourth, aside from policies that affect the general health of the economy, *should government promote or discourage particular types of economic activity?* Some people believe that government should subsidize heavy industry, such as steel mills and shipyards, because they are vital in time of war. A variation on this theme, often favored by the neoliberals discussed in Chapter 4, is the idea of developing a national "industrial policy," which plots out cooperation between government and industry in identifying and supporting particularly promising new products and industries. Others believe that certain industries, such as textile plants, need government help to protect them from foreign competition because these industries provide employment to many Americans. If necessary, government should engage in **protectionism** by restricting the flow of foreign goods into the United States. Advocates of **free trade**, by contrast, argue that a nation's economy will be better off in the long run if local producers who cannot compete with more efficient foreign producers are allowed to die a natural economic death. A recent twist has seen American corporations establish factories in foreign countries in order to take advantage of cheaper labor markets. While such practices often create inexpensive products for American consumers, many worry about the negative effect exporting jobs could have on employment rates in America.

The possibilities of success and failure suggest a fifth concern: *Should government foster economic equality among its citizens?* There is little support in this country for the idea that the government should ensure complete economic equality among all citizens. However, it is a principal tenet of contemporary liberalism that no citizen should be allowed to fall below a certain economic minimum. This view accounts for social welfare programs such as food stamps and medical care for the poor. A more conservative position is that government should see that every citizen has equal opportunity and then let economic forces work in their natural way. Extreme conservatives may find even this an unjustified intrusion into the economy.

Each of these five questions asks whether government should play an active or passive role. How each is answered has profound consequences for the kind of society in which Americans live. Should taxes be raised or lowered, should the supply of money be expanded or contracted, should social welfare spending be increased or cut, should the national government embark on a major program of capital investment or not? Such questions dominate most policy debate in the 2000s.

Fiscal and Monetary Policy

Economic policies are of two major types: fiscal and monetary. The two are conceptually and practically distinct, although political decision makers certainly must take the relationship between them into account. Some regulatory policy also involves economic issues, as discussed in the chapter on bureaucracies.

Determinations of how much and whom to tax, and how much and on what to spend, constitute the **fiscal policy** of the United States. The president makes tax and spending proposals and signs, if he agrees, legislation the Congress passes. The Constitution gives Congress the power "to lay and collect taxes, duties, imposts, and ex-

---

protectionism

Belief that government should protect American business and industry by restricting the flow of foreign goods into the United States. Opposite of *free trade*.

free trade

Belief that America's economic interests are best served by allowing foreign producers to sell their goods without restriction in the United States.

fiscal policy

Governmental decisions about taxing and spending that affect the economic life of a nation.

cises, to pay the debts and provide for the common defense and general welfare of the United States," and "to borrow money on the credit of the United States." Taken individually, decisions on these questions constitute much of the routine business of government. Should the savings from military spending cuts be put into constructing new bridges and highways? Should government raise the personal income tax or the corporate income tax to pay for new programs? Taken as a whole, these decisions by the president and Congress exert a powerful influence on the economic life of the nation.

monetary policy

Government decisions about how much money should circulate in the economy and what the cost of borrowing money, the interest rate, should be.

Monetary policy, the second major type of economic policy, is the determination of how much money should circulate in the economy and what the cost of borrowing money, or the interest rate, should be. The Constitution gives Congress the power "to coin money, regulate the value thereof, and of foreign coin." In the landmark case of *McCulloch v. Maryland*,[2] the Supreme Court recognized Congress's "implied power" to determine monetary policy when it held that the Congress could charter a national bank, even though the Constitution did not explicitly give it that power (see Chapter 2). In other words, Congress possesses the power to set monetary policy for the United States. Pursuant to this power, Congress created the Federal Reserve System and delegated to it the power to make these decisions on the supply of money and the cost of borrowing.

Office of Management and Budget (OMB)

An agency in the Executive Office of the President that provides the president with budgetary information and advice and is responsible for compiling the president's annual budget proposal to Congress.

The making of economic policy illustrates the classic interplay between institutions and ideas. In fiscal policy, the president and his **Office of Management and Budget**, an Executive Office agency that puts together the president's annual budget proposal, interact with Congress and its committees to produce a national budget. In monetary policy, the Federal Reserve shapes the economy by manipulating the money supply and interest rates. But, as the box "Politics and Ideas: The Ideology of Economic Policy" shows, officials in these government institutions choose from among competing economic doctrines in the proposals and decisions they make. Conflicting ideas are the roots of economic policy debate.

The Deficit and the National Budget

Grappling with fiscal policy choices—that is, what taxes to raise or lower, what spending to increase or cut—has dominated the policy agenda in the recent decades. Taxing and spending issues touch the president at almost every turn in his efforts to initiate and shape policy. Congress spends much of its time wrestling with the size and shape of the national budget. Sometimes elected officials find it easier to approve spending increases than tax increases, and the resulting budget deficits loom as a serious policy issue— American bristles at the prospect of making larger and larger payments for the interest on the national debt. Other times elected officials respond to budget difficulties and the

[2] 17 U.S. (4 Wheaton) 316 (1819).

Public Policy and Economics

economy by cutting spending programs and lowering taxes, pleasing some citizens but creating economic crisis for others. This chapter will analyze the former problem—deficit spending.

The Deficit as a Political Issue

College students can readily understand the concepts of deficit and debt. A **deficit** occurs when expenditures (tuition, room, meals, and so forth) exceed revenues (income from a part-time job and money from parents, for example). A student makes up the difference by borrowing money. **Debt** is the sum of the deficits of prior years. A student who borrows $2,000 each year for four years graduates with a debt of $8,000. This debt will not be erased until the student earns enough money to meet both current expenses and payments on those college loans.

The federal government today is in a similar position because the government's expenses routinely exceed revenues. Demands on government a century ago were not nearly so great as they are now. The national government in the nineteenth century had an almost embarrassing **surplus** (an excess of revenue over expenses) of funds. Difficult as it may be to believe, the national government had a budget surplus in 71 of the 100 years between 1800 and 1900. In 1834 the total public debt was about $37,000, a sum translating to less than a penny per citizen.[3] Even though the national government regularly ran surpluses in the nineteenth century, the existence of government deficits and debt today is really not a new phenomenon. What is new is the size and persistence of the debt—especially in the absence of war, which has always placed heavy demands for money on governments. Deficits have now become the norm in budget policy. Although a strong economy has allowed the national government to run a surplus again in recent years, there was a budget deficit every year between 1970 and 1997.

Annual deficits and the federal debt increased substantially from the 1970s through the 1990s. In 1965 the annual deficit was a relatively modest $1.4 billion, but by 1975 the deficit began to exceed $50 billion annually. By 1985 the deficit was more than $200 billion. Over the relatively short period of 10 years, annual budget deficits quadrupled.[4] Inflation accounts for some of this increase. But a tax cut pressed by President Reagan in 1981 and higher defense spending in the 1980s contributed substantially to the growth in deficits. The deficit for fiscal year 1992—the peak year for budget deficits—was $290.4 billion. As the economy improved in the 1990s, deficit levels shrank, resulting in a $69 billion surplus in 1998. The surplus grew to $236.4 billion in 2000, prompting calls for a tax cut. George W. Bush championed this cause in the 2000 campaign, and began to deliver on this promise in 2001.[5]

deficit
An excess of government expenditures over revenues.

debt
The total accumulated amount of money that the national government owes to lenders, such as banks, individual and foreign investors, insurance companies, and the variety of financial institutions that purchase government securities.

surplus
An excess of government revenues over government expenditures.

---

[3]Citizens for Budget Reform, "National Debt," http://www.budget.org/NationalDebt/Debt/ (25 September 2002).
[4]U.S. Office of Management and Budget, *Budget Baselines, Historical Data, and Alternatives for the Future* (Washington, DC: Government Printing Office, 1993), pp. 278–279.
[5]U.S. Office of Management and Budget, *The Budget for Fiscal Year 2002, Historical Tables* (Washington, DC: GPO, 2001), p. 22.

A budget surplus, however, does not mean the government is debt free. The accumulated federal debt—the total amount of money government owes to lenders, such as government trust funds, banks, insurance companies, and the various financial institutions that purchase government securities—has also increased sharply over the past three decades. Federal debt rose from $322 billion in 1965 to almost $1 trillion in 1980. The debt was $3 trillion in 1990 and grew to $5.8 trillion in 2001—over $20,000 for every person in the country. In 2000 the debt amounted to 57 percent of gross national product, an amount lower than it had been during the 1990s, but higher than any previous time since the late 1950s.[6]

Ronald Reagan. *(Library of Congress)*

http://www.budget sim.org/nbs/

Think it's easy to balance the budget? Try it yourself by playing the National Budget Simulation game at the address above.

Some of the debate over the deficit is colored by the belief that government ought to be guided by traditional values in the matter of money—"living within one's own means." However, as in other matters, economists disagree over the extent to which the deficit poses a problem. Some argue that government deficits are essential to stimulate consumer demand in a failing or even sluggish economy. That is, by cutting taxes or increasing spending, government pumps money into the private economy to allow the kind of consumer spending that counters a depressed economy. Some maintain that the nation has had large deficits in the past, particularly in wartime, and those deficits actually spurred the economy.

Many other economists argue, however, that large deficits that are the product of a fundamental imbalance between revenues and expenditures can have the effect of slowing down consumer spending and economic growth. Government borrowing to cover deficits results in government competition with all other potential borrowers in the economy, such as corporations that want to build plants or individuals who want to buy houses or cars. The deficit raises the cost of capital and the cost of doing business.

Most politicians and economists believe that persistent large deficits can lead to severe economic consequences. The long-term health of a society depends on its ability and willingness to save and invest for future growth. Resources must be invested in

---

[6]U.S. Office of Management and Budget, *The Budget for Fiscal Year 2002, Historical Tables* (Washington, DC: GPO, 2001), p. 122.

Politics and Economics
The Ideology of Economic Policy

In recent American history several philosophies of economic policy have vied for acceptance as official government doctrine. The dominant perspective among Democrats since the New Deal has been Keynesian economics. For many years the primary challenge has come from advocates of monetarism, usually traditional conservative Republicans. But beginning in the Reagan years, some less orthodox Republican conservatives embraced the new (or at least newly packaged) doctrine of supply-side economics.

Keynesian Economics

The brilliant British economist John Maynard Keynes saw the health of an economy as dependent on the relationship between overall supply and demand in the economy. Supply is the total amount of goods and services produced in the economy; demand is the total amount of goods and services consumed. Economic problems arose, he argued, when supply and demand were not in balance. If supply exceeded demand, businesses would build up a backlog of unsold goods, cut back production, and lay off workers. Thus, supply exceeding demand would lead to unemployment. If demand exceeded supply, buyers would bid up the prices of goods, and inflation would result. Only if supply

and demand were in balance would the economy experience maximum employment and minimum inflation.

Keynes argued that in complex modern economics, supply and demand would not automatically balance, and that the imbalance would lead to economic problems. Keynes's solution was to have the government use its fiscal policy to bring the two into balance. If supply exceeded demand and unemployment threatened, the government could spend more than it received in taxes—that is, it could engage in deficit spending and bring total demand and hence employment up to the optimum level. If demand exceeded supply and inflation loomed, the government could collect more in taxes than it spent—that is, it could run a surplus—and bring total demand and hence inflation down. In other words, Keynesians emphasize using government fiscal policy to adjust the level of demand to the point of balance with supply that will yield a low-inflation, high-employment economy.

Monetarism

Monetarists focus, as the name implies, on monetary policy. They see monetary policy rather than fiscal policy as the best way to control the level of demand

basic research, new products, new technologies, and education. If present consumption limits the amount of saving required for such investment, the society risks a decline in the standard of living. The Congressional Budget Office reports that among the world's most developed countries the United States has had the greatest decline in national saving as a percentage of gross domestic product.[7] Americans save three to four percent of

---

[7]Congressional Budget Office, *Assessing the Decline in the National Saving Rate* (Washington, DC: Government Printing Office, 1993), pp. 2–3. National savings rates were compared for the period 1960 to 1989. This downward trend continued throughout the 1990s. See Bureau of Economic Analysis, "Note on the Personal Saving Rate," *Survey of Current Business*, February 1999, pp. 8–9.

The Ideology of Economic Policy, *continued*

for goods and services. If the Federal Reserve lets the amount of money grow too large and the cost of money (i.e., the interest rate) fall too low, consumers and business managers will borrow and spend so much money that demand will exceed supply and inflation will result. If money is in short supply and interest rates are high, consumer and business spending and borrowing will decline, supply will exceed demand, and unemployment will result.

One widely recognized monetarist prescription, advanced by the prominent economist Milton Friedman, is that growth in the money supply should be steady and gradual, roughly in pace with the growth in the amount of goods and services the economy produces. Anything more will lead to inflation, anything less to unemployment. Further, many monetarists, being conservative and suspicious of active governmental involvement in the economy, prefer adherence to this general rule rather than "politically" exercised discretion about monetary policy.

Supply-Side Economics

As one might expect, supply-side economics focuses on how much is produced in the economy rather than on how much is demanded, as in the Keynesian and monetarist perspectives. According to supply-side economics leading theoretician, Arthur Laffer, government can affect the balance of supply and demand in the economy better by adjusting supply than by adjusting demand. In fact, government is seen as having created the imbalance by setting taxes so high (particularly for the highest income groups) that people have little incentive to work or to invest and thereby produce. Only if government reduces taxes sufficiently to restore incentives and make money available will people begin to work harder, invest more, and produce more. The stimulus to economic activity created by lower tax rates will, according to the supply-siders, be so great that tax revenues will actually increase as a result of higher employment and consumption.

Supply-side concerns have played an important role in recent debates over whether to reduce the deficit by taxing the rich. Rejecting liberal concerns about increasing inequality in income distribution, supply-siders have argued that income tax rates on the rich and rates for capital gains taxes on everyone should be kept low. Their argument is that the rich especially are more likely than the poor to invest their money (rather than spend it), thereby stimulating greater production and prosperity.

their disposable income.[8] Federal budget deficits and the national debt are major contributors to a low national saving rate.

Persistent deficits figured prominently as a political issue in the 1992 presidential campaign. Third-party candidate Ross Perot skillfully used television to criticize both major parties for inaction on the deficit and the resulting public debt. Perot clearly

---

[8]Bureau of Economic Analysis, "BEA News Release," 30 August 2002.

struck a chord with voters. He received 19 percent of the popular vote in the election, the best showing for a third-party candidate in 80 years.[9] Although he received less than half that vote when he ran again in 1996, the Reform Party that he and his followers created indicated the importance of economic reform to many Americans.

Perot's electoral strength placed pressure on elected officials to grapple seriously with the deficit. But the task is not easy. A booming economy, like the one the United States enjoyed in the mid and late 1990s, can replace deficits with surpluses for a time, allowing politicians to delay making difficult economic decisions. Eventually, though, the dynamic nature of a macroeconomy ensures that challenges will return. At the beginning of the 2000s economic downturns signaled the return of deficits and the tough policy choices that accompany them. Reducing the deficit is difficult because of the sharp conflict over the alternative ways of doing it, and the pain that lower deficits leave in their wake. Choosing among cutting expenditures, increasing taxes, or some combination of the two is really the essence of politics. For example, elimination of the revenue-sharing program through which the national government granted funds to local governments lowered the deficit somewhat. However, elimination of the program also forced local governments to decide whether to increase their own taxes or cut services for local residents. As another example, building an orbiting space station or the superconducting super collider will be of great economic benefit to some contractors and some states. Political leaders also face tradeoff decisions regarding Social Security and Medicare. As the baby boom generation retires these programs will need to pay out money to more individuals than they are collecting from, which may create a need to either increase the tax burden on working age Americans, or decrease benefits to those of retirement age. Neither option is likely to be popular. But these decisions also mean that either the deficit or taxes will be higher. Raising taxes will cut the deficit, but higher taxes also mean less money in the pockets of consumers. Researchers want more government money to do their work. Social welfare advocates want more spending on poverty programs. The beneficiaries of government spending, such as military contractors, researchers, and state and local governments, obviously press to maintain and even increase their benefits. At the same time, taxpayers do not welcome proposals to raise federal revenues by increasing taxes.

Major Components of the National Budget

Money's rise to the top of the policy agenda has deep roots in the past. Since the Great Depression of the 1930s government has treated the economic and social needs of groups such as the elderly, the disabled, and the poor as public problems. Meeting these welfare demands has meant the expenditure of huge amounts of public money. War and

---

[9]In 1912, after a split in the Republican party, Theodore Roosevelt, a former president, received 27 percent of the popular vote as the candidate of the Progressive party.

FIGURE 14.1

Federal Government Expenditures

Payments for individuals and national defense are the largest categories of federal expenditures. Net interest alone was estimated to consume 12.5 percent of the budget in 2001.

SOURCE: U.S. Office of Management and Budget, *The Budget for Fiscal Year 2002, Historical Tables* (Washington, DC: 2001), pp. 44–51.

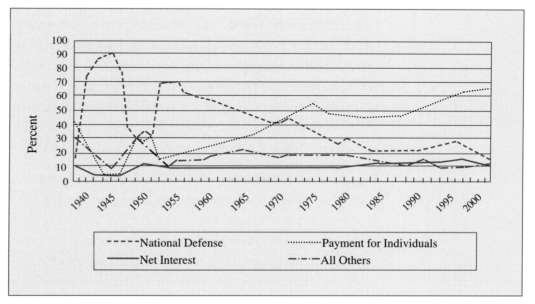

the threat of war have also made their own heavy demands on public funds. Paying interest on borrowed money has itself become a major category of spending.

Figure 14.1 offers a graphic and useful summary of major budgetary trends over the past half-century. The figure divides the budget into four proportional categories: national defense, payments for individuals, net interest payments, and all other expenditures, which include programs such as cancer research, space exploration, highway construction, and environmental protection.

National Defense The national government has constitutional responsibility to provide for the nation's security. Consequently, spending on defense has always consumed a significant portion of the budget. For example, of the $10.8 million that the national government spent in 1800, more than 55 percent went to the War Department (army) and the navy.[10] Figure 14.1 shows that at the height of World War II in 1945 almost 90 percent of the budget went to defense. After a postwar drop and then an increase in the

---

[10]U.S. Bureau of the Census, Historical Statistics of the United States: Colonial Times to 1970, pt.2 (Washington, DC: Government Printing Office, 1975), pp. 1114–1115.

early 1950s during the Korean conflict, the proportion of federal dollars going to defense began a general decline from almost 70 percent in 1954 to less than 23 percent in 1980. In absolute dollars, the amount spent on national defense increased over this period, but defense expenditures consumed an increasingly smaller proportion of the total budget. Other expenditure items in the budget were growing at a faster rate, and the proportional decline in defense spending became a major political issue.

One of Ronald Reagan's (1981–1989) priorities was strengthening defense, and, as Figure 14.1 shows, the proportional amount of federal spending going to national defense increased in the 1980s. However, the breakup of the Soviet Union and the end of the Cold War weakened the military's claim on the budget beginning in the early 1990s, and the proportion of the budget spent on defense went down accordingly. In 2000, the national government spent just 16 percent of its budget on national defense, but this percentage is likely to rise as President George W. Bush pursues plans for a missile defense shield, and as the nation retools its military and intelligence sectors to more effectively address the threat of terrorism.

Payments for Individuals   Payments for individuals, the second major spending category in the budget, includes social welfare programs that are primarily a legacy of the New Deal of the 1930s and the Great Society of the 1960s. Such programs include Social Security, Medicare, unemployment compensation, food stamps, Medicaid, and supplemental security income. Retired and disabled citizens receive monthly checks through the Social Security program. Medicare provides medical care for the elderly and the disabled. The short-term unemployed receive weekly checks through the unemployment compensation program. Needy individuals receive food, medical care, or cash through programs such as food stamps, Medicaid, or supplemental security income. In administering these programs, the national government takes money from some groups in the form of retirement contributions or taxes and transfers it to other groups either in the form of cash, such as Social Security checks, or in the form of in-kind payments, such as food stamps.

This category of spending, compared to national defense, is a relatively new one for the national government. Only within the past half-century has the national government administered social welfare programs on such a comprehensive scale. This category has grown proportionally faster than any other since the 1940s, as Figure 14.1 graphically illustrates. In 1940 payments for individuals comprised less than 20 percent of all federal spending, a proportion that increased to 33 percent in 1970. This category of spending consumed more than 60 percent of the budget in 2000.[11] Such growth has prompted reformers to suggest privatizing some of these programs. One study, for example, argues that transforming the government-run Social Security program into individually

---

[11]Office of Management and Budget, *The Budget for Fiscal Year 2002, Historical Tables* (Washington, DC: GPO, 2001), p. 51.

controlled private retirement accounts can reduce government spending while providing an efficient and solvent method for individual financial security during old age.[12]

net interest

Charges that the government must pay to the public for the use of money borrowed to cover budget deficits. Total interest costs include net interest plus interest paid to government trust funds.

Interest Costs   The third major category of spending, **net interest,** represents the cost that government must pay the public for the use of borrowed money to cover budget deficits. Most individuals have at one time or another encountered the inevitability of making interest payments on goods they purchase. For example, most people who wish to buy a new home simply do not have enough cash to cover the full purchase price. If they want to buy a $100,000 home, they may have to borrow $80,000 from a bank or mortgage company to add to the resources they have to make the purchase. Borrowing money is really nothing more than using money that belongs to others. Of course, the right to use this money comes at a price, which is the payment of interest.

Money is among the most expensive items individuals can buy, and how much it costs depends on interest rates, which are in constant flux. If a home purchaser borrows $80,000 at 9 percent interest to be repaid over 30 years, the total repayment at the end of that period will amount to more than $230,000, or almost three times the original $80,000 borrowed! The amount of interest paid will vary with interest rates and the time period of the loan, but this simple example illustrates the high cost of using other people's money.

Individuals borrow money because they want things that cost more than the cash they have on hand. Governments borrow money for much the same reason. Because the money demands on government exceed the amount of money government receives in taxes, the resulting deficit must be covered by borrowing money from individual investors and financial institutions that buy government securities. And as the deficits rise, so too must the cost of borrowing money. In 1965 government paid $8.6 billion in net interest, about 7 percent of total federal expenditures in that year. In 2000 interest payments alone were $223 billion, more than 12 percent of total spending.[13] The proportional amount of the budget consumed by net interest has doubled since the 1960s.

Mandatory Programs in the Budget

incrementalism

A model of decision making that holds that new policies differ only marginally from existing policies.

When the president and Congress begin to work on budget proposals every year, they do not begin with a clean budgetary slate. Present and future budgets build on past budgets in increments. This theory of **incrementalism** holds that "[t]he largest determining factor of the size and content of this year's budget is last year's budget."[14] Expenditures are difficult to control largely because present decisions are shaped by past decisions.

---

[12]See, for example, June O'Neill, "The Trust Fund, the Surplus, and the Real Social Security Problem," *The Cato Project On Social Security Privatization* No.26, 9 April 2002.

[13]U.S. Office of Management and Budget, *The Budget for Fiscal Year 2002, Historical Tables* (Washington, DC: GPO, 2001), p. 51.

[14]Aaron Wildavsky and Naomi Caiden, *The New Politics of the Budgetary Process*, 4th ed. (New York: Addison Wesley, 2000).

Budget makers cannot decide to reduce total spending from $1.9 trillion to, say, $500 billion in a single year. Just as a rapidly moving freight train cannot be stopped quickly (and without much screeching of brakes), so too budget expenditures cannot be massively and rapidly reduced from one year to the next.

mandatory programs

Government programs, such as Social Security expenditures, in which spending automatically increases from one year to the next without specific annual appropriations action by Congress.

Much of the budget is comprised of **mandatory programs** in which spending automatically increases from one year to the next without specific annual appropriations action by Congress. **Social entitlements**, programs in which eligible citizens receive benefits to which they are entitled by law, are a main source of mandatory programs, and include Social Security, Medicare, Medicaid, public assistance programs, unemployment compensation, and retirement programs for federal employees. The largest of the mandatory programs is Social Security, which alone accounts for over 20 percent of the total budget. According to the Congressional Budget Office, "[m]anaging the growth of federal spending . . . will be largely a matter of controlling the growth of mandatory outlays."[15] In a creative attempt at reducing these costs to the government, George W. Bush has recommended allowing individuals to retain control over a portion of their payroll taxes in personal retirement accounts.[16]

social entitlements

Programs, such as Social Security and Medicaid, whereby eligible individuals receive benefits according to law.

Social Security provides a good illustration of the concept of mandatory spending. Congress and the president do not decide every year whether or not the nation should have a Social Security program. Once the program was established, and it is now a solid rock on the political landscape, it continues to give eligible individuals benefits year after year. A person who has made contributions to the Social Security system via payroll taxes becomes automatically eligible for Social Security benefits upon retirement at age 65. Social Security expenditures are determined by the demographic movement of individuals into retirement age and by increases in payments because of inflation. Congress and the president could substantially reduce those benefits, but only at very high political and social costs.

A related program that illustrates the difficulty of cutting the budget from one year to the next is net interest. By law, interest on the debt must be paid. Failure to make such interest payments would destroy investor confidence in government securities and result in economic consequences too grave to contemplate. Thus, Congress and the president do not have much choice in the matter of paying interest. The amount paid in a given year will depend on interest rates and the size of deficits. Because of the necessity to pay interest and the existence of mandatory programs, budget makers cannot easily make proportionally large spending cuts from one year to the next.

In 2001 President George W. Bush's Office of Management and Budget estimated that over half of the 2002 budget would be comprised of mandatory programs. Net interest

---

[15]Congressional Budget Office, *Reducing the Deficit: Spending and Revenue Options* (Washington, DC: Government Printing Office, 1993), p. 225.
[16]*A Blueprint for New Beginnings* (Washington, DC: GPO, 2001), pp. 45–48.

payments and mandatory programs together would account for 64.7 percent of the total budget in 2002. Some changes can be made in social entitlements, but the programs cannot be cut drastically; and interest must be paid. The concept of mandatory spending illustrates the obstacles Congress and the president face in their attempts to cut deficits.

The President and Congress in the Budgeting Process

Most individuals know very little about the details of the national budget or how various governmental institutions work together to arrive at specific taxing and spending policies. However, taxpayers are acutely aware of the degree to which their salaries are reduced by withholding taxes, and beneficiaries of public programs notice even small changes in their benefits. From the perspective of individuals or specific groups, the politics of money is about maintaining or increasing the benefits of government spending while shifting the tax costs to someone else. If politics is the process of making choices among conflicting perceptions of national purpose, with different consequences for different people, then choices on the collection and use of public money are intensely political decisions.[17]

Budgets are essential because human wants must be tamed by the scarcity of resources. If human wants were limited, or if resources were unlimited, budgets would be unnecessary. However, because neither condition exists, the president and Congress are inevitably forced to wrestle with the necessity of coming up with a **budget**, or a planned statement of revenues and expenditures. One scholar has cited "the twin functions of a budget process as an opportunity for claiming resources and as a procedure for rationing limited resources among claimants."[18] Budgeting lies at the intersection of the inevitability of demands and the necessity to impose constraints on those demands. Continuing budget deficits are simply a reflection of the political fact that satisfying demands is more appealing than the distasteful business of imposing constraints.

Because the money pie cannot be expanded infinitely, making budget policy is a battle over the shares of the pie that different programs should receive. In addition to the inevitability of disagreement, putting together a budget is a complicated process for several reasons. First, determining how much government will collect in taxes and how much it will spend in a given year is largely a matter of estimation. Budget makers cannot accurately predict the flow of dollars into and out of the federal treasury in a particular year. Such dollar flows are greatly influenced by the performance of the nation's economy, a matter over which the president and Congress have little short-term control. Second, budgeting is complicated and difficult because constructing a budget is a highly

budget

A planned statement of expenditure that includes specific categories of spending.

---

[17]For the argument that "budgeting is at its very core political," see Donald F. Kettl, *Deficit Politics: Public Budgeting in Its Institutional and Historical Context* (New York: Macmillan, 1992), pp. 156–157.
[18]Allen Schick, *Congress and Money: Budgeting, Spending, and Taxing* (Washington, DC: Urban Institute, 1980), p. 570.

decentralized process. That is, a large number of individuals and groups, both inside and outside government, help to shape the budget. The president and his Office of Management and Budget, the executive agencies, Congress and a variety of its committees and their staffs, interest groups, and sometimes even the courts all contribute to the making of budget decisions. At the center of political conflict, the budget process reflects the decentralization inherent in the political system itself. The process would certainly be more tidy and efficient if only one individual or committee could make all budget determinations. But the framers of the Constitution did not intend such a system. Especially in the budget process, ambition counters ambition, resulting in inevitable disorder and complexity.[19]

The Stages of Budgeting

The most important governmental actors in the budgetary process are the president and his staff, Congress and its committees, and the executive agencies. Budgeting can be divided into three separate stages, with each of these three groups playing a primary role in one of them.[20]

1. *Presidential proposal*. The president and his staff compile agency requests for funds, shape those requests to fit presidential priorities, and then submit to Congress a proposed Budget of the United States Government.
2. *Congressional response*. Congress and its various committees review the presidential budget proposals and mold them to meet congressional priorities. If the president agrees with those congressional actions, they then become law.
3. *Agency expenditure of funds*. The executive agencies spend the money pursuant to budget laws enacted by Congress and signed by the president.

fiscal year

For budget and accounting purposes in the national government, the 12-month period beginning on October 1 and ending on September 30 of the following calendar year.

Each stage occurs every year. Actual expenditures take place during a **fiscal year**, which for U.S. government budget and accounting purposes is a 12-month period beginning each year on October 1 and ending on September 30 of the following calendar year. The calendar year designation given to the fiscal year is the calendar year in which the fiscal year ends. For example, fiscal year 2002 begins on October 1, 2001, and ends on September 30, 2002. Starting the fiscal year on October 1 rather than January 1 is based on the assumption that Congress will make budget decisions in the

---

[19]See "Madisonian Budgeting, or Why the Process Is So Complicated" in Joseph White and Aaron Wildavsky, *The Deficit and the Public Interest: The Search for Responsible Budgeting in the 1980s* (Berkeley: University of California Press, 1989), pp. 1–17.

[20]An excellent brief review of the budget process can be found in *The Budget System and Concepts, Budget of The United States Government, Fiscal Year 2003* (Washington, DC: Government Printing Office, 2002).

FIGURE 14.2

Major Steps in the Budgeting Process

The steps in the budgeting process for each fiscal year take two and a half years to complete. If appropriation action is not completed by September 30, Congress enacts temporary appropriations (i.e., a continuing resolution).

SOURCES: Adapted from U.S. Office of Management and Budget, *Analytical Perspectives, Budget of the United States Government, Fiscal Year 2003* (Washington, DC: Government Printing Office, 2002), p. 430, and information contained in U.S. Office of Management and Budget, *Budget System and Concepts, Fiscal Year 2003* (Washington, DC: Government Printing Office, 2002).

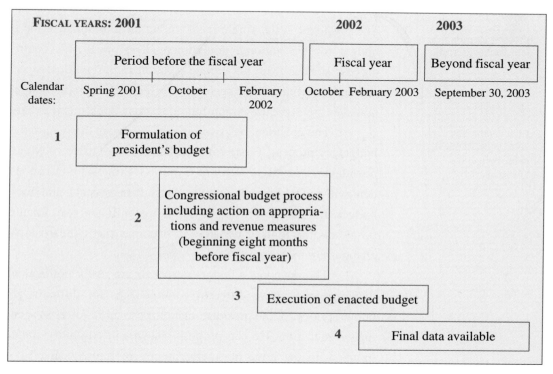

nine-month period between the beginning of its session in January and October 1, the beginning of the fiscal year. That Congress does not always meet this deadline exemplifies the problems Congress has in making difficult budget choices.

As Figure 14.2 shows, the three stages of the budgeting process take a total of more than two years to complete. For example, the president and his staff began to formulate proposals for fiscal 2003 in spring 2001, about 18 months before the beginning of the fiscal year in October 2002. Given uncertainties in estimating receipts and expenditures, planning for a fiscal year so long in advance is obviously no easy task. The second stage of congressional action begins in February 2002, eight months before the start of fiscal 2003. Agencies actually spend the money in the fiscal year itself, October 1, 2002, through September 30, 2003.

Not all budgetary action by all three sets of budgetary actors concentrates on a single fiscal year at a time. At a single point in a given calendar year, each of the three stages may be in progress for three different fiscal years. In spring 2001, for example, agencies were actually spending money in fiscal 2001, Congress was reviewing presidential proposals for fiscal 2002, and the president and his staff had begun to plan for 2003. The need for planning and executing money decisions seems to be eternal, and so does the process of putting together a budget.

The President in the Budget Process

The president is the single most important individual in the process of constructing a budget for the national government. The president's central role in the budgetary process springs from his unique position in the political system. More than the words and actions of any other person, what he says about the budget and the priorities he establishes are especially important in shaping subsequent debate about the budget.

The president has two important powers that guarantee him a central role in the budgetary process. First, with the help of the Office of Management and Budget, the president *proposes a budget to Congress.* Proposal power does not mean that the president will necessarily get what he wants. Congress can and does work its own will on the budget. But the power to propose is a significant one, for the president's budget proposal sets the tone of debate and becomes the standard against which congressional changes are measured.

The president's budget proposals are really political statements, for, if enacted, they inevitably have different consequences for different groups. Depending on his budget priorities, the president can propose more (or less) spending on defense or housing or education. He can propose changes in eligibility standards for entitlement programs with the hope of saving money in future years. He can propose tax cuts or increases with consequences for the general health of the economy, the size of the deficit, and the economic status of different income groups. And he can do all of these things with the great flair of publicity—natural to the office of the presidency—that brings guaranteed and immediate attention to his proposals. President George W. Bush announced his economic plan in a speech to Congress one month after his inauguration, thus illustrating a president's power to structure discussion of the budget. The plan contained a wide range of initiatives to pay down the national debt, improve America's schools, provide quality health care and a secure retirement, and strengthen national defense. Bush's proposals included tripling spending on education, developing an effective missile defense, and providing tax relief for all Americans who paid federal taxes. Members of Congress can oppose presidential initiatives, but the president's proposals define the budget policy debate.

http://www.public debt.treas.gov/opd /opdpenny.htm

The U.S. Treasury Department's Bureau of the Public Debt continually updates the national debt down to the last penny.

In addition to the authority to make budget proposals, the president has the constitutional power to *veto budget bills passed by Congress.* Appropriations bills go through the legislative process and must ultimately be signed by the president before they become law and actual spending proceeds. The president may decide that he is opposed to an appropriations bill that Congress sends him because it diverges too much from his original proposal. However, he must veto the entire bill rather than portions of it. Congress can try to override his veto with an extraordinary majority (a two-thirds vote in each chamber), or Congress may try to recast the bill in terms more agreeable to the president. No other person has such power to stop the budgetary process in its tracks than the president. The ever-present threat of a presidential veto dramatizes the critical role that the president plays in the budget process. But Congress has substantial powers of its own to shape budgetary choices.[21]

Congress and Budgeting

Congressional power to make decisions on the budget is firm and clear, for the Constitution states that "no money shall be drawn from the Treasury, but in Consequence of Appropriations made by Law." Presidential proposals cannot become law in the absence of congressional action. The first budgetary stage of presidential proposal is a triumph of simplicity compared to the second stage of congressional action.

Congress is a much more complicated institution than the presidency. By definition, the president is one individual to whom responsibility for budget proposals can be easily assigned. But Congress is a fragmented institution with 535 individuals representing different parts of the nation and inevitably reflecting conflicting views. By voting, each of these individuals can help to shape the budget that emerges from Congress.

Most of the important work of budget review and decision in Congress is done in committee. In addition to the authorizing committees (such as Agriculture and Armed Services), each chamber also has "money" committees, such as those on the budget, appropriations, and revenue (called Ways and Means in the House and Finance in the Senate). Each one of these committees can affect the budget in some way. Under the best of circumstances, the process of making budget decisions is never easy, because the demand for government services always outruns the supply of money to fund those services. But this fundamental difficulty is heightened in Congress by the large number of individuals and committees, each moved by diverse and conflicting interests, with the capacity to shape the budget.

---

[21]For a good review of relationships between the branches in the budgetary process, see see *The Federal Budget: Politics, Policy, and Process*, rev. ed. (Washington, DC: Brookings, 2000) by Allen Schick with Felix LoStracco.

Contemporary Controversies
Corporations and the Economy

Enron filed the largest bankruptcy in history and laid off thousands of workers who lost 401k savings loaded in Enron stock. *(AP Wide World)*

Throughout American political history government regulation of the private economic sector (or lack thereof) has been a source of conflict, and occasional corruption. One of the most famous incidents of economic misconduct, the Teapot Dome scandal of the 1920s, resulted in a prison sentence for a cabinet official. Secretary of the Interior Albert Fall leased federal oil reserves to his friends in the oil industry without seeking competitive bids and received kickbacks in return.

More recent examples of economic fraud are the corporate accounting debacles of the early 2000s. Created in 1934 as a response to the uncontrolled market forces that led to worldwide depression, the Securities and Exchange Commission (SEC) was designed to enforce laws requiring accurate and public disclosures of financial health by companies offering publicly traded securities, or stocks. One such rule requires companies to register with the SEC, a process that involves "a description of the company's properties and business; a description of the security to be offered for sale; information about the management of the company; and financial statements certified by independent accountants."[a] During late 2001 and early 2002 several corporations, including giants Enron and WorldCom, were found to have violated this rule by providing false financial reports. In other words, false accounting claims vastly overstated the projected earnings of the corporations, leading to artificially inflated stock prices. When the companies could no longer hide their insolvency, the false claims became public, the corporations filed for bankruptcy, many stockholders lost their investments, and many employees lost their jobs.

One of the most troubling aspects of this situation was that highly respected accounting firms, such as Arthur Andersen, played a big role in the fraudulent action. Accountants are supposed to provide independent audits of corporate financial claims, but in these cases the accounting firms shared in the guilt. In response to these corrupt practices, Congress passed, and the president signed, the Accounting Industry Reform Act in 2002, a measure designed to provide increased supervision over corporate accounting and stiffer penalties for misconduct—including 20 year prison sentences for chief financial officers certifying false reports. In signing the new law, President Bush warned: "No boardroom in America is above or beyond the law."[b]

Can the government prevent corporate corruption through tougher regulation? Does the government have a duty to protect citizens from fraud? What role should the government play in the economic sphere?"

---

[a]The Investor's Advocate: How the SEC Protects Investors and Maintains Market Integrity," Securities and Exchange Commission, December 1999, http://www .sec.gov/about/whatwedo.shtml (27 September 2002).
[b]Suzanne Malveaux, "Bush Signs Bill to Stop 'Book Cooking,'" CNN.com, 30 July 2002.

authorization

Congressional enactment that creates or continues a policy program and the agency administering it.

For most government programs, Congress must take two separate steps before money can actually be spent. The first step is program **authorization**, or the congressional decision to create (or continue) a program and the agency administering it. Such authorizations begin in substantive legislative committees, such as Agriculture, Armed Services, and Interstate and Foreign Commerce. Authorizing legislation ordinarily contains statements of program and agency goals as well as enabling powers to carry the program forward. Authorizations may be for one year, for several years, or open-ended. The legislation also contains a statement of money authorized to be spent on the program. For example, an authorization measure may state that an expenditure not to exceed $700 million is authorized for the following fiscal year for, say, certain pollution abatement activities carried on by the Environmental Protection Agency. However, no money can be legally spent as the result of such an authorization measure. Agencies do not have the legal right actually to spend money unless Congress takes the second step of appropriating funds pursuant to the authorization.

appropriation

Congressional enactment that funds an authorized program with a specific sum of money.

This second step is program **appropriations**, the congressional decision to fund an authorized program with a specific sum of money. Such appropriations decisions are shaped by recommendations from the Appropriations Committee in each chamber. The actual amount appropriated need not be the same as the amount authorized. For example, although $700 million may be authorized for pollution abatement, only $600 million may be actually appropriated.

The authorization-appropriations sequence does not apply to all government programs. For example, the authorization (creation and subsequent amendment) of most entitlement programs includes, in effect, a permanent appropriation to fund the program. By establishing the Social Security program, Congress has pledged that individuals reaching a certain age and meeting eligibility requirements will receive monthly checks. Congress can change the rules, but the amount of money spent in a given fiscal year is not dependent on specific congressional action for that year.

The Search for Better Budget Procedures

line-item veto

Power through which a chief executive reacting to a bill passed by the legislature may accept some items in the bill but may also reject other items in the same bill. Most state governors have the line-item veto power but the president does not.

The deficit is proof of the extraordinary difficulty Congress and the president have in coming to grips with decisions on cutting expenditures and raising taxes. The substantive issues are so difficult that policymakers have naturally considered whether different budget procedures might make their task easier. Would tough budget decisions be made more readily if procedures for arriving at them were different?

Proposed budget changes come in a variety of forms. The most controversial budget reforms are proposals to give the president **line-item veto** power, and to add an amendment to the Constitution requiring a balanced budget. Under current rules, the president must sign or veto an entire bill sent to him by Congress. An appropriations bill may contain many specific programs, and the president must either accept or reject all of them in the bill. The line-item veto would give the president the power to reject some items in the bill and to allow others to become law. Governors in 43 states have line-item veto power, which, proponents argue, increases the managerial capability chief executives must have. With this power, its supporters say, presidents would not be forced to accept wasteful spending projects that members of Congress pack into a bill. Riding a wave of reform, Republicans in the One-Hundred Fourth Congress passed the Line Item Veto Act in 1996 in order to provide the president with this power. President Clinton's first exercise of this power, however, was met with a legal challenge, and in 1998 the Supreme Court ruled the Act invalid for its circumvention of the lawmaking procedure set forth in the Constitution. Although the law was struck down, the idea remains alive. Amendments have been introduced in recent years to change the Constitution in order to allow for a presidential line item veto. Such a reform is not without its congressional detractors, though. Many members fear that the line-item veto would result in a discernible shift in budgetary power from Congress to the president. Given the much larger number of options the power would afford, presidential flexibility in determining the shape of the budget would greatly increase. Congressional ability to mold the budget would correspondingly diminish.

balanced budget amendment

A proposal for a constitutional amendment that would require the federal government to operate with a budget in which revenues equaled or exceeded expenditures.

The size of deficits and a growing public debt have also sparked interest in a constitutional amendment that would require a balanced budget. Proponents of a **balanced budget amendment** argue that only a constitutional mandate will force Congress and the president to produce balanced budgets. Opponents hold that the amendment risks tax increases and major reductions in a wide range of politically popular programs. Several times over the last decade, balanced budget amendment proposals have failed to get the constitutionally required two-thirds vote of the House and Senate before being sent on to the states for ratification. In 1992 Congress considered an amendment proposal that would have mandated a three-fifths majority in the House and Senate to allow deficit spending, except in a military emergency. The amendment did not receive the necessary two-thirds vote in either chamber. However, the amendment had substantial support, a sign that the political frustration of dealing with persistent deficits has led to a serious search for extraordinary constitutional remedies. Such efforts, though still pursued in every Congress, have lost some momentum in the past few years, as the government has proven capable of enacting balanced budgets without the looming threat of a constitutional amendment.

Although the line-item veto power and the balanced budget amendment remain proposals, Congress and the president have passed three laws resulting in fundamental changes in the process of deciding on budget expenditures while wrestling with the pain of reducing deficits.

continuing resolution

Legislative action taken by Congress to allow spending to proceed at the previous year's level when Congress has not met the deadline for reaching agreement on appropriations for the next fiscal year.

Congressional Budget and Impoundment Control Act of 1974

Legislation that significantly changed congressional budget procedures by creating budget committees, establishing a budget decision timetable, changing the fiscal year, placing limits on presidential impoundments, and establishing the Congressional Budget Office.

Congressional Budget Office (CBO)

A congressional staff unit that provides Congress with budgetary expertise, independent of the president's budget staff, to help Congress clarify budgetary choices.

The Congressional Budget and Impoundment Control Act of 1974   Before 1974, Congress reviewed the president's budget in a highly decentralized, piecemeal fashion. Budget totals resulted from a process of summing up the work of separate committees rather than any conscious effort to consider the budget comprehensively. Nor was there institutionalized consideration of the relationship between spending and expected revenue, a violation of sound budget practice.

With increasing frequency, appropriations bills were not enacted by the beginning of the fiscal year. In the absence of appropriations laws, some agencies were forced to operate under a **continuing resolution**, a temporary funding measure passed by Congress. In addition, the relentless growth of the budget produced demands for more budgetary information. And the regularity of annual deficits sparked heated battles within Congress and between Congress and the president over who was to blame for the budgetary "red ink." In fact, in an unprecedented use of presidential impoundment powers, President Nixon refused to spend billions of dollars already appropriated. He did so on the grounds that he was forced to take action to limit spending because Congress had not done so.

As a response to these problems, the **Congressional Budget and Impoundment Control Act of 1974** changed the fiscal year from a July 1–June 30 sequence to an October 1–September 30 sequence in order to give Congress more time to review the president's budget. The act also created the **Congressional Budget Office (CBO)**, a congressional staff unit with the responsibility of providing Congress with needed information about the budget and the analytical expertise to sharpen budgetary choices for Congress; placed limits on the president's impoundment powers; created budget committees in both the House and Senate to provide a mechanism for comprehensive budget review by Congress; and established a timetable (revised by subsequent legislation) for the congressional budget review process.

The president submits his proposed budget to Congress early in the calendar year. Congressional committees review the programs within their jurisdiction and offer budget estimates to the budget committees by mid-March. With the help of the CBO, the budget committees pursue a more comprehensive budget review and report to the House and Senate a budget resolution containing targets for total revenues, total expenditures, and money to be spent in functional categories across the budget for the next fiscal year. The resolution is to be adopted by the full House and Senate by April 15. Legislation on appropriations and revenue is then to proceed in light of the budget targets set in the resolution. Congressional money decisions and budget targets are to be reconciled in time for spending to begin at the start of the fiscal year on October 1. However, in some years Congress has not been able to meet these procedural deadlines required by law. For example, in the fall of 1990 not a single one of the appropriations measures was enacted by the time the new fiscal year had begun.

Gramm-Rudman-Hollings

Legislative enactment formally known as the Balanced Budget and Emergency Deficit Control Act of 1985, that mandated progressively higher annual cuts in the deficit to achieve a balanced budget by 1991. In 1986 the Supreme Court declared the act's procedure for automatic across-the-board spending cuts unconstitutional.

sequestration

The process through which the president makes budget cuts in government programs to meet the mandates in law requiring ceilings on specific categories of spending.

Budget Enforcement Act of 1990

Legislation that fundamentally changed budget deficit reduction efforts from the focus on deficit targets contained in Gramm-Rudman-Hollings to a focus on ceilings or caps on specific categories of spending.

Gramm-Rudman-Hollings   In response to the problem of deficits, Congress enacted the Balanced Budget and Emergency Deficit Control Act of 1985, more popularly known as **Gramm-Rudman-Hollings** after the senators who sponsored the legislation. The act as later amended mandated progressive annual cuts in the deficit and set into motion a process of automatic across-the-board spending cuts to achieve a balanced budget by 1993. The president ordered the cuts through the process of **sequestration**. Some programs, such as Social Security, Medicaid, and interest payments on the debt, were exempted from the cuts.

Gramm-Rudman-Hollings was enacted in the hopes of forcing Congress and the president to reduce the deficit. One problem with the deficit targets is that they encouraged the use of budget-reducing "gimmicks," which made it appear that cuts were made when in fact they were not. An example of a gimmick is pushing back a government payday several days from the fiscal year in question (say October 1) to the prior fiscal year (say September 29) so that the payroll will not be counted as an expenditure in the fiscal year under review. However, since the money was spent anyway, if only at a different time, the cut was not real. As the deficits continued, so Congress and the president tried a new law in 1990.

Budget Enforcement Act of 1990   Congress made fundamental changes in Gramm-Rudman-Hollings and tried a new approach to the deficit in the **Budget Enforcement Act of 1990**. The 1990 act shifts the emphasis of congressional action from deficit reduction to the control of spending.[22] Rather than being driven by overall deficit targets, Congress is limited by caps on discretionary spending and by constraints on changes in mandatory spending.

For fiscal years 1991 through 1993, the law placed caps on spending in each of the three categories of defense, international, and domestic discretionary—that is, nonmandatory—spending. The budget for the Federal Bureau of Investigation is an example of domestic discretionary spending, because Congress can change FBI budget amounts from one year to the next. Medicare payments to hospitals to fund health care for the elderly is an example of mandatory spending, because eligible individuals automatically and regularly receive benefits without specific congressional authorizing action from one year to the next. If discretionary spending exceeded the ceilings, then sequestration cuts were to be made within the category in which excess spending occurred. Under the law, all discretionary spending was combined into a single category in fiscal years 1994 and 1995. In addition, mandatory program increases had to be balanced by cuts in nonexempt programs or by revenue increases. Cuts were not required during war or a downturn in economic growth.[23] These complex budgeting limits have felt less restrictive since the economic upturn of the mid and late 1990s. Enacting budg-

---

[22]Congressional Budget Office, "The 1990 Budget Package: An Interim Assessment," December 1990, p. 2 (mimeo).
[23]U. S. House of Representatives, Committee on ways and means, *Background Material on the Federal Budget and the President's Proposals for Fiscal Year 1994* (Washington, DC: Government Printing Office, 1993), pp. 71, 82.

ets with surpluses rather than deficits and continuing to pay down the national debt have made some forget about the budget woes of recent past. Despite recent surpluses, however, it is crucial to have these rules in place for handling less rosy economic forecasts that could always be lurking around the corner.

Almost no one is satisfied with the procedures for considering and passing a budget. Elected officials and their staffs spend inordinate amounts of time dealing with budget issues. Congress has missed budget deadlines, government agencies have sometimes closed down temporarily for lack of spending authority, and the deficit continues. Critics wonder, "Is this any way to run a government?" Efforts to tinker with existing procedures will continue, and proposals for new ones are inevitable.[24] However, the tinkering with procedures is a symptom of a deeper political problem. Continuing entitlement programs at current levels, reducing the debt, and avoiding both tax increases and deep cuts in general government spending cannot all be achieved simultaneously. Such budgetary pressures have placed obvious strains on procedures for deciding budget policy. Ultimately, those pressures and strains emerge from the intense political resistance to spending cuts or tax increases. As President Bush's budget proposals illustrate, harnessing wants with available resources remains the quintessential challenge to government in the 2000s.

---

[24]For a summary discussion of budget process reforms, see Rudolph G. Penner and Alan J. Abramson, *Broken Purse Strings: Congressional Budgeting 1974 to 1988* (Washington, DC: Urban Institute, 1988), pp. 109–129.

SUMMARY

1. Conflict over economic policy has been at or near the top of the political agenda throughout American history. Government makes two major types of economic policy: fiscal and monetary. Fiscal policy assesses the impact on the economy as a whole of governmental decisions to tax, spend, and borrow; monetary policy concerns the availability and cost of money and credit in the economy.

2. Budget deficits, the dominant economic policy issue Congress and the president faced in for much of the past few decades, can be reduced by cutting expenditures, increasing taxes, or some combination of these two strategies. Payments for individuals comprise the largest category in the national budget. The cost of borrowing money has become a significant national expenditure. Much of the budget is comprised of mandatory spending.

3. Given the decentralization of power in the political system, no single individual or group alone can decide the size and shape of the budget. The

president has the power to make budget proposals, but money can be spent only after Congress reviews and revises those proposals and enacts them into law. Deficits persist despite procedural changes. Continuing calls to revise procedures are a consequence of the collision between the necessity to impose constraints and the political resistance to spending cuts or tax increases.

KEY TERMS

economic policy (411)

laissez-faire (412)

socialism (412)

recession (412)

depression (412)

protectionism (414)

free trade (414)

fiscal policy (414)

monetary policy (415)

Office of Management and Budget (415)

deficit (416)

debt (416)

surplus (416)

net interest (423)

incrementalism (423)

mandatory programs (424)

social entitlements (424)

budget (425)

fiscal year (426)

authorization (431)

appropriation (431)

line-item veto (431)

balanced budget amendment (432)

continuing resolution (433)

Congressional Budget and Impoundment Control Act of 1974 (433)

Congressional Budget Office (433)

Gramm-Rudman-Hollings (434)

sequestration (434)

Budget Enforcement Act of 1990 (434)

READINGS FOR FURTHER STUDY

For a thorough understanding of economic policy-making, there is no better starting point than a good text on economics, such as Paul A. Samuelson and William D. Nordhaus's *Economics*, 16th ed. (New York: McGraw Hill, 1998).

Analyses of current economic problems, along with an excellent compendium of useful economic data, are found in the *Economic Report of the President*, written by the president's Council of Economic Advisors, and available online at: http://w3 .access.gpo.gov/eop/.

Comprehensive information on the budget can be found in a document the Office of Management and Budget produces each year as the president submits his budget to Congress. *The Budget of the United States Government* contains extensive analysis of budgetary issues, detailed personnel and budgetary data for each agency in the government, and a variety of historical tables. The Congressional Budget Office also issues periodic reports that analyze the president's proposals, assess the state of the economy, and offer Congress spending and revenue options to reduce the deficit.

Aaron Wildavsky and Naomi Caiden's *The New Politics of the Budgetary Process*, 4th ed. (New York: Addison Wesley, 2000) is a superb analysis of the political environment of budgeting and the enormous changes that have taken place since Wildavsky first wrote on the topic in 1964.

An updated look at the budgetary rules and politics is *The Federal Budget: Politics, Policy, and Process*, rev. ed. (Washington, DC: Brookings, 2000) by Allen Schick with Felix LoStracco.

Two good recent texts focusing on economic policy are James J. Gosling's *Politics and the American Economy* (New York: Longman, 2000), and Jeffrey E. Cohen's *Politics and Economic Policy in the United States*, 2nd ed. (Boston: Houghton Mifflin, 2000).

Finally, *This War Really Matters*, by George C. Wilson (Washington, DC: CQ Press, 2000) is an inside look at the budget battles over defense spending in recent years.

CHAPTER 15

Domestic Policy

A/P World Wide

Chapter Objectives

Americans typically divide the substance of public policy into two categories—foreign and domestic. While foreign policy will be the focus of the next chapter, here we will explore a few of the thousands of domestic policies the American government enacts each year. In the 2003 fiscal year, domestic programs accounted for $1.5 trillion in government spending. As explained in the previous chapter, much of this money (over two-thirds) is committed to non-discretionary programs, such as social security, that have grown and changed incrementally over a long period of time. Some of the financial commitment, though, such as recent pilot programs in school vouchers, is dedicated to new and developing programs. Thus, on an annual basis, Americans must face tough decisions about which programs to expand and which to abandon, when to continue with an existing approach and when to change course, and when to embark on something entirely new.

Since we cannot address the entire gamut of domestic policies in the space of a single chapter, we will focus on two significant policy areas and explore them in detail. First, social welfare programs will be examined. Ranging from mandatory entitlements that benefit everyone directly, such as social security, to need-based efforts which are targeted at specific segments of society, such as welfare, these programs aim to ameliorate economic inequality. Second, this chapter will address environmental policy. As the human population continues to grow and consume resources, Americans will be faced with more and more challenges in our effort to devise a sustainable environmental policy that provides for the needs of human, plant, and animal ecosystems.

Debates over Public Purposes

Differences over what government should do beyond protection of the nation against external threat and protection of individual citizens from each other are at the core of political conflict. Should the government fund programs for farmers, for the elderly, for the poor? Should the government subsidize the work of defense contractors, universities, and medical researchers? Should the government give aid to the middle class in the form of favorable tax policies and pensions?

Over the past century, enormous changes in the role of government have produced new relationships between the government and citizens. How these changes occur is an important issue in the analysis of policies. What government should do, who should gain the benefits of government action, and who should pay the costs are common questions in policy debate.

As explained in the policy process chapter, new demands and new issues get on the policy agenda in a variety of ways. Changes in the social and economic environment produce new groups and new problems and, consequently, new issues. Industrialization, the rise of corporations, and the emergence of a national economy shaped the post-Civil War period. The resulting stresses and strains changed relationships among groups who then resorted to the government for help. Crisis can also indelibly change the policy agenda. The Great Depression in the 1930s so threatened the nation's political and social institutions that the government enacted welfare and regulatory policies radically different from those of the past.

Debate over the appropriate role of the government frequently begins in the perceptions of *self-interest* of various groups and individuals. Farmers want help in their battles against falling agricultural prices. Consumers want help in their battles against shoddy or dangerous products. The elderly want help in the economic uncertainties of retirement. Corporations want help in their battles against competitors.

Through political parties, the mass media, and political interest groups, demands for help are made on government institutions. In the process, self-interest is frequently cloaked in the mantle of *the national interest*. That is, groups often claim that what is good for them is really good for the nation. Determining whether groups are right in such claims is the substance of much political debate. Since most politicians desire reelection, they do their best to satisfy (or even create) demands that the government provide help. These demands are frequently in intractable conflict. Somebody must pay for farm programs, retirement pensions, and food stamps. Conflicts between the houses of Congress or between Congress and the president reflect these struggles.

Yet policies are not always the precise result of a collision of differing perceptions of self-interest. Some groups in and out of government favor certain policies because they are "right" and "fair." For example, the poor and the destitute lack the resources to exercise their economic claims on government. The idea that the government provide needy citizens with life's basic necessities has a powerful appeal and political support that goes beyond self-interest.

Social Welfare Policies

social welfare

Governmental programs, such as social insurance and poverty programs, directed specifically toward promoting the well-being of individuals and families.

The expression **social welfare** has no precise definition. It is burdened by the unfavorable connotations frequently attached to the word *welfare*. To some, welfare simply means public money given to people whose desire to live off the public dole is greater than their desire to work for a living. However, within this category of social welfare policy are a large number of public programs serving heterogeneous groups of people. The Census Bureau defines the concept of social welfare as "all governmental programs directed specifically toward promoting the well-being of individuals and families."[1] This definition catches within its net a large number of programs. The breadth of the concept signals the ranging presence of a government in the lives of citizens.

The data in Table 15.1 illustrate the growth of government social welfare spending since the start of the Great Depression. In 1929 government at all levels spent less than 4 percent of the gross national product on social welfare programs. By the 1990s this proportion had quintupled to just over one-fifth of GDP. At 9.8 percent, social insurance programs alone (including Social Security, Medicare, and unemployment compensation) constitute the largest category of social welfare spending. Education programs, the second largest category, are primarily the responsibility of state and local governments. Public aid, comprised of programs intended for the poor, such as food stamps and Medicaid, is the third largest category. These are means-tested programs and are discussed later in this chapter. Recipients qualify for support only if their income is below a certain level. Social insurance and public aid comprise **social entitlements**, which are programs in which individuals receive benefits they are entitled to by law.

social entitlements

Programs, such as Social Security and Medicaid, whereby eligible individuals receive benefits according to law.

Social insurance alone accounts for almost half of all social welfare expenditures. Social insurance, education, and public aid combined account for about 88 percent of total social welfare spending, while veterans', medical and health, housing, and other programs make up the rest. A review of how the national government became so heavily committed to providing social welfare offers insights on how issues move onto the policy agenda.

The Development of Federal Social Welfare Policy

At the beginning of the Republic in the late eighteenth century, the national government was miniscule. The pervasive presence of the national government at the beginning of the twenty-first century symbolizes the drastic changes in the relationship between government

---

[1]U.S. Bureau of the Census, *Historical Statistics of the United States: Colonial Times to 1970*, vol. 1 (Washington, DC: GPO, 1975), p. 332.

TABLE 15.1

Gross Domestic Product and Social Welfare Expenditures, 1929–1995

In 1929, government at all levels spent less than 4 percent of GNP on social welfare programs. By the mid-1990s, government social welfare spending accounted for more than 20 percent of GDP. The largest category of social welfare spending is comprised of federal social insurance programs, followed by education and public aid. Social welfare spending as a percentage of GDP gives an indication of how much society's total output of goods and services is devoted to these programs.

SOURCES: For 1929 and 1940, Social Security Administration. Data for 1950 and 1960 are taken from Social Security Administration, *Social Security Bulletin: Annual Statistical Supplement, 1990* (Washington, DC: GPO, 1990), p. 100. All other data are from Social Security Administration, *Annual Statistical Supplement, 2001 to the Social Security Bulletin*, (Washington, DC: GPO, 2001), p. 134.

	1929		1940		1950		1960	
Gross national product (GNP)	101,000	(100)	95,100	(100)	266,800	(100)	506,700	(100)
Total welfare	3,921	(3.9)	8,795	(9.2)	23,508	(8.8)	52,293	(10.3)
Social insurance	342	(0.3)	1,272	(1.3)	4,947	(1.7)	19,307	(3.8)
Education	2,434	(2.4)	2,561	(2.7)	6,674	(2.5)	17,626	(3.5)
Public aid	60	(0.1)	3,597	(3.8)	2,496	(0.9)	4,101	(0.8)
Health and medical programs	351	(0.3)	616	(0.6)	2,064	(0.8)	4,464	(0.9)
Veterans' programs	658	(0.6)	629	(0.7)	6,866	(2.6)	5,479	(1.1)
Housing	—		4*		15*		177*	
Other social welfare	76	(0.1)	116	(0.1)	448	(0.2)	1,139	(0.2)

	1970		1980		1990		1995	
Gross domestic product (GDP)	1,023,100	(100)	2,718,900	(100)	5,682,900	(100)	7,186,900	(100)
Total welfare	145,979	(14.3)	492,213	(18.1)	1,048,951	(18.5)	1,505,136	(20.9)
Social insurance	54,691	(5.3)	229,754	(8.5)	513,822	(9.0)	705,483	(9.8)
Education	50,846	(5.0)	121,050	(4.5)	258,332	(4.5)	365,625	(5.1)
Public aid	16,488	(1.6)	72,703	(2.7)	146,811	(2.6)	253,530	(3.5)
Health and medical programs	10,030	(1.0)	26,762	(1.0)	61,684	(1.1)	85,507	(1.2)
Veterans' programs	9,078	(0.9)	21,466	(0.8)	30,916	(0.5)	39,072	(0.5)
Housing	701	(0.1)	6,879	(0.3)	19,468	(0.3)	29,361	(0.4)
Other social welfare	4,145	(0.4)	13,599	(0.5)	17,918	(0.3)	26,558	(0.4)

Note: All monetary amounts are in millions. Percent of GNP/GDP appears in parentheses. Figures prior to 1970 measure Gross Nation Product rather than Gross Domestic Product.
*less than 0.05 percent

and individuals over the past 200 years. Such changes did not come gradually. Rather, the national government's presence grew in relatively short bursts of activity resulting in an ever-larger government that maintained its size in succeeding decades.

The domestic activities of the national government before the twentieth century were relatively limited. There were no Social Security programs, no health programs such as Medicare and Medicaid, no unemployment compensation programs, no food stamp programs, no poverty programs, and no programs to meet the special needs of the elderly or of individuals with disabilities. There were no public programs to help nineteenth century factory workers who lost their jobs or were disabled or to help families who lost a breadwinner. The national government taxed relatively little, spent relatively little, and did relatively little. It was, consequently, a shadow rather than an omnipresent force in the daily lives of most citizens. Today a widely held expectation is that the national government should assume major responsibilities for social welfare. However, this contemporary expectation contrasts sharply with political attitudes dominant a century ago.

The Philosophy of Social Darwinism

social Darwinism

A set of ideas applying Charles Darwin's theory of biological evolution to society and holding that social relationships occur within a struggle for survival in which only the fittest survive.

The dominant philosophy that shaped attitudes on the role of government in the late nineteenth century was **social Darwinism**, a set of ideas that applied Charles Darwin's theory of biological evolution to society. Darwin's theory held that physical changes in living organisms evolved as responses to the demands of survival and that organisms that adapted most successfully to their environments were most likely to survive. The theory of social Darwinism held that social relationships took place within a "struggle for survival" and that in this struggle only the "most fit" survive. Just as living organisms evolved to higher states, so too does society as a whole progress to a higher state as natural selection proceeds.

The theory seemed to offer intellectual justification for limited government and the unfettered growth and expansion of big industry and business in the late nineteenth century.[2] Since society could best progress to higher forms through its natural processes of competition and survival with no outside interference, government should not act on behalf of those too weak to survive on their own. Herbert Spencer, a British philosopher whose name is closely associated with social Darwinism, argued that government should limit itself to protecting the rights of individuals to pursue their own ends. In this view, government should not assume the role of providing for social welfare because such action would interfere with natural forces acting to improve society as a whole.[3]

The Progressive Era

Social Darwinism as a set of ideas about society and the role of government was dominant in the generation after the Civil War. Rapid urbanization, nationalization of the economy, and bigness in industry meant an end to the relative self-sufficiency individuals enjoyed in a less complicated agricultural society. The concentration of large numbers of people in urban areas strained the ability of local governments to provide

---

[2]Richard Hofstadter, *Social Darwinism in American Thought*, rev. ed. (Boston: Beacon Press, 1955), p. 44.
[3]Herbert Spencer, *Social Statics* (London: 1851; New York: Augustus M. Kelley, 1969), p. 323. For a review of the criticisms of social Darwinism, see Hofstadter, *Social Darwinism*, especially pp. 200–204.

essential services and bred a variety of social problems such as poverty and inadequate housing. Increasingly large and faceless companies provided goods and services to consumers who had little power to influence corporate decisions. Similarly, the availability of jobs and the quality of the work environment were matters over which workers had little control.

Such conditions gave rise to questions about the consequences of unfettered free enterprise. The limited role that government played at all levels increasingly became a matter of policy debate. It was in this environment of rapid social and economic change that reform movements began. This period of reform, named the **Progressive Era** by historians, generally spanned the last decade of the nineteenth century and the years of the twentieth century before World War I.

Progressive public policy goals included the replacement of corrupt politics by civil service systems, the regulation of monopolies, and the protection of consumers against unsafe products. Progressives also pressed for a more substantive role for government in aiding specific groups who suffered from rapid industrialism.[4] Most of the initiatives for such social welfare legislation came at the state rather than the national level. But laws on minimum wages, worker's compensation, and pensions all directly countered the social Darwinist view that government ought to play a minimal role in social and economic relationships. Progressive efforts at the state level to redress the economic and social imbalances created by rapid industrialization and urbanization laid the groundwork for the revolutionary change in the national government role that was to come.

The New Deal Policy Revolution

The **New Deal** spanned the first two terms of President Franklin D. Roosevelt (1933–1945). His revolutionary initiatives established the pervasive and active national government role taken for granted today.

The easy tranquility of the national government during the 1920s was exploded by the Great Depression, a period of massive and severe economic hardship that rivaled the Civil War in its cataclysmic impact on the nation's political institutions. Banks failed, companies went bankrupt, home and farm mortgages were foreclosed, industrial production plummeted, and unemployment soared. Millions of people lost jobs, homes, and bank accounts, with the attendant social misery such losses inevitably bring.[5] There were few government programs to cushion the shock of this economic disaster. Whatever government programs existed (almost entirely at the state and local level) were simply overwhelmed by the sharp and sweeping economic decline. In responding to the economic crisis of the Great Depression, the national government for the first time assumed the active and extensive role now so much expected.

Progressive Era

An urban reform movement of the late nineteenth and early twentieth centuries that called for direct primaries, restriction on corporations, and improved public services. Influential in the administrations of Theodore Roosevelt and Woodrow Wilson.

New Deal

The first two terms of President Franklin D. Roosevelt (1933–1945), whose revolutionary policy initiatives established a pervasive and active role for the national government.

---

[4]Richard Hofstadter, *The Age of Reform* (New York: Knopf, 1955), p. 240.
[5]See William E. Leuchtenburg, *The Perils of Prosperity, 1914–32,* 2nd ed. (Chicago: University of Chicago Press, 1993).

The Depression's impact on the public policy agenda was clear and unmistakable. Roosevelt was determined to take immediate and forceful action to bolster the nation's confidence in the government's ability to deal with the crisis. On the day after his inauguration as president, Roosevelt called Congress into special session, "convened in an atmosphere of wartime crisis." Congress gave every indication of wanting to be led, and the president accommodated this desire by sending to Capitol Hill a flurry of proposals for action. By the end of the special session, the famous "100 days," Congress passed every one of Roosevelt's 15 proposals.[6]

Enacted during the New Deal were the insurance of bank deposits by the Federal Deposit Insurance Corporation, Social Security for the aged, unemployment compensation, and minimum-wage and maximum-hours requirements. Designed to relieve the suffering of practically every social group touched by the Depression, these programs are all now embedded in the policy role of government. Public *expectations* that government "do something" about social and economic problems flowered during the Roosevelt presidency. An interlocking relationship between heightened public demands and government efforts to meet those demands developed. Government in Washington would no longer be distant, relaxed, and indifferent.

Expansion of the National Role in the Great Society

The New Deal firmly established the national government as the most important participant in ensuring the social and economic welfare of individuals. During subsequent decades major New Deal programs such as Social Security, federal insurance for bank deposits, and unemployment compensation have been changed in incremental steps, but the existence of such programs is no longer seriously debated.

Great Society

President Lyndon Johnson's term for an egalitarian society that aggressive governmental action to help the poor and disadvantaged would create in the 1960s.

The next period of major change in the role of the national government occurred during the **Great Society** of Lyndon Johnson's presidency (1963–1969). Johnson assumed office after the assassination of President John F. Kennedy in November 1963, an event that seared the nation nearly as much as the attack on Pearl Harbor in 1941. National grief turned into popular support for proposals that Johnson pressed as unfinished business of the slain president. This support combined with Johnson's landslide victory over conservative Barry Goldwater and huge gains by the Democratic party in Congress in 1964 to produce fertile ground for further growth of the national government role.

The Civil Rights Act of 1964 and the Voting Rights Act of 1965 finally provided by law rights long denied to African Americans. The Equal Opportunity Act and the Food Stamp Act of 1964 explicitly dealt with the plight of poor Americans. The Elementary and Secondary Education Act of 1964 provided federal aid for the disadvantaged in the nation's schools. And perhaps the most significant change in the social welfare role of the

---

[6]William F. Leuchtenburg, *Franklin D. Roosevelt and the New Deal* (New York: Harper & Row, 1963), pp. 43, 61.

national government was amendment of the Social Security Act in 1965 to provide health care for the aged (Medicare) and the poor (Medicaid).

The Great Society was the last major period in which the national government embarked on new social welfare initiatives. Growing budget deficits and foreign policy concerns, coupled with the election of conservative leaders such as Nixon, Reagan, and the two Bushes, made continued expansion of social welfare programs both unpopular and unlikely. In fact, by the mid-1990s efforts to reduce the scope of the federal role emerged. Most notably, attempts to reduce federal domestic spending focused on a restructuring of social insurance programs, which are described in the next section.

The National Government as Social Insurer

The principal consequence of the New Deal policy revolution is that the national government has assumed a major responsibility for the social welfare of individuals who are old, disabled, or unemployed. Rather than relying on private charities or state and local programs, people are, in effect, *insured* by the national government against the potentially harsh social and economic consequences that old age, disability, and unemployment can bring.

social insurance programs

Welfare programs that provide cash or services to the aged, the disabled, and the unemployed, regardless of income level.

A significant feature of **social insurance programs** is that they serve all eligible people, regardless of income levels. To be sure, millions of individuals would fall into officially defined poverty in the absence of these programs, but the receipt of social insurance benefits is not dependent on income. An elderly person need not be poor to receive Social Security benefits, and people who have lost relatively high-paying jobs can be eligible for unemployment compensation. The beneficiaries of social insurance programs are individuals from practically all income levels, a fact that helps to explain the staunch political support on which these programs rest.

Social Security

Social Security Act of 1935

Landmark legislation enacted in 1935 that firmly established for the first time a social welfare role for the national government by providing old age insurance, unemployment compensation, and grants to the states to provide cash assistance to dependent children and to the blind, disabled, and aged.

The **Social Security Act of 1935** was probably the most significant piece of domestic legislation ever enacted. Passed in the New Deal, the act provided for a system of old age insurance financed by taxes on workers and employers, a program of compensation for the unemployed jointly administered by the national and state governments, and a variety of categorical grants to the states to provide cash assistance to dependent children and to the blind, disabled, and aged. The 1935 act has been amended many times, but it is significant because it firmly established for the first time a social welfare role for the national government.

Administered by the Social Security Administration in the Department of Health and Human Services, "Social Security" is really a bundle of separate programs rather than a single one. Within the Social Security umbrella are insurance programs for retired workers and their spouses (old age insurance), survivors of retired workers (survivors' insurance), and individuals with disabilities and their dependents (disability insurance). The total package is generally known by the acronym *OASDI* (old age, survivors', and disability insurance). The evolution of these programs is a classic example of **incrementalism**, a process through which policies once established are changed piecemeal over time. The number of workers covered, the amount of benefits, and the level of payroll taxes to pay for these Social Security programs have changed incrementally (they have all increased) over the past half-century.

incrementalism

A model of decision making that holds that new policies differ only marginally from existing policies.

Elderly woman using the new card that replaces traditional paper food stamps. *(AP Wide World)*

In terms of expenditures, number of people receiving benefits, number of workers covered, and intensity of political support, the Social Security umbrella of programs is the national government's largest and single most important domestic policy. The old age, survivors', and disability insurance programs alone consumed more than 22 percent of all federal expenditures in fiscal 2002. More than 45 million people are OASDI beneficiaries. Benefits vary for different groups and are indexed to increase each year, but in 2001 retired workers received an average monthly benefit of about $878.[7] Figure 15.1 offers clues on the economic importance of Social Security to older Americans. Social Security benefits as a proportion of income rise as people get older and are the largest source of income for Americans over the age of 65, facts that help explain the potent political support for the program.

In the original 1935 act, only workers in commerce and industry were insured. But in classic incremental fashion, other occupational groups, including self-employed farmers, military personnel, self-employed professionals, and even the president and vice-president of the United States and members of Congress, have been progressively brought into the system. Coverage is now practically compulsory. Virtually every worker and employer in the United States must pay a payroll tax to fund the program.

These statistics suggest the potentially volatile political consequences that any change in Social Security can have. Practically no one can avoid being touched by the

[7]Social Security Administration, *Fast Facts & Figures About Social Security,* June 2002.

FIGURE 15.1

Shares of Income for the Older Population, 2000

Older Americans rely heavily on Social Security income. Social Security benefits are the principal source of income for Americans over the age of 65.

SOURCES: Social Security Administration, *Income of the Population 55 and OLDER, 2000* (Washington, DC: Social Security Administration, 2001).

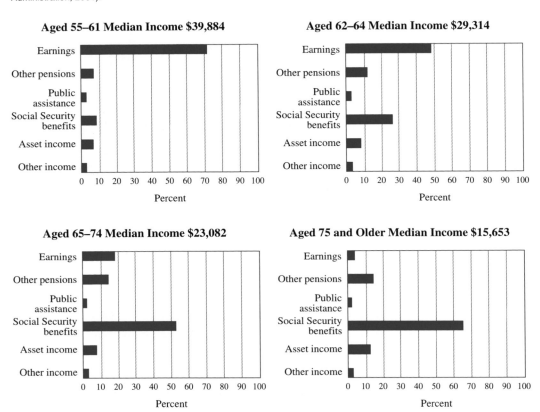

program in some tangible and specific way, either by receiving welcome benefit checks or by paying unwelcome taxes. The potential for intergenerational conflict in such a system is obvious. Younger workers may resent what they consider an increasingly rapacious payroll tax bite for a program that, they wonder, may not even still be in existence when they retire. Retired workers may view the program differently. Since they paid taxes into the system during their working years, they feel they are simply getting back in benefits what they rightly deserve. Given the very scope of the program, its crucial importance to so many people, and the potential for group conflicts, presidents and members of Congress pondering program changes are in a political mine field.

By the late 1970s and early 1980s it had become clear that major changes were essential if the program was to survive. Projections showed that expenditures (benefits) would soon exceed revenues (payroll taxes). A declining birth rate and a longer life expectancy meant that the number of retirees (beneficiaries) was growing faster than the number of workers paying taxes to fund the program. In addition, increases in benefit levels caused by inflation outpaced revenues.

The political consequences of the Social Security system "going broke" were too horrendous to contemplate. Unlike means-tested programs (to be discussed shortly) for which only lower-income people qualify, almost everyone expects to benefit directly from Social Security. This fact gives Social Security a political base far broader than that enjoyed by any means-tested welfare policy.

As a result of such concerns, the future of Social Security has been an almost constant topic on the American political scene for the past two decades. In the 1980s adjustments—such as raising the payroll tax rate and gradually increasing the retirement age—were made to insure solvency in the system as baby boomers began to approach retirement age. During the 1990s issues fluctuated between fears that the system would run out of money and concerns that the system's surplus funds were being used inappropriately. By the 2000 presidential election both major party candidates found themselves making pledges to assure the security of the Social Security system. One recent proposal suggests turning over control of at least part of the systems funds to individual contributors to manage as they see fit. This would make Social Security function more like a private pension plan. Such proposals are tempting because they offer contributors greater control; individuals could choose to invest in high yielding securities, for example. They are also hazardous, because high rates of return tend to be accompanied by higher risks as well. During economic downturns, pension plans often take a hard financial hit.

Medicare

The second major social insurance policy of the national government is Medicare, a program enacted in the Great Society in 1965 and administered by the Centers for Medicare and Medicaid Services in the Department of Health and Human Services. **Medicare** is essentially a public health insurance program for the elderly and disabled. Rather than providing cash benefits to individuals like other Social Security programs, Medicare pays the providers of health care (hospitals, physicians, and other health professionals) for services given to patients who are aged, disabled, or afflicted with terminal kidney disease. More than 40 million people are now insured by the program. In the past, the elderly and Americans with disabilities who were in need of medical care relied on families, private insurance plans, or the help of charities or friends—or, they went without medical care. However, Medicare has become a major source of health care funding for the elderly and disabled. In fiscal 2002 the national government spent an estimated $223 billion on Medicare, or almost 11 percent of total federal expenditures.

Medicare is a program with two parts. Part A is Hospital Insurance (HI), funded by a portion of the Social Security tax paid into a hospital trust fund. After a patient pays

Medicare

A public health insurance program in which government pays the providers of health care for medical services given to patients who are aged or disabled.

a deductible, Medicare covers hospital costs for two months, with patients sharing costs after that period. Part B of the program is Supplementary Medical Insurance (SMI); after the patient pays a deductible amount, SMI funds physician and outpatient services. SMI, which is voluntary, is funded by premiums paid by enrollees and general revenues from the federal treasury.[8]

Medicare was enacted after a bitter political struggle in which opponents of the measure argued that health insurance was "socialized medicine" and unwarranted interference in the relationship between patients and physicians. But providing health care for the elderly and people with disabilities has proved to be a highly popular program. Still, assumption of a major medical insurance role by the national government has inevitably created policy debates over costs—how high they should be and who should pay them. Efforts to ensure the financial soundness of Medicare are complicated by rising medical costs. Congress has attempted to control expenditures by placing ceilings on some of the medical costs the program will pay and by offering financial incentives to hospitals to keep costs low.

The original Medicare plan has been supplemented with additional coverage areas over the past few decades. One area in which many Americans would like to see the program expand is prescription drug coverage for the elderly. The rising costs of prescription drugs have placed a particularly large burden on the elderly, many of whom have modest incomes and require multiple long-term prescriptions. As a first step in the direction of coverage, the Bush administration developed a Medicare-Endorsed Prescription Drug Card Initiative—a plan that would allow Medicare beneficiaries to obtain prescription drugs at lower costs.[9]

Unemployment Compensation

unemployment compensation

A social insurance policy that grants temporary financial assistance to the unemployed.

A third major social insurance policy is **unemployment compensation, a** program of temporary financial assistance for the unemployed first enacted in the original Social Security Act of 1935 and administered by the states with the Office of Workforce Security in the Department of Labor. Massive unemployment was one of the severe economic and social problems that sparked the assumption of a much greater social welfare role by government in the Great Depression. The problem obviously continues, for changes in the economy and the decline of some industries mean that official unemployment rates exceeding 5 percent are not unusual.

One of the most significant public policy changes in the past half-century is that unemployed workers now receive cash benefits for a short period of time while they seek other employment. As foreign competition and changes in the international econ-

---

[8]For details on the program, see the Medicare web site, located at http://www.medicare.gov/.
[9]Centers for Medicare and Medicaid Services, "HHS Issues Final Regulation on Medicare-Endorsed Prescription Drug Card Initiative," 30 August 2002, http://cms.hhs.gov/media/press/release.asp?Counter=486 (9 October 2002).

omy have racked their industries, for example, unemployed steel and auto workers have been beneficiaries of the program. Unemployment compensation is designed not for the chronically unemployed but for those who need financial assistance to keep afloat between jobs. Employers are taxed by both the national and state governments to pay for the benefits and the administrative costs of the program. Eligibility requirements and benefit levels vary among the states. In general, an unemployed person receives weekly checks for a period of up to 26 weeks and up to 13 additional weeks in states where unemployment rates are particularly high.

Public Policy and Economic Inequality

In addition to social insurance, the second major category of social welfare policy at the national level is comprised of programs explicitly designed to aid the poor. Table 15.2 offers a summary portrait of both types of programs. Each of these two categories of programs serves different groups of people and is shaped by different kinds of political pressures. In general, social insurance programs tend to be the larger of the two types in terms of the number of beneficiaries and the amount of money spent. Given their broader constituencies, these programs also tend to receive much stronger political support.

means-tested program

Type of social welfare program in which government provides cash or in-kind benefits to individuals who qualify by having little or no income.

Programs specifically intended for the poor—and only the poor—are known as **means-tested programs** because the receipt of benefits is completely dependent on income level. Under these programs, individuals receive benefits only if they qualify by having little or no income. Unlike social insurance, beneficiaries of means-tested programs do not pay money into the programs before they receive benefits. Small children whose parents have little or no income and the chronically unemployed are among the beneficiaries of such programs.

Measures of Economic Inequality

Political equality amid sharp economic inequality remains one of the great ironies of the American experience. Economic inequality is a fact of life supported by even casual observation. Differences in the clothes people wear, the food they eat, the entertainments they pursue, the cars they buy, and the houses they live in all suggest great differences in economic status. One familiar measure of income disparity is a division of families into five groups (or quintiles) according to the proportion of total money income each group receives.

Perfect income equality would mean that each fifth of the population of families receives 20 percent of all money income—that each quintile of families receives an equal slice of the money pie. However, great income inequality persists. Table 15.3 shows that the lowest fifth of families received just 3.5 percent of aggregate income in

TABLE 15.2
Major Social Welfare Programs

Social insurance and means-tested programs are major categories of social welfare programs. *Social insurance programs* are generally funded by specific taxes and have the retired, the aged, individuals with disabilities, and the unemployed as their beneficiaries. *Means-tested programs* are designed for needy individuals, are funded by general revenues, and usually involve the states in their administration

Program	Date Enacted	Benefits	Funding Sources	Estimated Programs Costs in Billions, 2002
Social Insurance Social Security (Old age, survivors', and disability insurance)	1935	Monthly checks for retired and disabled workers, their dependents, and survivors of retired workers	Social Security tax, paid by workers and employers	$456
Medicare	1965	Medical care for aged and disabled	Social Security tax, premiums paid by beneficiaries, general revenues	223
Unemployment compensation	1935	Weekly checks for short-term unemployed workers	State and national taxes on employers	49
Means-tested Programs Temporary Assistance for Needy Families	1935	Monthly checks for needy children and parents	National and state general revenues	24
Supplemental Security Income	1972	Monthly cash payments for needy aged, blind, and disabled	National general revenues and state supplements	32
Medicaid	1965	Medical care for needy individuals and families	National and state general revenues	145
Food stamps	1964	Monthly food coupons for needy individuals and families	National general revenues and some state funds	15

*Social insurance and Medicaid data from OMB. TANF data from Administration for Children and Families (FY 2000 figures). SSI and Food Stamps data from the Social Security Administration (FY 2000 figures). Relevant figures include state funding.

2001, while the highest fifth received just over 50 percent in the same year. The table also shows that the lowest three-fifths of families have lost ground, from a combined 32 percent of aggregate income in 1971 to 26.8 percent in 2001. In the same period the highest fifth increased aggregate income from 43.5 to 501 percent. A domestic policy question is the degree to which such growing income inequality will develop into a trenchant political issue in the twenty first century.

Another measure of economic inequality is the proportion of the total population classified as poor in the United States. The term *poverty* is a human construct that does not have the same meaning in all societies. People are poor according to some eco-

TABLE 15.3

Aggregate Family Income by Quintiles

In the years between 1971 and 2001, the bottom four quintiles of families received a declining share of aggregate income, while the top quintile increased their share of aggregate income.

SOURCE: U.S. Census Bureau, *Money Income in the United States: 2001* (Washington, DC: GPO, 2002), p. 19.

	1971	1981	1991	2001
Lowest fifth	4.1%	4.2%	3.8%	3.5%
Second fifth	10.6	10.2	9.6	8.7
Third fifth	17.3	16.8	15.9	14.6
Fourth fifth	24.5	25.0	24.2	23.0
Highest fifth	43.5	43.8	46.5	50.1
Top 5 percent	16.7	15.6	18.1	22.4

relative deprivation

A definition of poverty that holds that individuals with less, regardless of their absolute income level, will feel poor or deprived relative to those who have more.

nomic standard against which they are judged, and those standards may vary greatly across the planet. A poor family in America may have a consistent diet of rice and potatoes, but such a diet may be considered rich by those in nations who have little or no food at all.

The concept of **relative deprivation** indicates how variable definitions of poverty can be.[10] According to this concept, individuals with less money will feel poor or deprived relative to those who have more. Of course, the greater the material wealth in a particular society, the more likely individuals will feel poor if they do not possess material goods in the same degree as others in the society. The substantial political and economic obstacles to fundamental changes in the distribution of income suggest the persistence of poverty defined relatively.

Another approach consists of some absolute standard below which individuals can be defined as poor. The United States government has constructed a standard to measure the extent of poverty and its changes over time. Based on a Department of Agriculture finding on how much families spend on food, the Social Security Administration in 1964 established a **poverty threshold**—an income level below which individuals are defined as poor. That income level is different for families of different sizes and changes each year with changes in the consumer price index (CPI). By 2001 the average poverty threshold for a family of four was $18,104. Families with money income below this level are defined as poor.

poverty threshold

Income level, different by family size and annually adjusted for inflation, below which individuals are defined by government as being poor.

Figure 15.2 shows the number of poor people in the United States between 1960 and 2001 on the basis of this poverty threshold. In 1960 almost 40 million people, or

---

[10]See Edward C. Banfield, *The Unheavenly City Revisited* (Prospect Heights, IL: Waveland Press, reissue 1990), pp. 129–130.

22.2 percent of the total population were defined as poor. Both the absolute number and the proportion of poor people declined until the early 1970s, before rising again in the 1980s and 1990s. In 2001 there were nearly 33 million poor people in America. At 11.7 percent, the proportion of Americans who were poor in 2001 was at one of the lowest rates since the 1970s.

Like almost all other social measures, the official definition of poverty has been subject to criticism. In particular, critics have charged that the income standard used by government overestimates the number of poor people. First, only money income (such as wages and cash benefits from government) is included in the standard. Not included are noncash benefits, such as food stamps, Medicare and Medicaid health benefits, and subsidized housing benefits, which many of the poor receive from the government. Counting such noncash benefits as income, critics argue, would greatly reduce the number of people officially defined as poor. On the other hand, when the Census Bureau makes adjustments for out-of-pocket costs, like those for medical care, the percentage of poor people shows an increase over the official measure, even when noncash benefits are included as income.[11]

---

[11]U.S. Census Bureau, *Poverty in the United States: 2001* (Washington, DC: GPO, 2002), p. 15.

FIGURE 15.2

Number and Proportion of Poor People in the United States, Selected Years, 1960–2001

Although the absolute number of poor people remains high, the percentage of poor in the population has been relatively low in recent years.

SOURCE: U.S. Census Bureau, *Poverty in the United States: 2001* (Washington, DC: GPO, 2002).

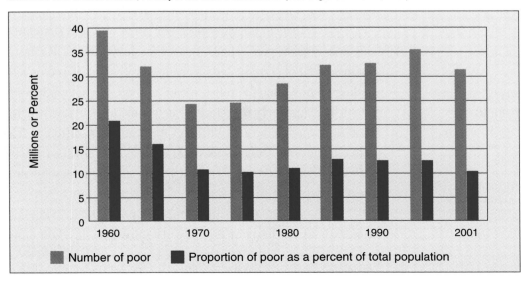

While aggregate numbers on poverty are open to criticism, no one questions the fact that poverty occurs disproportionately among different groups. Figure 15.3 displays poverty rates for selected groups in selected years since 1959. The graph shows that the poverty rate for whites tends to fall below the overall poverty rate, while the proportion of African Americans in poverty is consistently higher than the rate for the total population. The *absolute number* of whites in poverty exceeds the number of poor African Americans, but a higher *proportion* of the African American population is poor. In 1959 less than 20 percent of whites but more than 50 percent of African Americans were defined as poor. By 2001 less than 10 percent of whites but more than 20 percent of African Americans still fell below the poverty threshold. Persons identifying themselves as Hispanic or Latino have poverty rates higher than whites but slightly lower than African Americans. Poverty among children has fluctuated, but is consistently at a higher rate than among the population as a whole. The group that has experienced the most consistent positive gains over the past several decades is the elderly. Although this group has historically experienced poverty at above average rates, recently that trend has begun to reverse itself. Today, whites and the elderly are among the groups least likely to be poor.

FIGURE 15.3

Poverty Rates for Selected Groups, Selected years, 1959–2001

Although poverty rates are lower than they were in 1959, substantial differences among groups remain.

SOURCE: U.S. Census Bureau, *Poverty in the United States: 2001* (Washington, DC: GPO, 2002).

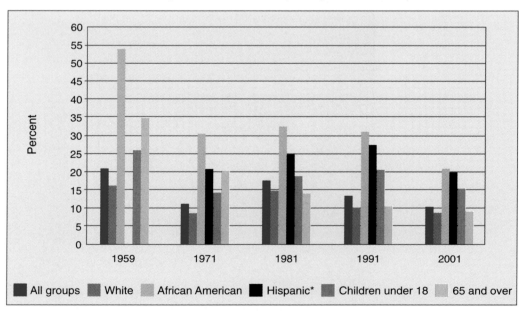

*Hispanic data was not available for 1959. The Hispanic data for the 1971 column is from 1972.

But, as Figure 15.3 indicates, poverty among children continues to exceed the overall poverty rate. The figure does not show that poverty rates differ among children of different races. The Census Bureau reports the startling fact that in 1989 more than two out of five (43.7 percent) African American children under the age of 18 were poor.

Poverty as a Political and Social Problem

Widespread poverty in a land of affluence has been a vexing political and social problem, especially since the national government assumed a massive social welfare role over a half-century ago. Economic inequality persists despite the huge sums of money spent by the national government over the past half-century to ameliorate economic distress among citizens in need. Why people are poor is an issue that has sometimes bitterly divided citizens, politicians, policy analysts, and academics. No single reason can adequately explain the existence of poverty among such a large number of people.

Social scientists have generally offered two sets of explanations for why people are poor. The first holds that people are poor because they lack *personal qualities,* such as ambition or intelligence, that make successful competition in the economic marketplace possible. A second explanation centers on the kind of social, economic, and cultural *environment* that is likely to be fertile ground for poverty. In this view, poverty is the result of, for example, the absence of a good education, a weak or crumbling family structure, disability, or the lack of job opportunities. Sorting out these distinctions is no easy task. As an example, continuing failure to find a job can weaken ambition to go on.

Homeless person sleeps on a bench. *(AP Wide World)*

The population of poor people in the United States is a constantly changing kaleidoscope, for individuals are falling into and climbing out of officially defined poverty from one year to the next. Personal crises, like the death of the family income-earner or loss of a job, can at least temporarily make some individuals poor. A rising unemployment rate increases the level of poverty, while falling unemployment has the opposite effect. Indeed, employment is no guarantee against poverty. In 2000 about 6.4 million Americans were classified as the **working poor.** These people worked or looked for work for at least half the year and yet were still officially defined as poor because their low earnings were not enough to pull their families above the poverty line.[12]

Some proportion of the poor are in what some poverty analysts call an **underclass,** comprised of individuals isolated from the rest of society and for whom poverty is a continuing way of life. Chronic unemployment, unstable family environments, welfare dependency, and a high incidence of crime are characteristics of underclass poverty. Whether the growth of the underclass can be attributed to systemic economic changes that have resulted in fewer blue collar jobs and more unemployment, or self-destructive behavior patterns among the underclass poor, or some combination of economic and behavioral factors, is an issue that reflects the general debate over the causes of poverty.[13]

Grappling with poverty in some way is the object of a range of government policies, including income transfer programs such as Social Security. But two categories of policy strategies illuminate government approaches. The first are **curative strategies** designed to get at the "root" causes of the problem, so that individuals can get out of poverty and lead productive, self-sufficient lives.[14] Expenditures on education, particularly targeted to the disadvantaged, are an example. In addition, employment training seeks to give individuals the skills necessary for a measure of economic success. Perhaps the most controversial example was the community action program of Lyndon Johnson's War on Poverty in the mid-1960s. That effort sought to involve the poor in initiating and coordinating local community efforts to combat poverty. The program began with the high hopes and optimism so characteristic of the Great Society, but political support evaporated when some local community action groups, in their efforts to exert political power, criticized what they saw as the insensitivity of elected officials.[15]

The second category of antipoverty strategies are **alleviative** in approach.[16] That is, they do not seek to cure poverty but simply to make it more bearable. Rather than trying to lift people out of poverty, such programs give cash or *in-kind* (noncash)

Margin glossary

working poor

Individuals who, despite being employed or seeking employment, are still defined as poor because their low earnings are not enough to put them above the poverty threshold.

underclass

A proportion of the poor comprised of individuals isolated from the rest of society and for whom poverty is a continuing way of life.

curative strategies

Policy strategies designed to reach the fundamental causes of poverty and to enable individuals to get out of poverty and lead productive, self-sufficient lives.

alleviative strategies

Policy strategies designed to make poverty more bearable for individuals rather than designed to attack poverty by reaching its fundamental causes.

---

[12]For more detail on the working poor, see U.S. Bureau of Labor Statistics, *A Profile of the Working Poor, 2000* (Washington, DC: GPO, 2002).

[13]See William Julius Wilson, *When Work Disappears: The World of the New Urban Poor* (New York: Vintage Books, 1997) and Herbert J. Gans, *The War Against the Poor: The Underclass and Antipoverty Policy* (New York: Basic Books, 1996).

[14]For a discussion of curative strategies, see Thomas R. Dye, *Understanding Public Policy,* 10th ed. (Englewood Cliffs, NJ: Prentice-Hall, 2002).

[15]For an interesting account of the community action program, see Daniel P. Moynihan, *Maximum Feasible Misunderstanding Community Action in the War on Poverty* (New York, Free Press, 1970).

[16]See Dye, *Understanding Public Policy.*

benefits to poor individuals or families to help keep them afloat financially. Various forms of housing assistance, the school lunch program, and emergency fuel assistance fall into this category. In terms of expenditures, these programs as a group make up the national government's principal policy strategy for dealing with poverty. Illustrations of major means-tested programs whose principal aim is the alleviation of poverty are discussed in the following sections.

Temporary Assistance for Needy Families

Temporary Assistance for Needy Families (TANF)

Social welfare program, administered by the states and jointly funded by state and national revenues, that provides cash assistance to needy children and an adult relative and, in participating states, an unemployed parent.

One of the oldest alleviative poverty programs at the national level is **Temporary Assistance for Needy Families (TANF)**, first enacted (under the name Aid to Families with Dependent Children) as part of the landmark Social Security Act of 1935. The program originally provided cash benefits for needy children under the age of 16, but subsequent amendments have raised the age limit and extended benefits to one adult relative or to both parents in needy families. TANF is a program administered by the states under the Office of Family Assistance in the Department of Health and Human Services and jointly funded about equally by state and federal revenues. The states themselves determine eligibility standards and payment levels within guidelines established by the national government. Monthly benefits vary widely among the states. For example, the maximum monthly payment for a family of three in 2001 was $164 in Alabama, $170 in Mississippi, $673 in Wisconsin, and $923 in Alaska.[17]

The number of TANF recipients grew tremendously from its beginnings until the reform efforts until the 1990s. Just over half a million individuals received benefits in the first year of the program in 1936, but that number increased to almost 8.5 million in 1970. In fact, the number grew by 3.5 million between 1969 and 1971. The rate of growth declined in the early 1970s, and even the absolute number of beneficiaries declined in some later years. In 1994 the program hit its peak with 14.4 million individuals receiving cash benefits. Due to the reform described below, the caseload figure declined to 5.3 million by September 2001.[18]

Welfare was among the most controversial poverty programs because of the widely held perception that it creates a "welfare dependency" that is passed on from one generation of families to the next, with little hope of breaking out of what seems like a vicious cycle. Conservatives saw welfare as subsidizing the undeserving, while liberals decried the insensitivity of bureaucrats administering the program and the insufficiency of resources devoted to it.

Concerns from both ends of the political spectrum and the goal of making welfare less of an alleviative and more of a curative anti-poverty strategy led Congress to

---

[17]Office of Family Assistance, "Specific Provisions of TANF State Programs," http://www.acf.dhhs.gov/programs/ofa/ (12 October 2002), Table 13:18.

[18]The Administration for Children and Families, *TANF Program, Fourth Annual Report to Congress,* April 2002, http://www.acf.dhhs.gov/programs/opre/ar2001/indexar.htm (12 October 2002).

Welfare Reform Act

A 1996 law that fundamentally altered the AFDC welfare program by renaming it TANF and placing work and training requirements, as well as time limits, on its use.

pass the Personal Responsibility and Work Opportunity Reconciliation Act of 1996. Known more commonly as the **Welfare Reform Act**, this piece of legislation fundamentally altered welfare. First, in changing the acronym from AFDC to TANF, the law stressed the temporary nature of the cash payment program. In an effort to break the cycle of poverty, the act placed a two consecutive year limit on receipt of benefits and a five-year lifetime limit. As recipients reached these limits, the states removed them from the rolls. The reform also required recipients to work at least part time while receiving benefits, providing some exemptions for education and job training. While the reform effort has been undeniably successful at reducing welfare caseloads and expenditures (at least partially as a result of its strict time limitations), it remains to be seen whether this harsh approach to poverty will be successful at reducing poverty in America over the long run.

Supplemental Security Income

Supplemental Security Income (SSI)

Social welfare program administered by the Social Security Administration whereby the national government guarantees a certain level of income for the needy, aged, blind, and disabled.

President Nixon's proposal to guarantee incomes for poor families seemed to violate a widely held public expectation that incomes should be earned rather than simply granted. In this view, both economic efficiency and simple fairness demand that incomes be rewards for contributions to society rather than guarantees unrelated to any such contributions. However, in 1972 Congress enacted what amounts to a guaranteed income program for certain groups. Under the **Supplemental Security Income** program (SSI), administered by the Social Security Administration, the national government guarantees a certain level of income for the needy among the aged, blind, and disabled. In 2001 the program spent over $31 billion to serve almost 6.7 million needy people. The national government's successful enactment of SSI shortly after the bitter battle over a proposal to guarantee incomes for poor families suggests the warm political support enjoyed by certain categories of individuals. In effect, SSI represents a national commitment to support aged, blind, and disabled poor people who are clearly unable to support themselves.

Medicaid

Medicaid

A means-tested medical care program providing in-kind medical benefits for the poor.

in-kind benefits

Noncash benefits, such as medical care services, that the needy receive from some social welfare programs.

Medicaid is a means-tested program, enacted in the Great Society, designed to provide medical care for the needy. Unlike TANF and SSI, **Medicaid** provides the poor with **in-kind benefits** rather than cash. That is, the needy receive a service (medical care) rather than cash, and money from the program goes directly to the providers (hospitals, physicians, etc.) of that service. The program funded medical care for more than 36 million needy people in 2001. Like TANF, Medicaid is funded jointly by state and federal revenues and administered by individual states within guidelines established by the national government. The Centers for Medicare and Medicaid Services is the unit in the

Politics and Ideas
Political Ideologies and the Welfare State

Policy debate is fundamentally a collision of ideas on what the appropriate role of government should be. Nowhere has the collision of ideas been more evident than in debate over social welfare. The scope of government expenditures, the number of people directly touched, and the shape of political discourse throughout this and most of the previous century all attest to the central place of the issue in our politics.

The contemporary *welfare state* is primarily the handiwork of political liberals, most of whom have been in the Democratic party. Viewing government as helper, provider, and protector of the disadvantaged, liberals successfully initiated and extended the programs that collectively make up the welfare state. In the liberal view, a significant government presence is right, just, and necessary to help redress the economic imbalances in a capitalist system.

Conservatives have generally opposed the creation and extension of social welfare programs, from the original Social Security Act in the New Deal to the Medicare program in the Great Society. They believe that such programs entrust government with decisions that should be left to individuals and groups in the private marketplace. Government intervention smothers initiative, risks values like independence, and threatens to overwhelm citizens in mindless bureaucracy and red tape.

Liberals and conservatives have been the major contestants in this battle of ideas. But other ideologies have contributed their own perspectives to the debate over government's social welfare role. Neoliberals see some welfare policies as too generous to middle-class recipients. Neoconservatives accept the necessity of a modest welfare state. But they argue that

government's capacity to solve social problems has often been overestimated and that public programs frequently do not make good on their promises. Ideologies on the margins of political debate raise even more fundamental concerns. Democratic socialists press for much greater government control of the economy and a comprehensive welfare system. At the opposite end of the spectrum, libertarians argue that government should be limited to protecting the nation from external attack and preserving the individual rights of citizens. They question the very existence of contemporary welfare state.

Today, few people seriously contest a fundamental social welfare role for government. Liberals and conservatives battle over whether more or less money should be spent on social welfare programs. However, social welfare policy debate has taken some new twists and turns. To maintain political support for welfare and to limit long-term dependency, liberals accepted a work requirement and time limit for welfare recipients in the Welfare Reform Act. Conservatives, by supporting, for example, voucher programs to allow the poor to purchase their own housing, have tried to blend their traditional support for market incentives with acceptance of social welfare policies.

The shape of social welfare lies at the center of battles over budget deficits now common in American politics. Budget makers wrestle with the question of whether deficits can be eliminated without some reductions in social welfare spending. Conflicting ideas over what is appropriate government action complicate this debate over deficits. On what criteria should judgments on cuts or increases in social welfare programs be made?

High tech debit card that replaces the food stamps. *(AP Wide World)*

national government responsible for the program. While specific rules of eligibility are highly complex, individuals who receive TANF and SSI benefits are generally eligible for Medicaid services. The rapid growth in Medicaid costs has become a political issue. In 2002 the program cost $145 billion, a hefty sum in a year of fiscal strains.

The Food Stamp Program

food stamp program

A means-tested program that provides the eligible needy with coupons that can be used only to purchase food.

Like Medicaid, the **food stamp program** was enacted in the 1960s to provide in-kind benefits to the needy rather than cash. This program is administered by the Food and Nutrition Service in the Department of Agriculture through state and local welfare offices. In this case, beneficiaries receive coupons that they trade for food items at grocery stores or supermarkets. The coupons represent money, but they can be used only to purchase food. The national government pays for the cost of the stamps but shares the administrative costs of the program with the states. Individuals and families who meet an income test qualify for the stamps. Like TANF beneficiaries, the number of food stamp recipients grew tremendously over time, from less than one-half million people in the mid-1960s to more than 22 million in 1981.[19] In response to charges of waste and fraud in the program, eligibility rules were tightened in the early 1980s and the number of beneficiaries declined. However, rules were made more liberal later in the decade. The program is highly sensitive to changes in the economy. With higher unemployment

[19]*Social Security Bulletin, Annual Statistical Supplement, 1989*, p. 343.

rates, more people depend on the program for help. In 2001, national and state governments spent almost $18 billion for about 17 million food stamp beneficiaries.[20]

Social Welfare Policy and Future Challenges

Since the late 1960s, social welfare debate has generally revolved not around new program initiatives but around the ways in which the nation can pay for existing programs, which consume ever-greater resources. If Presidents Roosevelt and Johnson attempted to expand the national government role in social welfare, Presidents Reagan and Clinton tried to find economically possible and politically acceptable limits to that role. Changing economic conditions and how policymakers like President George W. Bush decide to deal with budget deficits and demands for federal spending in other sectors, such as military and defense policy, will determine the shape of social welfare policies in the early twenty-first century. How much should social welfare cuts contribute to deficit reduction and other spending needs, or should social welfare programs be immune to cuts? If cuts are made, which groups, the elderly, or the working poor, or children, for example, should bear the brunt of the social and economic costs of the changes? The future shape of social welfare policies depends on how elected officials, interest groups, and individual voters respond to such questions.

Environmental Policy

While the previous section focused on the service-providing aspects of domestic policy via social welfare, this section will address the regulatory aspects of the government's role in domestic policy via the environment. Over the past several decades environmental protection has emerged as a highly visible political issue. Limiting pollution of the land, air, and water about us is a major policy objective at all levels of government. Public policies to protect the environment try to cope with the by-products of technological change, such as the air pollution in a nation so dependent on the automobile. At the same time environmental policy relies on scientific research and technological advances to limit pollution, such as the installation of catalytic converters in cars to reduce auto exhaust emissions. Science and technology can also help to identify environmental problems, but the uncertainty of risk complicates regulatory efforts to reduce pollution.

Environmentalism on the Policy Agenda

The imposing catalogue of threats to the environment helps to explain the deep well of political support for environmental protection efforts. Toxic waste dumps throughout

---

[20]Food and Nutrition Service, *National Level Annual Summary: Participation and Costs, 1969–2001*, http://www.fns.usda.gov/pd/fspmain .htm (12 October 2002).

the country contain used chemicals and other waste products of industrial production that can pose serious health threats. Burning fossil fuels to produce electricity emits into the atmosphere particles that are encircled by water droplets and carried by winds for hundreds of miles. They fall in the form of acid rain and kill forests and water life. Burning fossil fuels and the massive burning of tropical forest land for development dumps carbon dioxide into the atmosphere that traps the sun's heat and risks causing global warming with potentially dire consequences for the earth's climate. Scientists have also detected deterioration in the layer of ozone in the stratosphere high above the earth's surface. Ozone protects the planet from the damaging effects of the sun's ultra-violet radiation. Depletion of the protective ozone layer risks ultraviolet radiation damage to crops and an increase in the incidence of skin cancer.

Radon, a colorless, odorless gas, seeps into millions of homes from decaying uranium in the earth and threatens occupants with higher risks of lung cancer. The mountains of solid waste the nation produces pose a national problem touching every community. Great strides have been made in limiting air pollution, but the Environmental Protection Agency reported in 2002 that more than 133 million people live in counties where the air is unhealthy at times due to high levels of pollutants—a consequence of the 170 million tons of pollution released into the air annually.[21]

One reason why this catalogue of dangers seems so imposing is that we now have a more refined capacity to detect environmental changes and minute quantities of potentially harmful substances. Sophisticated instruments and procedures allow environmental scientists to detect radon, pesticide residues, and tears in the ozone layer. In part, environmental issues get on the policy agenda because new knowledge pushes them there.

Protecting the environment has potent political support in the first decade of the twenty-first century. Campaigning politicians from across the political spectrum seek to align themselves with the environmentalist cause. The 2000 presidential campaign featured both a major party candidate, Al Gore, who had made environmentalism a key feature of his political career, and the emergence of a formidable third party, the Green Party, which placed environmental policy at the core of its political agenda. Significant majorities of Americans judge that high environmental standards are necessary to deal with a deteriorating environment, even if that means setting higher emissions and pollution standards for business and spending more money on the development of renewable energy resources.[22] Whether such majorities persist in the event of a serious economic recession is an open question. Nonetheless, the executive agency that has the task of meeting these public demands may have the toughest job in Washington.

http://endangered .few.gov/wildlife .htm.

The Endangered Species Act created federal protections for species at risk of extinction. The U.S. Fish and Wildlife Service maintains a list of these threatened and endangered animals and plants at the above site.

---

[21]Environmental Protection Agency, *National Air Quality: 2001 Status and Trends* (Washington, DC: GPO, 2002).
[22]The Gallup Organization, "Environment-Unfriendly Policies Have Yet to Damage Bush's Ratings," 17 April 2001, www.gallup.com (12 October 2002).

Contemporary Controversies
Nuclear Power and the Environment

The high promise and menacing threat of nuclear energy have posed stark policy questions over the past sixty years. Flowing from basic research in particle physics, the ability to create nuclear fission reactions with enormous releases of energy led to development of weapons capable of almost incomprehensible destruction at the end of World War II. Nuclear technology also seemed to hold promise as a boundless source of energy to meet the nation's growing need for electrical power. But the bubble broke in 1979 when an accident at the Three Mile Island nuclear power plant led to a partial meltdown of the reactor. The accident so shook public confidence in nuclear reactor safety that the industry has not yet recovered. No new nuclear power plants have been ordered since. Anxieties about nuclear power were exacerbated by the more serious accident in 1986 at the Chernobyl nuclear plant in the Ukraine, which was then part of the Soviet Union.

In a classic illustration of the promise and threat that science and technology pose for public policy, nuclear power is at the same time pressed as a solution to some environmental problems but feared to be a creator of others. For example, many climatologists argue that extensive use of fossil fuels like coal and oil releases into the atmosphere carbon dioxide which, along with other gases such as methane and nitrous oxides, acts like a shield that traps heat from the sun. This global warming risks dramatic climatic changes that can turn fertile farm land into desert and, by melting polar ice and raising ocean levels, can put coastal regions under water. A greater reliance on nuclear power plants to produce electricity would reduce fossil fuel damage to the atmosphere. But public anxiety about the safety of nuclear plants makes greater reliance on nuclear energy a controversial option. In fact, at the same time that fears about global warming emerged, the State of New York negotiated with the Long Island Lighting Company to close down the Shoreham nuclear power plant. Long Island residents and state and local elected officials opposed the plant because of fears that evacuation of the surrounding densely populated areas could not be

The Environmental Protection Agency and Government Regulation

**Environmental
Protection
Agency (EPA)**

An independent agency that controls and abates air and water pollution and protects the environment from pollution by solid wastes, pesticides, radiation, and toxic substances.

The political environment of the **Environmental Protection Agency (EPA)** contains a mix of pressures and constraints that severely tax efforts to meet the policy goal of environmental protection. The agency must deal with a staggering array of potential threats to the environment, including thousands of sources of pollution throughout the nation. Public and environmental interest group expectations for agency action are high, but so are the anxieties of businesses and industries who see environmental regulation as an economic cost that someone must pay.

The Environmental Protection Agency was established in 1970 by pulling together into a single unit the anti-pollution programs then spread among several agen-

Nuclear Power and the Environment, *continued*

quickly and reasonably accomplished in the event of a nuclear accident. Thus, a newly constructed, $5.5 billion dollar plant never became operational. The decision not to use a facility that would reduce dependence on fossil fuels and that might help limit global warming illustrates the tough policy choices posed by nuclear energy. To many Long Islanders the decision was a wise move greeted by relief. To nuclear power advocates, closing down a perfectly good nuclear plant was folly.

Another tough environmental policy issue concerns the management of nuclear waste. Spent nuclear fuel remains highly radioactive, and potentially quite dangerous for several hundred thousand years. Since no one wants this dangerous by-product near them, finding locations for safe storage of nuclear waste has been a troubling domestic policy problem. After a decades long, $4 billion scientific study, in 2002 President Bush signed legislation establishing a new waste facility at Yucca Mountain, Nevada. The waste

depository will be maintained by the Department of Energy's Office of Civilian Radioactive Waste Management and will be the nation's "first long-term geologic repository for spent nuclear fuel and high-level radioactive waste."[a] Supporters of the project claim that a central location at a remote and secure site is the safest solution for the problem of radioactive waste. Critics argue that an accident could endanger millions of lives (Yucca Mountain is just 100 miles from Las Vegas) and that transporting radioactive waste from all over the country exacerbates risks of radioactive contamination. In light of the promise and problems of nuclear energy, should more nuclear power plants be built, or should more be closed down? Or, should we use less energy?

---

[a]Office of Civilian Radioactive Waste Management, "The Yucca Mountain Project," http://www.ymp.gov/ (13 October 2002).

---

cies. More than three decades after its creation the EPA is one of the biggest and probably the most visible regulatory agency, employing nearly 18,000 people and (in fiscal 2002) spending almost $8 billion annually. The agency must administer laws that try to protect air, water, and land, a daunting task that encompasses regulation of auto emission standards, toxic wastes, pesticides, radiation standards, and potentially dangerous substances such as asbestos, mercury, and radon. The demands on the EPA are a recipe of political passions, economic considerations, and scientific findings, a mix that makes the EPA's task at once fascinating and frustrating.

Since much of EPA's work is based on research and technological innovation, science and technology help to structure its decisions. For example, for fiscal year 2003 the EPA requested from Congress almost $330 million for a goal it identifies as "Sound

Science, Improved Understanding of Environmental Risk and Greater Innovation to Address Environmental Problems."[23]

Science and technology inevitably play a role in EPA decisions. Substances posing health and environmental threats are frequently invisible, their consequences long-term, and their structures and incidence discoverable only by highly trained investigators in fields such as chemistry and the life sciences. Does the runoff of pesticides into rivers ultimately damage human health? What will global warming do to climate patterns and ecosystems? How much of a carcinogen must an individual ingest before serious health effects occur? Ultimately, much of the EPA's work is comprised of **risk assessment,** or estimating the degree of environmental risk a pollutant or ecosystem change poses, and **risk management,** or making decisions that try to reduce or contain the identified risk.[24] Even with the trappings of scientific research, however, risk assessment retains a large measure of uncertainty. Different models and different data sets can produce different answers to the question of whether a contaminant in minute amounts causes cancer.

Scientific research can help the EPA ask the appropriate questions and frame the debate. But if action is to be taken and environmental goals are to be reached, the agency must issue specific regulations that limit pollution by trying to change the behavior of individuals, companies, and governments. Regulatory agencies such as the EPA ultimately receive all their power from Congress, which adopts policies through the statutes it enacts. As the policy process chapter explained, the implementation of policies or the translation of policy ideas into action is left to bureaucrats. Congress identifies problems and establishes policy goals but delegates to regulatory agencies the power to write rules that specify in greater detail the definitions, criteria, and standards of behavior necessary to meet congressional intent. For example, bringing to bear its highly technical expertise, the Nuclear Regulatory Commission issues detailed rules guiding the operation of nuclear power plants. As another illustration, the Environmental Protection Agency specifies maximum contaminant levels in drinking water. Congress may be very vague or very explicit in its statutes directing the work of regulatory agencies. But individuals in regulatory agencies with scientific and technical expertise are ultimately given the tasks of specifying, detailing, and defining in matters such as safe nuclear reactor procedures and acceptable drinking water contaminant levels.

Environmental regulations at once promise environmental benefits and impose monetary costs. Clean air and clean water are not free, and much debate ensues over who ought to pay how much. Heightened by media attention to toxic waste dumps, contaminated water, and carcinogens in the air, the EPA faces passionate demands from environmental groups to take aggressive action. At the same time, the agency is required

risk assessment

The process of estimating the potentially dangerous consequences of damage that might be caused by a particular practice, such as smoking, or by the use of a particular product, such as the impact of the burning of fossil fuels on global warming.

risk management

Process of making decisions that try to reduce or contain identified risks.

---

[23]Environmental Protection Agency, "Summary of the EPA's Budget, FY 2003," p.VII–1.

[24]These definitions are adapted from Science Advisory Board, *Reducing Risk: Setting Priorities and Strategies For Environmental Protection* (Washington, DC: Environmental Protection Agency, 1990), p. 2.

by law or by presidential executive order to take into account economic considerations to ensure that the presumed benefits of environmental rules outweigh their costs. The EPA is, therefore, frequently in the middle of the political struggle over the appropriate role for government in environmental regulation, an issue that reverberates in other areas of government regulation as well.

The Future of Environmental Policy

As America looks forward, environmental policy challenges abound. Our government's difficult task of balancing interests is, perhaps, highlighted best in this arena. The EPA and other federal agencies will continue to negotiate the conflicts between those seeking to preserve natural habitats and those wishing to pursue economic development of resources. Should we preserve the pristine environment of the Alaskan arctic wilderness, or should we utilize this resource by drilling for oil there? Should we increase regulations and raise environmental standards for industries, even if this means economic hardship for some businesses and more expensive products for consumers? These are among the difficult questions American environmental policy must confront in the coming decades.

SUMMARY

1. Government policies provide benefits to every income group. Social insurance and means-tested programs designed for the poor are the principal social welfare policies of the national government.

2. The philosophy of social Darwinism held that only a limited government role would allow society to progress, but substantial change in the activities of government began to occur in the Progressive Era. The real revolution in the social welfare role of the national government took place in the New Deal presidency of Franklin D. Roosevelt, who initiated a variety of new policies designed to cushion the economic hardship of the Great Depression. President Johnson's Great Society was the last period of major new social welfare initiatives.

3. Social insurance programs, including Social Security and Medicare, tend to be the largest social welfare programs. The size of social insurance programs and the fact that their beneficiaries come from across the income spectrum mean that such programs can draw on widespread political support.

4. Poverty can be measured either relatively or according to some absolute standard. The causes and extent of poverty are continuing matters of debate, but official estimates based on an absolute income standard indicate that 11.7 percent of the population in 2001 was poor. Programs designed to ameliorate poverty include Temporary Assistance for Needy Families, Medicaid, food stamps, and Supplemental Security Income. In these "means-tested" programs, the national government, in most cases in cooperation with the states, grants cash or in-kind benefits to individuals who qualify on the basis of income.

5. Spending on some social welfare programs has been the target of budget cuts over the past two decades, but resistance to further cuts indicates the well of public support for a substantial social welfare policy role for the government. Many social welfare problems persist, but the future shape of social welfare programs depends on Americans' willingness to continue to support them in the face of other perceived fiscal needs.

6. Environmental protection efforts draw on a deep well of political support to deal with the varied threats to environmental quality. The Environmental Protection Agency, with the unenviable task of administering the nation's environmental laws, confronts in its regulatory work a mix of political passions, economic considerations, and scientific data.

KEY TERMS

domestic policy (440)

social welfare (441)

social entitlements (441)

social Darwinism (443)

Progressive Era (444)

New Deal (444)

Great Society (445)

social insurance programs (446)

Social Security Act of 1935 (446)

incrementalism (447)

Medicare (449)

unemployment compensation (450)

means-tested programs (451)

relative deprivation (453)

poverty threshold (453)

working poor (457)

underclass (457)

curative strategies (457)

alleviative strategies (457)

Temporary Assistance for Needy
    Families (TANF) (458)

Welfare Reform Act (459)

Supplemental Security Income (459)

Medicaid (459)

in-kind benefits (459)

food stamp program (461)

Environmental Protection Agency (464)

risk assessment (466)

risk management (466)

READINGS FOR FURTHER STUDY

Michael Harrington's *The Other America: Poverty in the United States*, reprint ed. (New York: Touchstone Books, 1997) was influential in moving poverty onto the policy agenda when it was first published in the early 1960s.

William Julius Wilson, *When Work Disappears: The World of the New Urban Poor* (New York: Vintage Books, 1997) and Herbert J. Gans, *The War Against the Poor: The Underclass and Antipoverty Policy* (New York: Basic Books, 1996) are good discussions of poverty and public policy.

The history of social welfare policy is described in Walter I. Trattner, *From Poor Law to Welfare State: A History of Social Welfare in America*, 6th ed. (New York: Free Press, 1999). A good textbook approach to social welfare policy is Diana M. Dinitto, *Social Welfare: Politics and Public Policy*, 5th ed. (Boston: Allyn & Bacon, 1999).

An analysis of recent efforts to reform the welfare system is found in Alan Weil and Kenneth Finegold, eds., *Welfare Reform: The Next Act* (Washington, DC: Urban Institute Press, 2002).

Environmental Policy is explored from an historical perspective in Samuel P. Hays, *A History of Environmental Politics Since 1945* (Pittsburgh: University of Pittsburgh Press, 2000).

One of the most influential books in the development of an environmental movement in America when it was first released in 1962 was Rachel Carson's *Silent Spring* (Boston: Houghton Mifflin, 2002).

The process of environmental policymaking is explored in Daniel J. Fiorino, *Making Environmental Policy* (Berkeley: University of California Press, 1995).

A good text that explores the future of environmental policy is Norman J. Vig and Michael E. Kraft, eds., *Environmental Policy: New Directions for the Twenty-First Century*, 4th ed. (Washington, DC: CQ Press, 1999).

Finally, the relationship between technical experts and environmental policy advocates is examined in Frank Fischer, *Citizens, Experts, and the Environment: The Politics of Local Knowledge* (Durham, NC: Duke University Press, 2000).

CHAPTER 16

Foreign Policy

A/P World Wide

Chapter Objectives

Foreign and defense policy are central concerns of the American government. The president spends well over half his time on these issues. Defense spending consumes over 17 percent of the federal budget, and American military expenditures account for over 30 percent of all such expenditures worldwide.[1] The advent of nuclear, biological, and chemical weapons of mass destruction has raised the stakes of policy to enormous levels. Whereas a mistake in domestic policy can be serious, one in foreign and defense policy can be fatal.

During this period of endless crisis, personalities and events have influenced American policies and political institutions. Of particular importance are the roles of the president, Congress, and various agencies. This chapter also explores the effects of special economic and ethnic interests on defense and diplomacy as well as the major problems facing America as the world's twenty-first century superpower fighting a war on terrorism.

America's Role in the World

Prior to World War II American involvement in world affairs had been sporadic. American participation in World War I was followed by our rejection of the League of Nations treaty and a withdrawal from active leadership in world affairs. Until the Japanese attack on Pearl Harbor on December 7, 1941, George Washington's advice, given in his farewell address, to "steer clear of permanent alliances with any portion of

---

[1]U.S. Census Bureau, *Statistical Abstract of the United States: 2001* (Washington, DC: GPO, 2002), p. 327.

isolationism

A belief that America should not involve itself in the quarrels of Europe and Asia and should pursue a policy of military nonintervention.

internationalism

A foreign policy perspective that concludes that America's interests in peace abroad and liberty at home requires its permanent involvement in world affairs.

the foreign world" made good sense to most Americans. Especially in the 1920s and 1930s, **isolationism** was the American credo in foreign policy. This was the belief in noninvolvement in the affairs of other countries, especially staying aloof from armed conflict elsewhere in the world.

America emerged from World War II as the predominant industrial and military power. In the post–World War II era a new American credo was born: **internationalism.** This was the belief in the necessity of involvement in the affairs of other countries in order to protect the nation's political and economic security. Most Americans became convinced that peace abroad and liberty at home required our permanent involvement in global affairs. Accepting this new role, America took the lead in 1945 to form the United Nations. However, the breakdown of Soviet-American relations in 1946 and 1947 illustrated that the new era of internationalism meant not only responsibility but conflict and tension as well. After surviving a tense cold war that lasted for more than four decades, America emerged as the seeming victor of the struggle at the end of the 1980s. But the collapse of the Soviet empire did not mean smooth sailing ahead for American foreign policy. The post–cold war era has seen America's role in the world change and expand in unanticipated directions. Some have welcomed America's leadership in global policy, which has included foreign aid contributions intended to stimulate developing economies. Others have found America's new internationalism domineering, paternalistic, and unwanted. A few have even taken extreme and unjust measures to express their anger at America—such as the terrorist attacks on the World Trade Center and Pentagon. Today, the challenge of American foreign policy is to provide political and economic leadership while insuring national security.

The Cold War and the Post–Cold War Ear

Although the United States and the Soviet Union had been allies during World War II, the rupture of relations between them had numerous causes, steeped in mistrust and ideological division. Given the historic record, each nation had ample reasons to suspect the other.

With Britain and France, America had intervened militarily in Russia soon after the communist revolution of 1917 to obstruct that revolution and aid the Russian anti-communist forces. Although this intervention was brief and unsuccessful, it symbolized America's hostility toward this new revolutionary state. Finally, in 1933, America formally recognized the Soviet Union on the unrealized expectation of expanded trade, and during World War II the countries became allies. But the alliance was never easy. America delayed opening a second front in Western Europe and left the Soviets alone on the continent to face the German army. While the United States worked closely with Great Britain on the atomic bomb project, it refused even to inform the Soviets about the project until the bomb was used against Japan. Immediately after the war ended in

The first atomic bomb, which was detonated over Hiroshima in World War II. *(AP Wide World)*

Europe, President Harry Truman (1945–1953) abruptly curtailed military supplies, known as lend-lease, to the Soviet Union. Thus the Soviets contended that they were never treated as a genuine ally by the United States.

Ideological differences added to the lack of trust. From the outset of their revolution the Soviets believed that the Western capitalist states were hostile and would give them grudging acceptance at best. From the American perspective, Soviet communism presented a profound challenge to our institutions and values. The Soviets emphasized economic development above all and saw no function for representative democracy, freedom of speech and religion, free enterprise, or independent trade unions.

Through this prism of mutual distrust the United States and the Soviet Union found it difficult to resolve the complex issues created by the defeats of Germany and Japan. As the Soviet army pushed German forces out of Poland, Rumania, and Bulgaria in 1945, the Soviets imposed communist regimes on those countries. American suspicion of Soviet motives and hostility to the communist social system made it impossible to accept with tranquillity Soviet control of Eastern Europe, now described as being sealed from the West by an "iron curtain." Most American leaders were convinced by 1946 that Soviet domination of Eastern Europe was a first step toward the control of all Europe.

The Soviets resented American insistence on free elections in Eastern Europe, arguing that they had a legitimate claim to dominant political influence in bordering countries vital to their security. The failure of the two superpowers to agree on the Eastern European issue also meant failure to agree on the disposition of Germany. As a result, the occupation zones in Germany evolved into separate German states—one allied

Politics and Ideas
Contrasting Approaches to Foreign Policy: Idealism, Realism, and Isolationism

American foreign policy is a complex mixture of domestic pressures, geopolitical interests, and ideas. Over the course of this century several fundamental ideas about foreign policy have emerged and have found articulate spokesmen and advocates.

One of those ideas is the concept of *realism,* which accepts conflict as a permanent part of international politics. Realists believe that foreign policy can, at best, limit conflict, not eliminate it. Peace and national self-interest from the realist view are best assured by constructing a stable balance of power. Since not all conflicts threaten the balance of power, realists support a policy of limits: a nation should only commit itself to those struggles where vital interests are at stake and when it has the means to prevail. President Theodore Roosevelt (1901–1909) was one of the earliest exponents of realism.

Roosevelt asserted America's primary interest in the Caribbean, where he could exclude the European powers without dragging the country into a major war. In 1903, he promoted Panama's rebellion from Colombia and then acquired the Canal Zone from Panama. In 1905, he placed the finances of Santo Domingo under American control to prevent any European country from asserting authority over that beleaguered country. Critics argued that such realism had only short-term benefits, brought America few friends, and encouraged the belief that military threats could solve all problems.

The idealist approach to foreign policy begins with the assumption that human nature is basically good and that wars and other forms of conflict are not the normal condition of mankind. Political *idealism* holds that the goal of American foreign policy should be to promote the principles of universal peace, human rights, and democracy. President Woodrow Wilson (1913–1921) is the American statesman most closely identified with this school of thought. In the years 1914–1916, Wilson sent American troops to Mexico, Haiti, and the Dominican Republic—not, as had Roosevelt to stave off European intervention, but to establish democratic governments.

After war broke out in Europe in 1914, Roosevelt, then a private citizen, urged American intervention to prevent Germany from dominating Europe and thus upset-

Truman Doctrine

A policy, proclaimed by President Harry Truman in 1947, in which the United States would oppose the expansion of communism anywhere in the world.

with the West (the Federal Republic of Germany) and the other controlled by the Soviet Union (the German Democratic Republic). By 1947 Europe appeared to be permanently divided into an American sphere in Western Europe and a Soviet sphere in Eastern Europe. This cold war would produce several tense moments in the decades to follow. President Truman's approach to the situation was to send economic aid to countries at the risk of being influenced by or destabilized by the Soviet Union. His plan of opposing Soviet aggression came to be known as the **Truman Doctrine** and was a guiding principle of American foreign policy during the cold war. The Truman administration was also

Contrasting Approaches to Foreign Policy: Idealism, Realism, and Isolationism, *continued*

ting the balance of power on that continent. Wilson was reluctant to intervene until Germany began unrestricted submarine warfare against American merchant ships. Then he justified involvement upon the most lofty ideals. In asking Congress for a declaration of war, Wilson claimed that America would fight for "the ultimate peace of the world and for the liberation of its peoples . . . the world must be made safe for democracy." When World War I ended, Wilson insisted upon a peace settlement, known as the Fourteen Points, that would require a global peacekeeping entity (the League of Nations), arms limitations, open diplomacy, and the self-determination of nations. The eventual treaty, signed in Versailles in 1919, embodied few of these principles except for the creation of the League of Nations and was rejected by the United States Senate.

In twenty years Europe was embroiled in another war. Critics argued that Wilson's efforts at peacemaking did not end European habits of power politics, hostile alliances, and imperialist politics. Such moralistic policies, critics contended, only lead to futile crusades and endless wars.

The doctrine of *isolationism* has deep roots in American history, going back to George Washington's admonition in his farewell address. According to the isolationist credo, America should be a beacon light of liberty for all humanity, but not attempt to impose its way of life on other societies. America would only be contaminated by its involvement in the power struggles of the world. One of the leading spokesmen for isolationism prior to World War II was former President Herbert Hoover (1929–1933). Hoover saw no clear moral choice between Imperialist Britain and Communist Russia on one side and Nazi Germany and Fascist Italy on the other. Hoover feared that permanent involvement in the affairs of the world would so enlarge the role of the government and the military in the life of the nation as to constitute a threat to our liberty. Most Americans spurned Hoover's advice, believing that America must play a continual role in the international community.

Do you see the influences of realism, idealism, or isolationism in contemporary foreign policy?

Marshall Plan

A multibillion-dollar American program begun after World War II for the economic rehabilitation of Western Europe.

responsible for the **Marshall Plan** (named for Secretary of State George C. Marshall), a multiyear, multi-billion dollar program designed to help strengthen European economies, most of which had been devastated by World War II. The Marshall Plan became an American-Western European endeavor. After American aid of $12 billion over five years, European economies began to stabilize, forming the basis for a generation of Western European prosperity and democracy and further solidifying bonds to the United States.

The Soviets responded to the Truman Doctrine and the Marshall Plan by tightening their control over Eastern Europe, making both diplomatic and personal relationships between the two sides of Europe difficult. Such actions led America to develop a new foreign policy tack. Containment of the Soviet Union—holding communist political power within existing borders—became the hallmark of American foreign policy.

In April 1949 a total of 12 nations (the United States, Britain, France, Italy, the Netherlands, Belgium, Canada, Iceland, Luxembourg, Denmark, Norway, and Portugal) formed the North Atlantic Treaty Organization (NATO) and declared that an attack on one member would be considered an attack on all. NATO, the first mutual defense treaty signed by the United States since 1800, provided an American guarantee for the defense of Western Europe against a Soviet attack. The Soviet empire provided a counterbalance to NATO with the Warsaw Pact, established in 1955 and providing Eastern Europe with the same sort of alliance that NATO provided for the West. Interestingly, NATO never had to be used for the purposes of an all-out war during this era. Since the collapse of the Soviet empire, NATO has been expanded. It now contains 19 member states, including some from the former Soviet Union's sphere of influence.

Although it was called a cold war, this period also saw real military conflict, most notably in Korea and Vietnam. The Korean conflict (1950–1951) saw the American military deployed to the Korean peninsula when communist forces from North Korea crossed into South Korea. President Truman, following his containment policy, withdrew troops after the border between the two Koreas was re-secured. The Vietnam conflict (1961–1973) also involved discord between communist and non-communist factions in an Asian nation. This time the strategy was not as simple, and the result not as pleasing for the American military. After nearly a decade of heavy fighting, and the loss of more than 50,000 American lives, the Nixon administration reached a cease-fire agreement and began to withdraw the American military in 1973, leaving the war-ravaged country to continue the conflict on its own. South Vietnamese forces eventually fell to the communist North Vietnamese in 1975.

The Vietnam War profoundly altered the public's patience with the costs of containment policy. If America's leaders were to maintain some semblance of this policy, a new strategy had to be developed. President Nixon and his National Security Advisor, Henry Kissinger, attempted to shape a policy that would accommodate itself to these new realities. Known as **détente** (a French word meaning "relaxation" or "calm"), this approach was designed to ease tensions between the United States and the Soviet Union. Rather than containing Soviet influence by elaborate and costly means, Nixon and Kissinger hoped that diplomacy could persuade the Soviets to limit their own behavior. Though détente did not live up to the expectations of either side, it did result in some important outcomes. It established a precedent for arms limitations negotiations and it reduced American global commitments by advocating the **Nixon Doctrine**—a claim that America would no longer be responsible for providing, as it did in Korea and Vietnam, the military personnel to protect its allies.

détente

A French word meaning "relaxation" that was applied to Soviet-American relations in the early 1970s.

Nixon Doctrine

Proclaimed by President Nixon in 1969, a policy stipulating that the United States will support its allies with economic and military aid but that the allies should provide the bulk of the manpower for their own defense.

While American efforts such as détente had some effect at easing cold war tensions, the end of the war itself was largely a result of changes in Soviet policy. When Mikhail Gorbachev assumed power in the Soviet Union in 1985, Soviet-American relations began a period of profound alteration. With the Soviet economy in shambles, Gorbachev realized that his country required fundamental reform and could no longer afford the military and economic costs of competition with the West. In 1987, both countries signed the Intermediate Nuclear Forces Treaty (INF), which banned an entire category of nuclear weapons (missiles with ranges between 300 and 3400 miles) and provided for intrusive on-site inspection procedures. Gorbachev had made virtually all the concessions. Even President Ronald Reagan, who early in his administration had dubbed the Soviet Union an "evil empire," concluded, as he left office, that a fundamental shift had occurred in Soviet policy.

It was, however, a series of cataclysmic events in the first two years of the George H. W. Bush administration that altered the political map of Europe and brought the cold war to an end. In April 1989, with Gorbachev's consent, the Polish noncommunist Solidarity movement was legalized and swept to an election victory that June. Throughout the autumn and winter of 1989, Hungary, Czechoslovakia, and Romania followed suit. By the end of 1989 the governments of all the Soviet Union's East European allies had collapsed. New regimes asked the Soviet Union to withdraw its military forces. The Warsaw Pact was in shambles and for all intents and purposes ceased to exist.

Underscoring this was an agreement signed in the summer of 1990 between President and West German Chancellor Helmut Kohl for a united Germany within the NATO alliance. The division of Europe into two armed camps marked the ending of the cold war. But the end of the cold war did not mean the end of international conflict. The Iraqi invasion of Kuwait in August 1990 and the Gulf War that followed reminded the world of that grim fact. Without two rival superpowers, however, a major burden of responding to international politics seemingly fell to the United States alone—a reminder that American leadership in world affairs would not end with the cold war.

During the 1990s and the early years of the twenty-first century, America has been in the process of redefining its role to accommodate the changing international sphere. Presidents Bush, Clinton, and the second Bush established a large role for American diplomacy and military presence around the world. In addition to the Gulf War, the first President Bush involved America in military actions in Panama and Somalia. President Clinton continued American efforts in Somalia and sent troops to Haiti and Bosnia, in addition to continued bombings of Iraq. President George W. Bush campaigned for office as something of an isolationist, but when confronted with the tragedy of international terrorism responded by using the U.S. military in Afghanistan and Iraq. To be sure, some of these efforts were humanitarian in nature and many were

http://www.white house.gov/nsc/

Where does foreign policy come from? One of the most influential bodies in the development of American foreign policy strategy is the National Security Council, consisting of the president and key advisors, and headed by National Security Advisor Condoleezza Rice. See what this organization is up to at the above site.

multinational efforts. Their sheer quantity, though, underscores the growing burden of American foreign policy in the post–cold war world of the twenty-first century.

The Policy Machinery

Since the Vietnam War there has been no clear public consensus on foreign policy. Global containment was discredited by Vietnam, and the end of the cold war has left policymakers without a clear political strategy. Consequently, every major foreign and defense policy initiative is subject to searching examination. President Carter was barely able to get the Panama Canal treaty, which returned control of the canal to Panama, through the Senate; he had great difficulty in gaining Senate support for the SALT (Strategic Arms Limitation Treaty) II treaty. Despite his impressive election victories, President Reagan had no easy victories in Congress. His defense buildup was reduced, aid to the Nicaraguan *contras* was seriously circumscribed, and the MX missile program was severely limited. The vote to authorize the first President Bush to use military force against Iraq was marked by strong partisan cleavages. Even the second President Bush, who received incredible public support in the wake of the 9/11 attacks, faced significant opposition when he sought approval for large-scale military actions against Iraq.

Nonetheless, foreign policy in the nuclear age still carries a large presidential stamp. Since 1945 the major policy initiatives (the Truman Doctrine, the Marshall Plan, NATO, the Korean intervention, the Vietnam War, détente, the Gulf war, and the war on terrorism) have come from the White House. But gaining support for policy initiatives is increasingly difficult. Not only is Congress more independent, but the bureaucracy itself is not easily corralled. Each agency frequently has its own perspective, with a Cabinet secretary who may be its vigorous advocate.

The president, frequently operating through the National Security Council, attempts to control the play. The following sections explore and analyze the elaborate machinery of agencies and departments that the president seeks to dominate. They are responsible for the day-to-day operations of policy.

Department of State

Responsible for the routine daily functions of foreign policy, it represents the United States abroad, is involved in international negotiations, supervises foreign aid and programs, promotes cultural and educational exchange, and makes policy recommendations to the president.

Department of State

Although the conduct of crisis diplomacy and the overall direction of foreign policy come from the White House, the **Department of State** has the primary responsibility for the routine daily functions of foreign policy. The department's activities include maintaining diplomatic relations with over 180 countries; operating over 250 embassies, consulates, and other posts around the world; representing the United States in scores of international organizations; involvement in the negotiations of treaties and other agreements with foreign nations; monitoring human rights policies of both our allies and our

FIGURE 16.1

United States Department of State

In addition to its headquarters in Washington, known as Foggy Bottom, the State Department has over 140 embassies abroad, more than 100 consulates, and 8 special missions to international organizations. Yet as measured by its budget and personnel, it is among the smaller executive departments. Of particular importance are functional bureaus and geographic bureaus.

SOURCE: U.S. Department of State, *Diplomacy: The State Department at Work* (Washington, DC: GPO, 2001).

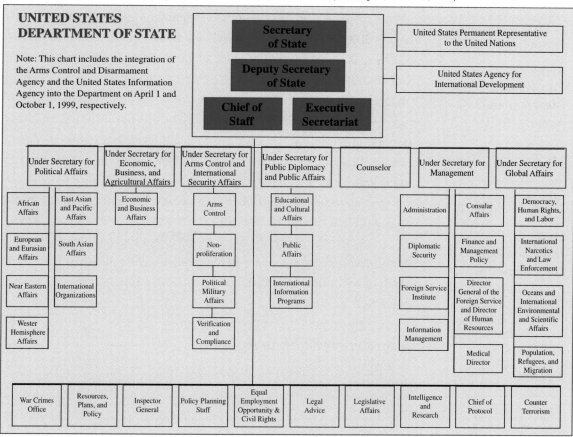

adversaries; supervising foreign aid programs; promoting cultural and educational exchanges; and making policy recommendations to the president and being responsible for their implementation.

Heading the department is the secretary of state, who reports directly to the president. Beneath the secretary is the deputy secretary of state, six undersecretaries, and a counselor. Below that level, the department is a mix of geographic and functional bureaus (see Figure 16.1). The *geographic* bureaus (such as African, European and Eurasian, Near Eastern, Western Hemisphere, and East Asian, and Pacific) have within them scores of country desks that are responsible for monitoring events around the world. The *functional* bureaus, which include Intelligence and Research, Political-Military Affairs, and Counter Terrorism, are responsible for specialized areas of policy. They inevitably involve other departments. For example, the Political-Military Affairs Bureau frequently interacts with the Pentagon and is crucial to State's participation in the development of military policy.

Attached to the State Department are the U.S. permanent representative to the United Nations and the **United States Agency for International Development** (USAID). In 1999 two additional organizations were integrated into the Department: the **Arms Control and Disarmament Agency (ACDA)** and the United States Information Agency, the latter of which became the **Office of International Information Programs (IIP)**. ACDA is responsible for research on arms control policy and is involved in those negotiations, USAID coordinates economic assistance programs, and IIP directs communications programs that provide information about the United States worldwide.

The State Department is staffed by an elite corps of employees known as foreign service officers (FSOs). They are selected through a rigorous series of written and oral exams. Few people would dispute the talent and ability of the FSOs, but they have been criticized for their caution, conformity, and elitism. These tendencies may be reinforced by the "up or out" promotion system in which a senior officer must advance beyond his or her present rank or be discharged.

Over the years the State Department has had difficulty leading foreign policy within the executive branch. In the modern age of diplomacy the State Department must share its own field of foreign policymaking with the Defense Department, the CIA, and the NSC.

Central Intelligence Agency

Established in 1947, the **Central intelligence Agency (CIA)** was originally charged with gathering information and coordinating all intelligence operations in the federal government. As tensions increased in the cold war, the CIA shifted its primary task from the collection of intelligence information to the conduct of secret political activities. Its most successful early operations involved aiding in the installation of pro-American governments in Iran (1953) and Guatemala (1954). Covert activities became such an important part of the CIA that between 1962 and 1970 they consumed 52 percent of the agency's total budget and 55 percent of its personnel.[2]

In the early 1970s public disclosure of CIA abuses put the agency on the defensive, thus weakening its political support. The abuses involved unsuccessful efforts to assassinate Fidel Castro in the early 1960s and an attempt to prevent Marxist-leaning Salvador Allende from taking office as president of Chile in 1970 after he had been

---

United States Agency for International Development

Agency of the State Department that coordinates economic assistance programs.

Arms Control and Disarmament Agency (ACDA)

Agency of the State Department responsible for research on arms control and often involved in the actual negotiations.

Office of International Information Programs

An agency of the State Department that directs overseas information programs.

Central Intelligence Agency (CIA)

Agency, established by the National Security Act of 1947, responsible for gathering information and coordinating foreign intelligence operations in the federal government.

---

[2]Charles W. Kegley, Jr., and Eugene R. Wittkopf, *American Foreign Policy: Pattern and Process*, 4th ed. (New York: St. Martin's Press, 1991), p. 389.

legally elected. Congress then took steps to limit such activities. The Hughes-Ryan Amendment of 1974 required that the president notify Congress when a covert action was undertaken and certify its importance "to the national interests of the United States."

Presidents Ford and Carter set firm limits on CIA operations by placing covert activities under close presidential control. They prohibited such extreme measures as assassination and forbade any CIA operations within the United States. President Reagan, however, felt that the CIA had been unduly restricted. In 1981, he appointed William J. Casey as director of the CIA with the explicit mandate to revitalize the agency. Reagan amended the Ford and Carter orders and allowed some domestic CIA operations as long as their focus was on gathering significant foreign intelligence data.

The Reagan administration was far less reluctant than its predecessors to approve covert operations. The CIA increased its flow of small arms and other military equipment to the Afghan rebels combating the Soviet invaders. It provided millions of dollars in arms to Iranian paramilitary groups opposing the Khomeini government in Tehran. It also trained the personal security forces of Liberian dictator Samuel K. Doe. But the CIA's most ambitious operation involved the support of Nicaraguan exile groups, known as *contras*, seeking to overthrow the Marxist Sandinista government. Congress raised serious objections to this operation and in 1982 barred funds "for the purpose of overthrowing the government of Nicaragua." However, in 1986 Congress, under considerable pressure from President Reagan, appropriated $100 million in *contra* aid. Only later did it come to light that some of the funds received from arms sales to Iran may have been diverted to the *contras*.

Although the current functions of the CIA are difficult to identify, due to the classified nature of much of the intelligence gathering work, the agency does make some of its activities public. For example, one recent effort has been the collection of intelligence on foreign terrorist groups. Although the budget of the CIA and its number of employees is not made public, in 1998 the aggregate budget for all intelligence gathering activities—of which the CIA budget is a part—was $26.7 billion.[3]

The dilemma that CIA covert operations pose for our democratic society is severe. Can the American government conduct a secret foreign policy without subverting the principles of democratic control? Yet should it stand by helpless if the Iraqis or international terrorists operate without constraints? There are no simple answers.

Department of Defense (DOD)

Established by the National Security Act of 1947, it is responsible for formulating military policy and maintaining the armed forces.

Department of Defense

The **Department of Defense (DOD)**, housed in the famous Pentagon building, is a mammoth organization. It was created in 1947 and reorganized in 1949 to reduce interservice rivalry and to provide more coherence for national security policy. DOD is comprised of three basic organizations: the Office of the Secretary of Defense (OSD), the

[3]Central Intelligence Agency, "Frequently Asked Questions," http://www.cia.gov/cia/public_affairs/faq.html (14 October 2002).

FIGURE 16.2

Department of Defense

The Defense Department is practically an empire into itself. The massive Pentagon office building covers 34 acres and contains a work force of over 25,000 people. Approximately 2 million people are employed by Defense, over two-thirds of them in the armed forces. The Defense Department is divided mainly into the Office of the Secretary of Defense, the Joint Chiefs of Staff, and the three service departments.

SOURCE: Department of Defense, *Organization and Functions Guidebook* (Washington, DC: GPO, 2001).

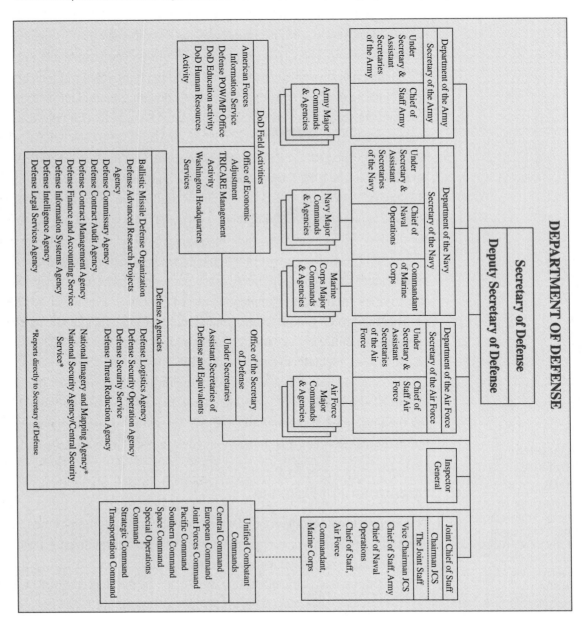

Joint Chiefs of Staff (JCS)

Heads of the various armed services and their chair who advise the president and the secretary of defense on important military questions.

Joint Chiefs of Staff (JCS), and the separate armed services, which are headed by a civilian service secretary and a uniformed service chief.

Overseeing this organization, the secretary of defense is one of most powerful Cabinet secretaries. The defense secretary has the challenging task of advising the president on crucial military decisions, serving as the link between the military leadership and the president, and building a policy consensus within the department. Frequently this task brings the secretary of defense into conflict with the secretary of state, who may emphasize diplomacy over force, arms control over military buildups, or alliance solidarity over unilateral U.S. military action.

Such conflict has been apparent from time to time in the second Bush administration. Secretary of Defense Donald Rumsfeld has demonstrated a preference for an aggressive military response in the war on terrorism, even when this means the United States must act unilaterally. This approach has sometimes been at odds with the more cautious, diplomatic route preferred by Secretary of State Colin Powell, himself a retired Army General and former Chairperson of the Joint Chiefs of Staff.

The Joint Chiefs of Staff consist of a chairperson, the chiefs of staff of the Army and the Air Force, the chief of Naval operations, and the commandant of the Marine Corps. Until recently, the JCS advised the president and the secretary of defense on important military questions and also served as heads of their various services. A former chairman of the JCS, General David Jones, argued that the service chiefs were unable to separate themselves from the interests of their individual service and to give objective advice on matters involving the defense budget. Another defense critic argued that the requirements of satisfying each individual service have weakened our capacity to prosecute war successfully.[4] Thus, giving every service a mission assignment often took precedence over designing strategy. The failure of President Carter's Desert One operation to rescue American hostages in Tehran in 1980 was attributed to the fact that every service had to be given a piece of the action.

To improve the situation, Congress passed the Goldwater-Nichols Defense Reorganization Act in 1986. It made the Chair of the Joint chiefs the principal military adviser to the secretary of defense and the president. Since the Chair headed no specific service, he or she was expected to provide objective military advice and to avoid the bland consensus that could come from the Joint Chiefs. To reduce service rivalry further, the actual command of combat forces rests with nine unified commanders. The 2002 Unified Command Plan, which revised the previous structure, divides responsibility between five geographic and four structural unified commands.[5]

[4]David C. Jones, "Why the Joint Chiefs of Staff Must Change," in *Understanding U.S. Strategy: A Reader,* ed. Terry L. Heyns (Washington, DC: National Defense University Press, 1983), pp. 304–325; Edward Luttwak, *The Pentagon and the Art of War* (New York: Simon and Schuster, 1985).
[5]Department of Defense, "Unified Command Plan," http://www.defenselink.mil/specials/unifiedcommand/ (16 October 2002).

Contemporary Controversies
Can Presidents Take the Country
to War on Their Own Authority?

The Gulf War was no minor military operation, certainly as compared to the American interventions in Grenada (1983) and Panama (1989). It involved over 500,000 troops, several carrier battle groups, and an extensive air armada. Could President George H. Bush have committed such forces to battle, as did President Truman in Korea, without prior congressional approval? The issue was never politically joined, as Congress did authorize President Bush to use military force against Iraq on January 12, 1991. Nonetheless, President Bush had maintained that he had ample constitutional authority to initiate such action without a congressional mandate. Was he correct? This question remains a vital one for American foreign policy. The second President Bush faced a similar question, ironically enough, also with Iraq. Like his father, George W. Bush took the constitutionally assured route, receiving permission from Congress to invade Iraq on October 10, 2002.

In the following selections, excerpted from the 1991 congressional debate on this question, Robert W. Merry argues that constitutional history and political necessity both require that the president receive authorization from the Congress before taking the country to war. On the other hand, Senator Jesse Helm (R-NC) in his speech to the Senate during the January 12th debate argues that the president had ample authority to make war without prior congressional consent.

Congressional Record—Senate

Jesse Helms

On August 27, 1787, the Constitutional Convention meeting in Philadelphia adopted without debate the words of Article II, section 2, clause 1, that the President is "Commander in Chief of the Army and Navy of the United States." He is also the head of the militia of the several States, if federalized.

Thus, the Constitution made the President the only Commander in Chief of the Armed Forces of this Nation. The President is therefore obligated to protect the interests of the United States, to defend the rights of its citizenry, and to preserve the national security by whatever means are necessary.

Thirteen years later, at the beginning of the second decade of the Constitutional Republic, Congressman John Marshall, before he was appointed Chief Justice, declared on the floor of the House of Representatives that "the President is the sole organ of the Nation in its external relations, and its sole representative with foreign nations."

There is no historical evidence that Chief Justice Marshall ever changed his mind. The phrase "sole organ of the Nation in its external relations" was emphatically restated by the U.S. Supreme Court in 1936 (*U.S.* v. *Curtiss Wright Corp.*). This view has never been repudiated by the Court.

On the other hand, the Constitution fails to provide for 535 other Commanders in Chief.

Article III, section 8, clauses 11–16, specifically enumerate the war powers of the Congress in the Constitution. Congress is given the power: First, to declare war; second, to raise and support armies; third, to provide and maintain a navy; fourth, to make laws regulating the Armed Forces; and fifth, to support the militia of the Federal States. These specific powers encompass the sole authority of the U.S. Congress with regard to war.

Thus, Congress can in no way limit or authorize the President's constitutional authority as Commander in Chief. Congress has attempted to do that in the War Powers Act, an act which I strongly opposed at the time of its passage in 1973, and which no Chief Executive

Can Presidents Take the Country to War on Their Own Authority?, *continued*

has ever accepted; but I believe that the War Powers Act is plainly unconstitutional.

In the short time that the Convention spent debating the subject, the Founders made a careful distinction between making war and declaring war. James Madison and Elbridge Gerry were responsible for enlarging the Presidential prerogative to enable the Chief Executive to meet the demands of national security.

As Madison warned in *Federalist* No. 48, encroachments by one branch upon another branch will upset the delicate balance of the tripartite constitutional system. Thus, it is exceedingly important to hold the branches to their intended functions with respect to the conduct of American foreign relations.

What the Framers originally intended . . . was to make a careful distinction between declaring war and making war. The Constitution is silent on whether the President is required to make war after Congress declares war; at the same time, it is silent on whether the President is prohibited from making war if Congress has not declared war. Clearly, common sense requires that the President seek the agreement and cooperation of Congress in any endeavor that commits the lives and fortunes of the American people.

The powers to declare and make war are inherent powers of national sovereignty. The President has welcomed the cooperation of the United Nations and our allies in the United Nations who have supported us with diplomacy and by conducting troops. But the U.S. Constitution is superior to any obligations that we may or may not have undertaken by assenting to the U.N. Charter. No treaty can compel us, either in fact or in intention, to set aside any provision of the U.S. Constitution. The power to declare and make war therefore remains with the United States, and has not been delegated to the United Nations.

The U.S. Constitution was carefully crafted to allow much room for judgment. And in matters of war, the power to declare war does indeed lie with Congress . . . nobody disputes that. But Congress has used that power only five times. On the other hand, the power to make war clearly belongs to the Commander in Chief, and we do not have but one Commander in Chief at a time.

From the *Congressional Record*, January 12, 1991, p. S387.

President, Congress, and War Powers
Robert W. Merry

When presidents commit the country to military campaigns of such force, should they seek from Congress a declaration of war?

There are two elements to the question: the constitutional and the political.

Though the president is the country's commander in chief, the Constitution vests with Congress the power to "declare war." This division was a bold innovation when the Founding Fathers wrote it; at the time, all other governments vested the warmaking power solely in the executive.

But the Founders considered that approach dangerous. As James Madison wrote, "The Constitution supposes . . . the executive is the branch of power most interested in war and most prone to it. It has accordingly, with studied care, vested the question of war in the legislature."

(continues)

Can Presidents Take the Country to War on Their Own Authority?, *continued*

Through the country's 200-year saga, Congress has declared war five times: the War of 1812, the Mexican War (1846), the Spanish-American War (1898), World War I (1917), and World War II (1941). And yet the forces of history have fostered a constant growth in presidential prerogative in this crucial area.

"With few exceptions, the power to initiate and wage war has shifted to the executive branch," historian Louis Fisher wrote in 1972. This was particularly true after 1945, when the cold war and the advent of nuclear weapons and intercontinental missiles raised questions about the ability of Congress to act with sufficient speed in a modern global crisis.

Thus, we had the Korean and Vietnam conflicts, two major wars waged without any formal congressional approval. Congress provided financial support, of course, and passed vague expressions of assent such as the 1964 Tonkin Gulf Resolution.

But at the base of all this was the question of whether the government had simply decided to ignore the Constitution. What precisely did the congressional power to declare war mean? Did it confer any obligation on the executive branch to seek formal congressional assent before going to war? Did it impose obligations on Congress to assert its prerogative in such momentous matters?

In light of the past 45 years, these might seem like mere academic discussion points . . . But the political dimension renders them far more serious than that. In the 1950s and 60s, with World War II fresh in the nation's consciousness, the American people were inclined to delegate to the executive broad discretion in the use of military force. And Congress pretty much went along. Thus, when President Dwight D. Eisenhower sent 14,300 marines to Lebanon in 1958, it caused hardly a political ripple in the United States. Johnson's Dominican Republic action generated far more domestic criticism, but the operation's success staved off any lasting political harm.

All that changed in the post-Vietnam era. Congress is more protective of its foreign policy prerogatives these days, more inclined to assert itself on operational matters and to criticize the president on delicate matters of state. In recent years, we have seen a House Speaker from the congressional majority party, Texas Democrat Jim Wright, virtually take control of the country's Central American policy.

All this underscores the political danger inherent in foreign military operations. When the stark realities become evident with the first signs of difficulty, the president becomes vulnerable to congressional second-guessing and naysaying. One could argue that the military challenge is daunting enough, without adding this political component.

And getting Congress aboard in the early days of national resolve is one way to lessen the political danger later on. It has been said that the postwar era was too dangerous and unstable to allow for consistent fealty to constitutional niceties such as the right of Congress to declare war. But that era is history now, and so perhaps it would be proper—and politically prudent—to return to the Constitution.

From *Congressional Quarterly Weekly Report*, August 25, 1990.

The Role of Congress

Given the different philosophies, interests, and objectives of the 535 representatives and senators, there are practical limits on congressional power in this field. Congress cannot forge a coherent foreign policy, it cannot negotiate with foreign powers, it cannot respond quickly to international crises, and it cannot conduct the day-to-day business of foreign relations. Congress can, however, tell the president what the executive branch cannot do. In the 1970s, it limited the president's authority to conduct arms sales, to intervene in Angola, to continue the bombing of Cambodia and Laos during the Vietnam War, and to send troops into combat for longer than 60 days without congressional approval. Congress serves as a check or constraining force in foreign policy, and to its critics it plays largely a negative role. As one pointed out, foreign policy is a geopolitical chess game, and chess is not a team sport.[6]

Congress is poorly equipped to conduct foreign policy for three reasons: *parochialism, organizational weakness,* and *lack of information.* Parochialism is found in the constituency focus of the members. As a result, their attention to foreign policy can be only brief and determined by the newsworthy nature of the issue. Organizational weakness is found in the fragmented and diffuse centers of congressional decision making. Over half of the standing committees in the House and Senate have jurisdiction over some area of foreign policy. No individual, set of individuals, or particular committee can speak for the entire Congress. Congress does not have the same resources as the executive branch for obtaining information and therefore often must rely upon the other branch.[7] It is in part because of these institutional weaknesses that Congress often abdicates the authority that it does have, turning over the reins of foreign policy almost entirely to the president. On October 10, 2002 Congress passed a joint resolution authorizing the President to deploy U.S. armed forced in order to conduct military actions against Iraq with very little congressional oversight. The fact that the House and Senate only asked the president to report his actions to them from time to time after the U.S. started a military campaign, and that they authorized a broad use of force, indicates how difficult Congress finds it to limit the president in foreign and defense policy.

Domestic Policy and National Security

In general, the public is more concerned with domestic questions than foreign and defense issues. But leaders cannot conduct national security policy in a political vacuum. Public opinion sets the outer limits of what is politically possible. Moreover, ethnic and economic interests exercise considerable influence on specific policies. The 9/11 attacks

---

[6]John G. Tower, "Congress Versus the President," *Foreign Affairs* 60 (1981–1982) 18.
[7]Martin E. Goldstein, *America's Foreign Policy: Drift or Decision* (Wilmington, DE.: Scholarly Resources, Inc., 1984), p.367.

brought foreign policy and national security to the forefront of national attention for the first time in a decade or more, but it remains to be seen what the long-term affect on the relationship between domestic policy and national security will be.

Public Moods and Foreign Policy

Public opinion surveys generally show the American people to be uninformed about the complexities and details of foreign policy. On specific issues public opinion changes frequently, is affected by current events, and in the short term accepts dramatic decisions made by the president. Does public opinion, then, have any influence on foreign policy?

Public moods or general attitudes, rather than opinions on specific questions, are what really influence policy. Such moods set limits within which foreign policy decisions are made. After the Japanese attacked Pearl Harbor in 1941 the public mood shifted from isolationism to internationalism. This internationalist mood became the broad consensus that provided the basis of public support for the United Nations, the Marshall Plan, NATO, and other initiatives of that period.[8]

The Vietnam War created a split in the internationalist consensus between liberal and conservative internationalists. Opposed to America's participation in that war and disillusioned with military power, liberal internationalists supported such cooperative goals as increasing assistance to the developing nations, reaching accommodation with the Soviet Union, negotiating arms control, and combating world hunger. Conservative internationalists stressed competition, opposed detente with the Soviet Union, and emphasized military defense and the use of force to protect our allies and interests abroad.[9]

In the years that have followed the Vietnam War the public mood has vacillated. In the mid-1970s less than 50 percent of the public approved of the use of American troops to support even such allies as Western Europe and Japan from a Soviet attack. But the seizure of American hostages in Iran and the Soviet invasion of Afghanistan in 1979 created a shift toward conservative internationalism; by 1980 a majority of Americans supported the use of troops to defend Western Europe and Japan.

The invasions of Grenada (1983) and Panama (1989) designed to oust dictatorships and install friendly democratic governments found broad public support. These actions, however, were brief, involved relatively few troops, and resulted in minor casualties. Although the Gulf war in 1991 involved an enormous commitment of land, air, and naval forces, victory was so swift and decisive that public support never wavered. On the other hand, the Korean and Vietnam experiences revealed that Americans soon become impatient with protracted and unresolved land wars. American support for the war on terrorism, in all of its evolving phases, has been mixed. Support for the initial

---

[8]Gabriel A. Almond, *The American People and Foreign Policy* (New York: Praeger, 1962), p. 53.
[9]William Schneider, "Conservatism, Not Internationalism: Trends in Foreign Policy Opinion, 1974–1982," in *Eagle Defiant: United States Foreign Policy in the 1980s,* eds. Kenneth Oye, Robert J. Lieber, and Donald Rothchild (Boston: Little, Brown, 1983), p. 45.

strikes against the Taliban government in Afghanistan in late 2001 was very high. In November 2001, 62 percent of Americans believed the U.S. should "mount a long-term war to defeat global terrorist networks."[10] As the scope of conflict broadened in the months that followed, however, support for military action decreased. By October 2002, only a slim majority (53%) supported an invasion of Iraq, and that majority disappeared entirely when qualifiers were added to the question. For example, only 37 percent of Americans would support such an invasion if the United Nations opposed the action, and only one-third would support the invasion if they knew there would be 5,000 U.S. casualties.[11]

How do such moods affect foreign policy? They can place limits on the choices available to policymakers. The American public is clearer about what they do not want than about what should be done. During the late 1960s and early 1970s public opinion opposed continued American involvement in the Vietnam War. But it gave no clear indication as to how the Nixon administration should end that involvement.

Multinational Corporations and Banks

multinational corporations

Large companies that carry on business in two or more countries simultaneously.

Multinational corporations are large corporations based in one country that have considerable assets and numerous subsidiaries in others. The leading American giants are Wal-Mart, Exxon-Mobil, General Motors, Ford, and, before filing for bankruptcy in December 2001, Enron.[12] These corporations command greater resources than many of the countries in the United Nations. Their sales today outrank all but the richest nations of the world.

In 1975, the United States, through the CIA, actively opposed the Soviet- and Cuban-backed faction in Angola, known as the MPLA. Yet the Gulf Oil Company, with extensive oil investments in Angola, made its royalty payments to the MPLA in amounts that far exceeded the budget of the CIA operation. When the State Department protested, Gulf temporarily suspended its payments. But they were eventually resumed after the MPLA had triumphed over the pro-Western faction, and Gulf Oil continued to develop a cooperative relationship with the Marxist MPLA government.[13] In 2000, multinational corporations successfully lobbied for the passage of a bill providing Permanent Normalized Trade Relations (PNTR) with China. America had held the giant Asian country at arm's length in the past, due to a poor human rights record, but corporations lobbied diligently for America to reduce trade barriers. These efforts, in addition to $58 million in campaign contributions, may have played an important role in the pol-

---

[10]The Gallup Organization, "Americans on Iraq: Military Action or Diplomacy?" 8 October 2002, http://www.gallup.com/poll/tb/goverPubli/20021008.asp (17 October 2002).]

[11]The Gallup Organization, "Top Ten Findings About Public Opinion and Iraq," 8 October 2002, http://www.gallup.com/poll/releases/pr021008.asp (17 October 2002).

[12]"The 2002 Fortune 500," *Fortune*, http://www.fortune.com/lists/F500/index.html (17 October 2002).

[13]Richard J. Barnet, *Real Security: Restoring American Power in a Dangerous Decade* (New York: Simon & Schuster, 1981), p. 69.

icy change. The new trade status resulted in $123.9 billion in trade between the two nations in 2000, a 22 percent jump over the previous year.[14]

American banks have also become heavily involved in overseas activities. In 1980 American banks had made $280 billion in overseas loans, a large portion of which went to developing nations and Eastern Europe. By the end of 2001 American banks claimed over $1.4 trillion in international investment, with some of the recent growth coming in the form of loans to Western Europe and the Caribbean.[15] Are loans of this nature and magnitude in the interests of the American people? Critics of the banks contend that loans to unstable developing governments unnecessarily risk important investment capital. Supporters argue they can help development schemes and add to stability in these parts of the world.

The volume of these debts underscores the growing interdependence of the world economy. For example, what would happen if a major debtor nation defaulted on its loans? Clearly it could throw many of the major banks and perhaps the entire international economy into turmoil. Indeed this was just the risk the world economy faced in the late 1990s when several East Asian countries became mired in economic turmoil. It was only the proffering of over $200 billion in aid packages from the International Monetary Fund that prevented a much deeper and more widespread crisis.

While foreign loans and investments gave American banks and corporations a stake in the economies of these countries, the leverage of the MNCs can work two ways, opening the door to foreign influence over the American economy. Japanese companies, for example, made large investments in the United States, buying Columbia Records and the Rockefeller Center. The Japanese automobile and electronics industries depend heavily upon their American customers. Japanese companies contribute to state political campaigns and the Japanese governments spend millions each year lobbying Congress against legislation that would limit the market for Japanese goods.

The Military-Industrial Complex

military-industrial complex

The Pentagon, defense contractors, unions in the defense industry, members of Congress whose states or districts receive considerable military funds, and academic strategists whose work is funded by the military.

In his farewell address President Eisenhower warned the American people "against the acquisition of unwarranted influence, whether sought or unsought, by the military-industrial complex. The potential for disastrous use of misplaced power exists and will persist." What is the military-industrial complex, and does its influence distort our national security policy?

Few observers deny the existence or importance of the **military-industrial complex.** It includes the Pentagon, major corporations whose profits depend on large defense contracts, members of Congress whose states and districts include these con-

---

[14]The Center for Responsive Politics, "A Passage to China Update: House Approves PNTR," 24 May 2000, http://www.opensecrets.org (17 October 2002), "Anxious Eyes on Beijing—and Washington," *Business Week*, 30 April 2001.
[15]Financial Markets Center, *Capital Flows Monitor,* 26 July 2002.

tractors or military installations, unions whose members depend on defense work, and the numerous defense scientists and academic strategists whose work is funded by the military.

Critics find that the influence of the military-industrial complex distorts defense policy and weakens our economy. They charge that by absorbing so much of the country's scientific and engineering talent, it erodes our ability to compete with other industrialized countries in the application of advanced technology to consumer products.

Second, critics argue that the military-industrial complex favors the production of weapons that are too expensive and often obsolete. Much of the blame for this centers on Congress, which frequently funds weapons systems regardless of their military value, simply because they are produced in the districts of influential members.

Several of the nation's largest corporations—Boeing, United Technologies, Lockheed Martin, Honeywell International, and Raytheon, for example—each have revenues in excess of $15 billion and gain a large percentage of their sales from the federal government, most of it related to defense.[16] These companies also operate some of the largest PACs in America and channel their contributions to members of Congress on the Appropriation and Armed Forces Committees. In the 2000 election cycle defense corporations PACs spent over $13 million in campaign and soft money contributions, 65 percent of which went to Republicans.[17] Although it is unfair to claim defense industry lobbying is the sole cause of defense spending, it certainly doesn't hurt. America spends an average of $500,000 per minute on defense.[18]

Although many Americans anticipated a decreased need for military spending after the end of the cold war, such a windfall has not occurred. Throughout the 1990s, Defense Department officials and defense industry lobbyists insisted that America's economic well-being depended on a smoothly functioning international system, which could require the use of military power. The 9/11 attacks convinced many of this need. In fiscal 2002 America devoted $19.5 billion exclusively to **Homeland Security**; that amount increased to 37.7 billion in 2003.[19]

Learning to live with the military-industrial complex is a formidable challenge to the American political system. In the era of the Founders, large standing armies, entangling alliances, and centralized governments were evils to be avoided, not accommodated.

Homeland Security

The effort of protecting of United States soil, particularly from foreign or terrorist attack.

Current Issues in Foreign and Defense Policy

Faced with the limits of power and yet still burdened with the obligations of a superpower, America confronts issues that defy any easy or quick solutions. Policymakers

---

[16]"The 2002 Fortune 500," *Fortune*, http://www.fortune.com/lists/F500/index.html (17 October 2002).

[17]The Center for Responsive Politics, http://www.opensecrets.org/industries/indus.asp?Ind=D (19 October 2002).

[18]George C. Wilson, *This War Really Matters: Inside the Fight for Defense Dollars* (Washington, DC: CQ Press, 2000).

[19]Office of Management and Budget, *The Budget for Fiscal Year 2003* (Washington, DC: GPO, 2002), p. 399.

face painful choices. They must recognize the demands of Congress and the public, the concerns of our allies, the unpredictable social forces in the developing world, and the ever-present dangers of nuclear arms and other weapons of mass destruction.

Shaping the defense budget in an era of fiscal austerity involves annual struggles with Congress. Dealing with the Western European allies who have grown prosperous and independent since the days of the Marshall Plan requires greater patience and tact. Confronting threats to the peace, such as international terrorist attacks, and the proliferation of nuclear weapons may take a measured balance of military force and shrewd diplomacy. Those problems will occupy our policymakers for some time to come.

9/11 and the War on Terrorism

When terrorists hijacked four airplanes to use as weapons against America on September 11, 2001, they did much more than kill thousands of innocent human beings. They prompted a new era of American foreign and defense policy, known generally as the War on Terrorism. In the months following the attack, the Bush administration used military force to drive the Taliban government (which had been harboring the al Qaeda terrorist network responsible for the attack) from power in Afghanistan, identified several other potentially threatening countries as an "axis of evil," and prepared for a military invasion of Iraq, which it accused of amassing chemical and biological weapons.

In addition to these highly visible actions, the Bush administration has also been busy developing a broad strategy for approaching world affairs. Unveiled in September 2002, President Bush's *National Security Strategy of the United States of America* calls for "a distinctly American internationalism that reflects the union of our values and our national interests."[20] The document sets forth three goals: political and economic freedom, peaceful interstate relations, and respect for human dignity. The Bush administration hopes to attain these goals through strong, worldwide military presence, encouraging free trade and economic development, and transforming national security institutions.

An example of this last point has been Bush's call for a Department of Homeland Security. Though President Bush was able to create an Office of Homeland Security within the executive branch, he needed congressional approval to make this office a permanent, cabinet-level department. The struggles he encountered in this effort are illustrative of the difficulty in changing America's formal institutions. Congressional Democrats opposed Bush's proposal, in part because, in reclassifying 170,000 federal employees, it removed their job security. President Bush argued that national security should not be hamstrung by labor disputes, but Democrats were concerned that the Republican administration would use the reduced job protection clause to unfairly weed out employees for political reasons. As late Senator Arthur Vandenberg (R-MI) famously noted in regard to

---

[20]George W. Bush, *The National Security Strategy of the United States of America* (Washington, DC: GPO, 2002), p. 1.

American foreign policy, "politics ends at the water's edge." While this claim may have held true in an earlier era, the shape and direction of American defense policy in the twenty-first century continue to be a matter of domestic political difference."

International Organization and the Developing World

developing nations

Nations whose standard of living lags far behind that of the industrialized states.

International Monetary Fund (IMF)

A specialized agency of the United Nations designed to promote international monetary cooperation.

World Bank

A specialized agency of the United Nations that makes loans to poorer nations for economic development.

Another challenge of twenty first century foreign policy is the great economic disparity between wealthy countries and poor countries. The latter group of countries, commonly referred to as **developing nations**, find themselves in the difficult position of attempting to gain an economic foothold, and maintain political stability, in a world where many other countries already have established themselves in the global market. Recognition of this difficult situation by the international community has resulted in two organizations whose mission is to help alleviate this problem. The two agencies, both part of the United Nations, are the **International Monetary Fund (IMF)** and the **World Bank**.

The International Monetary Fund was created in 1945 to help UN member nations overcome problems in their balance of payments and to help avoid another worldwide depression like to one that dominated the 1930s. Starting with just 45 member nations, the IMF today consists of 184 countries and has resources (which it calls quotas) of $280 billion. The IMF seeks to achieve its economic objectives through increased international trade, monetary stability and cooperation, and making funds available to nations experiencing debt crises.[21] Although its objectives are noble, some have criticized the organization and tactics of the IMF. For example, critics note that the decisions of the IMF Executive Board, which is responsible for conducting the organization's day to day business, are often controlled by the members representing the wealthier, industrialized nations. Some have argued that the United States, for example, takes a carrot and stick approach to funding decisions, rewarding nations that fall in line with American policy interests and punishing those which do not, regardless of the economic results on which the agency is supposed to focus.[22]

Closely related to the IMF, the World Bank was created in 1944 to provide loans to poor countries, with a goal of promoting worldwide economic growth and reducing poverty. In 2002 the World Bank loaned over $19 billion to developing nations. As signs of its success, the organization points to increases in life expectancy and literacy rates and decreases in infant mortality around the globe.[23] Like the IMF, though, this body has its critics. One charge is that the Bank's narrow focus on economic development sometimes causes it to make decisions that are at odds with other important concerns, such as environmental protection.

---

[21]International Monetary Fund, "The IMF at a Glance," 21 August 2002, http://www.imf.org/external/np/exr/facts/glance.htm (20 October 2002).

[22]Gustavo Gonzalez, "Aid to Brazil, Uruguay fails to dampen criticism of IMF," *Third World Network Online,* http://www.twnside.org.sg/title/twr143g.htm (20 October 2002).

[23]The World Bank, "At a Glance," http://www.worldbank.org (20 October 2002).

So, how does all of this affect American foreign policy? To start with, in an increasingly interconnected world, decisions that affect one nation, or group of nations, are likely to have an impact on every other country as well. If the problems of overpopulation, malnutrition, and underemployment go unattended in the developing world, the chances of civil wars, regional conflicts, and revolutions in those areas will increase. It is unlikely that such regional instability will fail to adversely affect the political stability of the industrialized world as well. Second, as the world's largest economy, the United States plays a particularly crucial role in shaping the global economy. With such power comes responsibility. One of the challenges for American foreign policy in the twenty-first century will be deciding which values should drive our economic relations with the rest of the world.

SUMMARY

1. The foreign policy consensus after World War II represented a shift from isolationism to internationalism. During the Cold War years this internationalism was characterized by the doctrine of containment. After the Cold War ended in 1989-90 the United States had to develop a new approach to foreign policy, this time as the world's primary superpower.

2. Although the president no longer monopolizes foreign and defense policymaking, he is the major actor and the primary initiator. Congress, though it cannot direct policy, can place important constraints on policy. Neither can the State Department dominate the foreign policy bureaucracy. As military action and covert activities have become an integral part of policy implementation, the Defense Department and the CIA have staked a permanent claim to much of the foreign policy turf.

3. A number of domestic constituencies, largely economic, have developed a strong interest in particular aspects of foreign and defense policy. Although their influence is considerable, it is difficult for them to overcome the determined will of the president.

4. Contemporary concerns, such as the War on Terrorism and the economies of developing nations defy solutions that can be reduced to simple formulas or doctrines. Every choice a policymaker makes may involve antagonizing an ally, a domestic constituency, members of Congress, or even part of the executive bureaucracy itself.

KEY TERMS

isolationism (472)

internationalism (472)

Truman Doctrine (474)

Marshall Plan (475)

détente (476)

Nixon Doctrine (476)

Department of State (478)

United States Agency for International
Development (480)

Arms Control and Disarmament
Agency (ACDA) (480)

Office of International Information
Programs (480)

Central Intelligence Agency (CIA) (480)

Department of Defense (DOD) (481)

Joint Chiefs of Staff (483)

multinational corporations (489)

military-industrial complex (490)

Homeland Security (491)

developing nations (493)

International Monetary Fund (IMF) (493)

World Bank (493)

READINGS FOR FURTHER STUDY

For a comprehensive overview of American foreign policy since 1945 see Steven W. Hook and John W. Spanier, *American Foreign Policy Since World War II*, 15th ed. (Washington, DC: CQ Press, 2000) and Walter Isaacson and Evan Thomas, *The Wise Men: Six Friends and the World They Made* (New York: Touchstone Books, 1997).

Joseph S. Nye, Jr.'s *The Paradox of American Power: Why the World's Only Superpower Can't Go It Alone* (New York: Oxford University Press, 2002) explores the difficulties of the United States emerging role as the world's sole superpower.

An excellent account of presidents' actions in foreign and defense policy throughout American history is Louis Fisher's *Presidential War Power* (Lawrence, KS: University Press of Kansas, 1995).

The process of defense budgeting is described insightfully in George C. Wilson, *This War Really Matters: Inside the Fight for Defense Dollars* (Washington, DC: CQ Press, 2000).

Emerging problems of a global economy are explored in Joseph E. Stiglitz, *Globalization and Its Discontents* (New York: W.W. Norton, 2002).

American policy toward developing nations is explored in Robert Chase, ed., *The Pivotal States: A New Framework for U.S. Policy in the Developing World* (New York: W.W. Norton, 1998).

The Appendix

The Declaration of Independence

When in the Course of human events, it becomes necessary for one people to dissolve the political bands which have connected them with another, and to assume among the Powers of the earth, the separate and equal station to which the Laws of Nature and of Nature's God entitle them, a decent respect to the opinions of mankind requires that they should declare the causes which impel them to the separation.

We hold these truths to be self-evident, that all men are created equal, that they are endowed by their Creator with certain unalienable Rights, that among these are Life, Liberty and the pursuit of Happiness. That to secure these rights, Governments are instituted among Men, deriving their just Powers from the consent of the governed, That whenever any Form of Government becomes destructive of these ends, it is the Right of the People to alter or to abolish it, and to institute new Government, laying its foundation on such principles and organizing its Powers in such form, as to them shall seem most likely to effect their Safety and Happiness. Prudence, indeed, will dictate that Governments long established should not be changed for light and transient causes; and accordingly all experience hath shewn, that mankind are more disposed to suffer, while evils are sufferable, than to right themselves by abolishing the forms to which they are accustomed. But when a long train of abuses and usurpations, pursuing invariably the same object evinces a design to reduce them under absolute Despotism, it is their right, it is their duty, to throw off such Government, and to provide new Guards for their future security.—Such has been the patient sufferance of these Colonies: and such is now the necessity which constrains them to alter their former Systems of Government. The history of the present King of Great-Britain is a history of repeated injuries and usurpations, all having in direct object the Establishment of an absolute Tyranny over these States. To prove this, let Facts be submitted to a candid World.

He has refused his Assent to Laws, the most wholesome and necessary for the public good.

He has forbidden his Governors to pass Laws of immediate and pressing importance, unless suspended in their operation till his Assent should be obtained; and when so suspended, he has utterly neglected to attend to them.

He has refused to pass other Laws for the accommodation of large districts of people, unless those people would relinquish the right of Representation in the Legislature, a right inestimable to them and formidable to tyrants only.

He has called together legislative bodies at places unusual, uncomfortable, and distant from the depository of their Public Records, for the sole purpose of fatiguing them into compliance with his measures.

He has dissolved Representative Houses repeatedly, for opposing with manly firmness his invasions on the rights of the people.

He has refused for a long time, after such dissolutions, to cause others to be elected; whereby the Legislative Powers, incapable of the Annihilation, have returned to the People at large for their exercise; the State remaining in the mean time exposed to all the dangers of invasion from without, and the convulsions within.

He has endeavored to prevent the population of these States; for that purpose obstructing the Laws of Naturalization of Foreigners; refusing to pass others to encourage their migrations hither, and raising the conditions of new Appropriations of Lands.

He has obstructed the Administration of justice, by refusing his Assent to Laws for establishing Judiciary Powers.

He has made judges dependent on his Will alone, for the tenure of their offices, and the amount and payment of their salaries.

He has erected a multitude of New Offices, and sent hither swarms of Officers to harass our People, and eat out their substance.

He has kept among us, in times of peace, Standing Armies, without the consent of our legislature.

He has affected to render the Military independent of and superior to the Civil Power.

He has combined with others to subject us to a jurisdiction foreign to our constitution, and unacknowledged by our laws; giving his Assent to their acts of pretended legislation:

For quartering large bodies of armed troops among us:

For protecting them, by a mock Trial, from Punishment for any Murders which they should commit on the Inhabitants of these States:

For cutting off our Trade with all parts of the world:

For imposing Taxes on us without our Consent:

For depriving us in many cases, of the benefits of Trial by Jury:

For transporting us beyond Seas to be tried for pretended offences:

For abolishing the free System of English Laws in a neighboring Province, establishing therein an Arbitrary government, and enlarging its Boundaries so as to render it at once an example and fit instrument for introducing the same absolute rule into these Colonies:

For taking away our Charters, abolishing our most valuable Laws, and altering fundamentally the Forms of our Governments:

For suspending our own Legislatures, and declaring themselves invested with Power to legislate for us in all cases whatsoever.

He has abdicated Government here, by declaring us out of his Protection, and waging War against us.

He has plundered our seas, ravaged our Coasts, burnt our towns, and destroyed the lives of our people.

He is at this time transporting large armies of foreign mercenaries to compleat the works of death, desolation and tyranny, already begun with circumstances of Cruelty & perfidy, scarcely paralleled in the most barbarous ages, and totally unworthy the Head of a civilized nation.

He has constrained our fellow Citizens taken Captive on the high Seas to bear Arms against their Country, to become the executioners of their friends and Brethren, or to fall themselves by their Hands.

He has excited domestic insurrections amongst us, and has endeavoured to bring on the inhabitants of our frontiers, the merciless Indian Savages, whose known rule of warfare, is an undistinguished destruction of all ages, sexes and conditions.

In every stage of these Oppressions We have Petitioned for Redress in the most humble terms: Our repeated Petitions have been answered only by repeated injury. A Prince, whose character is thus marked by every act which may define a Tyrant, is unfit to be the ruler of a free People.

Nor have We been wanting in attentions to our British brethren. We have warned them from time to time of attempts by their legislature to extend an unwarrantable jurisdiction over us. We have reminded them of the circumstances of our emigration and settlement here. We have appealed to their native justice and magnanimity, and we have conjured them by the ties of our common kindred to disavow these usurpations, which, would inevitably interrupt our connections and correspondence. They too have been deaf to the voice of justice and of consanguinity. We must, therefore, acquiesce in the necessity, which denounces our Separation, and hold them, as we hold the rest of mankind, Enemies in War, in Peace, Friends.

We, therefore, the Representatives of the United States of America, in General Congress, Assembled, appealing to the Supreme judge of the world for the rectitude of our intentions, do, in the Name, and by Authority of the good People of these Colonies, solemnly publish and declare, That these United Colonies are, and of Right ought to be Free and Independent States; that they are Absolved from all Allegiance to the British Crown, and that all political connection between them and the State of Great Britain, is and ought to be totally dissolved; and that, as Free and Independent States, they have full Power to levy War, conclude Peace, contract Alliances, establish Commerce, and to do all other Acts and Things which in-dependent States may of right do. And for the support of this Declaration, with a firm reliance on the Protection of Divine Providence, we mutually pledge to each other our Lives, our Fortunes and our sacred Honor.

John Hancock,

Josiah Bartlett, Wm Whipple, Saml Adams, John Adams, Robt Treat Paine, Elbridge Gerry, Steph. Hopkins, William Ellery, Roger Sherman, Samel Huntington, Wm Williams, Oliver Wolcott, Matthew Thornton, Wm Floyd, Phil Livingston, Frans Lewis, Lewis Morris, Richd Stockton, Jno Witherspoon, Fras Hopkinson, John Hart, Abra Clark, Robt Morris, Benjamin Rush, Benja Franklin, John Morton, Geo Clymer, Jas Smith, Geo. Taylor, James Wilson, Geo. Ross, Caesar Rodney, Geo Read, Thos M:Kean, Samuel Chase, Wm Paca, Thos Stone, Charles Carroll of Carrollton, George Wythe, Richard Henry Lee, Th. Jefferson, Benja Harrison, Thos Nelson, Jr., Francis Lightfoot Lee, Carter Braxton, Wm Hooper, Joseph Hewes, John Penn, Edward Rutledge, Thos Heyward, Junr., Thomas Lynch, Junor., Arthur Middleton, Button Gwinnett, Lyman Hall, Geo Walton.

The Constitution of the United States

We the people of the United States, in Order to form a more perfect Union, establish justice, insure domestic Tranquility, provide for the common defense, promote the general Welfare, and secure the Blessings of Liberty to ourselves and our Posterity, do ordain and establish this CONSTITUTION for the United States of America.

Article I

Section 1. All legislative Powers herein granted shall be vested in a Congress of the United States, which shall consist of a Senate and House of Representatives.

Section 2. The House of Representatives shall be composed of Members chosen every second Year by the People of the several States, and the Electors in each State shall have the Qualifications requisite for Electors of the most numerous Branch of the State Legislature.

No person shall be a Representative who shall not have attained to the Age of twenty-five Years, and been seven Years a Citizen of the United States, and who shall not, when elected, be an Inhabitant of that State in which he shall be chosen.

Representatives and direct Taxes shall be apportioned among the several States which may be included within this Union, according to their respective Numbers, which shall be determined by adding to the whole Number of free Persons, including those bound to Service for a Term of Years, and excluding Indians not taxed, three fifths of all other Persons. The actual Enumeration shall be made within three Years after the first Meeting of the Congress of the United States, and within every subsequent Term of ten Years, in such Manner as they shall by Law direct. The Number of Representatives shall not exceed one for every thirty Thousand, but each State shall have at Least one Representative; and until such enumeration shall be made, the State of New Hampshire shall be entitled to chuse three, Massachusetts eight, Rhode-Island and Providence Plantations one, Connecticut five, New York six, New Jersey four, Pennsylvania eight, Delaware one, Maryland six, Virginia ten, North Carolina five, South Carolina five, and Georgia three.

When vacancies happen in the Representation from any State, the Executive Authority thereof shall issue Writs of Election to fill such Vacancies.

The House of Representatives shall chuse their Speaker and other officers; and shall have the sole Power of Impeachment.

Section 3. The Senate of the United States shall be composed of two Senators from each State, chosen by the Legislature thereof, for six Years; and each Senator shall have one Vote.

Immediately after they shall be assembled in Consequence of the first Election, they shall be divided as equally as may be into three Classes. The Seats of the Senators of the first Class shall be vacated at the Expiration of the second Year, of the second Class at the Expiration of the fourth Year, and of the third Class at the Expiration of the sixth Year, so that one-third may be chosen every second Year; and if Vacancies happen by Resignation, or otherwise, during the Recess of the Legislature of any State, the Executive thereof may make temporary Appointments until the next Meeting of the Legislature, which shall then fill such Vacancies.

No Person shall be a Senator who shall not have attained to the Age of thirty Years, and been nine Years a Citizen of the United States, and who shall not, when elected, be an Inhabitant of that State for which he shall be chosen.

The Vice President of the United States shall be President of the Senate, but shall have no vote, unless they be equally divided.

The Senate shall chuse their other Officers, and also a President pro tempore, in the absence of the Vice President, or when he shall exercise the Office of President of the United States.

The Senate shall have the sole Power to try all Impeachments. When sitting for that purpose, they shall be on Oath or Affirmation. When the President of the United States is tried, the Chief justice shall preside: And no person shall be convicted without the Concurrence of two thirds of the Members present.

Judgment in Cases of impeachment shall not extend further than to removal from Office, and disqualification to hold and enjoy any Office of honor, Trust, or Profit under the United States: but the Party convicted shall nevertheless be liable and subject to Indictment, Trial, judgment and Punishment, according to Law.

Section 4. The Times, Places and Manner of holding Elections for Senators and Rep-

resentatives, shall be prescribed in each state by the Legislature thereof; but the Congress may at any time by Law make or alter such Regulations, except as to the Places of Chusing Senators.

The Congress shall assemble at least once in every Year, and such Meeting shall be on the first Monday in December, unless they shall by Law appoint a different Day.

Section 5. Each House shall be the judge of the Elections, Returns and Qualifications of its own Members, and a Majority of each shall constitute a Quorum to do Business; but a smaller number may adjourn from day to day, and may be authorized to compel the Attendance of absent Members, in such manner, and under such Penalties, as each House may provide.

Each House may determine the Rules of its Proceedings, punish its Members for disorderly Behavior, and, with the Concurrence of two thirds, expel a Member.

Each House shall keep a journal of its Proceedings, and from time to time publish the same, excepting such Parts as may in their judgment require Secrecy; and the Yeas and Nays of the Members of either House on any question shall, at the Desire of one fifth of those Present, be entered on the journal.

Neither House, during the Session of Congress, shall, without the Consent of the other, adjourn for more than three days, nor to any other Place than that in which the two Houses shall be sitting.

Section 6. The Senators and Representatives shall receive a Compensation for their Services, to be ascertained by Law, and paid out of the Treasury of the United States. They shall in all Cases, except Treason, Felony, and Breach of the Peace, be privileged from arrest during their Attendance at the Session of their respective Houses, and in going to and returning from the same; and for any Speech or Debate in either House, they shall not be questioned in any other Place.

No Senator or Representative shall, during the Time for which he was elected, be appointed to any civil office under the Authority of the United States, which shall have been created, or the Emoluments whereof shall have been increased, during such time; and no Person holding any Office under the United States shall be a Member of either House during his continuance in Office.

Section 7. All Bills for raising Revenue shall originate in the House of Representatives; but the Senate may propose or concur with Amendments as on other bills.

Every Bill which shall have passed the House of Representatives and the Senate, shall, before it become a Law, be presented to the President of the United States; If he approve he shall sign it, but if not he shall return it, with his Objections, to that House in which it shall have originated, who shall enter the Objections at large on their journal, and proceed to reconsider it. If after such Reconsideration two thirds of that House shall agree to pass the bill, it shall be sent, together with the objections, to the other House, by which it shall likewise be reconsidered, and if ap-

proved by two thirds of that House, it shall become a Law. But in all such Cases the Votes of both Houses shall be determined by Yeas and Nays, and the Names of the Persons voting for and against the Bill shall be entered on the journal of each House respectively. If any Bill shall not be returned by the President within ten Days (Sundays excepted) after it shall have been presented to him, the Same shall be a Law, in like Manner as if he had signed it, unless the Congress by their Adjournment prevent its Return, in which Case it shall not be a Law.

Every Order, Resolution, or Vote to which the Concurrence of the Senate and House of Representatives may be necessary (except on a question of Adjournment) shall be presented to the President of the United States; and before the Same shall take Effect, shall be approved by him, or being disapproved by him, shall be repassed by two thirds of the Senate and House of Representatives, according to the Rules and Limitations prescribed in the Case of a Bill.

Section 8. The Congress shall have Power To lay and collect Taxes, Duties, Imposts and Excises, to pay the Debts and provide for the common Defense and general Welfare of the United States; but all Duties, Imposts and Excises shall be uniform throughout the United States;

To borrow money on the credit of the United States;

To regulate Commerce with foreign Nations, and among the several States, and with the Indian Tribes; To establish an uniform Rule of Naturalization, and uniform Laws on the subject of Bankruptcies through-out the United States;

To coin Money, regulate the Value thereof, and of foreign Coin, and fix the Standard of Weights and Measures;

To provide for the Punishment of counterfeiting the Securities and current Coin of the United States; To establish Post offices and post Roads;

To promote the Progress of Science and useful Arts, by securing for limited Times to Authors and inventors the exclusive Right to their respective Writings and Discoveries;

To constitute Tribunals inferior to the Supreme Court;

To define and punish Piracies and Felonies committed on the high Seas, and Offences against the Law of Nations;

To declare War, grant Letters of Marque and Reprisal, and make Rules concerning Captures on Land and Water;

To raise and support Armies, but no Appropriation of Money to that Use shall be for a longer Term than two Years;

To provide and maintain a Navy;

To make Rules for the Government and Regulation of the land and naval forces;

To provide for calling forth the Militia to execute the Laws of the Union, suppress Insurrections and repel invasions;

To provide for organizing, arming, and disciplining the Militia, and for governing such Part of them as may be employed in the Service of the United States, reserving to the States respectively, the Appointment of the Officers, and the Authority of training the Militia according to the discipline prescribed by Congress;

To exercise exclusive Legislation in all Cases whatsoever, over such District (not exceeding ten Miles square) as may, by Cession of particular States, and the acceptance of Congress, become the Seat of Government of the United States, and to exercise like Authority over all Places purchased by the Consent of the Legislature of the State in which the Same shall be, for the Erection of Forts, Magazines, Arsenals, dock-Yards, and other needful Buildings; And

To make all Laws which shall be necessary and proper for carrying into Execution the foregoing Powers, and all other Powers vested by this Constitution in the government of the United States, or in any Department or Officer thereof.

Section 9. The Migration or Importation of such Persons as any of the States now existing shall think proper to admit, shall not be prohibited by the Congress prior to the Year one thousand eight hundred and eight, but a tax or duty may be imposed on such Importation, not exceeding ten dollars for each Person.

The Privilege of the Writ of Habeas Corpus shall not be suspended, unless when in Cases of Rebellion or Invasion the public Safety may require it.

No Bill of Attainder or ex post facto Law shall be passed.

No capitation, or other direct, Tax shall be laid unless in Proportion to the Census or Enumeration herein before directed to be taken.

No Tax or Duty shall be laid on Articles exported from any State.

No Preference shall be given by any Regulation of commerce or Revenue to the Ports of one State over those of another: nor shall Vessels bound to, or from, one state, be obliged to enter, clear, or pay Duties in another.

No Money shall be drawn from the Treasury, but in Consequence of Appropriations made by Law; and a regular Statement and Account of the Receipts and Expenditures of all public Money shall be published from time to time.

No Title of Nobility shall be granted by the United States: And no Person holding any Office of Profit or Trust under them, shall, without the Consent of the Congress, accept of any present, Emolument, Office, or Title, of any kind whatever, from any King, Prince, or Foreign State.

Section 10. No State shall enter into any Treaty, Alliance, or Confederation; grant Letters of Marque and Reprisal; coin Money; emit Bills of Credit; make any Thing but gold and silver Coin a Tender in Payment of Debts; pass any Bill of Attainder, ex post facto Law, or Law impairing the obligation of Contracts, or grant any Title of Nobility.

No State shall, without the Consent of the Congress, lay any Imposts or Duties on Imports or Exports, except what may be absolutely necessary for executing its inspection Laws: and the net Produce of all Duties and Imposts, laid by any State on Imports or Exports, shall be for the Use of the Treasury of the United States; and all such Laws shall be subject to the Revision and Control of the Congress.

No State shall, without the Consent of Congress, lay any duty of Tonnage, keep Troops, or Ships of War in time of peace, enter into any Agreement or Compact with another State, or with a foreign Power, or engage in War, unless actually invaded, or in such imminent Danger as will not admit of delay.

Article II

Section 1. The executive Power shall be vested in a President of the United States of America. He shall hold his Office during the Term of four Years, and, together with the Vice President, chosen for the same Term, be elected, as follows:

Each State shall appoint, in such Manner as the Legislature thereof may direct, a Number of Electors, equal to the whole Number of Senators and Representatives to which the State may be entitled in the Congress; but no Senator or Representative, or Person holding an Office of Trust or Profit under the United States, shall be appointed an Elector.

The Electors shall meet in their respective States, and vote by Ballot for two persons, of whom one at least shall not be an Inhabitant of the same State with themselves. And they shall make a List of all the Persons voted for, and of the Number of Votes for each; which List they shall sign and certify, and transmit sealed to the Seat of the Government of the United States, directed to the President of the Senate. The President of the Senate shall, in the Presence of the Senate and House of Representatives, open all the Certificates, and the Votes shall then be counted. The Person having the greatest Number of Votes shall be the President, if such Number be a Majority of the whole Number of Electors appointed; and if there be more than one who have such Majority, and have an equal Number of Votes, then the House of Representatives shall immediately chuse by Ballot one of them for President; and if no Person have a Majority, then from the five highest on the List the said House shall in like Manner chuse the President. But in chusing the President, the votes shall be taken by States, the Representation from each State having one Vote; a quorum for this Purpose shall consist of a Member or Members from two-thirds of the States, and a Majority of all the States shall be necessary to a Choice. In every Case, after the Choice of the President, the Person having the greatest Number of Votes of the Electors shall be the Vice President. But if there should remain two or more who have equal votes, the Senate shall chuse from them by Ballot the Vice President.

The Congress may determine the time of chusing the Electors, and the Day on which they shall give their Votes; which Day shall be the same throughout the United States.

No person except a natural-born Citizen, or a Citizen of the United States, at the time of the Adoption of this Constitution, shall be eligible to the Office of President; neither shall any Person be eligible to that office who shall not have attained to the Age of thirty-five Years, and been fourteen Years a Resident within the United States.

In Case of the Removal of the President from Office, or of his Death, Resignation, or Inability to discharge the Powers and Duties of the said Office, the same shall devolve on the Vice President, and the Congress may by Law provide for the Case of Removal, Death, Resignation, or Inability, both of the President and Vice President, declaring what Officer shall then act as President, and such Officer shall act accordingly, until the Disability be removed, or a President shall be elected.

The President shall, at stated Times, receive for his Services a Compensation, which shall neither be increased nor diminished during the Period for which he shall have been elected, and he shall not receive within that Period any other Emolument from the United States, or any of them.

Before he enter on the execution of his Office, he shall take the following Oath or Affirmation: "I do solemnly swear (or affirm) that I will faithfully execute the Office of President of the United States, and will, to the best of my Ability, preserve, protect, and defend the Constitution of the United States."

Section 2. The President shall be Commander in Chief of the Army and Navy of the United States, and of the Militia of the several States, when called into the actual Service of the United States; he may require the Opinion, in writing, of the principal Officer in each of the executive Departments, upon any subject relating to the Duties of their respective Offices, and he shall have Power to Grant Reprieves and

Pardons for Offences against the United States, except in Cases of Impeachment.

He shall have Power, by and with the Advice and Consent of the Senate, to make Treaties, provided two thirds of the Senators present concur; and he shall nominate, and by and with the Advice and Consent of the Senate, shall appoint Ambassadors, other public Ministers and Consuls, judges of the supreme Court, and all other Officers of the United States, whose Appointments are not herein otherwise provided for, and which shall be established by Law: but the Congress may by Law vest the Appointment of such inferior Officers, as they think proper, in the President alone, in the Courts of Law, or in the Heads of Departments.

The President shall have Power to fill up all Vacancies that may happen during the Recess of the Senate, by granting Commissions which shall expire at the End of their next Session.

Section 3. He shall from time to time give to the Congress Information of the State of the Union, and recommend to their Consideration such Measures as he shall judge necessary and expedient; he may, on extraordinary occasions, convene both Houses, or either of them, and in Case of Disagreement between them, with respect to the Time of Adjournment, he may adjourn them to such Time as he shall think proper; he shall receive Ambassadors and other public Ministers; he shall take Care that the Laws be faithfully executed, and shall Commission all the officers of the United States.

Section 4. The President, Vice President and all civil Officers of the United States, shall be removed from Office on Impeachment for, and Conviction of, Treason, Bribery, or other high Crimes and Misdemeanors.

Article III

Section 1. The judicial Power of the United States, shall be vested in one supreme Court, and in such inferior Courts as the Congress may from time to time ordain and establish. The judges, both of the supreme and inferior Courts, shall hold their Offices during good Behaviour, and shall, at stated Times, receive for their Services, a Compensation, which shall not be diminished during their Continuance in Office.

Section 2. The judicial Power shall extend to all Cases, in Law and Equity, arising under this Constitution, the Laws of the United States, and treaties made, or which shall be made, under their Authority;—to all Cases affecting Ambassadors, other public ministers and consuls; to all cases of admiralty and maritime jurisdiction;—to Controversies to which the United States shall be a Party; to Controversies between two or more States; between a State and Citizens of another States—between Citizens of different States,—between Citizens of the same State claiming Lands under Grants of different States, and between a State, or the Citizens thereof, and foreign States, Citizens or Subjects.

In all Cases affecting Ambassadors, other public Ministers and Consuls, and those in which a State shall be Party, the supreme Court shall have original Jurisdiction. In all the other Cases before mentioned, the supreme Court shall have appellate jurisdiction, both as to Law and Fact, with such Exceptions, and under such Regulations as the Congress shall make.

The trial of all Crimes, except in Cases of Impeachment, shall be by jury; and such Trial shall be held in the State where the said Crimes shall have been committed; but when not committed within any State, the trial shall be at such Place or Places as the Congress may by Law have directed.

Section 3. Treason against the United States, shall consist only in levying War against them, or in adhering to their Enemies, giving them Aid and Comfort. No Person shall be convicted of Treason unless on the testimony of two Witnesses to the same overt Act, or on Confession in open Court.

The Congress shall have power to declare the Punishment of Treason, but no Attainder of Treason shall work Corruption of Blood, or Forfeiture except during the Life of the Person attainted.

Article IV

Section 1. Full Faith and Credit shall be given in each State to the public Acts, Records, and judicial Proceedings of every other State. And the Congress may by general Laws prescribe the Manner in which such Acts, Records and Proceedings shall be proved, and the Effect thereof.

Section 2. The Citizens of each State shall be entitled to all Privileges and Immunities of Citizens in the several States.

A Person charged in any State with Treason, Felony, or other Crime, who shall flee from justice, and be found in another State, shall on demand of the executive Authority of the State from which he fled, be delivered up, to be removed to the State having jurisdiction of the crime.

No Person held to Service or Labour in one State, under the Laws thereof, escaping into another, shall, in Consequence of any Law or Regulation therein, be discharged from such Service or Labour, but shall be delivered up on Claim of the Party to whom such Service or Labour may be due.

Section 3. New States may be admitted by the Congress into this Union; but no new State shall be formed or erected within the Jurisdiction of any other State, nor any State be formed by the junction of two or more States, or parts of States, without the Consent of the Legislatures of the States concerned as well as of the Congress.

The Congress shall have Power to dispose of and make all needful Rules and Regulations respecting the Territory or other Property belonging to the United States; and nothing in this Constitution shall be so construed as to Prejudice any Claims of the United States, or of any particular State.

Section 4. The United States shall guarantee to every State in this Union a Republican Form of Government, and shall protect each of them against Invasion; and on Application of the Legislature, or of the

Executive (when the Legislature cannot be convened) against domestic Violence.

Article V

The Congress, whenever two-thirds of both Houses shall deem it necessary, shall propose Amendments to this Constitution, or, on the Application of the Legislatures of two-thirds of the several States, shall call a Convention for proposing Amendments, which, in either Case, shall be valid to all Intents and Purposes, as part of this Constitution, when ratified by the Legislatures of three-fourths of the several States, or by Conventions in three-fourths thereof, as the one or the other Mode of Ratification may be proposed by the Congress; Provided that no Amendment which may be made prior to the Year One thousand eight hundred and eight shall in any Manner affect the first and fourth Clauses in the Ninth Section of the first Article; and that no State, without its Consent, shall be deprived of its equal Suffrage in the Senate.

Article VI

All Debts contracted and Engagements entered into, before the Adoption of this Constitution, shall be as valid against the United States under this Constitution, as under the Confederation.

This Constitution, and the Laws of the United States which shall be made in Pursuance thereof; and all Treaties made, or which shall be made, under the Authority of the United States, shall be the supreme Law of the Land; and the judges in every State shall be bound thereby, any Thing in the Constitution or Laws of any State to the Contrary notwithstanding.

The Senators and Representatives before mentioned, and the Members of the several State Legislatures and all executive and judicial Officers, both of the United States and of the several States, shall be bound by Oath or Affirmation, to support this Constitution; but no religious Test shall ever be required as a qualification to any Office or public Trust under the United States.

Article VII

The Ratification of the Conventions of nine States, shall be sufficient for the Establishment of this Constitution between the States so ratifying the same.

Done in Convention by the Unanimous Consent of the States present the Seventeenth Day of September in the Year of our Lord one thousand seven hundred and Eighty seven, and of the independence of the United States of America the Twelfth. In Witness whereof We have hereunto subscribed our Names.

Go. Washington, President and deputy from Virginia; Attest William Jackson, Secretary; Delaware: Geo. Read,* Gunning Bedford, Jr., John Dickinson, Richard Basset, Jaco. Broom; Maryland: James McHenry, Daniel of St. Thomas' Jenifer, Danl. Carroll; Virginia: John Blair, James Madison, Jr.; North Carolina: Wm. Blount, Richd. Dobbs Spaight, Hu Williamson; South Carolina: J. Rutledge, Charles Cotesworth Pinckney, Charles Pinckney, Pierce Butler; Georgia: William

Few, Abr. Baldwin; New Hampshire: John Langdon, Nicholas Gilman; Massachusetts: Nathaniel Gorham, Rufus King; Connecticut: Wm. Saml. Johnson, Roger Sherman,* New York: Alexander Hamilton; New Jersey: Wil. Livingston, David Brearly, Wm. Paterson, Jona. Dayton; Pennsylvania: B. Franklin,* Thomas Mifflin, Robt. Morris,* Geo. Clymer,* Thos. FitzSimons, Jared Ingersoll, James Wilson, Gouv. Morris.

Articles in Addition to, and Amendment of, the Constitution of the United States of America, Proposed by Congress, and Ratified by the Legislatures of the Several States, Pursuant to the Fifth Article of the Original Constitution.

Amendment I [1791]

Congress shall make no law respecting an establishment of religion, or prohibiting the free exercise thereof, or abridging the freedom of speech, or of the press; or the right of the people peaceably to assemble, and to petition the Government for a redress of grievances.

Amendment II [1791]

A well regulated Militia, being necessary to the security of a free State, the right of the people to keep and bear Arms shall not be infringed.

Amendment III [1791]

No Soldier shall, in time of peace, be quartered in any house, without the consent of the owner, nor in time of war, but in a manner to be prescribed by law.

Amendment IV [1791]

The right of the people to be secure in their persons, houses, papers, and effects, against unreasonable searches and seizures, shall not be violated, and no Warrants shall issue, but upon probable cause, supported by Oath or affirmation, and particularly describing the place to be searched, and the persons or things to be seized.

Amendment V [1791]

No person shall be held to answer for a capital or otherwise infamous crime, unless on a presentment or indictment of a Grand jury, except in cases arising in the land or naval forces, or in the Militia, when in actual service in time of War or public danger; nor shall any person be subject for the same offence to be twice put in jeopardy of life or limb; nor shall be compelled in any criminal case to be a witness against himself, nor be deprived of life, liberty, or property, without due process of law; nor shall private property be taken for public use, without just compensation.

Amendment VI [1791]

In all criminal prosecutions, the accused shall enjoy the right to a speedy and public trial, by an impartial jury of the State and district wherein the crime shall have been committed, which district shall have been previously ascertained by law, and to be informed of the nature and cause of the accusation; to be confronted with the witnesses against him; to have compulsory process for obtaining witnesses in his favor, and to have the Assistance of Counsel for his defense.

Amendment VII [1791]

In suits at common law, where the value in controversy shall exceed twenty dollars, the right of trial by jury shall be preserved, and no fact tried by a jury, shall be otherwise reexamined in any Court of the United States, than according to the rules of the common law.

Amendment VIII [1791]

Excessive bail shall not be required, nor excessive fines imposed, nor cruel and unusual punishments inflicted.

Amendment IX [1791]

The enumeration in the Constitution, of certain rights, shall not be construed to deny or disparage others retained by the people.

Amendment X [1791]

The powers not delegated to the United States by the Constitution, nor prohibited by it to the States, are reserved to the States respectively, or to the people.

Amendment XI [1798]

The judicial power of the United States shall not be construed to extend to any suit in law or equity, commenced or prosecuted against one of the United States by Citizens of another State, or by Citizens or Subjects of any Foreign State.

Amendment XII [1804]

The Electors shall meet in their respective States and vote by ballot for President and Vice-President, one of whom, at least, shall not be an inhabitant of the same State with themselves; they shall name in their ballots the person voted for as President, and in distinct ballots the person voted for as Vice-President, and they shall make distinct lists of all persons voted for as President, and of all persons voted for as Vice-President, and of the number of votes for each, which lists they shall sign and certify, and transmit sealed to the seat of the government of the United States, directed to the President of the Senate; The President of the Senate shall, in the presence of the Senate and House of Representatives, open all the certificates and the votes shall then be counted; The person having the greatest number of votes for President, shall be the President, if such number be a majority of the whole number of Electors appointed; and if no person have such majority, then from the persons having the highest numbers not exceeding three on the list of those voted for as President, the House of Representatives shall choose immediately, by ballot, the President. But in choosing the President, the votes shall be taken by states, the representation from each state having one vote; a quorum for this purpose shall consist of a member or members from two-thirds of the states, and a majority of all the states shall be necessary to a choice. And if the House of Representatives shall not choose a President whenever the right of choice shall devolve upon them, before the fourth day of March next following, then the Vice-President shall act as President, as in the case of the death or other constitutional disability of the President. The person having the greatest number of votes as Vice-President, shall be the Vice-President, if such number be a majority of the whole number of Electors appointed, and if no person have a majority, then from the two highest numbers on the list, the Senate shall choose the Vice-President; a quorum for the purpose shall consist of two-thirds of the whole number of Senators, and a majority of the whole number shall be necessary to a choice. But no person constitutionally ineligible to the office of President shall be eligible to that of Vice-President of the United States.

Amendment XIII [1865]

Section 1. Neither slavery nor involuntary servitude, except as a punishment for crime whereof the party shall have been duly convicted, shall exist within the United States, or any place subject to their jurisdiction.

Section 2. Congress shall have power to enforce this article by appropriate legislation.

Amendment XIV [1868]

Section 1. All persons born or naturalized in the United States, and subject to the jurisdiction thereof, are citizens of the United States and of the State wherein they reside. No State shall make or enforce any law which shall abridge the privileges or immunities of citizens of the United States; nor shall any State deprive any person of life, liberty, or property, without due process of law; nor deny to any person within its jurisdiction the equal protection of the laws.

Section 2. Representatives shall be apportioned among the several States according to their respective numbers, counting the whole number of persons in each State, excluding Indians not taxed. But when the right to vote at any election for the choice of electors for President and Vice-President of the United States, Representatives in Congress, the Executive and Judicial officers of a State, or the members of the Legislature thereof, is denied to any of the male inhabitants of such State, being twenty-one years of age, and citizens of the United States, or in any way abridged, except for participation in rebellion, or other crime, the basis of representation therein shall be reduced in the proportion which the number of such male citizens shall bear to the whole number of male citizens twenty-one years of age in such State.

Section 3. No person shall be a Senator or Representative in Congress, or elector of President and Vice-President, or hold any office, civil or military, under the United States, or under any State, who, having previously taken an oath, as a member of Congress, or as an officer of the United States, or as a member of any State legislature, or as an executive or judicial officer of any State, to support the Constitution of the United States, shall have engaged in insurrection or rebellion against the same, or given aid or comfort to the enemies thereof. But Congress may by a vote of two-thirds of each House, remove such disability.

Section 4. The validity of the public debt of the United States, authorized by law, including debts incurred for payment of pensions and bounties for services in suppressing insurrection or rebellion, shall not be questioned. But neither the United States nor any State shall assume or pay any debt or obligation incurred in aid of insurrection or rebellion against the United States, or any claim for the loss or emancipation of any slave; but all such debts, obligations, and claims shall be held illegal and void.

Section 5. The Congress shall have the power to enforce, by appropriate legislation, the provisions of this article.

Amendment XV [1870]

Section 1. The right of citizens of the United States to vote shall not be denied or abridged by the United States or by any State on account of race, color, or previous condition of servitude

Section 2. The Congress shall have power to enforce this article by appropriate legislation.

Amendment XVI [1913]

The Congress shall have power to lay and collect taxes on incomes, from whatever source derived, without apportionment among the several States, and without regard to any census or enumeration.

Amendment XVII [1913]

The Senate of the United States shall be composed of two Senators from each State,

elected by the people thereof, for six years; and each Senator shall have one vote. The electors in each State shall have the qualifications requisite for electors of the most numerous branch of the State legislatures.

When vacancies happen in the representation of any State in the Senate, the executive authority of such State shall issue writs of election to fill such vacancies: Provided, That the legislature of any State may empower the executive thereof to make temporary appointments until the people fill the vacancies by election as the legislature may direct.

This amendment shall not be so construed as to affect the election or term of any Senator chosen before it becomes valid as part of the Constitution.

Amendment XVIII [1919]

Section 1. After one year from the ratification of this article the manufacture, sale, or transportation of intoxicating liquors within, the importation thereof into, or the exportation thereof from the United States and all territory subject to the jurisdiction thereof for beverage purposes is hereby prohibited.

Section 2. The Congress and the several States shall have concurrent power to enforce this article by appropriate legislation.

Section 3. This article shall be inoperative unless it shall have been ratified as an amendment to the Constitution by the legislatures of the several States, as provided in the Constitution, within seven years from the date of the submission hereof to the States by the Congress.

Amendment XIX [1920]

The right of citizens of the United States to vote shall not be denied or abridged by the United States or by any State on account of sex.

Congress shall have power to enforce this article by appropriate legislation.

Amendment XX [1933]

Section 1. The terms of the President and Vice-President shall end at noon on the 20th day of January, and the terms of Senators and Representatives at noon on the 3d day of January, of the years in which such terms would have ended if this article had not been ratified; and the terms of their successors shall then begin.

Section 2. The Congress shall assemble at least once in every year, and such meeting shall begin at noon on the 3d day of January, unless they shall by law appoint a different day.

Section 3. If, at the time fixed for the beginning of the term of the President, the President elect shall have died, the Vice-President elect shall become President. If a President shall not have been chosen before the time fixed for the beginning of his term, or if the President elect shall have failed to qualify, then the Vice-President elect shall act as President until a President shall have qualified; and the Congress may by law provide for the case wherein neither a President elect nor a Vice-President elect shall have qualified, declaring who shall then act as President, or the manner in which one who is to act shall be selected, and such person shall act accordingly until a President or Vice-President shall have qualified.

Section 4. The Congress may by law provide for the case of the death of any of the persons from whom the House of Representatives may choose a President whenever the right of choice shall have devolved upon them, and for the case of the death of any of the persons from whom the Senate may choose a Vice-President whenever the right of choice shall have devolved upon them.

Section 5. Sections 1 and 2 shall take effect on the 15th day of October following the ratification of this article.

Section 6. This article shall be inoperative unless it shall have been ratified as an amendment to the Constitution by the legislatures of three-fourths of the several States within seven years from the date of its submission.

Amendment XXI [1933]

Section 1. The eighteenth article of amendment to the Constitution of the United States is hereby repealed.

Section 2. The transportation or importation into any State, Territory, or possession of the United States for delivery or use therein of intoxicating liquors, in violation of the laws thereof, is hereby prohibited.

Section 3. This article shall be inoperative unless it shall have been ratified as an amendment to the Constitution by conventions in the several States, as provided in the Constitution, within seven years from the date of the submission hereof to the States by the Congress.

Amendment XXII [1951]

Section 1. No person shall be elected to the office of the President more than twice, and no person who has held the office of President, or acted as President, for more than two years of a term to which some other person was elected President shall be elected to the office of the President more than once.

But this Article shall not apply to any person holding the office of President when this Article was proposed by the Congress, and shall not prevent any person who may be holding the office of President or acting as President, during the term within which this Article becomes operative from holding the office of President or acting as President during the remainder of such term.

Section 2. This article shall be inoperative unless it shall have been ratified as an amendment to the Constitution by the legislatures of three-fourths of the several states within seven years from the date of its submission to the states by Congress.

Amendment XXIII [1961]

Section 1. The District constituting the seat of Government of the United States shall appoint in such manner as the Congress may direct:

A number of electors of President and Vice President equal to the whole number of Senators and Representatives in Con-

gress to which the District would be entitled if it were a State, but in no event more than the least populous State; they shall be in addition to those appointed by the States, but they shall be considered, for the purposes of the election of President and Vice President, to be electors appointed by a State; and they shall meet in the District and perform such duties as provided by the twelfth article of amendment.

Section 2. The Congress shall have power to enforce this article by appropriate legislation.

Amendment XXIV [1964]

Section 1. The right of citizens of the United States to vote in any primary or other election for President or Vice President, for electors for President or Vice President, or for Senator or Representative in Congress, shall not be denied or abridged by the United States or any State by reason of failure to pay any poll tax or other tax.

Section 2. The Congress shall have the power to enforce this article by appropriate legislation.

Amendment XXV [1967]

Section 1. In case of the removal of the President from office or of his death or resignation, the Vice President shall become President.

Section 2. Whenever there is a vacancy in the office of the Vice President, the President shall nominate a Vice President who shall take office upon confirmation by a majority vote of both houses of Congress.

Section 3. Whenever the President transmits to the President pro tempore of the Senate and the Speaker of the House of Representatives his written declaration that he is unable to discharge the powers and duties of his office, and until he transmits to them a written declaration to the contrary, such powers and duties shall be discharged by the Vice President as Acting President.

Section 4. Whenever the Vice President and a majority of either the principal officers of the executive departments, or of such other body as Congress may by law provide, transmit to the President pro tempore of the Senate and the Speaker of the House of Representatives their written declaration that the President is unable to discharge the powers and duties of his office, the Vice President shall immediately assume the powers and duties of the office as Acting President.

Thereafter, when the President transmits to the President pro tempore of the Senate and the Speaker of the House of Representatives his written declaration that no inability exists, he shall resume the powers and duties of his office unless the Vice President and a majority of either the principal officers of the executive departments, or of such other body as Congress may by law provide, transmit within four days to the President pro tempore of the Senate and the Speaker of the House of Representatives their written declaration that the President is unable to discharge the powers and duties of his office. Thereupon Congress shall decide the issue, assembling within forty-eight hours for that purpose if not in session. If the Congress, within twenty-one days after receipt of the latter written declaration, or, if Congress is not in session, within twenty-one days after Congress is required to assemble, determines by two-thirds vote of both houses that the President is unable to discharge the powers and duties of his office, the Vice President shall continue to discharge the same as Acting President; otherwise, the President shall resume the powers and duties of his office.

Amendment XXVI [1971]

Section 1. The right of citizens of the United States, who are eighteen years of age or older, to vote shall not be denied or abridged by the United States or by any state on account of age.

Section 2. The Congress shall have power to enforce this article by appropriate legislation.

Amendment XXVII [1992]

No law varying the compensation for the services of the Senators and Representatives shall take effect, until an election of Representatives shall have intervened.

Photo Credits

Unless otherwise acknowledged, all photographs are the property of North West Publishing, LLC.

The **Index**

S